T0345016

# STRATEGY
# FOR MANAGING
# COMPLEX SYSTEMS

*Fredmund Malik* is one of Europe's leading authorities on management. The bestselling author's work represents a standard of professional management that can be both taught and learnt. Malik's thinking goes beyond economics and draws inspiration from modern sciences of complexity, particularly cybernetics. He is an expert on corporate governance practice and an adviser to executives at the highest levels of international leadership. Fredmund Malik was Professor at the Swiss University of St. Gallen and Guest Professor at the Austrian University of Economics and Business in Vienna. He is Honorary Professor at three renowned Chinese universities and member of the European Academy of Sciences and Arts. His honors include the Heinz von Foerster Prize for Organizational Cybernetics and the Austrian Award of Honor for Science and the Arts, awarded for his wholistic management systems.

Fredmund Malik

# STRATEGY FOR MANAGING COMPLEX SYSTEMS

## A Contribution to Management Cybernetics for Evolutionary Systems

Translated from German by Jutta Scherer
(JS textworks – Munich, Germany)

Campus Verlag
Frankfurt/New York

The original edition was published in 1984 by Haupt Verlag with the title *Strategie des Managements komplexer Systeme.*
All rights reserved.

ISBN 978-3-593-50539-8 Print
ISBN 978-3-593-43349-3 E-Book (PDF)

Cover design: Guido Klütsch, Cologne
Printing office and bookbinder: Beltz Bad Langensalza
Printed in Germany

www.campus.de

# Table of Content

# Preface to the 1ˢᵗ German Edition

The present book, of which the original manuscripts for Chapters 1–3 were completed in August 1977 and accepted as a habilitation thesis by the University of St. Gallen in 1978, is committed to a long-standing tradition honored in St. Gallen. Since as early as the mid-1960s, a group of varying composition mentored by Prof. Dr. Dr. h. c. mult. Hans Ulrich had been trying to establish a management theory that focused on the design and management of complex socio-technical systems. Their intention was to reform business administration studies and the pertinent, very economics-centered way of thinking. At the same time, however, the group moved away from business administration, since, from today's perspective, it is highly questionable whether business administration and management theory have anything in common at all.

The way I see it, management theory attempts to solve a problem quite different from that which business administration deals with. Whereas Wöhe in his *Einführung in die allgemeine Betriebswirtschaftslehre* ["Introduction to general business administration"]*[1] points out that business administration deals with "the sum of all economic decisions taken in the context of a business organization," to then explain that its focal point is "not the business as such" but rather "the economic side of a business and of business processes,"[2] management theory aims to gain control over the entire system made up of the organization and its environment. As such, management theory, just like management practice, cannot limit itself to a particular aspect. The system has to be under control in all relevant dimensions.

---

\* Text in square parentheses indicates that the author is supplying his own translation of German book titles that do not exist in English.

1 Wöhe, Betriebswirtschaftslehre, pp. 2 (quotes translated by author).

2 Wöhe, Betriebswirtschaftslehre, pp. 6 (quotes translated by author).

The strive for multidimensionality is not the only element typical of this understanding of management theory: An even more significant aspect is the element of "getting something under control." Decisions like those analyzed in business economics studies can be one means to achieve this control, but they surely are not the only one.

As I hope to demonstrate in this book, management and management theory have strong foundations in systems science, and most specifically in a certain type of cybernetics. Note that I am not referring to the kind usually referred to as control theory or control engineering. What I am talking about is the cybernetics of truly complex systems, of organismic, self-organizing, and evolving systems.

You might ask yourself whether a mundane activity such as managing really needs and justifies using such a complicated approach to provide a foundation. I think it does. Even by human standards, our world has become a very organized world in rather short time periods, a network of institutions so complex it can no longer be captured by human dimensions. This world is the result of human action, and the explosive growth in the number of managers at all hierarchical levels plays an increasingly important role. Much of our present world is a result of managerial action. But is it also a result of managerial intention?

I am not sure which answer—yes or no—would imply greater problems. An essential part of this work is dedicated to finding out which of the answers is more accurate and what the consequences are. Today there are more people handling management tasks than ever before, and more people than ever are affected by and dependent on what managers do. As a result, it is becoming increasingly important to be able to tell what good or bad management means, who is a good and who is a bad manager, and what theory is best suited to solve present and future management issues.

As mentioned before, after having completed the first three chapters of this book I focused on application-related issues. In 1977 I took on the leadership of Management Zentrum St. Gallen, an organization specializing in management training, development, and consulting. I was driven to find out whether the thoughts and concepts described here could be applied in practice, whether the goings-on in organizations, the way people act, and so on, would be easier to understand if viewed from this perspective.

Based on my personal experience—which, of course, I do not claim to have evidentiary value—I am convinced that business enterprises, just like most other social institutions, are truly complex, self-organizing, and evolving systems and that only very specific ways of influencing, controlling, and shaping them will have a chance at being effective. Much of what happens in organizations is nothing but rituals that do not really have an impact or change anything. Many social institutions are not managed at all, even though it may appear otherwise, because they are simply not manageable. Quite often, decisions are not made—they make themselves. In many organizations, sensible things happen not because but in spite of management; and in many instances the past years have shown that it takes but a few changes for entire industries to get out of control. In many areas of society, the only way to conceal the fact that systems have never been under control is by resorting to semantics. Many problems can only be regarded as being under control because our expectations concerning their solution have been adjusted downward to reflect the status quo.

My efforts at practical testing and the dynamics these things tend to have—especially with regard to clients' specific needs and the associated time pressure—caused a greater delay in finalizing the print manuscript than originally expected. The experiences gathered during that time called for substantial changes and amendments. Chapters 0 and 4 were added; Chapter 3 was expanded and some essential aspects included. Chapter 1 remained unchanged for reasons I will explain later, while Chapter 2 was modified only marginally.

I would like to express my thanks to all the people that contributed to this book:

- those who influenced my thinking and my views about management, most notably Professor Dr. Hans Ulrich and my colleague Dr. Walter Krieg;
- the management practitioners with whom I had countless conversations at numerous seminars and consulting projects, and who taught me to see the world with their eyes;
- the client organizations which, apart from the immediate issues to be solved, were always objects of my research;
- my colleagues and staff at both Management Zentrum St. Gallen and St. Gallen University's Institute of Business Economics, who presented me with numerous management problems and helped me solve some of them;
- the Swiss National Fund for sponsoring my work;

- my publishers at Verlag Paul Haupt, who had almost given up hope of ever receiving my manuscript;
- Ruth Blumer, Felicitas Kurth, and my mother for producing and supervising the manuscript;
- Jochen Overlack for reading the proofs.

Last but not least, special thanks go to my family. Anyone who has ever written a book knows how much time and effort it takes, how everything else has to take a backseat. Every time my three-year-old daughter asked me, "Daddy, when are you going to play with me?" I would answer: "As soon as I'm finished here." "But when *will* you be finished?" she would ask. Over time, the children seemed to understand the nature and objective of evolution, for one day my five-year-old son, thoughtfully gazing at my crowded desk and the stacks of books, papers, and files on the floor, said to me, "Daddy, I think your book will never be finished."


St. Gallen, April 1984

*Prof. Dr. Fredmund Malik*

# Preface to the 2<sup>nd</sup> German Edition

In many fields, systemic thinking seems to have arrived at a point close to critical mass. There are more and more areas of human thinking and action where, by all accounts, people have begun to seriously consider the systemic nature of things. However, as encouraging as this may be, one must not underestimate the time required to implement an innovation like this. Fundamental innovations, whether they happen in an intellectual or technical realm, mature slowly.

If you try to understand development patterns over extended periods of time, you will find that it always takes around 50 years for a fundamental invention or discovery to turn into an innovation, that is, a change in behavior. At that point, new ways of thinking and acting will begin to replace the old ones, which will also take a substantial amount of time.

To this date, around 20 years have passed since the first St. Gallen papers on the systemic approach were published. This work is gradually beginning to bear fruit. Wholistic, integrative concepts have found their way into executives' minds. Conceptual thinking is at the fore, even for managers with a bias for pragmatic approaches. The complexity of management issues is an acknowledged fact; demands for simple recipes have abated. The majority of practitioners agree that it is far from sufficient to operate to the best of one's abilities within the limitations of given systems, and that the only way to control most organizations is by developing and shaping adequate systems.

In an increasingly interconnected world, the challenges of dealing with complex systems have rapidly gained importance. We are still a long way from having solutions to these problems, but it seems we are beginning to realize where we ought to look for them.

The first edition of this book was received favorably in particular by practitioners, and thus reprinted quickly. Major changes were neither possible nor necessary. I therefore confined myself to improving the wording in some places where I felt there was a risk of misinterpretation. I owe sincere thanks to Mr. A. Bossler lic. oec., for assisting me with this revision.

St. Gallen, May 1986

*Prof. Dr. Fredmund Malik*

# Preface to the 3<sup>rd</sup> German Edition

The second edition of this book sold out rather quickly, which actually surprised me because the book had originally been targeted at a primarily *scientific* readership, as is obvious from various details. I suppose the reason it appeals to practitioners as well is that these people know from first-hand experience that the complexity and interconnectedness of the systems surrounding them require them to adapt to events and circumstances they do not fully comprehend and perhaps never will. Most of the factors governing our behavior are basically unpredictable with regard to their future course. So the question is how best to design and control an institution in such a way that it will be functional, regardless of any turbulences, lack of predictability, and utmost complexity. This question was the starting point for my reflections on the management of complex systems.

In line with its original purpose, this book, now in its third unaltered edition, provides an (apparently still current) guide to the true nature of management, or in other words, to the design, development, and control of complex systems.

St. Gallen, March 1989

*Prof. Dr. Fredmund Malik*

# Preface to the 4<sup>th</sup> German Edition

If events since March 1989 (or the publication of this book's 3<sup>rd</sup> German edition) have proven anything, it is clearly this: that we really and truly live in a world of highly complex systems, that many of these systems are extremely fragile, that we do not have any substantial knowledge of their structure or behavior, and that we are far from really having them under control. It seems as though even minute occurrences can cause these systems to implode and/or gather alarming momentum, which our institutions are hardly prepared and equipped to deal with.

The cutting of a barbed-wire fence by a Hungarian border guard in the summer of 1989 eventually caused the Eastern Bloc to collapse—with breathtaking speed, in a way absolutely unforeseeable, and with consequences that to this date are impossible to survey. Ever since the summer of 1990, the world economy—after what appeared to be a never-ending abundance of liquidity and credits—has suddenly been facing a dramatic shortage of both, and after an eight-year boom phase finds itself in the midst of a severe downturn with no end in sight, regardless of all economic-political efforts. An out-of-control drug scene, unprecedented levels of organized crime, endless streams of refugees, and new waves of radicalization are shaking the foundations of the democratic constitutional state. Key elements of our social infrastructure—the U.S. educational system, the welfare systems in most countries, the healthcare system—are eroding, if not decaying; we are faced with new poverty even in developed economies. Not to mention the ecological situation.

All of these factors underline the urgency of studying complex systems more thoroughly, rather than indulging in quick fixes and can-doism. Only then will we adequately value the significance of modern society's most important function—the management of its institutions and organizations—and be able to implement necessary improvements. It is also the only way to recognize the charlatanism so rampant in this field.

St. Gallen, December 1991

*Prof. Dr. Fredmund Malik*

# Preface to the 5<sup>th</sup> German Edition

This fifth edition, which I could not have hoped and certainly had not planned to ever publish, is preceded by a few words on some recent developments—rather unfortunate ones in my view—in the field of systemic-cybernetic management. In addition, this preface presents some ideas on the problem-solving potential of this type of management, which is clearly underestimated even by many of the people that consider themselves proponents of systemic management. Last but not least, I have added an amendment to respond to some of the criticism that has been put forward.

Is it possible at all, you might ask, to stand behind a book that was published 10 years ago and whose three main parts date back almost 20 years? This was probably the key question that both the publishers and I as the author had to turn over in our minds when considering this new edition. It goes without saying that I still stand behind this book, in the sense that it reflects the knowledge and views I had at the time of its first appearance. What is more, I stand by it in a broader sense: I believe it still contributes to the better understanding of complex systems, their cybernetics, and how we deal with them—in other words, to their management. Even against the backdrop of recent developments, the views presented here seem arguable from both a theoretical and a practical point of view. What is more, they appear to be largely correct in the sense that they have withstood the criticism put forward so far—or so I believe—and much of what is said here has proved to be feasible in practice.

Some have criticized a lack of elaborate arguments to support the hypotheses in this book. They can all be found in the first volume of Gomez/Malik/Oeller, *Systemmethodik: Grundlagen einer Methodik zur Erforschung und Gestaltung komplexer soziotechnischer Systeme* ["Systems methodology: a basic methodology for researching and designing complex socio-technical systems"], or, for short: *Systemmethodik* ["Systems methodology"], Bern and Stuttgart, 1975. That first volume describes, explains, and discusses the terms, concepts, models, and areas of theory that I still consider the basis of a system-focused or systemic management theory. Just what these areas are and why I believe I can take the liberty of integrating them into a new whole will be explained on pages 57 and following of this book.

The book *Systemmethodik* has long been out of stock. I do hope, though, to soon republish the first volume—almost entirely written by me, except for a 14-page theoretical discussion of Ashby by co-author Peter Gomez— as a book in its own right. It would be both justifiable and useful because, first, the theoretical foundations are all discussed in the first volume of *Systems Methodology*[3] and, second, that volume would then form an entity with this book. Until then, anyone interested in the arguments and explanations not included in this book may want to resort to the sources listed at the end.

What matters much more to me than theory, however, is its *application in practice*. For a good 20 years now I have had the opportunity to work with executives as a mentor, trainer, and consultant. This has enabled me to meet another 500 managers or so every year, study their ways of thinking, problems, and solutions, and find out what mattered to them and why. I was also able to witness their successes and failures, to which—in both cases—I occasionally contributed my share. I learned both ways.

And while 20 years may not suffice to know all about business, I consider myself very privileged for not having to rely on my imagination as to what might be happening "out there." I have been able to experience it first-hand, both in the functions mentioned and as an entrepreneur in my own right. Admittedly, success and failure in practice have no evidentiary value for theory and thus cannot serve as arguments, which is why I do not rely on utilitarian or pragmatic arguments. Irrespective of that, I do find practical experience to be extremely valuable in helping to both identify priorities and gauge proportions and relative weights—which is something even "hardcore" theorists cannot avoid, although they usually lack a crucial dimension.

Heinz von Foerster[4] said many years ago that we ought to study cybernetic systems *in vivo*, not *in vitro*. I have had ample opportunities to do that and I took them. Von Foerster also said: "The laws of nature are written by

---

3 The second volume of *Systemmethodik* discusses various approaches to solving complex problems, and elaborates on systems methodology and some of its applications.

4 Fortunately, Heinz von Foerster's groundbreaking papers were also translated into German in the 1990s. I had compiled a complete collection of his work as early as 1977, including the legendary microfilms of all papers generated at the Biological Computer Laboratory (which were considered a best-kept secret at the time).

humans. The laws of biology have to write themselves," which he referred to as his Theorem Number Three. I would like to add a fourth:

*The laws of management practice also write themselves—and they are always good for a surprise.*

They will not be captured by any of the theorists' observations regarding possibility or impossibility.

Lamentably, in discussions on systemic management it has become fashionable to emphasize the most *complicated* aspects of systems theory and cybernetics. We hear and read about the risks of getting caught in logical paradoxes, about the impossibility of recognizing reality, about the general unpredictability of complex systems, about the non-trivial machines, undecidable issues, and the like.

Admittedly, these are intellectually fascinating things. Some of them appear in this book, and they are indeed crucial to the deeper understanding of complex systems. But do they have any practical significance? And if so, when, where, and why?

Practice will not be stopped by paradoxes, be it the Cretan Liar or the Medieval Barber, and I will spare you from rehearsing those stories yet again. If the matter is important enough, there will be pragmatic ways of finding out whether the Cretan is indeed a Cretan and whether he is lying or not. As to the question of whether the barber does or does not shave his own beard: This does not really have any practical relevance for anybody. Customers will accept him with and without a beard, as long as he does a good job shaving theirs, and if he fails to do that there will be others to take his place. Theoretically undecidable questions are resolved in practical action. Basically unpredictable systems are realigned. Unsolvable problems are something we can come to terms with—in the end we will all be dead anyway—while the world goes on. Alexander the Great failed to untie the knot, but that did not stop him.

Management and managers, whatever their relationships and names may have been or will be in the future, will continue to shape and direct systems as long as they exist. They will make the impossible possible, and they will fail to do the possible. All of that is part of *the practice of cybernetics*, and these managers do not care whether or not their actions are in line with relevant theories.

Irrespective of all the questions that have not been and perhaps cannot be solved in theory, managers can be helped in solving *practical* problems. One can sit down with them to jointly think about progress and regress, about better and worse solutions. With their shirt-sleeved ways, managers may have done more harm than philosophers have—but they have done more good, too. Good managers take their responsibilities very seriously and accept help when they need it. They are interested in better solutions and a better world. However, that help needs to be easily accessible, as they have other things to do than spend their time struggling with complicated theories.

The only thing I regret about this book and its reprint is that back in those days I put some things in more complicated terms than I would today and that at some points I lacked the courage to simplify and clarify things. Today I muster that courage based on my extensive practical experience. My gratitude goes out to all the practitioners who never let this stop them from working through these more than 500 pages, or at least some of them, and from testing some of the recommendations given. I was able to learn an incredible lot from them, far more than from all the theorists that picked out single sentences to criticize but ignored the context.

The only thing I can promise to my management friends in return is that I will not let them down. My plans to write a practical guide to management cybernetics, a book that will address not the theoretical topic but the *practice* of systemic management, are beginning to take shape.

St. Gallen, March 1996

*Prof. Dr. Fredmund Malik*

# Preface to the 7<sup>th</sup> German Edition

The publication of this 7th edition of my book comes at a time which highlights quite well, though somewhat tragically, the significance of cybernetics and a strategy for the management of complex systems. The year 2001 has dramatically proven the systemic nature of business and society. What may have been mere theory for many is now proving to be practice and reality—so forcefully that it can no longer be ignored.

Terrorism in the United States, the collapse of large corporations, the rise and fall of what had falsely been believed to be a new economic paradigm, increasing public awareness of the new situation in the stock markets and the entire economy, a growing skepticism vis-à-vis any kind of globalization after it was long believed to be the cure for everything: All these factors illustrate in various ways the enormous complexity of societal systems, their interconnectedness and interactive nature. They also illustrate the fact that the conventional concepts of management do not suffice to adequately deal with the basic phenomenon of any organization: its complexity.

Hardly ever has it been more evident how urgently we need to make use of the findings from systems science and cybernetics in order to design *robust*, *functional*, and *safe* systems in business and society—or indeed what the consequences are of ignoring these insights and leaving them for others to use, or even of systematically disregarding fundamental principles and laws of cybernetics.

Toward the end of the new preface to the fifth edition, which I wrote in 1996, I pointed out the risk of misuse of cybernetic findings, and how the extremely useful practical applications of cybernetics and systems science are recognized also by organizations pursuing unconstitutional goals. In that same preface I also expressed the notion that terrorist and criminal organizations probably have excellent system experts in their ranks. Back then there was no way of knowing when and how this assumption would prove correct; I did feel quite certain, however, that it would happen sooner or later.

Complex systems have their own laws, behavioral patterns, capabilities, and risks. Cybernetics and systems science provide us with enormous knowledge, enabling us to understand, design, develop, and control those systems; yet a lot of work remains to be done in terms of preparing theoretical insights for practical usability and transforming existing knowledge into tangible, value-adding results.

It was this search for scientific progress and its relevance for solving practical problems which caused Prof. Hans Ulrich, the founder of St. Gallen System-Oriented Management Theory, to consider cybernetics and system theory to be the key fundamental disciplines for management training with practical relevance. His collected writings were recently published for the first time, split into a total of five volumes.[5] They impressively demonstrate how far ahead of his time Hans Ulrich was.

In technology, medicine, and the natural sciences, far-reaching progress has been made by relying on cybernetic insights to solve practical problems. By contrast, much remains to be done in economics and social sciences. Part of the reason is that in some of these disciplines it has always been fashionable to ignore the methodological standards that brought success and progress to other fields.

St. Gallen, January 2002

*Prof. Dr. Fredmund Malik*

---

5 Hans Ulrich, *Gesammelte Schriften*, 5 volumes, Paul Haupt Verlag, Bern/Stuttgart/Vienna, 2001.

# Preface to the 10<sup>th</sup> German Edition

When writing the first preface to the first edition of this book in 1984, while I was convinced I was on the right track, I could not really be certain. I lacked the practical experience I have today. Now that I am writing the eighth preface and publishing the tenth edition, I have successfully completed numerous projects with a most diverse corporate clientele, which has confirmed my decision to take this radically different approach we call management cybernetics. What used to be an industrial society where many things were impossible to understand has turned into a society of knowledge and complexity which cannot function without cybernetic management.

It has certainly not become easier to capture the best knowledge about the management of complex systems. Nevertheless—or perhaps for that very reason—the demand for this book has risen from year to year. And while the theoretical knowledge has not become simpler, our firm has managed to simplify its practical application, in which I have gathered over 30 years' experience to date.

The manuscript for this book was completed in 1976. After that I dedicated all my efforts to developing, gathering, and integrating the models, methods, and tools required for the practical application of management cybernetics. It was only in 1984, after eight years of practical testing, that I published the book with corresponding amendments, specifically in Chapters 0 and 4.

I have written five other books since: *Die Neue Corporate Governance* ["The new corporate governance"], *Managing Performing Living*, *Uncluttered Management Thinking*, *Management: The Essence of the Craft*, and *Corporate Policy and Governance*. Every year, tens of thousands of managers familiarize themselves with my cybernetic management system for general management. A growing number of organizations use its contents and tools.

---

Cybernetic management means self-organization: *organizing a complex system in such a way that it will be able to self-organize.* This is the theme that will eventually prevail in our 21st-century society of complexity, if there is to be any more progress at all. That means we will migrate to completely new and different solutions. Our old methods and ways of thinking have created very poorly organized complex systems, which now fail to function due to these same ways of thinking.

Cybernetic management is the crucial paradigmatic step toward what I call *self concepts*: the step that takes us from regulation to self-regulation, from organization to self-organization, from structuring to self-structuring, from coordination to self-coordination, from developing to self-developing—or, in other words, to evolution. These solutions are the only ones that work, as we are no longer able to understand systems in their entirety. Due to their dynamics, interconnectedness, and indeterminateness—in other words, their complexity—they are non-analyzable, non-computable, and unpredictable in their behavior. This book shows how they can be controlled and shaped nevertheless. It contains the necessary theories and the reasoning behind them, as well as strategies, tools, and necessary steps for their application in practice.

For the new management, which is able to cope even with the most complex systems, I have put together elements from systems science, cybernetics, and bionics, configuring them so as to address the relevant issues, and integrating them into a new, coherent concept for managing the institutions of modern-day society. This has little to do with earlier concepts of management theory, and hardly anything to do with business economics and business administration. There is very little management can learn from these disciplines, or from economics in general, when dealing with complex systems. The potential of these disciplines—of whatever useful concepts they offer—has been exploited. Much has proved to be useless, in part even misleading. The issues that management has to deal with in our society of complexity differ greatly from those addressed by the economic sciences. Traditional, economics-based management theory is unable to cope with complexity, let alone take advantage of it.

Major references and rich sources of new insights can be found in the bio- and neuro-, computer, information, and communication sciences—which are all offspring of cybernetics and systems science. Existing knowledge about complexity has been used early and consistently in these disciplines, which is why they are the most successful in this field. Other disciplines have fallen behind because they keep within the narrow confines of simple systems and clearly defined areas of expertise. All they are good for now is lab research—in the real world they have lost most of their relevance. In medicine and technology, too, cybernetics has provided the foundation for spectacular advances. Some other fields would be virtually unthinkable without cybernetics: aeronautics, modern shipping, the intelligent automobile with its many self-regulating elements, computer technology, telecommunications, non-invasive surgery, and intensive-care units at hospitals—to name just a few.

Cybernetic solution systems exist in countless variations—which ultimately does not really matter because they are all outcomes of applying the laws of nature. There is no similarity whatsoever between Isaac Newton's falling apple and the positioning of a navigation satellite—yet they both follow the law of gravity. It is much the same with cybernetic laws of nature, no matter whether they work through proteins, computer chips, or the master controls of complexity-adequate business management: "There are many possible manifestations; there is one cybernetic solution," as Stafford Beer, the founder of management cybernetics and my long-time friend and partner, once summed it up.

Many fail to understand the significance of the natural laws at work in complex systems, which were discovered in the 20th century, because—contrary to those of physics—these are not perceptible to the senses via matter and energy. The laws of cybernetics describe the effects of the third basic quantity in nature: information. Information originates in the brain. So the only way to explore the effects of cybernetic laws of nature is by reflection. This is precisely what keeps the complexity-focused sciences, specifically cybernetics and bionics, from unfolding their full potential. To this date, some people still believe it is a mere illusion harbored by early pioneer thinkers, something impossible to implement. This kind of thinking is a sign of ignorance, especially when absurd allusions to totalitarian surveillance systems are used to stir vague fears.

Cybernetics is the science of functioning; management cybernetics is its application in practice to all organizations of business and society as well as to society itself. Crises and conflicts are always consequences of malfunctioning systems and management failures. All attempts to keep systems like these alive with outdated, simple, linear ways of thinking are bound to fail for reasons rooted in cybernetics and natural law. Functioning organizations in a functioning society are the purpose, the objective, and the outcome of scientifically based, professional, ethical and

This book has mobilized valuable support for me in direct and indirect ways. I thank everyone that has contributed, if unknowingly. First and foremost my heartfelt thanks go to the numerous readers who have bought this book and worked their way through it. Many have corresponded with me for years; some have become cooperation partners and even friends.

To the tens of thousands of managers from all areas of business and society, I owe sincere thanks for the courage and trust it took to test cybernetic management models, principles, methods, and tools together with me and keep improving them. This practice has been and still is my research lab, where the strategy for the management of complex systems continues to be tested on a day-to-day basis. It is the ideal empirical platform for my scientific work, something I wish my colleagues from academia could have.

Special thanks are owed to the Swiss National Fund, which years ago funded the research project on "system-oriented cybernetic management of complex systems," enabling me to do the research for this book, as well as to my long-time academic mentor and superior, Prof. Dr. Hans Ulrich, who established this kind of management thinking at the St. Gallen University in the 1960s, and my colleague and friend Prof. Dr. Walter Krieg. Together with Hans Ulrich he created the St. Gallen Management Model, which was first published in 1972 by Management Zentrum St. Gallen. The model was presented to the global public in 1973, together with the Club of Rome's first report on the "Limits to Growth," at the 3rd St. Gallen Management Symposium hosted by the ISC (which I co-chaired at the time). I am very grateful to Walter Krieg and to my colleague Dr. Karl-Heinz Oeller, co-author of my doctoral thesis, for continuing to provide the most valuable support in the developments at Malik Management Zentrum St. Gallen. I also owe sincere thanks to all my staff, some of whom have been with me for over 30 years, as well as to Haupt Verlag in Bern, specifically Dr. Manuel Bachmann for managing this new release of the book.

Last but not least I thank my wife Angelika and my two children. The final paragraph of the first preface still holds true: Anyone who has ever written a book knows how much time and effort it takes, how everything else has to take a backseat. Every time my three-year-old daughter asked me, "Daddy, when are you going to play with me?" I would say to her: "As soon as I'm finished." "But when *will* you be finished?" she would ask. Over time, the children seemed to understand the nature and objective of evolution, for one day my five-year-old son, thoughtfully gazing at my crowded desk and the rather chaotic stacks of books, papers, and files on the floor, said to me, "Daddy, I think your book will never be finished."

St. Gallen, April 2008

*Prof. Dr. Fredmund Malik*

# Preface to the 11<sup>th</sup> German Edition

A strategy for managing complex systems is now more important than ever, much more so than in 1984, when this book first came out. I had actually written it from 1976 to 1978, as my habilitation thesis. This was in the context of a large research project conducted by the Swiss National Fund for Basic Research, which focused on the design and control of complex productive systems. Ever since then there has been a continuous process of self-reinforcing global complexification.

More recently, this process has developed a very distinct pattern: A fundamental transformation of businesses and societies around the world is going on, affecting more and more areas of our lives at increasing speed. This became apparent quite early: Back in the 1980s, I addressed the first signs of the transformation in my lectures and speeches. After the stock market crash in 1987, I started exploring strategic deflation scenarios with my corporate clients; in 1991, my book *Krisengefahren in der Weltwirtschaft* ("Risks in the global economy") came out. In 1997, I described the key characteristics of this transformation, which were quite visible by then, in my book on corporate governance, referring to it as the "Great Transformation." This choice of wording is a tribute to two great Austrian thought leaders, Karl Polanyi and Peter F. Drucker, who have both studied the transformation of global social and economic systems.

The Great Transformation 21, as I call it now, is not simply "change." Change always happens. Rather, it is a very specific kind of change: the replacement of something that exists by something completely new. It is the kind of change that has regularly occurred in history, and which constitutes a key element in the brazen logic of social evolution: substitution by basic innovation. Joseph Schumpeter, the famous Austrian economist, introduced the term "creative destruction" to refer to this very phenomenon. He realized that innovative managers and entrepreneurs played a key part in this kind of transformation, and he was the first to incorporate this insight into his economic theories.

Perhaps the most well-known example of a major transformation is the change from agricultural to industrial society some two hundred years ago. Collapse, revolution, and a new order are all features of such transitions. The fundamental shock to existing ways of life affects everything, down to the minute details of everyday life. Other examples of substitution through innovation include the replacement of the horse carriage by the automobile during the years from 1890 to 1930, and more recently the replacement of conventional telephony by smartphone technology. Substitution processes like these have invariably caused the demise of formerly thriving economic empires within a very short time. On the other hand, they have created new empires which have often risen to much greater significance. Examples of the former include Kodak and Nokia, and of the latter Apple and Google.

The survival and–much more importantly–the *viability* of a system fundamentally depend on its ability to realize its potential for the future, which also requires exploiting its present potential. Furthermore, the fact that we do not know where a specific development begins or where it ends creates enormous challenges to the management of complexity–in particular when considering that there is not one single future development but usually a set of competing potential developments.

In view of the growing number of economic, political and social crises we have witnessed over the past years, it is becoming increasingly obvious that this is the beginning not just of a new era but, literally, of a new world with a new order. What most people believe to be the coincidence of a number of individual crises is easier to understand if we consider these crises as the systemic dimensions of the Great Transformation 21. The exploding complexity of global systems, the increasingly dense network of interconnections between them, the accelerating dynamics of global change, the resulting turbulences–all of these phenomena are, in a sense, the "birth pangs" associated with the emergence of a new world.

To master this epochal change I call the Great Transformation 21, all organizations in society will need complexity-compatible management systems and innovative tools. Both businesses and society as a whole will have to shift their focus to the new *functioning of organizations in the 21st century's society of complexity*. The existing economic and social sciences alone will not be able to produce the new solutions we need. Rather, the sciences of complexity will provide the basis: system sciences, cybernetics, and bionics.

Disciplines such as engineering, medicine and the natural sciences have used cybernetic findings intensely and successfully for many years to create feasible solutions. Economics and the social sciences have taken much longer to recognize their inherent solution potential. Slowly but surely they are coming around, however, and we are seeing an almost Copernican turn. Yet while the significance of management cybernetics is generally recognized now, the scope of its impact is not.

What we are experiencing is not simply a paradigm change but a change of the categories in which we view those paradigms. The categorial dimensions of the new world are complexity, system, functioning, control, self-organization, information, nonlinearity, knowledge, and cognition.

Truly effective solutions to the questions raised by the hyper-complexity of business and society will only materialize if the old ways of managerial thinking and acting are replaced by cybernetics–the science of functioning. In going through this fundamental change, organizations' capability to adapt to completely new things and to function under any kind of circumstance will safeguard their survival.

We are not at the mercy of that complexity–provided we accept it and incorporate it into our thoughts and actions. By looking into the nature of complex systems, we will recognize what is impossible, and thus improve our ability to implement the possible and feasible. We will also realize that there is no reason to be afraid of growing complexity. On the contrary: Complexity provides the raw material for intelligent solutions at a higher level of effectiveness.

The systems, methods and tools required as well as the rules for their application are all described in the books I have written (see a complete list in the preface to the 10th edition). This book provides the basics on how to create robust, functional, and sustainably viable systems. One of the reasons why it has become a classic on management cybernetics, now in its 11th edition, is that the strategies and heuristic principles of complexity management are still relevant–now more than ever.

My thanks, which I have expressed extensively in the preface to the last edition, still hold true. I owe them to all the managers and clients mentioned there; to my partners and colleagues at the Malik Institute, who, with the combined expertise and skill of an interdisciplinary team, repeatedly and thoroughly scrutinized my theories–and who were sometimes hard to convince even by what I thought were excellent arguments; to Campus Verlag, and in particular Jutta Scherer for her professional translation services and numerous improvement suggestions, which helped me to better communicate to an English-speaking audience; to my friends who, in many intense discussions, challenged me to put my thoughts in clearer words; and last but not least, to my family.

St. Gallen, January 2015

*Prof. Dr. Fredmund Malik*

# Introduction to the 5<sup>th</sup> Edition

## Is This the Final Breakthrough?

When in the mid-1960s Hans Ulrich, together with other faculty of St. Gallen University, began developing a management theory based on systems science and cybernetics, great hopes were attached to both these fields—but less so with regard to the practical application of the abstract knowledge. When the first edition of this book was published some 20 years later, I was personally convinced of the value of systems science and cybernetics-based methods and concepts—but there was little to indicate they would ever find circulation and acceptance outside a small circle of experts.

Now that another 10 years have passed, we are presented with an entirely different picture. Triggered and driven primarily by the explosive developments in electronics and computer sciences, what used to be technical jargon from the pioneer field has all but become common usage. Everybody talks of (w)holistic approaches and networking; "information" and "communication" have become household terms; surfing the web has become a hobby not only of youngsters but of your average office clerk; cyberspace and virtual realities, the Fractal Factory and the information highway have made the headlines.

Whether this actually aids the cause is a different question. But the fact remains that complexity, systems, networks, and cyber-whatever have become an issue. As questionable as this trend may be in some aspects, it also entails an opportunity. Above all, it involves a certain degree of *compulsion*: It is no longer possible to deny or ignore the *relevance* that systems science and in particular its core concept, complexity, have for the design and control of institutions—at least not in good conscience and without consequences. No one today can afford to not deal with these matters in a meaningful way.

This is not to say that every manager needs to be an expert in the theory of complex systems. But many will need an excellent understanding of the opportunities, limitations, and consequences that these systems bring to management practice. Most institutions, whether in business or in the ever-growing non-profit sector, will have to have at least a few systems theory and cybernetics experts in their ranks. It will be a key prerequisite for them to avoid the risks of complexity and take advantage of its opportunities. In the business sector it will be inevitable for those who want to prevent competitors from gaining major advantages by engaging in these activities; in the non-profit sector it will be necessary because many modern-day organizations have increasing difficulties executing their tasks and, unless there are fundamental reforms, may soon be forced to give up.

As business and society are going through one of the greatest transformations ever, almost all institutions face the need for fundamental, sometimes radical changes to their structure and mode of operation. In my view, systems science and cybernetics provide essential foundations and aids for coping with the current and future problems associated with this change. I am not saying they will provide a solution for *any* problem, let alone a simple and convenient solution, but they have a potential we cannot afford to ignore.

It will be all the more important then to separate the wheat from the chaff. Not everything published on the subject, which currently attracts quite some attention, is actually useful. Quite to the contrary: The growing general interest in systems science and cybernetics is bound to cause undesirable developments and misunderstandings, errors and misinterpretations[7]

---

7 Please also consider my statement in the attachment concerning the critique.

As far as I can tell, a particularly serious risk seems to be arising at the interface between systems science and the humanities, and it seems to be greatest in the field that has always intrigued me the most: management. There may be many reasons for this. A particularly important one, in my view, is the severe lack of critical analysis and debate in this area. The methodological principle of critical examination, absolutely indispensable and a clear driver of progress in the natural sciences and in engineering, is still underdeveloped in large parts of the humanities, despite all the debates over methodology. In management and management science it hardly exists at all. Despite the abundance of publications, there is hardly any critical discussion. In the natural sciences, by contrast, new findings are often tested by other, independent researchers within a matter of weeks or months; the underlying data are examined and hypotheses and experiments challenged. Similar things hardly ever happen in management.

Below I will summarize some of the misdirected developments that have particularly caught my attention.

## Misdirected Development

### 1. Lack of Specificity

First of all, I cannot help noticing that a large part of the relevant literature is rather vague and superficial. It is not very helpful, least of all to practitioners, when terms like "system," "subsystem," "element," "interaction," "self-organization," "self-reference," "autopoiesis," "feedback" and "complexity" keep popping up in theoretical contexts while their practical impact and application is hardly referred to. Some authors—at least this is my impression—keep writing the same books on fundamental topics over and over again, without ever moving beyond the basics to deal with the practical side. However, as systems theory and cybernetics are rather abstract, I consider it extremely important to work to make them concrete, in particular if their problem-solving potential is to be captured. In the absence of such efforts there will be little chance of widespread adoption in practice.

On principle, many practitioners, entrepreneurs, managers, politicians, chief executives, and so on are very open to and interested in these things—which is hardly surprising, as they increasingly realize that traditional approaches are reaching their limits. Much of what systems science and cybernetics have to offer is in line with their own intuition and experience, even though they are often unable to find the words for it.

Seasoned practitioners—not the inexperienced ones, obviously—are very well aware that many things in their organizations self-regulate, self-organize, and evolve on their own. But experience has also taught them that the results of this "self" process are not always satisfying, and sometimes lead straight into disaster. As a result their attitude tends to be ambivalent. On the one hand there is a vital interest in better understanding complex systems, be it out of necessity, lack, or disorientation; on the other hand there is considerable skepticism and distrust—and for good reasons, I might add. Practitioners need to be given practical aids. They also need to be shown, based on a few examples, that systems science thinking can provide solutions to several of their problems and that these solutions can be better than others.

It makes little sense, for instance, to keep emphasizing the significance of interaction when referring to management practice. It is quite obvious that many aspects of complex systems—including their complexity—result from interaction. Practitioners know that, even if they do not use the term, but they do not have the time to wait until science has explored every single interaction. Rather, their situation is such that they have to do something on Monday morning. If they do not launch any actions, the actions will launch themselves. And it will often be for the worse.

Let me illustrate what I mean by using an example which, in the broadest sense, belongs in the area of motivation. The past 30 to 40 years have been marked by what we could call the theory of job satisfaction. Put somewhat pointedly, it can be summed up in one phrase: *Keep employees happy and they will perform.* Certainly no one could say that nothing has happened in this field. But what are the results? If we look at international benchmarks, differences in productivity, market share shifts, and so on, my feeling is that results have not been as good as they could be. Of course, proponents of the job satisfaction theory would immediately object that my summary of their theory is incorrect, that there are interdependencies between satisfaction and performance, and that this is an "interactional" problem. Well, perhaps that is so... But what should practitioners actually do? How much longer can they afford to wait?

They do not have the time—for systemic reasons, no less—to await the results of interaction research and the corresponding publications. Precisely *because* they deal with "dynamic" systems that keep changing from day to day, or even by the hour, and might be in a totally different constellation tomorrow, they *must* act. They cannot afford to sit back in contemplation.

That is why my suggestion to practitioners is a different one: To begin with, I tell them I am not convinced the job satisfaction theory is correct. The evidence and findings we have so far leave room for legitimate doubt. Historically, performance has probably never arisen from satisfaction but, on the contrary, from dissatisfaction. Had the Stone Age man been satisfied with his damp and cold cave, he would hardly have left it to eventually build a family home with central heating. In response to this, I am then usually asked whether I am suggesting we keep people dissatisfied to elicit good performance? Certainly not. But there is an alternative option: *Give people the chance to deliver the kind of performance that is great from both a relative and their individual perspective—and many of them (not all) will achieve an astounding degree of satisfaction.* That, in rough terms, is what I suggest.

Just like anyone else studying this problem, I am aware that this is still not 100 percent to the point. It is probably too simple to represent the "real" situation, and we are probably dealing with a much more complex interaction, a cybernetic or systemic interdependency involving many more variables. But this realization does not help anyone. When managers ask me, "what should I do Monday morning: Which way should I intervene with the system in order to shift it to another, hopefully better state or at least get it on the way?" I will still suggest the above, as I am convinced it will help them in an essentially system-adequate way. It will give them the chance to spend the weekend thinking about how to enable their people to deliver strong performance and how to shape their tasks accordingly. Last but not least, instead of thinking about how to do this for *everyone* in the organization, they will focus on the eight, twelve or fifteen people directly reporting to them—for this is the problem they will actually be facing, rather than how to make the world a better place. Some systems scientists may regard this as being too simplistic and modest an approach, and it may indeed lead to a suboptimal solution. However, if all or at least a majority of managers acted that way, this would be an enormous step forward.

I feel there are good reasons (though not final evidence) for this viewpoint, which can be derived from cybernetics and systems science. It is owing to these precise cybernetic reasons and the fact we are dealing with a complex system that I am making this suggestion.

There are many other examples to illustrate similar points, for instance with regard to cooperation, coordination, coexistence, and coevolution—which many systems theory papers claim should replace competition. I am not sure we are doing practitioners a great service by permanently insisting they should network. After all, they know from everyday experience that it is sometimes better to disentangle things, even keep them from interacting. Why else would it be that organizations are decentralized, independent entities formed, responsibilities delegated to other hierarchical levels or external providers? A system where everything is interconnected will *block itself* so nothing will work anymore. Perhaps all those that permanently talk about networking, and in much too general terms, would do well to read some works by the early cybernetics pioneer W. Ross Ashby, who masterfully explained these things back in the 1960s.

## 2. Difficulties Being Blown Out of Proportion

Much the same is true for a habit that has become fashionable in systems science literature, which is to overstrain the philosophy of (radical) constructivism[8] beyond all reasonable measure. The basic message of this school of thought is that our picture of the world is a construction of our minds. As such, this fact can hardly be denied by anyone having studied the basic schools of philosophy and epistemology, and of course it has significant effects on the management of organizations. I have left no doubt about that in this book.

Some proponents of constructivism, however, seem to be taking it much further, claiming that the world "out there"—reality—does not exist at all.

---

8 Seeing as there are enough misunderstandings already, perhaps I should mention that the term "constructivist," which I frequently use in this book, has nothing to do with the constructivism I am referring to here. When I use the terms "constructivist" in connection with "technomorph," it is to express the opposite of "systemic/evolutionary." In doing this I adopt the terminology used by Friedrich von Hayek, which, to my knowledge, dates back further than so-called (radical) constructivism. As far as I can tell, the term was introduced into the discussion much later, in the 1970s, by Ernst von Glasersfeld. In subsequent years, however, it was used by several authors publishing works about systems theory, cybernetics, and systemic management, and always with the meaning Glasersfeld had introduced. I always felt that this was creating a great deal of confusion, which is why I wish to call readers' attention to the potential misunderstanding that would completely distort my meaning.

The ultimate question is not just whether our image of the "world" is a construction of the mind, but what this construction has to do with the reality that possibly exists, independent of the perceiving subject—or in other words, whether our image is completely subjective or correct, at least with regard to some aspects; whether it can be improved; whether or not we can get it to come close to what we might call reality.

If these were *only* philosophies, perhaps we would not have to deal with them in the management context. However, the different varieties of this type of constructivism are introduced to organizational practice in many ways: through communication theory and training, through training on leadership, motivation etc., and most recently through an ever-increasing number of publications on "systemic management," including one by the Heidelberg Institute for Systemic Research. Of course I am all in favor of dealing with these questions thoroughly, and I am hoping for results that will add some momentum to the joint concern we may have, which is to contribute to improving the management of organizations.

But we will hardly succeed—at least not with the arguments put forward so far—in convincing practitioners that the world is just a figment of their imagination. Perhaps not all managers but many of them will readily admit that they sometimes make mistakes, that their image of reality is often incorrect or incomplete. Why else would they dedicate such effort to gathering information, gaining a clear understanding, driving market research, studying competitors, and so on? But they will hardly believe us when we tell them that currency rates are not a reality, that the superior product or the promotional campaign that enabled a competitor to win market share and turnover from them is just a phantasm, and that the shareholders' meeting where people got furious over low dividends and sinking stock prices was just a product of their imagination.

Especially good managers will be willing to reflect upon the issues raised by this school of constructivism, particularly since they apply its findings on a daily basis (and had done so long before constructivism even existed), for instance in advertising or negotiations. And they have always known that balance sheets never reflect reality, which is why anyone who learned the trade will never be bluffed by them. He or she will not only have learned to use a balance sheet as a tool, but also have carefully studied the connections between balance sheets and economic reality, between "map" and "territory."

Issues like these, which are systemic in nature, have been observed, studied, and applied in practice much longer and much more intensely in the business sector than they have been studied by philosophers. We can trace them back to the supposedly Sumerian scripts, which actually appear to have been Chaldean:[9] rather than recording heroic deeds, as many historians have claimed, their main purpose was to document debtor-creditor relationships. So if we want to change, perhaps even improve the management of organizations based on findings from systems science and cybernetics, it will be essential to get practitioners' attention. That, in turn, will only be possible by being more specific, by using examples and providing practical advice.

And whether we like it or not, this will take some compromising with regard to the language used, the examples selected, and the specific recommendations made. Every example has its limits and raises its own ifs and buts; not every wording will stand up to purist semantic analysis; not every recommendation can be fully substantiated. On the other hand, if systems science and systemic management degenerate into an intellectualistic playground, this may be interesting to observe but it will remain *ineffective*. Also, practitioners will reject it, perhaps even aggressively, and justifiably so: first, because it is no help to them; second, because it causes even more confusion for them and their staff than they are already dealing with every day; third, because they are keenly aware that they—the business sector—are expected to create value before any tax money is spent on intellectual pursuits.

## 3. Small or Large System?

There is yet another observation to be made. A substantial share of recent literature on systemic thinking and systemic management deals with the type of system we refer to as a *small system*. It is the face-to-face group, the team, the workgroup, the family, and so on. Almost the entire field of organizational development, human resource management, and what is usually referred to as people leadership is influenced by these systems and by so-called systemic therapy. I certainly do not intend to question the sense and value of engaging with these elements; we owe significant insight to the research done in this area. Of course, small systems are systems, too. That said, they

---

9 See G. Heinsohn, *Die Sumerer gab es nicht* ["The Sumerians Did Not Exist"], Frankfurt, 1988.

are not the main field where systems science and cybernetics will prove fruit-ful.

While there is nothing to be said against using systemic terms, concepts, and ways of thinking in this field, they are rarely needed. Common sense and some experience will get you quite far here.

The practical context of this kind of systemic management, systemic therapy, and so on is usually a *small* number of people: a couple or a group of, say, 20 or 25 individuals. With this system size and the corresponding degree of complexity we have the essential advantage that the structure and behavior of the system and its elements—that is, of the individuals and the groups they form—are accessible to sensory perception. Of course this perception is influenced by constructions of the mind and might not be able to get beyond it (if we believe the proponents of radical constructivism)—and yet the situation is completely different and in my opinion much simpler than it is with large systems. The true difficulties will occur *beyond* the limits of a small system, that is, when we deal with organizations comprising thousands or even hundreds of thousands of people. Systems of this kind are no longer accessible to sensory perception. Here, we face dimensions of complexity that require entirely different methods and ways of thinking: those that appertain to systemic management. Systemic management must not be confined to the field of small and/or simple systems, and we have to avoid the impression that this was the most important or preferred or most productive application.

Perhaps this is the right place to recount a personal experience that is still very vivid in my memory. Years ago I attended a small symposium entitled "Evolution and Management" in Vienna. The hosts had managed to win keynote speakers from different scientific disciplines; there were also quite a few senior and top managers of business organizations, some of them as speakers, most as participants. It was quite obvious that the practitioners present were very interested in possible applications of evolutionary (systemic) management. One of the scientific speakers, a business economist, gave an interesting and comprehensive presentation on a real-life case he considered best practice, explaining how systemic thinking was being applied at a company. He impressively outlined the methodology, presented complex network diagrams that had been developed in the course of the business diagnostic, explained an equally comprehensive matrix of influencing factors, and gave the time and HR expenditure required by the project. It had spanned several person-months. One of the managers in the audience asked him—obviously quite impressed—what kind and size the company had been. The speaker readily provided the desired information: It was a trading firm with eight employees… Disappointment was written all over everyone's faces. The same manager went on to ask—and justifiably so—what use this method could be to him, the head of a corporation of over 100,000 employees, with several dozens of associated companies and over 500 business units worldwide …!

Well, obviously it does not work this way. You cannot take minor issues that might serve as case studies for a third-year term paper and present them to seasoned practitioners faced with completely different dimensions, in hopes of persuading them to give your suggested management approach a try. And there is yet another point to consider: The influences of systemic therapy have led to the emergence of what I would call a dominance of pathological cases. Therapists deal with *sick* people and systems. If systemic thinking helps their therapies, all the better.

In organizations, however, we typically deal with *healthy*, normal people. Or, to be more precise: We are probably all sick or abnormal in some way—if only because it is impossible to define normality. Most of us, however, are probably abnormal to a perfectly normal extent. We may all be "sick" or "crazy," but we are so in an ordinary way. We all have our problems and neurotic traits, but we are able to deal with them more or less. In that same sense, many organizations are "sick" in that they have their shortcomings, structural and functional deficiencies, and thus are in need of reforms and restructuring. In other words, people and organizations both have their difficulties, but treating them as illnesses is wrong in my opinion.

It seems to me that some therapists and organizational developers take ordinary problems, disagreements, and the occasional, perfectly normal and inevitable conflict and turn them into severe pathological cases. We may face such severe cases every now and then, but they are rare. By far the most difficulties occur because people are people—a fact we are obviously losing sight of. Many problems result from simple misunderstandings and from a certain degree of neglect in performing essential management tasks. To solve or eliminate such "problems," we do not have to bring in the heavy artillery of therapy, least of all systemic therapy.

## 4. Mystification of the Systems Approach

Another trend to be observed—a rather unfortunate one, I might add—is what we might call the "mystification" of the systems approach. From a scientific perspective it is hardly worth the trouble dealing with it, as the arguments supporting it are rather weak. Surprisingly, however, this line of thought holds plenty of emotional appeal for many people. It is tightly linked to what is sometimes referred to as the "psycho-boom."

In the course of this development, the systems approach is closely associated with the most diverse doctrines, be they of Chinese, Indian, or Tibetan origin, be they rooted in Taoism, Hinduism, Buddhism, or Confucianism, be they of the esoteric, spiritualist, or other mythological variety. Proponents of this line of thought sometimes refer to authors who used to be known as serious scientists before they started "tripping." Their former scientific reputation often gives their mystifying musings enormous power of persuasion, and thus broad dissemination to a degree never justified by the quality of their metaphysical thought labyrinths. Well, we all know that scientists are people, too; like everybody else they have their ups and downs, their emotions, doubts, and self-doubts, and along with pronounced rationality we often find a remarkable degree of irrationality.

It is no exception, for example, for highly skilled physicians who have made major contributions to their discipline to develop a strong bias towards metaphysics and mysticism, either as part of their reaching old age or due to their personal situation. This is not objectionable, of course, nor can it be avoided. But the question is what impact this has on others, what intellectual movements it sparks, how it can be abused, and how it can put a dent into a scientific discipline's thinking.

If these were all questions arising inside the science community only, one could calmly rely on their self-correcting forces. Not so in the world of media. Mystifying salvation doctrines are a favorite media product, not only due to their emotional appeal but also because they sell so well. As a consequence, the impact of such doctrines is far greater than we would like it to be, especially when they have the power to discredit a discipline to the point of being rejected by everyone outside those "esoteric" circles, for the very reasons that it is popular with them.

Interestingly, mystifying beliefs that resemble salvation doctrines often meet with a great deal of sympathy in entrepreneurial and management circles, sometimes even fervent support—so fervent in fact that it bears all the hallmarks of sectarianism. Perhaps it is the sometimes very exposed positions of these people, the loneliness at the top of organizations, the decision-making pressures and considerable stress associated with management positions, which makes them so susceptible—not only to the usual temptations of modern society, such as alcohol, stimulating and tranquilizing substances, and other drugs (things that are much more common on executive floors than one might think, even though they are rarely discussed), but also to said mysticism—be it in the form of systemic theory or not. Fortune-telling, astrology, swinging the pendulum, and other magic rituals are "methods" which, lamentably, are firmly established in some companies—no matter whether they have proven untenable, and regardless of the damage they do.

The very least we should ask about these doctrines, be they camouflaged as systemic theories or not, is what their followers have actually achieved. No matter whether we are talking about Indian, Chinese, transcendental, or other metaphysical concepts—what are their accomplishments? I, for one, am not impressed. Even if we consider that there have been historical high cultures which were allegedly based on these philosophical or religious foundations that are recommended to us again, one question should be permitted: Was everyday life really influenced by these philosophical-religious doctrines, and if so, to what extent?

Why did these cultures perish, if their spiritual foundations were so superior, so much better than ours, to the extent that they are recommended to us now? Why is these peoples' recent history, their economic, social, and political situation, anything but impressive? And even if our overall judgment is positive, would it be possible at all for us to transplant those doctrines to a totally different tradition, apply them to a totally different mentality?

I have always had my serious doubts about Japan's owing its economic success of the past 30 to 40 years to Far Eastern culture and mentality, and I am having the same doubts about modern-day China. In my view, a much simpler and more convincing explanation for their achievements lies in the fact that these countries, after decades and even centuries of political and social maldevelopment, had reached a point where they had to face a few truths, and that they then adopted the very philosophies and approaches which in the Western world led us if not to Paradise, then to a way and forms of living that their populations found much more desirable than what they had at the time. Whatever the Japanese economy has accomplished, it has accomplished by means of Western approaches—methods that the Japanese have demonstrably adopted from the West. These approaches had often been developed in the West but, having largely been ignored here, were implemented more rigidly and effectively by the Japanese. The same goes for China.


## The Potential of the Systems Approach

As we have seen, anyone studying and dealing with systemic and systems-based management had better watch out for potential aberrations. Properly understood, however, systemic management holds considerable potential. We will simply need it, and those that master it will make substantial progress. They will be able to master much more complexity, and they will also achieve greater personal and economic success.

Systems- and cybernetics-based approaches and findings help you, for example, come up with a better and more precise assessment of given situations and their future evolution. It is largely due to my many years of studying complex systems that in the late 1980s I arrived at a completely different—and eventually much more correct—assessment regarding probable developments to be expected in the 1990s than almost anyone else that spoke or published on the subject.[10] Neither did I join in with the universal euphoria about Europe, nor did I share the general view on the future of the collapsed communist world. From a systems-cybernetic perspective, I was fully aware that these hopes could not come true unless there was a miracle. It was equally obvious to me that the entire global economy would experience major turbulences in the 1990s and that there would be severe downturns, if not worse.[11] As a result I was able to forecast that in the economic and thus the political and social climate, changes for the worse were much more likely than the scenarios drawn up by most economists, futurologists, managers, and politicians, who had basically predicted lots of good things for the 1990s. If you read the headlines and publications of that time you will quickly realize that none of the predictions have come true; much to the contrary. The study of complex systems allowed even more forecasts: that

---

10 See, e.g., my book *Krisengefahren in der Weltwirtschaft* (co-author: D. Steiler), Zurich, 1991, p. 13.

11 I had expected this as early as in the late 1980s, but even systems theory and cybernetics do not allow for such precision, even though this forecast proved correct for Japan.

Europe was not going to work like that (neither in the given nor in the planned structures), that the U.N. would face a severe crisis and either become meaningless or break apart. In both these cases (and many more), a rough system analysis sufficed to show that the architecture of these systems was wrong and that they lacked crucial tools and regulations to ensure coherence and integration.

Complex systems have their own laws. If you are aware of them you will be able to understand, explain, and forecast their basic options and probable evolution much better than, say, with the techniques and tools used in economics and trend research. You will be able to organize and direct them more effectively, and in a certain sense, to better control them—if that is what you want.

Most importantly, once you have studied and understood complex systems you will find it easy to abandon the naïve can-doism that so dominates the minds of a certain kind of managers and politicians, always in the erroneous belief that they are masters of their systems. It will enable you to judge quite reliably whether or not an enterprise will be successful with a certain strategy, and under what circumstances. It was clear to see back then—and my view, which I expressed quite early, is "on the record"—that some of the strategic maneuvers in business would fail and thus produce severe consequences, even though at the time they met with general applause from the "experts" and were presented as showcase examples of entrepreneurial savvy and vision. There is this naïve type of managers—a result of poor personnel decisions—but then there are also many others who are well aware of the complexity of the systems in and for which they do business.

Being aware of the regularities of complex systems enables you to form an educated opinion on what a system is *not* able to do, what will *not* work, and that helps eliminate the naïve belief that anything is doable. It also enables you to assess what a system *can* do and what *will* work.

Just because you have dropped the attitude that anything is doable, there is no reason whatsoever to succumb to the other, equally naïve belief that there is hardly anything or nothing you can do. That attitude, which we might call the non-doability attitude, seems to enjoy unfortunate popularity among the proponents of system management. In my opinion, neither are they right nor are they doing the cause a favor. There is, for instance, the hypothesis that social relationships (in social systems) cannot be organized by managers because they are part of the same organization.[12] Others see managers and management in the role of catalysts and facilitators, or would expect them to "give process-based suggestions, 'disturb' and irritate."[13] Well, the range of managerial behaviors does include that—amongst other things. I have occasionally used the terms "catalyst" and "cultivator" myself to express the degree of caution sometimes required, for example, in negotiations. But of course the fact that executives' repertoire should include such practices does not mean there cannot or should not be other, very directive ways of shaping things.

This would not only mean that the possibilities of shaping, changing, and even improving systems—for which I think there is solid evidence—are massively underestimated. Also, such models of managerial behavior are hardly suited to persuade executives to study systems and systemic management, on which basis they could possibly change their dysfunctional understanding of their role. There will, however, be no way around winning managers over as allies to the cause—and once again, it is for systemic and cybernetic reasons.

There are numerous examples to prove that it is very well possible for executives to change and manage systems, and to direct them in a positive and desirable sense, in a way that serves the system's interests or purpose. There have been mergers that were approached in a very professional, skilled, clever, and quite systemic way, including that of the Swiss pharma companies Ciba and Geigy in the 1960s. And it very much looks as though the most recent move, the merger of Ciba-Geigy and Sandoz, will result in a new system that in many ways holds attractive potential for success.

Every successful cooperation between companies is another case in point, and there are many of them. Systems like these do not simply emerge. There are decisions to be made, and they are made by managers in their function as members of legal or statutory bodies. Even if implementation requires plenty of self-regulation and self-organization—and it is often (or rather: always) deliberately organized that way—the fact remains that this has to be preceded by some decision-making.

---

12 See, e.g., H.R. Fischer, "Management by Bye?" in: C. Schmilz, P.W. Gester, and B. Heitger (eds.), *Managerie—I. Jahrbuch für Systemisches Denken und Handeln im Management*, Heidelberg, 1992, p. 28.

13 See Schmilz, p. 67, who referred to this as "stimulation mode" and contrasted it with what he called the "control mode" (author's translations).

Of course there is no denying that for every positive example there are many more negative ones. But that, precisely, proves my point that these things can be done the right way—, in line with system requirements—or the wrong way. By the same token, it is certainly possible to change and improve the structure and function of, say, top management—undoubtedly a social system—by appropriately designing contracts, company bylaws, and in particular one of the most effective systemic interventions: managerial pay.

Let me give you another example. Take European air traffic control, a poorly functioning system comprising several dozens of autonomous local and national centers which, although interconnected and interacting, mainly produce plenty of cumbersome complexity. There certainly is no doubt that this system could be changed—which would have enormous positive effects on almost every system variable (except for a somewhat childish variety of national prestige). In the U.S., a new solution has long been implemented, and the same will happen in Europe, although it will take a bit longer—again, for systemic reasons. Technical structures and conditions play a crucial role here; yet the fact remains that it is a social or socio-technical system.

These examples should suffice to show that systems and their structures can indeed be shaped, even on a daily basis, which sometimes requires more and sometimes less systemic know-how, and it goes without saying that mistakes can happen. So when systems are shaped in this way, this clearly changes the conditions under which self-regulation, self-organization and a further evolution of the system take place, and it also contributes to the management of social relationships in a system—not in detail, but in their patterns. That has always been the meaning of "control" in a cybernetic sense, be it cybernetics of the first or second order.

So it *is* possible to act and do something—and I feel that this also implies an obligation. That does not mean you can act everywhere and any time, nor does it mean that your actions will always be faultless.

As I said earlier, business and society are currently undergoing one of the greatest transformations of all times. Almost all systems have fundamental changes coming. Almost everything we do and how we do it will change over the next 10 to 15 years: the way we produce and consume; the way we distribute and finance; the way we do research, teach, learn, and innovate—that is, the way we gain, disseminate, and use knowledge. The work we do and how we do it will all change.

All of this happens through and by means of organizations—that is, systems that are often difficult if not impossible to comprehend. That is why certain reactions of people are easy to predict. Some will resign and wish they could return to the romantic environment of the closed tribal societies of ancient times; some may even make aggressive attempts to bring them back. Others will be fascinated, dreaming of new worlds to come. Yet others will begin to coolly take advantage of these developments, perhaps use or abuse them.

Whatever one's attitude may be, the fact remains that we are going to have those systems. We will not be able to ignore or escape them. It will be up to systemic management to make sure these systems serve people, not the other way round. We will need system architects, system regulators, and system organizers, and not only will they need to know a lot about complex systems, but they will need ethics and morals suited to the complexity of these systems, in order to recognize potential abuse early on and prevent it.

One of the most important and most difficult issues to be solved will be the question of *responsibility*. How can we effectively implant responsibility in a complex system, what does it mean, what does it have to mean? Solving this issue has to take top priority. This also includes the responsibilities of the systemic consultant and of the therapist. There may be no *general* solution for these questions, but there are definitely *specific* solutions for individual situations, and a cumulation of individual cases would be a step forward. Effective responsibility will also have to include *liability*, as otherwise we would never get beyond the point of mere appeals.

As we learn from the quote from Gregory Bateson, which has headed this book since the first edition, a good understanding of complex systems can also be put to terrible use. Sometimes I cannot help the impression that those most knowledgeable about systems include the "Godfathers" in Mafia-like organizations and the masterminds of drug cartels and terrorist organizations. We just cannot afford to ignore the efficiency of these systems, and it is common knowledge that this efficiency does not spring from intuition alone; rather, these organizations have experts on their payrolls. It goes without saying that this is abuse.

It is all the more important for us to have large numbers of managers, in the broadest sense of the word, with profound knowledge about complex systems and who use this knowledge in a responsible and ethical manner. No philosophy, no theory, no discipline is immune to abuse, and as long as we do not have computers capable of taking ethical decisions and bearing responsibility for these decisions, it is humans who take and are responsible for them. I therefore think it is extremely important that the knowledge about complex systems is disseminated as widely as possible, so that a maximum number of people will be able to gain a better understanding of them and competently work on their design.

# 0. Introduction: Construction and Evolution[*]

> "... we create the world that we perceive, not because there is no
> reality outside our heads, but because we select and edit the reality
> we see to conform to our beliefs about
> what sort of world we live in"
>
> *Mark Engel*

## 0.1 Premises, Frames of Reference, and Illusory Worlds

Depending on the premises that a scientific discipline uses with regard to its object of research and the problems studied, that discipline will come to different conclusions and even maintain a totally different theoretical understanding. It is normal for assumptions concerning the nature of the object and its central issues to appear so obvious, even trivial, that they are often perceived to be unproblematic. Many of these assumptions are not based on explicit knowledge but tacitly accepted. Some cannot even be put in words because they are implicitly inherent in the way we get our bearings in the world, in particular in the language we use to describe the structure of the world.

The dispute among scientific schools of thought can often be traced back to different basic assumptions, which their representatives may use subconsciously. The conclusions drawn by opposing parties and the resulting recommendations may be utterly irreconcilable and contradictory, and related discussions tend to be highly emotional because both parties proceed from the assumption—which in itself is based on assumptions—that they are referring to the same object, while upon thorough analysis it often turns out that a common understanding is impossible because they are talking about different things.

We tend to fall into a semantic trap here in that we automatically assume that identical names are used for identical objects. Alfred Korzybsk[8] is

---

* A very condensed version of this introduction entitled "Two Kinds of Management Theories: Construction and Evolution" was published in H. Siegwart and G. Probst (eds.), *Mitarbeiterführung und gesellschaftlicher Wandel*, a festschrift for Charles Lattmann, Bern/Stuttgart, 1983.
8 Korzybski (Science).

known for his observation that a map is not identical to the respective territory and a name is not the same as the object it refers to. These observations only appear trivial. Together with the laws of human communication, ignoring these insights can cause us to create illusionary worlds which—and this is what is hellish about them—are not recognizable as such.

This is due to the fact that recognizing reality is more difficult than generally assumed, in particular because the human brain has the ability to construct different realities, each of which can be consistent in itself, so that under certain conditions we are unable to see which construction is the best. Rather than having a "picture" of reality, we have to learn to recognize it. This is true for both the human organism and science. Wherever we deal with a reality that can basically be shaped, and wherever we face the phenomenon that people think reality is what they consider to be real, the question as to what premises result in what constructions of reality and how we can recognize illusory worlds gains particular importance.

These questions are probably even more important to social sciences than they are to natural sciences. When people think that reality is what they believe to be real, they will act accordingly. A key aspect of the "social" is that, as a result of our expectations and opinions on our fellow humans, we act in a way that conforms to these opinions. That, in turn, influences others' expectations, opinions, behavior, and so on, which enables socially constructed realities to emerge. In conjunction with modern-day technology, these constructed realities can then become *the* reality for us in those parts of the world where things can be shaped, and they may grossly conflict with other areas so far unaffected by our construction. Sciences with a strong application focus have particular responsibility in this context because the "images" of the world that they convey increasingly influence people in their actions—in particular when acting on behalf of organizations.

Large parts of business economics seem to be based on such deceptive views of the word, and for various reasons they are impossible or at least difficult to debunk. The main reason is that it depends on the nature of our cognitive tools what kinds of insights we are able to gain. One of these tools is language—above all, the structure of the language game prevalent in a science, of our frame of reference (or universe of discourse) we impose on an object and in whose light we see that object. Another aspect is the structure of language in a broader sense, the structure commonly referred to as object language or meta-language. This refers to the logical layering of language due to which it is not completely impossible to transcend a frame of reference, difficult as it may be to break it. Confusing the object- with the meta-level of language is the main reason why certain phenomena cannot be recognized.

Here, the frame of reference is defined as a system of premises that together form an "image" of reality, which may or may not be consistent in itself. A frame of reference is comparable to a system of coordinates, defining what is considered relevant; how perceptions, observations, statements, allegations, and so forth should be interpreted; what kind of question is or is not "permissible," and so on. What I refer to as a "frame of reference" here is sometimes given other names, such as framework, background knowledge, image of the world, world view, or universe of discourse. Despite all the variations that the paradigm concept according to T.S. Kuhn comprises, the core of this concept seems to correspond to what I call frame of reference.

Another enormous difficulty we face when discussing the usefulness and appropriateness of a certain frame of reference is a philosophical one. This is because the discussion inevitably leads us to ontological issues: As these are deemed inadmissible from some epistemological standpoints, many scientists believe these issues have to be avoided in strictly scientific procedures. My view is a different one: I believe that much of our thinking on the nature of the object of cognition is empirical rather than philosophical, in that we actually develop an empirical theory regarding the nature of the problem under study. Consequently, at least some of the premises initially mentioned represent not logical axioms but empirical statements. Again, due to a certain use of the word "premise" the word is often exclusively used for *logical* premises of the kind discussed by scientists when doing fundamental research on mathematics or formal logic. Those kinds of premises represent unquestionable assumptions of an often tautological nature (such as $p \rightarrow p$), or assumptions of a defining nature. While in the empirical sciences we probably face quite a number of premises of that nature, too, a considerable share of premises is purely empirical and can be validated by empirical means.

## 0.2 Systems-Oriented Management Theory

Business administration studies seem to be dominated by a set of empirical key assumptions which on closer inspection appear rather questionable. Some of them are clearly wrong.

Admittedly, the term "business administration" itself can be understood in a range of ways. It would lead us too far to discuss the whole spectrum of teachings and their widely varying viewpoints. This book focuses on the kind that thinks of itself as a *theory of management*. The question as to whether it is correct and useful at all to consider management theory one variety of business administration has deliberately been excluded from the analysis. There is plenty of evidence suggesting that management theory should be considered an independent and entirely different discipline, at least compared to the business administration theory taught in German-speaking countries, which largely presents itself as a sister discipline of economics.

One key point to remember is that in business enterprises, economic problems and their solutions never occur on their own. They are always linked to problems of *business management*. This immediately raises the question as to what "business management" actually is, as the assertion I just made is only true if we assume a very specific idea of business management applies. In the following paragraphs I will try to carve out the basic assumptions underlying this idea, in order to avoid the semantic trap of calling different things by the same name.

Some remarks on the historical development of management theory may facilitate readers' understanding. In 1968, in the context of a reform of St. Gallen University's Business Administration course, Hans Ulrich published his book *Die Unternehmung als produktives soziales System* ["The enterprise as a productive social system"]. The business administration theory it described, and to which a sizeable number of university faculty had contributed, was designed as a *general theory of business enterprise*—or so the subtitle read—a theory that explicitly referred to general systems theory and cybernetics as its basis and viewed the enterprise as a multidimensional entity. It was as early as in that book that business economics was perceived as the theory of *shaping and managing systems*.[9]

---

9 Ulrich (Unternehmung), p. 45.

In the years to follow, the so-called "systems approach" was studied by PhD students, scientific assistants, and postdoctoral candidates, who attempted to further expand and substantiate it as well as drive its application in practice. Ulrich started from the assumption that business administration, being a sister discipline of economics, had only limited potential in terms of helping to solve real-life problems. Specifically, questions of corporate management were largely excluded, which was mainly due to the fact that problems were reduced to their economic dimension. In Ulrich's view, however, the *management* of organizations was the most important problem of all, and he essentially judged the usefulness of business studies based on their ability to help solve problems of corporate management.

For Ulrich, business management could not be reduced to questions of personnel management; his main interest was focused on the comprehensive, practice-oriented, and viable design and control of the enterprise as such. This was obviously a multidimensional problem which could not be solved from a merely economic perspective, so executive training had to include aspects above and beyond what business studies offered.

Seeing a business enterprise (and ultimately any social institution) as a complex, multidimensional, open, and dynamic *system* seemed to be a fruitful approach that opened up a series of new perspectives, raised new issues, and, despite its abstract foundations, seemed to come closer to executives' real-life problems and situation than the purely economistic business studies did. Due to this approach, business administration seemed to gain social relevance instead of degenerating to a purely pragmatic artificial doctrine. On the contrary, it appeared likely that an attempt at providing it with a scientific-theoretical foundation would render compelling results.

When the issue of business *management*—in the sense of shaping and directing the enterprise as a whole—took center stage, this raised new and different questions: first, because this view also included the way an enterprise is embedded and positioned in its relevant environment (such as markets, political and social environment, etc.), which could not be assumed to be known a priori but remained to be determined; second, because it was clear from the start that the enterprise had to be understood as a part of a much larger network of institutions which also had a layered structure and that reducing that network to the enterprise as such would be an unacceptable simplification, even a fundamental mistake in defining the system. And third, because in the course of refining the approach it became very clear that the problems faced by the people acting in and on behalf of an enterprise were obviously very different from the way classical business administration assumed them to be.

In particular, when an essential characteristic of enterprises—their complexity and dynamic nature—was taken seriously, rather than being ignored by reductionist assumptions and the *ceteris paribus* clause, it was obvious that many of the issues that classical business administration theory focused on were of minor importance or represented rather specific cases. It also became clear that some highly relevant problems had received little or no attention so far. Examples abound, and they start with very basic questions: Is it possible at all to truly understand business management when regarding it from a profit maximization or optimization perspective? Does the question of factor combination really present itself in the way described in business administration theory? For instance, do the pricing models and hypotheses discussed in industrial marketing have any practical relevance at all? Are investments really judged against the criteria suggested by investment theory?

As is generally known, a key element of conventional approaches is the notion of optimizing business operations or decision-making under certain conditions, and the typical approach to this is to use economic, quantifiable parameters. But do the assumed conditions really exist? Does it suffice to use economic-quantitative parameters? Observations in practice suggest that there are many other factors of much greater importance to business management, and they rarely have to do with optimization. As a matter of fact, it is often quite an achievement to get things under control.

Management—and this is something that various Anglo-Saxon authors, most notably Peter Drucker, realized early—is not so much about optimizing things as it is about keeping them in balance. Analyses do play an important part, but what matters much more is the integration and synthesis of various aspects; also, developing a set of non-conflicting objectives is much less important than the tireless effort to reconcile conflicting intentions and expectations in everyday business. Quite possibly, it would be much better to consider management to be a permanent striving to get and keep a very complex system under control: a system characterized by probabilism and constantly changing elements, with regard to both their state and—much more fundamentally—their kind and number; a system that is difficult to influence, often only with undesirable side effects, due to its very own dynamics.

So the key task consists in controlling a system, and this tasks varies along with the structure and mechanisms of that system. By the same token, ensuring or improving the controllability of systems is one of the most significant design challenges for managers. Consequently, the shaping and controlling of complex dynamic systems is the overall perspective of systems-oriented management theory.

Over time it became increasingly clear that the step from economics-focused business administration to a systems-focused management theory would have much further-reaching impact than the fathers of this new approach might have been able to imagine. To meet the high demands of a wholistic, multidimensional enterprise and business management theory, it was and still is necessary to include certain areas of knowledge that have absolutely nothing to do with business administration. In fact, they cannot even be counted among the economic and social sciences.

Using the term "system," which is largely formal and certainly very broad, and trying to build a corresponding business economics theory on this foundation has been both an advantage and a hindrance. The advantage is that the orientation by general systems theory has enabled a much broader perspective, so that even sciences that had formerly been excluded were now explored in the quest for possible solutions to business problems. A sizeable number of papers that have since been written on systems-oriented business economics in a broader sense, both in St. Gallen and elsewhere, have provided numerous examples of authors engaging with disciplines that must appear rather exotic from a classical business administration standpoint. The most noteworthy example is cybernetics in all its varieties, from regulation theory to bio- and neuro-cybernetics and on to the research on artificial intelligence, linguistics, and evolution theory.

Major obstacles have resulted from the fact that the study of these disciplines often involves misunderstandings. Efforts to adopt concepts, theories, and findings from totally different disciplines in business administration have involved various difficulties: Both the relevance of those disciplines for the newly emerging systems-oriented business economics and the correct understanding of those new or different disciplines raised a number of questions.

Among other things, these difficulties also triggered a research project to develop a so-called "systems methodology," which was carried out from

1972 to 1974 at the Institute of Business Studies at St. Gallen University.[10] The aim was to develop immediately applicable methods and tools, in the sense of a basic procedure, as well as rules, principles, techniques, and so on for the shaping and controlling of complex systems—proceeding from the status quo in systems-oriented management theory. In rather general terms, the basic idea was to create a methodology for *managing* complex systems, explicitly taking into account that dealing with them in reality would always involve considerable imperfections as compared to the standard of logical reasoning, that our efforts would often remain far from the theoretical optimum, and that the criterion for success would usually have to be whether the system could be influenced enough to produce a halfway satisfactory result while key characteristics of the system, such as its adaptability, would remain unaltered.

The outcome of this project was based on my attempt to integrate several very different areas of human knowledge which, while at first seeming to have little in common, on closer scrutiny gave us reason to hope that they might be able to contribute to the solution of the problem posed (for details see Vol. 1 of the book)—an attempt that might have seemed a bit daring and which provoked some criticism of various aspects.

One of the key elements was Popper's Theory of Knowledge in its 1972 version; that is, including and with references to his then newly published book *Objective Knowledge*. As I had thought to establish in part A of the mentioned book, Popper's epistemology—which he basically considered to be a *problem-solving methodology*—is particularly relevant for solving problems that arise in the context of shaping and controlling complex systems. I still believe that Popper's philosophy and epistemology, correctly understood, provide an essential basis for management practice in social institutions. Studying the scientific writings of Friedrich von Hayek then confirmed my view. To Hayek I owe probably my most important insights for the purposes of this book, with regard to both the way complex systems function and the question as to what requirements a theory on complex systems would have to meet.[11]

---

10 Peter Gomez, Fredmund Malik, and Karl-Heinz Oeller: Systemmethodik: Grundlagen einer Methodik zur Erforschung und Gestaltung komplexer soziotechnischer Systeme, 2 volumes, Bern/Stuttgart, 1975.

11 A very convincing explanation, in my opinion, of why Popper's methodology is so relevant to rational practice can be found in a book written by Hans Albert, which was published after the main sections of the manuscript of this book had been completed: Traktat über rationale Praxis, Tuebingen, 1978. Further important arguments are presented in a

Further key elements were certain cybernetic disciplines, and in particular the writings by Stafford Beer, Gordon Pask, Ross Ashby, and Heinz von Foerster. They seemed essential in that they went far beyond the concept of cybernetics that prevailed in the German-speaking part of the world, specifically with regard to the topic of high complexity.

This broader concept of cybernetics is based on three articles published as early as 1958: "Organic Control and the Cybernetic Method" by Gordon Pask[12], "The Irrelevance of Automation" by Stafford Beer[13], and an essay by Heinz von Foerster entitled "Some Aspects in the Design of Biological Computers"[14]. One of the key objects of study in this type of cybernetic research is the free organism in its natural environment, with its ability to adapt to constantly changing conditions, to learn, and to evolve—or perhaps, in more general terms: to live successfully. Another key source was Ashby's book *Design for a Brain*, in the first chapter of which he formulates the problem as follows: "Our problem is, first, to identify the nature of the change which shows as learning, and secondly, to find why such changes should tend to cause better adaptation for the whole organism."[15]

These first attempts, which were rather rudimental, were developed further by said authors in a way that is quite remarkable and which has considerable significance for this book. Pask's thinking laid the groundwork for a comprehensive theory on learning systems, based on the model of a freely evolving conversation process.[16] Stafford Beer's thinking found its preliminary culmination point in his Viable Systems Model,[17] which is presented in the first part of this book; his cybernetics theory has provided an essential foundation for my work. Heinz von Foerster was doubtlessly one of the great pioneers of systems theory and cybernetic thinking. His work is so diverse and multifaceted it is impossible to sum it up in just a few words. An

---

1980 epilog to the German original version of Hans Albert's Treatise on Critical Reason ["Traktat über kritische Vernunft"], 4th edition, Tuebingen, 1980. The epilog is entitled "Kritizismus und seine Kritiker" ["Criticism and its critics"].

12 Gordon Pask: Organic Control and the Cybernetic Method, *Cybernetica* 1 (1958), pp. 155–173.

13 Stafford Beer: The Irrelevance of Automation, *Cybernetica* 1 (1958), pp. 280-295.

14 Heinz von Foerster: Some Aspects in the Design of Biological Computers, proceedings of the 2nd International Congress on Cybernetics, Namur 1958, Paris 1960.

15 W.R. Ashby: Design for a Brain: The Origin of Adaptive Behaviour, London, 1952, p. 12.

16 G. Pask: The Cybernetics of Human Learning and Performance, London, 1975; Conversation, Cognition and Learning: A Cybernetic Theory and Methodology, Elsevier Press, 1974.

17 S. Beer: The Heart of Enterprise, London, 1979.

insight of particular significance for this book is his cybernetic epistemology for observing (as opposed to observed) systems.[18] The gist of it is that the perceiving subject and its cognitive apparatus have to be factored in to the explanation if we want to understand the cognitive process, its outcomes, and the behavior resulting from it. This school of thinking coincides with the most recent developments in the field of biology: evolutionary epistemology and the theory of autopoietic systems, which attempt to view life as a self-producing (not *re*producing) cognitive or ordering process.[19]

I am mentioning these developments because, too often, general systems theory is believed to be just a special branch of mathematics (which it is indeed—among other things) while cybernetics is equated with regulation theory, in particular the kind that focuses on systems with known or identifiable transfer functions (which it includes—among other things). For complex social systems, however, the much more relevant cybernetic concepts are those developed around organic control.

Another significant source for the systems methodology project was Jean Piaget's work on genetic psychology. I found Piaget's thinking to be clearly related to the concepts of organic cybernetics, a view that was confirmed only recently by a compelling article by Heinz von Foerster.[20]

In my opinion, Piaget's work provides an essential empirical complement to Popper's epistemology. It is also a major step towards empirical epistemology of the kind formulated by Warren McCulloch—another great cybernetics pioneer—in the 1940s. McCulloch postulated that philosophical views must ultimately be supported by corresponding insights on anatomy and on the function of organisms' cognitive apparatuses, or brains and central nervous systems.[21] This postulate is impressively confirmed by studies conducted by Eccles[22] and, of course, by evolutionary and biological epistemology.

---

18 H. von Foerster: Objects: Tokens for (Eigen-)Behaviours, ASC Cybernetics Forum 8 (3&4), 1976, pp. 91–96.

19 See, e.g.: R. Riedl: Die Ordnung des Lebendigen: Systembedingungen der Evolution, Hamburg/ Berlin, 1975; and R. Riedl: Biologie der Erkenntnis, Hamburg/Berlin, 1980; as well as H.R. Maturana and J.F. Varela, Autopoiesis and Cognition, Dordrecht, 1980.

20 See footnote 17.

21 See his essay collection Embodiments of Mind, MIT Press, 1965, which he had started as early as in 1943, and in particular the introduction to that book by Seymour Papert, where connections to Piaget's theory are also highlighted very well.

22 See J.C. Eccles: The Human Psyche, Berlin/Heidelberg/New York, 1980; Eccles: The Human Mystery, l.c., 1979; Eccles: Pacing Reality, l.c., 1970; as well as K.R. Popper and J.C. Eccles: The Self and Its Brain, l.c., 1977.

Furthermore, I applied the TOTE concept and the associated theory of cognitive processes by Miller/Galanter/Pribram, with obvious links to both cybernetics and epistemology, as well as Goerge Kelley's Theory of Personal Constructs, which is an interesting attempt at interpreting cognitive and learning processes as the formation of a system.

The result of these efforts at integrating different approaches was a problem-solving method comprising several steps. It started by stating a problem in Popper's sense while limiting it to one category: *control problems*. The basic idea behind it was that managers, as mentioned before, ultimately always face the same question: how to gain and keep control of the area (or system) they are in charge of. In the course of that research it became quite obvious that the word "control" was used in a very specific sense. Briefly and metaphorically speaking, it is roughly the same meaning as in expressions such as "being in control of an orchestra" or "mastering a language or sport."

If the basic problem was assumed to be control over a system in the sense outlined, the next key component of the methodology was obvious: The answer to the question as to whether and to what extent it is possible to have control over a system is largely dependent on the characteristics of the systems involved—the system you want to get under control and the system that is faced with that task. Some systems are very easy to control, for example because they are simple and uncomplicated; others, perhaps by nature, may not lend themselves to any form of human control.

The problem seemed determined mainly by the complexity of the systems involved, and by the question as to what conditions offered so much as a chance of bringing a system under control. In the context of that research project, this led us to thoroughly study the characteristics and nature of systems, as well as the typical approaches to controlling them, or *control models*. The final key element of the methodology was to define actions that, considering the nature of the system and its control mechanisms, would offer the greatest chances of influencing that system. In line with the cycle thinking so typical of cybernetics, the effects of those actions—or rather, our corresponding expectations—were starting points for defining further control measures. Our concept of the underlying problem, which provided the basis for this systems methodology, might best be illustrated by some examples:

1. *Herding a flock*: Depending on what kind of animals we are dealing with, the terrain, the weather, the dangers they are exposed to, etc., solving this problem in detail will present greater or lesser difficulties. Keeping a herd

of half-wild horses under control is one thing, and herding a flock of sheep is another; both require specific methods and tools. Still, the basic problem—keeping a herd under control—is clearly visible in both cases.

2. *Training a mixed group of big cats*: Again, the overall strategy and the behaviors, techniques, and tricks to be used depend on the nature of the system and its elements. The key is to maintain control at all times, using a maximum of concentration and physical and mental presence. The animal trainer needs to adequately respond to a variety of influences and disturbances, his goal being to perform the entire act while staying alive and healthy and taking care not to ruin his animals.

3. *Ecological balance*: In nature, the interaction of different species of animals and plants creates states of equilibrium that are typical of ecotopes. A special feature here is the absence of a person to lead and guide the process, such as the shepherd and the animal tamer in the above examples. Instead there is some kind of system-immanent control resulting from the way interactions take place. This form of control is particularly important for the present paper. In part II it will be discussed and explained in detail.

4. *Building and maintaining a happy family*: The cohesion and "climate" in a family depend on a range of factors. In the course of a lifetime the task keeps presenting itself in new ways, depending on the influences and events in the family members' lives. Nevertheless, the pattern underlying the general problem is easy to see.

5. *Business management*: As mentioned in the beginning when I sketched out the evolution of a systems approach in business economics, the problem of managing a business demonstrates the same characteristics as the other varieties of the problem. Of course there will be very different variables and influencing factors compared to other examples; but if we abstract from the specifics of individual situations, the same basic pattern of cybernetic problems is clearly visible.

The systems methodology published in 1975 was described in very general terms. There were but few references to practical problems associated with the management of institutions. One of the reasons was that many issues cannot be addressed in a research project of limited duration; another resulted from a dilemma that often arises in dealing with systems-theoretical approaches: the question as to whether statements should be kept general to include any kind of system, or limited to a certain category of systems, such as enterprises, in order to address their problems as precisely as possible.

In view of the very general nature of systems methodology at the time, it seemed advisable to launch a follow-up project to clarify and operationalize its contents for the field of business management. The project plan comprised three separate but closely linked subprojects: In the first and second we were to apply systems methodology to problems from operations management and strategic management, respectively, to make it clearer and more specific. In the third subproject we were to develop a special cybernetic communication system, initially sketched out roughly by Beer and based on specifically designed indices and parameters. We would thus be able to process information in a way that was compatible with the structures of the viable system.

The members of the research group—P. Gomez, who was to focus on operations management issues,[23] K.H. Oeller, who was to develop a set of indices,[24] and myself—agreed that it might be useful to write a common chapter for all three subprojects. To provide a foundation for all further activities on the subject, this chapter was to describe a cybernetic model which we considered particularly helpful and which would serve as a reference for our subsequent development work.

These considerations were perfectly in line with the concept of systems methodology: After all, one of its key elements is the insistence on modeling the respective problem in terms of the options available to the problem-solver for steering and influencing it—which essentially means you identify and describe all the control-relevant mechanisms driving or causing the problem situation.

The cybernetic model we found to be the most advanced and richest in structure was Stafford Beer's *Viable Systems Model* (VSM). It seemed to offer three essential advantages: First, it implicitly or explicitly included the largest possible number of control-relevant questions; second, it allowed us to neatly localize and categorize operational and strategic problems and divide the research work accordingly in our group; third, in the context of his model Beer had developed a few intriguing approaches we could work with when developing a set of indices. By using this model as a common basis, we could hope to achieve a maximum of integration of our insights on the partial

---

23 See P. Gomez: Die kybernetische Gestaltung des Operations Managements, Bern/Stuttgart, 1978.

24 K.H. Oeller: Grundlagen und Entwicklung kybernetischer Kennzahlensysteme, 1976, manuscript as yet unpublished.

problems we worked on, based on a shared structural understanding and, along with it, a common language.

The result of these shared ideas is the chapter preceding each of our three papers, of which I wrote paragraphs 11 through 14 while P. Gomez was in charge of the 15th and K.H. Oeller the 16th paragraph.

However, integrating such diverse fields of human knowledge is by no means the only difficulty one encounters when setting out to advance systems-oriented management theory with its rather ambitious objectives. Over time it became clear that there were more obstacles. To begin with, we had to learn to really understand the world of practitioners, capture it with scientific means, and finally, after numerous transformation processes which might not be retraceable later, make a contribution to the solution of practical problems—again, in a practice-oriented way. We were always aware, of course, that the focus was not to be on the current understanding of practice, or even a certain kind of practice, but that we had to take a much broader view. Although we never undervalued the everyday understanding of things and attached great importance to it, we were also aware that any *science* of the design and control of productive social systems would have to transcend and challenge practice, offer solutions where problems had yet to be identified, and discover problems where obvious solutions appeared to exist.

A key criterion, however, has always been the practical relevance or application focus. This very criterion involved considerable difficulties, as it soon turned out that the systems-oriented perspective on business administration, which is strongly influenced by systems theory and cybernetics, initially was not understood by practitioners. Hence, it was not enough to develop a system-oriented business administration theory; we also had to understand the mechanisms for transferring this new theory into practice. Related questions included: How do practitioners view the scientific community? What do they expect of it? How do practitioners view their own activities? How are knowledge, thoughts, behaviors, even entire paradigms adopted and implemented in practice?

In the course of dealing with such questions, we quickly realized that in both practice and science very specific assumptions and beliefs prevailed which basically resulted from the economic environment of the 1950s, 60s, and early 70s.

These were deeply rooted assumptions influenced by the accomplishments of economically stable decades, and they concerned the basic possibilities of doing business, the prerequisites for successful management, and the "right" methods and principles of corporate governance. Many of them were not compatible with the basic assumptions used in systems-oriented management theory and thus prevented it from spreading further. In line with scientific approaches, system-oriented management theory attempted to deal with the *generalized* case, while practitioners were focused on the specific case and the current economic situation. And since this economic situation in its fundamental structure spanned a whole generation, the illusion took hold that the particular and the general case were identical and that the methods and principles useful in the particular context—the upturn following the Second World War—provided universal solutions to general problems.

This trend among practitioners had its analogy in the scientific community, where concepts and thought patterns were also built on very specific assumptions, as I hope to demonstrate at a later point. In a sound economic environment this kind of thinking may be justified and acceptable; however, it can be misleading, even dangerous, once underlying assumptions are no longer correct.

These historical beliefs, which back in those times were confirmed by visible accomplishments year after year, have recently begun to erode. More and more people are beginning to realize that we live in a period of structural change and fundamental turnaround.[25] Although this realization has yet to reach the cognitive level, the changes emerging in corporate balance sheets and nations' insolvency statistics are clearly having an impact. There is a general awareness that the foundations of business and society, which were long considered unshakeable, may soon undergo fundamental change, and that essential conditions for a certain kind of business management have ceased to exist. As a result, for the first time since the great economic upswing there is a real chance of the true nature of that social function we call management being thoroughly revisited.

Yet, a glance at the past decade's literature on strategic management issues reveals that certain ways of thinking—notably, the premises or frames of references discussed at the beginning of this chapter—still prevail. Even worse: The fact that such constructed realities have a tendency toward perpetuation prevents people from realizing they are caught in a mental prison.

Although a more intense study of strategic problems has provided a series of valuable insights, one key phenomenon continues to be left out of

---

25 Kneschaurek (Unternehmer).

the equation: the *issue of complexity*. Depending on whether you assume circumstances to be complex or simple, strategic problems will manifest themselves in very different ways—and the same is true, of course, for their solutions. Nevertheless, my observation that the issue of complexity is largely disregarded in writings on strategic management issues also applies to a remarkable share of management literature in general.

Depending on how the issue of complexity is dealt with, there are two very different types of management theory, which I will briefly outline in the following paragraphs, as the clear distinction between them is of fundamental importance for the understanding of this book. One kind is still dominant, yet I consider it outdated and even dangerous, and I believe it to be one of the main causes of the difficulties we are currently facing in business and society.

The second type of management theory seems to contain at least the seed of an opportunity and, due to a deeper insight into the true social nature of humankind and society, more effectively contribute to solving the problems of our time—whereas the other type of management theory only claims to be based on behavioral and social sciences. In fact, as the first kind applies biased or even misunderstood criteria for scientific scrutiny, it resorts to forms of social sciences that are actually antisocial at heart in that they slavishly copy the concepts and methods of natural sciences, and even asocial when it comes to their practical application and its consequences.

This first type of management theory is a result of the *Pretense of Knowledge*,[26] as Friedrich von Hayek so accurately called and described it: humankind's premature and illusory assumption that it is possible to get anything under control, no matter what the degree of detail, if only enough time and effort are invested, along with the superstitious belief that basically anything is possible and that every problem has a solution. As long as this illusion was nourished by the achievements of an era, based on an unparalleled coincidence of favorable factors, and as long as the consequences of disregarding systemic laws and relationships were not visible, it was virtually impossible for the second type of management theory to meet with attention or interest.

---

26 See, e.g., F. von Hayek: The Errors of Constructivism and The Pretence of Knowledge, both in New Studies in Philosophy, Politics, Economics and the History of Ideas, London/Chicago, 1978.

Meanwhile, chances have increased that humankind will learn to accept the limits to our knowledge, reason, and power, and that we will therefore use these tools more prudently and more effectively. We are just beginning to understand that there are other realities besides those conveyed by our educational system, which is itself incapable of learning; we are slowly beginning to understand the systemically interconnected nature of events; it is increasingly clear that the methods and ways of thinking which appear to be the most scientific are actually the least suited to help us understand the world, and that they instead create pseudo-insights that are not much better than historical myths.

## 0.3 Two Types of Management Theory

The changes we are experiencing do not only concern the world of business. We are not solely and perhaps not even primarily dealing with what is currently dominating the public debate and especially the media: the issue of economic environment or economic cycles. It is remarkable how much this debate is based on the assumption that we are dealing with an economic-political problem. The common belief seems to be that changing one or several of a set of economic variables—inflation rate, money supply, employment, public expense, tax revenue, social security benefits, etc.—could improve the situation or at least introduce a general tendency toward the better. Accordingly, the debate is dominated by financial journalists, economists, and economic policymakers.

But the current plight can also be viewed from a totally different perspective—for instance, that of *management*, which is at least as legitimate as the economic-political one. If nothing else, our present difficulties are due to the malfunctioning or non-functioning of institutions and their interaction. The way an institution operates, however, is primarily an issue of its organization or "architecture" and the resulting behavior. It is therefore the problems of design and control, or the management of institutions, that cause a major share of our current difficulties.

I will go as far as to surmise that the difficulties of our time are probably owed to the way in which our society is organized, to its control and regulatory mechanisms and the underlying management ideas. In light of this hypothesis it is all the more remarkable that the general debate about these issues hardly ever involves management scholars; as a result, the question of how management theory could contribute to a possible solution to these problems is not even considered.

However, in order to recognize the reach of management theory and assess its potential relevance, it is necessary to distinguish between two fundamentally different approaches, or types of theory: the *constructivist-technomorphic* and the *systemic-evolutionary* approach. The two are fundamentally different: They differ in their views of what the logical and empirical characteristics of management are, about the nature of the problems addressed by management theory, about what does and does not count as solutions, and about what options people have in terms of perception and action.

If we extricate management from the prevailing context, which is primarily business-oriented and equates management with the management of business enterprises, and if we generalize management in accordance with the notion that it is about the design and control of institutions in general, or of socio-technical systems, we will ultimately realize that the basic problem of management is how to *control complexity*.

Complexity, as an empirical characteristic of socio-technical systems, refers to these systems' diversity in terms of states and sets of states, a diversity that basically results from the interaction of systems and system elements.

The greater the number and diversity of the states of a system, the more difficult the problem of management will be, because no matter what criteria you apply, not all states will usually be acceptable. After all, it is a key element of management to eliminate unacceptable states and create or maintain acceptable ones. As mentioned, this is irrespective of what criteria are applied to judge particular states and what these criteria refer to in detail. The problem's nature remains the same, for no matter what criteria are used, they all involve a distinction between desirable and undesirable, acceptable and unacceptable states. Hence, choosing certain criteria may make management easier or more difficult in the particular case, but it will not change the nature of the task, which is to get complexity under control. Usually this complexity manifests itself in an immense number and variety of system states, and the purpose of said control is to ensure that only certain states will occur while others will not.

Along these lines, the problem of how to control complexity can only be solved in two very different ways: in the *constructivist-technomorphic* or the *systemic-evolutionary* way.

The basic paradigm of the first approach, hereafter referred to as the *constructivist-technomorphic* kind of theory, is the machine in the sense used by classical mechanics.[27]

The basic idea about a machine is that it has to be designed in keeping with a specific, predefined purpose and plan, and that its function, reliability, and efficiency depend on the function and qualities of its individual parts. Another key concept is that all individual parts have to be designed according to detailed, very precise plans and assembled in a specific, predefined way. Consequently, a machine has to be well thought out and controlled in advance by its designer; nothing must remain undefined. In a similar way, machine building requires complete knowledge of all the details of all individual parts as well as complete information on the interaction of these parts. The accomplishments we have seen in the area of technology which are based on this way of thinking are so convincing that at some point people began to believe that the underlying concepts and ideas could be generalized. The result was a kind of paradigm which seemed applicable far beyond the realm of engineering, and which actually began to be transferred to other areas.

According to this paradigm, controlling complexity means creating an order (of elements, processes, etc.) that can be assessed and whose rationality can be measured against certain predefined objectives. This is done by way of deliberate human action, in such a way that the result of this action will meet those predefined intentions and objectives due to the purposefulness and rationality of said action. Also, the paradigm entails the idea that this is the only possible way to create anything useful, so that any order that meets humanly defined purposes could have only emerged through purposeful, rational, and intentional action in the sense described.

---

27 The fact that I am referring to machines in the classical mechanical sense warrants emphasis because in modern science a very different meaning of "machine" has emerged which, while encompassing the classical meaning as a special case, is not subject to the limitations inherent in it. This modern machine concept largely resulted from the developments in cybernetics and the general system sciences: In these sciences it refers to any system with a regular behavior, or one could almost say, to regular behavior as such. This means that the very qualities originally considered constitutive of the term—i.e. being determined, in the sense of physical determinism, and tied to matter—have lost all meaning or at least become special cases. This new machine concept has yet to catch on in the general debate, and particularly in common usage the classical machine concept is much more widely used, which is why it appears permissible here to use this concept to illustrate the technomorphic type of management theory.

The second type of management theory, which is referred to as *systemic-evolutionary*, works on very different assumptions. Its basic paradigm is the spontaneous,[28] self-generating order, of which the most striking example—and probably the one most obvious to common sense—is the living organism. Organisms are not really created by anybody—they evolve. The same is true for the social sphere: Here, too, we have spontaneous orders that evolve, rather than being made by anybody. They may emerge as a result of human action, but they do not necessarily conform to predefined human intentions, plans, or purposes. Still, they can serve a rational purpose even when they have not been designed with a rational purpose in mind. According to current scientific knowledge, biological organisms are the preliminary results of a self-organization process. Nobody would seriously deny this nowadays, although we are still far from having solved all the problems of evolution theory—one possible reason being that all alternative attempts at explanation raise even greater problems. Likewise, no one would deny that biological order is extremely useful for humankind, although it brings both advantages and risks. So, at least in this area we have one case of a self-generating order that has emerged without any human intervention yet does serve humankind's purposes—if only because humans have learned to take advantage of it.

The more controversial applications for this type of theory can be found in the social rather than the biological sphere. The reason why the Theory of Spontaneous Orders is particularly interesting for social scientists and management is that it attempts to explain social achievements—ultimately, civilization and culture as such—based on a theory of spontaneous, self-generating orders.

The essence of this theory is that humans have not really created or invented all the social institutions that are so helpful in coping with life, such as custom and morals, language, law, family, money, credit, business, and enterprises: things that, in their totality, are generally referred to as civilization and culture—or at least humans have not created or invented them in the sense that they have invented and created machines and tools. It was not

---

28 The term "spontaneous" is primarily used by Friedrich von Hayek. He does point out, though, that due to the progress made in systems sciences and in cybernetics, two disciplines that have contributed greatly to the understanding of self-generating systems, the terms "self-generating" and "self-organizing" might prove to be much more useful in the future than the term "spontaneous" (Hayek, Political Order, pp. xi et seq.).

human reason that created social institutions to meet certain predefined purposes; rather, human reason has evolved along with the development of social institutions. In very extreme and somewhat exaggerated terms, we might say that humans are not cultural beings because they are endowed with reason—it is the other way round: they are endowed with reason because they are cultural beings. As extreme as this way of thinking may appear, it is less dangerous and misleading than the constructivist view, according to which humans have created purposive institutions by means of their reason, through purposeful action, and in line with their purposes and intentions.

Due to this very view, which so contradicts the everyday understanding of social phenomena, the discussion is often conducted at a rather emotional level. Some people simply find it difficult to comprehend that it is possible for something useful to emerge in the social sphere unless there is specific human action aimed at creating, initiating, or shaping its purpose. What seems even less comprehensible is that, in this way, not only is it *possible* for very rational and purposeful systems to have evolved—it is even the *only* possible way they can have evolved, because, according to the Theory of Spontaneous Orders, they are much too complex and serve to cope with much too complex circumstances to be entirely an object and outcome of human intervention.

Under the systemic-evolutionary paradigm, the emergence of spontaneous orders is attributed to the fact that humans, apart from being guided by goals, align their behavior with *rules* that, irrespective of the goals relevant in the specific case, determine the *way* they act. And while the objectives of human action have been given much emphasis in management theory, particularly in the field of business, the rules governing our behavior have largely been left unconsidered—apart from some rather unsatisfactory attempts in the context of the leadership style debate, which, for its part, is rather constructivist and not systemic-evolutionary by nature. After all, "style" does not refer to a certain, specific action but to a *kind* of behavior. It refers to the fact that, irrespective of the specific circumstances and the goals pursued in the individual case, a manager's behavior is—or should be—guided by certain rules and standards. So, a person with style, or a certain style, is someone that observes certain rules and standards in his or her behavior and who aligns that behavior with those rules and standards.

Style, understood this way, can only be learned in a specific sense: It can be cultivated and can thus develop further. Playing a crucial role here seem to be role models and imitation, or the process we call internalization—a process that largely takes place in our subconscious. My feeling is that, for example, Piaget's theory of accommodation and assimilation might be much more helpful here than the notion of instructive learning: This theory regards leadership style as something we can influence deliberately, through appropriate training, although in practice the results of training sessions give little cause for optimism.

Rather, it appears as though leadership style cannot be changed through deliberate intervention, once we have reached a certain age and development phase.

Most rules governing the *kind* of behavior are negative. Instead of telling us what to do, they tell us what to avoid. These rules resemble bans, and they define the scope of admissible or risk-free behavior. Rules of this kind and their determinant character are an extremely important, perhaps even the most important mechanism of managing complexity, for they are particularly useful wherever there is no or not enough positive knowledge on cause and effect, because the specific circumstances of the individual case are unknown.

As mentioned before, orders in the sense of the systemic-evolutionary approach emerge as a consequence of their elements (i.e. individuals) obeying general rules—without necessarily being aware of those rules in the sense that they could name them. As a consequence, there will be patterns that—and this is the crucial point—enable us to *orientate ourselves* and form educated opinions regarding other people's behavior, expectations with a high probability of being met, and thus to coordinate our own behavior with that of an undefined, basically unlimited number of other individuals.

It is this orientation effect which allows us to manage any kind of complexity to a certain extent, a complexity that would otherwise result from the unpredictability of other people's behavior, or the lack of knowledge that would inevitably result if those regularities did not exist. This orientation is why order makes sense—quite literally, for individuals' behaviors are only meaningful within this order and its context, and by the same token this same order is maintained through those behaviors.

Not all rules and control systems[29] will result in one type of order that will have the effects described. It is quite possible for control systems to

---

29 The effects of different types of rules and control systems can easily be simulated, by computer or "manually," to find out what kinds of order will result, whether these orders are stable, and whether they will eventually converge to certain states (Eigen/Winkler (Game)).

exist that cause disorientation in the individuals following the rules. But that also means that historically the only orders and control systems that have prevailed have facilitated the orientation and coordination of the individuals in a social collective, as all other collectives, groups, societies, and so on would have had to fall apart and perish for good.

In the competition among different groups, the winners had to be those whose control systems offered better orientation and coordination to solve arising problems, and in the process of socio-cultural evolution these order and control systems were bound to prevail. At this point, let me briefly comment on the stereotypical argument that this is social Darwinism. The fact of the matter is that the Theory of Spontaneous Orders, or the systemic-evolutionary approach, has never referred to the direct competition between individuals but only to a competition between different types of order and different control systems. "Survivors" in this competition were the orders whose rules were handed down because the groups that followed them had competitive advantages.

Goal-rationality in the usual sense requires us to have sufficient knowledge on the causalities determining whether or not we will reach a certain goal. However, the kind of behavior that will preserve a certain order, or type of order, is also possible when we only have some general rules to guide us and if we do not pursue any specific goals, apart from avoiding a behavior that would disturb or endanger that order. So these rules will enable us to act sensibly or appropriately in a certain sense, even if we do not have sufficient knowledge of the specific circumstances to behave rationally and in accordance with the causalities of the specific case.

It can be stated, then, that in the context of complex systems we usually lack positive knowledge of the specific circumstances of the particular case—the kind of knowledge that would allow us to behave in a way that is adequate for the particular case, or rational in the particular case; usually we cannot acquire that knowledge either. This is true for the individual who in numerous social situations has to act in certain ways to reach very specific goals, without having sufficient knowledge, or access to knowledge, about the causalities of the particular situation. It is also true for the representatives or groups acting on behalf of institutions. To name just one of many examples in the area of management: Decision-making would be no problem at all if we had or could obtain all the information we needed to make rational decisions. But even under the given circumstances, following certain rules in the sense described here will enable us to give some coherence to a number of sequential decisions on different aspects. In fact, it is probably the only way to accomplish this. The practical relevance of this mechanism is illustrated, for example, by the phenomenon of prejudice.

As pointed out earlier, the constructivist theory type is based on the assumption that it is empirically possible to fulfill the requirement of complete information. That said, even under this type of theory the occurrence of incomplete information is dealt with. In line with the paradigmatic nature of the constructivist approach, however, this case is considered a particularly difficult obstacle to constructivist rationality, not a basic crossroads where a decision between very different theory types might be called for.

But while the constructivist approach includes in its paradigm the problem of the inevitable incompleteness of our knowledge, the systemic-evolutionary approach uses it as a starting point for a completely different solution. This solution is centered around the notion that, by specifically addressing the complexity manifested in human ignorance, social institutions have emerged as evolutionary adaptations to this ignorance.

"Rational" in the sense used by constructivist theories essentially means acting economically in accordance with a specific, predefined goal based on causalities that have been recognized or are considered recognizable. Under the systemic-evolutionary theory type, "rational" means behaving in a way conducive to maintaining a given type of order, which in itself does not serve any specific purpose or goal except to provide maximum orientation for all individuals who orientate themselves by it. So the latter involves much more modest aspirations which, however, are much more fundamental in nature, as they provide essential conditions for constructivist goals.

Now if the constructivist paradigm prevails in situations where it is applicable only because a social order has evolved which can absorb enough complexity to enable the pursuit of specific goals based on a general orientation, there is a substantial risk that this very basis—general orientation—will be destroyed by the notion of the dominance and priority of human reason, a theory according to which the spontaneous order that provides orientation is a product of human reason and purposeful human action.

So under the constructivist paradigm, and with the form of rationality defined by it, it is not even possible to question the assumptions underlying this paradigm. In fact, the question does not even arise because the constructivist view considers rationality to be the creator of the very systems that, under the evolutionary theory, pave the ground for the emergence and application of this same rationality.

Allow me some further comments to facilitate the understanding of the Theory of Spontaneous Orders, and to enable readers to see its possible relevance for management. To avoid misunderstandings, among the rules of behavior mentioned we have to distinguish at least three different kinds.[30] First of all, we have rules that are followed in effect but have never been put in words, and perhaps cannot be. One example is a child's ability to use language correctly long before he or she can understand or express the rules of grammar. What we might call a feel for languages is this very ability to adhere to the rules of language without being explicitly aware of them. Putting these rules in words requires special training, and most people use language more or less correctly all their lives without being able to name its rules. Communication processes are one case in point, as they illustrate that it might not even be *possible* to express rules in words. Thanks to the research done in this field, today we know that the meaning of any single communication depends of the context and that the context is determined by rules that appertain to the meta-level of communication and which are mostly of the non-verbal kind.[31] Another example is the way the human brain works: While scientists have attempted to determine the underlying rules, these rules cannot be identified by the human brain because they determine the way it works.[32]

The second type of rules are those that have been articulated and put in words; however, prior to that there have often been long periods during which these rules were obeyed in effect, thus creating a reality that enabled their formulation. One example is the codification of the rules of law, which were long followed before they were put down.

The third kind of rules are those that are first formulated and then followed, often after a formal and ritual act of enactment.

While the systemic-evolutionary approach uses all three kinds of rule to explain social phenomena, the constructivist approach only considers the third category to be relevant. According to this view, anything purposeful has to be the result of deliberate, purposive action. As a consequence, not only the goals have to be known in advance but also the rules that govern our behavior, usually through instructions, directives, and commands. These instructions—and this is where this approach differs most from the evolutionary one—have to be designed so as to regulate every detail, just as the

---

30 Hayek (New Studies), pp. 8 et seq.
31 Bateson (Ökologie), pp. 530 et seq.
32 Hayek (Primacy and Order).

smooth functioning of a machine requires all its components and parts to be designed down to the last detail. By contrast, the rules defined in a systemic-evolutionary approach only refer to the general nature of behaviors, certain traits, and qualities. They only refer to certain *kinds* of behavior, not their details: These will result from applying the rules to the specifics of the individual case. Usually these specifics will only be known to the individual; they certainly cannot be captured in a complete system of behavioral rules.

So the reason why detailed instructions and general rules are so different in nature is rooted in the problem of complexity. Instructions concerning and determining the concrete detail are only suitable as control tools, provided the matters to be controlled are so simple they can be captured in advance.

This condition certainly does not apply to social systems. People's behavior is influenced by so many factors that, for information-theoretical reasons alone, they cannot be regulated in detail—unless the nature of social interaction would be changed completely and its diversity diminished.

If we apply this insight to management, a closer look will reveal that the choice between the control of details through corresponding instructions and the control of general behavioral elements through general rules is not so much a question of social acceptance, motivation, and leadership style as it is a matter of de facto possibilities, taking into account the existing complexity of facts and situations.

This aspect is largely disregarded at present, as the public debate is dominated by topics such as humanity, motivation, and values. The general perception is that if we only make a big enough effort, possibly supported by state-of-the-art technology, we could control and regulate everything in detail if we only wanted to, and the only reason we refrain from doing that is for lack of social acceptance. This is blatant constructivist thinking.

The systemic-evolutionary approach, by contrast, starts from the assumption that it is simply impossible to control everything in detail, regardless of whether it would be socially acceptable or not. In other words, the two paradigms encompass very different expectations as to the options we have for managing and controlling social systems. The constructivist approach basically assumes that everything can be controlled in detail, that social systems, just like machines, can be designed, regulated, and controlled completely. These assumptions may not always be stated openly, but they implicitly underlie the tools and methods suggested. Take, for instance, the writings on corporate planning systems: For most of them it could be demonstrated that their creators have—knowingly or not—based their thinking on said assumptions.

The evolutionary approach assumes complete control to be impossible. Installing general rules of behavior may help to provide more orientation than we would have without any rules, but the details cannot be controlled. Under this approach, the order-creating effect of general rules facilitates some degree of regulation in the area of extreme complexity; this effect, however, has a price in that it leaves the details undefined. So, contrary to what some people seem to think, the evolutionary approach does not call for the general abandonment of regulation, intervention, and thus management. Rather, it proposes other tools and methods, based on the empirical facts regarding the extreme complexity of real situations and the resulting inevitable limitations to our knowledge. It also leads to other ways of thinking and other expectations.

The predominantly constructivist nature of current management theory and the almost complete negation of systemic-evolutionary thinking result from the fact that the constructivist approach is based on certain premises regarding the subject of management. As outlined in section 1, these premises lead to a self-reinforcing paradigm that makes it more and more difficult, if not impossible, to see precisely those elements of management reality that would raise justifiable doubts about the validity of the paradigm. Attempts are directed at getting a systemic reality under control with constructivist methods, and whenever there are symptoms pointing to a lack of control this is not understood to mean that constructivist thinking and methods might be wrong, but merely regarded as a preliminary lack of constructivist control. In response to it, there will usually be even more attempts at increasing this same form of control. In other words, a failure of regulation is countered with even more regulation; out-of-control costs are battled with even more budgeting and cost control; planning errors are responded to by doing even more planning; and so forth.

A key characteristic of constructivist management theory is that it primarily deals with *small* (in the sense of *simple*) systems, selecting the relevant context so it will correspond to a small, simple system. A typical example, which will repeatedly be referred to in this book, is the dominance of the small face-to-face group as a subject of management theory. A very large part of management theory obviously assumes management to take place in the context of a rather small group, even in cases where it does not explicitly focus on a certain field of application but is said to apply to large-scale systems, such as entire business enterprises of any conceivable size. This becomes particularly obvious when questions of employee motivation, leadership style, or job satisfactions are addressed.

But even issues like planning, decision-making, management by objectives, and performance monitoring, which are addressed quite frequently in business literature, are placed in contexts with all the characteristics of small, manageable, non-complex systems. In such a context, the necessary conditions for successful application of constructivist thinking may actually exist, as in small, non-complex systems it is basically possible to have or obtain the information needed for what the constructivist approach believes to be controllability. However, this self-chosen context blocks the view of the real situation, which is often very different and bears the characteristics of large-scale or complex systems.

My feeling is that one key reason why large parts of business administration and management theory are irrelevant for everyday practice—an observation increasingly made by practitioners—is precisely this: the fact that in developing a theory, the context is defined in such a way that problems and possible solutions are depictable in constructivist-technomorphic ways. A theory built on this foundation, however, is bound to fail when in real-life cases the conditions assumed do not apply. In most cases, the choice of a certain context is not a conscious decision but strongly influenced by implied premises, which often seem so banal they are never even questioned.

Seemingly banal or obvious premises are not the only thing to block skepticism and critical thinking. There is also the fact that the constructivist type of theory appears to be very common-sense. As mentioned before, so convincing are the achievements in the area of technology that it will hardly occur to anyone that anything could be wrong with the *type* of theory put forward. Consequently, the failure of a theory will be attributed to its needing to be refined further, modified in a few points, or tailored to the specific case. It hardly ever occurs to anyone that the problem might be much more fundamental and to do with the underlying theory type—not only for the reasons described but also because truly relevant criticism would have to be expressed at a meta-level, rather than being targeted at the content of the theory or its object-related statements.

These two levels of criticism have to be clearly distinguished: criticizing the assertions a theory makes, or its content, without ever questioning its basic nature—or criticizing the essence of a theory, the way in which it approaches the problem in question. Even so, it is quite conceivable that certain material statements of a theory may be acceptable; in most cases, however, such meta-criticism will lead you to very different statements, or at least to different interpretations of given statements.

The various immunization strategies mentioned before were effective as long as there was reason to believe that the approach was essentially right. This is no longer the case. Now that a majority have become acutely aware of the profound changes and turbulences that have been going on for too long, now that their consequences have become too serious to be concealed or glossed over in hopes of quick fixes, the situation has started to change. Now there are increasing doubts as to whether conventional methods and ways of thinking are correct at the core, and alternatives are being sought.

However, as the dominant constructivist management culture has been able to evolve largely undisturbed, the underlying premises are deeply rooted. Until these roots are exposed and the assumptions implied are made transparent bit by bit, all we can hope for is a cure for the symptoms. In the next chapter, I will therefore single out some of these premises, with no claim to being exhaustive, and use them as examples to show how the two types of management theory are positioned vis-à-vis each other and what their implications are.

## 0.4  Seven Dominant Thinking Patterns

To make the premises underlying the two theory types as clear as I possibly can, I will express them as pairs of dichotomous statements. I am aware that the result will be a rather coarse picture and some fine distinctions will be lost. That said, I believe it is more important for the purpose of this introduction to achieve a clear picture than to deal with fine differentiations, as might be necessary in other cases.

There are seven premises that I consider particularly important with regard to the paradigms described in section 0.3:

| *Constructivist-technomorphic* | *Systemic-evolutionary* |
|---|---|
| Management is about... | Management is about... |
| ... people leadership | ... shaping and steering entire institutions in their respective environment |
| ...managing a few people | ...managing many people |
| ...the responsibility of a few people | ...the responsibility of many people |
| ...influencing directly | ...influencing indirectly |
| ...aiming for optimization | ...aiming for controllability |
| ...essentially having sufficient information | ...never having sufficient information |
| ...pursing the goal of profit maximization | ...pursing the goal of maximizing viability |

*Figure 0.4*

## 0.41 Management: Shaping and Steering Entire Institutions in Their Respective Environments (S), Not Just Managing People (C)

A considerable share of management and leadership theories in the English- and German-speaking parts of the world more or less explicitly assume that management is basically people leadership. Management is understood to be influencing people—individuals or groups—with certain objectives in mind.

The underlying assumptions warrant being called "technomorphic," as in many instances the view prevails that, if only you study very thoroughly what people best respond to, you will ultimately be able to control them. At this point I should emphasize that it is not my intention to pass judgment regarding the notion of controllability. It is one thing to discuss attempts at management (in the sense of influencing, guiding, and controlling people more effectively) from an ideological point of view; it is quite another thing—regardless of all the appeals for incorporating values in management theory—to analyze the issue of people's controllability and directability from a factual-empirical perspective.

I do not wish to adopt a position on this issue; rather, it is my concern to highlight the aspect most crucial for any management theory. In systemic management theory, a completely different question has to be addressed: Can we understand the function of management if we exclusively focus on the individual or group perceptible to our senses? Under systemic management theory, the answer to this question is no. The people-focused perspective falls short of the mark, as people's behavior—whether we consider it controllable or not—cannot be understood based on the interactions between the person managing and the person managed. Rather, an additional factor to be considered is the context in which people management takes place. While people-focused management theories increasingly acknowledge this, they fail to realize that this context is usually defined by the characteristics of the overall system.

From an individual's point of view, the overall system—the order governing the behavior of many—is not manifest as an entity nor is it perceptible to the senses. It does manifest itself, however, in that individual behaviors would not make sense if they were not elements of an overall pattern. Employees do not act on a case-by-case basis, as though there were no past and no future. Rather, the particular case is a part of an overall system of interrelated events.

In other words, when an employee acts a certain way today, it is not only because it seems appropriate and reasonable but also and especially because he or she has acted in a certain way yesterday and hopes to be able to act in a certain way tomorrow. For the same reason, he or she will often be prepared to respond in a way that might seem inappropriate from the perspective of the particular case but is certainly appropriate in a greater context.

A systemic management theory will never negate the importance of insights on the immediate personal interaction between the manager and the person managed, and would not want to refrain from analyzing these personal forms of interaction. However, as a general rule it will be possible, and often even necessary, to interpret the same behavior and interaction pattern in different ways, depending on whether our frame of reference is the interpersonal relationship or the context of an entire system.

Another factor, obviously, is that a management theory aimed at shaping and steering entire systems will have to be fundamentally different because it faces very different tasks. As a consequence of this underlying premise, none of the aspects needed to solve the problem may be neglected or denied.

The conclusion is that the conventional division of scientific disciplines is losing relevance. Shaping and steering an overall system is neither a scientific problem nor a technical or psychological one. It is all of these. However, rather than representing an aggregating, interdisciplinary construct, it forms a *new discipline of its own*. This alone is what makes cybernetics so important in solving the problem: It is that new discipline, albeit at a rather abstract level. Cybernetics is the science of the control of systems. The term "control" is used here in the sense of mastering an ability or having control of something. We use it in the same way as when we might say that someone masters two languages or has control of his skis. As these examples may illustrate, we do not refer to the constructivist form of control—it cannot be our key focus.

Cyberneticists' claim to wholism, often attacked and sometimes mystified, does not mean that we are out to research and analyze everything under the sun. Rather, it refers to what I have just described: the objective of getting systems under control. Not just anything is relevant—but everything required to get a system under control.

If we attempt to keep a business enterprise under control, it will not be sufficient to have control of one aspect or the other, one dimension or the other—it has to be *every* aspect and *every* dimension of relevance. If we make profit today but fail to ensure tomorrow's profits we have not solved the problem. If we have control of the costs but not the market, of human resources but not of finances, of finances but not of human resources, and so on, we will not have control of the enterprise overall.

In a world of specialists, controlling an enterprise is not an easy task, as anyone knows who has been at the helm of an organization long enough to see the impact of his or her own mistakes. Still, there is the chance and hope that, in addition to all the experts we have for various things, we can train and school experts in the control of institutions. This, precisely, is the purpose of management theory. Note that its focus is not on financial management, human resources management, marketing management, and so on, but simply on *management*.

## 0.42 Management: Leading Many People (S) Rather Than Just a Few (C)

This premise pair is directly related to the one discussed under 0.41, and you might say it follows from it. If we focus our attention and efforts on the system as a whole, the question immediately arises as to how the actions of so many people can be coordinated. In direct interaction with individuals or small groups, a manager or leader will always be able to intervene directly. His or her personality and the possibility of sensory perception and experience—both ways: of the manager by the managed individual, and vice versa—largely determine the context of the interaction. Management and coordination of many, however, means you need to resort to certain aids in order to be effective. Management will then become impersonal, as it will no longer or hardly lend itself to sensory perception. The sensory modalities that can be addressed by management will become fewer; the range of possible experiences will decrease; ultimately, management is performed through anonymous directives and abstract regulations.

In a sense, the situation is comparable to the situation of modern warfare: The prevalence of high-tech devices and remote-controlled weapon systems prevents a personal encounter of combatants, as opposed to the hand-to-hand combat of earlier times. It is common knowledge that the experience of killing someone is very different in the two cases, and that the leadership situation will differ accordingly.

An obvious key issue here is how to define "few" and "many." What is the number marking the transition from one to the other? It would certainly be nice if we could determine it precisely; however, for several reasons I suspect that this might not be possible, because we are dealing with a variable rather than a constant. Some situations permit involving more people in the immediate interaction than others. Some tasks require interaction so close it will not be feasible with more than three or four individuals—others require less interaction and coordination, so that in a given time frame you can have personal contact with a larger number of people.

It would exceed the scope of this book to elaborate on these things, so a few comments will have to suffice. This is about the so-called *critical group*, defined as the "maximum possible total of single elements (people, things, connections) to permit the proper functioning of an organization of a certain structure."[33]

Friedman explains very clearly that, although the size of the critical group varies for every species, each critical group has its own characteristic size. Key determining factors are the individuals' biological characteristics and the topological structure of society. The former determine the individual's *valence* (number of interest centers accessible or addressable in conscious attention) and *conductivity* (ability to absorb and pass on influences). In other words, they determine the number of different things someone can deal with at any one point, and the influences he or she is exposed to or exerts. This delineates his or her scope of interaction. Beyond its boundaries, the world starts

---

33 Friedman (Utopien), pp. 38 et seq.

becoming incomprehensible to the individual, or no longer accessible to sensory perception. The individual will then depend on a mental, abstract reconstruction of his image of the world, based on a decreasing number of fading signals, and will have to resort to reinforcing tools in order to exert an influence. That, in turn, will alter the quality of the means of control available, of deviation and error signals, of feedbacks, and so on. We reach the limit of comprehensibility and controllability, which we can metaphorically call the "barrier to complexity."[34]

Managing many is fundamentally different from managing within the confines of a critical group. It would be great if every manager could be taught early on—before he or she actually gets into the situation—the sometimes traumatic experience of absolute helplessness that you feel when you are put in a position that requires you to manage, influence, control, and so forth beyond the confines of the critical group.

With the exception of very traditional, well-established organizations which have been able to develop appropriate forms of management over extended periods of time, most organizations are not really prepared for that situation. Also, most executives have spent by far the longest part of their lives *within* the confines of the critical group. Specifically, our earliest experiences in life are something that usually occurs in the context of perceptible and influenceable small systems—be it our family, our peer group at school, the different forms of personal friendship and enmity, the small group of colleagues at work, and so on. On the other hand, the systems that increasingly take hold of our lives have been growing beyond comprehensibility, while our knowledge about how to shape and control such systems has not grown at a corresponding rate.

## 0.43 Management: A Task for Many People (S) Rather Than for Just a Few (C)

Under the constructivist management theory type, one dominant idea is that management in any organization is executed by a relatively *small* number of people. Quite often, the term "management" is used for the small group of individuals that hold the most senior positions in an organization. So, "management" under this theory type usually refers to so-called top management.

---

34 Beer (Decision), pp. 256, 258.

Likewise, in everyday language the term mostly refers to the top executives and representatives of an organization.

Although it is usually clear who the top management members are de jure, de facto the group is not that well defined or definable. Apart from the purely legal, statutory, and organizational regulations in a company, there are always additional rules and rituals that define that membership. So there is no *universal* answer to the question as to who is part of top management; however, there definitely are specific answers, as in any given organization it will usually be very clear who does and does not "belong."

Despite this indeterminateness, we can safely assume that management, in the sense used in constructivist theories and in an operational context, comprises a small group.[35]

Once again we are faced with the phenomenon discussed earlier: In order to create a theory, a context or situation is assumed which will make the constructivist-technomorphic theory type appear reasonable. By contrast, if we assume management to be a task of many rather than a few, as we would under the systemic-evolutionary approach, we face a very different kind of challenge. There are sound reasons to assume that, at both a business enterprise and an institution, anyone expected to enable others to make productive contributions can basically be considered to be a manager. It does not matter so much what position and job title, legal competencies, and organizational rank this person has. The crucial factor is his or her function in the overall network. Simply put, we could say that everyone that manages is a manager. Everyone that takes responsibility for and exerts influence on others' performance is a manager according to this definition. Her work will have many of the characteristics addressed in management theory today. She will do some sort of planning, which does not necessarily have to include a lot of paperwork but simply means that she will try to organize her work as sensibly and economically as possible. She will also take decisions which, even though they may not be particularly important from a top-level perspective, are required for a certain process to run smoothly.

This analysis could be carried on much longer. It would reveal that management takes place on many, perhaps even most of the levels of an organization, and that it is actually performed not by a few senior or top executives alone but by numerous people through their interactions.

---

35 The operational context is emphasized here because large corporations structured as affiliated groups usually have several, often numerous management teams that meet at certain occasions. These groups, however, will not perform operational tasks.

Except for very small companies, our concept of management cannot be limited to a small group of people, which also raises questions about the effectiveness of the technomorphic type of theory.

There is no such thing as a clearly identifiable center that possesses all the relevant information and makes all decisions required for controlling the company. Even when control seems to be exerted from a center, due to a certain organizational structure, allocation of competencies, and self-image, and even when that center exerts an objectively strong, perhaps even dominant determinative effect on events in the organization, it will still turn out that actual, complete control requires much more information than is available to that center, and that the number of relationships to be continuously adjusted is much too large to be managed through the directives issued by one center.

The arguments are essentially the same as those governing the debate between the centrally controlled and the market economy theories. As in the case of the two different orders governing the economy and ultimately society, the key question is whether central control is *possible at all*. As this discussion shows, the problem is not a question of values but a problem of empirical qualities of the world we live in, and ultimately a problem of the laws of human and systemic communication.

Admittedly, central control of any system would be better than any other kind of control, perhaps even optimal, if a series of conditions could be met: *if* it were possible to provide the center with all necessary information on both permanent and preliminary circumstances; *if* this could be done timely, that is, faster than things could change again; *if* it could be done in a way that would exclude errors and distortions—or at least eliminate the effects of inevitable transmission errors; *if* the center could use incoming information, which would inevitably arrive in fragments, to obtain an accurate picture of the overall situation; and *if* the center could then issue appropriate directives which—despite the information transmission problems mentioned—would trigger the right behaviors in their many recipients, whose work would still be based on a division of labor and knowledge.

The fact is that the information problems this kind of control brings are unsolvable and will continue to be, even if we manage to multiply the computing power of latest-state computers. Not even the technological control of elementary particle physics and the continued micro-miniaturization of computer parts will enable us to provide the quantities of information required to solve the problem.[36]

Like it or not, we have to depend on the vast majority of relationships to adjust themselves on the spot, as it were, taking into account the momentary and often rapidly changing circumstances at the respective time and place. The only way for us to achieve anything useful, an appropriate order of events based on the multitude of continually self-coordinating elements, is to apply abstract, general rules of behavior (as discussed in section 0.2) when dealing with the evolutionary approach.

It would be a mistake to think that this was only valid for the system types discussed in the theory of political-economical orders. Admittedly, business enterprises are usually not as large as a whole economy (although there are corporations which, measured by the usual yardsticks, are as big or even bigger than small or medium-sized economies), but with the exception of very small enterprises they are generally complex enough to exceed by far the scope of possibilities given under constructivist control systems.

Perhaps this is the core of the error committed by current management theory: Its proponents acknowledge the great complexity of an economy and are prepared to thoroughly discuss the resulting problems of control and coordination; however, they automatically assume circumstances at business enterprises to be simple by comparison—so simple, indeed, that any insights on the regulation problems posed by economic and social types of order cannot be relevant for them. One reason for this misjudgment may be that the problem of complexity is not understood very well to begin with—in particular the fact that even when there is only a limited number of elements, the complexity of possible states will explode once these elements start to interact. (See my related comments in section 0.2.)

If we accept the underlying premise of the evolutionary approach, according to which management is a task performed by many rather than just a few people, the consequence is that much more attention must be paid to a company's code of conduct. Above all, I consider it an essential requirement to thoroughly research the three categories of rules—those not articulated at all, those articulated ex post, and those set ex ante—including their possible effects, both in a general, theoretical context and for the individual enterprise, taking account of its specific situation. Another aspect is that this will bring into focus the mechanisms by which *general rules* in companies are

36 Ashby (Bremermann).

created. Management tools such as guiding principles and general policies will be given higher priority, and will probably have to be studied much more thoroughly than before in theory. At least in this regard there is a lot to be learned from the legal and political sciences, in that these are the only disciplines of social science that seriously deal with the nature, logic, and impact of rules. This is not to say that each of their findings is important to management theory or should be adopted by it. But the approach to dealing with these phenomena can surely serve as a model.

In the light of thorough studies of such forms of control, coordination, regulation, and ultimately government, it would turn out that current management theory basically follows the archaic models of a closed tribal community, or perhaps an analogy to an ancient Greek polis, which, although I would not call it archaic, can certainly be considered to have been the kind of system closed enough to permit the information-related problems of control and coordination to be solved. To achieve the effectiveness required, however, management theory will definitely have to orientate itself by the idea of an open, abstract, or larger society.[37]

## 0.44 Management: Indirect Influence on a Meta-Level (S) Rather Than Direct Influence on an Object Level (C)

As we have seen in various contexts, the constructivist-technomorphic paradigm is centered around the notion that it is basically possible to control the activities and events in a company by specifying in detail the functions of and relationships among its individual elements. This would require interfering with the processes themselves, at the level of real activities. Specifically, one assumption is that the faulty output of a process can be corrected by directly adjusting that very output and by intervening in the process itself. Other possibilities, while not explicitly excluded, are not specifically highlighted.

By contrast, the systemic approach starts from the assumption that the output of a system always depends on the structure of that system, on the rules governing its behavior, and especially on the pattern of interaction between system elements and subsystems. So if the output is not acceptable,

37 Popper (Gesellschaft); Hayek (Law), p. 57.

under this approach it would make little sense to correct that output or intervene in the process producing that output; instead, the structure of the system and the interaction pattern of its elements have to be changed.

Now if we call the level of events producing the output the *object level*, in analogy to the term "object language," and the level of structures and rules determining the output the *meta-level*, in analogy to the term meta-language in linguistics and logic (or the term meta-communication, coined by Gregory Bateson[38] and subsequently used by him, Watzlawick, and the Palo Alto Group), we will find that the constructivist approach operates at the object level while the systemic-evolutionary one operates at the meta-level.

In simple cases this distinction is unproblematic. If in a manufacturing process a machine keeps producing parts that need rework, those in charge will quickly adjust the machine's settings to minimize rework costs. And if a shipping department keeps misrouting shipments, management will also look for basic solutions rather than accepting the fact that individual shipments have to be corrected.

Distinguishing the object from the meta-level becomes more difficult, and at the same time relevant, once things get complicated. As an example from practice, let me briefly recount the case of a medium-sized electromechanicals company of 550 employees which kept having deadline problems. Although the company's operations were organized quite well by business administration standards, and with process engineering and a unit in charge of production planning and process supervision doing all they could to closely monitor and control order throughput, they could not get the problem under control. Depending on the importance of the specific order and customer, the company kept taking ad hoc measures to avoid or at least minimize delivery delays. These measures were often quite extreme and they caused other factors, such as overtime, to get out of control. Increasingly, individuals and their presumed incapability or unreliability were blamed for the mistakes that happened. There was growing mutual distrust and the blame was passed around.

Even though the company had capable experts and good managers by common standards, and despite the considerable efforts made, the problem could not be solved. Introducing a computer-aided production control system which management had hoped would improve the situation only made things worse, as it eliminated certain possibilities of improvisation that had

---

38 Bateson (Ökologie), pp. 24 et seq.

sometimes saved the day. In this case, the solution to the problem definitely could not be where it was presumed to be: in manufacturing and warehousing. Its actual root cause lay in the *interaction patterns* between procurement and manufacturing. Manufacturing was very capable of keeping the delivery dates agreed on under the service level the company had set for itself. However, due to the increasingly difficult economic situation of the industry, the company's customers had changed their ordering and material planning behavior as compared to earlier years. The company's sales management had been aware of this change, but instead of communicating it to manufacturing as a major change to their overall situation, they had only passed on bits and scraps of it, relating to individual order situations. In fact, the company's specific form of planning permitted communicating changes within one pattern, but not communicating a change of patterns. So while the sales department had noticed the transition from one basic kind of customer behavior to another, the mode of interaction between sales and manufacturing—with information being transferred and filtered by a planning and IT system—made it impossible to communicate such meta-change. The only thing it permitted was to enter new changes at the object level again and again, which caused increasing instability and disorientation because these individual entries and changes no longer made sense from a manufacturing point of view.

The first step toward a true solution was to suspend the planning system for these departments for the time being, thus bypassing certain IT procedures. A steering committee was established which comprised people from sales, manufacturing, process engineering, operations scheduling, and warehousing, and which met twice daily for short, usually half-hour meetings. This personal interaction served to bring back into the process the wealth of information that had been diminished by formal procedures. The objective was for everyone involved to regain a feel for the new interaction patterns, so they would be able to put single entries and pieces of information into perspective, attach the right meaning to them, and interpret them appropriately.

The established mechanisms of production scheduling and control, which may appear reasonable from a constructivist perspective and which kept being reinforced and expanded, caused an increasing inability to define the problems of interaction between key subsystems and elements, which were much more fundamental than the many individual planning steps discussed.

So, in this rather complex case the distinction between the object and the metal-level was anything but trivial, nor was it immediately obvious. After long years of practical experience in management consulting and management training, I tend to believe that a major share of the problems encountered almost daily in business organizations can only be solved if this distinction between the object and the meta-level is kept in mind. It happens much more frequently than you would think that the fundamental question as to whether a problem can or cannot be solved is answered at the meta-level. In my view, this applies to most problems of motivation, work climate, and job satisfaction. Only seldom will the solution lie with individuals, or even in the behavior of all persons involved; in most cases it is a question of people's *interaction modes*, and thus of meta-communication. Here we find all the phenomena so masterfully analyzed and described by Gregory Bateson, such as "double bind," "deuterolearning," "culture contact," and "schismo-genesis."[39]

While I am not one to sweepingly accept just everything, I think there is no way around such research findings if we want to establish a truly effective and relevant management theory. Admittedly, many of the relevant papers were not written in a terminology directly applicable to management; also, the relevant research was often carried out in a context far away from management, such as the anthropologic studies of indigenous peoples. But these difficulties can be overcome, thus clearing the path for significant insights.

I would like to conclude this section as follows: Behavior, the output of a system, is a function of system structures. These structures essentially emerge from the way key subsystems interact; they are continually produced or perpetuated by said subsystems and can only be modified at this level.

### 0.45 Management: Controllability (S) Rather Than Optimality (C) as a Key Criterion

A dominant motive in constructivist thinking is the strive for optimality, or the assessment of problem solutions based on optimality criteria. This strive forces the constructivist theory type to call for information as complete as possible. Almost inevitably, the consequence is that its proponents work on assumptions that imply situations where this requirement can be fulfilled.

---

39 Bateson (Ökologie).

The notion of optimality, such as of decisions, operations, organization, and structures, is clearly fascinating and even seems rational in an economic context, as economic behavior is closely connected to ideas of optimality.

But what is it that should really be optimized? Under what circumstances can we reasonably define what we are talking about when we use the term "optimum?" is it rational at all in a management context to aim for optimums, and if so, of what variables should these optimums be?

In a sufficiently stable context, where the necessary information on relevant variables is given or available, working on this notion is not objectionable. But the question remains as to whether the constructivist theory type, in its strive for optimality, has caused a development that is getting increasingly dangerous, now that the conditions of context stability and availability of information no longer apply.

Together with the fixation on the object level as discussed under 0.44, companies have invested plenty of money and effort in the optimization of their production plants, production processes, operations, logistic systems, and so on, and they have done so with a focus on the key criterion of optimizing an enterprise's economic viability.

From a technomorphic perspective, however, optimization mostly means eliminating flexibility. A machine is more effctively laid out, the more stable the input is—that is, the lesser the fluctuations in material quality and quantity, in delivery dates, and in processing cycles. Continued efforts to determine optimal lot sizes in manufacturing, with a minimum of retooling, are one case in point. All the variables around a machine that is expected to work optimally, in the usual sense, are increasingly determined or regulated with very narrow tolerances. By doing this the overall system seems to have been made more stable—while it has really been made increasingly instable. If serious structural changes occur in external conditions outside management's control, management will no longer be able to respond adequately because it lacks the necessary flexibility.

This is the problem we seem to be facing at present. Long years of a relatively stable economic situation have led us, in our strive for optimality, to adapt—or rather: overadapt—everything to the circumstances prevailing at the time. More and more relevant variables of relevant systems, production capacities, production processes, distribution systems, price and volume ratios, organization structures, salary structures, and so on, were increasingly fixed in a system of mutual interrelations; agreements and contracts were concluded in an attempt to stabilize the variables that might cause fluctuations and require corresponding measures; vested rights were defended more and more fiercely; every previously unorganized group did everything in its might to become a stakeholder group capable of lobbying—until the systems had finally lost all of their flexibility.

The changes in global oil prices have shown how in such a system a sudden massive change in even one variable can cause uncontrollable waves of reverberation. Another example concerns the changes that have been going on in microelectronics: The reason they are so profound is that our systems are not flexible enough to absorb these new forms of complexity.

The reason is that flexibility is an economic commodity which incurs costs. Under the constructivist type of theory, these costs are equated with potential for rationalization, rather than resources. So, in approaching the goal of optimality—in the constructivist meaning—we have lost more and more flexibility. Consequences are obvious from insolvency statistics.

A systemic-revolutionary management theory does not assume the set of circumstances to be more or less invariable and stable. Rather, it starts from the underlying premise that historically, every constellation we have seen has been temporary. It has to do with the problem of complexity, as well as with the momentum inherent in complex systems. The conditions under which optimization at the object level is possible are treated as a special case in systemic types of theory, while constructivist theories tend to assume them as given.

So, if we assume that we have to continually adapt to changing circumstances, optimization will only make sense at the meta-level. Instead of optimizing an adapted state, we will then have to optimize something entirely different: the *ability to adapt*.

This idea applies to a broad range of situations. It opens completely new perspectives once it is considered carefully. Take, for instance, our educational system: Does it not have an inherent tendency at all levels to optimize the mastery of concrete learning content, while it would be just as important, or even more important, to optimize the *ability to learn*? After all, no teacher or planner of learning content is ever able to know exactly what skills and knowledge our children will need tomorrow to cope with the problems they will face then. Also, do we not try to optimize companies' organization structures instead of optimizing their *organizability*; and do we not experience over and over again how the organization structures that were optimal yesterday now prevent the adjustments required today—precisely because they were so optimally tuned to yesterday's requirements?

From the perspective of systemic management theory, which has gained much relevance due to the structural changes that occurred over the past decade, the key is not to optimize specific states at the object level but to *optimize the controllability* of an organization, or its *manageability*. If this criterion is applied when assessing decisions, processes, capacities, and so on, things will suddenly appear in a very different light. The key question will then have to be: How will this or that decision affect our flexibility, our adaptability, the manageability of our company?

Obviously, this question will also influence the economics of a decision, as all capabilities or potentialities cause costs, as mentioned before. At this point, a constructivist critic would object that everything has remained as it was, except that now an additional condition—the cost of flexibility—will have to be taken into account...

## 0.46 Management: Never Having Sufficient Knowledge (S) Rather Than Assuming Information to be Complete (C)

By now the problems related to the information base have been discussed in various contexts, so a few brief comments should do. Under the constructivist type of theory, the existing information base is usually assumed to be sufficient to solve the problems discussed. Planning systems, accounting, controlling systems, target-setting, and so on are designed in such a way that, based on their architecture, one would conclude that the information required for their use is available or at hand.

Even the case of decision-making under conditions of uncertainty, which is addressed in decision theory, is discussed to the effect that information blanks only have to be filled with subjective estimates of probability. Again, apparent certainty is gained by presuming a context, at least implicitly, which only seldom mirrors real-life situations.

By contrast, the systemic type of management theory explicitly starts from the assumption that we never—or only in very specific instances—have enough information to really be able to justify our decisions. The conclusion from that is that it is wrong to even want to justify them.

Now this latter remark could be construed as my speaking in favor of arbitrary decisionism. In fact, the position taken by systemic-evolutionary theories represents a *revisionist* attitude: It proposes that wherever possible decisions should be made in such a way that they can later be revised if necessary—or at least their effects can largely be mitigated. Except for a few very atypical cases, we can never be certain that a decision that may be right today will still be right tomorrow. Even the best decisions are overtaken by events, and thus become obsolete.

Above all, we never have enough information to be able to make forecasts. It is remarkable to what extent the management systems, tools, and methods discussed in literature are still based on the predictability of relevant variables. In management practice, too, most planning systems are still designed so as to require forecasts on key variables, such as sales volumes and prices, in order to be able to do any "planning" at all.

Although the past years' changes in this area have raised serious doubts and caused numerous companies to make changes to their planning systems—sometimes even to abandon planning overall—under the constructivist type of theory there are still attempts to develop and refine forecasting methods.

The systemic theory type consistently assumes that forecasts (those of the kind usually referred to) are impossible. We cannot predict the gross national product, or industry production, or the rate of inflation, or currency rates, and so on, with the precision required in business management. Also, consumer behavior—no matter whether we assume it to be rational or irrational—tends to be a surprise game.[40]

The systemic approach assumes planning to be not a mental anticipation of future states but an activity aimed at making decisions in the present while taking account of their future-determining or, if you will, prejudicial effects; or exploring the future-determining effects of past decisions; or—and this is where the main focus will have to be—ensuring that the organization keeps adapting to changing circumstances.

In any case, the systemic approach implies utmost suspicion regarding the correctness of plans and decisions, thus shifting the focus to preventive measures that address, among other things, the company's manageability (as discussed in the previous section).

There is a series of examples that illustrate quite well the attitude that should be cultivated. A particularly illustrative one, perhaps, refers to alpine mountaineering, which despite all the technical progress still involves considerable risks. One key factor for mountaineers is the weather, so reliable

---

40 Drucker (Changing World), p. 81 ff.

weather forecasts would be highly desirable. There are macro-weather situations that permit such forecasts, such as large and stable high-pressure zones. Still, every experienced alpine climber knows how fast the weather in the mountain area can change and how often the specific local micro-climate differs from the macro-weather situation. But there are numerous further risks that alpine mountaineering involves, ranging from falling rocks and ice to injury and on to the subjective dangers inherent in the physical and mental skills of every individual—all of these things can turn even a meticulously planned and carefully prepared tour into an outright disaster. Experienced climbers, just like experienced entrepreneurs or managers, know that it is in the nature of the undertaking that you cannot have complete control of it. Even at the risk of taking much too much equipment (which is something you can only know from hindsight), an experienced climber will therefore never leave without certain pieces of equipment that might be vital in cases of emergency.

In planning the route he will pay close attention to the points where he can turn around if necessary; during the ascent he will use these points to carefully check once more all the conditions affecting the outcome of this climb, and in the event that any of them has changed he may decide to turn around rather than carry on in an act of would-be heroism. The key is to survive, not to win at any cost.

German Field Marshal Rommel is said to once have provided an acute analysis of the difference between a great commander and a reckless daredevil, which is relevant in this context. According to Rommel, while both will make every effort to win, the great commander, in preparing an offense, will make sure his planning also covers the risk that his troops might have to withdraw. In the event that the offense does not turn out as planned, whatever the reasons may be, the daredevil will end up with a disaster while the great general can command an orderly withdrawal and await another opportunity.

My observations of management practice lead me to assume that only a minority of managers are aware of this difference.

But the climbing example can be continued further. Many difficult climbs have points beyond which you cannot return in the event of an injury or change of weather. The parallels to business management are obvious: Regardless of all the care and circumspection applied, managers often face the problem of having to make irreversible decisions that involve major risks, perhaps even the risk of company decline. In both cases, the art is in avoiding such situations as far as possible, and, if you cannot avoid them, in venturing the project with the best preparation possible and in full awareness of all risks involved. There are no "methods" in the usual sense to handle such situations; we have to accept them as our fate. Parallels to politics and warfare are obvious, and history is full of case examples from which we can learn a lot.

In management literature, however, we will hardly find a thorough discussion of these issues. Most efforts are dedicated to refining methods that do not come anywhere near the heart of the problem.

## 0.47 Management: Aiming to Maximize Viability (S)
## Rather Than Profit (C)

The constructivist type of management theory is still aimed at profit maximization. There have been numerous modifications in detail, but the underlying concept has remained unchanged. It is not my intention here to discuss the details; rather, the question is what parameters will enable us to minimize the risk of *systematic* errors in decision-making.

Here, too, it was the long years of economic prosperity after the Second World War—with unsaturated demand in all sectors, commercialization of the technological progress achieved by military research and the war economy, stable economic-political conditions, and a fundamental consensus in society regarding core values—which, having prevailed for a whole generation, gave rise to the illusion that whatever had proven effective in this fortunate constellation of circumstances just had to be right.

The few years of economic turbulences we have experienced so far have sufficed to show how misleading profit orientation can be, and how little even profit-maximizing strategies can do to safeguard a company's existence. Even large reserves will usually not suffice to save a company that has failed to keep pace with technological development.

Almost for decades now, Drucker has tirelessly pointed out that there is no such thing as profit, only costs: costs of the *existing* business and costs of *staying in business*. Consequently and quite logically, he pointed out that "the proper question for any management is not 'What is the *maximum* profit this business can yield?' but 'What is the *minimum* profitability needed to cover the future risks of this business?'"[41]

---

41 Drucker (Changing World), p. 52.

In the relatively few years that the issue of strategic (not just long-term) planning has been explored in theory and practice, the relevant arguments have become substantially clearer—and they reveal how the orientation toward profit maximization will lead to a dangerous kind of blindness.

There is no doubt that profit never arises unconditionally. A series of conditions have to coincide for profit to materialize. There must be marketable products, a useable distribution system, consumers that are willing and able to buy, and so forth. In short, there must be present *profit* potential,[42] that is, potential that can be captured here and now.

In a business economics sense, profit is a result of exploiting present potential. This can obviously be done more or less effectively, and in this sense we can speak of profit maximization. But the closer this goal moves to the focus of managerial efforts, the greater the risk that management loses sight of the conditions on which profit depends.

This is not so much a business economics problem as it is a psychological one, or more precisely, a problem related to the psychology of perception. It is exacerbated by the fact that we are only just beginning to develop some kind of "bookkeeping" to record profit potentials, while classical accounting is hardly able to identify even traces of them. So, quite literally, profit potentials are elusive to perception. This is true not only for present profit potentials, which are not recorded even when they must be an economic reality already—it applies even more to the *future* potentials every company needs, that is, all the conditions that have to be created to achieve profits not only today but also "tomorrow."

The better current profits are, the higher the probability that another psychological effect will ensue: the immediate feeling of having succeeded, of having done all the right things, and of controlling everything. It is the false sense of security that materializes under the constructivist paradigm: It will have the strongest impact whenever there are hard facts and figures to work with.

At this point, an excursus would be warranted on the problems associated with quantification as a pseudo-criterion for economic viability, as well as with operationalism, but I am afraid this would take us too far. Another

---

42 Terminology is not consistent in the area of strategic planning. I stick to the terms used by Gälweiler (Unternehmenssicherung), (Marketingplanung), whose concept I find to be extraordinarily clear and useful for both theoretical and practical purposes.

excursus would be required to address the subject of social rewards or punishments, which, in using profit as a criterion—be it as earnings per share or cash flow per employee—do their bit to mislead managers by drawing attention to the wrong variables.

The systemic-evolutionary approach is centered around the idea of an organization's viability. Admittedly, this idea has only just about taken hold and there is still a lot of work to do; however, some initial steps are possible based on certain—by no means all—approaches to strategic planning and strategic management. Liquidity, profit, and present and future profit potentials all have to be balanced simultaneously. Their influenceability and controllability are subject to different rhythms and time horizons. Liquidity can be pre-controlled using profit information; profit information can be pre-controlled using information on present profit potentials; the latter can be pre-controlled using information on future success potentials. All these parameters are assessed and controlled based on different key variables, from receipts and expenditures for liquidity to potential trends in technological substitution for future profit potentials.[43]

But this is just a first step to get a grasp on the problem of a company's viability. Implementing strategies requires certain structures, and certain structures imply certain strategies—or, perhaps more to the point, they prevent certain strategies.

As discussed in section 0.44, the structures depend on the way the relevant subsystems and elements interact. In that section and in 0.45, I pointed out that the key objective cannot be to change states at the object level but to focus management theory and practice on certain potentials, capabilities, and qualities that are more likely to be located at the meta-level. While in those sections we were dealing with the optimization of manageability and flexibility, we will now address yet another meta-variable: viability. It seems to be superordinate to the variables mentioned so far, in that it is located on a higher, second-order meta-level.

It is important to emphasize that the idea of viability does not relate to or imply any forms of biologism. Viability is a structural quality of systems: It refers to their ability to maintain their existence for an indefinite amount of time. Hence, the issue of viability is closely related to the issue of identity and its preservation. Relating it to companies and putting it in very simple terms, we could speak of the ability to stay in business for an indefinite

---

43 See Gälweiler (Marketingplanung) for individual points.

amount of time. This necessarily includes the ability to modify operations, if changing conditions call for it. For instance, companies in the watch industry have preliminarily proved their viability by managing to change from watch manufacturers to electronics companies.

The viability criterion is not limited to organizations but can be applied to any kind of system—not as a formal criterion but as an empirical one. Some systems are able to solve this problem, others are not. And almost as in section 0.45, where I recommended to judge decisions, actions, and so on based on a company's manageability, we can now take another step and explore their impact on viability. Retaining viability is preliminary evidence that the complexity relevant for a system can be brought under control.

However, this does not imply anything for the future; at least it does not guarantee that in the future it will still be possible to solve the problem of existence. This is exactly why strategic management in its current form is not enough. Similarly to what has been said in section 0.45, which did not address the optimal state of adaption but the general idea of adapt*ability*—the ability to create new states of adaptation over and over again—our objective in terms of viability cannot simply be to develop a good strategy for tomorrow but must be to maximize the ability to change *any* strategy as soon as it turns out to be obsolete: the ability to keep developing new strategies over and over again, all aimed at preserving the system's viability.

## 0.5  A Chance to Rethink

The premises underlying the constructivist type of management theory almost inevitably lead to the idea that systems are essentially manageable. The premises underlying the systemic-evolutionary approach destroy these hopes. Based on these, the only form of control to be expected is what could be called soft or fuzzy control.

Hence, the aspiration level associated with this type of theory is much lower. It accepts that many, perhaps even most things cannot be controlled. This type of theory seems to reflect the current state of the world much better than the constructivist type, as we keep observing symptoms that indicate that the course of events is much less controllable than the corresponding rituals would lead one to believe. The non-governability of the world, the impotence of politicians and managers, the unmanageability of economic processes, the helplessness of economists, and the proliferation of new forms of complexity speak for themselves.

It does not take a major effort, though, to regard all these things not as symptoms of a world that has gotten out of control, a world consisting of unmanageable systems and their different, unpredictable forms of interaction, but as deficiencies and shortcomings we will temporarily have to accept as we proceed towards an increasingly effective coordination of these systems.

This, precisely, is a function of paradigms and their language. Depending on the paradigm used, the world appears different and we arrive at a different interpretation of the events we observe.

The systemic-evolutionary approach, however, in a certain sense leads to a paradox. On the one hand, all we can expect is a moderate form of *soft control* when dealing with truly complex systems. On the other hand, does not this very fact give us critical power over the course of events? Can we not form completely different expectations on this basis which offer much greater fulfilment probabilities, because they are orientated by the realities of our world? And can we thus not eliminate the risk that theories created for a totally different context will be applied outside that context?

It seems to me that these very opportunities are an essential element of systemic management theory. The starting point for reasonable action is to understand how systems are connected, and on this basis form realistic expectations that will provide the foundation for any kind of orientation. Once we have understood the nature of complex systems, we may also expect to find new *kinds* of solutions for many of problems that will arise. However, whether or not the prevailing paradigms and concepts of the world actually permit new solutions to be implemented is an open question. Systemic analyses of the application context do not really warrant optimism. We are all an output of our systems; we are products of these systems; and according to everything we know about complex systems, our own nature has to be adapted to the nature of these systems.

Perhaps technomorphic thinking and technomorphic systems have mutually adapted to an extent where everything is considered normal and in perfect order. Historically, it would not be the first time that this has happened. The illusory worlds created by human reason, with its limitations and its presumptuousness, can lead to collective, self-perpetuating realities that can only be changed by a general collapse.

> "The nature of the trap
> is a function of
> the nature of the trapped ..."
> *Geoffrey Vickers*

Large parts of this book were written six years ago in hopes of making a modest contribution to a better understanding of systems, and thus to a more effective but also more responsible management theory. My key concern was to uncover the reality behind official teachings and constructed perceptions, buried under the debris of a concept of reality that certain communication mechanisms had created and that everyone thought to be true. It was the reality of highly complex systems, of the emergence of order patterns, of gaining orientation and understanding through learning and problem-solving processes reaching out into the unknown; the realities of viable systems; and finally the reality of meta-systemic control and of the seeming paradox that by refraining from defining all the details we can gain even stronger creative forces.

As mentioned earlier, Chapter 1 deals with Stafford Beer's Viable Systems Model. According to the systematic approach this book takes, this discussion should have belonged in Chapter 2. The reasons why it has been placed at the beginning have been pointed out before. Some comments on this chapter are necessary, though. Honesty and fairness towards my colleagues of that time, as well as considerations related to printing require me to leave this chapter unchanged, although I no longer fully agree with it. It reflects the way our research group understood Beer's model in 1974. As of today, I find it to be too mechanistic, too constructivist. In the years since I have had ample opportunity to work with the model in practice, which has convinced me of its effectiveness; so I regret even more that the chapter cannot be changed for the reasons mentioned and that a new description reflecting a more current view will have to be left to another publication. Based on my own experience with the model in helping to solve companies' problems, and in particular due to Beer's book *The Heart of Enterprise*, which provides the most comprehensive and, as far as I am concerned, clearest description of the model, I am convinced that this is one of the most significant contributions to the understanding of complex systems and a major breakthrough from the perspective of both cybernetics and management. This model represents one way of structuring complex systems; it is also a language system enabling us to see management problems in a logically consistent, completely new way.

Although in this introduction and in further parts of this book, as well as in Beer's own publications, the term repeatedly used is the Viable Systems "Model," I believe that it is in fact—in particular in the version described in *The Heart of Enterprise*—a *theory* in the true sense of the word. What is more, I believe it is actually the first management theory that really deserves the name, while the literature we have so far, as interesting and helpful as it may be in some cases, actually represents approaches, attempts, opinions, and views most of which are highly arbitrary. I have to admit, however, that it was only after the manuscript of this book was finished—and specifically in the course of my attempts to apply Beer's thinking in practice—that my present perspective on his work crystallized. This is one of the reasons why I believe that the description of his model rendered here does not really do justice to the significance of his work. It does take some effort, however, to understand the model, because Beer does not really make it easy for readers to approach his way of thinking. So, although the next chapter is not fully satisfactory in itself, I find this deficiency to be remedied by the two chapters following it.

Chapter 2 deals with the problem of complexity and two additional ways to get it under control: *order* and *problem solving*. The chapter will discuss two kinds of order and two kinds of problem-solving processes, which are required to understand the Viable Systems Model the way Beer wanted it to be understood. The problem of addressing and managing complexity is considered to be *the* key problem of management, and the most important ways to solve it are order, or system structures, and the resulting *problem-solving capacity* of the system.

In Chapter 3 I will try to provide a rationale for my view that a promising approach to dealing with complexity will have to focus on the *meta-systemic* level. This term corresponds to the distinction between the object and the meta-language, which initially seemed to be relevant only for formal logic and basic mathematics. Today we know that complex systems are impossible to understand unless you distinguish between the object and the meta-system. From a systems theory point of view, effective management is essentially a meta-systemic activity. The discussion will show that there is a series of meta-systemic principles of crucial strategic importance. In Chapter 3 I will also try to synthesize the individual parts of this book into a systems methodology of a meta-systemic nature, which can be construed as strategy for managing complex systems.

# 1. The Cybernetic Organization Structures of Management Systems[*]

## 1.1 Introduction

Due to the increasing complexity of their tasks, managers at all levels of business organizations and other socio-technical systems face problems no longer amenable to traditional methods and ways of thinking. Increasing complexity requires them to develop new approaches to the design and management of socio-technical systems, focusing on the *organization* or the activities to be managed. This, in turn, requires developing an organization model to serve as a grid for localizing and addressing problems of both operational and strategic management. In this chapter, such an organization model will be presented: It is the *Viable Systems Model*, which was developed by Stafford Beer in two decades of cybernetic research. We will begin by explaining the general structure of viable systems and their invariance, as well as the distribution of the necessary functions in this structure. Next, we will look at the principles of the model's structure and use, most specifically the principles of recursion, divisional autonomy, and viability. The VSM will then be explained in detail, with analysis of system functions 1 through 4 and descriptions of their components. Finally, the overall model will be depicted at several different levels of recursion in order to make it easier for you to understand the fundamental interconnections. All this will be preceded by a few brief remarks on management cybernetics to shed some light on the background of using this cybernetic organization model.

---

[*] This chapter has been written in collaboration with Dr. Peter Gomez and Dr. Karl-Heinz Oeller, in order to ensure a common basis for the cybernetic discussion of operations managements (P. Gomez), strategic managements (F. Malik), and key business figures (K.H. Oeller). An identical version of it is therefore incorporated in the works of both P. Gomez and K.H. Oeller; see Gomez (Operations Management) and Oeller (Kennzahlen). Sections 11 through 14 were written by me, while P. Gomez was in charge of the 15th and K.H. Oeller the 16th section.

## 1.2 Management Cybernetics

To understand the cybernetic organization model described below, it is helpful to form a general idea of the role that cybernetics plays in the area of management. The basic significance—or potential, if you will—that cybernetic and system-theoretical ideas can have was recognized quite early. The expectations associated with these new ideas were very high, sometimes bordering on the fantastic.

Meanwhile, some results have been achieved. A general awareness of the multidimensional nature of events in an organization has largely replaced the former, rather one-sided perspectives. An integrated, synthetic way of looking at things has gained as much importance as the analytical one that used to prevail; the notion of feedback is widely accepted and applied; there is general agreement on the importance of communication processes; business enterprises are no longer analyzed in isolation but in the context of their relationships with their environment; questions of methodology are being discussed, in particular with regard to solving highly complex problems; and on the whole, system ideas have gradually loosened some of the rigid principles of structure and organization. In addition to these general characteristics of the cybernetic and systems-theoretical thinking that is slowly but steadily gaining ground, there is a series of cybernetics-based approaches to solving specific problems. Apart from the actual automation efforts, attempts include everything from integrated production planning and control to warehousing systems and the like and on to integrated planning and management information systems. All these concepts are more or less influenced by cybernetic ideas. Some are applied in practice; others are under development. Needless to say, there are also a vast number of concepts that only seem to be related to cybernetics and systems theory, and which hardly get beyond the surface of sheer terminology.

However, except for the cybernetics-oriented *thinking* mentioned earlier, the problem-solving approaches targeted at very specific problems have hardly gotten closer to the *core* of the overall problems management faces. One reason is that they address *parts* of problems, while management always has to keep sight of the entire organization. Another reason is that partial problems can often be studied using simplified assumptions. In other words, the very characteristic of problems that calls for cybernetic concepts to be applied—that is, their complexity—is eliminated. Cybernetics, seeing itself as the science of system control and explicitly taking into account the complexity of real systems, is the discipline one would first expect to bring new impulses to the development of management theory and practice.

The most promising approach is clearly presented in the works of Stafford Beer, who has to be considered the preeminent pioneer of management cybernetics. Beer mainly focuses on analyzing the actual core mechanisms of management and summarizing them in one consistent theory. His findings culminate in an overall model on the structure of any system capable of subsisting in a dynamic—that is, continually and unpredictably changing—world. Problems such as adaptability, flexibility, the ability to learn, self-regulation, and self-organization are his main concern. Generally speaking, the key problem of cybernetics is the question as to how systems of any kind can cope with the complexity of their environment, which, above all, results from permanent changes and the speed of change. The answer lies in the *structure* or *organization* of the systems in focus. Organization is the key means of dealing with explosively growing complexity.

However, not every organization form has the potential to cope with complexity: Solving this problem requires extremely complex structures. Even a very superficial cybernetic analysis impressively shows that most social systems have organization structures whose foundations were developed at a time when just a fraction of today's complexity existed, and which therefore appear rather anachronistic when analyzed from the perspective of complexity management.

The need for fundamental changes in the way social systems are organized is recognized widely, yet there is no consensus as to where these changes should be headed. The solution Stafford Beer has developed for this problem in 20 years of cybernetic research is the Viable Systems Model, which is described in the following sections. Above all, the model includes the results of bio- and neuro-cybernetic studies which are transferred to the humanities, specifically to management theory, using the invariance theorem, which will be discussed in more detail later. It essentially says that all complex systems, regardless of their substantial manifestation, have isomorphic control structures. In the history of evolution, the most highly developed governance structure is clearly the human central nervous system, including the brain. Although the functioning and organization principles of the central nervous system are yet to be fully explored in detail, the findings of neurophysiologic and neurocybernetic studies suffice to define a general model of structures and functions. Due to the invariance of the governance structure of all complex systems, one could use any random complex system for illustration, such as an ecosystem comprising several interacting populations. And since a certain level of knowledge on functional connections in the human central nervous system is generally available and understood, the human central nervous system provides the best starting point and reference for the following description of a viable system.

Allow me a word on terminology at this point. Cybernetics boasts a host of terms that have been transferred from the research of organic problems to other areas, or were adopted from those, because this made it possible to discuss problems that had gone unnoticed before, if only for reasons of language. It is neither possible nor desirable to do without cybernetic terminology. In some cases a cybernetic term can be replaced with a term from management theory, but in many cases this is impossible. So if the vocabulary used in the following chapters seems a bit biologic and the term "viable system" is used even when referring to a socio-technical system, this is not a sign of neglectful use of analogies or metaphors. It does make sense to use cybernetic terminology here, and in the further course of describing the model it will become clear that the terms used have very precise meanings.

The VSM and the theory behind it have had far-reaching consequences for the design and management of systems of every kind. In the light of this theory, large parts of conventional organization and management theory lose much of their significance; many elements turn out to be wrong. Hardly a view held in conventional theory will remain unaffected. Of course, the VSM must not be understood as a simple recipe for the solution of all problems of organization and management theory; the model requires careful consideration in both developing and applying it. Given a careful approach, it will prove to be an enormously powerful tool.

Above all, it is safe to assume that certain solutions to organizational problems have been developed in practice which make much more sense when viewed in the context of the overall model and are cybernetic in the best sense of the word. The mere fact that a business organization or any other social system is able to exist and function over longer periods of time is an indicator that within this system, mechanisms have been developed that strongly contribute to the viability of the overall system. This does not necessarily mean that the members of a social system will always be aware of the cybernetic significance of these mechanisms, such as codes of behavior, organizational rules, and the like. What it means is that both the description of the VSM and its application for specific problems of analysis and design do *not* assume a social system to be a structural vacuum. A specific business organization under analysis does exist. It operates in the environment relevant to it, more or less successfully, and that alone indicates—as mentioned before—that there are certain mechanisms at work that safeguard the viability of that system. It would make little sense to negate everything developed so far, an organization's entire history and tradition, its staff's experiences, knowledge, and skills, and to set about building the whole system from scratch. Beer's model is so valuable because it enables us to determine, based on "hard" analysis, which of the behaviors and rules practiced are useful from the Viable Systems point of view and should thus be continued, and what other mechanisms have yet to be developed in order to expand certain, perhaps rudimentary functions and to introduce mechanisms that may still be lacking. In other words, although a major part of traditional organizational theory is proven obsolete by the VSM, another part of theoretical and especial practical organizational and management know-how may continue to be useful. The model provides a consistent frame of reference they can fit into, and permits evaluating the relative strengths and weaknesses of given practical insights.

## 1.3  The Structure of Viable Systems

A key outcome of cybernetics, perhaps the most important of all, is the insight that all viable systems have an invariant structure, or in other words, that only systems with that structure are viable. Of course, the term "viable" is used in a broad sense here. It does not refer to biological-organic viability in its everyday meaning. "Viability" here means that systems with this kind of structure are able to adapt to changing circumstances in their environment, to absorb and utilize experiences—that is, to learn—to maintain their identity and to develop further.

An objection frequently made is that the term "viability" is not permissible when referring to social, cultural, and socio-technical systems. This view is based on the assumption that a system's viability results from very specific qualities of its components. Cybernetic research has shown, however, that this is not the case. In fact, the truly crucial factor is their structure, that is, the specific interrelationship of its components.

"The fundamental discovery of cybernetics is that the structures of large complicated systems are what cause them to behave as they do. To take an important example, if we can find a structure which of its nature learns, as we can, then any system informed by this structure will proceed to learn ... Structure within the system is exactly what makes it the system that it is."[44]

The cybernetically relevant qualities and functions of systems are never located at certain points in the system—they are a result of the system's being organized in a specific way. This is why they are qualities and functions of the system as a whole—although not as *constitutive* characteristics of the entity system, but as characteristics of the way its components are linked. From this we can conclude that the same organization structure can be implemented in very different systems with different components,[45] and that these systems—which would otherwise be considered to be very different—can be classified in one category based on their identical organization structures.

1.31 The Viable Systems Model (VSM)

The following paragraphs will describe the basic structure of a (any) viable system. This description will focus on the most essential aspects. Later sections will deal with the details of each element. The purpose of this section is just to form a general idea of the nature of the model and its usage, and to introduce a few terms that will be required to follow the argumentation.

The paradigm of a cybernetic system is the living organism, as it develops in constant interaction with its environment, learning and achieving a steady state with its environment. The cybernetic paradigm of *control* of a living organism is, in popular terms, everything that innervates it; so, basically that would equate the central nervous system including the brain with its respective characteristics at the different stages of evolution. Its formal structure is that of a homeostat, and its basic mechanism is homeostasis. The mechanism of homeostasis is able to maintain one or several simple or complex

---

44 Beer (System Approach), p. 30.
45 See Varela, Maturana, and Uribe (Autopoiesis), p. 188.

variables within specified behavioral limits.[46] Homeostasis is the most important form of a control mechanism, or controller.[47]

The closest management equivalent to the cybernetic paradigm of the living system or organism is the small company managed by the individual entrepreneur. This prototype, the pioneer-entrepreneur, possesses all necessary information on any aspect of the company; she knows what happens in the organization; she knows her customers; she is aware of the strengths and weaknesses of her products; she more or less fulfills all functions herself and is the "spiritus rector" of the enterprise, in the true sense of the word. In this context, problems such as centralization versus decentralization, delegation of tasks, responsibilities and competencies, complicated forms and documentation systems, time-consuming meetings, and so on, will not exist. There will be no sub-optimization of sub-functions and the problem of competing institutional priorities is not very likely to arise. The general management of the company is integral, indivisible, and a task that can be performed with utmost efficiency because its dimensions allow an individual, or perhaps a small team, to keep an eye on virtually all issues at the same time. As the company grows, however, and the complexity of its internal and external situation increases, its integral management by a person or a close-knit team is no longer possible. The problem of delegation will arise, and so will the problem of distributing functions over several people, the problem of the division of labor and thus knowledge, and—immediately associated with it—the problem of re-integrating the tasks and functions that have been divided.

The transition from an integrally managed organization to one managed by division of labor[48] is tantamount to the crossing of a complexity barrier.[49]

---

46 On the functioning of the cybernetic mechanism of homeostasis, see Ashby (Brain), pp. 80 et seq.; Beer (Decision), pp. 277 et seq.; Beer (Brain), pp. 184 et seq.; Beer (Platform), pp. 426 et seq.; Gomez, Malik, and Oeller (Systemmethodik), pp. 558 et seq.

47 On the cybernetic terms "control" and "controller," see Gomez, Malik, and Oeller (Systemmethodik), pp. 113 et seq., and the sources indicated there.

48 Of course, even in an integrally managed organization there can be a division of labor at the execution level. What I am referring to here is that management as such can only be performed in a division of tasks once a certain level of complexity has been reached.

49 It is usually not possible to determine precisely the point where a critical level of complexity has been reached or exceeded. The mere increase of certain indicators, such as headcount, sales, and so on, is not tantamount to an increase in complexity. Peter Drucker has often discussed this question (see (Praxis), p. 278f. and (Management), p. 664f.) and he came to the conclusion that "small" enterprises can be very complex regarding its structure and management requirements, whereas "big" enterprises are often surprisingly easy

Once a certain point in the complexity scale is exceeded, most tasks—at least those related to the management of the organization—change completely. Whereas beyond that complexity barrier the exact same laws continue to govern the management, control, and design of systems, they now refer to the overall structure of the organization, its governance as such, not to the way specific tasks are performed by the individual members of the organization.

Below the critical complexity barrier, the VSM is not entirely useless, but there is no need for the explicit application of cybernetic concepts. Due to the limited dimensions of all matters, the laws mentioned are usually complied with, implicitly or intuitively, by everyone concerned. Only after the critical mark has been crossed will management and organization become a key issue; only then will management require more than intuition, experience, and tact. Beyond the complexity barrier, management turns into an explicit application of cybernetic laws. From this point on, management is the profession that is based on the science of cybernetics.[50]

The most preeminent characteristic of social systems located beyond the critical mark of complexity is none other than their complexity, which by far exceeds any measure the human brain can capture. The only way to quantitatively describe it is by referring to the explosively growing functions of the variables characterizing the system. In a management context, complexity means that the formal management bodies of an organization can never have all the information, skills, and know-how they would need to control and shape an organization located beyond the complexity barrier *in its details*. The major part of the decisions adding up to from the overall activity of the organization cannot be made by its actual formal management bodies, because they lack the information required for reasonable decisions. One key reason is that the matters on which management bodies have to be informed will have changed long before this information reaches its destination.

The formal management bodies can define a *general line of conduct* for the organization through certain kinds of decisions and by setting rules that concern the organization as a whole and provide a frame of reference for the numerous and diverse detail decisions. Nevertheless, the organization is

---

to manage. Generally speaking, complexity depends on the interaction between the different aspects and variables of an enterprise and on the speed and predictability of changes.

50 See Beer (Decision), p. 239.

largely self-regulating and even self-organizing from the perspective of the formal management bodies.

Now, organizing and controlling a system that largely regulates and organizes itself—that is, that is intrinsically managed—is very different from shaping and controlling a system which largely depends on explicit or extrinsic control[51] and which is below the complexity barrier.

With the following comments on the VSM I hope to establish the basic control structure of every system of this kind, which in most social systems is concealed by rampant complexity; further, I will show how a basically self-organizing and self-regulating system has to be organized and controlled. Since this shaping and control goes beyond the system's self-organizing and self-regulating characteristics, we can speak of meta-organization and meta-control in the logical sense of the words.

### The Overall Structure of the Viable System[52]

As mentioned before, we use the human central nervous system as a starting point and a reference. Figure 1.31(1) shows a control-relevant depiction of the most important parts of the central nervous system. Figure 1.31(2) shows the general control relationships abstracted from these specific structures of the nervous system, which will be used to illustrate the explanations given in the further course of this book.

---

51 On "intrinsic" and "extrinsic" control, see Gomez, Malik, and Oeller (Systemmethodik), pp. 123 et seq.
52 For the following, see Beer (Brain), pp. 135 et seq.; I will refrain from providing detailed reference here.

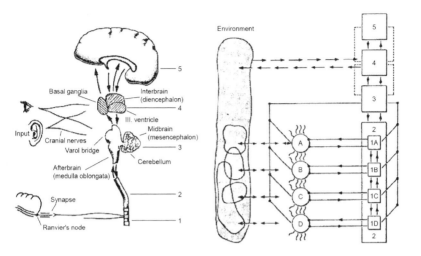

*Figure 1.31(1): Central nervous system*[53] *Figure 1.31(2): General control relationships*
*of the viable system*[54]

Five structural elements, or subsystems, can be distinguished. We will refer to them as systems 1 through 5. They are represented by rectangular symbols. Each viable system has to perform certain operational activities, which in figure 1.31(2) are represented by the circles marked as A, B, C, and D. Each of these activities—which in the human body would correspond to the individual organs and limbs, and in business organizations to the various departments and divisions—is performed in an environment relevant to this activity, which can be linked to other environments and, in addition, is part of the environment that is relevant to the system as a whole and connected to it through system 4.

To give you a rough idea of how this abstract, formal structure can be read, figures 1.31(3) through 1.31(6)[55] show several possible interpretations. Studying them will aid understanding of the following description of the individual components.

### System 1
Systems 1 are the bodies controlling the viable system's main activities, subsystems or areas, as represented by circles A through D. In the human body,

---

53 See Beer (Brain), p. 129.
54 See Beer (Brain), p. 168.
55 See Beer (Prerogatives), pp. 6 et seq.

the equivalent to the systems 1 would be the 31 vertebrae of the spinal column, which have specific control functions for defined organs and limbs. In the organizational context, circles A through D stand for quasi-autonomous entities or divisions, with systems 1A through 1D representing the divisional *management*; in hospitals these would be the different departments and facilities.

Two principles are crucial for structuring a viable system in system 1 areas:

- the principle of viability
- the principle of recursion.

Both will be dealt with at a later point. For the moment it should suffice to gain an impression of the basic ideas inherent to both principles.

According to the viability principle, the system has to be broken down into elements which are also viable, that is, basically able to form independent systems in themselves and exist independently in their environments. So the division cannot be arbitrary; it has to follow the principle of viability. In organizational theory, what best meets this criterion is the divisional structure. In any case, the formation of subsystems requires thorough analysis.

At the beginning of this section I said that every viable system has the same structure or organization. Now if the basic structure of a viable system has to meet the criterion of viability—that is, if each area is a viable system within a viable system—the conclusion is that every subsystem formed according to this principle has to be organized in the same way as the total system. This is basically what the *principle of recursion* says. Every viable system is a structural copy of the viable system it is a part of. This also means that all of the areas A through D (see figure 1.31(2)) with their systems 1A through 1D are *organized in the same manner* as the total system.

### System 2

Every single system 1 *on principle* has absolute freedom of action. However, as it is part of a greater system, its room for maneuver has to be restricted for the sake of the greater entity, and for the sake of the other systems 1 which are also part of the overall system. Coordinating and harmonizing the actions of all systems 1, within the restrictions given in the overall system, is a coordinating function performed by system 2. It essentially consists of balancing existing dysfunctionalities and oscillations between the systems 1.

The problem is rather common in the business context. A decentralized corporation will have its quasi-autonomous divisions. Based on corporate planning, target setting, personal consultations, meetings, and so on, each of these divisions, or their management, will have more or less clear ideas on what top management expects of them. In these ideas, other divisions' existence and the fact that each of them has to make its own contribution to the greater whole are included, at least implicitly. These explicit guidelines reach the divisions through the vertical command axis. Within these guidelines, each division is called upon to optimize its own performance. Each division operates in the environment relevant to it; each has its own specific problems which it tries to solve as effectively as possible, without paying much attention to the other divisions. If everything went according to plan in the execution of divisional tasks, there would hardly be any coordination issues. But since there is no guarantee of that and any kind of disturbance—both of the external and of the internal kind—has to be reckoned with, greater and smaller conflicts between the divisions are almost inevitable.

The difficulties depend on a *minimum of three factors*:

1. the complexity of the environment relevant to the division—that is, the kind and frequency of unforeseeable developments;
2. the intensity of the divisions' interdependencies. The division can be very tightly linked, for instance if there are mutual supply relationships in that one division processes the products delivered by the other division. In that case, disruptions in one division will immediately and fully affect the other divisions as well. By contrast, if the total system is a conglomerate of divisions that are largely unrelated, disturbances or disruptions in individual divisions will hardly affect the remaining ones;
3. the quality of divisional management—that is, the quality of the control mechanism referred to as system 1.

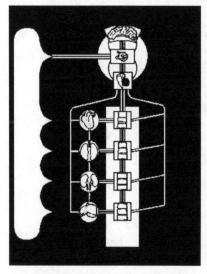

*Figure 1.31(3): Control-relevant struc-tur business organization*

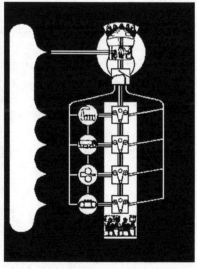

*Figure 1.31(4): Control-relevant struc-ture of a business organization*

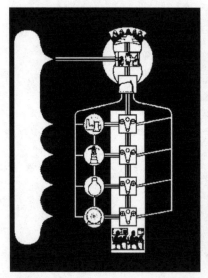

*Figure 1.31(5): Control structure of an industrial system*

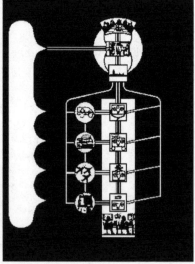

*Figure 1.31(6): Control structure of government activities*

It is the task of system 2 to settle these conflicts, no matter what their causes or sources, through *interdivisional* coordination. Its function is to exploit the synergies that the overall company intended to create by passing plans, guidelines, and instructions to the divisions. What the individual divisions and their managements (systems 1) perform are divisional tasks, while the coordination between the divisions and the synergy effects they are intended to create is a task of the overall organization.[56] How this coordination task is to be accomplished in practice can only be decided based on detailed analysis of the individual organization. In essence, all kinds of coordination tools and mechanisms can be used, such as committees, meetings, planning, and budgeting systems, but also informal communication relationships among the individual divisions, both at executive and at staff level.

*System 3*

Although system 2 coordinates the systems 1 interactions, there is no guarantee that the coordinated systems 1 will jointly have a better or stronger effect than the sum of their individual activities. Ensuring that is the task of system 3. When describing systems 1 and 2, I pointed out that the divisions' basic freedom of behavior is restricted by the guidelines and rules governing the overall system. System 3 works out this overall operational plan, based on information from the systems 4 and 5—which will be described at a later point—and from systems 1 and 2. Hence, system 3 is best understood as the *optimization of resource allocation*, including their assignment to the divisions, as well as the *monitoring of the purposive use* of these resources. To fulfill this task, and to do so under continually changing circumstances reported from both the lower- and the higher-level systems, three key communication links are available:

1. the central vertical command axis extending to each system 1, or to the divisional management systems;

---

56 Distinguishing the divisional and the corporate perspectives is of utmost importance for the correct understanding of the model. The following remark by A.P. Sloan, referring to the problem of allocating and evaluating individual divisions' activities, shows that this is not just cybernetic sophistry: "It was not ... a matter of interest to me only with respect to my divisions, since as a member of the Executive Committee, I was a kind of general executive and so had begun to think from the corporate viewpoint." Sloan (General Motors), p. 48.

2. a channel connected to system 2 and, similar to the corresponding part of the human nervous system, representing the sympathetic system. Through this channel, system 3 receives information on the coordination efforts of system 2 and the results achieved;

3. a channel providing a direct link to the divisions, and which corresponds to the human parasympathetic nervous system. This channel directly conveys to system 3 special information on what is going on in the divisions, in particular information that has no counterpart in the company's official planning, such as on the workload and stress level in the divisions, or on new developments that cannot be included in the planning system and that "official" tools such as progress monitoring cannot take account of.

Systems 1 and 2 are *inward-focused* on the overall organization. Divisions A, B, C, and D operate in an environment relevant to them as divisions, and so have to process environmental information from a divisional perspective; but from the perspective of the overall company, these are matters of its internal stability. System 3 is also largely focused on maintaining the internal equilibrium, on internal harmonization and optimization—except for its connection to system 4.

*System 4*
The overall system cannot exist without any information about the outside world—the environment in which it operates as a whole. Even the internal equilibrium can only make sense as long as external factors are also taken into account. It is the task of system 4 to receive, process, and forward information on the environment. If we imagine a group of associated companies operating in different industry sectors, perhaps even different industries, it is obvious that environmental information received by each division has to be distinguished from the corporation's relationships to its environment. There is a series of transactions with the environment which only the company as a whole can perform in a meaningful way, and which transcend the divisions' relations with their environment.[57] In later sections we will deal with the environmental relations maintained by system 4. At this point, suffice it to say that all environment information relevant to the company as a whole enters the organization via system 4. Its physiological analogy is the

---

57 See, e.g., Drucker (Management), pp. 611 et seq.

main sensory organs, from which signals are passed on to other parts of the brain only after highly complicated processing.

Information is forwarded to both the top-level system 5 and system 3. A balance between the internal and the external steady state is attempted through the interaction of systems 3 and 4, under the influence of and monitored by system 5. While system 4 has something of a classical staff function, its functions by far exceed the quasi-objective, merely advisory kind of information processing that staff functions are usually assumed to have. This is why system 4 is located on the central vertical command axis (see figure 1.31(2)).

*System 5*

This system represents the chief decision-making body of the overall system, both by providing the basic standards and rules in which the other systems operate and by determining and selecting the general options for action, thus actively shaping the future for the total system. This is where corporate policy is crafted—albeit not through authoritative, lonely, top-management decision-making but in close interaction with systems 3 and 4 (note the interconnectedness of all of these systems in figure 1.31(2)), which bring their specific information on internal and external events and prospects as well as their views and presumptions to the policy-making process. If we try to provide a concise description of the function of each stage in the vertical command axis, what we get is the following framework:

| System 1 | What is happening here and now? |
|----------|----------------------------------|
| System 3 | What will happen shortly, and in the circumstances cannot be changed in the short term? |
| System 4 | What could happen, taking into account the development trends that are |
| System 5 | What should happen, based on all these considerations? |

*Figure 1.31: System 2 cannot fit into the framework because, as we have seen, its task is to coordinate systems 1.*

The five systems described very briefly here, together with the links between them as shown in figure 1.31(2), form the structure of the viable system. As mentioned before, only their abstract basic functions and connections have been outlined, and of course a deeper understanding of the model, its practical use, and the actual functionality of the overall system requires a closer look at its details. In sections 15 and 16 we will get to another level of detail.


## 1.32 Invariance of Structure

In the previous section, two principles governing the system structure were mentioned: the viability principle and the principle of recursiveness. Both principles are expressions of a basic cybernetics theorem, according to which all complex organizations are mutually isomorphic when regarded as systems under control, and their control structure is an invariant characteristic of all viable systems.[58]

In literature, the term "system" is frequently criticized for being too general and devoid of content. In its usual definition, or so the argument goes, the term can include virtually anything. Attempts at depicting matters by means of system diagrams, critics argue, often result in network diagrams where all elements are interconnected, rendering the whole depiction rather devoid of meaning.

These and similar objections do not apply to the VSM. Of course it is true that it is also a totality of elements connected by relationships, which makes them a system in the general sense. *However, it is equally clear that not every system meeting these criteria has to be a viable system.* The structure of a viable system is very specific; any analysis of a real system, if performed with expertise and appropriate care, will quickly reveal whether that system has exactly that structure, what components are missing overall or in part, what channels are incomplete, and so on. Likewise, designing a viable system in line with the model is anything but a matter of random or arbitrary relationships between its elements. Rather, it requires very thorough consideration of how the structure defined by the model can be implemented in the specific case.

The theorem of invariance has, deliberately and intentionally, not been phrased in a *normative* manner. Rather than stipulating that all viable systems *should* be structured according to the model, it states that they *are* in fact structured that way.[59] This is an apparent contradiction to the organization forms we find in practice. Social systems obviously have a variety of very

58 See Beer (System Approach), p. 30.
59 See Beer (Brain), p. 198, and (Plan), p. 413.

different structures, and if there is invariance at all, it is the hierarchical structure expressed in the organization charts used in organizational theory.

As such, the Viable Systems Theory clearly implies a refutation of major parts of traditional organizational theory. The organization chart, as the graphical manifestation of this theory, illustrates the way organizations *allegedly* function. In fact, they do not entail even a single mechanism that is *truly* significant for the existence and function of an organization. By contrast, the cybernetic VSM covers precisely the structures and mechanisms that are relevant for the viability and functionability of an organization. When using the model to analyze existing social systems we find precisely the structures to be expected according to the invariance theorem, though in part only in rudimentary form, stunted, or embryonic. In most cases, the members of an organization are not aware of the cybernetic meaning of their activities. In some cases, vital functions are performed in passing rather than consciously, and they seem to be emergency measures, ad hoc regulations, and improvisations. For instance, even a superficial diagnostic of a social system will often reveal a completely insufficient divisional structure, systems 2 and 4 in a very atrophied state, and system 5 degenerated to a largely operational system somewhat similar to system 3.

When system structures are revealed which appear pathologic when compared to the frame of reference provided by the VSM, this obviously permits immediate conclusions on the *possible behavior* of that system and above all on the pathologic behaviors of the total system. For instance, a company whose system 4 has degenerated can hardly be expected to adapt to environmental changes quickly, proactively, and in a reasonable way. In pathological structures, such changes are noticed only after they have started affecting the individual areas (divisions/systems 1). In an organization with a defective system 2, one would expect strong fluctuations of all kinds, such as of inventories, capacity utilization, delivery times, and so on.

Due to the fact that in larger social systems hardly anyone possesses an adequate model of how the system works, many activities performed with the best intentions and a great deal of skill create dysfunctional effects. In most cases, these negative effects are noticed rather late, and in completely different places, because tasks performed with shared responsibility are poorly integrated and there is a lack of quick, responsive feedback mechanisms. As a consequence it is impossible to determine the causal relations between activities and their effects, which leads to interventions that only appear to make sense but actually create even more unexpected and unintended effects. But even if the source of certain dysfunctionalities can more or less be located, attempts are usually made to correct the mistake by trying to "improve" the respective employee's behavior. However, as employees' behavior is determined by the specific structural context in which they act, any appeals to improve their performance will only create even greater dysfunctionalities—unless structures are changed so as to improve the company's viability.[60] So the changes required have to aim for the implementation of the VSM.

The fact that there are pathological system structures and system behaviors which analysis can reveal by means of the cybernetic model does not represent a contradiction to the invariance theorem. It only proves that the structures that make a system viable—that is, adaptive, responsive, capable of learning, self-regulating—are *underdeveloped* in many social systems. The reasons are manifold. Most important among them is certainly the general lack of understanding of the mechanisms, structures, rules, and processes that make a system viable. As pointed out in the introduction, cybernetic—specifically bio-cybernetic and neuro-cybernetic—research has impressively shown that systems are viable not due to certain specifics of their organic components, as is generally believed. Rather, it is the organizational and informal links or connections between their components that make them viable. The VSM comprises these links and connections.

## 1.33 Distribution of the Functions

Every pictorial representation of content has to observe certain graphical conventions. The previous graphical depictions of viable systems suggest a clarity of individual system components and their interconnections which we cannot expect to find in real situations. Every graphical or verbal depiction has to apply some form of abstraction and idealization. One example of this is my repeated use of the human central nervous system and brain as an object of reference. Although it is possible to group the structural elements of the brain by anatomical, physiological, and neuro-cybernetic criteria, and thus to get a grasp of them in verbal and visual communication, this could never mislead anyone about the enormous structural complexity of

---

60 Regarding the dysfunctionalities discussed here, see, e.g., Forrester's work on contraintuitive system behavior (Social Systems).

the brain. The connections between the individual components of the brain are so numerous and rich in kind that even the clear distinction between structural components and brain components per se poses a problem.[61]

Parts of these structures merge seamlessly; some functions overlap and, in order to be complete, require the parallel or sequential interaction of numerous structural components. It is the same with social systems. Regardless of the seeming clarity and neatness of structures implied by the organization charts for social systems, any member of such an organization will know from experience that the actual goings-on, the information channels actually used, the distances to be traveled until a decision can be made on important matters, the social groupings within and across organizational departments, the complicated fabric of roles, and so on, much rather correspond to the complexity of neurophysical matters than to the seemingly clear structures depicted in org charts. Not only is this known to the people working in social systems; it has been a much-discussed phenomenon in organizational theory ever since informal organizations were discovered.

The views on this problem of both organization theoreticians and organization practitioners are still very ambivalent. Many scientific papers concede that informal organization structures are a necessary complement to any formal organization structure and that any attempt to remove informal structures or their function will immediately render the organization dysfunctional.

However, the "chaos" organizational insiders seem to face often causes them to try to improve organizational matters, clarify relationships, simplify mechanisms, and "streamline" the organization. What these attempts usually ignore is that the wealth of structures found in every real organization—the apparent chaos—is absolutely essential for the system's functionality. This is not to say that the structures of a company or any other social system could not be improved. However, this issue has to be approached with utmost care and, above all, to be based on a thorough understanding of how companies *really* function, for example, what mechanisms and structures their viability is *really* based on.

Consequently, the *actual structural diversity* of every real system cannot be expressed by either organization charts or graphical depictions of the viable system. The difference between the two depictions is that the organization

---

61 The human brain consists of roughly $10^{10}$ nerve cells (neurons) linked together by approximately $10^{12}$ synapses, which means that each neuron is connected to about 100 other neurons through circuits.

chart at best includes the formal reporting relationships in a social system, while the VSM explicitly shows the mechanisms relevant to the viability of systems. In both cases, applying the tools requires translating the abstract depiction into concrete structures and relationships. If, however, the VSM is used to analyze and shape a real organization, this ensures that the system's fundamental control characteristics will not be disregarded—whereas the latter can easily happen if the analysis is based on organization charts.

In the graph (see figure 1.31(2)), the functions any viable system needs to have are located in each of the systems 1 through 5. In a real social system, these functions can be either located somewhere or distributed over the whole system, with the latter being the much more significant version. For instance, the function of system 4—receiving, analyzing, assessing, and passing on information on the organization's environment and bringing this information to the process of stabilizing the overall organization—can very well be supported by a market research team, reports from the sales people in the field, and periodical visits of production staff to industrial fairs. At the same time, the formal and informal relationships of top management to government authorities, major competitors, and so on, will contribute their share to the completion of the system 4 function. Last but not least, the company's purchasing agents, members of the labor council—via their trade union links—and a large number of other employees at various levels and in various areas of the organization obtain a wealth of information that, from a cybernetic point of view, is system 4 information. So the VSM must not be understood to mean that the respective system functions are performed by one gigantic corporate department each, and that the connections between these departments have to be designed as formalized communication channels. Rather, it is the management cyberneticist's task to explore which of the everyday activities in the organization also fulfill the functions of the viable system, implicitly or explicitly. He or she has to filter out the cybernetic core content of all activities at all hierarchical levels and in all functional areas, departments, and so on, and summarize these activities in accordance with the functions of the viable system.

Note that this only means that activities are linked *functionally*—the staff concerned does not necessarily have to be centralized in one location.

Physical centralization *can* be one of several means of coordination: for instance, when a group of employees is thus given the opportunity to develop into a self-controlled, autonomous work group. Figure 1.33(1) illustrates some aspects of this analysis and design process.

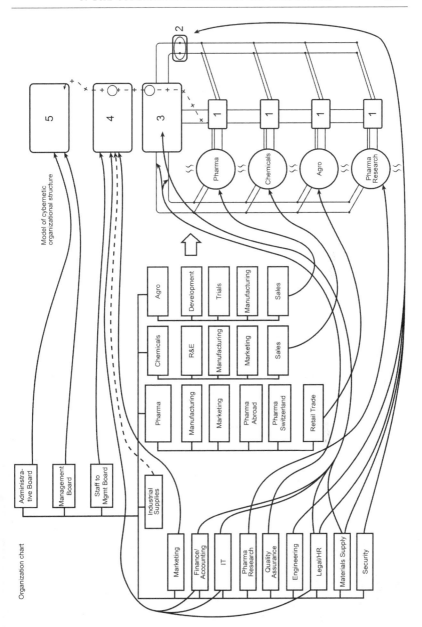

*Figure 1.33(1): Model of the cybernetic organization structure*

## 1.4  Principles of the Model's Structure and Application

Section 1.3 provided a first overview of the structure of the VSM, as well as a few remarks to enable a general understanding of the model's structure. This section will deal with the basic principles of the model's structure and application. These principles are so important to the understanding of the model and its application in practice that a detailed discussion of their content appears in order. Specifically, this refers to the principles of recursion, to divisional autonomy, and to systemic viability.

### 1.41  The Principle of Recursion[62]

When describing system 1 in section 1.3, I already mentioned the principle of recursiveness, or recursion. It is one of the key principles in *structuring a system*. As explained in that section, it basically says that in a constellation of systems, which in general systems terminology can be referred to as systems, subsystems, and supersystems, *each system, no matter what level it is on*, is structured the same way. The recursion principle can only be understood in connection with the principle of viability; that is to say, it applies if and when the systems, subsystems, and supersystems under consideration are structured according to the VSM. Consequently, the basic structure of a system hierarchy structured according to the recursion principle does not follow a pyramid-like structure, as known, for example, from depictions in organizational theory. Rather, it consists of systems that are nested within each other, almost like Chinese boxes or Polish dolls.

Figure 1.41(1) shows the recursiveness principle, illustrating the structure of the viable system. As has been mentioned before, every sub-entity of a viable system—which in a business context would be a division—has to be

---

62 The term "recursion" is used here in the strict sense of algebraic number theory: "A function f(n) is said to be defined by recursion if, instead of being defined explicitly (that is, as an abbreviation for some other expression) only the value of f(o) is given, and f(n+1) is expressed as a function of f(n). In other words, a recursive definition does not define f(n) itself but provides a process whereby the values of f(o), f(l), f(2), f(3) and so on, are determined one after the other." Goodstein (Recursive Number Theory), p. viii. On the use of recursive functions in cybernetics, see, inter alia, von Foerster (Memory), pp. 39 et seq. On applying the recursion principle to the design of viable systems, see Beer (Science), p. 11, and (Brain), p. 287.

a viable system in itself. This means that each division has to have the overall structure of a viable system; that is, at the divisional level there will also be systems 1 through 5. Now, since the division itself, being a viable system within the overall organization, comprises systems 1 as quasi-autonomous entities within the division, this means that at this level (i.e., within the division) systems 1—or the divisions of the divisions—must again be structured as viable systems.

A very rudimentary form of the recursion principle is not entirely alien to organizational theory. If, for instance, organization charts are drafted for the management structures of large corporations, in particular those with a group structure, it is clear that each of the entities appearing in the chart would have to be depicted with its own org chart if the details were to be captured. For the sake of clarity and simplicity, however, such level of detail is usually avoided and general structural overviews are used.

But as I said, this is just a very rudimental manifestation of the recursion principle, especially because in an organization chart it may be possible to break down some of the boxes and depict them as organization charts in their own right, but other boxes cannot or must not be broken down. So there would be a confusion of several logical levels, which would conceal the true interrelations and interconnections in the organizational fabric. Another key difference, and a quite obvious one, is that the *cybernetic* recursion principle requires that structures at all levels follow the VSM, based on the specific five-level structure described in section 1.3.[63]

This principle of recursion has very far-reaching consequences for both systems theory and management theory. It leads to a complete reorientation in the way social systems are structured. When considered at *one* recursion level only, the viable system is structured *hierarchically*. This is necessary for logical reasons—the five system components of the viable system are related to one another in a similar way as object language and meta-language; that is, the "higher-level" system component is a meta-system to the "lower" one. Authority-based relationships play a much less important role here than they do in conventional, pyramid-like structures, because "higher" means "meta;" that is, a meta-component is responsible for other kinds of information,

---

63 See figures 1.33(1) and 1.33(2).

other variables, other system aspects.[64] Now, if a system constellation is analyzed at *several* recursion levels, it turns out that—although each level has hierarchical structures—the recursion principle does not create hierarchy in the traditional sense. Rather, it leads to the "lower-level" system being comprised or closed in by the "higher-level" one, or in other words, its *being embedded* in the overall context of the next "higher-level" system. Likewise, the mutual relationships of systems at successive recursion levels are not predominantly relationships of super- or subordination—in the sense of wielding power—but they are *meta-systemic in nature*. Even a cursory glance at the configuration resulting from the recursion principle (see figure 1.41 (l)) reveals that it permits extremely complex system constructions which are much better suited to reflect the complexity of business and social realities than conventional organization charts are.

Thus, the recursive structuring based on the VSM is one of several tools that enable us to comply with Ashby's Law of Requisite Variety. This law,[65] which expresses one of the absolutely fundamental insights of cybernetics, says that the problem of control can only be solved if the variety of the systems in question is in balance. Variety, as a measure of complexity, can only be coped with or absorbed by variety. In simple terms, this means that the only way to get a complex system under control is by having just as much complexity, which, in turn, means that the model we create of a system has to be similarly complex as that system, if the model is to provide a useful reference for control measures.

In addition, recursive system design offers a series of further advantages:

- The subsystems at each level of recursion are systemic entities, as they comprise all structural elements of the viable system.
- As each viable system has at least some degree of autonomy and independence, every system structured according to the principle has considerable potential in terms of coping with complexity.
- Due to the recursiveness of system structures, the same thinking, detailed structuring principles, methods, techniques, programs, and so on can be

---

64 On the logical problem of object and meta-language, or object and meta-system, see, inter alia, Gomez, Malik, and Oeller (Systemmethodik), pp. 308 et seq.; Beer (Platform), pp. 7 et seq., 145 et seq., 236 et seq., 255 et seq.

65 See Ashby (Introduction), p. 206; Beer (Brain), pp. 109 et seq.; Beer (Freedom), pp. 18 et seq.

applied at each level. As a result, there is a much greater variety of possible designs, along with considerable rationalization effects.

– As mentioned before, the principles of recursion and viability do not permit just any kind of system structure, so this may well be the first time the problem of structuring principles can be discussed in a meaningful way, perhaps even solved once and for all. That means that the VSM and the principles for its application provide an extremely valuable diagnostic and design tool.

Beer has formulated two versions of the recursion principle, which both express the underlying design idea very well:

1. "If a viable system contains a viable system, then the organizational structure must be recursive."[66]
2. "If we decide to define a social system by recursion we shall find that every viable system contains a viable system."[67]

Let me illustrate the recursion principle using an example from genetics/biology. As is generally known, each of our body cells contains our entire genetic blueprint. In perfect analogy, a business organization of, say, ten different hierarchical levels designed according to the recursion principle would have the viable system structure at every level—from the company's top all the way down to each of its shop-floor units. Even the individuals working at that company will carry the entire viable system structure in themselves: After all, as I have just mentioned, the model was built after the human central nervous system. So, every viable entity of an organization contains the blueprint of the overall organization, or in other words: The overall organization has been reproduced in each of its viable units.

---

66 Beer (Brain), p. 287.
67 Beer (Science), p. 11.

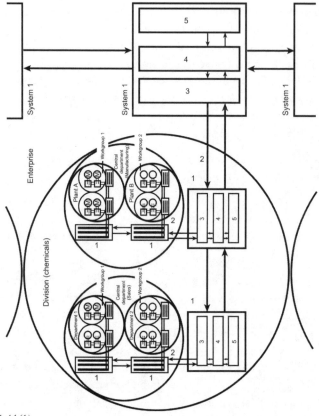

*Figure 1.41(1)*

## 1.42 The Principle of Autonomy: Centralization versus Decentralization[68]

In my general description of the structure of the viable system I have already mentioned that the individual divisions (systems 1) *on principle* have full freedom of behavior. At the same time, these divisions are parts of a greater entity and, according to the recursion principle, embedded in a greater system, which is why their freedom of action *cannot be total and absolute*. We are faced with the classical problem of centralization and decentralization here.

Apart from very few exceptions, in the literature this problem is discussed assuming strongly simplified conditions. The basic model that the discussions of this issue refer to can be depicted as a straight line the ends of which represent the two extremes: total centralization and total decentralization. Everyone knows that neither one can be a reasonable solution. So, if the underlying assumption is that the solution has to be at some point between the two ends, the problem consists in defining a point on that line (see figure 1.42(2)).

The Viable Systems Theory completely refutes this paradigm. Neuro-cybernetic research has shown that a meaningful discussion of the issue of relative autonomy—that is, of identifying the right point between the two extremes—requires a model with *at least two dimensions* (see figure 1.42(2)). In the horizontal dimension, the individual subsystems or divisions, which on principle have freedom of behavior, are arranged almost like the lines of a text. The vertical dimension represents the authority of the system as a whole, which, on principle, is in a position to prevent certain potential behaviors of the divisions.

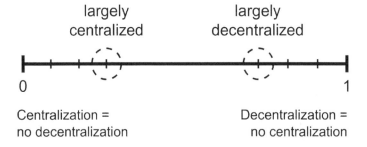

*Figure 1.42(1): Classical paradigm of the problem of centralization versus decentralization*

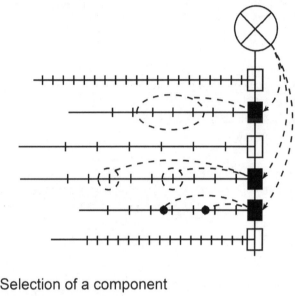

■  Selection of a component
( ⁻ )  Variety reduction for a component
●  Variety increasa for a component

*Figure 1.42(2): Cybernetic interpretation of the problem of centralization versus decentralization*

Interventions in the vertical dimension are characterized by two key aspects:

1.  A choice is made between the components represented in horizontal order
2.  Certain behaviors of the selected, horizontally represented components are prevented or made possible.

Both aspects—the choice of horizontal components and the choice of behaviors permitted or banned—change constantly, depending on the situation of the horizontal components (divisions) and the situation of the overall system.

Both dimensions are subject to a certain variety, which, of course, cannot be described in general but needs to be based on analyses of each particular case. The variety of horizontal components is in proportion to their range of behaviors, which in turn depends on a number of factors. The variety of vertical dimensions is proportional to the power and ability of the total system to reduce the horizontal components' behaviors. For the design of this two-dimensional model of autonomy it does not matter whether the varieties involved can somehow be measured empirically.[69] Although in real-life cases it is certainly possible at least to estimate the scope of these varieties, our objective at this point is just to develop a model that will permit an adequate discussion of the issue of autonomy. Within this model, a definition of autonomy becomes possible:

"If a system regulates itself by subtracting at all times as little horizontal variety as is necessary to maintain the cohesion of the total system, then the condition of autonomy prevails."[70]

The only way to discuss this cohesion of the total system in a meaningful way is in the context of the VSM. Key points are the characteristics and detailed design of systems 1 through 5, as well as the specific layout of the channels connecting them. The problem of *system cohesion* is directly connected to the problem of *system identity* and the system's ability to maintain that identity, irrespective of disturbances and external influences. The system's ability to respond to external disturbances with identity-preserving behaviors immediately follows from the way it is structured. Every viable system is capable of responding to a certain range of disturbance so as to preserve itself, and every system also has a specific level beyond which it will no longer be able to cope with the complexity of disturbances. Consequently, the criterion of total system cohesion which the autonomy of each of the subsystems depends on is a *variable*. Its variations are subject to the environmental pressure on the overall system.

The usefulness of this two-dimensional autonomy model, in which the relative autonomy of each division continually changes depending on the cohesion of the total system—which, in turn, responds to environmental pressures and stress—is illustrated by a rather simple observation: The general

---

69 It is important to point out that the issue of quantification of the aspects discussed here, while potentially significant in real-life settings, is of minor importance for theoretical validity. In the area of *organized complexity*—as opposed to the unorganized complexity which can be addressed with statistical means—it is important to avoid the scientific error of only accepting quantifiable aspects as scientifically significant. Regarding this extremely important issue, see Hayek (Studies), pp. 3 et seq., 22 et seq.; Hayek (Vernunft), pp. 11–142; as well as Weinberg (General Systems), pp. 17 et seq.

70 Beer (Development), p. 7.

willingness to accept central directives and interferences with one's own freedom of behavior is much greater in times of crisis than in situations that experience has taught us can be considered normal. In normal situations, the divisional subsystems' claim for autonomy is a permanent problem; in crises and exceptional situations, divisional freedom is readily abandoned for the sake of the greater whole.

The autonomy of a given level of recursion is guaranteed by the next higher level. In the context of the cybernetic model, this is a question not only of voluntary self-restraint or mutual consensus but especially of the information filters installed—that is, of the actual information the next higher recursion can have, or in other words, of the information rights and duties between the two recursion levels. The fact that a given recursion level in a Viable System can intervene in the divisional freedom of the logically and systemically next lower level must not be understood to be something purely negative. The reduction of the variety of behaviors is both a constraint and a support. It provides support to the divisional entities in that, when the variety is reduced through general rules, this aids their orientation—which is essential to the survival of any system.

There are three basic kinds of interventions by the vertical dimension:

1. general rules of conduct, which apply to one horizontal component in its totality, but can differ for several horizontal components;
2. resource allocation;
3. interventions in the detailed operations of horizontal components.

For the purpose of this paper I will refrain from elaborating on the specific contents of these three interventions and focus on their general aspects instead. The *first* kind of intervention at the intersection of the dimensions is primarily aimed at integrating the respective component into a greater whole. General rules of conduct, directed at the integrity of the whole without eliminating the identity of its parts, define the "partness" of each component. They do that without interfering with the internal operations of that component or with its own inner cohesion and wholeness, which it has to have according to the principles of recursion and viability. Key examples include federal structures in which independent entities (states, cantons) join to form a federation—although in practice, discussions around federalism hardly ever come to an end because the counterparts usually base their ideas on one-sided, over-simplified models.

The *second* kind of intervention by the vertical dimension is the allocation of resources of any kind which the total system has access to. Here it is quite obvious that interventions can contain both an element of constraint and an element of support. Cutting back resources has a constraining effect; allocating resources has a supporting one. A key issue in this context is the way in which resource allocation is handled: that is, how the respective decision-making process is organized, how the horizontal components compete for their shares of the resources, and what responsibility they have for the resources allocated. In practice, such problems are often seen as the "adversities of everyday business" and "bargaining over one's share of the cake." In the context of the VSM, however, it turns out that these are key issues in the overall control of a system, in terms of its viability, or to be more specific: the question of how to ensure greatest possible autonomy for the parts while preserving the integrity of the total system and exploiting synergies. As a matter of fact, the negotiation and decision-making processes to be organized in this context are important information filters and variety management tools which have to be designed with utmost care so as to keep the overall system viable.

The *third* kind of intervention, which is very common in practice, is highly questionable in terms of the system's viability. Within the framework of general rules of conduct and allocated resources, subsystems have to be enabled to use their own mechanisms to cope with complexity. For this purpose, they comprise the whole viable systems structure at their respective recursion level. As I explained earlier, in complex systems you cannot expect all the information needed for detailed decisions to be passed to the formal management bodies unadulterated and in time. But since in a viable system, due to the principles of recursion and viability, each recursion level is equipped with the mechanisms and structures needed to deal with variety, there is no reason for any level to interfere with the detailed operations of the next lower level, apart from the intervention forms already discussed. Should there be apparent or true reasons for such an intervention, the reasons are likely to be found in structural defects of the systems involved.

"The confusion about autonomy is founded in a structural defect of the system, in that the filters are not correctly designed to prohibit horizontal diffusion. The crisis usually arrives when the bosses of the total system perceive the organization as a veritable chaos that they can barely influence, while at the same time the individuals running the parts perceive an autocratic regime that ties their hands. The bosses see themselves as uttering genuine policies—mere prescriptions; those at the lower level receive inhibiting rules—genuine proscriptions. This situation is explosive. The bosses may go so far as to say that their people are anarchists, that no one takes any notice of them any longer, or that they are reduced to an advisory role in the interest of "permissive" notions put about by social scientists. The managers of the parts may go so far as to say that their jobs could be done by a well-trained poodle, whereupon they start to look through the job advertisements. And both of these sets of people are describing *the same* situation … in less dramatic forms it seems to me endemic to contemporary management. The only people who are going to get any joy out of it are the consultants who will advocate more centralization, and then return later to advise decentralization."[71]

The description I have so far given of the two-dimensional model of relative autonomy of viable systems within a viable total system may appear very complicated at first. But as the real matters discussed are highly complex, a simple model would hardly be suited to capturing the problem. Also, the practical solutions developed for this problem are anything but simple.

Careful analysis of the reorganization that General Motors underwent in the 1920s, under the guidance of Alfred P. Sloan, will illustrate the degree of complexity. With respect to this subject, Harald Wolff notes:

"When reading Sloan's book very carefully, it is striking that the restructuring that Sloan and his staff carried out at GM was not a decentralization in the usual sense. On the contrary, it was a much more complex and multi-layered mix of carefully allocated responsibilities. Even within the GM organization, some of the most important and successful units were actually strictly centralized. Moreover, there is a growing number of cases to prove that the kind of decentralization commonly (erroneously) referred to as being characteristic of GM has led to failure just as often as it has led to success for other companies. That is why decentralization and the "profit centers" associated with it are, at least in their simple from, far from being considered universal management principles. They only prove effective under very specific conditions, and only if they are implemented with particular care—as was the case with GM."[72]

The fact that Sloan was aware of the enormous complexity of the problem discussed here is obvious from a remark he made with regard to the issue of a company's size:

"It should be clear that I do not regard size as a barrier. To me it is only a problem of management. My thoughts on that have always revolved around one concept

---

71 Beer (Crisis), p. 328; emphasis as in the original.
72 Wolff (General Motors), p. 98 (author's translation).

which contains considerable complexity in theory and in reality—the concept that goes by the oversimplified name of decentralization."[73]

At another point—in the chapter headed "Concept of the Organization"—Sloan clearly addresses the core of the problem. He reports that the fundamental organizational study he made was based on two principles, which I quote here:

1. "The responsibility attached to the chief executive of each operation shall in no way be limited. Each such organization headed by its chief executive shall be complete in every necessary function and enabled to exercise its full initiative and logical development.
2. Certain central organization functions are absolutely essential to the logical development and proper control of the Corporation's activities.

   ... looking back on the text of the two basic principles, after all these years, I am amused to see that the language is contradictory, and that its very contradiction is the crux of the matter. In point 1, I maximize decentralization of divisional operations in the words "shall in no way be limited." In point 2, I proceed to limit the responsibility of divisional chief executives in the expression "proper control." The language of organization has always suffered some want of words to express the true facts and circumstances of human interaction. One usually asserts one aspect or another of it at different times, such as the absolute independence of the part, and again the need of coordination, and again the concept of the whole with a guiding center. Interaction, however, is the thing, and with some reservation about the language and details I still stand on the fundamentals of what I wrote in the study. Its basic principles are in touch with the central problem of management as I have known it to this day."[74]

At General Motors, Sloan managed to solve the fundamental contradictions associated with the idea of centrally coordinating decentralized units with positively brilliant logic and intuition. Still, he did not succeed in developing universal principles for structuring organizations. With regard to this problem, Peter Drucker writes:

"Despite Sloan's pioneering work, we still do not know what structure most large business organizations should have. In my mind, Sloan's method of decentralizing operations while, at the same time, centralizing policies and control does not apply to more than two out of five large corporations—specifically, to those where identifiable economic units are manufactured and sold separately. They are not applicable

---

73 Sloan (General Motors), p. xxii f.
74 Sloan (General Motors), p. 53.

to a bank or insurance company. Neither are they applicable to the materials industry—e.g., steel or aluminum—where the whole production output is generated by the same process. If fate had put Sloan at the helm of U.S. Steel, his first-class intellect might have worked out an appropriate organization structure for a steel group. However, he did not work on setting up a universal theory for structuring major corporations. The conclusion is that this is a task we have yet to accomplish. And this can only happen by developing general ideas and principles that will enable us to deal with structural problems."[75]

This is precisely the problem that is solved by the cybernetic VSM. Of course, it is not a solution to be adopted by just any company without further checking. As with most cybernetic solutions, its value lies at the structural level. As has been demonstrated, cybernetics can identify the problem within the general viable system structure and determine w here it is located. With the two-dimensional autonomy model, it provides a language rich enough to permit objective discussion of the problem. If neuro-cybernetic research findings are included, it permits determining the direction in which nature itself has found a solution for this problem of relative autonomy.


1.43 The Principle of Viability[76]

In the course of my previous remarks on the structure of viable systems, the basic idea of viability has already been presented. Still, a few specific remarks seem warranted, especially since the concept of survival, which in cybernetic literature is often presented as the superior and ultimate purpose of every system, often meets with misunderstandings.

It is extremely important to be aware that the concept of viability, as used in the cybernetic context, is a typically meta-linguistic or mega-systemic idea to assess the structural effectiveness of a system. This means that the assertion that a system is viable says absolutely nothing about the state or configuration of states the system is in. Rather, "viability" means that the specific configuration of states the system is in can be maintained for an indefinite amount of time.

As mentioned before, many cybernetic studies postulate that survival is the system's ultimate goal or purpose. Although this postulate is generally deemed adequate for other, in particular less sophisticated biological systems, it is considered rather unsatisfactory for many other systems, especially

---

75 Drucker (Großunternehmen), p. 324 (quote translated by author).
76 See Beer (Brain), pp. 283 et seq.; Beer (Platform), pp. 423 et seq.

for humans and most other social systems. The reason seems to be that "survival" always seems to imply surviving on the edge of livelihood.

"Surviving" is construed to mean "pure survival," which in turn—and justifiably—is considered a restrictive, necessary condition or prerequisite for a system's further development and prosperity, not its superior and ultimate goal. Every system, in particular a social system, can take a number of configurations, one of which is "pure survival." In might just as well be in a configuration of continued wealth, a low or a high cultural level. The crucial question is whether these are permanent configurations, that is, whether specific configurations can be maintained for a specific amount of time. That is nothing else but the question of the viability of a system, in general terms. This is not cybernetic sophistry. It conforms to a point of view and an approach to judgment that is also expressed in realistic, pragmatic everyday judgments. For instance, it is manifest in statements such as, "He won't be able to keep up this extravagant lifestyle for long," and "With this project, they have bitten off more than they can chew," and "They have not managed to find a workable compromise as yet." When at times of economic crisis someone says that an industry is not going to survive long if it keeps on like this, or that a given line of business or profession is not viable, that usually does not mean that the entire industry will disappear. Rather, people making serious statements like these usually try to express that a certain area needs profound, drastic structural changes that might well lead to the demise of certain businesses or companies, but that after a structural improvement the industry or industrial sector will be able to continue its existence in a new configuration. This is precisely how the cybernetic concept of viability is to be understood. Some considerations will quickly reveal that the concept is universally applicable and in this sense, the attribute of viability—not of survival as such—can indeed be considered the highest goal for every system. Of course, the mere survival of a system is included as a marginal case.

Whatever the specific efficiency or effectiveness criteria may be for the individual processes running in a system (technical efficiency, economic efficiency, etc.), *structural* or *systemic* effectiveness can only be assessed based on the criterion of viability. This observation is confirmed by managers' behavior in practice. The one-sided optimization of processes or functions in a company cannot solve a problem for good. A partial optimum is only sustainable for an indefinite period of time, if it can be integrated in the company's overall steady-state equilibrium. These considerations rarely center around the "mere survival" of a company. Rather, they focus on the question of how to achieve a permanent balance of all corporate activities. Any over-emphasis on some activities at the cost of other areas or functions can be nothing but a preliminary state.

Of course, a firm's general management cannot assume to know *in advance* what configuration of states will be viable in the meta-systemic sense. Rather, this is a continuous process of searching and assessing which, however, can only be carried out adequately if management and the overall organization have the right structure. So, "viability"—as repeatedly mentioned—is a matter of systemic structures. Not every system is viable. In the generalized cybernetic meaning referred to here—that is, as a metaphysical criterion—"viability" only comprises the five-level system structure described in section 1.3.

Depending on the level at which this system structure is applied, permanent configurations can be very different. A small business can be just as viable as a large conglomerate, even though their balance sheets and P&L statements will reflect very different sets of states. Whatever indicators may be used to assess businesses, there will always be a great variety of configurations of states. Structural *cybernetic* viability is not a function of the different states that systems can adopt; it is a matter of the individual organizations' invariant system structure or organizational structure. And the latter is not a question of the organization charts, job descriptions, and so on that may officially be in effect in the organizations studied. Rather, it depends on whether careful and thorough analysis of these organizations based on the VSM will reveal the five-level structure.

As is implicit in my earlier remarks on the principles of recursion and of relative autonomy, the viability criterion, or the principle of designing based on the viability criterion, has to be applied at all recursion levels. Each individual recursion has to be viable in itself, which means that the units concerned (body organs, corporate divisions, social institutions, autonomous work groups, military units, university departments, etc.) have to have the viable systems structure as well. Since, however, the viable subsystems at a given recursion level are parts of a viable system at the next higher recursion level, their autonomy can only extend to where they start interfering with the system at the next higher level, and vice versa.

## 1.44 Summary

As has been explained in the introduction to this section, the principles of recursion, relative autonomy, and viability are of crucial importance for the structure of a viable system, and especially for using this structure as a model for socio-technical systems.

On the other hand, it is important to understand the detailed structure of the viable cybernetic system in order to be able to understand the significance of those general principles.

The next section therefore describes the details of the system, while in section 1.6 the overall context is depicted graphically

## 1.5  The Detailed Model for the Cybernetic Organization Structure of Management Systems

### 1.51 System 1

Every business organization has different areas of activity which, within the context of the overall organism, perform specific tasks in relative autonomy. These areas differ by the kind of firm. However, if such a unit is a viable system, it can be integrated in the company's management hierarchy as a *division*. In this hierarchy, *system 1* controls the division in accordance with the corporate policy and the instructions derived from it. System 1 responds to developments in the environment relevant to it, and coordinates with other divisions in order to ensure its own stability in keeping with the overall company's stability.

Its neurophysiologic counterpart is the *reflex arc* with its peripheral ganglion, which is integrated in the total organism as part of the vertical command axis (the spinal cord).[77] The reflex arc embodies the principle of a control mechanism which, through feedback, corrects undesirable developments in the division controlled and ensures the stability of that division. Relating to the business organization, these matters can be schematically depicted as follows:[78]

---

77 See Beer (Brain), p. 139.
78 See Beer (Brain), p. 161.

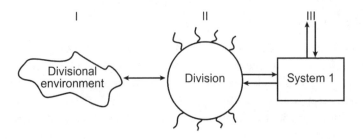

*Figure 1.51(1a): The division's position in its environment*

The *division* to be controlled is exposed to the stimuli from its environment, which force it to adapt permanently (I). In addition, it has to deal with the inflow and outflow of materials, energy, and information to and from other divisions (II). All these coordination tasks have to be performed in line with corporate policies (III), which requires system 1 to exert a great deal of control variety. How is this variety generated so as to enable the division to cope with unpredictable disturbances, or in other words, ensure its *ultrastability*? Beer[79] has demonstrated that system 1 is to be understood as an "anastomotic reticulum"—a network of multiple interconnections which is fed by bundles of input channels and from which bundles of output channels emerge. These things become clearer when we consider the management of a corporate division. The multitude of information inputs and outputs, decisions, directives, and controls cannot be shown in detail, so in any model of these activities the existing variety has to be drastically reduced. Nevertheless, such models have to be built in order to explore the basic mechanisms of information processing and decision-making which can provide useful pointers for an adequate design of system 1.

One way to describe the functionality of system 1 in general terms is by comparing it to a servomechanism. Beer specifies the requirements of this control mechanism as follows:

"What the system needs, and all it needs, is a way of measuring its own internal tendency to depart from stability, and a set of rules for experimenting with responses which will tend back to an internal equilibrium ... To be aware of something happening and label it disturbance, and to be able to alter internal states until the effects of the disturbance are offset, is enough."[80]

---

79 See Beer (Brain), p. 42.
80 See Beer (Brain), p. 38.

Hence, the servomechanism—which follows the principle of negative feedback—has to have the following components:[81]

- An *initial plan*, positioning the division in the overall organism and providing a *standard* against which to assess the division's current development within its environment,
- *sensors* capturing its real-time development, permitting an immediate response to sudden disturbances,
- a repertoire of *plans* for a variety of environmental constellations,
- *motor* channels permitting the execution of the plans selected.

In a servomechanism, undesirable developments trigger corrective action (or plans) themselves, in that these developments themselves will initiate the necessary feedback loops.

So how should a servomechanism be designed if it is to execute the functions of a system 1 controller? First of all, we need a *model* of the division in focus, in order to determine the variables to be monitored and their optimum values. This is a key prerequisite for building sensors and the error-detection mechanism.

In this context, Beer[82] calls for building both a structural and a parametric model. The *structural model*[83] characterizes the division in focus using a number of variables and the relationships between them; that is, it describes their structure without providing any characteristic values of individual variables or relationships. A model of this kind can be very detailed, for instance when it captures a manufacturing process in an arithmetic formula. Often, however, variables are qualitative and the relationships between them comprise whole bundles of channels, allowing only a basic structure to be drafted. The model fulfills its purpose if it permits the identification of the variables which, if closely monitored, will provide all control-relevant information. These are the points where the sensors of the servomechanism have to be placed.

The *parametric model* specifies numerical values for the variables of the structural model. These values are defined as optimal values. They represent

81 See Beer (Brain), p. 165.
82 See Beer (Decision), pp. 313 et seq.
83 On the structural and parametric model, see detailed description in Gomez, Malik, and Oeller (Systemmethodik), pp. 1003 et seq.; as well as Gomez (Operations Management), section. 2.332.117.

*capabilities*, which—as opposed to capacities—signify the best possible outcome for a given set of conditions and resources. This specific feature of the model serves two purposes: First, it significantly reduces the variety of the graph, whereas capturing all the values possible would require too much data storage capacity. Second, it permits generating indices, as quotients of actual versus optimal values of the variables, which will always range between zero and one, as actual values can never be higher than the optimal ones. These indices provide the foundation for developing a mechanism to detect disruptions in the system.

Generating *indices* to detect disruptions is a crucial part of building system 1, which is why I will briefly outline some basic points.[84] Indices are "neutral" measurement units reflecting the developments in a business organization, free of any specific context, as for instance the term profit would have with regard to the measuring unit "money." Indices are dimensionless quantities which always range between zero and one, indicating the ratio of a possible (e.g., 100 units) versus an actual output (e.g., 50 units)—which in this case would be 0.5. Beer distinguishes three levels of achievement which, when put in relation to each other, can provide indices for the monitoring of business operations.

- Reality: What is currently achieved with given means and at given conditions.
- Capability: What could currently be achieved with given means and at given conditions, if all opportunities were exploited.
- Potentiality: What would realistically be achievable if all existing means were fully utilized and enhanced and hampering factors were removed.

Putting these levels of achievement in relation to each other results in three *indices*, the evolution of which will offer clues as to possible disruptions in the system: productivity, latency, and total output.[85]

---

84 See Beer (Brain), pp. 206 et seq. For an elaborate explanation of indices, see Oeller (Kennzahlen).
85 See Beer (Brain), p. 209.

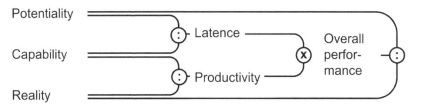

*Figure 1.51(1b)*

So if we put the optimal values (capabilities) of the parametric model in relation to the actual values, we get the productivity of the parameters to be monitored for the division. The evolution of these parameters is a key indicator of possible disruptions in the system. Upon closer scrutiny of the above indices, it turns out that a fully fledged system 1 should comprise a model of potentialities, in addition to the structural and the parametrical one, in order to monitor the latency and the total output of the division. We will get back to this subject when we deal with the detailed description of the functions of system 1.

Having outlined the first two prerequisites for building a system 1—the *variables to be monitored* and the *indices* required to detect disruptions—we now have to determine the *standards* that enable us to assess any disturbances occurring and which trigger corrective actions. Standards are *stability criteria* which enable us to identify any deviations of the system from its internal equilibrium. These stability criteria are set in the *initial plan*, which locates the division in focus within the overall organization. Possible criteria include precisely defined targets but also vaguely phrased "reference conditions,"[86] largely depending on the recursion level selected, as well as the overarching corporate *policy* that each division has to comply with in performing its coordination tasks. The stability criteria determine much of the information flow in the network, and if there are any disturbances, such as a change in productivity, they are countered with corrective actions (plans).

But how can this network be interpreted? Simply put, it can be understood as a *transfer function* assigning outputs to certain inputs.[87] Outputs in this case are *plans* to eliminate disruptions (inputs). To be able to eliminate a great variety of disruptions—even unforeseeable ones—there has to be a *repertoire* of plans. These plans have to be available "on demand," so in case

---

86 See Powers (Behavior), pp. 44 et seq.

87 See Beer (Brain), p. 41.

of emergency they only have to be adapted to the specific situation (programming). The assignment of plans to disruptions can partly be done in advance. This ideal case, however, requires that all possible disruptions be known in advance, so that nothing but their timing remains uncertain. Usually this will not be the case, so when disruptions occur, plans have to be selected from the repertoire and introduced. It is a step-by-step approach. Every newly implemented plan is tested for its impact on internal stabilization, and replaced again and again until the desired outcome—equilibrium— is achieved. Above all, this evolutionary approach[88] will be required for all divisional environments where discontinuities occur.

Finally, the plans selected have to be translated into control activities. This happens via motor channels and effectors. The question as to where to place *effectors* can be answered with the aid of the structural model, by identifying the division's controllable parameters. Even motor channels—just like the sensory ones—have to be interpreted as bundles through which information is transported in various ways to the centers of activities.

After this brief description of the preconditions for designing system 1, we shall next look at how this system operates, specifically dealing with its components and the *information flow* between them.[89]

In this context it should be noted that controllers will again be mentioned in the descriptions of systems 2, 3, 4, and 5. These controllers also have to meet the requirements outlined here in order to function properly. So when in the further course of this book the subject of controllers is addressed, these preconditions will be assumed as given, and only the respective system's specific requirements for the controller will be discussed.

A detailed depiction of the organization of system 1 *from the perspective of the overall organization* reveals that two essential components of these controllers have to be distinguished: the divisional management and the division's regulatory center. These are connected to each other and to their environment through information channels, enabling them to fulfill the function of a servomechanism: maintaining the division's stability. The *divisional management* is responsible for managing the division. Being a part of the vertical command axis, it derives normative plans for the division from corporate policy and monitors implementation. To accomplish this task, the *divisional regulatory cen-*

---

88 See also Malik and Gomez (Entscheide), pp. 308 et seq.
89 See figures 16(1) through 16(10).

*ter* serves as its managerial toolset. It monitors the evolution of certain divisional variables and responds to undesired developments by making short-term plan adjustments, but always within the frame set by the normative divisional plan.

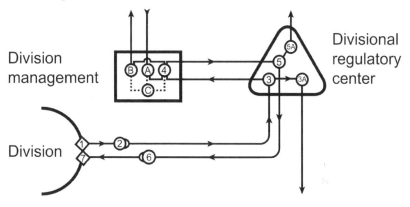

*Figure 1.51 (2): System 1[90]*

The mechanism of system 1 can be characterized by the following components of divisional management (A, B, C, 4), of the divisional regulatory center (3, 3A, 5, 5A), and the information channels connecting them (1, 2, 6, 7):

(1) *Recording mechanism*
To be able to assess the stability of a division, its development has to be checked based on the behavior of selected parameters. This requires the recording of *data* that characterize parameter behavior. These data then have to be *codified*, that is, translated into a language the control system will understand. For the system-1 controller, this two-fold task is performed by recording mechanisms referred to as "transducers." According to Beer,[91] a transducer is "a machine, device, protocol or rule by which information is changed to an appropriate form and introduced into a system." So these mechanisms transduce the raw data into "system language" following a specified procedure, for instance by generating ratios such as pcs/hr.

---

90 See Beer (Brain), p. 216.
91 See Beer (Brain), p. 307.

### (2) *Input synapse*

Via the transducers, a multitude of codified data enters the regulatory center's information channels, especially if recording goes on permanently. To avoid overload of the monitoring mechanisms, information flows have to be controlled by something resembling a synapse of the human nervous system. It collects and stores certain data until there is a data set that is meaningful to the monitoring mechanism, which is then transmitted completely. In terms of the detailed design of system 1, this means that the data collected are reduced according to a *sampling plan* and the remaining data are gathered as *samples*. So the sample size chosen determines the value at which data are transferred.

### (3) *Monitoring mechanism*

The function of this mechanism is to calculate and monitor *indices* indicating significant changes in divisional behavior and triggering corrective actions. Such indices can only be generated if *model values* are available to which data samples can be put in relation. As the foregoing explanations have shown, capability models permit calculating the evolution of the productivity of divisional variables and potentiality models permit calculating their latency, and thus—together with productivity—overall output.

The calculation of indices is followed by their statistical *monitoring*. To accomplish this, the first thing we need to do is establish populations to serve as a measure $(x, \sigma)$ for any new development. Every newly calculated index is compared to that measure and statistically significant results are reported to the division's management. The details of this approach to designing and operating this monitoring mechanism have been dealt with in various publications;[92] section 3.2 will illustrate it with an example. At this point, let me remind you once more that the monitoring mechanism is able to forecast *trend changes* in index behavior at relatively short notice. Based on the mathematical theory of short-term forecast,[93] Beer developed a program ("Cyberstride") that responds sensitively to trend changes of the indices and enables system 1 to counter undesired developments quickly.[94]

---

92 See Beer (Decision), pp. 299 et seq.; Gomez, Malik, and Oeller (Systemmethodik), pp. 993 et seq.; Oeller (Cybernetic Process Control), passim.

93 See Harrison and Stevens (Forecasting).

94 See Beer (Platform), pp. 439 et seq.; and Beer (Development), passim; as well as the elaborate explanations in Oeller (Kennzahlen).

(4) *Directive trigger mechanism*

When there are significant deviations from normal index behavior—characterized by x and σ of statistical distribution—or trend changes, relevant information will get to the directive trigger mechanism. This mechanism is part of divisional management: It comprises behavioral standards based on which deviations can be evaluated and corrective action triggered. So its purpose is to evaluate, in meta-language, the impact of deviations on the division's *stability*. As a result of this process, an instruction is issued to either adjust short-term divisional plans to the changed situation or to confirm current plans.

(5) *Planning mechanism*

The divisional regulatory center has a repertoire of plans specifying adequate behaviors for the most diverse constellations. One set of *plans* is being implemented at any point in time; the *programs* derived from it determine the division's behavior at given environmental conditions. So, whenever the trigger mechanism calls for a change of plans, the regulatory center does not have to draft them from scratch but simply *selects* from its repertoire and makes *adjustments* for the current situation, translating the plans into programs. Plans are formulated as capabilities—just like the models of the monitoring mechanisms—which means that prior to implementation they have to be weighted with the *reciprocal* value of current productivities (as determined in 3) in order to get realistic values to work with. *So, planning* means the selection by the divisional regulatory center of short-term plans from a given repertoire, based on the instruction received from the directive trigger mechanism, and combining these components into a program.

(6) *Output synapse*

Just as the input synapse collects and organizes incoming data, the output synapse arranges groups of programs to be forwarded for implementation. This ensures a certain continuity in the adjustment process: As interventions in ongoing operations occur batch-wise, this gives the system a chance to adapt to new developments—which would not be the case if it were continually "showered" with individual programs.

(7) *Execution mechanism*

The program packages transmitted by the output synapse will then have to be translated into concrete action, that is, interventions in the division's ongoing operations. This requires *transducers* to read the program code and trigger or issue commands for the corresponding action.

The components 1 through 7, which have been discussed, constitute the control process for divisional operations. This process, however, has to be controlled as well. To do this, the following components are crucial:

(A) *Information intake by divisional management*

The construction of a monitoring mechanism and the development of short-term plans in the divisional regulatory center have to conform to an overriding frame of reference defining the division's function and long-term goals. Divisional management formulate this frame of reference, deriving from the corporate policy a *normative* or *initial plan* for the division and adjusting it for its environmental constellation and the requirements from other divisions. In order to be able to devise an initial plan, and to ensure it will permit the evaluation of divisional control with regard to its consistency with overall corporate goals, the divisional management has to have a *sensorium* capturing the following information:

– Information on corporate policy
– Information on relevant developments in the environment
– Information on other divisions' normative plans
– Information on index deviations in the division.

This information has to be integrated and coordinated, thus making the necessary preparations for the *decision* in C on the normative divisional plan.

(C) *Normative divisional plan*

This is where the actual decision on the normative divisional plan have to be made and *behavioral standards* have to be set up, thus permitting the evaluation (in 4) of the impact that behavioral deviations have on the division's stability. It would be wrong, though, to regard C as the only decision-making authority. The decision is worked out by the entire divisional management (A, B, C, 4), with C having a primus inter pares role.

(B) *Information release by divisional management*

In addition to being a part of the decision-making process, the function of this component of divisional management is to *communicate* the normative divisional plan and behavioral standards defined to higher-level authorities on the command axis, as well as to other divisions and to the divisional regulatory center. If the divisional management is unable to implement the principles of corporate policy, this will also be communicated to the command axis via B.

In addition to the central command axis, there are further points connecting the division with other divisions and the superordinate control system. These points are located in the divisional regulatory center and their functions are as follows:

(3A) *Connections to other divisions*

Undesirable developments in the division, which are reflected in deviations from indices, are communicated to other divisions. The intended coordination is achieved via system 2, which will be discussed in the following section. Communicating deviations from *indices* has a key advantage: The fact that just the deviation as such is communicated, without passing judgment, makes it easier to mandate appropriate responses.

(5A) *Connection to the divisional coordination center*

This is where selected plans and programs are communicated to an entity that will compare them to the company's general synergy concepts to prevent oscillations. This, too, is a system 2 function that will be discussed later.

Summarizing all system 1 components with their respective inputs and outputs, we get the following list of functions and information flows:

| | Component | Function | Input | Output |
|---|---|---|---|---|
| 1 | Recording mechanism | Systemic re-cording and encoding of the variables to be moni-tored | Raw data of rele-vant vari-ables | Codified data |
| 2 | Input synapse | Selection and collec-tion of re-lated data and trans-mission as samples | Codified data | Data samples |
| 3 | Monitoring mechanism | Aggregation of data, cal-culation and monitoring of indices | Data samples | Information on devia-tions (4), (3A) |
| 4 | Directive trigger mecha-nism | Behavior-re-lated analysis of deviations in the light of divisional standards, is-suing of or-ders to ad-just plans or confirmation of plans | Standards (B), infor-mation on deviations (3) | Orders to follow through with or adjust plans Information on plan adjustment (A) |
| 5 | Planning mechanism | Selection of routine plans and programs; adjustment for specific situation | Orders to follow through with or adjust plans | Programs to (6) and other divi-sions (5A) |
| 6 | Output syn-apse | Collec-tion and commu-nication of pro-grams | Programs (codified) | Aggregated programs |

| 7 | Monitoring mechanism | Releasing program action | Aggregated programs | Actions (manipulations) |
|---|---|---|---|---|
| A | Information receipt by division management | Integration and coordination of information to prepare decision-making of C and monitoring of 4 | Information on corporate policy, environment, other divisions, deviations (4) | Information to B and C |
| B | Information release by division management | Contribution to integration/coordination of information and forwarding of normative divisional plan and standards | Decisions on divisional policy (C), A-information | Information on: Standards (4) Compliance with corporate policy (higher-level authorities), divisional policy (other divisions) |
| C | Normative divisional plans | Decision-making on divisional initial plans and standards | A, B, 4 information | Behavioral standards and divisional plan |
| 3A | Connections to other divisions | Communication of deviations | Information on deviations | Aggregated and addressed information on deviations |
| 5A | Connection to the divisional coordination center | Communication of selected programs to center and other divisions | Divisional plans and programs | Plans and programs |

*Figure 1.51*

## 1.52 System 2

From the perspective of the overall organization, system 2 represents the meta-system that coordinates all systems 1. In neurophysiologic terms, it is the sympathetic interaction of the peripheral ganglia of the reflex arc which are located in the spinal cord.[95]

The *purpose* of system 2 is to prevent oscillations between the divisions. This phenomenon—which is referred to as "uncontrolled oscillations" in engineering and as "ataxia" in neurophysiology—can occur when the individual divisions' behavior is not coordinated. As every division has to remain as effective as possible—that is, as though it were competing with the other divisions—difficulties of collaboration are inevitable. However, it is the collaboration between the individual divisions that constitutes a total organism, which is why a mechanism to prevent oscillations is necessary.

This mechanism has to have the form of a *controller* measuring the behavior of each division against defined standards and taking appropriate action in case of deviations. That, in turn, means that the following information is essential for its design and operation:

– Information on significant *deviations* in individual divisions' behavior
– Information on short-term *plan changes* in the divisions
– Information on the general *synergy concepts* of the overall company, making it possible to derive *standards* for assessing the collaboration between the divisions

Another requirement is that the controller not operate through the central command axis to prevent overload. If the central command axis is defined by those line functions in an organization between which there is a flow of hierarchical information (e.g., on corporate policy and compliance with it), system 2 represents the connection between the peripheral management at the individual divisions, represented by the divisional regulatory centers. In many firms, this connection consists of informal contacts among staff members of different divisions which create a "management sub-culture." What is often lacking, though, are the synergy concepts mentioned above, embodied in standards for collaboration among the divisions.

---

95 See Beer (Brain), p. 142.

System 2 can schematically be depicted as follows:[96]

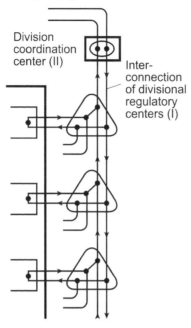

Division coordination center (II)

Inter-connection of divisional regulatory centers (I)

*Figure 1.52(1): System 2*

Two *components* are characteristic of the system: the connection between the divisional regulatory centers and the division coordination center.

(I) *Connection between the divisional regulatory centers*
This is a network of information channels through which two kinds of information flow:

Information on significant *deviations* in the *indices* of individual divisions. This information *automatically* gets into the information loop through the divisional regulatory centers' connecting node 3A.

Information on short-term *divisional plans* and any modifications to them, as well as behavioral programs which are tapped at the divisional regulatory

---

96 Beer (Brain), p. 221; see also figures 1.6(3) and 1.6(4) in section 1.6, where these interrelations are also depicted for different recursion levels.

centers' connecting node 5A and transmitted to the division coordination center.

The connection between the divisional regulatory centers is to be regarded as an information loop comprising all relevant deviations from indices and plans, and which communicates them to other divisions so they can check the impact on their own planning. Hence, it serves the *coordination* of short-term, tactical divisional plans, with the main emphasis laid on *speed and completeness.*

(II) *Division coordination center*

Creating an information loop to support the coordination between the individual divisions is a first step to prevent oscillations that would put the company's stability at risk. However, two potential sources of risk will not be captured by it, although they have enormous significance. First, the fact that there is information on deviations does not mean that appropriate adjustments will be made. If a division reports index or plan deviations, another division may or may not react—at least until a coordinating entity issues directives to that effect. Also, while some kind of coordination can be performed between the divisions, in many cases this will not correspond to the goals of the overall organization. Here, a coordination center has to introduce the corporate synergy concepts.

So the division coordination center's *function* is to assess the different divisions' interaction from a "higher" vantage point. This implies the following tasks:

Comparing the short-term divisional plans to *standards* derived from the company's general synergy concepts.

Ordering local *corrections* to divisional plans, if coordination fails to work. *Communicating* significant deviations from synergy concepts to system 3, so it can intervene through the vertical control axis.

In this way, the division coordination center represents a *servomechanism* monitoring the synergy between the divisions based on a plan or paradigm; this plan reflects the ideas of systems 3 as to how the company's *internal* stability can be achieved.

In practical implementation, the division coordination center can be a *monitoring entity* with precisely specified standards. Quite possibly, however, it may just be a certain "house style," such as a consistent policy for warehousing or advertisement, or a uniform dress code or image that performs the coordination function.

In sum, system 2 can be characterized as a managed connection between the different divisions, coordinating their interaction in addition to the central command axis. The information flowing between the individual divisions' regulatory centers and the division coordination center is not hierarchical or directive in nature. It is intended to "inform" in the true sense of the word, and it is a contribution of the divisions' peripheral management to the overall company's stability. It would certainly be wrong to institutionalize these information relationships completely; their key advantage is their social component, for computers, unlike people, do not have the possibility of capturing the current state of operations in just a gesture. So, system 2 is the link between systems 1 and 3, with the division coordination centers as its input synapse. In neurophysiology, this whole connection is referred to as the sympathetic nervous system; we will get to that when we discuss system 3. The functions of system 2 and its components can be summarized as follows:

| Component | Function | Input | Output |
|---|---|---|---|
| (I) Connection between the divisional regulatory centers | Coordination of short-term, tactical divisional plans and actions | Information on significant index changes, short-term divisional plans and changes to them, behavioral programs | As before, due to information loop |
| (II) Division coordination center | Aggregated divisional plans<br><br>System 3 input | Comparison of short-term divisional plans to general corporate synergy concepts, derivation of local corrections or forwarding to system 3 | Addressed corrections to divisional plans or actions, or information to system 3 |

*Figure 1.52*

## 1.53 System 3

The function of system 3 is to preserve the organization's *internal stability*. This internal stability comprises more than local homeostasis at the level of individual divisions, with regard to individual environmental segments, and is aimed at preventing oscillations between these divisions. As systems 1 and 2 are only capable of settling *local* imbalances, while the organization has to be able to respond to environmental developments *as a whole*, system 3 is introduced to coordinate all internal operational activities with the overarching goals of the total organism. Thus, it is also a liaison between the autonomous management—of which it represents the most senior level—and corporate management, of which it is the lowest level. Its *function* is to optimize the organization's overall internal performance within a generally accepted scope.

In neurophysiologic terms, system 3 can be compared to the pons and the medulla, as well as to the sympathetic and parasympathetic nerve cords.[97] The latter will be addressed in greater detail with regard to their interpretation for management, as they are crucial for the control function of system 3. Before that, however, let us have a look at the general *functionality* of system 3.

The purpose of systems 3 is to enter relevant information on the company's operations in a kind of input-output matrix, and to optimize this information in the light of the organization's primary goals.[98] Hence, the question is how to design and optimize the matrix, and what information is needed. As for the *information* required, three kinds can be distinguished:[99]

Information on *corporate policy* and *compliance*. This information flows through the central command axis: as corporate policy provisions from systems 4 and 5 and as reports from systems 1 on the compliance with the corporate policy.

Information on compliance with the organization's *synergy concepts*. This information is a result of the activities of the division coordination center and system 2, and the corresponding channel is the sympathetic nervous system.

Information on *overload phenomena* and new developments in the individual divisions This information gets to system 3 through the parasympathetic system's direct access to the divisional operations.

---

97 See Beer (Brain), p. 170.
98 See Beer (Brain), p. 401.
99 See also figure 1.6(5) in section 1.6. The following numbering relates to this graph.

Integrating and coordinating the incoming information in the input-output matrix, optimizing this matrix, and deriving measures are all parts of a very complex process which—as we will see later—can be depicted as the interaction of four homeostats. Depending on the complexity of the organization and the recursion level chosen, this process can take very different forms. It can transpire in the discussions at department manager meetings, or it can be carried out based on expanded OR models, for instance of warehousing theory or mathematical programming. In any case, it is crucial to have a dynamic model of the organization's *internal* functioning so as to be able to manage the organization for internal stabilization. It does not matter so much whether this model is located in the mind of the manager in charge or whether it actually exists in writing, as long as it permits incoming information to be combined and associated correctly.

After these general remarks on the functionality of system 3, next I will try to break down the system into its *components* to better explore its mechanism. This analytical approach should not lead us to oversimplify its functionality. Each of the four homeostats addressed in the following should be regarded as a network with multiple interconnections, and the interaction between the four homeostats is a network of the higher order. So the analytical approach only serves illustrative purposes.

The following diagram shows system 3 with its basic structure:[100]

---

100 See Beer (Brain), p. 226.

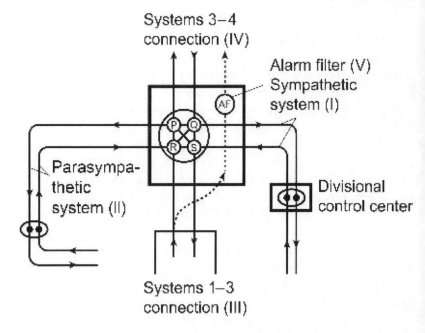

*Figure 1.53(1): System 3*

System 3 comprises five key modules:[101]

- I sympathetic system: homeostat Q-S
- II parasympathetic system: homeostat P-R
- III systems 1–3 connection: homeostat R-S
- IV systems 3–4 connection: homeostat P-Q
- V alarm filter 1

The interaction of the first four components creates the homeostat , which constitutes system 3. Its function will be dealt with later. At this point, the individual homeostats will be described, calling to mind my earlier explanations regarding system 1. Homeostats are *controllers* which have to meet certain requirements to be functional. These requirements have been described above. Their specific characteristics shall be discussed next.

(I) *Sympathetic system: Homeostat Q-S*

---

101 See also figure 1.6(6) in section 1.6.

The sympathetic system can generally be described as the monitoring mechanism of the division coordination center, or system 2. The information on the division's *synergy*, which is sent to system 3 by the division coordination center, is processed in Q–S, with S absorbing the filtered information and Q requesting further information if required. This information relates to significant deviations in the divisions' collaboration as compared to the overall organization's synergy concepts. This information is *stereotypical*, as it only refers to deviations that can be expressed in the language of the model, that is, the synergy plan of the division coordination center. In every organization there are unpredicted deviations or "emergencies" that the sympathetic system is unable to cope with. This is where the parasympathetic system (II) comes in. The homeostat Q-S enters the deviation information in the input-output matrix. One result of this optimization is countermeasures to correct the significant deviations from the organization's synergy concepts. These are *instructions* via the central command axis, ordering the individual divisions to change either their normative or their short-term plans. The double function of S becomes very obvious here: It receives information on deviations from the synergy plan, and forwards plan-change instructions to the divisions.

Another possible way for system 3 to respond is to *adjust* the organization's synergy concepts and thus the division coordination center's synergy plan. This leads to changes in the model of collaboration between divisions, in that deviations will be weighted differently or other deviations will become relevant. Communicating these new *standards* for system 2 is a function of Q.

Just as the management of an organization maintains its stability through checks and counterchecks, system 3 has the option to complete the stereotypical information from the sympathetic system in direct contact with the divisions. This function is performed by the parasympathetic system, which will be described next.

### (II) *Parasympathetic system: Homeostat P-R*

As we have seen, the limitations of systems 2 and the sympathetic system consist in their inability to perform anything but *routine* tasks. Just like system 1, system 2 represents a servomechanism gauging the developments in the relevant environment—which, in the case of system 2, would be the divisions' indices—against a model of *standard behavior*. That is why the sympathetic system only carries clearly specified information on deviations to system 3. But how does information on unforeseen events in the divisions, or "emergencies," get to system 3? And how can possible *overstrain* of individual divisions—resulting from the multitude of control requests from the command axis and the sympathetic system—be recognized and countered in time?

In the human nervous system, the solution for that is the *parasympathetic* system. It has two basic functions which, when relating to organizations, can be characterized as follows:

– Creating an *antithetical mode of control*[102] to complement the control activities taking place in the sympathetic system. To implement the organization's synergy concepts, divisions may be overstrained by the demands coming from the sympathetic system; possible symptoms of overstrain include excessive overtime. This calls for corrective action, and it has to be taken *directly* at the source: in the divisional operations.

– Directly *recording* developments that are new and evolutionary, and can therefore not be captured in the models of systems 1 and 2. It should be noted, however, that these developments have to be relevant to the overall organization, for the parasympathetic system only acts with regard to corporate synergies.[103]

To obtain the information needed in order to fulfill these functions and to be able to launch appropriate measures, each of the divisions has to have a point of contact with the parasympathetic system—an "audit ganglion"[104]— which immediately forwards both new developments and indications of overstrain of the division and which translates the corresponding corrective action or reinforcement of system 3 into the division's language.

So, the homeostat P–R of the parasympathetic can be construed to be entering in the system 3 input-output matrix any *new developments* as well as *symptoms of overstrain* of the divisions that are relevant to the organization's synergy and are not captured by system 2. Its outputs are corrective or reinforcing measures which have a direct effect on the individual divisions' specific operations. These measures then have to be translated into the divisions' languages by their audit contact points.

---

102 See Beer (Brain), p. 225.

103 See Beer (Brain), p. 227.

104 See Beer (Brain), p. 227.

(III) *Systems 1–3 connection: Homeostat R-S*
The homeostats described above of the sympathetic and parasympathetic systems represent a complex network of checks and counterchecks of control activities, which is crucial for maintaining the organization's internal *synergy*. In the management of business enterprises, this principle of mutually balancing control mechanisms is often applied. In engineering they occur rather infrequently; usually they are joined in one mechanism.[105] The key point in this context is that both homeostats *do not* function via the central command axis but complement its control function. The question now is what information is fed into the input-output matrix via the central command axis.

The homeostat R-S directly connects systems 1 and 3. Its *function* is to check whether the divisional normative plans are in agreement with each other and with corporate policy. Via S, the individual divisional managements receive the provision of *corporate policy*, any changes to them, and additional special instructions. The divisional managements derive their normative divisional plans and thus the *standards* based on which divisions' development and stability are assessed. If these standards cannot be complied with, this is communicated to system 3 via R; as a result, the incompatibility of normative divisional plans and the requirements resulting from corporate policy are accounted for in the input-output matrix. By optimizing the matrix, requests to change the normative divisional plans are sent to the individual divisions via S, together with the corrections triggered by the sympathetic system. At the same time, suggestions to change corporate policies can be sent to system 4, if it turns out that the autonomous management is unable to meet the targets set. This, however, is a task performed by the homeostat P-Q.

(IV) *Systems 3–4 connection: Homeostat P-Q*
Whereas the R-S homeostat ensures compatibility between corporate policy and the normative division plans, the P-Q homeostat integrates information on the organization's internal and external stability. Via Q, the homeostat delivers to the input-output matrix corporate policy guidelines as well as information on external stability (see the description of system 4). P, on the other hand, reports on the degree of *internal* stability and submits suggestions for modifying the corporate policy. The degree of internal stability reported

---

105 See Beer (Brain), p. 148.

to system 4 is the actual *result* of the complex interaction process, which in the course of these descriptions has been referred to as the optimization of the input-output matrix. However, as stability can only be discussed in a very specific *context*, it is clear what the function of the systems 3–4 connection must be: It combines information on corporate policy and on external stability and derives *specifications*, or a frame of reference, for internal stability.

After this description of the four homeostats of system 3 and the way they work, we can describe the functional complex in $\begin{smallmatrix} \text{ESE} & \text{EME} \\ & \times \\ \text{ISE} & \text{IME} \end{smallmatrix}$ general terms.

As mentioned before, its *function* is to optimize the organization's overall internal performance within a generally accepted scope, which is corporate policy and external stability. In more detailed terms, its function is to

– make sure countermeasures are tailored to the deviations from synergy concepts, and the planning of stabilizing measures is tailored to overstrain symptoms and new developments in the divisions.
– coordinate corporate policy, divisional plans, internal corporate events, and the current information on the whole organization's environment.

All these activities amount to a complex *bargaining process* which can often be supported by optimization techniques and other procedures. The only thing about this process to be captured in general terms is its objective: achieving internal stability for the organization.

### (V) *Alarm filter l*

As the top level of autonomous management, system 3 tends to be very sensitive to what happens "below," that is, to information about the control activities in systems 1 and 2, whereas it tends to suppress information to the levels "above" in its interaction with systems 4 and 5. This mode of operation makes sense from the perspective of the overall organization, for systems 4 and 5 should not permanently be showered with insignificant information, such as about local goings-on at the divisions. It does happen, however, that system 3 absorbs *too much* information and sums up a large amount of information relevant to systems 4 and 5 by tersely stating that "internal stability is provided." To ensure that important pieces of information on divisional matters is not simply absorbed, system 3 has an *alarm filter*. From the information flow going through the central command axis, it *singles out* those pieces of information that appear relevant to systems 4 and

5, based on statistical criteria. It is *algedonic* information, which means that—in analogy to the principle of reward and punishment—specific developments are rated "good" or "bad," and forwarded directly, along with this categorization.[106] Just as the human organism immediately evaluates certain local events (for instance, when we eat, as "abdominal *pain*" or "feelings of *pleasure*") and this information is directly communicated to the cortex, rather than being processed by the autonomous nervous system only, important single events in an organization have to be transmitted directly to system 5, labeled as "bad" (pain) or "good" (pleasure), so that system 5 can immediately issue corrective or affirmative action.[107]

Exactly which events are captured by this alarm filter depends on how the underlying *management by exception* principle is handled in practice. In any case, the key point is that the individual events are labeled as "pain" or "pleasure" in this information, thus making it easier for system 5 to fulfill its function.

After these detailed comments on system 3, the following graph summarizes the functions of its individual components as well as their inputs and outputs:

---

106 See Beer (Brain), pp. 181 et seq., 228.
107 That is why the algedonic information channel is depicted as a +/- chain in figure 1.6(6), section 1.6.

| Component | Function | Input | Output |
|---|---|---|---|
| (I) Sympathetic system Q-S | Monitor and evaluate deviations from synergy concepts as well as their effects on the organization's internal stability, launch corrective action | Deviations from synergy concepts, P-R input, and information to command axis | Change instructions for normative and short-term divisional plans Instructions to adjust synergy plan output to P-R |
| (II) Parasympathetic system P-R | Direct access for system 3 to the operations of individual divisions, in order to gain paradigm-free entrepreneurial synergy information and launch stabilizing interventions | Company-related info on overstrain symptoms, new and otherwise unforeseen developments in divisions Q-S input information of command axis | Stabilizing measures not taken via system 2 or the command axis |
| (III) Systems 1–3 connection R-S | Compatibility check between divisions' normative plans and against corporate policy, maintaining compatibility | Divisional normative plans Corporate policy P-Q input | Instructions for corrections to normative plans, suggestions for alterations to corporate policy (to P-Q) |

| (IV) Systems 3–4 connection | Integration of information on corporate policy and external stability, derivation of frame of reference for internal stability | Information on corporate policy and external stability, R-S input | Information on corporate policy and external stability R-S input requirements for internal |
| X System 3 ho-meostasis | Optimize the internal performance within a generally accepted scope | See above | See above |
| | Align countermeasures for deviations from synergy concepts as well as planned stabilizing measures with overstrain symptoms and new developments in the divisions. | | |
| | Coordinating corporate policy, divisional plans, internal corporate events, and current information on the organization's environment. | | |
| (V) Alarm filter 1 | Directly transmit significant, algedonic divisional information to systems 4 and 5 | Evaluated pieces of information on divisions | Number of evaluated pieces of information on divisions |

*Figure 1.53 (2)*

## 1.54 System 4

In system 3, the organization has a mechanism to maintain its *internal stability* in a given environment, with a given technology, at the present time, and with its own control facilities. But what about the future? Most organizations face dynamic change in their environment and the continuous emergence of new technologies. They cannot simply expect to "keep the situation under control" with their present control facilities. Moreover, when individual divisions are stable in their *local* environmental segments that does not automatically mean that the total organization can subsist in its environment, for these environments are not necessarily identical. To solve these problems, the organization has to have a mechanism to address possible future developments and identify necessary adaptations to environment and technological dynamics. This is what system 4 does.

From a neurophysiologic perspective, system 4 is characterized by its structural diversity. Its function is distributed over different nerve cords and areas of the brain, making it difficult to localize. Broadly speaking, it can be compared to the diencephalon, the basal ganglia and the third vetricle.[108]

The *functions* of system 4 are to:[109]

– *connect* the organization's top-level decision center (system 5) with the autonomous management represented by system 3 via the central command axis,
– receive and process information on the *corporate environment* and pass it on to the top-level decision center as well as to its autonomous management,
– integrate internal and external *algedonic* information from the alarm filters and pass it on to system 5 through special channels.

Hence, system 4 fulfills the function of a *staff unit* for top management, although the term must not be interpreted too strictly, as traditional staff units have no decision-making competencies. The system 4 staff unit plays a key role in the organization's decision-making process. Just as the human cerebrum has no direct connections to the outside world, an organization's top

---

108 See Beer (Brain), p. 170.
109 See Beer (Brain), p. 183.

management is relatively isolated from current developments in the environment, at least as far as details are concerned. System 4, however, monitors these developments with its sensors. It is therefore able to evaluate information with regard to its significance, select and summarize it, or even withhold it. Moreover, it has information on the internal stability of the organization, which it coordinates with the incoming information on the outside world before notifying system 5. Hence, with its "information policy" system 4 can strongly influence the corporate decision-making process, so the notion of a staff unit with purely advisory functions does not really work.

The task of system 4 can basically be described as executing *corporate planning* in the broadest sense. To be able to achieve the required integration of the various bits of information on internal and external events and developments, system 4 has to use a *model* representing the organization's internal structure and its relations with the outside world.

This model exists in most organizations, though usually only in rudimentary form and distributed over various units and people in the organization.Beer[110] has impressively demonstrated what a good corporate model can look like in condensed form. At this point, the most important aspects to be discussed are the prerequisites for gathering information, and thus for building the corporate model that will provide the basis for corporate planning.

As far as the *function* of system 4 is concerned, it has to reconcile the following four aspects:

- Internal sensory events
- External sensory events
- Internal motor events
- External motor events

The delineation of these areas is based on the distinction between sensory and motor aspects of decision preparation, and on separating internal from external events and developments. The *sensory* component of system 4 perceives certain states in both the organization's environment and the organization itself, processes these states according to certain rules, and brings them to the process of preparing decisions, which is characterized by mutual interaction between all four areas. The *motor* component transmits to the

---

110 See Beer (Brain), pp. 233 et seq.

center concerned the behaviors that have been set as standards for gathering environmental information or for achieving internal stability through divisions' and units' homeostatic interaction. The *function* of system 4 is illustrated by the following graph:[111]

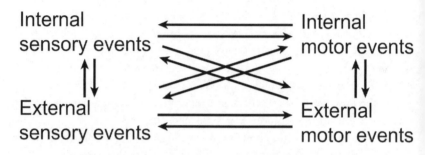

*Figure 1.54(1): The function of system 4*

This shows that we again have a strongly interconnected network here which prepares the decisions of system 5 in a complex negotiation process.

As for the *information* that the individual components need in order to fulfill their functions, it will also be described as a series of *modules*. This is due to the fact that both the human organism and organizations clearly distinguish between the four areas, although it is only the result of their interaction—a certain state of affairs—that actually has relevance for the organism.

Taking into account what has been explained so far, which results in a modified version of Beer's diagram,[112] system 4 can be depicted as follows:[113]

---

111 See Beer (Brain), p. 184.
112 See Beer (Brain), p. 231.
113 See also figure 1.6(7) in section 1.6.

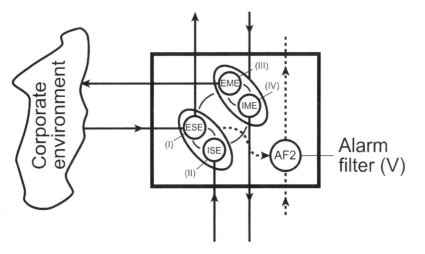

*Figure 1.54(2): System 4*

**(I) *External sensory events (ESE)***
One of the key functions of system 4 is to gather *environmental information*, process it, and enter it to preparations for decision-making. In his theoretical and practical presentation of the *T-machine*, Beer[114] has demonstrated what this process looks like. Three questions are raised in this context:

– What *variables* in the environment should be monitored?
– What *sensors* are best suited to capture the evolution of these variables?
– How does sensory information have to be *transformed* to be useful in the decision-preparing process?

To determine what relevant *environmental variables* are, every organization needs to build a model of relevant relationships and interdependencies, and explore by way of simulation what variables could be critical to its future development. Whether this process is carried out by a manager's mind or a sophisticated simulation model (which could be based on the System Dynamics approach developed by Forrester[115]) largely depends on the organization's possibilities. The evolution of the key variables determined is monitored by *sensors*, in this case exteroceptors. In analogy to the human organism, *telereceptors* are used which are comparable to the eye or ear, and

---

114 See Beer (Factory), pp. 51 et seq.
115 See Forrester (Industrial Dynamics), passim.

which are able to capture economic, political, technological, or societal developments.[116] Finally, this information has to be translated into bases for decisions, which in sophisticated cases are compiled in keeping with statistical procedures, as described in detail by Beer.[117] Alternatively, they can be simple "translation rules" to translate, for example, technological developments in management language.

In this context, a phenomenon may result which we have already observed for system 3: that key pieces of information of major relevance for the organization are suppressed by the sensory apparatus. This is why *algedonic* information is extracted once again and sent directly to system 5 through the alarm filter 2, together with the information from alarm filter 1. This alarm filter 2 will be dealt with specifically.

### (II) *Internal sensory events (ISE)*

In addition to environmental information, the sensors of system 4 have to bring to the decision-preparing process some information on the organization's *internal* functionality. Coming from the central command axis, this information will be in condensed form; it indicates whether the organization's *internal stability* is or is not guaranteed. As mentioned before, system 3 is responsible for internal stability, and it communicates its success or failure to system 4 via P. If internal stability within the specified scope is guaranteed, system 3 just needs to confirm this fact. If internal stability is not achieved, the *rationale* for that has to be transmitted through the central command axis, possibly with the autonomous management's suggestions for modifications to corporate policy. How internal sensory events are processed in practice—in particular if the organization's stability is lacking—is something that differs from one company to the next. Beer[118] has demonstrated a possible approach; his "Operations Room" comprises two tools ("Cyberstride" and "Datafeed") that shed light on the details of undesirable internal developments.

### (III) *External motor events (EME)*

Whereas the sensory component delivers information on the environment and on the organization's internal stability to system 4, contributing to the decision-making preparations, the *motor* component specifies and forwards

---

116 See Beer (Brain), p. 131.
117 See Beer (Decision), pp. 383 et seq.
118 See Beer (Development), pp. 14 et seq.

codes of behavior implementing the guidelines received from system 5. Beer[119] has illustrated this process in his theoretical derivation of the *V-machine*. For the external motor events, this means that system 4 has to specify *codes of behavior* for gathering environmental information and for carrying out operations in the environment relevant to the organization. These instructions represent *corrections* to current approaches, as reflected in the decisions taken and directives issued by system 5. These corrections also affect the sensory component, as critical environment variables might change.

### (II) *Internal motor events (ISE)*
Finally, system 4, in its function as mediator between systems 5 and 3 on the central command axis, has to translate system 5 decisions into codes of behavior for system 3, that is, formulate and issue corporate policy as a specification and reference framework for the organization's internal stability. In addition, the internal motor mechanism also transmits information on the organization's *external* stability to the autonomous management. This information results from the complex interaction of all parts of system 4, completing the frame of reference for internal stability.

Having described the individual components of system 4 in detail, we will now have a closer look at their *interaction*. Its purpose is to:

- *Prepare* the decisions taken by system 5. This includes not only coordinating and integrating the sensory information received, but also taking into account the motor limitations and possibilities.
- Translate the decisions taken and directives issued by system 5 into *codes of behavior*. Again, consequences for sensory configuration are taken into account and evaluated.
- Achieve and maintain *external* stability for the organization. Sensory and motor activities have to be coordinated so as to provide the basis for the organization's continued viability in its environment.
- Perform *corporate planning* in the broadest sense, balancing the organization's internal and external stability.

An analysis of the possible interactions between the different areas of system 4 will reveal *six* different interfaces, which means that six homeostats have to be coordinated in order to ensure system 4 can fulfill its function. It is quite obvious that this process cannot be captured *analytically*. It is a complex, *self-organized* process that can only be controlled if certain *basic conditions*

---

119 See Beer (Factory), pp. 52 et seq.

are created. Beer[120] has described this process at length. Some of these conditions are provided by specifying the information processing tasks that the individual areas have to perform. Another requirement is that a *model* be used which will match internal events and developments with the organization's external relations. A possible layout of this model has been described in detail by Beer.[121]

The model of the enterprise is the starting point for *corporate planning*, which, based on the model, builds a bridge from the organization's current situation to possible future developments. System 4 is "positioned" ideally for this task. On the one hand, it receives foresights and instructions from system 5; on the other hand, system 3 sends information on the current internal situation as well as exception signals. On top of that, it receives sensory input from the organization's environment. The key criterion that corporate planning has to meet is *adaptability*, as relevant internal and external developments have to be integrated immediately. This is the only way it can fulfill its double control function: optimizing profits and matching product features with market demand.[122]

To conclude, *system 4 homeostasis* is a permanent process of mutual adaptation—aided by simulations—to the continuously changing status reports on the environment and internal constellations, as influenced by general rules, and its purpose is to achieve and calibrate the organization's internal *and* external stability.

(V) Alarm filter 2

When describing system 3, particular emphasis was laid on alarm filter 1. It collects algedonic information about special divisional events, which are of interest to the organization, and passes it on to system 4.

Here—specifically, in alarm filter 2—the internal algedonic information is reconciled with the information on external events. The system checks whether internal events and external developments are related and whether the triggering factors are located inside or outside the organization. For instance, a seemingly erratic internal behavior can be declared adequate if it is justified by external developments. So the purpose of this alarm filter is to reevaluate information on single events that has already been evaluated, thus creating a balanced foundation for decisions to be taken by system 5.

---

120 See Beer (Brain), pp. 185 et seq.
121 See Beer (Brain), pp. 233 et seq.
122 See Beer (Brain), p. 411.

By summarizing all system 4 components, we get the following list of functions, inputs, and outputs:

| Component | Function | Input | Output |
|---|---|---|---|
| External sensory events | Receive, process, and enter environmental information into the overall organism of decision preparations Forward to alarm filter 2 | Environmental information Information from the motor events segment | Descriptions of environmental situation |
| Internal sensory events | Receive and process information on internal stability, enter it into the overall organism of decision preparations | Internal information Information from the motor events segment | Descriptions of internal situation |
| External motor events | Instruct on what to do to gain environmental information and how to carry out operations in the environment | Decisions by and instructions from system 5 Information from the sensory event segment | Instructions on behavior |

| Internal motor events | Issue instructions on what to do to achieve internal stability; provide frame of reference (corporate policy, external stability) | Decisions by and instructions from system 5 Information from the sensory events segment | Instructions regarding behavior, corporate policy, information on external stability |
|---|---|---|---|
| System 4<br><br>ESE—EME<br>$\boxed{\times}$<br>ISE—IME<br><br>homeostasis | Permanent process (aided by simulations) of mutual adaption to continuously changing descriptions of the system's state, as influenced by general rules, to achieve and balance internal and external stability | See above | See above |
| Alarm filter 2 | Reconcile significant divisional algedonic information with environmental information and | Environmental information Alarm filter 1 information | Evaluated and agreed-on information on individual internal events |

*Figure 1.54(3)*

## 1.55 System 5

System 5 represents the highest level in the control hierarchy of both human organisms and organizations. This is where fundamental thinking processes take place, and where decisions are taken which will guide the organism's future course. Whereas the function of system 4 was to prepare information on internal and external events and support decision-making, system 5 has to take the *decisions* that will determine the organization's *policy* and thus its future activities. With the foresight only top management is able to have, it develops a *set of guiding principles* and philosophy for the organization, which the remaining management levels can translate into activities that will maintain the *viability* of the organization in its environment.

In neurophysiologic terms, these system 5 functions are performed by the *cortex*[123]—an analogy that seems quite appropriate for business organizations: Corporate top management, just like the cortex, is the place where critical thinking processes take place, in a complex network of interactions that will yield optimal results even if individual elements are faulty. We will get back to this common characteristic of the brain and top management at a later point.

The *function* of system 5 can basically be described as dealing with the organization's possible future development, evaluating alternative corporate strategies, and formulating corporate policies.[124] Comparing these tasks with the functions of systems 3 and 4, the key differences are revealed in the underlying *models*. While system 3 can be assigned a cost-benefit model enabling it to optimize internal constellations, system 4 models aspects such as the organization's marketing, its position in the money market, and a series of other external aspects. By contrast, the model underlying system 5 has to be able to reflect any important aspect of the organization in its environment that could influence its *future* development. Hence, the model has to permit examining totally new directions in corporate policy.

Before going on to deal with the functions of system 5 in greater detail, we first have to specify the *frame of reference* within which the system has to act. It comprises the requirements communicated by systems 3 and 4, as well as restrictions associated with the information channels.

With their activities to maintain internal and external stability, systems 3 and 4 put the organization in very specific general states which can be construed as overall *behavioral modes*. These modes can include, for instance, states of permanent growth or of crisis. At any given point in time, the organization is in *one* of these mutually exclusive states (Beer distinguishes six of them[125]) which result from the interaction of systems 3 and 4. The details of this interaction will be addressed at a later point. The *behavioral mode* prevailing at the time represents a frame of reference for system 5, which also

---

123 See Beer (Brain), p. 170.
124 See Beer (Brain), p. 410.
125 See Beer (Brain), pp. 294 et seq.

restricts its actions. For instance, an enterprise afflicted by strikes and facing take-over by another company will not have full freedom of decision, even at the top, so its policy will strongly depend on the current stage of its crisis. Hence, the organization's given behavioral mode creates a first restriction to system 5 actions.

Another restriction consists in system 5's relative *isolation*. Just like the cortex in the human organism, top management does not have *direct* access to information on the environment and internal developments; in the case of top management, this is true, at minimum, for the details of these developments. System 5 does receive condensed information via the central command axis, as well as pieces of algedonic information from alarm filter 2. But due to its lack of direct access there can be distortions, especially if systems 3 and 4 do not work properly. System 5 has to take account of this in its decisions; in addition, it has the option of monitoring the *functionality* of systems 3 and 4, as we will see later.

The *functions* of system 5 are illustrated by the following graph.[126]

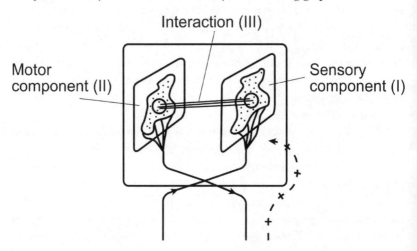

*Figure 1.55(1): System 5*

Through the central command axis and alarm filter 2, information on sensory events—prepared by system 4—is sent to system 5, where it is registered and categorized (in the sensory component). Categorization is based

126 Beer (Brain), p. 231; see also figure 1.6(8) in section 1.6.

on certain criteria, checking sensory events as to their fit with the state preferred by system 5. This *preferred state*—marked by a circle in the graph—is the result of a complex bargaining process combining top management's long-standing experience, the organization's current external and internal development trends, and existing ethical and moral concepts concerning the role of the organization and the entrepreneur, and turning them into a *mission statement* to guide the organization's activities. If sensory events do not conform to this preferred state, system 5 can influence the other systems via the motor component. The objective is to ensure that the great variety of control actions will ultimately result in sensory events that can be matched to the preferred state. The motor activities of system 5, however, have their own preferred states which preclude certain actions. The whole mechanism is to be regarded as a sophisticated homeostat that, both on the sensory and on the motor side, aims to implement the preferred states.

To facilitate readers' understanding of this mechanism, three of its *elements* will be described in greater detail: the sensory component, the motor component, and the interaction between the two.

## (I) *The sensory component*

To get an impression of internal and external developments, system 5 receives sensory information via the vertical command axis and alarm filter 2. Every sensory event determines a *point* in the sensory component, which is depicted as ameboid due to the uncertainty of the amount of possible events. The sensory events can now be grouped in two categories: those that correspond to the preferred state and those that do not. This way, the variety of incoming information is reduced drastically, each piece of information comprising one *bit*.

So, formulating a *preferred state* is a "trick" for top management to cope with the diversity of incoming information. But what can this preferred state be understood to mean? As we have seen earlier, it is the outcome of a complex negotiation process combining the most diverse ethical, moral, economic, social, and technological aspects. Thus, it is a *mission statement* of what the organization's (internal and external) output should be. Put in more operational terms, it is the *corporate policy* which determines the operation's future leeway of action and against which future actions are measured. Of course, the corporate policy is not carved in stone. It changes, depending on the exceptional internal and external developments reported to system 5 as well as on the *veto* issued by the motor component. The latter might not be able to implement the policy demanded, which means that the policy has to be modified. In the above graph, this possible need for adjustment is reflected in the existence of several circles.

### (II) *The motor component*

The depiction of the motor component resembles that of the sensory one, with the points representing *instructions* or directives demanding certain behaviors from systems 3 and 4. From the total amount of possible instructions, some are selected and defined as the preferred state. Likewise, some instructions are defined as undesirable for ethical, moral, economic, social, or technological reasons. This *preferred state* can change, too, if required due to additional information; this means that the corporate policy is in need of modification. This makes it quite obvious that the organization's vision or policy can only be discussed within the framework defined by the sensory *and* the motor components.

### (III) *Interaction between the sensory and the motor component*

As mentioned above, the interaction of the two components consists in homeostatic balancing, thus creating a corporate policy that conforms to the organization's limitations and possibilities. This process, which takes place in the complex network interconnecting the motor and sensory components, is not amenable to analysis. However, Beer[127] has defined the *basic conditions* to guide the self-organizing process in a desired direction, designing top management as a *multinode* and applying the *search paradigms* for decision-making, which will be dealt with later.

Summing up, system 5 has to define preferred states and formulate an adequate corporate policy, adapting these states to the changing internal and external development of the organization, in order to ensure the organization's *viability* in its environment. Formulating corporate policy requires a complex negotiation process that involves both the sensory and the motor components. Corporate policy has to be communicated to the subordinate systems in the form of instructions, so these systems can align their control activities accordingly. Their success in complying with corporate policy is reported back to system 5.

---

127 Based on Beer (Systems Approach), p. 290.

In addition to its core functions, system 5 has to monitor the *functioning* of systems 3 and 4. The associated links are shown in the following graph:[128]

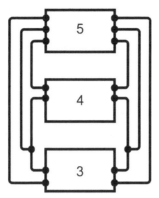

*Figure 1.55(2): System 5 has to monitor the functioning of systems 3 and 4.*

While the purpose of monitoring *system 3* is to ensure the proper operation of the homeostat $\begin{smallmatrix} P-Q \\ |\times| \\ R-S \end{smallmatrix}$, which is responsible for the organization's internal stability, monitoring the system 4 homeostat $\begin{smallmatrix} ESE-EME \\ |\times| \\ ISE-IME \end{smallmatrix}$ aims to ensure permanent control of the operations maintaining external stability. The reason the homeostats of systems 3 and 4 have to be monitored is that they are unable to assess their own function, as this would require a *meta-language*. They are certainly able to capture all internal aspects, such as delays in the arrival of information or a lack of interaction between their elements; however, the question of whether or not a homeostat *as a whole* fulfills its function in the organization is exclusively for system 5 to judge, as only system 5 has access to the meta-linguistic criteria required. Whenever it is uncertain as to whether 3 and 4 function properly, system 5 has to be able to ascertain this in order to issue appropriate instructions to modify the control activities in these systems. These instructions, which are sent through the central command axis, specify how to reprogram the relevant control mechanisms. What becomes very obvious here is that the functional monitoring links only serve *monitoring* purposes—reprogramming takes place via the central command axis.

---

128 See Beer (Brain), pp. 253 et seq.

The most important of system 5's monitoring functions is to monitor the *interaction* of systems 3 and 4. The purpose of this interaction is to reconcile the organization's internal and external stability, thus determining the organization's basic *behavioral mode*. As mentioned before, Beer[129] distinguishes six basic behavioral modes, which are mutually exclusive, and which define the frame of reference for system 5 actions. By monitoring the interactions of systems 3 and 4, system 5 is aware of the actual behavioral mode at any time, and thus able to initiate—via the central command axis—the steps required to either maintain this condition or introduce another behavioral mode. These steps consist in reprogramming the control mechanisms of systems 3 and 4.

The following table summarizes the components of system 5 and their functions, inputs, and outputs:

| Component | Function | Input | Output |
|---|---|---|---|
| Sensory component | Evaluate and determine preferred states, in the form of corporate policy, by which to maintain viability | Information on sensory events, alarm filter-2 information, veto from motor component | Preferred state as corporate policy |
| Motor component | Determine preferred motor states and derive instructions to lower systems | Information and veto from the sensory component | Instructions on codes of ehavior |
| Interaction SC-MC | Design corporate policy in a multimode and apply the search paradigm, coordinate preferred sensory and motor states | Information on sensory and motor components | Corporate policy |

---

129 See Beer (Brain), pp. 294 et seq.

| Monitoring the functioning of systems 3 and 4 | Maintain the function of systems 3 and 4, balance internal and external stability | Information on functionality, information on interaction between systems 3 and 4 | Instructions on how to adjust control activities |
|---|---|---|---|

*Figure 1.55*

## 1.6  The Overall Model: Graphic Depiction at Several Levels of Recursion

This section comprises graphical depictions of the structures and functions of the viable system and its subsystems, as well as of the principle of recursion, in order to provide an overall perspective on the organization structure and facilitate readers' understanding of the composition of systems 1 through 5. Figures 1.6(1) through 1.6(8) are intended to complement the descriptions of the individual systems. Figures 1.6(9) and 1.6(10) illustrate the overall organization and its recursiveness. Captions and labels have been matched to the wording of section 1.5.

The following graphs warrant some brief comments:

*Figure 1.6(1): Functions of System 1 from the perspective of the overall organization*
This diagram shows two recursion levels, although internal functional links in System 1 are only depicted *roughly* that is only those that are significant from the point of view of the overall organization.

*Figure 1.6(2): System 1 as a viable system*
Again, two recursion levels can be distinguished. The lower one comprises the *complete* structure of system 1, which makes that system a viable system. This is obvious from the fact that *all* five system functions are present in system 1.

*Figure 1.6(3): Functions of system 2 from the perspective of the overall organization*
In this graph, system 2 is depicted as linking the divisional regulatory centers to each other and with the division coordination center.

*Figure 1.6(4): System 2 as coordinator for the viable systems 1*
This graph shows the recursiveness of the organizational structure from the perspective of system 2.

*Figure 1.6(5): Functions of system 3 from the perspective of the overall organization*
System 3 is depicted with its informal links to systems 1 and 2, so the main emphasis here is on the information channels linking it to the other systems, rather than on its internal structure.

*Figure 1.6(6): Internal structure of system 3*
This graph shows the mechanism of information integration and coordination which is responsible for the organization's internal stability.

Rather than the information flow between the systems, the focus here is on how this information is integrated.

*Figure 1.6(7): Functions of system 4*
This graph shows the mechanism of information integration and coordination which is responsible for the organization's internal stability.

*Figure 1.6(8): Functions of system 5*
This graph shows the mechanism to design and enforce corporate policy.

*Figure 1.6(9): Basic structure of the viable organization*
This graph combines systems 1 through 5 into an organization structure for the viable system. The recursiveness of this structure is hinted at, but the main focus here is on the mechanisms working at one recursion level only: the level of the overall organization.

*Figure 1.6(10): Recursiveness of the organizational structure of the viable organization*
This graph further breaks down the corporate divisions and their control systems, thus demonstrating that not only these contain the entire organization structure of the viable system but so do their divisions and systems 1.41.

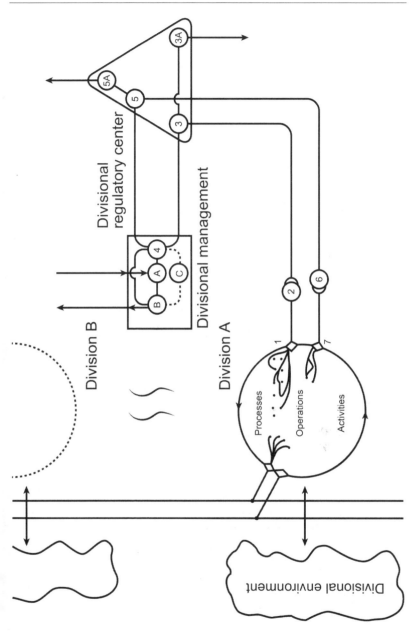

*Figure 1.6(1): Functions of System 1 from the perspective of the overall organization*

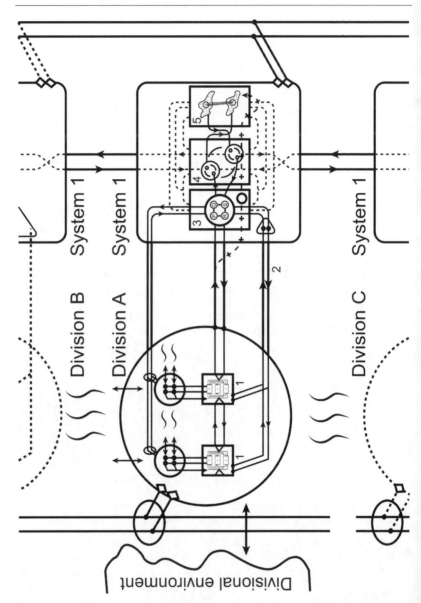

*Figure 1.6(2): System 1 as a viable system*

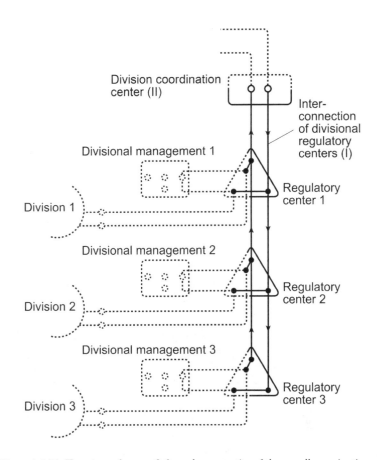

*Figure 1.6(3): Functions of system 2 from the perspective of the overall organization*

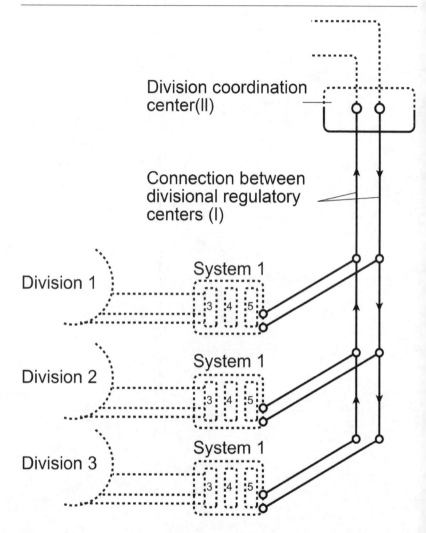

*Figure 1.6(4): System 2 as coordinator of the viable systems 1*

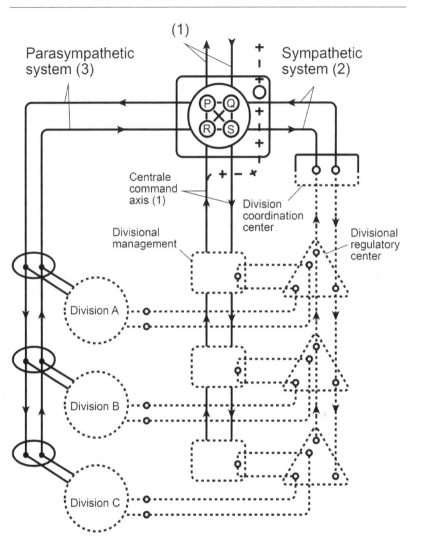

*Figure 1.6(5): Functions of system 3 from the perspective of the overall organization*

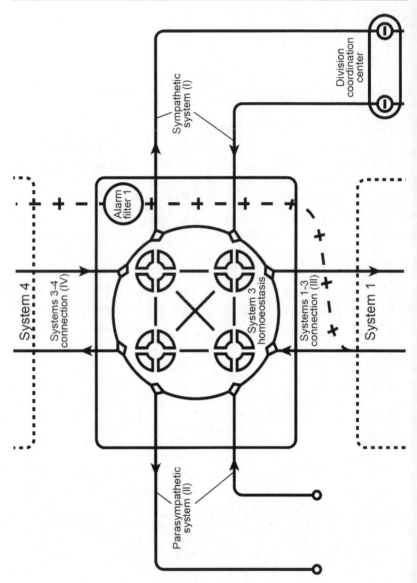

*Figure 1.6(6): Internal structure of system 3*

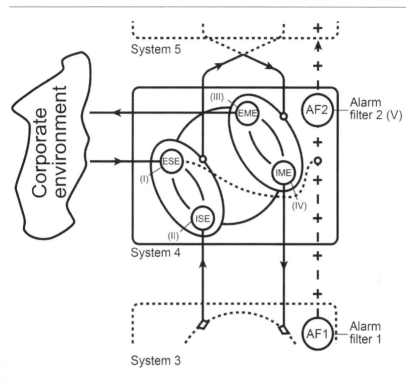

*Figure 1.6(7): Functions of system 4*

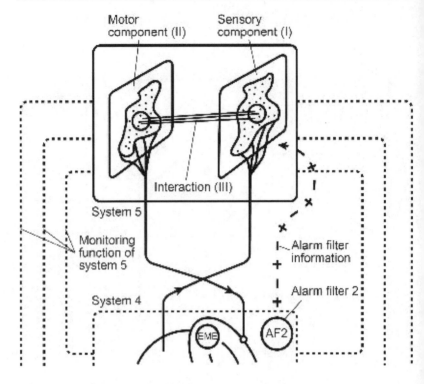

*Figure 1.6(8): Functions of system 5*

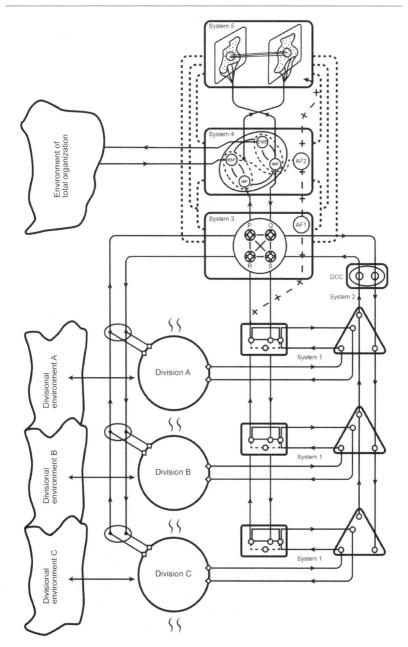

*Figure 1.6(9): Basic structure of the viable organization*

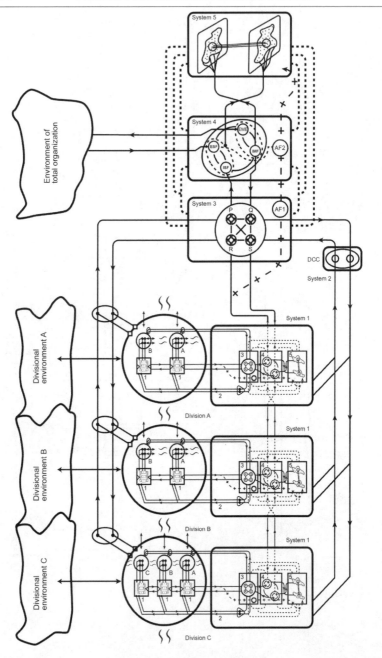

*Figure 1.6(10): Recursiveness of the organizational structure of the viable organization*

# 2. Strategic Management and the Problem of Complexity

## 2.1 Strategic Management as a Means of Managing Complexity

> "[C]ybernetics is the science of control,
> management is the profession of control."
> *Stafford Beer*

### 2.11 The Problem

Like any other kind of socio-technical system, enterprises can be viewed from various angles. Depending on what aspects, functions, qualities, and so on you consider relevant, you will end up with different theories as to the structure and behavior of the system you are studying. Some of these theories complement each other; some are antagonists. Apart from explanatory approaches based on *different views*, there have also been repeated attempts at establishing a *consistent* perspective that embraces and *integrates* the different approaches to socio-technical systems. Cybernetics and systems theory in general, and specifically the cybernetic Viable Systems Theory, are examples of such attempts at reconciling and integrating different perspectives. The key question is what the structures, functions, tasks, problems, goals, and so on of the different systems have *in common*. According to various findings by the scientific disciplines mentioned, there seem to be considerable similarities between different systems, permitting the development of *consistent solutions* to a number of problems these systems are supposed to solve.

Specifically, the writings by Ashby und Beer[130] suggest that the *key problem* any organism faces is how to gain control over the complexity that is relevant

---

130 See Ashby (Introduction), pp. 195 et seq.; Beer (Decision), pp. 270 et seq.; Beer (Heart), passim.

to its survival. That is to say, it needs to find ways to reconcile its own complexity, as manifested in its variety, with the complexity of its environment, again manifested as variety. No matter what configuration of states the system is in, it will only be able to survive if (and to the extent that) this problem of balancing complexities can be solved[131] Figure 2.11(1) shows a metaphorical and very general depiction of this situation.

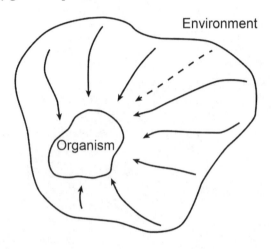

*Figure 2.11 (1)*

The organism under discussion, O, is permanently exposed to a large though usually not ascertainable number of influences in its environment. Metaphorically speaking, the organism is constantly "bombarded" with complexity by its environment. As a result, it is under permanent pressure to cope with that environment and its influences—which may keep changing in terms of kind, number, and intensity—in order to maintain its structure, function, and identity. This happens in various ways, ranging from passive adaptation to active interventions with the environment. The different biological, social, and socio-technical systems use many different tools—so diverse are these tools, in fact, that this diversity in detail tends to keep observers from seeing the fundamental similarities that exist or even the true nature of the problem.

---

131 The terms "complexity" and "variety" will be explained in section 2.2.

A look at the relevant literature on strategic problems of corporate management will confirm this. Most publications focus on specific elements of the problem associated with particular business functions—such as marketing issues or problems of longer-term financing—and usually they present very specific tools to solve these particular problems. Of these studies, most are dedicated to the product-market problem. Questions are usually examined from the technical-economical perspective, more or less tacitly assuming that the problem under study—doubtlessly a very central one—can be analyzed in isolation of other (e.g. political or social) aspects, and that the basic internal requirements for implementing product-market strategies are essentially met. Ansoff, Declerck, and Hayes place this entire range of activities in the category of strategic *planning*, as opposed to strategic management.[132] They also point out that this approach will capture part of the problem at best.

According to Ansoff, Declerck, and Hayes, the strategic problem has undergone tremendous changes over the past 20 years: They now define it as the *overall positioning* of a system in its environment, taking into account all existing linkages and including the design and development of the internal abilities that an organization needs to continually adapt its position to changing circumstances.

"… the strategic planning problem … has undergone significant changes in emphasis. From an instrument for correcting a partial strategic imbalance with the environment, it is coming to concern itself with the changeability of *all* economic and social linkages with the environment, with increasing incidence of major surprises and with ecological and resource constraints … internal configuration of resources is evolving from the problem of essential preservation of the firm's strength into a problem of fundamental redesign of the internal capability of the firm in order to preserve harmony with its internal linkages … from a technology designed to correct partial deficiencies in an organisation to a technology of "design to order"—an ability to define, structure and put into action a new organisation which is responsive to a specific social need." [133]

From a cybernetic perspective and particularly under the Viable Systems Theory, it is clear that strategic management has to be located somewhere at the top of the structure—that is, in systems 3, 4, and 5 and the interactions between them—and that it has to concern itself with precisely those subsystems

---

132 See Ansoff, Declerck, and Hayes (Strategic Management), pp. 1 et seq.
133 Ansoff and Hayes (Strategic Management), pp. 3, 4.

that are responsible for the overall positioning of the system in its environment, for the fundamental linkages between system and environment, and for the mechanisms required for positioning and repositioning.

As established in part 1, system 3 comprises all the functions and activities that stabilize the system internally, while system 4 is responsible for its external equilibrium. The overall balance of the enterprise can only be achieved, however, if its internal and external equilibria are permanently matched and if the measures required to maintain a partial balance can be adjusted in line with changes in the remaining partial balances. System 5, on the one hand, operates as a top-level normative authority; on the other, it has the eminently important task of constantly balancing the two partial equilibria.

As mentioned earlier, the core of the problem is how to manage complexity, or put the complexity of the enterprise in balance with that of the environment. So the enterprise needs to find a way to anchor itself in its environment, to an extent where it will be able to take in sufficient information about relevant environmental aspects and their changes, while developing sufficient behavioral codes to adequately respond to environmental changes. These matters can be depicted schematically as shown in figure 2.11(2) and, in line with a common cybernetic convention, figure 2.11(3).

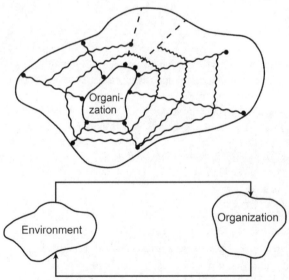

*Figures 2.11(2) and 2.11(3)*

In the former, the idea is that of an enterprise which, much like a spider, sits at the center of a huge web of environmental changes which it monitors, and to which it responds based on the information gathered and according to its own complexity, immediately restoring or improving defective or disrupted connections and introducing new ones whenever required. In the latter (see figure 2.11(3)), environment and enterprise are depicted as homeostats with the corresponding communication channels. In this graph, two simple channels represent the multitude of permanent, web-like linkages. Whatever depiction one may prefer, the solution to the problem of mutually balancing complexity is based on two components:

1. existing organizational system structures and
2. the control processes they permit.

A system's control capacity, and thus its ability to manage complexity, depends on its basic structures. Some system structures facilitate the mastering of complexity; some make it difficult or entirely impossible. So when it comes to controlling complexity, a system will behave according to what its structure permits. This insight is a fundamental result of systems theory research, and Stafford Beer has repeatedly emphasized its significance. Still, it is yet to receive the attention it deserves. Due to the inability to build on this insight in analyzing and designing socio-technical systems, attempts to reform social institutions often focus on the wrong points.

In particular, when it comes to addressing the strategic problem of enterprises, it seems crucial to have profound knowledge of basic control-optimal system structures. When strategy design fails to take proper account of the options an organization has or the system structures associated with them, either these strategies will not be implemented or any attempt at implementation will cause the system to exhibit dangerous signs of stress. A substantial share of the social resistance to strategic planning frequently deplored in literature may be due to this very fact: that strategies designed without taking account of existing options lack the basis for implementation. Quite possibly, these resistances—which usually manifest themselves in the social sphere—are only surface symptoms indicating deeper, structural defense mechanisms of a system. Analogous mechanisms in the field of biology would be immune reactions.

Given the interdependency between a system's structure and control-relevant behavior, we can further conclude that every system will display its normal behavior, as related to its particular structure, and that this behavior will generally be very stable and resistant to change, precisely because it is structurally dictated. Anyone that ever experienced the difficulty of reforming a social institution will know what I am talking about. One example out of many is the task of restoring the profitability of a loss-making business—although in this case the task is facilitated by the fact that a single look at the P+L statement will reveal to all involved that something must be wrong. Another example would be the task of transforming a conservative, sluggish operation into a dynamic and aggressive enterprise. It is precisely in those situations where it is not obvious to everybody that something is wrong, when a business even seems healthy by outward appearances and at a cursory glance, and when its behavior is construed as perfectly acceptable and normal by most of the people concerned, that it is most difficult to achieve a fundamental behavioral change. In most cases it will require major interventions in both the way business is done and the way human resources are handled, and often there will be *modifications* but no real *change*.

Consider the following remarks by Stafford Beer:

"The message is just this. Institutions are systems for being what they are and for doing what they do. No one believes this: it is incredible, yet true. People think that institutions are systems for being and doing what they were *set up* to be and do, or what they *say* they are and do or what they *wish* they were and did. The first task of the systems scientist is to look at the fact: What is the system? What does it do? If the answer turns out to be something no one wants, do not go around repeating the popular but fictitious belief in a very loud voice. Do not hire a public relations campaign to project the required image. *Change the system.*" [134]

Consequently, interventions in a system will always have to be of a structural kind if they are to be effective. As anyone with some experience in this kind of task will know, "structure" here does not refer to the organization chart; essential structural components include the pattern of mindsets, underlying behavioral codes (no matter whether or not they have been written down), power structure, the network of relationships of both sympathy and antipathy, and the usually very complex fabric of material and immaterial advantages.

From a cybernetic perspective, "structure" is not a static but a dynamic term. In this context it must be emphasized that structural relationships are not only those more or less immediately perceptible to the senses, or even visualized, but all kinds of relationships that contribute to the formation of

---

134 Beer (Crisis), pp. 319 et seq. (emphasis in original).

certain connections, patterns, or orders, no matter whether they are directly perceived and visualized or not. Above all, the structure of a system includes all kinds of abstract rules, irrespective of whether or not they can be captured in words.

As demonstrated in part 1, cybernetic researchers have managed to identify and conceptually describe the structures that are necessary and sufficient for the viability of any system. If properly applied, the structures of the viable cybernetic system create optimal conditions for solving the problem of mastering complexity. Hence the structural model of the viable system provides the basic paradigm for any kind of organizational design, and thus for locating all problems to be solved by management.

In addition to the structural requirements, however, the second element that is essential for solving the complexity problem, and thus for the design of strategic management, is the control processes that the respective structure permits (as mentioned before). The most important control processes with regard to the general problem of mastering complexity are *problem-solving processes*. These control processes, which are targeted not at specific, defined purposes but, in the sense of multi-purpose processes, at solving or dealing with any kind of problem, have particular significance in the field of strategic management. Therefore they are not to be judged from the perspective of specific, defined purposes but with regard to a *meta-purpose*: their general *problem-solving capacity*. The development of general system-related problem-solving capacity, which is closely related with institutional learning capacity, leads to a strong increase in systemic variety. Control processes which are not directly purpose-driven, and which explicitly aim to solve entirely new problems or gain control over environmental variety, even when its form or pattern is yet unknown, seem to be the institutional analogon to what behavioral science would call an "open program."[135] Open programs, as opposed to closed ones, are needed whenever the survival of an organism is not guaranteed by genetically pre-programmed solutions, so that appropriate solutions are subject to environmental circumstances that *cannot* be known in advance. The openness of genetic programs is a prerequisite for systems' *adaptive modifiability*, a quality which in complex environments has to be structural or genetic and is a result of earlier selections.[136]

The greater a system's expected environmental complexity, the greater the importance of this kind of control process. So, after having addressed

---

135 See Lorenz (Rückseite), p. 94.
136 See Lorenz (Rückseite), pp. 93. et.

the basic *structural* components of the viable system in part 1, as a next step we now need to take a closer look at these particular control processes, hereafter referred to as "evolutionary problem-solving processes." We will compare these *evolutionary problem-solving processes* with so-called *constructivist problem-solving processes*, and at the end we will see how these fundamentally different kinds of control process can be merged into one *systems methodology* which can be used to solve strategic management problems.

As the present writing consistently treats strategic management as a problem of how to master complexity, we will also need to have a closer look at the basics of viable systems. The Viable Systems Model is an end product (at least for the time being) of cybernetic research in this area. With regard to the structure of a viable system, two important kinds of system or order have to be distinguished: the so-called *spontaneous* or *polycentric* systems and the so-called *taxic* systems. Only by integrating these two forms of system we will achieve the result presented in this chapter: the Viable Systems Model.

By combining the structures of the viable system and the processes of systems methodology we obtain the *cybernetic concept of strategic management*. These interrelations are visualized in figure 2.11(4).

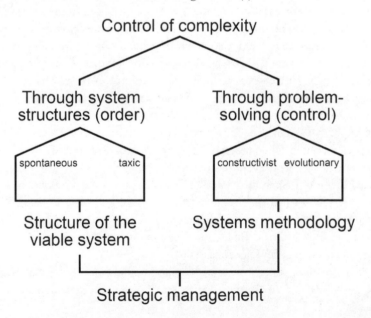

*Figure 2.11 (4)*

## 2.12 Strategies and Strategic Management

In cybernetics, systems are studied at a relatively high level of abstraction, which is why the connections between abstract structures and their application to individual real-life cases are not immediately obvious. This is a major obstacle to its proper understanding and application: although every manager—no matter whether he or she is heading a small or large business, a division or a whole organization, a school, a hospital, or a political party—ultimately faces the same problem, which is how to master complexity, this problem manifests itself in countless varieties, and the methods and ways to master complexity are just as varied.

The situation can perhaps be compared to a problem everyone is familiar with. Every human being has to find a way to make a living, but there are countless ways to solve the problem. Although this puts the problem in very abstract terms, it bears a very concrete meaning for every single human being: Everybody will be able to say for each of their actual or possible actions whether they help solve their specific problem or not. And it is certainly possible that, depending on the situation of the individual and on that person's standard of living, *equal behaviors must be judged differently and vice versa* with regard to solving the problem. When two men at a blackjack table lose the same amount of money, the impact this loss has on their lives will be very different if one of them is rich and the other is poor.

While one's individual sphere of life and the problem of making a living is usually tangible for the individual—that is to say, manageable and controllable—the same cannot be said of the level of social systems. The mere fact that social systems are multi-person entities, and that they have to serve purposes far beyond the capacities of an individual, suggests that the complexity to be considered by far exceeds the scope comprehensible to the individual brain. So, with the exception of very trivial cases, the problem of balancing varieties cannot be the task of one individual. Rather, the *organizational set-up* of a system, no matter what its components, has to enable the system as a whole to solve that problem.

And since the organization of a complex social system also exceeds the individual's capacity for comprehension, even when that person resorts to abstraction, the connection I pointed out before between the abstract formulation of the problem of managing variety and the concrete tools to control variety is often lost. As a result there is a tendency to focus on those qualities of the tools used which are irrelevant to the actual solution to the problem, while the truly important qualities are neglected. For instance, in many organizations budgeting is viewed from a financial perspective only, while the question as to whether and to what extent the budget and budgeting process will help to manage complexity—or whether they might even have an adverse effect—is hardly ever discussed. Along the same lines, questions about the "right" leadership style are hardly ever regarded in terms of whether and how a certain kind of management behavior will produce or reduce variety, what components of the system will be affected, and whether this will impede or promote the overall system's viability. As a result of that, discussions on leadership style are regularly carried on from consistent perspectives, such as efficiency, humanity, the just treatment of staff members, power, authority, and so on, but these considerations do not necessarily extend to the core problem, which is coping with variety and thus the system's viability, but focus on the mere epiphenomena of that problem.

Due to the fact that an individual is unable to survey all relevant circumstances, but also because the problem is hardly every discussed systematically with regard to its general structure, practitioners' interest tends to focus on solving their specific, immediate problems—and sometimes justifiably so—so they are not (or not immediately) interested in a universal problem-solving approach. In other words, rather than asking themselves, "How can I solve problems?" practitioners will ask themselves, "How can I solve problem X or Y?" Much the same is true for the general attitude toward strategic management. Questions asked will usually be located at a very concrete level: What should textiles company A, machine works B, retail chain C, hotel D, bank E, and so on, do in this or that situation?

Indeed, problems as *specific* as these do not have a *universal* solution. Each individual case requires special consideration, and there will usually be a special solution to it. The question to be answered with regard to strategic management is rather general by comparison. It is not, What does company X have to do in situation Y in order to reach objective O at the point in time T? Rather, it is, What kind of mechanism is needed to produce specific strategies, no matter for what industry and company? Consequently, a paper on strategic management will have to deal with these kinds of general questions, although their solutions should also help solve the specific problems managers face in concrete situations.

The whole situation can be compared to drawing a map of a specific territory. As an orientation tool, a map should, among other things, help to select destinations and identify appropriate routes to those destinations.

However, precisely what destinations and routes the different users will select is something the map's creators cannot know. In a sense, the map represents a potential to solve many different problems of the same *kind*, but of course the questions that the geographer faces upon creating the map will differ from those that, for example, a father faces when planning a family outing, or a military commander faces when devising an operational plan. A map, together with the rules for its use, can be considered a machine or mechanism for solving problems of a specific category. It is similar to the ability to play a musical instrument: Together with the rules for its use, the instrument provides a mechanism for creating results of a certain category— but these are not limited to certain compositions. On the contrary, it is even an essential feature of mastering a musical instrument to be able to play not only one musical piece or a list of pieces, but all compositions written for that instrument.

Similarly, it is a characteristic of management to be applicable not only to *one* specific enterprise in *one* situation but to the management of organizations in general, in almost any conceivable situation.

It is much the same with strategic management. What is normally referred to with this term mostly belongs to the categories of strategies of product, marketing, HR, R&D, and so on. From a cybernetic point of view, strategic management means something completely different. The central question is not what principles a company's manufacturing or marketing should be based on but how these manufacturing or marketing principles are created— that is, what principles the process of defining those manufacturing or marketing principles should be based on. So the focus is clearly on the *meta-level*, as its design and mechanisms determine processes at the object level—and very comprehensively so.

Rather than asking, What strategies should we pursue over the next few years?, typical key questions include these: What are key characteristics of successful strategies? What processes need to be launched to develop a strategy? What structural requirements have to be met so that necessary processes can run smoothly? Rather than striving to produce a concrete strategy, which would be an output of a specific system, these questions are aimed at the *strategy-producing system* itself. Likewise, the problem primarily consists not in developing a specific strategy but in designing a system capable of producing strategies.

So, strategic management is a nucleus of mechanisms which ultimately generates concrete strategies: Its *output* are strategies. And although strategies should essentially be designed for the longer term, there is always a probability they will have to be modified. By contrast, the strategy-producing core of management mechanisms will remain effective for a much longer period of time. Hence, the often-heard proposition that management theory should entail statements on concrete strategies can hardly ever be satisfied. It is in the very nature of strategies—at least successful ones—that, viewed from a general perspective, they tend to represent the exceptional case and be difficult to comprehend. After all, a strategy just anyone could pursue, or actually pursues, is not very likely to be successful. By contrast, it is quite conceivable that the *strategy-producing mechanism* could be the same for all organizations, which is why general statements, in the sense of a theory, are often only possible for this strategy-producing mechanism, not for the strategies produced by it.

The fact that strategic management, the way it is understood here, is primarily meta in the sense described does not mean it is impossible to make concrete statements on specific types of strategies. For example, strategies aimed at diversification, growth, focus, and so on, have common characteristics that can be clearly described for a multitude of companies, perhaps even for several industries. Certain types of strategies can be so dominant in certain periods that scientists and practitioners concentrate their efforts on working them out in detail, which may cause them to temporarily disregard the actual core problem. However, once the situation changes and the current strategy appears questionable the core problem will re-emerge. At that point it will be clear that anyone concentrating on one strategy or one kind of strategy is comparable to a singer who can only sing one kind of song while his or her audience's taste has changed. As the economic, social, and political situation grows more and more complex, involving continuous, fast-paced change, business enterprises and other social systems increasingly face the problem that their strategies become questionable or even obsolete, forcing them to develop fundamentally new modes of behavior. As a result, it gets increasingly important to deal with the characteristics, qualities, components, and functions of the strategy-producing mechanism available to the particular organization.

To sum up, the subject of a theory on strategic management is the mechanism or combination of mechanisms that enables an organization at any given time to develop a system of basic rules for both its current and its probable future environmental situation—which in most cases cannot be known in advance—to guide the behavior of its elements, including its employees, for an indefinite amount of time.

In the literature and everyday language, what we usually call strategy is the behavior that *actually results* from such rules, or is intended or expected based on people's awareness of those rules. It would make much more sense, however, to use the term "strategy" for the (set of) rules themselves, rather than the behavior guided by them and *de facto* resulting from them. Thus, a strategy is a *set of rules* produced by the management mechanisms existing in an organization, and which is to guide the future behavior of a—not necessarily predefined—number of people in unforeseeable numbers and kinds of situations.[137] It takes a certain kind of rules to fulfill this function of regulating future behaviors in situations that are unknown at the time of rule creation. The problems associated with such sets of rules will be discussed in later sections. These rules or sets of rules form by far the most important mechanism that an organization or, in more general terms, a socio-technical system can use to master complexity.

As has been established in the foregoing sections, a scientific paper on strategic management has to deal with both: a rule-generating mechanism and the set of rules it generates. These are the two components for which general statements are possible. The actual behavior resulting from those sets of rules cannot be described by general statements, mainly because rules *alone* will not suffice to specify the entire behavior of individuals and systems: An additional key factor is their respective situation, that is, the facts and circumstances known to the individuals or systems at any given point in time. Metaphorically speaking, the particular set of rules represents a filter separating actual from potential behavior. However, as at any given time both potential and actual behaviors are strongly influenced by continually changing environmental circumstances, it is obvious that the result of this filtering process can only be predicted in part, that is, with regard to its general aspects determined by the "filter." To the extent that the set of rules governing a social system is known, the resulting behavior can be forecast at least in part. To the same extent it is also possible to determine the general characteristics of behavior that, at least in retrospect, have been shown to be effective in the long run, which is what led to the term "strategy" being used for actual behavior. The situation is comparable to having a computer and being familiar

---

137 See Beer (Decision), p. 90; and Ansoff (Strategy), pp. 118 et seq.

with its program but unable to specify the kind of input it needs for its computing processes. If we know a system well enough to know the kind of input it requires, though not the specific details, we will be able to make forecasts regarding its behavior or results. We can then predict that, given a certain kind of input and a certain *kind* of program, there can only be certain kinds of results, while other kinds are not to be expected for this system. This is a typical case of an in-principle prediction, or pattern prediction: It is possible to predict the general behavior of a system but not the details. This kind of forecast will be explained in greater detail at a later point.

I will conclude this section with some comments on the use of terms such as "successful" or "good" strategy. Some thoughts on the basic problems of strategic management suggest that at a strategic level, there can be no certainty of success for socio-technical systems. Even the most sophisticated methods hold no guarantee that a company will find and apply the right strategy at any given time. Consequently, the purpose of developing a concept for strategic management cannot be to solve this unsolvable problem, but to increase the probability that any strategies developed under this concept will be superior to others. Hence there is always a possibility that an enterprise will be able to operate successfully even without full-fledged strategic management—at least temporarily—and, vice versa, that an enterprise will fail despite its having a sophisticated strategic management in place.

The implementation of any strategy is always a high-risk endeavor. It is the trial element in a trial-and-error process which may have been preceded by numerous mental and other trials (e.g., in test markets), which means it is not entirely random, but all the same, in essence it is a trial without a success guaranty. This is not necessarily a reason for resignation, though. Instead, upon recognizing the facts and setting straight any illusions that might prevail, responsible managers will take various structural measures allowing them to detect potential undesirable developments early and create a maximum of room to maneuver.

## 2.2 Complexity

> "Greater skill only arises from greater complexity."
> *Carsten Bresch*

### 2.21 Complexity and Variety

As mentioned before, this book addresses the idea of strategic management from the perspective of controlling complexity. No matter what aspects of management initially appear to be the focus of analysis—setting targets, organizing, taking decisions, leading people, planning, monitoring, and so on—at the end of the day, management is always about managing complexity. The many different aspects of management addressed in *literature are nothing but means to that end. In a manner of speaking, they are the* epiphenomena (or concrete manifestations) of the core task of management, and it happens too often that they cover that actual task with insignificant details.

Hence, management is only required when matters are characterized by a great degree of complexity. This is particularly true for the approaches and concepts of strategic management: In simple situations they are not appropriate and can even appear trivial and absurdly complicated, as the problems arising in these cases tend to have obvious solutions. So, given that the complexity or simplicity of matters is the key criterion for the use or non-use of the principles, methods, and tools of strategic management, we obviously need a much deeper understanding of the idea of complexity than can generally be assumed to exist.

### *Complexity as a Buzzword*

It has almost become fashionable to use the term "complexity" as an opener for scientific essays and papers, for instance by emphasizing that the matter at hand is complex. In most cases this is mere lip service, a concession to what is perceived to be the zeitgeist. Only in the rarest of cases are matters really discussed in their full complexity. More often than not, reference to the enormous complexity of a phenomenon is even used as an excuse for pursuing reductionist scientific approaches: "We are dealing with a complex phenomenon here, so for the sake of simplicity, let us assume that…"

### *Complexity as an Everyday Experience*

The term complexity is often also used in its colloquial meaning, which is something like "complicated," "intransparent," "incomprehensible," or the like. Now this use of the term may basically be correct in that it expresses the human being's impotence vis-à-vis what is going on around him—his incapacity to understand, comprehend, and influence matters—but this is the farthest that everyday experience will take us. What remains is a feeling of uneasiness. And while this sentiment often triggers ideological-political attitudes, perhaps even actions, such actions usually come to nothing for lack of a foundation; or when they do have an impact it is due to a demonstration of power. The problem remains, and so do basic solution approaches (examples: the controversy around nuclear power, terrorism, alternative ways of life, various manifestations of resistance against specific government actions).

### Complexity as a Scientific Problem

It is no exaggeration to say that the way in which the problem of complexity is addressed marks the segregation of two scientific worlds. Depending on whether you follow an analytical-reductionist or a systemic-interactionist approach, your focus will be on very different

- questions,
- approaches/methods
- answers.

One might even say that two very different world views and thus very different understandings of science come with this distinction. They also involve very different concepts of humankind, society, and the role of humankind in the world.

### Complexity as a Management Problem

A further consequence is a different attitude towards any issue associated with human beings' influencing their environment. What can we influence? How can we exert influence? What results can we expect? What side effects should we be prepared for? What is basically possible or impossible to accomplish?

These are just some examples of questions, and the answers will differ depending on whether we examine the problem from a scientific or an analytic-reductionist approach.

To understand the idea of complexity in its entirety, we have to resort to what one might call a *theory of complex phenomena.*[138] A theory that explicitly

---

138 Regarding this term and the following explanations, see Hayek (Studies), pp. 22 et seq.

deals with complex phenomena has to be fundamentally different from the much more common theories dealing with relatively simple phenomena, such as most natural sciences. It is these fundamental differences in the handling of simple and complex phenomena that require very specific approaches and ways of thinking. Without a comprehensive understanding of the specifics of complex phenomena, it is impossible to understand the specifics of the approaches and the ways of thinking applied in this field.

The term "complexity" refers to the fact that real systems can be in an enormous number of states. Even in relatively simple cases, this complexity is usually greater than what the human mind can comprehend.

Complexity can be quantified and measured in terms of *variety*:

Definition: Variety is the number of distinguishable states of a system, or of distinguishable elements of a given quantity.

Complexity is caused mainly by the *interactions* of elements. The approach to determining complexity is essentially based on mathematical combinatorics.

To get a sense of the complexity of matters, it usually helps to go through a number of examples. Take, for instance, chess. It is considered complex because there is an enormous number of possible moves and an even greater number of possible configurations on the chess board. According to quantitative analyses as to the potential orders of magnitude to be reached, enumerative computation of all possible moves and combinations is impossible, not only for the human brain but also for computers. This is why strategic approaches are so important in chess.

Another example is economics: The extent of complexity we deal with here is obvious when you consider that there are millions of exchange-of-goods relationships among millions of economic subjects, be they households, businesses, or other organizations. Changes in some areas of such systems will transfer to other areas in very complicated ways, or in other words, every single relationship can potentially respond to changes in other relationships, which, in turn, can cause more changes in further relationships. While it may be possible to develop universal theorems for these matters, it is impossible to observe or describe each and every one of them specifically.

For reasons to be explained later, it seems appropriate to move beyond the level of mere intuition and develop a deeper understanding of the characteristics of systems, in order to see how complexity is created and what orders of magnitude it can reach. The following examples should help to make this clearer:

*Example 1*

Let us assume the system comprises five light bulbs, each of which can be on or off. How many states can the system be in?

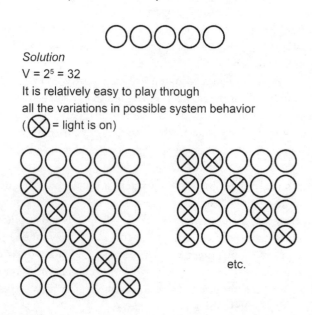

*Solution*

V = 2⁵ = 32

It is relatively easy to play through
all the variations in possible system behavior
( ⊗ = light is on)

etc.

*Example 2*

How many states can the system be in, if each of the bulbs can not only be switched on or off but also be lit in five different colors, e.g. red, blue, green, yellow, and white?

*Solution*

V = 5⁵ = 3125

While it is relatively easy to play through the system behaviors in the first example, it is hardly possible for this system, which has been modified just a bit.

*Example 3*
This time, let us assume the system has 25 light bulbs, each of which can be on or off.

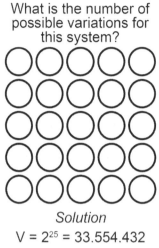

What is the number of
possible variations for
this system?

*Solution*
$V = 2^{25} = 33.554.432$

*Figure 2.2: Complexity and Variety-Example 1-3*

Now this is a rather complex system. Its overall variety would suffice to clearly identify each of the inhabitants of, for example, the U.S. state of Massachusetts, and even to assign four additional characteristics to each of them.

As we have seen, this basically rather simple system has an enormous potential of possible behaviors.

In general, when a system comprises n elements and can take k states, its variety is $k^n$. Exponential functions like these are explosive in nature and can quickly reach astronomical dimensions, even with small values for n and k.

*Example 4*
What is the variety of the system in example 3 if one of the bulbs is defective?
*Solution*
$V = 2^n - 1 = 2^{24} - 1 = 16,777,216 - 1$

*Example 5*
How do varieties change for the system from example 3 if we have ten switches by which we can switch ten bulbs on or off at random, thus coupling and decoupling them from the system?

*Solution*
In this case, V can be reduced to 32,768 states, which shows that even minor changes to a system can drastically change its complexity.
*Example 6*
How does system variety change if we gradually add more light bulbs to the 25 we had originally?
Solution
Again, we have the same effect: Each new bulb doubles the system's variety.

$$n = 26 \quad \rightarrow \quad 67{,}108{,}000$$
$$n = 27 \quad \rightarrow \quad 134{,}217{,}000$$
$$n = 28 \quad \rightarrow \quad 268{,}435{,}000$$
$$n = 29 \quad \rightarrow \quad 536{,}870{,}000$$
$$n = 30 \quad \rightarrow \quad 1073{,}471{,}000$$

*Example 7*
The human brain has approximately 10 billion (= $10^{10}$) brain cells. Neurophysiologic research has shown that each of them can be in one of two states: It can be either stimulated or not stimulated. This adds up to an enormous degree of variety for this system: It is $2^{\wedge}10^{\wedge}10$.

## 2.22 The Cybernetic and Systems-Theoretical Standpoint

The study of the phenomenon of complexity impressively shows what the core of the cybernetic/systems-theoretical perspective is, apart from the differences between analytical and systemic approaches discussed before.

While most scientists look into matters as they *actually are*, the starting point for cybernetics is the question of what matters *would be like if they were at their maximum variety*. So, the starting point is always an imagined *number of possibilities* (which in subsequent phases we generate by way of experimenting).[139]

The key questions and approaches in cybernetics, in particular the approaches of communications theory, seem pointless as long as this fundamental difference is not acknowledged and included in scientific research. Only by mentally contrasting what is and what could be will cybernetic problem-solving approaches unleash their full power.

---

139 See Ashby (Introduction), pp. 121 et seq.

*Communication* requires a set of *possible* messages that *could be* exchanged. Information content can never be an intrinsic characteristic of the individual message (statement, signal, and so on) but will always depend on what else could have been said but in fact was not—which also explains why "nothing" can be information.

*Regulation, steering, and control:* For an in-depth understanding of these, we have to imagine what things would be like without them. What the regulation content or the control effect of a certain measure is will only become clear when we realize what would happen without it. So the key cybernetic question is not: "How will a maple tree grow from this seed?" but "Why will a maple tree grow from this seed—and why not a lime tree, or a rabbit, or a human being?"

*Coordination and Integration:* Again, we never start by asking what exists (apart from the fact that it provides an initial impulse, a dissatisfaction with facts), but always start by asking what could be, in order to then ask why things are as they are and not as they could be.

Hence we always have to distinguish between the *potential* variety of a system and its *actual* variety. We also need to carefully examine each of our actions as to whether it will further reduce the actual variety or even increase it, thus enabling more potential variety to unfold.

This is why *cybernetic* explanations are often *negative*,[140] while a *causal* explanation is *typically positive*. For instance, when we see a billiard ball move in a certain direction we explain that by saying that another ball has hit it from a certain angle and with a certain momentum. By contrast, in cybernetics we would ask what other things could have happened alternatively, then explain why in fact they did not. This approach permits a more and more in-depth understanding of matters, as one has to examine more and more thoroughly what the constraints were that have influenced the situation in such a way that, out of a whole range of possibilities, it was this particular one that has ultimately materialized (or been selected). So, a cause in the cybernetic sense is never a one-dimensional effect of A on B, but always a network of constraints that determine the context of what can be observed.

---

140 See Bateson (Ecology), pp. 399 et seq.

Any failure to take proper account of this distinction between the possible and the actual will result in limitless confusion.

## 2.23 The Law of Requisite Variety

Why, you may wonder, is it so important to study the phenomenon of complexity? What is the point of playing around with numbers like that? Its significance follows from the key insight that we can only control a system to the extent that we keep it from moving to states we consider undesirable. Systems that "behave as they please" are obviously out of our control.

This observation may seem trivial at first, but this notion will quickly fade once we start thinking about how to solve this particular problem: How do we prevent systems from doing what they please (or whatever they are able to do)?

The universal solution to this problem is one of the key findings of cybernetics. To wit: The only way to gain control of a system with a given degree of complexity is by using a system at least as complex—or, as the discoverer of this law, British cyberneticist Ross Ashby, very aptly put it:Only variety can absorb variety.[141]

This observation, which is claimed to be equivalent to a natural law, is backed by strict scientific evidence, at least with regard to its formal part. It is also easy to understand and intuitive. A good soccer team will have plenty of variety in terms of possible actions—if it is really first-class—and it will take a team with a comparable degree of variety to beat it. A good chess player can only be beaten by one that plays just as well. It takes a well-trained hound to hunt down an old, experienced fox. In combat with a well-equipped, strong army you will only have a fighting chance if your army is equally strong. All the terms I have used here—"strong," "well-trained," "experienced," and so on—are merely synonyms for high variety, manifest in a broad range of possible behaviors.

The following sections will describe the basic structure of the situation, including all the elements that, from a cybernetic point of view, are required to depict this insight and its "technological" application.

---

141 Ashby (Introduction), pp. 202 et seq.

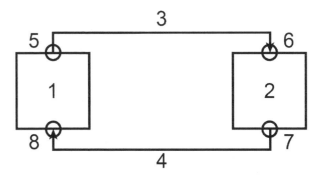

*Figure 2.23(1)*

The key components in this graph are numbered from 1 through 8. The following conditions are required to ensure a balance of varieties between the two systems:

1. The two systems (1 and 2) have to be on a par in terms of variety.
2. It must be possible to transmit the available variety of each system via transmission or communication channels (3 and 4), which means these channels have to have sufficient capacity.
3. The transduction elements (5 through 8) as interfaces between the communication channels and the systems also have to have sufficient throughput capacity.

This system structure (homeostat), with the variety-related connections shown here, is the cornerstone of cybernetic analysis and design.

At this point you might rightfully ask why the significance of system complexity has been *underestimated for so long*. First off, complexity or variety can take *many different forms*. In specific situations in the past, for instance in assessing the military power of a potential adversary, decision-makers were well aware of the inherent variety and of the fact that the key challenge was to counter the enemy's complexity with a matching degree of complexity. Of course, this analysis was carried out in a military context; its general background—the insight that applies to all complex systems—was hidden by the details of the specific problem at hand. This situation is actually similar to what happened with other scientific findings. For instance, people had taken advantage of gravity long before Newton was born, and they had found solutions to overcome gravity in specific situations. But it took a Newton to figure out that this is a law of nature.

A second point to keep in mind with regard to the above question is that all natural systems are under *some kind of control*, so that the large numbers of states theoretically possible are rarely or never actually reached. For instance, we all take it for granted and as a not very remarkable fact that our nervous system functions well, as long as it does. Only when coincidence or a disease causes individual functions to fail do we realize how many undesirable states our organism can take.

Thirdly, many people lack both the education and the *imagination* required to think of what *possible behaviors* a system could display, apart from what we are already familiar with.

According to Ashby's Law of Requisite Variety, complexity can only be controlled by complexity. In other words, the variety of control options available for the goals pursued has to be at least as great as the variety of the system to be controlled. Or, putting it yet another way, one might say that the system states actually occurring depend on both the system variety and the control variety available.

In the context of simple systems, the Law of Requisite Variety will not pose any major problems. When matters get really complex, however, it becomes enormously difficult to comply with this law and generate the control variety needed to meet *specific goals*. Of course, Ashby's law is always fulfilled in one way or another because is it a law of nature; however, the system states resulting from the respective varieties may not always be acceptable. For instance, if juvenile crime increases in a country due to prevailing conditions whose effects are partly known and partly unknown, this is formally a result of the varieties involved. In theory one could accept this situation as a necessary evil; most governments will try to do something about it. This is a nice example to show what dimensions the problem of requisite variety can have: It will be very difficult in this case to generate the necessary control variety, and enacting new laws will hardly do the trick, considering that the key problem here is the very fact that laws are disregarded. So the challenge lies in finding a control mechanism that forces young people—or better yet, motivates them—to respect the law.

A similar problem concerns the enforcement of speed limits in road traffic. A law stipulating a maximum speed level on highways will hardly suffice to generate the desired results. Also, in most countries it is highly doubtful whether the available police resources, radar equipment, and so on suffice to generate adequate control variety for a system whose variety is determined by the overall length of the country's highways, the number of drivers, and so on. Of course—and fortunately so—the control mechanism available to limit driving speeds comprises much more than police staff, who could never fulfill that task on their own. Further components include social control amongst traffic participants, the basic attitude of system elements (i.e., drivers) towards compliance with traffic laws, and so on. Social control and traffic morals help to reduce system variety, thus facilitating the task of the official control mechanism. Control variety can be enhanced further by using a sophisticated system of random checks, along with adequately strict sanctions, and so on. Still, it remains doubtful as to whether the resulting balance in varieties will generate and maintain the desired state.

Let us go back to figure 2.23(1) and the quantitative variety examples. The fact that it is possible to precisely define variety and, under certain conditions, determine the relevant quantities must not lead us to believe this is the core of the variety concept and the ideas behind it. That would be utterly wrong. Of course, just because we can precisely define something and it is possible *in principle* to measure it (by way of counting), this does not mean that we can measure it in every single case; likewise, if something cannot be measured, this does not mean that the respective concept is useless.

Perhaps the non-quantitative examples suffice to show that it is all a matter of *balancing* varieties: This is the regulative effect, or rather, it is regulation. Two soccer teams have to have about the same variety—while obviously nobody could say exactly how much that would be—to deliver an exciting match. If one of them has much less variety than the other one, we can make rather sound forecasts as to the outcome. This constellation can be depicted graphically (in line with Beer's concept[142]), as shown in figure 2.23(2).

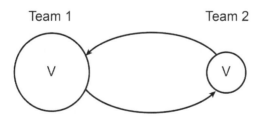

Team 1                    Team 2

*Figure 2.23(2)*

---

142 Beer (Freedom), p. 31.

Relative to the criteria of good soccer, this system, which is made up of two teams, is not well balanced. Team 1 can practically be expected to win every match, and it does not matter so much how many goals are scored. The match will tend to be rather boring, and lack exciting situations and gambits.

As a general rule, there will *only be the following options for restoring* the (soccer) balance of this system:

1. Team 1 reduces its variety
2. Team 2 increases its variety
3. a mixture of both.

A graphical depiction, again based on the conventions introduced by Beer, can be found in figure 2.23(3).

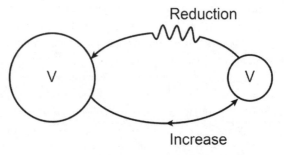

*Figure 2.23(3)*

Of course, the two new symbols for variety reduction and variety increase which have been added in figure 2.23(3) do not give us any clue as to how exactly that is supposed to happen. For now, we have only stated and localized a problem. We now know—and that is the purpose of cybernetic modeling—that in the situation represented by the model shown in figure 2.23(3), the elements to be considered are systems, interaction, variety, variety reduction, variety increase, channel, and transduction.

Option 1 would result in a well-balanced but probably rather mediocre game, for what could you do to reduce the variety available to Team 1? You could exchange good players for not-so-good ones, create conflict in the team, cause them not to play to their strengths, and so on. Option 2 would result in exciting, high-class soccer. Team 2 would have to train hard, exchange bad players for better ones, and so on.

This example, which can be refined ad libitum with some imagination and some knowledge of soccer, suffices to show most of what is important from a cybernetics standpoint:

1. In a sense, Ashby's Law is always fulfilled; however, the equilibrium reached does not necessarily correspond to the observer's criteria.
2. In real life, it rarely happens that varieties can actually be measured. Nevertheless, the idea and the concept are indispensable. It is all about balancing varieties, that is, a matter of comparative parameters.
3. There are basically two options to alter varieties: reducing or increasing them. These are the only truly relevant modes of regulation. By mixing them we can generate a third option which, as it is based on the other two, is obviously not an option in its own right.
4. Controlling complexity means nothing else but performing this regulating act.
5. The truly relevant facts about regulation are usually disguised by the specific measures taken to reduce or increase variety. The key challenge, however, is in determining the regulation-relevant aspects behind the specific contents, which can vary greatly from one system to the other. These aspects are referred to as the cybernetics of the particular situation, that is, the cybernetics of soccer, nuclear armament, food security, or marital fidelity—just as we might speak of the physics of elementary particles or of the physics of the alpine body harness.

I would like to place particular emphasis on the last point, as in my experience it is the greatest barrier to accessing systemic or cybernetic thinking: the ability to recognize cybernetic invariance behind the details of the particular case. When it comes to improving a soccer team, an experienced coach will quickly think of a range of possible measures. The same is true for a tennis coach, a piano teacher, or a priest, each faced with their respective challenges. Of course, the methods applied by the soccer coach and the piano teacher will seem to have nothing in common at first; from a cybernetic perspective, however, both increase the variety of their systems, that is, of the soccer team and the piano player.

This may seem like a simple insight, perhaps even trivial. In more complex situations, however, it is far from trivial. What impact do the countless management techniques in corporations actually have? Where do they reduce variety, and where do they increase it? Does this happen at the right points?

For instance, where exactly does cooperative management style increase variety? Questions of this kind are not that easy to answer.

The problem of controlling complexity is further exacerbated by a second set of problems: the *insurmountable limitation of human knowledge*, that is, the fact that complexity sets boundaries to human knowledge. It is impossible to obtain the same amount of knowledge about complex matters as about simple ones. This is not a preliminary state, resulting from the fact that certain scientific disciplines are at an underdeveloped stage. Human ignorance with regard to complex matters is an absolute fact, and cannot be overcome with even the greatest advances in computer sciences.

## 2.24 The Bremermann Limit[143]

Why the astronomical number of system states resulting from the interaction of elements or why the fulfillment of the law of variety should represent problems at all is not immediately obvious. For a better understanding you have to be familiar with a proof for Bremermann's Limit. Bremermann managed to prove as early as in 1960 that, due to the fact that matter consists of atoms, information processing has an upper limit that cannot be exceeded by any computer or brain made up of matter. This limit is comparable to the speed of light, which, according to today's state of science, is also an upper limit that cannot be exceeded.

Bremermann's Limit says that
"No material system can process more than $mc^2/h$ bits per second."

$m$ = mass of the system
$c$ = speed of light
$h$ = Planck's Constant

Based on Bremermann's finding, we can determine an upper limit in the order of $2 \times 10^{47}$ bits per gram per second.

---

143 See Bremermann (Optimization); as well as Ashby (Informational Measures), p. 84; Ashby (Bremermann), passim; and Ashby (Models), pp. 102 et seq.; as well as Beer (Brain), pp. 62 et seq.

The interesting point is what we can conclude for the size of computers and their resulting information processing capacity. Let us assume that the entire globe, or its mass, could be transformed into a gigantic computer, and let us further assume that this computer would have processed information throughout the entire geological history as we know it—what quantity of information would we have?

1 year      $\cong \pi \times 10^7$ sec
Geological history $\cong$ 1,000 million years $\cong 10^9$ years of masses of earth   $\cong$ 6 x $10^{27}$ grams
The resulting information quantity is
IQ = $(2 \times 10^{47}) (t \times 10^7) (10^9) (6 \times 10^{27})$ bits $\cong 10^{92}$ bits

This shows that even relatively small and simple systems have a potential variety far beyond Bremermann's Limit. Consequently, it is also clear that even the ever-continuing micro-miniaturization in computer technology will not change anything about this absolute limit.

Against this background, the key question for the management of complex systems is this: How can we gain control over the potential variety of systems that are within physical limits? This is the problem that all brains, all computers, all management bodies, all governments, and even nature itself are faced with.

As we will shortly see, it is achieved through *organization* or *order*. Some readers may have already wondered why in some examples the mere number of states has been treated as the relevant phenomenon, and they may have objected that the number itself does not mean much, and that it is the significance of states that matters. With very few exceptions, the states of a system do not come about randomly or chaotically, but follow a pattern and have certain regularities, or an order. This creates the conditions for the reasonable and economic interaction of systems, and is a prerequisite for their ability to adapt, learn, be regulated, and evolve.

"A pattern is the result of a *chain* process in which at any given time the existing pattern determines the probability that any of the different options encompassed in the following coincidence will actually transpire. Hence, patterns grow and change by way of random events that are linked together. Patterns are arrangements of modules which develop in "self-limiting freedom."[144]

---

144 Bresch (Zwischenstufe Leben), p. 60 (quote translated by author; emphasis as in original).

What we refer to as the state of a system is another pattern, of course, a specific constellation of all aspects relevant for the characterization of the system, at a specific point in time. Variety is the number of patterns that can emerge in this way. And since these patterns—the system states—do not occur at random, as explained, we are looking at patterns of patterns. This raises the question about a variety of a higher order, and we could think about how many patterns can be formed from the patterns (system states).

The following example may help to illustrate this point. The current state of a soccer match depends on the positions that the players and the ball are in at any given time. It keeps changing in the course of the match, which is one of the factors that make soccer so exciting and popular. A match is a specific sequence of states. This sequence is unique. The next match and other matches to follow will be different even when they involve the same teams. This is an assumption which will certainly meet with general approval—and the reason is variety. The number of possible combinations of states that will add up to different matches is so huge that the probability of two matches taking exactly the same course is nil. Even if we apply generous criteria and describe soccer matches in very broad terms—as happens in sports reporting, where details are left out even when they may have added a lot to the excitement—we will still be left with an enormous number of different sequences, or matches.

So the question is not only of how many states can occur in the course of *one* match but also of how many different matches are possible. This question has quite some practical significance for the coaching of teams and the training of referees, and also for the business opportunities associated with soccer.

If, for instance, only 100 different games were possible, it would be possible to design the training so as to have the team train all of these 100 different combinations, just as a ballet or theater company would rehearse their repertoire. The only uncertainty and apprehension involved would then arise from not knowing beforehand which of the 100 combinations would be played in the particular match. Perhaps we would have to find some kind of lottery procedure for that purpose.

In reality, however, there are not only 100 possible combinations but an astronomical number of them, which is why soccer training—being the key regulation problem in balancing varieties—has to be structured differently: It has to ensure that players will be enabled to respond adequately to the multitude of combinations emerging in the course of the match. This example has all the characteristics of the management of an evolutionary process, which does not mean, of course, that certain tactical moves (offside trap, dashes from the penalty area, certain corner kick combinations, penalty kicks, and so on) won't be trained more intensely, thus making sure they will be available as components, or subroutines (in computer language), or pre-coordinated, semi-automatic behavioral programs (in ethnology terms). These examples also help to visualize the difference between potential and actual variety—between what could be and what is or was. There is a huge difference between the actual variety of a concrete, historically unique match such as the 1978 World Championship final and the potential variety this same match could have had. The finalists had to be prepared for the latter, and that makes for a much greater regulation problem.

## 2.25 The Limits to Human Knowledge and Their Consequences

The fact that our knowledge about complex phenomena is so limited has significant consequences for our ability to *predict* events and to *influence behaviors* of people and situations. As pointed out earlier, complexity can theoretically be measured by the number of states a system can have, or its variety. Its cause is the interaction of a large number of different and largely independent variables. Reducing them to just a few, allegedly typical variables in an attempt at "scientific" analysis would mean that the key characteristic of complexity is lost—on the other hand, if we used statistical techniques to summarize the multitude of interacting variables in statistical collectives we would lose the complexity resulting from their diversity. In other words, both these approaches would limit the key characteristic of the phenomena under study that they are supposed to explain: complexity.

From our above analysis of complexity, or the variety of things, based on several examples we can conclude that its key characteristic is the number of *possible configurations* that result from the interaction of many variables. If we can neither reduce the number of variables involved nor apply statistical techniques, the only solution we have is to look into the *kinds of configurations* that emerge and try to sort them in an appropriate classification scheme. The question is, then, what kinds of patterns or regularities can emerge from the interactions among variables. Some scientific disciplines—in particular those that are commonly referred to as "natural sciences"—are able to assign numerical values to the individual variables joining together to form configurations.

This enables them to provide very precise descriptions of concrete, individual manifestations of each configuration. Unfortunately this option will only work when matters remain below a certain level of complexity. Disciplines dealing with very complex phenomena cannot achieve this kind of precision (let alone numerical precision). Contrary to what is often claimed, however, this does not mean that these disciplines are in underdeveloped stages.

Typically, sciences of this kind, while unable to state the specific manifestations—let alone numerical ones—of individual configurations or patterns, are certainly capable of describing the *types* or *kinds* of configurations generated by the interaction of variables. Now, describing or predicting the *kind* of configuration occurring under certain conditions is no less scientific or useful than precisely describing or predicting specific manifestations of configurations. Above all, it is this distinction between describing, explaining, and predicting *classes* or *types* of patterns and describing, explaining, and predicting *manifestations of specific kinds of patterns* which has utmost significance for the understanding of sciences and of phenomena at different levels of complexity.

As we can see, the terms "describe," "explain," and "predict" refer not solely to individual events or occurrences, as is customary, but also to configurations of events, even if these cannot be specified precisely and numerically in the individual case. In the field of complex phenomena, these terms

1. mostly refer to certain classes or types of events,
2. usually relate to just a few rather than all characteristics of the phenomena under study,
3. assign to the variables involved a whole range of possible values rather than specific individual values.[145]

It is also typical of the analysis of complex phenomena that *positive* statements are often impossible. It is only possible to state what kinds of configurations *cannot* be expected.

It would be wrong to assume that explanations on a specific matter are only scientifically sound or useful if they are positive statements. Rather, knowing what a mechanism of interacting variables *cannot* do can be just as interesting and useful as being able to state what kinds of phenomena it can generate. So, the differences between these kinds of explanations and predictions are not fundamental but gradual, as they concern the degree of ex-

---

145 Hayek (New Studies), pp. 9 et seq.

planation or prediction possible. Hayek makes this very clear when he explains that while positive statements such as "We will have a full moon at 5:22:16 a.m. tomorrow" are to be sharply distinguished from negative ones such as "Tomorrow we will not have a full moon," both are predictions that can be falsified.

And there are many more kinds: For example, any statement excluding even one configuration from a number of possible configurations is a falsifiable prediction. Such predictions are far from being useless, as despite their general nature and poor precision they may render valuable contributions to our state of knowledge. For instance, it is very useful to know that on a certain journey we will not encounter any water even though the information is both very general and negative.[146]

Probably every business manager will know some examples from experience. For instance, it is enormously useful to be familiar with the general economic trend or the general development of an industry, even if details are not known and perhaps never will be. Any information on whether the market is growing or shrinking strongly influences what business enterprises and their executives do, even when they know little or nothing about what the concrete rate of expansion or shrinkage is, what specific products it concerns, how consumer behaviors will change, and so on. Similarly, in everyday life the knowledge of patterns strongly and directly affects people's behavior, as their entire thinking, actions, decisions, and so on are aligned with those patterns. For instance, when we expect winter to come we will take a series of measures to be prepared, even though we won't know any details as to the temperatures, snow levels, and so forth. We know the general characteristics of the period we call winter, but not the details. This is enough, however, to guide our behavior, and so the limited knowledge we have significantly helps us master complexity.

As is widely known, a prediction is the inverse of an explanation. So, in order to be able to make even general predictions of the kind described here, we need a theoretical explanation of the phenomena observed. If there are predictions with different degrees of precision, it is very obvious that their inverses have to have degrees of precision that differ just as much. These are so-called *in-principle explanations*: Instead of explaining individual events with numerical precision, as usually—and wrongly—expected by the so-called exact

---

146 See Hayek (Studies), p. 10.

sciences, they merely state a mechanism that is able *in principle* to generate phenomena of a certain kind.

A typical example that Hayek presents in this context is general evolution theory. To recognize its scientific nature, it is necessary to correct a very common misunderstanding regarding the content of this theory. Irrespective of assertions to the contrary, evolution theory does not state that certain kinds of organisms originate from certain other kinds of organisms. Instead, it says that a specific process or mechanism, which in essence consists of re- production with transmittable variations and the selection of viable variations, will generate a great variety of structures over time which will be well adapted to their environment.[147][148] Consequently, the validity of this in-principle expla- nation does not depend on whether or not humankind has descended from apes; nor does it matter whether this process has taken place in a terrestrial or other environment, for it is valid for any kind of environment. Of course, the theory—and this is typical of any in-principle explanation—cannot ex- plain the occurrence of specific organisms but only the occurrence of nu- merous varieties adapted to the respective environmental conditions. In or- der to explain why we have these precise kinds of organisms on earth, rather than other ones, we would have to include all the drivers at work in the course of millions of years. Since it is clearly impossible to include all of these factors and their specific effects, we will have to make do with an ex- planation of the *principles* of action.

A more detailed analysis and elaboration of the action mechanism of evolution, taking into account some additional factors, would certainly be desirable. That said, I sincerely doubt anyone would regard evolution theory as useless from a scientific point of view just because it is general in nature and an in-principle explanation. However general such an explanation may be, and however great the number of possibilities it leaves for the evolution of concrete, specific organisms, it certainly does preclude a sizable number of possibilities. For instance, if we were to observe that dogs were born with wings all of a sudden, or that the continuous amputation of a four-legged animal's hind legs over several generations would lead to pups being born without hind legs, then our understanding of evolution theory as we know it—the purported action principle being the evolution of a large number of well-adapted kinds—would be shaken to the core. Often, it is only a lack of

---

147 See Hayek (Studies), p. 32.

148 Certain amendments and clarifications with regard to the essence of evolution theory will be dealt with at a later point.

imagination that keeps us from seeing how many theoretical possibilities are precluded by an in-principle explanation.

Just because the evolution mechanism creates an enormous range of varieties, we must not forget that an even greater range of varieties are precluded by this same evolution theory and the way it is said to work. The empirical content—that is, all events "prohibited" by the theory—is certainly much lower with such an in-principle explanation than it is with the laws of mechanics. While mechanics theory teaches us a lot about relatively simple phenomena, an in-principle explanation teaches us about very complex phenomena, though it may not appear as rich in empirical content and involve major difficulties in application, considering that every application has to take into account an enormous amount of specifics.

Given these connections, in-principle explanations and their inverses, for example, predictions regarding certain *kinds* of configurations of events, can be regarded as both a *limitation* and an *expansion* of scientific possibilities. The limitation consists in the fact that the statements we can make are less specific; the expansion consists in our being able to access the sphere of complex phenomena.

My above remarks about evolution theory equally apply to all other disciplines dealing with complex phenomena. In particular all disciplines of biology as well as all social sciences face the same problem: They all deal with phenomena caused by an enormous number of variables interlinked in complicated ways and the interactions of these variables. Although it can be possible in these disciplines to determine the basic mechanisms of action, that is, the structure of the variables configuration, it is usually impossible to attach numerical values to each of the relevant variables to achieve numerical solutions for the configurations that occur. But even if we could insert numerical values for thousands or millions of variables in the structural equations, the equations could not be manipulated to the point where we could derive more information than we already have. Typical examples of such in-principle explanations—or perhaps we could also call them "pattern explanations"—are the economic equation systems created by Pareto and Walras: While they point out the structural connections between the variables determining exchange ratios, their most important result is doubtlessly the insight that it will *practically* never be possible to attach numerical values to the variables appearing in the equations.

Just because there are limits to our knowledge in exploring complex phenomena, there is no reason to assume that disciplines dealing with complex matters are in need of further development or imprecise; nor should the limitations to human knowledge make us despair. As mentioned before, much of the precision of what we refer to as exact natural sciences is owed to the fact that the phenomena analyzed are relatively simple, measured against the above definition of complexity. But we must not forget that despite the greater precision and specificity owed to the simpler nature of the phenomena under study, even in these disciplines the numerical values of variables can only be expressed as orders of magnitude, though narrower ones. The second aspect associated with the fundamental limitation of human knowledge is the common assumption that the disciplines in question are profoundly unable to obtain scientific insights. This assumption is completely unsubstantiated. The only sound conclusion is that in these complex fields we will have to make do with *in-principle explanations* and *predictions giving ranges* of values. It would be a fundamental error, however, to assume that these disciplines are less scientific or their findings less useful.

This is not to say that the different ways of describing, explaining, and predicting simple phenomena here and complex ones there will not have various consequences in different areas. For instance, it is very obvious that different kinds of explanations and predictions facilitate or require different actions. A rocket directed at the moon would have to be equipped with completely different control systems if, instead of precise positioning data for the moon, we could only loosely define the area where the moon would be located over a certain period of time. It is equally obvious that a company's financing policy will differ greatly depending on whether or not its future cash needs can be accurately forecast. If based on the precise knowledge of all the drivers influencing the company's cash requirements, it could be accurately predicted for, say, a 12-month period as to what funds that company would need on a daily basis, and its financial strategy could be determined with equal precision. The complexity of the situation most companies are in, manifest in the immense number of often vague and partly unknown factors that drive their financial needs, makes it impossible to make precise forecasts of their cash needs; consequently their financing policies have to follow their own laws, which are rooted in this very complexity. As a consequence, safety margins have to be calculated, credit limits cannot be exhausted, banking relationships are cultivated with care to ensure that the temporary exceeding of credit limits will be pardoned, and so on. The usually enormous complexity permits only certain kinds of problem solutions—that is, of procedures and approaches—also in other areas of the business. We will get back to this at a later point.

The most significant consequence we have to consider in the area of complex phenomena is the inevitable and irremediable limitation of our knowledge. The deeper we dive into the sphere of complex matters and the more we learn about them, the greater our ignorance. So, one of the key findings of all theories on complex matters is that our knowledge about these matters is bound to remain limited. "We have indeed in many fields learnt enough to know that we cannot know all we would have to know for a full explanation of the phenomena."[149]

The limits to our knowledge, however, relate to the specific details of an explanation of complex matters. As pointed out earlier, we simultaneously expand our possibilities of cognition if we are prepared to accept the restricted objective of providing in-principle explanations and order-of-magnitude predictions. It would be totally incomprehensible if in areas where no detailed explanations are possible we were also to dispense with in-principle explanations, just because some people claim that only numerically precise statements as in physics and similar sciences are strictly scientific. In-principle explanations and order-of-magnitude predictions can provide extremely valuable guides for organismic and in particular human behavior. They can enable us to draw conclusions as to what kinds of behavioral categories make sense in certain situations—which can also be categorized by means of in-principle explanations—and what kinds do not, and they can provide information on what situations we should avoid overall.

As Hayek brilliantly points out,[150] one should perhaps not refer to the accomplishment of an order-of-magnitude prediction as a prediction or forecast but rather use the term "orientation." He writes:

Although such a theory does not tell us precisely what to expect, it will still make the world around us a more familiar world in which we can move with greater confidence, that we shall not be disappointed because we can at least exclude certain eventualities. It makes it a more orderly world in which the events make sense because we can at least say in general terms how they hang together or are able to form a coherent picture of them. Though we are not in a position to specify precisely what to expect, or even to list all

---

149 See Hayek (Studies), p. 40.
150 See Hayek (Studies), p. 18.

the possibilities, each observed pattern has meaning in the sense that it limits the possibilities of what else may occur.[151]

It is quite obvious that especially in the areas of corporate and strategic management, having such orientation and, even more important, a methodology to systematically create and adjust such orientation is of utmost importance. As mentioned several times before, it would of course be desirable and useful in strategic management to be able to form precise—perhaps even quantitative—expectations as to coming events and clusters of events. However, the complexity of matters in many (if not most) cases only permits a more or less substantiated orientation.

As Hayek[152] further points out—and as is widely known from numerous cybernetic studies—the possibility of controlling or determining events is directly correlated with the possibility of predicting them. Among other things, this is expressed in the fact that a *control* mechanism can only be as good as the model of the environment that is available to that mechanism. So, if based on in-principle explanations only order-of-magnitude predictions can be made, in the sense of an orientation that is limited to the kinds or types of events, and which often can only provide information as to what kinds of events are *not* to be expected, then the possibilities of controlling such events will, of course, be subject to the same limitations regarding both their nature and scope.

As Hayek writes,[153] even when we cannot control external events in any way, we can still adapt our behaviors to them. Of course, what we are talking about here is the passive kind of adaptation—the kind that is often (erroneously) understood to be the only possible one. That said, the fact remains that in situations where we cannot influence external events because it is impossible to make precise forecasts, passive adaptation is extremely useful for any organism or organization. In addition, however, Hayek also mentions a special way to influence external events: Rather than control, it can best be described as "cultivation."[154] It means that even when we are not in a position to directly create specific events or circumstances, we still have the option to *create conditions that are favorable for a certain kind of events.*

Hayek uses an excellent example to illustrate his point. The term "cultivation" means something largely similar to what a gardener or planter does:

151 See Hayek (Studies), p. 18.
152 See Hayek (Studies), pp. 18 et seq.
153 See Hayek (Studies), p. 19.
154 See Hayek (Studies), p. 18.

While she can hardly influence how the different attributes of plants—their sizes, colors, fertility, and so on—will turn out, she can always create the conditions in which they can be expected to thrive. Likewise, parents will hardly be able to determine all the features and characteristics of their child. Instead they will have to content themselves with creating a family climate that is favorable to the child's development and education. So, we are talking about a kind of indirect control aimed at making sure that the matters under discussion are guided intrinsically, and that they self-regulate and self-organize while leaving certain possibilities of exerting extrinsic influence. In view of the extraordinary importance of the two ideas discussed here—creating general orientation and guiding in the sense of cultivating—we will get back to this problem at a later point.

## 2.3  Controlling Complexity by Means of Order

> "Many of the patterns of nature we can discover only after
> they have been constructed by our mind."
> *Friedrich von Hayek*

### 2.31 Spontaneous Orders

In the previous section we established how the term "complexity" is to be understood and what factors every study of complex matters should take into account. Also, we looked into some important consequences of behavioral options in the area of great complexity. However, as the matters to be considered are not static by nature but, for various reasons, subject to continuous change, a constant process of complexity creation and reduction takes place—or, to use the precise terminology, a process of variety creation and reduction. Above all, it is the problem of permanently ongoing variety production—that is, a permanent process of complexification that poses enormous difficulties for any kind of management. In this context, Stafford Beer speaks of "*proliferating* variety,"[155] which is nothing else but the permanent sprawling and growing of new system states.

There are basically two reasons for the existence of this process of complexification. The first is that practically all systems go through either a natural or

---

155 See Beer (Decision), p. 246 f.

a manmade exchange of energy. This exchange process drives the internal metabolism of the systems. The second reason—and this is much more important for the mechanism of proliferating variety—is that both the elements of the same system and the elements of different systems interact. More than anything else, it is the *possibility of interaction* which drives the complexification process. In the previous section we saw several examples of how the increase of both the number of elements involved and, even more, of the *possibilities of interaction* cause the number of possible states to grow explosively. It is not very surprising, then, that systems such as the human brain and also social systems are prime examples of the process of proliferating variety. In both cases we are dealing with an enormous number of elements that can potentially interact.

Stafford Beer writes in this context:

The brain of the firm, just as man's brain, has more potential states than can ever be analysed or examined by an enormous factor—an unthinkably large factor. Information, then, has to be thrown away by the billion bits all the time, and without making nonsense of control. It must be noted at once, most especially, that there can be no question of finding absolute optima of behaviour—either for men or companies—because all the alternatives cannot be examined. It is, by the laws of nature, fundamentally impossible.[156]

In another passage he writes: The fullscale handling of proliferating variety is completely impossible for the brain of the man or for the brain of the firm. Yet both men and firms actually work. They do so, they *must* do so, by chopping down variety on a mammoth scale. It takes more than an act of faith in electronic computers to achieve this. The question is: how does a system conveniently and effectively undertake this fearful task? The answer is: by *organization*.[157]

So the linchpin of the problem of how to control complexity seems to be *organization*. This does not necessarily refer to the teachings of conventional organization theory, however, for organization means something else in the context of truly complex systems. So the question to be addressed next is: When we explicitly take into consideration the proliferation of variety, *how can order emerge and be created?* Understanding of this problem is just as crucial as understanding the problem of complex phenomena. The different views of

---

156 See Beer (Brain), p. 65.
157 See Beer (Brain), pp. 65 et seq.; emphasis in original.

how order emerges or is created—that is, the different perspectives on the problem of organization—are the starting point of a number of social and philosophical theories and, furthermore, for a long series of very fundamental misconceptions with serious consequences.

At this point it is necessary to address a few works by Friedrich von Hayek, who thoroughly studied the problem of different kinds of order as well as their formation and creation. Hayek's works are very cybernetically oriented in both their thinking and their results. However, since Hayek studied these problems primarily in the social sciences context, they are much easier to understand than the usually very abstract and formal cybernetic works from areas like abstract automata theory, neurocybernetics and the like, and which might not immediately be comprehensible to management scholars or social scientists.

As Hayek points out, "The discovery that there exist in society orders of another kind which have not been designed by men but have resulted from the action of individuals without their intending to create such an order, is the achievement of social theory—or, rather, it was this discovery which has shown that there was an object for social theory. It shook the deeply ingrained belief of men that where there was an order there must also have been a personal orderer."[158] Hayek further notes that the consequences of this discovery reached far beyond the field of social theory and, in particular, permitted "a theoretical explanation of the structures of biological phenomena."[159]

The following considerations are centered around the relation between those institutions commonly referred to as "organizations," which, as I hope to prove, are erroneously understood to be exclusively created by humans with deliberate intentions, and the structures commonly referred to as "organisms"—as well as, above all, the similarities and differences between the two. It goes without saying that this discussion will have to be limited to those aspects of Hayek's related works that are indispensable for understanding the systems methodology of strategic management, as described here. Hayek's theory of the formation and creation of order has numerous implications for nearly all social sciences which have to be disregarded here,

---

158 Hayek (Studien), p. 34 (translation by author) also see Hayek (Kinds of Order in Society), also see Gomez, Malik, and Oeller (Systemmethodik), pp. 117 et seq.
159 See Hayek (Studien), p. 32 (translation by author) also see Hayek (Kinds of Order in Society).

even though they are highly interesting and bear great significance for a number of problems so far considered unsolvable. However, a few summarizing comments have to be made which are of crucial importance for the development of a systems methodology for strategic management.

1. As mentioned before, the idea of order is a crucial point in the following discussion. The concept of order has the same significance for studying complex phenomena as the concept of law or natural law does for studying relatively simply matters.[160]

2. The term "order" refers to a state or matter in which a multitude of diverse elements are related in such a way that knowing a spatial or temporal part of the total will enable you to form correct expectations as to the remaining parts—or at least expectations with a high probability of proving correct.[161]

3. Order in this sense is often referred to as "structure," "pattern," "configuration," or "system."[162] As Hayek explains, it was the key discovery by the great social sciences thinkers of the 18th century that they recognized the existence of such spontaneously forming orders and described them as 'the result of human action but not of human intention'. It was this discovery of spontaneous orders and, closely associated with it, the insight into the development processes that generate the institutions to secure the maintenance or permanent formation of such orders, which showed that there certainly is a specific object of explanation for theoretical social sciences and, what is much more, which has become extremely important especially for biology. Only recently, cybernetics has created something similar in the area of physical sciences, which goes by the name of self-regulating or self-organizing systems.[163] According to the above definition, the concept of order is a *gradual one*: as orders can be implemented to a greater or lesser degree, related expectations can be fulfilled to a greater or lesser degree. We can also conclude from the definition that "order" is not related to specific, defined purposes here. At best, we could consider the basic possibility of acting rationally to be the purpose of such order.[164]

---

160 See Hayek (Rules), p. 35.
161 See Hayek (Rules), p. 36, Hayek (Studien), p. 164.
162 See Hayek (Rules), pp. 35, 155.
163 See Hayek (Studien), pp. 163 et seq.
164 See Hayek (Studien), pp. 164 et seq.

4. A certain degree of order or regularity is necessary for the survival of any kind of organism. As has been set out in detail before, organisms cannot evolve in a disordered environment.[165] It is all the more necessary, then, in a society where most needs of individuals can only be met through cooperation with other individuals, that expectations regarding other individuals' behavior can be formed which will prove correct in many cases and thus provide a basis for one's own behaviors or intentions. After all, we refer to a number of people as "a society when their actions are mutually attuned."[166] Successful, meaningful, or reasonable behavior in a society is possible exactly because we know more or less what to expect of our fellow human beings.

   The *general* possibility of forming expectations that are largely correct results from *some* expectations being systematically frustrated. In other words, the fact that in an order a majority of expectations are largely fulfilled is based on the fact that a minor share of expectations are systematically falsified and must continually be corrected. Although it seems a paradox that a maximum fulfillment of expectations has to be frustrated and corrected, this is nothing else but an operation of negative feedback processes.

5. Two different kinds of order have to be distinguished. While they both fall into the category defined above, they are fundamentally different in another aspect. The first kind of order can be regarded as *manmade* or *designed* order; the second kind is referred to as *grown* or *spontaneously formed* order, or *polycentric* order.[167] In literature, both kinds go by a variety of names. Given the excellence of Hayek's analyses, we will stick to the terminology he suggested: he uses the Greek terms "taxis" for a made or designed order and "cosmos" for a grown or spontaneously formed order. In literature, order in the taxis sense is often referred to as "organization," which is why it must be emphasized here that in cybernetics— particularly the works by Stafford Beer—the term "organization" is used in the cosmos rather than the taxis sense.

6. Order in the taxis sense forms as a result of exogenous causes; order in the cosmos sense results from endogenous causes. The terms "exogenous" and "endogenous," which are adopted from Hayek, are closely

---

165 See Gomez, Malik, and Oeller (Systemmethodik), pp. 126 et seq., pp. 375 et seq.
166 See Hayek (Studien), p. 32.
167 Concerning the term "polycentric order," see, above all, Polanyi (Liberty), pp. 170 et seq.; as well as Watkins (Unity), p. 389.

related to the two kinds of control discussed elsewhere, that is, extrinsic and intrinsic control.[168]

The following remarks by Hayek are essential to the understanding of spontaneous or polycentric orders:

"While a cosmos or spontaneous order ... has no center, every taxis (arrangement, organization) calls for a specific goal, and the people forming such an organization have to serve the same purposes. A cosmos results from the regularities in the behavior of the elements it is comprised of. In this sense, it is an endogenous system that grows from inside or, as cyberneticists say, a 'self-regulating' or 'self-organizing' system. A taxis, on the other hand, is determined by a force outside the order, and in that same sense is exogenous or imposed.

Such external force can also stimulate the formation of a spontaneous order by instructing its elements to respond to environmental occurrences with such regularity that a spontaneous order forms. Such an indirect approach to ensuring the formation of an order has major advantages as compared to the direct method: It can be applied even when no single person can know everything impacting the order. Also, it is not necessary for the behavioral rules that apply in the cosmos to be created deliberately. They, too, can emerge as a result of spontaneous growth or evolution. Hence it is important to differentiate between the spontaneity of an order and the spontaneous origin of regularities in the behavior of the elements that determine it. A spontaneous order can partly be based on regularities that are not spontaneous but imposed. For purposes like these, we thus have the options either to build an order using a strategy of indirect means, or to assign to each element its particular place and specify its task in detail."[169]

The fact that we understand the forces driving spontaneous orders also means that there are possibilities to make use of them. As we will see later, applying the indirect strategy of creating and designing an order involves a considerable expansion of human freedom of scope, as it enables us to create extremely complex orders that would be impossible to create by way of commands to individuals.

Simply speaking, the indirect strategy of designing order corresponds to an approach in which the elements are given ground rules, so to speak, but within these rules are free to behave as they please. From a cybernetic perspective, the totality of all rules forms a *meta-system*.[170] As will also be explained in greater detail at a later point, the key problem in this context is that not all ground rules automatically result in an order; rather, there

---

168 See Gomez, Malik, and Oeller (Systemmethodik), pp. 113 et seq.
169 See Hayek (Studien), p. 209.
170 See Beer (Platform), passim.

are rules that will even hinder or prevent the forming of an order. It can thus be very important for orders—irrespective of their concrete manifestation—to have certain abstract attributes; and while it is in our power to create these abstract attributes, we cannot influence the concrete manifestations of the resulting order.

7. Deliberately designed orders in the sense of taxis are relatively simple, compared to spontaneous orders of the cosmos type. As the positions of the elements in these structures as well as their possible behaviors are subject to instructions from a planning authority, the complexity of any manmade order can never exceed the complexity of its planning or controlling authority. Spontaneous orders are not necessarily more complex than manmade orders; they do, however, have the potential to reach any degree of complexity. The reason is that both the positions of the elements and their behaviors are determined by a much larger number of concrete circumstances than could ever be made available to a directing or planning authority. The more complex an order is or is meant to be, the more likely are we to be dependent on spontaneous order-creating forces. Also, the more complex an order is, the more limited are we to merely directing and determining its abstract characteristics.[171]

8. Broadly speaking, the attributes of orders in the taxis sense depend on what facts and circumstances are accessible to the controlling and planning authority, while the attributes of spontaneous orders depend on a much greater number of facts, since every single element processes in its behavior all the fact-based information *it* has access to. Hence, spontaneous orders are designed to have a much higher amount of knowledge integrated in their design compared to planned orders. At the same time, their permanent existence depends on their ability to process more information. In other words, spontaneous orders would not be what they are unless an enormous amount of knowledge and information was available for their precise design.

9. Examples of spontaneous orders include the formation of crystals and organic chemical compounds. It would be impossible to deliberately determine and arrange the specific positions and shapes of all connections between elements. Instead, the elements of crystals and chemical compounds arrange themselves under the influence of precisely those laws and forces that lead to the formation of spontaneous orders. (Note that

---

171 See Hayek (Studien), p. 33.

these examples should not lead us to believe that all spontaneous orders are relatively static or immediately perceptible to the senses.)

Another example used by Hayek[172] is equally enlightening: Iron shavings on a sheet of paper placed above a magnet will arrange themselves in complicated configurations under the influence of that magnetic power. Although it is possible to forecast the general, abstract pattern of this arrangement, it is absolutely impossible to predict what precise position each of the shavings will assume along the unlimited number of curves defining the magnetic field. The precise position of an element in this case depends not only on the form or pattern of the magnetic field, but also on its starting position, its direction, weight, size, and surface condition, as well as on the precise condition of the paper surface in each individual point. In addition, a number of environmental influences would have to be considered to predict exactly how a given pattern would manifest itself. While we can predict the general, abstract pattern based on our knowledge of certain forces and laws, the precise order emerges as a result of interactions between these laws and a multitude of concrete, specific environmental states that are temporary in nature.

It is due to this usually enormous number of concrete, continually changing facts affecting the behavior of the elements and to which they adapt (apart from the universal forces and patterns they follow) that most spontaneous orders are much more complex than deliberately designed or manmade orders. It would be impossible for any central controlling authority to know the totality of all circumstances to which elements have to be adapted.

There is a series of further examples of spontaneous orders, particularly in the social realm, such as language, scripture, morals, law, money, and credit. Hayek notes:

"For some social phenomena, such as language, it is an established fact today that the order they exhibit has not been deliberately designed and we are yet to discover it. In these areas we have finally grown out of believing that behind any order of elements that supports man's pursuit of his goals there must be a personal creator. There was a time when people believed that all useful institutions serving the interaction between humans, such as language, morals, the law, scripture, and money, had to be owed to a specific inventor or legislator, or to an express agreement among wise men as to the use of certain useful practices.

---

172 See Hayek (Studien), p. 37.

Today we understand the process in which such institutions have gradually taken shape, which was through people's learning to act in accordance with certain rules, and they knew to follow them long before they felt a need to put them in words."[173]

10. Probably the greatest obstacle to propagating an understanding of spontaneous polycentric orders—or what one might call self-organizing systems—is the fact that such orders are *not perceptible to the senses*, at least in the social realm, but can only be captured in an act of rational reconstruction. For instance, a market in the economic sense is impossible to observe or perceive directly; instead we can only conclude from the concrete occurrences we observe, such as barter transactions, changes in ownership, and the like, that there must be a certain totality of relations which we call a market, but which cannot actually be captured by the senses. The system we call "monetary and credit system" is another type of order not immediately perceptible to the senses. The same goes for language. What we are able to perceive or observe are, at best, concrete manifestations of such systems, individual occurrences or outputs of these systems, but not the orders as such. Those can only be reconstructed, more or less completely, in a rational act.[174]

11. While spontaneous orders do not result from a planning authority's intentional act, they are not completely independent of human action. Spontaneous orders in the social realm are, as Hayek so aptly phrased it, the *result of human action but not of human design.*[175] In this context, the distinction between *nature* and *convention*—or between *natural* and *artificial* orders or systems—comes into play. It is due to the inadmissible dichotomy expressed here, coupled with the above-mentioned difficulty in grasping spontaneous orders, that in the social realm the orders or systems of probably the greatest importance were long ignored, then poorly understood.[176] The following matrix illustrates that at least *three* kinds of orders have to be considered, with the highly complex systems of modern, civilized societies simultaneously covering fields 2, 3, and 4. Of these, the phenomena predominantly belonging in field 4 have received little attention so far; as a result, our knowledge about this field, as well as about the interaction among the phenomena in all three fields, is still very inadequate.

---

173 See Hayek (Studien), pp. 35 et seq. (translation by author).
174 See Hayek (Studien), p. 33; Popper (Historizismus), p. 106.
175 See Hayek (Studien), pp. 97 et seq.
176 See Hayek (Rules), p. 20 f, and (Studien), p. 97 ff.

| Formation of systems and orders | As a result of human intention | Without human intention |
|---|---|---|
| Without human action | 1<br>Do not exist. | 2<br>Purely natural systems, such as planetary systems, Earth's development in pre-human times |
| As a result of human action As a result of human intention | 3<br>Predominantly technical systems and very simple social systems | 4<br>Most complex social systems and institutions, such as money, language, the law, morals, family, society, enterprise, church, etc. |

*Figure 2.31 (1)*

Apart from the fact that spontaneous social orders can emerge in the absence of any design or plan, as mentioned before, and that most social institutions can be assumed to have emerged that way, this phenomenon is also illustrated by everyday experience: Even when there is a desire to shape and influence events, the concrete results of human action will usually deviate somewhat from the original intention or plan, as the numerous factors at work in the social sphere cause human actions to have unintended and even undesirable side effects over and over again.[177]

12. When I use the terms "general patterns" or "laws" or "order-producing forces" in this book, it is in reference to the fact that the behavior of elements of an order or structure follows certain rules. The problem of the perception of and compliance with rules has been discussed at great length in other publications,[178] so I will just address a few essential aspects here. As Hayek points out,[179] the reason why the actions of organisms, including human beings, are successful—that is, well adapted to their

---

177 See also Popper (Historizismus), p. 52 f.
178 See Gomez, Malik, and Oeller (Systemmethodik), p. 232 ff., and the sources cited there.
179 See Hayek (Rules), p. 17 ff., and (Studien).

environments—is not just that we have some insight into cause-and-effect relationships, but above all that organismic behavior is guided by rules determined by both the experiences gathered by the individual and, as an outcome of an evolutionary process, the experiences of thousands of generations before us. There can be no doubt that organisms, including humans, know how to act successfully long before they are able to reflect rationally on what happens in their environment. The genetic and—at least in the case of humans—the cultural heritage that the organism obtains forms a cumulated act of adaptation, which is effective even when we are not aware of it in the sense that it is articulated or verbalized.[180]

In the case of spontaneous orders, their elements are defined by the different behavioral rules they follow. Transmittable mutations of these rules result in new elements, or cause an increasing change in the characteristics of all elements of a group. Depending on the complexity of elements, we can distinguish between simpler and more complex spontaneous orders. The elements of societies are very complex structures themselves, and their chance of subsisting depends, at least in part, on their being elements of that particular order. Here a distinction must be made between the behavioral regularities of the elements at an individual level and the overall order resulting from them. These two levels interact: On the one hand, certain individual regularities contribute to the formation of an overall order; on the other hand, the overall order requires or facilitates certain individual regularities and prevents others. "This means that the individual element with its special structure and behavior owes its existence in this particular form to a society with a distinct structure, for only in such a society has it been advantageous for that individual to develop some of its specific traits, whereas the social order itself is an outcome of this regularity in behavior that the society's individuals have developed."[181]

13. Behavioral rules of the kind discussed here have a few specific features:
   a. Their mode of action with regard to the individual elements and their contribution to the formation of a spontaneous overall order do not in the least depend on whether they are or could be articulated. The individuals acting do not have to be *aware* of them. It is perfectly sufficient for them to *de facto* determine elements' behaviors. For instance, an animal defending its territory against members of its own kind, thus contributing to the regulation of the overall number of

180 See Lorenz (Rückseite), passim.
181 See Hayek (Studien), p. 155.

animals in a certain region, does not have to know either the rules governing its behavior or the overall order based on them.[182] Of course, every highly civilized society has a multitude of behavioral rules, which the acting individuals are aware of in the sense that these rules can be and often are articulated, and in many cases have been designed and created very deliberately. These facts, however, are not constitutive to the effectiveness of behavioral rules; or in other words, the regularities in an individual and the resulting overall order do not depend on the individual's ability to verbalize these regularities.

b. The reason such rules are followed de facto is that they involve certain advantages—essentially, in terms of survival—for the group of individuals that follows them, even if the single members of that group do not actually know them. The formation of systems of behavioral rules happens in accordance with the laws of evolutionary processes. It is important to note, however, that the evolutionary selection process impacts not individual, separate behavioral rules but always the order as a whole, as the effect and the advantages of a single rule always depend on their interrelation with other rules leading to that order.

c. In general, behavioral rules do not align individuals with specific goals; that is, they are not aimed at the creation of concrete, specific states. Rather than determining what has to be done, behavioral rules stipulate *how* it is to be done. The key characteristic of organismic behavior is often said to be its goal orientation. And it is doubtlessly an important aspect. However, we must not forget that organismic behavior is governed by rules at least as much as it is influenced by goals. R.S. Peters writes:

"Man is a rule-obeying animal. His actions are not simply directed towards certain ends; they also conform to social standards and conventions, and unlike a calculating machine he acts because of his knowledge of rules and objectives. For instance, to certain machines we assign certain traits of character like honesty, punctuality, considerateness, or meanness. Such terms do not, like ambition, hunger, or social desires, indicate the sort of goals that a man tends to pursue; rather they indicate the type of regulation that he imposes on his conduct, whatever his goals may be."[183]

---

182 See Hayek (Studien), p. 156; see also Wynne-Edwards (Dispersion), passim.
183 Peters (Motivation), p. 5.

Hence, behavioral rules determine a certain range or scope within which the individual will act. Quite remarkably, a scope of behavior is often not defined positively but by *exclusion* of certain behaviors, so rules of behavior or conduct are often *negative* in nature. From an evolutionary perspective, the reason is that those rules that specify what must not be done define the scope within which the *consequences of actions are largely known*. Within this scope, the so-called factual knowledge, which is sometimes erroneously believed to be the only legitimate kind of scientific finding, is rather useful because it helps predict the consequences of our behavior. However, as factual knowledge in a complex environment is bound to be limited, the rules of conduct that prohibit certain behaviors on grounds of their unknown consequences are equally important. Along these lines, it is remarkable how behaviors are selected: first, actions with predictable consequences are given priority over those where consequences are unknown; next, from all the options with known consequences we select those that in a specific sense are superior to all the others.[184]

14. Although the emergence of orders, in particular spontaneous orders, requires de facto compliance with rules of behavior, *not all* rules will lead to the emergence of such order. Rather, it is very specific kinds of rules that lead to the emergence and formation of a spontaneous order, or cosmos. On the other hand, there are rules that prevent the formation of spontaneous orders. One of the key challenges of social theory, or of a theory of self-organizing systems, is therefore to answer the question as to what rules the elements will have to follow to ensure an order will emerge. The answer partly depends on the particular cases, that is, the concrete system in focus; in part it can be formulated generally. This, precisely, is the subject of the cybernetic theory of self-organizing systems: It attempts to find a general solution to this problem by studying information behavior, the different ways in which elements and systems can be coupled, elements' learning capacity, and so on.

15. The fact that the individual behavior of the elements of a system is bound by rules has been recognized as the key force driving the emergence of a spontaneous order. In most cases, however, a spontaneous order cannot simply be construed to be the totality of regularities in individual behav-

---

184 See Hayek (Studien), p. 159.

iors; furthermore, much of the structure of the overall order is determined by the interaction of individual elements and the whole with an *external environment*. Consequently, changes in the environment of spontaneous orders can call for changes in the rules of behavior given to the individuals, if the order as a whole is to be maintained. This, in turn, will usually lead to certain changes in the spontaneous order itself and its environment, which will have repercussions on the individual rules of conduct. This is a classic case of homeostatic coupling.

16. The rules of behavior which lead to the emergence of spontaneous orders—through compliance with these rules and consideration of specific, in part temporary circumstances—*may emerge spontaneously themselves*. We even have to assume that a very large, albeit unknown number of rules of behavior had formed long before societies in the current, highly civilized sense existed; that these rules created the conditions for the formation of groups, tribes, and such; and therefore that—contrary to what is often assumed—the need for rules of behavior did not emerge because there were societies but that societies formed because there were rules of behavior of the kind discussed.

Quite arguably, the conclusion from this is that the same rules of conduct leading to the formation of societies were selected in a natural evolution process. It is important to keep in mind, however, that the selection mechanisms at work in such an evolutionary process do not impact the individual but the order of behavior emerging from the individuals' behavior. As every spontaneous order is an adaptation to numerous specific circumstances, and any knowledge of these circumstances can never entirely refer to one individual but will always be distributed over the entirety of individuals—while it is the total order, rather than the individual and its behaviors, that constitutes an adaptation—evolutionary selection impacts the order as such. Consequently, what is selected in an evolutionary process of natural selection is not the individuals or individual behaviors, as erroneously assumed by so-called social Darwinism, but the *systems of behavioral rules* and the corresponding spontaneous orders. This is irrespective of the fact that rules of behavior are genetically—and partly culturally—transmitted from one individual to the other.[185]

17. Despite the fact that orders and the behavioral rules leading to their emergence can form spontaneously, it is possible to *deliberately change* and

---

185 See Hayek (Studien), pp. 145, 149 et seq.

*improve* said behavioral rules. It is even conceivable for spontaneous orders to be based exclusively on rules that have been deliberately defined. Whether or not spontaneous orders will emerge on that basis depends on the degree to which the elements or individuals are permitted to make use of *their* knowledge about the specific circumstances. As explained earlier, the question as to what order will emerge from a set of rules depends not only on the rules themselves but also on a number of specific factors that, together with the rules, determine individuals' actions. Although spontaneous orders can be improved by changing the rules determining them, it will never be possible to challenge all of those rules at the same time. Rather, at any given time the majority of them will have to be accepted more or less uncritically because, in view of the complexity of spontaneous orders, recreating them will always be out of the question. Improving spontaneous complex orders is fully consistent with the kind of influence discussed earlier and referred to as *cultivation*.

18. Interestingly, the control of behavior through abstract rules is not only a means to coordinate the actions of *large numbers* of people, thus leading to the emergence of spontaneous and complex orders in the social realm. Following abstract rules is also the only way to bring some coherence, and thus some meaning, to the behavior and successive decisions of *individuals and individual organizations*. If plans for the future are to have more than a random chance at being implemented, the set of individual decisions required for implementation must have a certain order or coherence. These decisions will have to integrate a multitude of details that cannot be known at the time of plan generation. "The method by which we … manage to bring some coherence to our actions is by setting a framework of rules for our guidance, which make the general nature though not the details of our lives predictable. It is these rules, which we sometimes are not even aware of and which are often very abstract in nature, which bring order to the course of our lives. Many of these rules are simply 'customs' of the society in which we grew up; only some of them will be individual 'habits' we have accidentally or deliberately adopted."[186]

The rules leading to mutual adaptation of individual persons' or organizations' successive decisions and actions, thus creating coherence and a sense of meaning in individuals' lives, are abstract in nature; indeed, they

---

186 See Hayek (Studien), p. 45 (translation by author).

have to be abstract as they only concern certain aspects of said decisions or actions. Only certain categories of facts are selected as noteworthy by these rules, and only these facts determine the general decision-making and behavior. "This includes our systematic disregarding of certain circumstances we know of, and which would be relevant to our decision making if we knew all circumstances of this kind; however, neglecting them is actually rational as they represent accidental pieces of information which do not alter the probability that, if we knew and could process more circumstances of this kind, the bottom-line benefit would still be with rule compliance."[187]

Cybernetically speaking, we bring coherence to the multitude of individual decisions by systematically reducing variety. This reduction of variety is achieved by complying with abstract rules which, however, represent cumulative adjustments (as pointed out before); that is, the extent of knowledge and experience they entail by far exceeds an individual's capabilities, thus representing an enormous increase in variety from the individual's perspective.

19. This peculiar relation between variety reduction (referring to the details to be considered) and variety increase (by complying with abstract rules) is closely associated with is generally called the *rationality of action*, and which represents a permanent practical and philosophical problem. This point is best illustrated by the following quote:

"It is ... the limited horizon of our knowledge of concrete facts which requires us to coordinate our actions by complying with abstract rules, rather than trying to decide on each individual case based on the limited number of relevant single facts we happen to know. It may sound paradoxical that rational action requires deliberately ignoring some of the knowledge we have; but this is part of the necessity to deal with our inevitable ignorance of many facts that would be relevant if we knew them. When we know that the unfavorable effects of an action are likely to outweigh the favorable ones, we should not let our decision be influenced by the fact that in this particular case, some of the effects we happen to be able to predict will be favorable.

The fact of the matter is that in what appears to be a strive for rationality by weighing all predictable consequences more thoroughly, we will actually get more irrational in that we will give less consideration to the more distant consequences and achieve a less coherent result in total. It is the great lesson from science that we have to resort to abstracts where we are unable to master the

---

187 See Hayek (Studien), p. 45 (translations by author).

concrete. Preferring the concrete means abandoning the power that thinking gives us."[188]

Hence, abstract rules or norms are the most important tool humans have found to date for gaining control of the complexity of their world. Understanding and controlling orientation and cultivation beyond the realms of concrete knowledge—or the knowledge of concrete facts—are only possible by applying abstract rules of conduct: These rules are a precondition for the emergence of spontaneous orders, which, in turn, are required to manage the complexity arising in systems greater than the individual.

20. With the exception of extremely simple and primitive organizations whose complexity does not exceed an individual's or small group's means of control (which are limited to the issuing of commands or instructions), the two kinds of orders—designed orders in the taxis sense and spontaneous orders in the cosmos sense—can only be controlled or designed through the kind of rules discussed. The reason is that organizations (except for the most simple ones), in order to be able to function, need to make use of a greater amount of knowledge than can be made accessible to a single person or group. When the members of an organization only execute orders, the complexity of this organization and thus its functionality, in an absolute sense, will be limited by the complexity of the person(s) issuing those orders. This limitation can only be overcome by giving the members of the organization some leeway within which to commit their own ideas, knowledge, specific modes of behavior, and so on, to their organization. Consequently, an organization's degree of complexity can only increase as a result of more general or more abstract rules of conduct; that is, rules that only govern general attributes of behavior, general objectives, and so on, while the individual persons can determine the necessary details based on their skills and the information available to them. According to Ashby's Law of Requisite Variety, an organization must grow more complex as the complexity of its environment grows. From the aforesaid we can conclude that increasing complexification of an organization is only possible by applying new principles of order consistent with the laws of spontaneous orders.[189]

21. Every complex society will always comprise a combination of orders in the taxis sense—that is, organizations—and orders in the cosmos sense.

---

188 See Hayek (Studien), pp. 45 et seq.
189 On businesses being spontaneous orders in the "cosmos" sense, see Tullock (Corporations).

Although my previous statements about abstract rules of conduct to some degree apply to both kinds of orders, there are some important *differences* between the rules of an organization and those of a spontaneous order:

a. An order in the taxis sense (an organization) is usually geared towards a *defined* goal or purpose, so its members will have to fulfill *defined, specific* tasks or provide defined, specific services. These tasks have to be assigned to the individual members of the organization, at least in a general manner. These assignments are aligned towards specific goals and resemble commands. To a certain extent, they serve to fix the individual's position within the order, and the rules of behavior the individual is expected to follow also depend on that position.

b. In a spontaneous order, rules of behavior are *not* aligned towards a specific objective or purpose. They are much more abstract and valid for entire categories of individuals that are not known beforehand, and for unforeseeable numbers and kinds of circumstances. In complying with these rules, individuals not only make use of their own information but also pursue their *own* goals and purposes.

c. The more complex an organization is, however, the more general will these rules of behavior have to be, or to put it the other way round: The more general the rules of behavior in an organization, the more complex that behavior can be. Organizations that depend on the use of knowledge distributed over numerous individuals in order to function, and organizations that need to adapt to circumstances that no one can know in their entirety *must* have many of the features of a spontaneous order. Therefore, in very large and complex organizations, the specific instructions issued by a senior authority will regulate little more than the general allocation of a loosely defined function as well as a general purpose statement, while all actions, the way functions are executed and goals achieved, will be governed by a set of general, abstract rules of behavior of the kind that is known from spontaneous orders.

In structures like these, it is the primary task of those authorized to issue instructions to stipulate general functions and goals and also lay the *ground rules* for individuals' behavior; the taxic forms of order mainly serve to ensure that these rules are enforced, not to bring about specific facts or results. The key problem in this context consists in developing and enforcing rules of behavior which, when applied, permit individuals to use a maximum of skill and knowledge while guiding their behavior towards the general objectives defined. This problem is identical to the creation and maintenance of a viable system.

22. It should be stressed that the rules of behavior which have led to the emergence of spontaneous orders, such as the civilized societies, have not been "invented" with the intention of producing this particular result. It would probably not even have been possible to conclude just from the knowledge of certain rules that their application would lead to the emergence of systems this complex. Hence, as Hayek points out,[190] it would be more than paradoxical to claim that modern societies require full-fledged, deliberate planning and control because they have grown so complex. It is the other way round: Their complexity is an outcome of the lack of deliberate planning and control. As has been pointed out before, the spontaneously formed rules of behavior that have contributed to society's current complexity can certainly be improved. The way to do that is through deliberate design—not by directly influencing the resulting system states. Improvements can only be achieved the indirect way, that is, by further developing and enhancing the rules that will the formation of a spontaneous order, based on a deep understanding of the relationships between order formation and order creation. In other words, by developing system structures which, in view of proliferating variety, are capable of conforming to the Law of Requisite Variety.

This way of influencing a spontaneous order, or a self-organizing system, aims to steer that system onto a *development path* and keep it there, although the final stage and the intermediate stages of that development cannot be known, as they depend on both the effect of said rules and factors located in the future. In other words, the objective of design is not to reach any kind of specific system state, but to achieve certain qualities of order or of the system, in particular the qualities of *adaptability*, of learning *capability*, and of the *ability* to develop further. At the time a system is designed, it is impossible to know exactly what it will have to adapt to in the future or what it will have to learn. If the system is enabled to learn, or even to learn how to learn, the overall design objective has been met.

23. Any attempt to improve or correct the actual states occurring in a spontaneous order through direct commands or interventions is certain to have a multitude of unintended and possibly undesirable consequences.

---

190 See Hayek (Rules), pp. 50 et seq.

The reason is that the states occurring in a complex, spontaneous order emerge as a result of the consideration of countless factors as well as the complex process in which these factors are weighed against each other. As in complex orders it will never be possible to consider all undesirable consequences of an action or decision, and since we accept our ignorance of most concrete circumstances as an irreversible fact, we can conclude that in the area of great complexity, "finding a way to adapt to the facts of irremediable ignorance [may well constitute] greater progress than acquiring more positive knowledge."[191]

As pointed out initially, this section was not intended to describe the Theory of Spontaneous Orders or, cybernetically speaking, of self-organizing systems. Rather, its purpose is to single out some aspects that are important to the understanding of order formation and order creation. The problem of complexity and how to control it cannot be dealt with in a meaningful way without some fundamental knowledge about spontaneous orders and abstract rules of behavior.

## 2.32 The Manageability of Orders

In the first part of this book the structures of the viable system were described in detail, and it was pointed out that they are necessary and sufficient for the viability of systems. In this second chapter, the remarks I have made so far have been intended to characterize the problem situation for which the viable system structures were developed. Key characteristics of such situations are their *immense complexity* and the irremediable *lack of knowledge* associated with it. In this context, I repeatedly had to point out the impossibility of doing things, such as giving detailed explanations, making precise forecasts, and controlling complex orders without using abstract rules.

Assertions of impossibility will also play a key role in the topics to come, as this whole book is essentially based on the view that many of the solution concepts and methods for management problems recommended in the literature can be defined, discussed, and described but not *applied*. Such assertions of impossibility tend to be viewed with skepticism, and justifiably so because they have often been refuted by scientific discoveries.

---

191 See Hayek (Studien), p. 171 (translation by author).

On the other hand, Popper has shown that all natural laws are actually assertions of impossibility of one kind or another.[192] In this context, Hayek writes:

"It is fashion today to sneer at any assertion that something is impossible and to point at the numerous instances in which what even scientists represented as impossible has later proved to be possible. Nevertheless, it is true that all advances of scientific knowledge consists in the last resort in the insight into the impossibility of certain events. Sir Edmund Whittaker, a mathematical physicist, has described this as the "impotence principle" and Sir Karl Popper has systematically developed the idea that all scientific laws consist essentially of prohibitions, that is, of assertions that something cannot happen."[193]

Ashby, too, has repeatedly pointed out that it has often been scientists' conscious recognition of factual impossibility—or in other words, the conscious destruction of the illusionary belief in certain possibilities—that provided key impulses for scientific research by revealing the true problem. For instance, Ashby explains that it was only after scientists had acknowledged the impossibility of building a perpetuum mobile that the power machine was developed. Similarly, or so he argues, only after we take into account that neither our brain nor the largest computer can solve certain information processing problems will truly meaningful brain research be possible, and thus a solution to the fundamental problems associated with this topic.[194]

In view of these facts—on the one hand, assertions of impossibility are viewed with skepticism; on the other hand, illusionary feasibility hopes can seriously hamper progress—I will address the problem of complexity from yet another angle: by providing evidence that certain systems cannot be controlled and certain kinds of problems cannot be handled with certain methods. The fact that there are such things as non-manageable systems and problems would not have that much significance if we did not encounter these phenomena in everyday practice. Unfortunately, it is precisely the systems and problems we deal with every day which are not amenable to the methods commonly recommended. In other words, what I am referring to is the *question of manageability of social institutions*, an issue addressed far too

---

192 See Popper (Logik), pp. 39 et seq., and (Historizismus), p. 49.
193 Hayek (Studies), p. 146.
194 See Popper (Logik), pp. 39 et seq., and (Historizismus), p. 49.

rarely in management literature.[195] Instead, the open or tacit assumption is that management—undoubtedly a social function of many merits—can solve any problem that might arise and thus effectively guide social institutions. Managers are too often depicted as "doers and fixers" who, while perhaps not familiar with the latest technology and its applications, have the potential to cope with the difficulties they face.

With the following considerations I hope to show that the problem of manageability of social institutions and problems is of crucial importance. I will attempt to demonstrate that the methods usually discussed in literature, which are mostly of the analytical variety, are not suitable for managing complex systems and solving the problems that come with them. A possible alternative will be described in the following section; it deals with the evolutionary problem-solving paradigm. However, in order to ensure that evolutionary problem-solving processes can operate in the structures of a viable system, certain operating principles have to be described beyond what has been discussed in Chapter 1. These operating principles concern the operation of the homeostats at work in systems 3, 4, and 5, which represent the only mechanism so far known to guarantee the manageability of social systems.[196]

In essence, a homeostatic control system's mode of operation is consistent with the spontaneous orders discussed here, which—as explained before—result from the process where their elements, under general rules of behavior, adapt to the behavioral changes of all other elements and this adaptation impacts all other elements. In these cases, interventions of a superordinate control authority—in management, for example, of a superior—cannot influence the individual elements' behavior in its details, only create the conditions to guide that behavior in certain directions.

---

195 There are examples, of course, including Drucker (Management), pp. 664 et seq.; Taylor (Future), pp. 129 et seq.; and Beer, whose central hypothesis is that all social institutions risk becoming unmanageable.

196 This is a rather bold statement, which, however, is substantiated by the Viable Systems Theory. In particular, Beer's "Heart of Enterprise," published as late as in 1979—that is, more than two years after the manuscript of this book was completed—contains what I consider the critical rationale for why the structures of Beer's model are necessary and sufficient for viability, and thus for the manageability of systems. Other, apparently equally suitable mechanisms will, upon closer analysis, probably turn out to be variants of the cybernetic structures demanded by Beer. For an elaboration of this view, see Beer (Heart), p. yi and passim.

When superordinate authorities refrain from dictating elements' behavior in detail, this increases rather than diminishes their influence. In a spontaneous order or homeostatic control system, the span of control—the number of manageable and adjustable relationships between elements—is much higher than it is in systems where superordinate entities determine elements' individual behavior. Consequently, homeostatic control systems or spontaneous orders are able to solve problems of much higher complexity—that is, adapt to far more complex changes in their environment—than orders of the taxis kind, or deliberately controlled system.

The following examples should help to illustrate this point.[197] Imagine two teams of five people, each representing one of the two kinds of order. Let us assume that one is a team of five strikers in soccer: In their efforts to score goals they mutually align their actions, based on both the rules of the game and the rules of behavior they have been trained to follow. Let us further assume the other team to be the crew of a small ship in heavy seas: Here, each crewmember's actions are determined by the captain's commands and coordinated with all other crewmembers' actions. If the number of effective adjustments or reactions each soccer player can accomplish per minute in response to the other four players' actions is f, and the number of effective directions or commands to the crew that the ship captain can issue per minute is c, the number of adjusted relations per minute per soccer player will be f, while the respective number per crewmember will be c/5.

As the adjustment resulting from self-coordination will be quicker and smoother than the commands-based adjustment even a close-knit team can accomplish—due to the absence of certain communication barriers—f is bound to be greater than c, and thus five times greater than c/5. It is clearly an acknowledged fact that a soccer team has to self-coordinate to solve its problems, and a soccer coach would never even think of trying to steer his or her team's game with direct commands and instructions. The problem that the ship crew has to solve is no less complex, yet people usually try to solve problems of this kind by way of deliberate, direct interventions.

The adjustment and control-related advantages of spontaneous orders based on self-coordination may be relatively small for systems this small, with only five elements, but they grow enormously as systems get larger. When a taxis system (or a deliberately controlled system) such as the ship crew is expanded, this is usually done by setting up more hierarchical levels.

---

197 See Polanyi (Logic), pp. 114 et seq.

In the above example you would have five people reporting directly to the captain, and assuming this span of control was maintained throughout the hierarchy, each of those five direct reports could have another five direct reports, so the result would be the pyramid-shaped organization structure we are all familiar with. Now if the number of hierarchical levels is e (from the German *Ebene*—level), and, with a span of control of five, each level comprises five times more people than the level above it, the overall number of people or elements in such an organization can be expressed in the following formula:

$$p = 1 + 5 + 5^2 + 5^3 + ... + 5_{e-1}$$

The number of superiors in such an organization is $v = p - 5^{e-1}$ (v standing for *Vorgesetzte*/$r$ = superior), and at the base of the organization pyramid, $5_{e-1}$ elements or persons carry out the actual task. The number of relationships to be adjusted by way of direct instructions remains c for each superior, as in the ship crew example, and c/5 per staff member directly reporting to this superior. Now if we assume that in this system, which has been expanded by e hierarchical elements, each superior makes full use of his or her command capacity c, the resulting command capacity—or control variety—per person and minute for the overall system will be

$$k = c \, \frac{p - 5_{e-1}}{5_{e-1}}$$

Considering that this value is not much greater than c/5, this means that the manageability and adjustability of this system *do not grow relative to its size.*

Next, let us look at what happens when we enlarge a system that has formed spontaneously, that is, by self-coordination. Let us assume individuals' adjustability to remain the same. In the above example of soccer strikers, the self-adjustment rate was f: This value referred to a group of five, each player having to coordinate his or her actions with what the other four players did. There is no reason to assume that the team members could not coordinate their actions with more than four fellow team members—on the contrary, a soccer player will usually align his or her actions with a much larger number of fellow players. Hence, despite unchanged adjustability, f, the number of adjustable *relationships*, grows rapidly when the number of system elements increases, and can easily reach an order of several thousand times f. This is conditional, however, on system elements staying in informal contact, as this provides the basis for their adjustment responses. For instance, it goes without saying that a defense player in soccer will hardly be able to adjust his actions to those of a striker he cannot see. Thus, cutting information channels between elements will allow subsystems to form which can each have a higher degree of adjustability than would be possible *between* subsystems. The adjustment behavior of elements linked to more than five other elements, and which are thus able to adjust to more than five relationships, is illustrated by figure 2.32(1).[198]

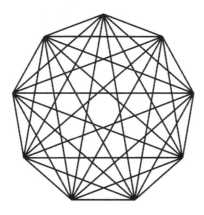

*Figure 2.32(1)*

Here, let us imagine the individual elements, represented by the nine points arranged in circular order, to be connected by elastic bands. If the position of one element changes, its connections to all other elements will change accordingly—provided that the relationships concerned ensure effective coupling. In a cybernetic system, effective coupling means that an element's behavior is effectively changed by the information exchange with other elements. If this is not possible, we are not dealing with coupling in the cybernetic sense. So, the adjustability of a spontaneously formed system is many times greater than that of a taxis system. The soccer example nicely illustrates that the managing or organizing of systems regulated spontaneously, or by self-coordination, cannot be based on dictating each element's position and behavior. Rather, elements that already have a great variety of behaviors are embedded in an organizational framework which, in essence, permits them

---

198 See Polanyi (Logic), p. 120.

to implement this variety, then uses rules to limit the overall variety to the point where the overall system's behavior will comply with certain criteria.

The advantages of a problem-solving methodology based on spontaneous orders and self-coordination are based on the fact that such orders comprise a multitude of decision or problem-solving centers, all of which are interdependent and contribute their share to the solution of the problem. That is why, as has been mentioned before, spontaneous orders are also referred to as *polycentric orders* or *polycentric systems*. Each of the decision centers in a polycentric system—that is, each system element—changes its behavior in response to the behaviors of all other system elements, thus contributing to an overall state of adjustment. By contrast, taxis systems have only one decision center, and as we have seen, the overall rate of adjustment in such systems equals that of a single decision-making authority. As a result, the management task is comparable to a man having nothing but his hands to operate a machine with thousands of levers and buttons: As he will have limited options to intervene, chances are he will disturb the overall process rather than contribute to its effective management.

The phenomenon of polycentricity can be illustrated as shown in figure 2.32(2).[199]

Once again, let us assume all elements arranged hexagonally to be connected by elastic ties. Further, let us imagine this polygon to be fixed by a nail at its top end, and loaded down by a weight at its bottom. This weight will disturb the previous state of adjustment in a very specific way, requiring corresponding adjustment processes in each connecting element. This adjustment occurs in such a way that the forces at each corner element will offset each other, except for the elements fixated at the top and loaded down at the bottom, where forces are equal but opposite. The adjustment processes triggered by the load to the polygon are polycentric; that is, each element adjusts to the changes in all other elements, and vice versa.

In this particular case, however, we are facing a very specific polycentric problem commonly referred to as a *formalizable* polycentric problem: Due to the relatively small number of elements, it would be possible to set up a system of mathematical equations that represent the polygon, and the parameters of which can be quantified empirically.

---

199 See Polanyi (Logic), p. 170.

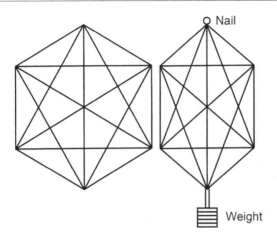

*Figure 2.32(2)*

As a result, it would be possible to instruct each element on how to act, and thus to create an overall equilibrium. Demonstrably, however,[200] the probability of precise and complete calculation decreases as the number of equations increases, and the approximate upper limit is at 150 linear simultaneous equations. Even for a polygon of just 20 vertices or elements, it will take around 150 equations to properly represent the relations given.

Besides calculable systems there are also systems that can be determined by *successive approximation* only, or *not at all*. As we can see from the brief considerations laid out here, the limit to exact computation is quickly reached even with relatively simple systems. Beyond that point, deliberate management interventions must give way to polycentric adjustment, spontaneous order, or cultivation of a self-organizing system. So, a system's manageability is directly dependent on its complexity, and above a certain limit it requires very specific types of control. As complex systems cannot be formalized or computed, it is clearly not possible to base their control on an analytical model. Rather, any model existing, explicitly or implicitly, can only represent certain characteristic traits of the system to be managed.

In essence, the method of polycentric adjustment or successive approximation consists in having each decision center solve its immediate problem without involving the remaining decisions centers. This solution is only preliminary and tentative, however: In the following round, the other centers'

---

200 See Polanyi (Logic), pp. 172 et seq.

problem solutions are taken into consideration as well, and in the light of this new situation a new solution is developed, again for the individual decision center. This way, several rounds will generate an overall solution or state of adjustment, which would not be possible with any other approach, least of all central decision-making and adjustment. Polanyi provides a simple example:[201] The problem he describes consists in solving a very large puzzle which would take one person several weeks. Under the polycentric approach, a number of people work on the puzzle simultaneously, each placing the pieces according to his or her situation and progress. Quite obviously, this method requires a maximum of information and feedback, as well as considerable adaptiveness on the individuals' (or elements') part.

However far the improvement of computational methods may extend that range, there will always lie beyond it a vastly greater range of more complex polycentric problems, which can be solved only by approximation from centre to centre. This method can be effectively organized and speeded up by using a team of independent calculators, one for each centre. The proper method of managing a polycentric task is therefore not by collecting all the data at one centre and evaluating them jointly.

The much more powerful and more accurate method is to solve the problem in respect to one centre at a time while pretending blindness in respect to all other conditions set by the problem as a whole, that is to the overwhelming majority of relations to be fulfilled.[202]

Note that this method can only produce satisfying results when the solutions developed at one center are taken into account by the other centers, that is, when the state of each center is communicated to the others (in the cybernetic sense).[203] Another important aspect is that each adjustment at a single center has to be integrated in an overall concept, which will either emerge implicitly through the individual adjustments as such, or will have to be introduced by way of general rules. One way to accomplish this task is to ensure that adjustments, decisions, problem solving, and so on happen in the structures of the viable system—based on a consistent strategy or vision communicated or dispersed across the entire structure. *Hence it is the method of decentralized problem solving at the object level, combined with central control by a metasystem, which permits one common direction with a maximum of adaptiveness and flexibility.*

---

201 See Polanyi (Logic), p. 35.
202 See Polanyi (Logic), pp. 180 et seq.
203 See also Jay (Management), pp. 106 et seq.; and Jay (Man), pp. 199 et seq.

Based on these considerations, three key forms of adaptation[204] can be depicted graphically (see figures 2.32(3)).

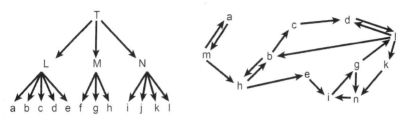

Figure 2.32(3a)                    Figure 2.32(3b)

In this graph, we see the taxis type of system and its adjustment on the left-hand side, and the spontaneous, polycentric order, which is based on the mutual adaptation of elements, on the right. Each of the letters represents a problem solver or decision maker, or simply an element of the system. x → y means that the decisions or the behavior of element y are adapted to the behavior of element x, or aligned with it.

With regard to central management, there is no need for detailed explanations at this point.

A closer look at figure 2.32(3b) reveals, however, that numerous complex and interlinked processes can take place here. As the graph also shows, contrary to earlier examples of regular polygons, not every element is linked to all other elements. The quality of polycentricism, or spontaneity of a type of order, does not necessarily require a fully interconnected structure. What it does require is rich interconnectedness, or the possibility of intense interaction. Total interlinkage of all elements will not occur very often in practice, or at least there will be different degrees of intensity; that is, it must be taken into account that some elements' behavior can be more autonomous than others'. In this context, a key point is that whenever the behavior of an element is effectively influenced by that of another element, an information channel in the cybernetic sense exists between the two elements. And it does not matter whether there are actually any messages—in the usual sense of the word—exchanged between the two elements. The only fact truly relevant for the characteristics of the overall system and its cybernetic qualities is that changes in an element's behavior will modify that of another element.

---

204 See Lindblom (Intelligence), p. 26.

The following two graphs show a comparison of the two types of management from the business context. Figure 2.32(4) is a typical organization chart implying a more or less typical taxis form of control, while figure 2.32(5) shows for a section of that chart how polycentric control relations should connect the individual components to permit smooth adaptation to changing circumstances.[205] A change in any component has to be able to trigger changes in other components, although with various delays and to different extents. A relatively significant deviation in the actual production time of an item has to be able to modify the production schedule; it has to have an effect on costing, delivery time estimates, and the earnings estimate. In addition, depending on the system relations, certain effects on warehousing, production planning, and the sales system have to be possible.

It does not matter whether these changes are transmitted and recorded by means of computers, through ordinary forms, through oral communication, or simply in the head of the manager of a small firm: The only thing that really matters is that the changes in a component will propagate across the remaining components to ensure overall adaptation of the system to current circumstances. Effectively implementing these actual connections is a major problem in most business organizations, due to the departmental thinking that is so common.

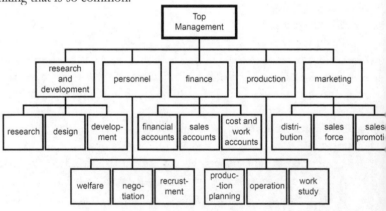

*Figure 2.32(4)*

---

205 See Beer (Governors). From the graphs 2.32 (3a and 3b) we can derive a third form in which both "pure" forms of adaptation are mixed (see figure 2.32(6)).

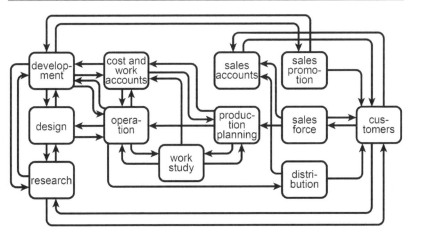

*Figure 2.32(5)*

From graphs 2.32 (3a and 3b) a third shape can be derived in which the two "pure" forms of adaptation are mixed (see figure 2.32(6)).

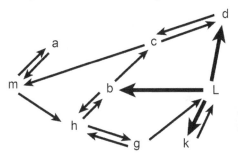

*Figure 2.32(6)*

The graphs in figures 2.32(3b) and 2.32(6) are not identical but are rather similar. It should be noted, however, that in the former, element l de facto triggers behavioral adjustments in other elements (such as b or k), but its role is that of a superior. In the latter, the letter L has been capitalized to indicate that this element has more power to intervene and direct other elements' behavior. This is also expressed in the differing thickness of the arrows originating from L: It indicates that the directions issued by L have more impact, or a greater probability of success to the benefit of L (in the sense of propensity). Metaphorically speaking, we could say that L plays with marked cards, and thus wins more often than the elements that influence L.

Next, figure 2.32(7) shows how combining such mixed control systems will generate extremely complex types of order and forms of control in which elements' behavior is mutually adjusted in very complicated ways, with certain elements—which in the graph are marked with capital letters—having greater importance than others. It does not take much imagination to realize how such a system is permanently kept in motion by the extremely complex interactions, how behavioral changes in subsystems or disturbances from the external world will propagate through the system in complex ways, fade out, or cause permanent fluctuations. And it is just as easy to imagine how different kinds of structural interventions in the systems will work. In this context, structural interventions are those that directly affect either the elements themselves (for instance, by eliminating them) or the arrows between them (thus changing information or adaptation streams between elements). These illustrations help to demonstrate that interventions intended to work on one arrow only can trigger extremely complicated and absolutely unpredictable changes of behavior in the overall system.

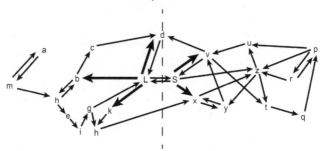

*Figure 2 32(7)*

Note that the graphical depiction of the different forms of adjustment just shows differences in weight between the elements; it does not take into account the different ways in which influence can be exerted or adjustments achieved. These particular options have to be included as well if we want to approximate real-life situations.

For example,[206] in one type of mutual adaptation the decision maker (or element x) adjusts his behavior to y without expecting any response. This may be because x adapts his or her decisions or behavior to y without ever taking into account the consequences for y. Another variety may be that x adapts his or her behavior in such a way as to prevent any negative consequences for y. Another, diluted variant would be that x is not really determined to avoid any kind of negative consequences of his or her adjustment for y but designs his or her own adjustment based on considerations as to the negative effects for y. A fundamentally different type of behavior would be for x to try to trigger a certain behavior in y, and to make this a condition for his or her decision making and adjustment behavior. There are a series of variants for this type of adjustment, the simplest one being the kind in which both x and y try in various ways to trigger behavioral responses to their own behaviors from the other element.

There are, of course, innumerable other forms of adaptation, which cannot all be addressed in detail here. The point is not to demonstrate that there are different variants, but to show that in the case of complex systems with numerous elements, it is impossible to accurately predict the effects that interventions will have. One possible solution obviously is to redesign the structure of such a system so that it will permit a centralistic type of control. As our analysis has revealed, this can be accomplished by cutting selected information and adjustment ties. When doing that, however, one must beware that the overall system's potential for adaptation shrinks considerably, so the system loses much of its flexibility and range of behaviors.

This is further complicated by the fact that in reality, subsystems are not separated from each other as cleanly as shown in figure 2.32(7). It must rather be expected that two or more subsystems will permeate each other, as indicated in figure 2.32(8). Typical examples of such forms of control include all natural ecosystems, such as predator-prey systems, in which predators normally live not in isolation from their prey but, more or less disguised, in the midst of the prey population. The predator and the prey populations control each other, thus regulating their respective density, penetration of a geographic territory, etcetera. Of course it is possible to separate the two subsystems of predators and preys by way of mental abstraction, and depict them in two distinct boxes in line with cybernetic conventions, but this is not consistent with reality. On the contrary, the interpenetration of both

---

206 See Lindblom (Intelligence), pp. 33 et seq.

populations—that is, the infiltration of the prey population with predators—is an essential precondition for the viability of the entire control system. For instance, in order to have one animal population control another one, it is usually necessary to trigger that infiltration process and ensure that the predators have an opportunity to mix with the prey population.

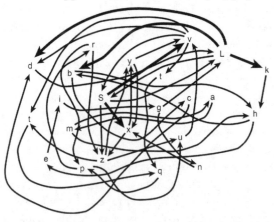

*Figure 2.32(8)*

By analogy, according to modern marketing theory, companies developing a new market need to ensure a very intense interaction of their promotional activities with potential consumers or buyers. Promotions are therefore usually aimed at achieving maximum market penetration for the respective advertising messages, and ensuring that potential buyers will encounter the company's product or message wherever they go. In view of the complexity existing even in a relatively simple system with only 22 elements, as shown in figure 2.32(8), it is obvious that it takes new ways of thinking and new methods to effectively influence and control such systems.

The following section will deal with some questions of meaningful problem solving in complex systems, in particular the *evolutionary* approach to problem solving. Again, these questions will be addressed exclusively from the perspective of how to manage complexity. After that, we will look at how, in the viable system structure, these components can be *integrated in a consistent concept of strategic management.*

## 2.4  Managing Complexity by Solving Problems

> "We are the product of a strategy
> of emerging regularity."
> *Rupert Riedl*

The last two sections were dedicated to the problem of complexity and theoretical treatment of complex phenomena, as well as to the problem of the formation and creation of order. In dealing with these two problems, certain methodological aspects have been addressed which can now be integrated to provide a description of a methodological approach that is suitable for complex situations. The term generally used is "problem-solving methodology," although it would be just as well to use terms such as "decision-making methodology" or "policy-making methodology." For the present discussion of the basic characteristics of the approach, all these names will be used synonymously.

### 2.41  Introduction to the Evolutionary Approach to Problem Solving

This section is dedicated primarily to describing the general characteristics of the approach, regardless of the specifics it will have in certain situations, that is, in solving specific problems. In this general discussion a distinct focus will be on the *evolutionary character of the methodology*. I hope to demonstrate that there are close correlations between the biological and social evolutionary process and the general problem-solving process in complex situations, in that both can be referred to as evolutionary processes. We will discuss both the *basic performance* and the *fundamental limitations* of the process. It is often more effective to know what a certain approach *cannot accomplish* than to make positive statements about its performance, as any information about the performance limits of a method is much better suited to identifying potential applications.

#### 2.411  *Misperceptions about Evolution Theory*

Before discussing the evolutionary approach to problem solving, some comments on general evolution theory seem warranted which transcend the assertions made in earlier sections and above all serve the purpose of resolving common misunderstandings about this theory. The first refers to the nature of the so-called evolutionary laws, the second to the school of philosophy commonly referred to as social Darwinism.

The *first fundamental misperception* about evolution theory is that it has generated assertions we might call *laws of evolution*, or that the quest for such laws of evolution was the subject of evolution theory. According to this misconception, such laws of evolution would describe evolutionary processes that necessarily (that is, by law of nature) have to take place and will lead to a predetermined or historically necessary succession of evolutionary stages or phases. Another misconception is that knowing these laws of evolution will enable us to forecast future events, that is, predict the future course of evolution. If these assumptions were true, the stringent conclusion would be that exploring the laws of evolution is part of the overriding subject of science itself.

Although it must be admitted that occasionally, even in studies based on a correct understanding of evolution theory, we find the notion of evolution taking a preprogrammed course and passing through possibly predetermined stages or phases, evolution theory in fact has nothing to do with these things. As such, it can only provide knowledge about a certain kind of process whose results we can predict with regard to their general attributes but not their specific manifestations. The results of the process of blind, transmissible variation and selective preservation depend on a much higher number of concrete, though partly temporary circumstances than we could ever comprehend or even predict. Unsatisfactory as this explanation may seem to some, it does provide an extraordinarily fruitful and comprehensive explanation of the evolutionary processes. It is an "in-principle explanation"— which in some situations is the only way to explain complex matters. As Hayek points out, the basic message of evolution theory is that a reduplication mechanism, comprising transmissible variations and the competitive selection of elements with superior survival chances, over time will produce a great diversity of structures that have been adapted to permit continuous adjustment to both the environment and each other.[207] Hence, Darwin has demonstrated with his evolution theory that the mechanism of natural selection can "in principle" simulate the accomplishments usually attributed to a creator.[208]

Darwin thus shows—as Popper points out—that it is possible *in principle* to "reduce" ideological explanations to causal ones by explaining the seem-

207 See Hayek (Studies), p. 32.
208 See Popper (Knowledge), p. 267.

ing existence of a purpose-oriented plan in the world based on purely physical principles. Although the term "in principle" represents a great enough
restriction for some people to consider the entire approach to explaining
complex and well-adapted structures unacceptable, and although to this date
nobody has managed to provide an actual causal explanation for the formation of organisms, we must not forget that Darwin's achievement was
nothing less than to demonstrate that such true causal explanations of evolutionary processes are indeed possible, that is, they are not a *logical* impossibility.[209]

Providing evidence for the *logical* possibility of explaining evolutionary
processes that have actually taken place is a considerable scientific achievement; yet it must not lead us to ignore that we are dealing with a *factual* impossibility, as any rationale for why this or that organism or kind of organism
actually exists would have to take into account all the different circumstances
that have existed in millions of years, either permanently or preliminary, and
which thus have influenced the evolutionary process.[210]

As Hayek explains—and as has been mentioned earlier—this is a situation one just has to accept in all disciplines dealing with complex matters.
"The theoretical understanding of the growth and functioning of organisms
can only in the rarest of instances be turned into specific predictions of what
will happen in a particular case, because we can hardly ever ascertain all the
facts which will contribute to determine the outcome. Hence, 'prediction and
control, usually regarded as essential criteria of science, are less reliable in biology.' It deals with patter-building forces, the knowledge of which is useful for
creating conditions favourable to the production of certain kinds of results,
while it will only in comparatively few cases be possible to control all the relevant circumstances."[211] So, although it would be wrong to interpret evolution
theory as a historical course following the laws of evolution—as I am hoping
to demonstrate—evolution theory does comprise an important historical element. This may be the reason why so many scientists have been led to misinterpret evolution theory in the ways described. As explained above, every
actual explanation of an evolutionary process would have to deal with all the
past facts that have contributed to the emergence of the subject under study.
Although we have reason to believe that under repeatable conditions the

---

209 See Popper (Knowledge), p. 267.
210 See Hayek (Studies), p. 33.
211 See Hayek (Studies), pp. 33 et seq.

mechanism of evolution would lead to repeatable results, many actual results of evolutionary processes—if not most of them—are outcomes of *singular* events or processes. "The theoretical disciplines that deal with the structures of such complexes thus have an object of experience, the existence of which is owed to circumstances (and an evolutionary process determined by them) which, although basically repeatable, may in fact be unique and non-recurring. Therefore, the laws determining the behavior of these complexes are, though 'universally valid in principle' (whatever that may mean) actually only applicable to structures that will occur in a limited space-time area of the universe."[212]

Popper holds a similar view regarding the scientific nature of evolution theory: According to him, the theory of natural selection is a *historical* one, and it constructs a situation just to show that when this very situation is assumed, exactly the things whose existence we are trying to explain will happen. He then goes on to explain, however, that an equally important characteristic of evolution theory, distinguishing it from other disciplines, is that it tries to reconstruct a *typical* situation rather than a unique one. That is why it is possible to model evolutionary processes.[213]

Consequently, the true theory of evolution, properly understood, should not lead us to assume that there are any laws of (historical) evolution allowing us to extrapolate the present into the future. Even if the mechanism of evolution, which is described in general terms here, was explored further in an attempt to establish how different variation mechanisms work or what specific selection criteria have permanently or temporarily been applied—which is certainly desirable and the object of intense research—this would not generate evolutionary laws in the sense described above.[214]

The *second error* with regard to evolution theory, which has discredited it and needs to be rectified in order to remove another barrier to understanding, is the idea commonly referred to as "social Darwinism." Much of the error

---

212 See Hayek (Studies), p. 153.

213 See Popper (Knowledge), p. 270.

214 It was long after the manuscript for this book had been completed that Rupert Riedl's writings came to my attention—above all, his book *Order in Living Organisms: A Systems Analysis of Evolution* (Wiley, New York, 1978), which offers what I consider a very convincing explanation of why evolution itself creates the conditions of its future course, in a sense, and argues that we are dealing with a strategy of emerging regularity. To me this seems a considerable step forward in evolution theory thinking, the consequences of which are yet to be fully understood. Nevertheless, I believe that it does not refer to the same historicist laws of evolution which are subject to the misconception discussed here.

is probably due to the fact that, although the evolution mechanism works the same way in both the biological and the social sphere, there are significant differences. The mere statement that a process based on transmissible variations and selective preservation will produce rich and complex structures is not enough: It does not tell us anything about the *object* of that variation of selection. It is important to note, therefore, that the mechanism of evolution in the social sphere usually works at the level of social *institutions*, not individuals, and that selection works on culturally transmitted behaviors rather than innate ones. "The error of 'Social Darwinism' was that it concentrated on the selection of individuals rather than on that of institutions and practices, and on the selection of innate rather than on culturally transmitted capacities of the individuals."[215] It is of utmost importance to note that in the social sphere, it is not the individuals themselves that are mutated as what we might call evolution's objects of experimentation: It is individuals' behaviors, habits, customs, capabilities, and so on—or in other words, the very rules of behavior we have discussed before.

Another point to be noted is that it is not primarily individuals that fall victim to the selection process. Rather, it is the social institutions resulting from the rule-compliant behavior of individuals. So, contrary to what is sometimes claimed, the selection pressure of evolution leads not just to the formation of certain organs, extremities, or specific tool-like features such as teeth, claws, and such, but also and particularly to the formation of certain *modes of behavior* and certain *institutions* in the sense of orders.

### 2.412  Two Kinds of Methods

> 1. The information you have is not what you want.
> 2. The information you want is not what you need.
> 3. The information you need is not what you can obtain.
> 4. The information you can obtain costs more than you want to pay!
> *Finagle's Laws of Information*

As you may remember, the purpose of this section is to provide a general description of a problem-solving methodology adapted to the specifics of the subject matter. These specifics consist in the immense complexity of the areas under study, and in the existence of certain types of order and of special processes producing these kinds of order. It was stated earlier that this method is closely related to general evolution theory in terms of its general

---

215 See Hayek (Rules), p. 23.

characteristics. It was therefore necessary for the understanding of the method, which is described below, to discuss two profound misconceptions about evolution theory.

The nature of the evolutionary problem-solving method, which is both a decision-making method and an approach to strategy design, can best be illustrated by contrasting and comparing it to an opposite approach. In line with Hayek's writings, the counterpart of the *evolutionary method* will be referred to as *constructivist method*.[216]

As always in cases like these, there is a great variety of names for both approaches. Lindblom, for instance, speaks of a "method of successive limited comparisons" or—metaphorically—of the "branch method" when referring to an approach that is essentially similar to the evolutionary method discussed here. On the other hand, what I here refer to as "constructivist method" he calls the "rational-comprehensive," "synoptic," or—again, metaphorically—"root method."[217]

Steinbruner uses the term "analytic paradigm" for the constructivist approach and "cybernetic paradigm" for the evolutionary approach.[218] In the following sections I will use the two terms mentioned above. The main reason I chose to speak of "evolutionary" and "constructivist" approaches is that I wish to remind readers that these terms are not random but represent two very different theoretical approaches, rooted in two very different philosophical or epistemological schools. In addition, I hope to make very clear that they are associated with two completely different approaches to explaining biological and especially social phenomena—a fact that is rather significant when it comes to explaining management as a social institution with a shaping and guiding function.

The *constructivist* view, put in broad terms, assumes all social institutions to be the result of deliberate, purpose-oriented, rational planning and design, constructed by humans for very specific purposes, and that all social actions are or should be guided by rational, purpose-oriented considerations. The effectiveness of both behavior and organization is considered to be a result of the thorough and comprehensive understanding of all problems by human reason, as well as of rational design. *Evolutionary* conception, by contrast, is based on the assumption that social institutions are the result not of rational

---

216 See Hayek (Rules), pp. 8 et seq. (Konstruktivismus), passim.
217 See Lindblom (Muddling Through), p. 158.
218 See Steinbruner (Cybernetic Theory), passim.

plan and design but of a growth and evolution process: While a human creative intention is always involved to some extent, the formation of social institutions cannot be explained by it. From an evolutionary point of view, the effectiveness and rationality of social institutions and behaviors results primarily not from rational insight into cause-and-effect relationships and deliberate goal-setting, but from largely unconscious compliance with rules that have emerged from an evolutionary process themselves.

From an evolutionary point of view, any insight into cause-and-effect and purpose-and-means relationships, which constructivism or constructivist rationalism claim to be a basis for rational behavior, is practically impossible. The evolutionary approach is therefore aimed at exploring the *methods* to enable successful behavior, especially given the very serious circumstance of a lack of insight, knowledge, information, and understanding of correlations—in short: under conditions of great complexity.

Constructivist rationalism is pseudo-rationalism, or actually irrationalism, as the complete alignment of social institutions and social behavior with reason, along with the negation of the limits of human reason, is equivalent to the demand to try the impossible.

### a) Basic principles of the constructivist method

All efforts at developing problem-solving and decision-making approaches to be categorized as constructivist are centered around the idea of *rational choice* or *rational decision*. Although this category of methods comprises many variations, there is one thing all of them have in common: They all attempt to develop principles, approaches, techniques, and so on intended to lead to rational decision making or problem solving.

Evolutionary methods pursue the same objective, of course. The key difference between the two is what "rational" is understood to mean. Roughly speaking, and anticipating the results of the following discussion, if what the constructivist method demands of a rational decision or solution were fulfilled, this would clearly lead to a better decision than the evolutionary method could. The problem is, however, that the demands and requirements defined by the constructivist method *cannot be fulfilled*. In other words, the constructivist method calls for things that would be better indeed but are actually impossible to achieve. By contrast, the evolutionary method focuses on developing rational problem-solving principles that seem possible to apply. So, while these principles may seem less rational in an absolute sense, compared to those of the constructivist method, they have the advantage of being practical. It would exceed the scope of this book to address all variations of the constructivist method. Instead, I will try to outline the basic idea common to all variants. According to Lindblom's analysis,[219] the following four characteristics can be considered constitutive of the constructivist or synoptic method:

1. To solve a problem rationally, a problem solver identifies and analyzes all the goals and values that in his view determine the selection of a solution, and ranks these goals in an unambiguous and stable order.
2. He thoroughly examines all conceivable means and ways to reach these goals while taking into account existing value systems.
3. He also thoroughly explores all possible consequences of each individual means or way.
4. He chooses the alternative that, in the light of this analysis, promises a maximum or at least a satisfactory degree of goal fulfillment.

Hence the core elements of the constructivist or analytical decision-making and problem-solving approach:

1. sets of goals and priority ranks postulated in advance, based on the assumption that they are unambiguous and will remain stable;
2. the view that the problem-solving process is a process of assigning means and ways to goals;
3. very comprehensive analysis of all available options and their consequences; and
4. sufficiently exact assessment criteria which can be operationalized and appear stable.

A choice is considered to be a good or rational decision if it can be demonstrated that under the given conditions the best of the options available has been chosen. Consequently, a constructivist problem-solving method is a procedure leading to such a choice. As the constructivist decision-making and problem-solving methodology is often mathematically-quantitatively oriented, it seems appropriate to describe the method under discussion with regard to this particular characteristic. The following five steps are constitutive:[220]

---

219 See Lindblom (Intelligence), pp. 137 et seq.
220 See Steinbruner (Cybernetic Theory), p. 32.

1. For each option or alternative, a variable measure of value (v) is estimated for every possible state, resulting in a series of values ($v_1$, $v_2$, $v_3$, ..., $v_n$).

2. Next, the probability that each state will actually occur is estimated, resulting in a series of values ($p_1$, $p_2$, $p_3$, ..., $p_n$).

3. Now the probability values are used to discount the values of each alternative. The result is a series of values ($p_1v_1$, $p_2v_2$, $p_3v_3$, ..., $p_nv_n$).

4. The sum of this series ($p_1v_1 + p_2v_2 + p_3v_3 + ... + p_nv_n$) is referred to as expected value.

5. Finally, the option with the highest expected value is selected.

It is neither possible nor necessary at this point to elaborate on the numerous difficulties associated with applying this concept. The key difficulty I will address here is that this problem-solving concept requires an extent of information not achievable in practice. The constructivist or analytical method is strongly based on a causal model of the decision-making situation, assuming the decision maker to be comprehensively informed about all circumstances relevant to the situation.[221] (This does not only apply to the models that require full information, in the sense of making decisions under conditions of certainty.)

As explained in the sections on complexity and order, in complex situations it cannot be reasonably assumed that the amount of information required by the constructivist approach is in fact achievable. This limitation of our knowledge makes it impossible to apply the constructivist decision-making and problem-solving methodology. The limitation of information on complex matters is both inevitable and irreversible. One could even say that many phenomena are so complex just *because* we do not have enough information about them and never will. This, in turn, means that complexity is irreversibly associated with uncertainty. A rational choice or decision in the constructivist sense requires, however, that decisions be made in the light of information as complete as possible. Demonstrably, this perspective on rationality is based on the philosophy of Descartes, and "[since] for Descartes reason was defined as logical deduction from explicit premises, rational action also came to mean only such action as was determined entirely by known and demonstrable truth. It is almost an inevitable step from this to the conclusion that only what is true in this sense can lead to successful

---

221 See Steinbruner (Cybernetic Theory), p. 35.

action, and that therefore everything to which man owes his achievements is a product of his reasoning thus conceived."[222]

Due to the detailed discussion of the problem of complexity and of the emergence and creation of order, it is not necessary at this point to elaborate further on the problem of inevitable limitation of human knowledge, which is the key argument to invalidate the constructivist decision-making and problem-solving methodology. It is certainly understandable that there are efforts to develop this kind of method, and also that such efforts to overcome the limits to human knowledge usually hold a great fascination. Still, they are attempts to make the impossible possible. As Lindblom remarks, a method like this can be *described but not practiced*, except in the area of relatively simple problems, because the method requires intellectual capacities that humankind does not possess, as well as sources of information that do not exist.[223]

As we have seen, the constructivist failure to recognize the fundamental limitations of human knowledge determines not only the decision-making methodology under discussion but—perhaps even more—a frequent attitude towards the problem of designing social institutions, and thus society as such. The basic limitations of information on complex matters do not trigger any attempts to search for new, different methods that could help manage complexity; instead, people keep trying to plan and design more and more areas of human life, and to limit the effects of spontaneous forces of order. This is not least a consequence of the attempt to research societal phenomena using so-called scientific, thus seemingly precise methods.

Hayek has thoroughly analyzed this attitude and thinking, which he called "scientism," and revealed a number of interconnections with some fields of social sciences, political theory, and several other disciplines. Put very simply, Hayek's findings can be summarized by saying that scientism is an attempt to research very complex matters with simple methods. However, as this is not possible, complexity is simply ignored; that is, it is somehow pretended that it is simple. It comes as no surprise that any "insights" into complex matters gathered this way will have little or no relevance. *Constructivism*, then, is an attempt to influence societal dynamics so they can be managed with simple methods, or in other words, so they can be fully surveyed and managed by individuals. That, in turn, would make social systems lose all their capability of self-regulation and self-organization.

---

222 See Hayek (Rules), p. 19.
223 Lindblom (Muddling Through), p. 156.

*b) Errors underlying the constructivist method*

Instead of providing an abstract analysis of the constructivist problem-solving approach, it may be better to openly address some points disregarded by the constructivist theory.[224]

1. The analytical approach fails to take into account human beings' limited mental capabilities, in particular their limited ability to process information, as well as other specific characteristics of the way the human brain functions.

2. It also disregards the basic openness of virtually all complex problems and decision situations, that is, the fact that it would usually be impossible to list all relevant variables and their interrelations.

3. Further, the theory fails to consider the inseparable interconnectedness of facts, opinions, and judgments that is characteristic of all complex problems.

4. It fails to take proper account of the fact that all available information on facts, opinions, and judgments is incomplete and subject to change, and also that the facts, opinions, and judgments themselves are uncertain and subject to change.

5. The possibilities of setting up stable sets of goals and evaluation criteria, as well as scales of preferences and priorities, are enormously overestimated.

6. The number of options basically available tends to be underestimated. Along with the demand for comprehensive analysis of all options and their consequences, this results in information-processing problems that are unmanageable in terms of sheer quantity.

7. Another factor hardly ever taken into account is that a complex problem usually cannot be specified at the outset; at best you will have some phrased statements of intent regarding the solution aspired to; often, you will only know that things "cannot go on like this."

8. The analytical approach focuses mainly on the quantifiable aspects of a problem. Even in rather verbally oriented variants, there are usually efforts to apply point systems and similar things to achieve a degree of accuracy that, upon closer analysis, turns out to be pseudo-precision. The underlying attitude is basically scientistic.

---

224 With regard to the following, see Lindblom (Intelligence), pp. 138 et seq.; and Malik and Gomez (Entscheide).

9. Time and cost limits, which often play a key part in actual decision-making processes, are hardly taken into account.

10. The uncertainties and "irrationalities" of human behavior are disregarded or deliberately ignored.

11. Discontinuities and surprising developments are almost impossible to capture with the analytical approach.

12. Under the analytical approach, it is difficult if not impossible to take account of the fact that every solution to a problem has to be preliminary in nature, and that there will always be a risk of undesirable side effects, which, in turn, will pose new problems.

13. Finally, the analytical approach does not take into consideration the fact that truly complex problems hardly ever have a "correct" solution; often, the term "solution" is not even applicable.

*c) Characterization of the starting point for developing the evolutionary method*

By reversing the deficits of the constructivist approach, we can essentially derive the key factors calling for the development of an evolutionary approach. Still, some characteristics of the situation warrant special emphasis.[225]

1. There is a great, or at least not immediately manageable, number of options, which in the course of the problem-solving process is gradually diminished by eliminating entire categories of options.

2. It is initially unclear or unknown what characteristics the decision should ultimately have. They have to be clarified or identified in the course of the process.

3. Goals and means are closely interconnected. As a general rule, several goals have to be considered at once. Different alternatives are associated with different *combinations of goals*, as a result of which an empirical analysis of options will meet with an additional difficulty: As each option changes, so does the basis for its evaluation.

4. The effects of a decision are not completely predictable. There is always a risk of undesired side effects which cannot be predicted but will strongly affect the desired outcome. 5. The required decision is not an isolated, nonrecurring act, but embedded in a continuous course of events. Consequently, even the best decision can only temporarily be "good" or "right," and at the time of its implementation it may have been rendered obsolete by the latest events.

---

225 See Malik and Gomez (Entscheide).

6. The number and kind of factors relevant to the decision are not fully known. They keep changing and, to the extent that they are known, their future development can rarely be predicted.

The first two points—the facts that the number of options to be examined is usually much greater than expected and that the target characteristics of the decision are initially unknown, or difficult to specify—can be illustrated by a graph (see figure 2.4(1)). It makes very clear what the basic problem of any problem-solving method is: The process of problem solving or decision making has to be designed so as to ensure its course will follow the extended curves as closely as possible. This is not so much about the question as to how this illustration can be quantified and the actual course of the curves determined.

It is about a conceptional insight with regard to the question as to what problem is to be solved by an appropriately designed problem-solving methodology. Asking this question may seem a bit peculiar, as it seems to have an obvious answer. It is usually answered at the level of concrete, specific, content-driven problems—problems such as setting up a spatial development framework for a municipality, determining the funding requirements of a business for a certain period, developing a promotional concept for a product, obtaining an import license for a country, registering a patent, fixing a technical problem in a machine, and so on.

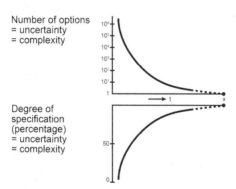

*Figure 2.41 (1): Fundamental problem: All options except one have to be eliminated and 100 percent specification of all conditions has to be achieved.*[226]

---

[226] See Tarr (Problem Solving), p. 4; and Beer (Brain), p. 281

Upon asking what methods are used to solve such problems, the answers will almost certainly be tailored to the nature of a specific problem. This fixation on the concrete subject of specific problems usually makes it difficult if not impossible to recognize the basic structure of the problem-solving process. It goes without saying that it takes different methods, techniques, and ways of thinking to determine the funding needs of a business from those needed to fix a technical problem in a machine. But if you try to transcend the level of specific content of individual problems and to get to the general characteristics of the problem-solving process, you will find that the different approaches to solving a problem share certain basic elements which are amenable to description and exploration, and hence to deliberate design.

Especially in the area of highly complex problems, it is essential to focus on these general structural characteristics of problem-solving processes. The lack of concrete knowledge with regard to complex matters is inevitably associated with a lack of concrete content, which means that the problem-solving process has to be aimed at producing the level of concreteness that usually exists in the area of simple problems, and which provides a starting point for all further problem-solving efforts. Since the characteristics common to all complex problems consist in that very complexity, the uncertainty associated with it, or generally speaking a fundamental lack of knowledge, it is possible to make general statements about the solving of problems in the realm of great complexity. Consequently, we can also speak of a general theory of problem solving in this area, while this would not equally be possible in the realm of simple problems.

The task of designing the problem-solving process in such a way that the curves shown in figure 2.41(1) are approximated has been referred to as the core problem to be addressed by a theory of problem solving. It is a problem of *steering the problem-solving process*, which is immediately obvious when you consider what alternative curves would be possible. These alternative curves are shown in figure 2.41(2). As we can see, both the number of options and the degree of problem specification can be subject to strong fluctuations—and they do fluctuate in practice—which is mainly due to the fact that there are continuous changes in the problem solver's situation.

I have pointed out in earlier sections that complex matters are characterized by strong dynamics, or, in other words, that the dynamics of the situation are one of the reasons why it is so complex. This means that due to the continuously changing situation and the resulting changes in the state of information, the issue of problem solving or decision making keeps presenting itself in a new light over and over again. It is entirely possible, and happens quite frequently in practice, that under circumstances like these there will never be a decision or solution. It is the very task of a problem-solving process (that is, of a systematic procedure aimed at taking decisions in complex situations) to guide the activities of everyone involved so that a solution will be found, despite all the chances to be expected, and so that the actual curves will be as close as possible to the ideal ones.

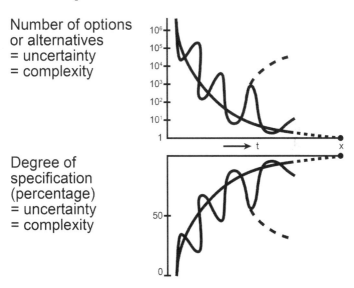

Figure 2.41 (2)[227]

As pointed out earlier, in the realm of very high complexity this is not possible by way of direct intervention into the problem-solving process. Instead, you will have to resort to indirect methods of controlling or managing complexity, as has been described in the section on the emergence and creation of orders. In other words, the only way to solve complex problems usually is the deliberate, planned, and targeted creation of *conditions* that will create or improve the chances of effective problem solution. The outcomes to materialize under such conditions are driven mainly by the forces of spontaneous orders.

---

227 See Beer (Platform), p. 295.

These general remarks about the situation calling for the development of an evolutionary problem-solving methodology should suffice to set the frame. In the next section, we will have a closer look at the evolutionary problem-solving process itself.

## 2.42 Basic Structure of the Evolutionary Problem-Solving Process

### 2.421 Description of the Process

Solving problems in complex situations resembles a blind variation and selective retention process. As this process and its epistemological background have been discussed at length elsewhere, I will assume the state of discussion to be known.[228] In a nutshell, it is a trial-and-error process which—as I hope to demonstrate in detail at several points—is the only way to eliminate ignorance, or gain information. As complex situations are strongly marked by the fact that we have insufficient information about the relevant facts, the trial-and-error process is one of the key tools to manage complexity.

As is generally known, the trial-and-error process or (synonymously) the blind variation and selective retention process has the following structural components:

a) as a starting point: problems to be studied in a situation analysis;
b) tentative problem solutions which, from an epistemological perspective, are always hypothetical in nature;
c) the elimination of errors;
d) new problems which can be the outcome of a preceding process and a starting point for further problem-solving activities.

According to Karl Popper, the process in its simplest form can be visualized as follows:[229]

---

228 See Gomez, Malik, and Oeller (Systemmethodik), vol. 1.
229 See Popper (Knowledge), passim; and Gomez, Malik, and Oeller (Systemmethodik), pp. 54 et seq.

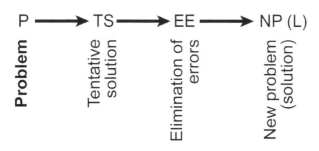

*Figure 2.42(1)*

In slightly amended form, taking account of the fact that every problem might have several solutions, so that the elimination of errors will have to be fanned out accordingly and there will be a greater number of newly emerging problems, the graph looks like this:

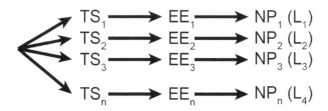

*Figure 2 42(2)*

The problem-solving approach shown here is of fundamental importance from an epistemological point of view. However, it is only when you apply it to your own situation, thus establishing the various interactions and inter-dependencies between the individual steps, that the full effectiveness of the method is brought to bear. Although that does not affect the basic structure of the problem-solving process, in reality that process will rarely have the clarity and simplicity indicated in the symbolic depiction. Instead, the practice of problem solving is rather like a dense network of steps and practical steps, some of which merge into one another while others abruptly displace one another, and which together form a complex dynamic system that can best be compared to a labyrinth the structure of which changes continu-ously—that is, with walls rising where there were passageways just moments before, and with new paths opening where there has been nothing. What further adds to the intricacy of the problem-solving labyrinth is that while problem solvers can sometimes determine where "walls" should be set and "paths" opened, they cannot know how this will affect their further progress through the labyrinth.

To get an impression of the complexity of a real-life problem-solving process, we can expand the simple graph above by adding another dimension to form a kind of matrix, thus making visible how we apply the process to our own situation. A general, formal description of this approach has been provided elsewhere.[230] The key point about this structure is that it operates at two levels, an object-language and a meta-language level, with the hierarchies of both levels defined by pragmatic considerations rather than logic. As there has been a detailed description of the cross-linkages between the two process levels, it seems in order at this point to restrict the discussion to the essentials.

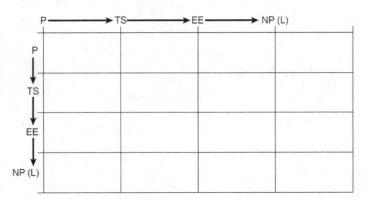

*Figure 2.42(3)*

The first step in this scheme is to recognize a problem and put it in words. For instance, the problem might be: How can I increase my return on equity? Once the problem has been phrased that way, and provided the phrase really captures the true problem, an essential step has been taken. As a general rule, however, the process of recognizing the problem is a difficult problem in itself, and there are usually several, if not many methodological approaches to it. It is therefore necessary to apply the entire problem-solving process to the problem of recognizing and formulating the problem. This is what the first column of the matrix refers to. For the problem of problem recognition,

---

230 See Gomez, Malik, and Oeller (Systemmethodik), pp. 94 et seq.

tentative solutions have to be developed, gradually eliminating the errors contained in them to finally arrive at a solution, if only a preliminary one at first, which can then provide a starting point for the next step in the horizontal dimension. In all probability, along with this preliminary solution there will be a series of new problems emerging in the context of recognizing and formulating the problem.

The remaining columns of the matrix must be interpreted in much the same way. However—and this is an important aspect of solving problems—it is neither mandatory nor necessary to take these steps successively or in a linear order. On the contrary, the process can be started with any one of the steps, and it is also possible to change between steps ad libitum. Each step in the scheme essentially represents a tool for the problem solver, a kind of testing probe to scan the entire problem space, and it is not necessary to stick to a certain sequence in using the different probes. The crucial point, however, is that *all* steps are completed and not a single step is *systematically* neglected. This is very important in particular for the expanded variants of the problem-solving process.

In essence, the theory of evolutionary problem solving is based on the following hypotheses:[231]

1. A blind-variation and selective-retention process is necessary and sufficient for any expansion of knowledge, that is, for any information gain, and thus for any kind of adaptation and problem-solving process.
2. Such a process comprises three essential components:
   a, mechanisms producing variations or mutations,
   b, consistent and persistent selection processes, and
   c, mechanisms to retain and/or disseminate the variants selected.
3. All information gathering processes or methods which do not apply the trial-and-error principle are themselves an outcome of earlier trial-and-error processes, which may have taken place at another logical level and which may have used information that was also gathered in earlier trial-and-error processes.
4. Information-gathering or problem-solving processes which from a specific or superficial point of view are not trial-and-error processes are

---

231 With regard to the following, see Campbell (Creative Thought), (Blind Variation), (Epistemology); as well as Popper (Autobiography); and Lorenz (Rückseite).

based on a preceding or underlying trial-and-error component which, however, takes place at another level and uses substitutes.

5. Variations of trial-and-error processes are usually small, incremental changes. When several such trial-and-error levels are overlaid which by design permit mutations to be simulated at another level with regard to their consequences by means of substitutes (models) before actual implementation, it can happen that many small changes "accumulate" into greater changes as the variation selected can become a starting point for further variation processes. This way, the overall process can be steered in a certain direction.

6. In this process, the range of possible variations (variability) is in itself a variable whose concrete manifestation is an outcome of previous trial-and-error processes.

7. Likewise, the selection criteria at work in such processes are results of earlier trial-and-error processes.

8. The aspects subject to variation and selection—that is, the elements, variables, and so on to be modified—and thus the overall modifiability of a system are results of trial-and-error processes.

These hypotheses probably raise more questions than they answer because when the terms "variation mechanism," "selection criteria," "retention and propagation processes," and so forth are used, it is far from clear what each of them encompasses, how they actually work, and so on. Still, the key outcome of studies of evolutionary problem-solving processes has to be that you can explain targeted, insightful, and intelligent problem-solving behavior by means of the trial-and-error paradigm.

For instance, Campbell[232] uses the following ten-level hierarchy of problem-solving processes to show how increasingly complex forms emerge from earlier results and the way they work:

1. Non-mnemonic problem solving: basically by carrying out blind locomotoric activities to explore the environment.

2. Problem solving by carrying out motion substitutes to simulate activities before actually carrying them out.

3. Problem solving by forming habits.

4. Problem solving by forming instincts.

---

232 See Campbell (Epistemology), pp. 422 et seq.

5. Problem solving by visually supported thought.
6. Problem solving by mnemonically supported thought.
7. Problem solving by observational learning and imitation.
8. Problem solving by using language.
9. Problem solving by accumulating cultural experience.
10. Problem solving in the sense of scientific research.

As the individual elements of this hierarchy of problem-solving processes—all based on the paradigm of blind variation and selective retention—have been described at length elsewhere, the details are assumed to be known.[233]

These studies, together with modern epistemology's finding that the only logically possible way to gain insight is by trial and error, provide the *starting point* for the development of problem-solving methods. The conclusion from that is that the deliberate design of such methods in the context of complex socio-technical systems should not focus solely on finding methods that will help reveal the philosopher's stone, as it were, but should seek methods that make the trial-and-error processes and their structural elements as efficient as possible.

Starting points can be a number of factors, as illustrated by the list Campbell has put together:

"...some 6 to 14 or more separately variable parameters are implied. These include:

a. A mnemonic representation of environment, varying perhaps in scope, accuracy, and fineness of detail;
b. A mnemonic search or thought-trial process, varying in the accuracy with which it represents potential overt exploration;
c. A thought-trial generating and changing process, varying in rate, heterogeneity, idiosyncrasy, and lack of repetitiousness among successive thought trials;
d. Selective criteria, varying in their number, accuracy of representation of environmental contingencies, and precision, sharpness, or selection ratio;
e. A preservation of propagation process, providing a retention for selected thought trials of a quite different order from the memory traces of the nonselected ones, varying perhaps in accuracy and accessibility;

---

233 See Campbell (Epistemology), pp. 422 et seq.; and Gomez, Malik, and Oeller (System-methodik), pp. 54 et seq.

f. A reality testing process in which the selected thought trials are checked out by overt locomotion in the external environment, varying perhaps in sensitivity to disconfirming feedback.

... Manipulation of any one of the 14 variables just listed should increase the number of creative products, providing the other variables can be held constant.[234]

Of course, the view taken here on the fundamental significance of the trial-and-error paradigm does not imply that there are no such things as methods and techniques for the direct utilization of knowledge; it just implies that such methods cannot be applied in the area of *high complexity*. They do remain applicable for relatively simple situations. High complexity and, along with it, a high degree of uncertainty—or lack of information—is highly characteristic of the problem of strategy design in management. Hence, the well-thought-through design of trial-and-error processes to determine business strategies is of crucial importance.

### 2.422  Discussion of Counter-Arguments

Some difficulty for the understanding of the evolutionary problem-solving paradigm based on blind-variation and selective-retention processes emerges when the trials in trial-and-error process are interpreted as *random* trials. This interpretation is wrong, which is why Campbell speaks of "blind" rather than "random" variation. Apart from the fact that the concept of randomness in itself requires a certain kind of order, and that only relative to that order is it possible at all to speak of randomness, there is no contradiction between the observation that the trials in the context of trial-and-error processes are blind within a *certain range*, and the observation that the fact that the trials take place in a certain range give the overall process a kind of direction. It must be stressed, however, that the selection of a range, again, is the result of a blind-variation and selective-retention process.[235]

The use of the term "blind" warrants some explanation. As Campbell points out,[236] an essential aspect of the meaning of "blind" is that the variations created are independent of the environmental conditions leading to

---

234 Campbell (Creative Thought), p. 68.
235 See Popper (Autobiography), pp. 35 et seq.
236 Campbell (Creative Thought), p. 58.

their creation. Another aspect is that no individual trial, or no individual variation, is correlated with the solution to the problem; that is, the probability of occurrence is not systematically higher for successful trials or variants than for those that fail. (If appearances are different, this is a result of earlier blind trial-and-error processes. This does not mean that we should assume an even distribution of probabilities; it just means we should not assume that trials which *in retrospect* turn out to have been successful or correct are systematically favored.) The third essential aspect of "blind" is that it would be unsubstantiated to assume that a variation following an incorrect or unsuccessful one has to be a correction of that earlier variation. Successive trials in a trial-and-error process are not correlated with the correctness or incorrectness of earlier trials. (Wherever appearances are different, this is an indication of a substitution process which—at another level—also operates with trial-error variations and is able to select adequate variations.)

To illustrate the problem of information gain, Popper has occasionally used the metaphor of a blind man searching a dark room for a black hat that might not even exist.[237] This is clearly a situation where very little directional information is available. Still, searching efforts will not be completely random even in such a situation; instead they will have a certain orientation resulting from the fact that the person searching acts as though he has a certain problem. So, his search behavior will have a certain order which, however—and this is important—is not simply a given fact but results from earlier trial-and-error processes. Now, the situation when designing a strategy may not be as lacking in information as the situation of the blind man searching for a black hat. Any directional information that is available will be used. However, to the extent that explorations into unknown territory are required, there will be no other option but to apply the method of blind (not random) variation and selective retention.

Apart from these common misunderstandings about the random component of the trial-and-error method, there are several other frequent objections to this paradigm of problem solving which will be discussed in the following. Regarding the assertion that any kind of information gain, including creative problem solving, can be explained by a trial-and-error process in the sense described, the following three arguments are often put forward:

1. the argument of gestalt psychology concerning the phenomenon of sudden and spontaneous insight;

237 Popper (Replies), p. 1061.

2. the argument associated with the possibility of a spontaneous inspiration, in the sense of a creative act, and which can be referred to as the "myth of genius"; and

3. arguments from the area of heuristic problem solving.

*Regarding item 1.*

I will be brief in addressing the arguments of gestalt psychology. The trial-and-error paradigm is not contradictory to the gestalt school of psychology's assertions concerning formative mechanisms and the insightful problem-solving behaviors associated with them. From a descriptive perspective, it may seem reasonable to use gestalt terms to describe certain phenomena. Nevertheless, it must be noted that from an epistemological standpoint or from the perspective of *gathering* information, the trial-and-error principle remains fundamental to any discovery or gathering of new information. Specifically, the example of sight—which is often quoted as a model of the way formative mechanisms function—is useful to illustrate how any information we gain by means of our visual sense is only superficially direct, and that sight a) is itself a result of evolutionary processes and b) also makes use of trial-and-error operations.[238]

Furthermore, it is important to remember that evolutionary processes are multifaceted and, as mentioned before, there are substitution processes at many levels which in a manner of speaking perform simulations using substitutional internal selection criteria, before at another level the respective trial is implemented in actual behavior. To the extent that the internal variation medium and the internal selection mechanisms are adequate representations of the relevant ambient conditions, it is obvious that the variations selected this way will be considered insightful, intelligent, targeted, and so on when implemented. Many of the qualities quoted by the gestalt school, such as wholeness, symmetry, structure, and so forth, may well be considered to be such internal selection criteria; however, they must also be regarded as results of evolutionary processes at a previous level.[239]

Incidentally, another point to be taken into account is that the evolutionary paradigm of solving problems does not specify the kind of variant created. It is therefore easily conceivable that at a given level, for example the level of creative thinking, the gestalt qualities themselves have to be varied, or that general abstraction principles undergo blind variation, or that general search

---

238 See Campbell (Blind Variation), (Creative Thought), (Epistemology).
239 See Campbell (Creative Thought), p. 63.

rules are experimented with. Quite obviously, trial-and-error processes differ greatly in terms of effectiveness, depending on whether they take place at the level of locomotoric behavior or the variations just described are made use of.

*Regarding item 2.*
The second argument against the explanatory adequateness of the trial-and-error principle, metaphorically referred to as the "myth of genius," results from an illusion similar to a delusion of the senses. When someone has a great idea, or a specific thought that for whatever reason is of extraordinary quality, people tend to assume that this person has found that idea by applying a *special method*. This is probably due to a deep bias toward causal thinking, that is, a tendency to explain remarkable outcomes by equally remarkable causes. Even though this kind of cause-and-effect thinking may be biologically significant and genetically embodied, it does lead to a post-hoc-ergo-propter-hoc error.

Of course, the theory of evolutionary problem solving does not negate the existence of creative ideas, flashes of genius and such. It does negate, however, that the distinctiveness of a creative idea has to be due to distinctive elements in the methods leading to it. If ten people guess the points achieved in the next roll of the dice and one of them guesses correctly, that does not change the fact that it was pure guesswork.

Variations of presumptions (in this example regarding the roll of the dice) have to be regarded as equally "good" at first, that is, *before* selection criteria are introduced. Only by applying a selection mechanism or criterion can one of the presumptions be singled out as superior, or correct. Often, however, selection criteria are not within the reach of the "creative genius"; instead they are characteristics of the environment that cannot be controlled. In many cases we will have to assume that an idea is considered creative simply because adequate selection criteria happened to exist in its environment. In many cases it would probably be much better to speak of good or bad luck, rather than of particular creativity or the lack of it.

This post-hoc-ergo-propter-hoc interpretation of results of evolutionary processes also causes misunderstandings about biological evolution. The fact that plants and animals have a very complicated and even miraculous structure and are able to perform remarkable functions often leads us to assume that there must have been equally miraculous processes to create these structures. However, we must remember that when we make such statements, our attention is always focused on the organism, never—or very seldom—on its environment also. If we were to explore the features and properties of that environment we would unearth plenty of evidence to prove that under certain ambient conditions the corresponding organismic features simply had to emerge, as organisms with other characteristics would not have survived in this particular environment. Thus, the distinctive features of the results of evolutionary processes that we encounter are not owed to anything more miraculous than the fact that all other, less adequate variations have been eliminated. As has been discussed at length before, this is precisely the explicative content of evolution theory, and you probably remember that the fact we cannot identify or describe all relevant environmental properties does not suffice to refute evolution theory. The complexity of matters simply reaches an order of magnitude where we are faced with practical impossibilities. As demonstrated, the interplay of relatively simple rules of the evolution mechanism and a virtually unlimited number of distinctive features can lead to outcomes whose existence could ex post be understood to be the result of a highly complicated plan, or at least of a very special mechanism.

Of course, the theory of evolutionary problem solving is far from denying that some people are more creative than others, or that some have great ideas and inspirations all the time while with others it happens very rarely. Under the evolutionary paradigm, this is explained not based on specific qualities, capabilities, or talents of those concerned but based on *differences in applying the evolutionary methodology*. The structural components of the trial-and-error method provide clear indications as to where we can expect to find the differences. If one of two otherwise comparable individuals studies a problem very thoroughly and intensely while the other only deals with it sporadically, we can assume the former to have better chances at solving the problem. Studying a problem intensely will usually lead to a greater number of idea variations, or solution variants, than sporadic efforts. There will be differences as to the number and kind of selection criteria, in the precision and details of how the environment is represented, in the kind and scope of background information, and so on.

All these factors, and a substantial number of additional ones to be discussed later, are much more helpful in explaining the different degrees of creativity than the postulation of exceptional qualities and capabilities—unless those exceptional capabilities are in some people's tendency to produce a very large number of idea variations before they even consider a problem solved, or present their proposed solution to the public. Hardly anyone will doubt that along with the intensity of studying a problem a person's familiarity with that problem will increase, possibly leading to an accumulation of *negative knowledge*, or information on what solution variants have to be considered unsuccessful or at least not very promising.[240] From the previous discussion it is obvious, however, that under the evolutionary paradigm the accumulation of information about dead ends is a result of trial-and-error processes, rather than being owed to particular talents of the problem solver.

*Regarding item 3.*
The third argument against the fundamental significance and the explanatory power of the blind-variation and selective-retention paradigm stems from a field known as artificial intelligence research or heuristic problem solving. The arguments put forward there are based on the view that in most cases— that is, under somewhat complex circumstances—it would take so many trials to successfully conclude a trial-and-error process, that capacity and time considerations preclude the trial-and-error paradigm as a possible problem-solving approach, and that other, better explanations are called for to shed light on the matter of successful problem solving. The same category of views also comprises the statistical calculations that attempt to prove that, for reasons of time, the postulated variation and selection process of natural evolution could never have produced the diversity of species we have today.

In response to any arguments of this kind, the following should be noted:[241]

a. The way language is used to discuss problem-solving processes must not blind us to the fact that both organic and intellectual evolution are far from having solved *all* problems. The fact that everyone speaks of problem-*solving* processes can tempt us to believe that these are all promising or even successful attempts at solving problems. It would generally be better to speak of problem-*handling* processes and approaches, as we have to be keenly aware that there can be no guarantee of successful problem solving. We do not know all relevant problems, nor can we solve all the problems we know, nor can we presume that, once we have solved them, we have found a good or even the best solution. On the contrary, it seems

---

240 At this point I remind the reader of the explanations provided in section 2.22, concerning negative rules of behavior to prohibit certain areas of possible behavior as being risky, not adequate, etc.

241 See Campbell (Blind Variation), pp. 222 et seq.

appropriate to work on the assumption that most problems are not even known to us (which does not mean they are irrelevant), that most of those we know are not solved yet, and that those solved do not have good or even the best solutions. We can thus conclude that with some problems it would take more attempts than is actually feasible to find a solution. That, however, is not an argument to refute the evolutionary approach; it rather illustrates the trivial, but often forgotten fact that some problems (perhaps even most) remain unsolved.

b. Although at first glance it may seem as though the number of attempts required to solve a complex problem under the evolutionary paradigm is beyond any reasonable dimension, we must not underestimate the number of attempts actually made. In a social system in which millions of people deal with the most diverse problems every day and every hour, on the whole we may expect an enormous number of attempts, although most of them will eventually fail. For instance, if in the field of science we look at how much thought is given to a certain set of problems within a certain period of time, and how much of this deliberation is put in words, how much of it is printed, and what part of that eventually proves significant, it seems obvious how small the share of success (or the share of successful attempts) actually is. In view of this ratio it hardly seems necessary to demand specific methods of gaining insight, apart from the evolutionary paradigm.

c. It has been pointed out before that the call alone for a trial-and-error process does not include any details on what the related efforts should entail, or what is experimented with. From an evolutionary perspective, we basically have to randomly allow anything as a potential trial component in the process; that is, we must not exclude any areas, objects, principles, and so on beforehand. This can result in certain difficulties, for it is far from obvious whether each distinct mode of behavior can in itself be regarded as an attempt, or trial, or whether entire behavioral programs comprising a multitude of individual behaviors represent that trial. This circumstance further complicates the problem of the number of necessary trials. However, this difficulty is offset by the fact that there are elimination criteria which are used in every single step, including the *parts* of a large-scale trial program. In any phase of a larger, multi-part trial, once it becomes clear in the light of the selection criteria applied that there is sufficient reason to preclude the trial in question, that trial will be eliminated. Quite obviously, this way an unknown number of variations will be rejected in an early phase, although in the further course of the trial it would have turned out that the trial as a whole would have been better than could have been expected based on those partial results. The immediate application of selection criteria, and thus the rejection of trials in any phase of experimentation, considerably reduces the number of necessary variations, but at the same time causes a large, not specifiable number of potentially successful variations to be excluded early on. The following example should help to illustrate this point. As is generally known, in the field of information theory there have been considerations as to whether, if all conceivable permutations of the alphabet including punctuation marks were used, it would be possible to create a kind of "universal library" comprising everything ever written by humans, as well as anything ever to be written. This universal library would clearly entail all past and future masterpieces of world literature, but also all past and future scientific findings, to the extent that they lend themselves to being articulated in a language. In addition to that, this universal library would contain all kinds of nonsense, as not any combination of letters, words, and punctuation marks adds up to a grammatically acceptable sentence, regardless of whether its content makes sense or is even true. Apart from the fact that according to calculations, the physical size of such a universal library would exceed any realistic dimension, even if it were computerized, and that any related considerations are little more than thought experiments, the example helps to visualize the effect of immediate selection in each individual step. To check which of the volumes of the universal library do make sense and which do not—or in other words, to select the meaningful ones—each volume would have to be eliminated the moment it turns out that this cannot be meaningful language. It is very well possible, however, that a particular volume would begin with a few pages of meaningful text, followed by one or several grammatically unacceptable or meaningless sentences, which would again be followed by meaningful, perhaps even very valuable text. Due to the way the evolutionary paradigm works, however, a volume like that would be eliminated as soon as the first meaningless sentence were detected, regardless of any previous or subsequent text passages. While organic evolution adamantly follows that principle—which explains how a rather reasonable number of variations will produce evolutionary results that may not be optimal in an absolute sense but are still superior to any other results that exist—the principle can of course be attenuated for the areas of creative thinking or problem solving, and generally for the realm of intellectual evolution. Under such a modified approach, one would view negative partial results of experiments in the greater context and consider whether, in the light of the overall experiment, those seemingly negative results might perhaps turn out positive in the end. This modified approach has its limits, of course, for in complex situations or complex series of experiments we must never expect to have all the information required to complete the big picture. So there are certain variation options, yet we have to remember that the strict insistence on applying selection criteria to entire experiments, not to their partial steps, is a clear element of the constructivist or analytical paradigm. The evolutionary method clearly is focused not on finding the best of all possible alternatives, but on obtaining a result by immediately examining each variation for its "value for survival," singling out the first viable variant, and creating new variations on this basis or level. The effects of this approach are illustrated by a set of experiments carried out by Prof. Rechenberg (see figure 2.42(1)). A plane surface consisting of several parts is to be arranged so as to offer minimal aerodynamic resistance. The angular positions of the individual parts vis-à-vis each other can be modified by means of adjustable hinges; at each kink a defined number of settings is possible. For instance, if two parts can be in 30 different angular positions to each other and there is a total of 7 kinks in the surface, this will result in over 21 billion combinations ($30^7$, to be precise). Each combination is a potential solution option. In Rechenberg's experiments, the individual settings for each kink were selected at random. For each setting aerodynamic resistance was measured, and in the case of improvement the setting was retained; further variations were now carried out starting from that level. According to these experiments, this process of approximation, which led from the latest stage of evolution to the next stage, required 300 trials to produce the optimal aerodynamic resistance. That value had been known in advance, of course, as it was clear that an overall plane surface would offer the lowest resistance. Rechenberg carried out a number of related experiments in this context, and was able to demonstrate that the number of 300 trials was relatively stable. If we compare the original complexity—over 21 billion options—with the relatively small number of 300 trials, the effectiveness of the evolutionary approach becomes very obvious.

Figure 2.42(1)

In more complex situations, the optimal solution to a problem will obviously not be known in advance. Still, the logic of evolutionary problem solving and the experiments described here support the assumption that this approach to problem solving can be trusted to be an effective means to manage complexity. So, although we cannot be certain that the results of evolutionary processes are absolutely optimal, there are many indications that the results will be good, and that the evolutionary process described here has a high probability—in the sense of propensity[242]—of producing good results. In view of the great complexity of real-life problem situations, there is not much more one could expect; indeed it seems extraordinarily much already.

d. Regarding the argument that the evolutionary approach cannot be feasible due to the high number of trials required, resulting from the possible number of permutations, the following should be noted. Problem-solving processes are often discussed based on the tacit assumption that every problem-solving process occurs, or is performed, against a *predefined objective*. Relative to a predefined objective, it is certainly possible—irrespective of the three considerations discussed above—for the number of permutations to be still too large to allow performing enough experiments, or trials, in a trial-and-error process. It should be taken into account, however, that many problem-solving processes—first and foremost those in organic evolution—are distinctly "opportunistic" in nature. In many cases, the solution to a problem or the result of a problem-solving process has not been set as a goal beforehand, but the *de facto outcome* is said to have been a goal in retrospect, or at least accepted as a fact to be used as a starting point for all further efforts. The "opportunistic" nature of problem-solving processes is owed to the fact that these processes are usually multipurpose; that is, in most cases they permit applying several selection criteria at once. What is considered negative under one criterion may appear positive under another. Practically speaking, this means you do not only look for solutions to problems raised but also identify a fitting "problem" for "solutions found"—which basically means you try to make use of actual results. A good example of this "opportunistic" aspect of problem solving is so-called fundamental research. A scientist may start on her research effort (e.g., a certain experimental analysis) with a certain purpose in mind; however, in the course of her experiments it may turn out that the outcome originally hoped for cannot be produced, while other results—which may be equally or *also* interesting—are achievable. In that case, nobody can stop that scientist from publishing those unexpected outcomes generated, and it is largely subject to her personal assessment as to whether she wishes to mention that the experiment had been started with other expectations in mind. Both certain human qualities and possibly certain constraints inherent to scientific publications seem to support the assumption that only results actually achieved are published in the end. The effect from that is that

1. a possibly very large number of failures are not mentioned at all and
2. the multi-purpose character of problem-solving processes also remains unmentioned.

That, in turn, may support ex post the common assumption that the scientist has not followed the trial-and-error principle but found her solution in a targeted approach, possibly equipped with extraordinary talent and applying specific, promising methods. These mechanisms, which operate at a totally different level completely unrelated to the actual problem-solving process—such as scientists' personal qualities or certain customs and traditions of the publication system—tend to camouflage the real structure of problem solving, creating a superficial illusion that may lead methodical design efforts gravely astray.

Of course it must be conceded that both in science—specifically in fundamental research, which is often believed to be free of purpose—and in organic evolution there is much more room for the multi-purpose character of problem solving than, for instance, there is in applied research or business management. But even though there will be a much greater degree of restrictions, there is no denying that this principle is often applied here as well. It is particularly obvious, for example, in the area of trade: Although a trading firm will do everything in its power to market a certain, potentially lucrative product, it will hardly hesitate to switch to other products if it turns out—perhaps even as a result of its effort to solve the original problem—that the first product sells poorly, or even just that other products sell better. After all, the solution to a problem often consists not in selling a certain product but in identifying— basically at random—a product that will sell. Of course, this approach is only possible within certain limits, as no company in the world is absolutely free in its actions. HR issues, financing issues, market position issues, and so on set "natural" limits here, although it is certainly possible to act according to the *opportunity principle—as we might call it—within those limits.* The same possibilities are open to manufacturers and service providers, although perhaps not to the same extent. One example here is that it is not always helpful to cling to the objective of creating a profitable product for a certain market; instead one might want to try to find markets for existing products.

In view of the opportunistic character of problem-solving processes, the obvious conclusion is that not every problem is solved, or at least many problems are postponed for an indefinite length of time. Of course, this leaves the question as to whether and to what extent it may become necessary to solve a very specific problem known in advance, and what the consequences would be if that problem could not be solved. Here, I remind you that it would be absolutely unrealistic to expect that *every* problem can be solved. Experience shows that even problems that have vital importance to particular organizations remain unsolved, causing some of these organizations to decline. From that we cannot conclude, however, that there must be a more effective method than the blind trial-and-error process—as desirable as that would be. The only valid conclusion is that there can be *no guarantee* of *successful* problem solving and that, even for a method that has proven remarkably effective over millions of years, there are problems that persistently defy all attempts at solution.

As initially mentioned, the problem of the number of trials required, or of the permutations possible, first arose in the course of research in the field of heuristic problem solving. As doubts about the constructivist approach were raised on several occasions and as the realization spread that a method based on rigorous requirements would hardly ever be feasible, scientists began working on methods that would represent a systematic and well-thought-through *advancement of a set of rules of thumb.* The intention was to use said rules to reduce the enormous search spaces in which potential solutions to complex problems generally have to be sought. Studies on the heuristics of problem solving are of utmost importance, of course, as they represent a major step forwards compared to the constructivist paradigm.

However, related research was often performed with the intention (or secondary motive) to refute the evolutionary paradigm of the trial-and-error process. So far, these efforts have not been successful. After all, while a heuristic rule—*once found*—is a huge step forward compared to a pure trial-and-error process, the act of searching for heuristic problem-solving rules requires trial-and-error processes. Heuristic problem-solving rules are not simply given; they have to be identified, and whenever such a rule appears to have been found the question is whether the underlying assumption proves true. In other words, rules have to be tested and good rules must be distinguishable from not-so-good ones—possibly by applying tentative selection criteria which, again, have to be identified in an evolutionary approach.

In other words, there are blind-variation and selective-retention processes which themselves deal with heuristic rules. As pointed out several times before, it is not defined upfront what the *subject* of trial-and-error processes is or could be, and since heuristic rules usually contain information on the possible *solution space to be explored*, the investigation of heuristic principles clearly implies some sort of intelligence amplification (or variety amplification, to use a cybernetic term). After all, the more or less substantiated selection of search spaces (using tentatively proven heuristics) will give all further problem-solving activities the *directedness* commonly regarded as a sign of intelligence. However, as also pointed out repeatedly, it would be naïve to assume that trial-and-error processes can only be one-level processes. On the contrary, we have to assume that there are entire hierarchies of such processes and that the trial-and-error process at each hierarchical level deals with other elements than the process before. Thus, the fact that search activities are directed to some extent does not necessarily mean there are direct, insightful, and immediately goal-oriented problem-solving processes; instead, it is an indicator that a major part of the job has already been completed by the blind-variation and selective-retention processes at upstream (higher or more abstract) levels. In sum, we could either say that trial-and-error processes can *stimulate* intelligent behavior or intelligence, or else that such processes *are* mechanisms of intelligence.

## 2.43 Special Aspects of the Evolutionary Problem-Solving Methodology

The previous discussion seemed necessary because these two arguments against the universality and effectiveness of the evolutionary method, although refuted, keep coming up again and again. They are intellectual traps which keep people from truly understanding the power of the evolutionary paradigm, and which result in the frequent objection according to which trial-and-error processes are a primitive and trivial approach that makes sense at the level of primitive forms of life—if at all—and at higher levels, particularly that of human beings, has to be replaced by other methods.

With my above remarks I hope to have shown that the evolutionary approach is of fundamental importance for the management of complexity in its most challenging form, that is, when genuine lack of knowledge is to be eliminated. Nevertheless, we must not forget that in the course of natural evolution, this very evolutionary approach has produced various heuristic principles. It can be a considerable advantage to know and apply these principles, as this can help to abbreviate trial-and-error processes considerably. Research in this field is still in its infancy, but some principles and tricks are known and will be discussed in the following paragraphs.

Mechanisms and procedures to manage complexity have several characteristics in common. To understand and assess them, it is necessary to first identify the difficulties posed by the problem of complexity management itself. As I have repeatedly pointed out here, the problem of managing complexity is located at a higher level than the solution of specific, content-driven problems. Upon superficial scrutiny, the problems faced by both organisms and institutions are all content-driven. That, however, blocks the view of their *general* characteristics. However, since simple and complex problems require fundamentally different modes of behavior and strategies, as I hope to have shown, successful problem-solving behavior in organisms can be expected to have different general characteristics depending on whether the situation is complex or simple—regardless of what the specific problem is.

The following three aspects are relevant here:

1. While under the constructivist method all attention is sort of outward-focused, that is, at a comprehensive analysis of the environment, much of the evolutionary paradigm's logica is *inward*-focused, that is, at the organism's (institution's) internal functions and structures.

2. As is generally known, complexity can take two forms: numerical uncertainty or structural uncertainty. In the case of numerical uncertainty, it is largely unknown what values the variables involved will have, but the relevant variables themselves are known and so may the connections between them be. So, complexity is located at the detail level while there is some structural information available. In the case of structural uncertainty, the problem is much more difficult, as almost nothing is known about the relevant structures, that is, about the relevant variables and their connections. In both cases, the evolutionary method aims to eliminate uncertainty by introducing *conventions*, that is, by *imposing a structure* on the situation, thus making it manageable and possibly even predictable. This method—or trick, if you will—of imposing a structure is largely alien to the constructivist paradigm, which is focused on analysis, and has caused a number of misunderstandings.

3. From a cybernetic perspective, while it would be incorrect to maintain that decision making or problem solving is located exclusively in the human brain, the brain's function undoubtedly plays an important part. As the human brain (or generally any kind of brain) is a prime example of a complexity-managing organ, and since it has clearly emerged from an evolutionary process, we can assume certain structural commonalities of cognitive processes to be important to the understanding of the evolutionary problem-solving methodology. These commonalities will now be discussed.

### 2.431 Internalization of Process Logic

The prototype of a problem-solving mechanism with an internalized process logic is the homeostat described by Ashby.[243]

This non-teleological stabilization mechanism is able to function in an environment where it has absolutely no information or theoretical understanding in the sense of the constructivist paradigm, and thus to survive in a very general sense. Rather than relying on a comprehensive causal analysis of its environment, the homeostatic mechanism operates based on *internal stability criteria*, or in Ashby's terminology, "essential variables."[244] The basic principle of the homeostatic mechanism, or the ultra-stable system, is that every disturbance in internal equilibrium criteria is countered with behaviors

---

243 See also Beer (Brain), p. 38 and section 1.51.
244 See Ashby (Brain), pp. 80 et seq.

from a standard repertoire. If these behaviors succeed in returning critical variables to an acceptable range, the system will reach a steady state; if they fail, other possible behaviors from the repertoire will be tested one by one. The mechanism goes on like this until the necessary degree of stability is achieved.

I suppose it is not necessary to elaborate on the functions of the ultra-stable system at this point, as it has been described in detail elsewhere.[245] I will just mention its two key characteristics: First, based on internal stability criteria established in a previous evolutionary process it can determine whether the organism is in an acceptable state relative to its environment; second, if that is not the case it can respond with a behavior from its standard repertoire. Behaviors in that repertoire are well-programmed, established behavioral routines which are selected as appropriate responses to regain stability.

In Ashby's basic model, this selection happens at random statistically. However, in view of what I have explained earlier regarding the problem of evolutionary selection, in this case we should rather imagine this selection to be blind in Campbell's sense, and of course with several overlaying levels of logically similar processes it is possible to achieve the directedness of processes discussed earlier. The point is that in the basic model possible modes of response do *not have to be developed anew* but are available and ready for use as behavioral programs.[246] Another key point is that a behavioral program is selected and triggered by *changing internal states* of equilibrium criteria, and not, as erroneously assumed, by performing an anticipatory analysis of causal relationships in the environment. As Stafford Beer points out in several places, the term "ultra-stability" refers to the system's very ability to resist even disturbances that have not, indeed could not have been foreseen by its designer.[247]

Under the constructivist paradigm this would be considered to be impossible. From a constructivist perspective, to construct a mechanism that is stable or can reach stable relations with its environment, it would be necessary to have all the relevant information. Cybernetics has shown, however—and that is probably its greatest achievement—that there are control mechanisms capable of responding even to unforeseen and unpredictable disturbances or threats to the system, and of doing so in ways that will preserve the system's existence. Centrifugal governors and gyroscopes are examples of such

---

245 See Ashby (Brain), pp. 80 et seq.; Gomez, Malik, and Oeller (Systemmethodik), pp. 558 et seq.
246 See also Lorenz (Rückseite), pp. 67 et seq.
247 See inter alia Beer (Platform), p. 108; see also Beer (Brain), pp. 35 et seq.

mechanisms: They keep machines, ships, airplanes, and so forth on a defined course, regardless of what the causes of possible deviations may be. As Beer explains, they achieve this not by analyzing the causality of the situation to get to the root of the problem, but by determining pathologic symptoms within themselves that they can use to define control measures. Beer referred to this principle as the principle of intrinsic control.[248]

Although Ashby's basic model of the ultra-stable system and its functional principles has not been refuted to this date, one must not commit the error of using this cybernetic-evolutionary mechanism as a standard model for highly complicated problem-solving processes in social systems. As explained several times before, wherever causal knowledge is available and the necessary environment models can be filled with sufficient information, this will permit a problem-solving behavior superior to the evolutionary paradigm. The question is, then, what a meaningful approach would be in situations too complex to set up the required causal models. Between the purely evolutionary model, represented by Ashby's homeostat in its simplest form, and the purely constructivist model, where a comprehensive causal model permits the necessary calculations to determine the optimal decision, there is a broad range of intermediate forms. We must not overlook, however, that the evolutionary method has more points in its favor, as it helps address both simple and complex problems, while the constructivist approach can only be used in relatively simple situations.

A single-cell organism such as an ameba is certainly able to find its way through a territory strewn with obstacles by applying the evolutionary approach. From a higher-level perspective, it would clearly be possible to achieve effective behavior by means of constructivist methods. However, with the control and behavioral options available to the ameba, such territory is so complex that its problems can only be solved with the evolutionary approach. Now while humankind and its social systems are equipped with much more information and intelligence, the problems to be solved are much more complex, too. That is why even at this level, applying the evolutionary approach is often the only way to deal with problems adequately.

As Beer points out, in business management we are often expected to eliminate disturbances without knowing the causes. "This idea is very important in management, because it may often take too long to identify the cause of trouble and to correct it at source. The common belief that this is the only

---

248 See Beer (Platform), p. 108; see also Powers (Behavior), pp. 44 et seq.

scientific way of proceeding is mistaken, and derives from a very old-fashioned view of science itself."[249] When we dispense with a full causal analysis and concentrate on the internal monitoring of stability criteria or critical variables, as well as on a sophisticated, well-programmed repertoire of responses, this translates into an enormous reduction of the varieties involved and enables the organism or institution to comply with Ashby's Law of Requisite Variety. The large quantities of information required for causal analysis are reduced to those pieces of information that are captured by the channels immediately associated with stability criteria. In other words, information is used not to analyze the environment but to monitor internal events. Under this paradigm, the only information relevant is the kind that supports the internal monitoring. As Steinbruner observes, the secret of managing variety is that, at least in the simplest of cases, cybernetics mechanisms are not even faced with the problem of variety because they do not analyze the environment. All they do is monitor some internal variables; they are completely blind to the environment.[250]

This does not mean, of course, that the Law of Requisite Variety can be evaded or considered invalid here. If environmental variety is relevant to the organism or institution, there must be ways to cope with that variety in order to survive. Consequently, the focus of the problem is on the question as to how environmental variety can be reduced or organismic variety increased. Any organism that manages to replace causal environmental models and their enormous information requirements with internal stability criteria has increased its own variety. On the other hand, when all information is ignored that is not captured by the established channels, the result is a considerable reduction of variety. A focus on internal stability criteria and on the associated information channels, which provide a link to specific segments of the environment considered relevant, tends to have a stereotypical character and may even lead to very rigid system structures.

Even when an organism may have survived this way until a certain point, this is no guarantee of future survival because there is always a possibility that new environmental variety will emerge that proves detrimental to the organism. Of course, it is conceivable—and has to be assumed for complex systems—that these processes, like any evolutionary process, do not occur at one level only. While from a certain perspective an organism's behavior may seem rather stereotypical due to the internal stability criteria used and

249 See Beer (Platform), p. 109.
250 See Steinbruner (Cybernetic Theory), p. 57.

the largely preprogrammed repertoire of behaviors, it is certainly possible to monitor the adequacy of processes, critical variables, and behavioral repertoires by means of other processes occurring at a higher or meta-systemic level and in which logically superordinate stability criteria and behaviors are applied. At a later point I hope to show that management can largely be explained by focusing on these higher-level monitoring processes, and by implementing detection processes to identify and eliminate the inadequacy of lower-level processes.

A critical variety problem arises from the richness of the behavioral repertoire. When we speak of highly programmed behaviors here, it should be noted that there are at least two kinds of programming:

a. one focusing on the concrete result of a behavioral routine, and
b. one that, irrespective of the result, only programs the way in which the behavior is to occur.

Based on what has been said earlier about the phenomenon of rule compliance and in general on the role that behavioral rules play, it is evident that the second kind of programming will enormously increase an organism's variety. For instance, human language is very highly programmed structurally, which says nothing about the specific content of what is being said. Similarly, the motion sequence required for walking is almost entirely programmed, while the concrete purposes or results to be achieved are largely open and only depend on the programming in a very general sense. This also means that an organismic repertoire of behaviors focuses not on any concrete results to be achieved in the environment, but on the rules that have proven to produce successful behavior, which means they are a product of previous evolutionary processes.[251]

Steinbruner points out that a decision maker following this kind of cybernetic approach will use information processing techniques and methods which *de facto* produce decisions and results, without actually having dealt with the desired results psychologically. "Cybernetic mechanisms which achieve uncertainty control do so by focusing the decision process on a few incoming variables while eliminating entirely any serious calculation of probable outcome."[252] The reason it is possible to ignore the concrete results of behaviors is that behavior is programmed in a specific sense discussed earlier. As pointed out before, rules of behavior govern areas of behavior, and only in those areas will

---

251 See section 2.22 for relevant remarks on the emergence and creation of order.
252 See Steinbruner (Cybernetic Theory), p. 66.

the concrete result be uncertain. In other words, programming gives behaviors a specific direction and their adequacy is a result of evolution; however, determining the concrete outcome would require more information than can be processed. In this context it should also be clear that the critical or essential variables monitored internally can be variables of a very specific kind, namely *those very rules of behavior*, or sets of behavioral rules.

It is all too easy to fall for the assumption that such mechanisms require variables such as temperature, blood pressure, blood sugar levels, oxygen concentration, liquid funds, profit, cost, sales, and so on. On the other hand, the way things are done, or the *principles of behavior*, can be variable, too, and can thus be potential monitoring objects in an ultra-stable system. One of the most obvious examples is the legal system in a civilized society: Rather than being focused on specific content-related results, it will stipulate certain rules of behavior that help legal subjects achieve desired results. For instance, apart from a few exceptions, contractual law does not stipulate any specific content for the different types of contracts (such as a purchase contract). After all, legislators cannot create specific rules for just any conceivable thing that could ever be the subject of a purchase contract. That would clearly be an attempt to violate the laws of managing variety. Instead, legislators will stipulate in contractual law that in the case that legal entities wish to conclude a purchase contract, no matter what the subject, there are specific rules to be observed. Hence, the judiciary is largely an institution that has to ensure that certain critical variables—here: the rules of contractual law—are observed inside the system (that is, in society). At a later point I hope to demonstrate that in management, too—at least at the senior levels—the critical variables to be monitored (and, in a wider sense, designed) internally consist not so much in concrete results as in the way certain behavioral routines have to be adhered to.

## 2.432 Imposing a Structure

Let me reiterate here that besides what we call numerical uncertainty, *structural* uncertainty is of crucial and even greater importance. Structural uncertainty exists when in a given situation not only are the concrete values of the variables are unknown, but it is also unclear what variables are relevant and how they are connected. To give you one example: When you flip a coin you cannot know in advance whether it will land heads or tails, but you do know that it has to be either one or the other. It is a very different kind of uncertainty when you do not even know whether the next toss will be done with a coin or with, say, a die or several dice, several coins, combinations of dice and coins, or any other result-producing machine.

There is no doubt that many situations, particularly in the management of social systems, are characterized by this structural uncertainty. Even the most laborious and intense analysis will hardly provide us with full certainty that not even one of the variables, drivers, and so on potentially relevant for the decision—and none of the interdependencies between them—has been left unconsidered. When all attempts to gather all the relevant information cannot produce the desired result, the only way to deal with the situation is to impose one's own structures on the environment. In other words, whenever we are unable to *identify* any kind of order that will enable us to behave in a meaningful way, we still have the possibility of *creating* that order in the environment. This can happen, for instance, by setting up organizational procedures, routines, programs, and so on—in short: rules of behavior. As this topic has been discussed at length elsewhere, at this point it should suffice to highlight just one aspect. Opponents of the creation of order, the imposing of structures, and the setting of rules often argue that this is nothing but decisionism and it will never be possible to justify why one specific rule was chosen over another. However, if this line or argument were continued in perfect logic we would have to be opposed to any kind of organizational procedure, as there is always a multitude of *possible* rules and it will hardly ever be feasible to provide evidence as to why one specific rule *must* be accepted. You see, this way of thinking culminates in what Hayek calls "scientism," an attitude where any normative design of systems is rejected as being non-scientific.

This basic attitude can be countered in two ways:

1.  One is by showing that order can only emerge when certain rules are followed by the elements of that order. Here, I refer to the related discussion in earlier sections. It may be the case that the very first rule defined to create order in a complex situation is chosen arbitrarily; however, if it is to create order it cannot be modified arbitrarily at a later point. Imagine you are rowing across a lake in a rowboat: You will usually choose a point of orientation to stay on course, which can be just any fixed point within a larger area. It may be a church tower, a very tall tree, a telephone pole or any other landmark clearly visible to you. In other words, to control

your course it is not relevant whether your point of orientation is chosen at random but whether and to what extent it can be modified. Similarly, in business enterprises it is often much less important whether a decision, a rule, or the like to structure a complex situation is or is not determined at random; what matters much more is that a decision is taken at all, and that there are such things as procedures and rules allowing the formation of stable expectations.

2. The problem of decisionism occurs not only in disciplines commonly accused of producing normative distortion, but also in the natural sciences, which are generally believed to be objective. Popper has shown that in all sciences, the question as to whether or not an observation is acceptable contains a conventional element, and hence a decision. That, however, does not justify the widespread conclusion that such decisions are *arbitrary*.[253] Just as in courts of law the question of innocence or guilt is answered after lengthy deliberations and in accordance with certain rules, in science the decision on whether to accept or reject an observation is generally preceded by active debate. One might therefore refer to the acceptance or rejection of an observation as a decision or convention, as there will never be full certainty as to the truth or falseness of an observation; however, it would be wrong to call that decision arbitrary. Instead, it is made to the best of the decision makers' knowledge and belief, and in the light of all information available to them at the time. Of course, errors can never be fully excluded, but that cannot be regarded as arbitrariness.

It is similar with behavioral rules. You will hardly ever structure unknown territory by means of rules. In most cases, some rules already exist (as a result of an evolutionary process) and any change or creation of rules will have to consider that the outcome will also be influenced by the existing rules. If you want to generate abstract attributes of order (which can demonstrably cope with complexity), it is definitely possible to furnish scientific proof of the need for very specific rules—even though they are clearly normative in character. Although this point should be clear from the previous discussion, it will be discussed in further detail below when we deal with discovery processes. For instance, if complexity analysis reveals that certain pieces of information can only be gathered if the systematic conditions for discovery processes

---

253 See Popper (Replies), pp. 1110 et seq.; and Popper (Society), pp. 380 et seq.

are created, we can conclude that very specific rules—those that drive discovery processes—have to be set.

Order is necessary for survival, that is, to be able to form stable expectations regarding certain classes of events. To the extent that order cannot be identified in the environment, in an objectivist manner if you will, it is necessary to create order, that is, impose a structure on a situation. As will be shown at a later point, one way for this to happen is based on cognitive functions, in that the individual construes the particular situation to entail certain subjective categories; but more than anything else, structure is created by establishing institutions. As far as subjective cognitive biases are concerned, it is safe to assume that the categories used must have made sense in the past at the very least, given that they are a result of an evolutionary process. However, whether structuring by social institutions, and in particular under a constructivist social theory, makes just as much sense is another question. I seriously doubt it. Based on the latest research in this field, the cybernetic or evolutionary paradigm—which was long relatively open in this aspect, for reasons not entirely acceptable—can now be completed. I am referring to the social theory established by Friedrich von Hayek, and to Stafford Beer's research of the viable system. The fact that we have considerable knowledge today about the design of adaptive structures allows us not only to keep evolution going but also to give it the direction it needs to produce and retain viable structures.

### 2.433 Cognitive Functional Principles as Elements of Evolutionary Problem Solving

As an outcome of an evolution process that has taken millions of years, the human brain has found ways to cope with complexity on earth. That does not mean it could not be exposed to situations whose complexity would overstrain its capacity. On the contrary, it is relatively simple to set up experimental situations in which a person loses much or all of the control over him or herself, which ultimately drives him or her to a nervous breakdown or something of the sort. Even in everyday life we often face situations where the human brain is strained to the limits of its capacity in dealing with complexity. One example everyone knows from first-hand experience is street traffic at certain times of the day, or during certain times of the year; typical indicators include accidents due to lack of response or inappropriate reactions. And there is a series of other behaviors typically found in stressful situations like these, such as people refusing to deal with a problem any further, people caught in stereotypical ways of thinking, killer phrases, and so on.

While criticism of these behaviors is certainly in order, the question is whether they could be expressions of specific cognitive processes in dealing with complexity. Indeed, some research findings in this field support the assumption that they are extreme manifestations of perfectly normal, highly efficient mechanisms of complexity management which serve us well every day, although we never even give them a thought, let alone fully realize how they help us manage complexity. The "tricks" for mastering complexity which have been "devised" by evolution in the course of developing the human brain can give us valuable hints as to how problem-solving processes should be designed in general. If the constructivist paradigm were valid, extreme complexity would have to put decision makers and problem solvers in a state of indecision and inactivity, as by definition there would be too little information to permit the kind of rational choice required by that problem-solving paradigm. According to Steinbruner, that is not the case. Using the U.S. involvement in the Vietnam War and the Cuban Missile Crisis as examples,[254] he shows that while governments tend to delay decisions, which is understandable in view of the inherent uncertainty, they do not become inactive. The same is true for any decision maker. In the course of active, possibly hectic information search processes, stable opinion systems as to how the situation is to be assessed will form relatively quickly. These opinions are partly results of people's earlier experiences, education, and current state of information; but of course, aspects such as personality and cultural links can be relevant as well.

Hardly ever will there be sufficient knowledge available in such situations to reach a decision that is acceptable from a constructivist point of view. To explain the formation of relatively stable opinions about a problem situation, influenced by very incomplete knowledge and the other factors mentioned, one has to assume that certain cognitive operations occur which—unnoticed by the decision maker—artificially close existing information gaps. From an evolutionary point of view, the cognitive processes operating here have obviously been successful, considering that the human race has survived so far. Of course, that does not tell us anything about the future, as nothing can guarantee that these cognitive processes will also be appropriate complexity-

---

254 See Steinbruner (Cybernetic Theory), pp. 88 et seq.

controlling tools when new problem situations with new dimensions of complexity come up. Regardless, as the human central nervous system including the brain is a prime example of an adaptation mechanism, representing a survival machine that works on evolutionary principles itself, we can expect to derive valuable insights from the knowledge of cognitive mechanisms when it comes to analyzing and designing complex problem-solving and decision-making processes.

Although in both cognitive psychology and cybernetics there are plenty of controversies to this date, some basic principles of cognitive processes can be listed that are widely recognized.[255] These principles are:

1. the inferential principle,
2. the consistency principle,
3. the reality principle,
4. the simplicity principle,
5. the stability principle, and
6. the abstraction principle.

These six functional principles of cognitive operations help to explain a series of distinctive features of evolutionary problem solving; at the same time, they can be observed in designing such processes, either in general or in specific manifestations. To facilitate your understanding of the following, I should emphasize that the discussion will not focus on the content to be processed either by the human brain in general or by any specific human brain: Such content occurs in such numerous and diverse variants that it appears impossible to capture it in a general statement. The question rather is what processing rules govern that content and what processing mechanisms are required for any content to be produced at all. To give an example, it will hardly ever be possible to know what a person X will think or feel in a situation Y at a point in time Z. It does seem possible, though, to establish in-principle statements and forecasts of the kind discussed earlier: for instance, that a type A person faced with a type B situation will respond with type C behavior.

*The Inferential Principle*
In epistemology it was long a widely held opinion that the human brain or mind more or less passively receives incoming signals or perceptions, from

---

255 Regarding the following, see Steinbruner (Cybernetic Theory), pp. 88 et seq.

which an image of reality is formed. Today it is an established fact that this view was wrong, and that we can assume the human brain to play a very active role in the process of acquiring knowledge. This is also confirmed by psychological and cognitive research. We further have to assume that many signals are even created by the organism's activities.

Hence the brain can be understood to be a kind of conclusion machine, capable of creating and completing information. It is thus able not only to perceive patterns but also to form them. Of course, we cannot automatically assume the conclusions the brain uses to form patterns to work the same way as a conclusion in formal logic. The latter, as is generally known, is to be understood as a transformation of truth and falsehood values: By making a logically admissible deduction, one will always derive true conclusions from true premises. The same cannot be assumed for the way in which the human brain works. The patterns that the brain forms from fragments of information, by way of constructional operations, do not necessarily have to be correct, not even when each of the fragments is definitely correct.

So, the key aspect of the inferential principle with regard to problem solving and decision making is not that the brain draws the right conclusions but that it is capable of drawing conclusions at all. It must be considered, however, that these conclusions can be either true or false, and in a stricter sense it has to be assumed that most conclusions drawn this way will probably be false. Nevertheless, cognitive operations based on the inferential principle are very important mechanisms to manage complexity and eliminate uncertainty. From an uncertain situation where only fragmented information is available, the brain sort of creates a subjectively certain situation by supplementing the missing pieces of information. In a logical sense, these are mostly inadmissible leaps in the chain of logical deductions; from a psychological perspective the organism eliminates the uncertainty inherent in a situation.

*The Consistency Principle*

In formal logic, admissible deductions are limited by the requirement to transform truth values. While this is not the case for factual deduction mechanisms in the human brain, these mechanisms obviously follow a kind of consistency principle. This means that of two contradicting pieces of information, one is eliminated and the other retained. It is enormously difficult to say what kind of consistency criteria are applied in each case, what kind of information is retained and what is eliminated. Yet it is a common, almost everyday observation that most people will hesitate to let go of the opinions they have formed even when the opposite proves to be true. Opinion and conviction structures are very stable, at least for grown-ups (see the stability principle discussed further below), and the cognitive operations are constantly working to ensure that stability will not be threatened by the constantly emerging incompatibilities between new and old information content.

Again, it is obvious how this operation helps to master complexity. In truly complex situations, we always have to be ready for contradicting messages and pieces of information, and it is typically very difficult to form a halfway sustainable opinion about the situation. Consequently, the brain operates according to the motto "better to have an incorrect opinion than to have no opinion at all."

As in individual cases in the context of complex matters, it is very difficult, if not impossible, to furnish proof of truth or correctness, and since in such situations there are at least possibilities to actively influence matters, this cognitive principle of operation is not as irrational as is sometimes assumed.Holding on to certain systems of convictions and opinions and eliminating any information that contradicts them enables the organisms to achieve the orientation in its environment that it needs to survive. So, the consistency principle can be understood to be a variant of the principle of imposing a structure that has been discussed earlier. In sum, the brain performs what one may call active inconsistency management (by eliminating inconsistencies) based on mechanisms which are not justifiable from a constructivist point of view, but which, together with the other principles yet to be discussed, form a very powerful instrument of complexity management.

Bearing in mind Steinbruner's findings,[256] within this inconsistency management three key mechanisms can be distinguished:

a. Use of similarities, metaphors, and analogies
b. Wishful thinking
c. Impossibility statements and devaluation of alternatives.

Regarding item a).
*Analogies*: When observations on complex matters are contradictory and it is impossible to form a meaningful impression based on the information

---

256 See Steinbruner (Cybernetic Theory), pp. 115 et seq.

available, people often resort to analogies or similarity statements. The complexity of the current situation is neglected by resorting to simpler, better known, more familiar situations and using them as a model for dealing with the problem at hand. There are numerous examples from history to show how military commanders have tended to apply formerly proven formations or strategies to current situations without doing a careful analysis of the matters at hand, in particular potential differences compared to those past situations. This phenomenon particularly occurs in times of crisis, that is, in situations requiring quick and determined action and leaving little time for lengthy deliberations. But even longer-term political concepts can be based on very simple analogies, as recent history's political doctrines have impressively shown.

For instance, the domino theory has caused America's post-war foreign policy to largely ignore the inherent complexity of the political situation in the Middle and Far East, basing political decisions on a rather simple—in this case too simple—model. One situation was used as an analogy for another, thus disregarding the numerous subtle yet, in retrospect, crucial differences between them. The requirement to consider all details and minute differences between the particular situations would have probably overstrained the decision-making and intellectual capacities of the individuals and institutions involved. The fact that in many cases this and other principles of evolutionary problem solving have produced results that must be regarded as negative in retrospect cannot be used as an argument to support the constructivist approach. Situations like these are always much too complex for constructivist methods; however, as has been pointed out several times before, neither can there be any success guarantees for the evolutionary approach. Above all, however, it has to be stressed that a peculiar and almost tragic mix of constructivist claims and factual-evolutionary approach produced precisely the negative results which would not in the least be inherent to the evolutionary problem-solving approach itself.

*Regarding item b).*
*Wishful thinking:* Lately there has been an increasing call for long-term thinking and concepts of longer-term relevance. Still, decision makers' thinking is often focused on relatively short time spans, precisely because long-term perspectives tend to add a lot of complexity to the decision-making process. In complex situations, however, even with short decision-making horizons there are often inconsistencies, in that a situation takes a different course

from what decision makers have expected. These inconsistencies are eliminated by assuming that short-term negative developments will turn positive
in the longer run. One typical example is the activities at international stock
and commodity exchanges: Indecision in the face of downward price trends,
which would actually require a very quick response, can be rationalized by
"transforming" what was originally intended as a short-term engagement
into a long-term investment. Of course, the expectation that the long-term
trend will be positive is frustrated just as often as it is confirmed. Nonethe-
less, what we have here is a fundamental mechanism of inconsistency management, or complexity management, for speculative stock exchange operations are subject to so much uncertainty—particularly in times of hectic
price fluctuations—that an escape into wishful thinking often appears to be
the only way to cope with the complexity at hand.

*Regarding item c).*
*Impossibility statements and devaluating alternatives:* According to the consistency principle, the "correctness" and "tenability" of opinions, views, and
beliefs formed in the course of a problem-solving process is often defended
and maintained by describing their alternative as being unfeasible or inadequate. Often, the only justification decision makers have is that they have
already made up their minds concerning essential aspects of the problem.
Considering further aspects or options that might collide with the opinions
they have formed would create instabilities in their opinion structures, thus
adding to the complexity of the situation, which is why it is perceived as
emotionally irritating and unpleasant. If the requirements of the constructivist paradigm had to be met, in many cases it would be impossible to ever
reach a decision due to the enormous number of potential alternatives. Often it is the mechanism of claiming unfeasibility or devaluating alternatives
that enables decision makers to reach a decision at all. The motto here is,
"Better to take a suboptimal decision than to take no decision at all." Hence,
cognitive operations of this kind—which, as has to be emphasized here, usually occur subconsciously—also help to cope with complexity.

Undeniably, the mechanisms of complexity management discussed here,
which are based on subjective or cognitive operations, sometimes lead to
very poor results and can even have devastating consequences for the organism. Still, it must be reiterated that this is not an argument in favor of the
constructivist paradigm. If the situation that an organism or an institution
faces were simpler, if there were more information available on the matters

at hand, these mechanisms of complexity management would clearly not be necessary. Better or rational decisions would certainly be possible if situations were not subject to continuous change and if the necessary information could be gathered. These conditions cannot be provided. Consequently, the need for more rationality in problem solving and decision making cannot be fulfilled by demanding impracticable methods and pointing to the undoubted shortcomings of complexity-managing mechanisms; instead, we should try to specify the field of application for those mechanisms by clearly identifying their strengths and weaknesses so they can be used appropriately.

*The Reality Principle*
Irrespective of all philosophical thought loops conceivable in this context, it is a cybernetic basic principle for the organism to be in close contact with its environment. Even if it is impossible to say precisely what "reality" is, based on an evolutionary perspective we must assume that organisms would not have survived if their cognitive functions had developed regardless of the environment. We have to assume that the brain, as initially mentioned, has superbly adapted to the realities of the environment and its operations are adequate for these realities. The inferential principle and the consistency principle are only understandable when combined with the reality principle, that is, when the basic functional mechanisms of cognitive operations are limited by including the given realities. Hence, consistency also means "consistent with reality," for consistency alone, for its own sake if you will, would not suffice to ensure the organism's survival—even if it is an extremely important principle. We can expect, then, that the cognitive mechanisms are connected to the outside world by selective but highly efficient information channels, and that they possess critical correction capabilities to correct the internal consistency of the system of opinion and belief.

*The Simplicity Principle*
Another cognitive mechanism to master complexity consists in simplifying matters, even when there is no objective justification. This is partly due to the fact that information is taken in and processed selectively, and that it is never possible to take account of all aspects of a matter. The simplicity principle works with the inferential principle and the consistency principle to simplify both the conclusions and the retention or creation of consistency of cognitive structures. Above all, it is the studies in gestalt psychology which

have revealed that, for instance, visual perception tends to produce simple rather than complex structures.

The same is true for the cognitive assumption, opinion, and belief structures that serve to explain and interpret reality: Here, too, simple explanation and interpretation formulas are usually preferred to complex ones. To give you one example: In complex problem-solving and decision-making processes—which, among other things, typically have large numbers of competing values and objectives—decision makers, instead of weighing and thus integrating these competing values and objectives, tend to act as though the individual values and objectives could be pursued simultaneously and independently of one another. This is not to say that there is no weighing of competing values and objectives; it certainly does occur. My observation here is that in very complex situations the brain tends to resort to simplification strategies to be able to gain control of complexity, or in other words, to keep up its own operation. The fundamental difference between the constructivist and the evolutionary paradigm is very obvious here: There is no doubt it would be more rational in a sense (a constructivist sense) to consider the full complexity of matters in a decision-making process, instead of ignoring parts of it and adopting simplification strategies; however, the reason that the cognitive mechanisms work that way is that when we are faced with extreme complexity, what matters is their functionality rather than their rationality. There are basically two options: becoming dysfunctional due to overstrain of cognitive capacity, or continuing to be operational, although at a lower level of rationality.[257]

### The Stability Principle

The way cognitive mechanisms work tends to uphold the cognitive structures themselves. Or in other words, all other principles have the effect of safeguarding the stability of the cognitive systems. It is difficult to say what particular content of cognitive structures is stabilized that way, one reason being the enormous diversity of concrete cognitive content, as pointed out earlier. Yet in the particular case it should be possible, at least to some extent, to find out a person's stable views and convictions by way of smart questions and appropriate experiments.

---

257 See Hayek (Studien), pp. 44–46.

Although in individual cases—for example, when putting together a management team—it may be of utmost importance to know the stable contents of individuals' minds, it is even more important for the design of decision-making and problem-solving processes to know that there are stabilization mechanisms and that stable thinking categories can be used to structure uncertain situations. There is hardly a real-life situation so simple and certain that the human brain would be nothing but a receiving mechanism or a registry machine. In almost every case, information and signals have to be organized actively. Internally stable interpretation formulas and cognitive categories are used to structure the environmental information, transforming it into orders and thus making it understandable and meaningful.

For the time being, it remains an open question as to what kind of information leads to the stabilization or destabilization of internal cognitive systems. One frequently held view is that the stability of opinion structures is a function of previous reinforcing operations; that is, opinions will be more stable, the more often a certain opinion structure has proven valid. That would mean there is some kind of induction mechanism at work which can accumulate information about the successful use of cognitive structures and, as the number of positive cases grows, increases the stability of the structures concerned. Based on modern epistemology, in particular Karl Popper's work,[258] it must be assumed that this stabilization results from unsuccessful attempts at refutation. Hence, the only way a new piece of information could have a stabilizing effect is if it could potentially have challenged the cognitive structure.

Whatever the answer to the question about specific stabilization mechanisms will ultimately be, the key fact is that problem-solving processes function based on internally stabilized cognitive structures whose purpose it is to interpret and organize situations.

### The Abstraction Principle

It has been described in earlier sections how general or abstract rules work in organizing social systems. To understand the mental processes that are an essential and defining element of social systems and the problem-solving processes occurring there, it is important to note that the phenomenon

---

258 See Popper (Logik), (Conjectures), (Knowledge).

known as the human mind is subject to the same laws as all other spontaneous orders. This is particularly important in the context of the problem of abstractness or concreteness of mental processes and operations.[259]

It is generally assumed that *concrete* experiences are a primary factor in terms of time, logic, and cause-effect relations, and that abstract thinking categories, *abstract* concepts, and explanation patterns are *derived* from these concrete experiences. This view further leads to the assumption that concrete thinking is closer to reality, and that thinking in abstract categories is poorer in content, further from reality, and less pragmatic in a certain sense. In particular under the constructivist paradigm, the use of abstractions—such as creating order in a system by means of general rules—is frowned upon, or at least considered inefficient.

This view is wrong. As Hayek points out,[260] abstractions are not something the mind derives from perceived reality by means of logical processes; on the contrary: They are one characteristic of the categories that the mind operates with—or in other words, they are a requirement rather than a product of the mind.

Our everyday language makes it difficult to use the term "abstract" because people tend to tacitly assume there has to be something to be abstracted from. Hayek notes:

We just do not have any other appropriate term to describe what we refer to as "abstract." The word implies, however, that we refer to something "abstracted," or *derived* from one or several other mental entity or entities that have existed before and are richer or more "concrete" in one way or another. ... appearances keep us from realizing that these concrete[261] particularities are a product of abstractions the mind has to perform, in order to be able to experience certain sensations, perceptions, or imaginations. When we are aware of the concrete details, that does not exclude that the only reason we are aware is because our mind operates according to abstract rules, which clearly must have existed before we could even notice the particulars we assumed to be the basis of any abstraction. In short, it is my assumption that the human mind must be capable of performing abstract operations in order to be able to notice individual things, and that this ability exists long

---

259 Regarding the following, see Hayek (Primat).
260 See Hayek (Rules), p. 30.
261 See Hayek (Primat), pp. 301, 302 *(author's translation)*.

before we can speak of conscious perception. Subjectively, we live in a concrete world and we often have our difficulties even identifying just some of the abstract relations that enable us to distinguish between things and respond differently to them. However, to explain how our perception works we need to start from the abstract relations that determine the order in which each individual thing has its place.

Abstract concepts—and this is a frequent subject of misperceptions—are the only way to gain some control over the complexity of concrete reality, which the mind could never control completely. So, abstracts are an essential tool to get one's bearings in a reality that is impossible to grasp in its totality because it is too diverse and rich in details—or too complex. Consequently—and paradoxically—an organism's ability to succeed in an environment not completely identifiable is based not on its exploring as many details as possible, but on its adjusting to the inevitable non-knowledge of details by applying abstract behavioral rules and interpretation patterns.[262] In other words, "abstractness" is not, as is often erroneously assumed, a quality of higher-level thinking processes or logical thinking; it is a characteristic of all processes determining organismic behavior, long before parts of these processes enter into our consciousness.

What are generally referred to as concrete experiences, perceptions, emotions, and so on are the product of a number of overlapping abstractions, each of which is focused on very specific aspects only, but which in total are capable of producing these concrete experiences. This process of "specification by superimposition," as Hayek calls it, is of utmost importance for the design of problem-solving processes. Quite obviously, decision-making and problem-solving processes are designed very differently depending on whether they are based on the constructivist assumption that the understanding of a problem requires concrete details or on the evolutionary paradigm according to which that understanding has to focus on the abstract relations of order. While the former may seem intuitively plausible, it cannot be successful in view of what has been discussed. The latter—concretization by way of progressive structuring based on abstract relations of order—appears to be the only way to gain control over complexity.

---

262 See also section 2.22.

*Interrelations among the Cognitive Principles*

None of the principles briefly outlined here must be regarded on its own, even if they are discussed successively. The key points are their interaction and the behavioral tendencies they cause. Each of them can undoubtedly lead to absurd results in extreme cases. The occurrence of extreme cases, however, is partly prevented by the other principles. Moreover, extreme cases have obviously been rather rare in the environment where these cognitive principles have evolved, as otherwise the systems operating on these principles would not have survived. Insofar as extreme cases do occur—for instance, when real facts are oversimplified on grounds of the simplicity principle, or when the consistency and stability principles lead people to stabilize self-consistent cognitive structures that bear no relation to reality—it is highly questionable whether that organism will survive. When an entire species thus runs into an ecological impasse it will sooner or later die out.

First and foremost, however, the cognitive principles described here work at the level of the individual. This is also where extreme cases such as the failure of complexity-managing mechanisms occur most frequently.[263] By combining numerous individuals into a social system where additional rules will be in force, new mechanisms of complexity management will emerge in addition to the cognitive principles, which will work as security mechanisms preventing the shortcomings of individual principles from affecting the total system.

One of the most obvious security mechanisms is that the extinction of individual elements is also an opportunity for survivors to learn to avoid specific behaviors. So, the individual organism sort of spearheads the development of the entire social system, or in other words, of the species. In cases like these, the trial-and-error process can be considered to take place at two levels: that of the individual and that of the social system.

At the level of the overall system, the success or failure of the individual organism is the internal criterion by which the selection of behaviors, habits, and so on takes place. In this way, any problems the individual is unable to solve can be solved by the social system: New behaviors can be tested at the individual level, and, if they prove successful, they can then be adopted by the other individuals as well.

This does not require the *causes* of individual organisms' decline to be analyzed. It is sufficient that negative behavioral rules are obeyed, and thus

---

263 See, e.g., Bateson (Ecology).

certain behaviors no longer practiced, no matter what has actually caused the decline. The complexity-managing mechanisms of the individual are enhanced by the rules of the social system. Problem-solving mechanisms like these do not relate to primitive forms of life but are used on a daily basis in highly civilized societies. Examples include military patrols, research expeditions, large parts of modern art, and a series of sports whose key characteristic is to explore the limits of what is possible, such as car racing and mountaineering. Even the intense safety measures usually taken for such endeavors do not change the way these mechanisms basically work. The key aspect is: Despite previous studies of all possible sources of danger, and despite the extensive safety measures taken, at the end of the day the complexity-managing mechanisms do not suffice; instead, a few people actually have to undertake an attempt so the social system can learn from their success or failure.

## 2.44 Systematic Design of Discovery Processes

Out of everything that has been said so far, the most important observation is that we rarely have sufficient knowledge or information to make a rational decision or find a rational solution to a problem in the constructivist sense. This view leads to a certain modesty with regard to the capabilities of human reason, which is no longer considered to be a tool with unlimited possibilities. Our knowledge and reason are subject to inevitable limitations.

However trivial it may seem when stated openly, this view is hardly accounted for in conventional theories. Many theories on individual and social, in particular institutional, behavior are more or less explicitly based on the assumption that it is essentially possible to gather the information required for rational behavior in the constructivist sense, and vice versa: that behavior is only rational if it builds on a comprehensive information base. In fact, the behavior of both individuals and institutions is quite far from this utopian ideal—not only because this ideal is very ambitious and hard to fulfill but because it is not feasible in practice. On the other hand, it must be admitted that the utopian ideal of constructivist rationality strongly impacts decision makers' thinking, leading to a remarkable ambivalence between what they actually do and what, under the impression of constructivist views, they believe they should be doing.

The widening gap between feasible decision-making and problem-solving behavior on the one hand and the constructivist-normative views on the other hand leads to disastrous uncertainty and frustrations and, above all, causes attempts to improve decision-making behaviors to head in the wrong direction. As the concept of rationality is claimed by the proponents of the constructivist paradigm, all non-constructivist views are *a priori* considered irrational, which means they are automatically deleted from the list of possible approaches to improving decision-making behaviors.

Once it is understood that it can be proven with those rational means that both reason and knowledge are subject to the fundamental limitations discussed, there are very far-reaching consequences for the design of decision-making and problem-solving processes. Contrary to what is often assumed, being aware of the limits to what is possible does not necessarily lead to resignation. On the contrary: It has turned out that, while the fact that our knowledge is limited will force us to dispense with detailed statements and forecasts, at the same time the creation of spontaneous orders by applying general rules and, equivalent to these, in-principle statements and forecasts will enhance our possibilities to influence the course of events to an astonishing degree.

The following paragraphs will outline a specific kind of problem-solving process that follows directly from these views, but which is often misunderstood completely because from a constructivist perspective it must seem inadequate.

When there is something you do not know, you do not necessarily have to resign yourself to that state of uncertainty. You can search for the unknown; you can explore it. In the individual sphere it is largely clear what the conditions are that have to be met so that search process will be successful. For instance, when you have lost or misplaced something in your apartment you will hardly sit down and wait for inspiration to strike. You will much rather look for that item in all the places you can think of. This approach does not guarantee you will actually find it. It does guarantee, however, that the probability of success will be higher than if you remained passive.

Similarly, in a company facing specific problems, management will hardly sit and wait for inspiration to hit them; instead they will actively search for a solution to those problems, for instance by applying creativity techniques, studying the problem more intensely, and so on. Again, there is no guarantee an effective solution will be found—as should be clear from my earlier explanations on the evolutionary paradigm—but again, active search in compliance with certain conditions will involve a greater probability (or propensity) of success. As has been pointed out in the context of the emergence and creation of order, in cases like these there is often no other option but to create optimal conditions for search or discovery processes, while being aware that there can be no certainty of success.

While the examples from the individual sphere (or from areas a single brain is halfway able to grasp) make perfect sense after they are given some thought, and the specifics and success factors of search processes are somewhat clear, in complex situations it seems much more difficult to achieve a similar understanding of such processes. Typical examples of such discovery processes include criminal proceedings (in particular under Anglo-Saxon law), all kinds of competition—especially in business—and the procedure of scientific research. In a paper of outstanding significance, Friedrich von Hayek has systematically examined economic competition as a "procedure for the discovery of facts," pointing out that these facts would remain unknown, or at least unused, if it were not for that competition.[264] Using business competition *as an example*, it is possible to discuss the general characteristics of discovery procedures to be used in all situations where no one can know the relevant facts in advance.[265]

Procedures like these will probably gain importance for business leaders in the future: As the complexity of situations increases, it will become more and more important to incorporate the maximum possible number of relevant facts and findings in the problem-solving process, while at the same time it is impossible to tell in advance which facts will be relevant, which of them *are* facts at all, or who has the information required. It does not matter for the general structure and design of discovery processes whether—as with creativity methods—it is a competition of ideas or opinions, procedures, assumptions, capabilities, skills, and so on. In particular when it comes to designing a specific business strategy in conditions of complexity and permanent change, such discovery procedures must be applied at least in part.

Contrary to the discovery processes in scientific research, which essentially focus on finding out what could be referred to as *"general* facts"—that is, discovering the general and permanent laws of the universe—business competition primarily aims to "discover specific temporary circumstances."[266] As Hayek explains, market theory presumes a state that, if it really existed, would make competition superfluous. Paradoxically, this state is

---

264 See Hayek (Studien), p. 249.
265 Also see Hayek (Individualismus), pp. 103 et seq.; and Hayek (Mirage), pp. 107 et seq.
266 See Hayek (Studien), p. 251.

called the "perfect competition," although it does not even permit a competitive *process* and thus prevents competition to fulfill its true function. As a general rule, market theory is based on "the assumption of a 'given' quantity of scarce resources. But exactly what resources are scarce or what things are considered resources at all, or how scarce or valuable they are—these are among the matters that competition is supposed to discover. The preliminary results of the market process tell the individual player what is worth looking for."[267]

As the different economic subjects always have to base their economic planning on incomplete information, an adaptation mechanism is required to allow the plans of many different subjects—which are likely to contradict or at least affect each other—to be mutually adapted. On the one hand, it is only possible to do business successfully when you can form expectations concerning your transactions with other individuals that have a high likelihood of being met. However, the necessary mutual adaption of individual plans requires some economic subjects' expectations to be systematically frustrated. As Hayek impressively shows, this seeming paradox—the fact that overall high consistency among individual economic subjects' economic plans can only be achieved if some individuals' plans systematically remain unfulfilled—represents a negative feedback process of the kind typically studied in cybernetics, specifically when dealing with the theory of self-organizing systems.[268]

Hayek managed to show that the term "balance" would not be fitting for this kind of competitive theory. According to him, balance can only exist when competition comes to a complete stop after all the facts relevant to individuals' economic plans have been discovered. However, as in a complex social system the so-called relevant facts keep changing, the only thing competition can bring about is a spontaneous order in the sense discussed earlier. By being established to a greater or lesser degree, this spontaneous order can provide the individual players with some orientation to base their expectations on. In an order like this, the only thing that can be in balance, or stable, is *not the concrete results* of competition but the *conditions* in which competition, as a discovery process, takes place.

As discussed in previous sections, the formations we refer to as spontaneous orders do not have consistent objectives or sets of objectives of the kind we find in organizations. Such orders are designed to achieve specific

---

267 See Hayek (Studien), p. 253.
268 See Hayek (Studien), p. 256 and section 2.22.

abstract rather than specific single purposes. In the case of economic competition, the abstract purpose is to ensure that a multitude of diverse individual purposes—which cannot be known to anyone in their entirety—can be achieved or at least pursued. Rational and successful action is only possible for individuals in a world that has some kind of order; so it obviously makes sense to try to create conditions in which the prospects of pursuing one's goals effectively are as good as can be—even when we cannot predict which specific individuals are favored by them and which are not.[269]

If the facts relevant for business did not change or were known in advance, a procedure such as competition would obviously be superfluous and above all extremely wasteful. Hence it is doubtlessly possible to devise models operating on more rational procedures. In all of them, however, the complexity of real matters is greatly underestimated, or blocked by setting adequate theoretical conditions. As a result, these models will only provide solutions—if at all—to problems very *different* from that which the competition-type discovery procedure is supposed to solve. If the winner of a sports competition were known in advance, the competition would obviously not be required at all. Of course, it is quite conceivable that a list of favorites can be compiled in advance, but experience has shown too often that even with such a list there can be great surprises when the actual competition takes place. The reason is that the number of influencing factors to be considered is so large, even in relatively simple situations such as sports competitions, that even the biggest computers are unable to capture all interdependencies and determine the outcome—unless the competition actually takes place.

The unpredictability of results is common to all discovery processes. So, all anyone can do to discover the facts of interest—in this case the outcome of a discovery process—is to maximize chances for all candidates and not to tolerate any preferential treatment. Clearly, this cannot happen by allocating specific events to specific individuals. Instead, conditions have to be designed so as to ensure that this allocation is performed by the impersonal competition process. One point to be considered here is that there is no guarantee the rules of competition will cover all factors potentially influencing the outcome. It is very well possible that even with very carefully designed conditions individual candidates will be systematically disadvantaged and so the result of the discovery process will be distorted. Of course, the conditions of the competition can be successively improved, though not by

---

269 See Hayek (Studien), p. 255 (translation by author).

improving the disadvantaged candidates' results ex post but by introducing further rules.

For instance, it would quite obviously be a glaring mistake if in a high jump competition, the smaller athletes were to have a few inches added to their actual results. If there really was evidence that height was a key factor in high jumping that could not be offset by other factors such as superior technique, one adequate way to prevent the systematic distortions of results would be to classify jumpers by height and have separate competitions for each class.

When people say that competitions, in particular economic competition, will identify a "maximum" or "optimum," careful thought must be given as to what particular aspects are maximized or optimized. Rather than directly maximizing concrete results, discovery processes like these are aimed at maximizing *chances*. Referring to economic competition, Hayek says:

"Of course, the so-called "maximum" we can achieve this way must not be defined as a sum total of specific quantities of good things; rather, it only refers to the chances it offers to unknown individuals to gain a maximum equivalent for a share of the whole, which is partly determined by coincidence." [270]

In another passage he writes:

"all we may expect of the use of an adequate discovery procedure is that it will increase the chances for unknown individuals, but not any specific results achieved by specific individuals. The only common objective we can pursue when choosing this technique, the order of social matters, is the abstract structure or order that will emerge as a consequence." [271]

For the problems discussed here, it is not necessary to discuss in greater detail the numerous implications of this understanding of competition as a discovery procedure in general economic and social policy. There is just one point I will briefly address: When viewed from this angle, the idea of social justice has aspects that, while not entirely unknown, have largely been forgotten or neglected and which, together with my earlier remarks on the problem of order emergence and creation, shed new light on the design of social systems.

At the same time, the systematic design of discovery processes which are structurally similar to business competition is of crucial importance for many

---

270 See Hayek (Studien), pp. 257 et seq. (translation by author).
271 See Hayek (Studien), p. 255 (translation by author).

business management problems at a lower level. For instance, corporate planning, according to Kami,[272] is a system that is supposed to make employees think. Exactly what they are supposed to think, what factors they should focus on, which aspects in their environment are or could become relevant, what indicators are significant, and what changes harbor the greatest chances or risks are all things that are not clear from the start, and nor can they be stipulated by decree. So, corporate planning can be considered a discovery procedure for all of these and a number of other factors, which is why a theory of corporate planning cannot focus on plan contents—it will rather have to deal with the structural conditions in which discovery has to occur, in order to optimize the chances that the relevant factors will be discovered. This does not mean, of course, that in each individual case—that is, for a specific company or industry—the procedure should not be reconciled with the specific plan content.

Not only should discovery procedures be used to tackle large problem complexes, such as corporate planning; they could also be used to improve a number of smaller yet important issues. One typical example is the set-up of conferences. In business practice, meetings are called for all kinds of reasons and purposes, and problem solving is clearly among the most important ones. It goes without saying that problem-solving meetings can be organized in such a way that no problem whatsoever will be solved. On the other hand, it is possible to create conditions that will improve the chances of finding solutions. Such conditions include the composition of the group, the way the meeting is convened, its preparation, general working conditions and ambiance, the way the meeting is chaired, and so on. Much the same is true for any other type of group work, for the organization of decision-making processes in top management, for certain areas of intra-company information exchange and in-house processes of will and opinion-forming, for the organization of research and development functions, for certain marketing issues, for the design of incentive systems, for democratic election processes, and for a number of other issues.

The common denominator of all these examples is that they are processes aimed at unearthing or identifying specific facts or results which cannot be known or determined in advance, due to the complexity of the situation, the speed of change, the lack of information, the lack of certainty, and so on, and which may therefore have to be newly determined day by day in

---

272 See Kami (Planning).

a permanent discovery process. In cases like these, management faces at least two specific tasks: It has to focus its attention on the discovery process itself—that is, on the design of the conditions in which desired results are produced—and subsequently evaluate the results produced.

Thus, with regard to the processes taking place, management operates in a typical *meta-systemic* sense: The organization of a process is located at a higher logical level than the process itself; likewise, the evaluation of process results can only be based on meta-criteria resulting from the overall context the process is embedded in.

Here, the structure of an ultra-stable system becomes very evident, for it is obvious that two feedback channels are required to stabilize the overall structure. To give an example, let us assume we are looking at a team that a manager has put together to solve a specific problem. If it is a complex problem—and that is the kind we are talking about here—the manager himself will only have some vague ideas as to its actual nature, and be able to name a few general characteristics the solution should possibly have. Really identifying the problem, exploring various solution alternatives, developing a solution concept—those are tasks he will leave to the team, for this is what the team has been established for. So, this manager puts a system in operation to find out something, or in other words, he or she initiates a discovery process. In the team itself, depending on its structure, there will be more or less numerous and intense feedback and interaction processes which in themselves represent a very complex matter in the sense of a network. All these feedbacks can be depicted as one single feedback channel with a correspondingly great variety, which forms the first feedback loop. Now there are numerous ways to have a group of employees work together. The term "team" alone does not tell us anything about the approach taken. In many cases, managers will leave the topic to their staff—in other cases, they will specify the procedures to be applied. Usually this happens in passing, as people will focus on the issues to be solved and consider group organization to be a minor issue. However, managers' actual task would be exactly that: thinking about the approach the group takes and the way they organize themselves; so there has to be a second feedback loop running from the group's results to its structure (see figure 2.44(1)).

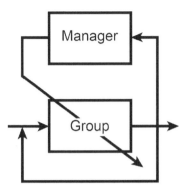

*Figure 2.44 (1)*

Now the characteristic feature is that the group's results—that is, the solutions they propose—is assessed at a meta-language rather than an object-language level. For example, if the issue to be solved consists in working out a marketing plan, the group's proposals will be assessed based on how realistic, well thought-through, accurate, innovative, creative, risky, cost-efficient, and so on they are. These are obviously all *meta aspects*, as they can be applied to *any* marketing plan, while the contents of the plan itself will differ greatly for, say, an insurance company and a chemicals group. Based on his assessment of meta-criteria, the manager then has to change the team's organization until results correspond to his meta-ideas, which are also subject to change. In this context, "organization" includes the composition, rules to be followed, interpersonal relations, and so on, not just the question of group leadership. This reorganization is itself a continuous search process, as indicated by the arrow running through the "Group" box.[273]

This task of continuous reorganization can be performed in two ways. The first is to intervene in the details of group activities and tell individual members what to do, who should lead the group, how sub-issues should be structured, and so on. The second is to merely define the conditions that will enable the group to self-organize and reorganize. This could be achieved, for example, by eliminating hierarchical ranks or bringing together people of the same rank only, and by creating conditions for a maximum of interaction, such as physical proximity, identical "language," ensuring that team members are freed from other tasks and shielded from disturbances, and so

---

273 Regarding the graphic symbols, see Gomez, Malik, and Oeller (Systemmethodik), passim; see also Pask (Approach), passim.

on. In cases like these, the actual leadership of the team by its manager would be limited to sheer pain or pleasure signals, or expressing satisfaction or dissatisfaction based on his meta-assessment. Expressions of dissatisfactions, or pain signals, would trigger internal rearrangement of the group, with the manager exerting no influence on the what and how. All he would do is assess the new output, and express whether or not he is satisfied with it. Of course there are mixed strategies, too, because management by pain or pleasure signals might turn out to be too slow. That is to say, active interventions in the group's detailed organization can be mixed with those aimed at restoring the group's self-organizing capability. The problem here, however, is that in the absence of cybernetic knowledge any interventions in the group's detailed organization can easily render it unable to self-organize, or block its respective capabilities.

Of course, the manager could also provide input on content aspects, even to a point where he is the one to solve the problem. In that case, however, he is no longer a manager but an expert in, say, marketing. Another potential problem here is complexity management: Whereas before, that manager would have had to focus on his control variety and leave it to his team to eliminate any variety related to the actual problem, he would now have to gain control over the complexity existing at both levels—a challenge either that would either totally absorb him or that he would be unable to cope with, as he would have additional tasks to perform.

A lack of understanding of these matters tends to mean people concentrate on results only, and disregard the conditions in which these results are produced. As we have seen, however, the results of discovery processes are clearly determined by the structure of the respective process, so the way to permanently improve them is not by tinkering with them after the fact, but by shaping the structure of the systems or processes generating them.

Although this was not specifically pointed out at the beginning, it should be reasonably evident that the discovery processes discussed here are of the evolutionary variety. Their concrete results evolve from the interaction of the rules governing the processes, that is, their structure, and while knowing this structure may permit an in-principle forecast of the types or kinds of results, it does not allow a detailed forecast of the results themselves. These can only be registered in retrospect.

As explained before, discovery processes cannot be the best of all conceivable procedures to solve specific problems. From a constructivist perspective, they will even be considered rather primitive decision-making and problem-solving approaches. Discovery procedures of the kind discussed have one key advantage at least: Under conditions of complexity they are the only ones that are feasible. Once again, what Hayek says about the analysis of economic competition holds true:

"The discovery procedure we use comes at a considerable cost. But we would be doing injustice to the accomplishments of the market if we assessed them "top-down," comparing them to an ideal standard that we simply cannot reach in any way known to us. If we follow what appears to be the only permissible approach and assess them "bottom-up," comparing them to what we could accomplish with any other method available to us, in particular with what would be generated if competition was prevented—e.g., if only those could manufacture a good that were granted permission by the authorities—then what the market accomplishes will appear enormous. All we need to remember is how difficult it is in an economy with effective competition to find new ways of supplying consumers with better or cheaper goods than we presently do. Whenever we believe we have found such unexploited opportunities, we usually find that they have remained unexploited because it has been prevented by some authority or some highly undesirable private power being exercised." [274]

As mentioned earlier, much the same is true for all discovery procedures. They are not as good as may seem desirable or imaginable according to some utopian ideal, but they are the best that is available to us under the given circumstances (that is, under conditions of high complexity). The shortcomings doubtlessly found in very many cases are usually due to the fact that not enough attention has been paid to their functional requirements; that is, there is no *feedback* from these inadequate *results* to the *structures*.

## 2.45 Characteristics of Evolutionary Problem-Solving Processes [275]

The situation typically requiring an evolutionary strategy has been described in an earlier section. In the following paragraphs I will summarize and briefly

---

274 See Hayek (Studien), p. 257 (author's translation).

275 With regard to the content of this whole section, see also the excellent works by Quinn, specifically his book *Strategies for Change* (1980). Published only after the manuscript for the present book had been finished, this work contains extraordinary illustrations of the different viewpoints regarding the evolutionary approach. Quinn has analyzed a series of case examples in large U.S. corporations, and has essentially come to the same conclusions I am presenting here. In my view, his book is one of the key publications taking an opposing view to most of the literature on strategic management, which is almost exclusively constructivist oriented.

outline the key characteristics of the evolutionary problem-solving process. It must be emphasized, however, that they are what you might call superficial phenomena, or in other words, a description of how the process works. An explanation of why an evolutionary problem-solving process looks the way it does has been provided in the foregoing sections. Now if we assume the structure and mechanisms of evolutionary decision-making and problem-solving processes to be given, results of their operation will be the characteristics described below. The chapter to follow will then describe how evolutionary processes can be integrated in the structure of the viable system—which was described in Chapter 1—and what distinctive features or improvements will result from that. Key features of an evolutionary strategy are these:[276]

1.  Only a limited number of options are taken into consideration.
2.  Only a limited number of key consequences are taken into account.
3.  Key factors for decision are not the options as such, but the marginal, often incremental differences between them.
4.  There are intense interactions between objectives and options.
5.  The available data are subject to permanent restructuring.
6.  The analysis and evaluation of a problem are successive steps.
7.  Both the analysis and the evaluation are aimed at eliminating shortcomings and errors.
8.  The problem-solving process is socially fragmented.

The following subsections deal with each of these points.

### 2.451   Only a Limited Number of Options Considered

Problem-solving hardly ever happens out of the blue. Every problem arises in a certain context. As pointed out elsewhere,[277] a problem is always a disturbance in a preliminary state of adaptation, which means that this state has considerable influence on what aspects the problem will have. In most cases, this also defines a range within which a solution can reasonably be sought, and from which the options to be considered can be selected.

It can certainly happen that in the course of a problem-solving process the selection range has to be varied—that is, that some variation happens in

---

276 With regard to the following, see Braybrooke, Lindblom (Strategy), pp. 83 et seq.; and Lindblom (Intelligence), pp. 143 et seq.
277 See Gomez, Malik, and Oeller (Systemmethodik), pp. 7 et seq., 49 et seq.

the heuristic rules discussed earlier. However, if we were to take at face value what many papers say about the art of problem solving—that is, that *all* conceivable options are to be considered—we would quickly realize that this is an impossible task, as the number of options is usually unlimited. This is also in line with practical experiences gained with problem-solving teams: Often they limit their search space to relevant fields, deliberately or subconsciously, although the criteria that make them relevant or irrelevant have not always been defined. As has been repeatedly emphasized, the risk of this approach is that a number of promising options will never make it to the shortlist. That, of course, is the key objection raised against the evolutionary strategy by proponents of the constructivist view. After all that has been said so far about complexity-controlling mechanisms, it should be reasonably clear that a claim to evaluate *all* options is unrealistic, and that the options to be evaluated will always have to be selected from a defined reasonable range. Hence, it is to be expected that in the course of a problem-solving process there will be some degree of oscillation between evaluating options from a tentatively preselected range and evaluating the ranges themselves.

### 2.452 *Limited Number of Key Consequences Taken Into Account*

Just as it is impossible to analyze all options, it is equally impossible to consider all potential consequences of an option. Part of the reason is the number of possible primary consequences; in addition, each primary consequence will have a series of other consequences that, by interacting with other factors outside the decision makers' control, cause side effects that are impossible to track. These unintended, unplanned, and usually unexpected side effects and backlashes represent an essential component of complexity and make it impossible to apply the constructivist approach.

Only in fields describing more or less closed systems, such as in some disciplines of natural sciences or technology, might it perhaps be possible to grasp the consequences of an action in their entirety. It is absolutely impossible in all the fields that can only be described as open systems. In this context, some remarks by Peter F. Drucker are highly pertinent:[278]

"… entrepreneurial decisions must be fundamentally expedient decisions. It is not only impossible to know all the contingent effects of a decision, even for the shortest

---

278 See Drucker (Technology), p. 121.

time period ahead. The very attempt to know them would lead to complete paralysis. But the determination of what should be considered and what should be ignored, is in itself a difficult and consequential decision. We need knowledge to make it—I might say that we need a theory of entrepreneurial inference."

An obvious conclusion from my earlier remarks on the problem of complexity and on cognitive mechanisms is that the constructivist method cannot be applied, although it can certainly be described. With regard to evaluating the consequences of actions, this leads to fundamentally different attitudes in the evolutionary and the constructivist problem solver. While under the evolutionary strategy we are fully aware that our actions may have undesirable side effects, which will cause us to apply due caution and take adequate measures, a constructivist problem solver—being under the illusion of having considered all possible consequences—will usually be surprised by unexpected side effects. There are basically three ways out of this: maintaining an attitude of "what must not be cannot be," taking hectic ad hoc measures, or deliberately switching to an evolutionary strategy.

### 2.453 Decisions Based on Marginal and Incremental Differences

As mentioned above, problem-solving processes always occur in a specific context. In most cases, situations will be structured to some degree; there will be some initial thoughts on what is doable, achievable, and implementable, as well as some ideas on what would be desirable. But as much as I have to emphasize that all this information, these views, and these opinions are of a preliminary or tentative nature and that in the course of a problem-solving process each individual aspect—or all of them—may be altered, there can be no denying that these tentative opinions represent the starting point of the problem-solving process and lead to some kind of prestructuring.

That is why evolutionary variations or mutations usually result in small, step-by-step changes (as mentioned before). Nature generally does not do anything by jumps and leaps, and collapse-type discontinuities are usually indicators of disastrous conditions. Incremental changes make the best use of the experience accumulated historically (through evolution), and they involve the smallest possible risk. It therefore comes as no surprise that in truly complex situations, the options considered are usually not radically different from the status quo.

Of course it is a historical fact that revolutions can happen, and it is equally undeniable *that in some situations, radical changes seem the only adequate solution.* It should be taken into account, however, that revolutions of any kind are not so much part of the ordinary course of things, but belong in the category of catastrophic events. Another question is, after revolutions subside, whether and to what extent situations will really be radically different from before. In many cases there are changes but not a fundamental change, which does not mean that these changes could not have initiated a new, revolutionary path—but again, in most cases that path will unfold step by step.

Another issue to be examined here is the assertion that under the revolutionary paradigm, radical changes such as revolutions cannot be explained, while necessary radical and great changes cannot be implemented. When assessing the scope of a change, the level at which this evaluation takes place is of crucial importance. Incremental changes at the meta-level, for example in the behavioral rules governing a meta-system, can result in profound changes at the object level or in the object system. For instance, an incremental change in an article of the constitution can trigger major changes at the "lower" levels of a state's government structure. Likewise, marginal changes in a company's corporate policy can require considerable adjustments.

So any statement on the scope of a change will have to take into account the relevant system levels. On the one hand, this reflects a key aspect of so-called *system thinking*: it always takes place at several system levels, as only the embedding of a system in a greater context will permit reliable statements on the system. On the other hand, it highlights a feature of *system control*: the so-called "judo effect."[279] If you focus on the right factors, even small changes building on the inherent dynamics of the situation will have strong effects. Of course, the problem is what key factors to look for. In this context, cybernetic studies have shown that it is usually the *meta-systemic components* that can trigger the necessary leverage.

Some examples should help illustrate this key aspect of system control.[280] The cybernetic structure of a soccer game is based on two homeostats—the two teams—which are rather balanced in their varieties, provided the teams play at the same technical level, and which try to gain control over each other. Each of the teams has access to the same range of behaviors;

---

279 See Beer (Platform), pp. 111, 148.
280 See Beer (Platform), p. 112.

each knows the other's tricks and tactics; the teams have comparable training, identical numbers of players, the same environmental conditions, and
so on. A key purpose of the rules of the game, among others, is exactly that:
ensuring a balance of varieties. (By the way, note that these rules were not
invented by anyone but have evolved over time.) A club manager or coach
will obviously be anxious to lead his own team to victory. Now if his team
are in a match that is tied, he would theoretically have the option of throwing
on a jersey and intervening directly, for example by replacing another player.
But that would not help much because his own variety would not be much
greater—probably smaller—than that of the other players. In any case, it is
not something he could bring to the object level of the match to improve
things. If he had *real authority* over the situation, the smartest solution
would surely be to intervene in the *meta-system* and change the rules so as
to favor his own team.

The example is absurd, of course, as no team representative has the
power to change the rules of the soccer game. Business managers usually
have that power, though to varying extents and relating to larger or smaller
areas of responsibility. Managers can certainly influence the "rules of the
game" for their staff, they can shape the context in which they operate as a
complex, homeostatic, and self-organizing system, and they can define the
criteria against which to assess the output of that system.[281] Although managers may sometimes be strongly tempted to intervene in the detailed operation of a system, their actual task is to shape the meta-system in their roles
as "referees" and designers of the "rules of the game."

"A senior manager often has the notion that he may intervene in the homeostatic systems
which operate under his aegis. He has the authority to do so, of course. But the
minute he directly engages in a highly complex situation, on level terms as it were
with those whose interactions are performing the balancing activity of the homeostat itself, the senior manager abandons his olympic role. His own personal variety is
that of a human being, however elevated his status. No: the role of the senior manager is to remain above the homeostatic fray, and to consider what is happening in
terms of his higher level understanding. Because he is outside the system, in fact, and
because he partakes in another system which is no concern of his subordinates his
method of control is explicitly to alter the criteria according to which the lower level
system is operating. ... This illustration seeks to define the notion of *metasystem*. A
metasystem is a system over-and-above the system itself. Its major characteristic is that

---

281 Drucker has expressed this aspect very clearly in his definition of "management": "if there
    is one right way to define management it is as the work and function that *enables* people
    to perform and to achieve." Drucker (People and Performance); author's emphasis.

it talks a metalanguage; and this is a richer, better informed way of talking than is available to the system lower down. It should be noted that the raison d'être of the metasystem is given in logic: it is not necessarily anything to do with the hierarchy of status." [282]

It is of crucial importance that the "judo effect" be used at a meta-systemic level to control a system. In this context, it becomes clear why the actual or alleged meta-systemic factors of a society are the subject of such hot political debates, and why everyone monitors everyone else's respective activities with so much suspicion. It also becomes clear why in high-level political negotiations the disputes over seemingly minor organizational details often carry on for months on end. In the context of the extent of changes, another point warrants mentioning. In the course of the evolutionary development of systems, which in itself progresses at incremental speed, it may happen that two systems which before were separated and operating in isolation are merged into one comprehensive system, which then shows a radically different behavior. Konrad Lorenz refers to this process as "fulguration." As is rather evident, what basically happens is that a new meta-system emerges.

"Cybernetics and systems theory have shown that the sudden emergence of new system characteristics has nothing to do with miracles, thereby absolving phylogeneticists from the reproach of vitalism. There is nothing supernatural about a linear causal chain joining up to form a cycle, thus producing a system whose functional properties differ fundamentally from those of all preceding systems. If an event of this kind is phylogenetically unique it may be epoch-making in the literal sense of the word."[283]

Thus it is also possible that what initially were two incremental steps of evolution result in radical changes. Note, however, that this "docking maneuver" of two or more subsystems can be incremental in itself and probably will be; also, an unknown and probably very large number of fulgurations are eliminated by natural selection due to their failure to adapt to the environment, precisely because they change so radically.

It is therefore conceivable that an incremental evolutionary development of fulgurations, or system-docking processes, takes place. After all, as has been observed earlier, there is a risk of committing the post-hoc-ergo-propter error: Whether a fulguration will or will not be a "big stroke" in terms of

---

282 See Beer (Platform), p. 112; also see my remarks regarding figure 2.23(4).
283 See Lorenz (Rückseite), p. 30 (translation by author).

evolution history cannot be predicted in advance; it can only be verified in retrospect.

The other aspect mentioned above, that radical measures sometimes seem the only adequate solution to a problem, can often be explained by the fact that various circumstances have prevented the necessary marginal adaptations in earlier phases. In cases like these, evolutionary development has been forced in a completely wrong direction, usually because the need for continuous adaptations was not understood, resulting in a crisis situation over time. But even if this is revealed by a situation analysis, and even if radical changes seem called for, one must not forget the risk generally associated with radical measures. So, even in cases where a profound change would make a lot of sense, the unmanageable consequences and side effects will usually cause decision makers to defer it and pursue a policy of small steps instead—that is, meta-systemic changes that will gradually take effect on the object system. In most cases it seems more reasonable, in view of the risks, to allow a social system of whatever variety some time to make the necessary changes towards the new direction, rather than exposing it to the enormous tensions usually associated with a "big stroke" policy.

## 2.454  Interactions between goals and behavioral options

Under an evolutionary strategy, comparisons not only to the status quo but also among the options available will focus on incremental differences. Some papers on problem solving call for a strict separation of values or goals from the means or options to achieve them. In complex circumstances such separation is illusionary. Goals and means are closely interconnected. In most cases it is not even possible to rank the goals or values affected by a decision-making process. For instance, any attempt to weigh and rank factors such as profit, market share, and liquidity, or employment and inflation, is bound to fail unless the concrete options available are included in the consideration.

Ongoing efforts to set up such rankings, for instance in the context of studies on a social welfare function, are made under such restricted conditions that they are absolutely meaningless for real problem-solving processes. As Baybrooke and Lindblom point out, individuals are not even capable of ranking two factors such as unemployment and inflation. Almost anyone will have a preference for inflation, as long as it is low enough, and consider unemployment the greater evil if it is high. Conversely, anyone will prefer unemployment, as long as it is in a tolerable order of magnitude, and consider high inflation to be the greater evil. In other words: The question "Do you consider inflation or unemployment the preferable option?" cannot be answered in that general form, and the same is true for the question "What is more important: profit, market share, or liquidity?" It all depends on the situation and the options available. The complexity inherent in questions of this kind is reduced by making only a marginal comparison of the parameters discussed, that is, by evaluating them based on the differences in goal achievement.

As goals and means are closely intertwined, it would be misleading to view the problem-solving or decision-making process as a goal-means process, the logic of which is based on determining goals first and then searching for means to achieve those goals. If there were not a risk of exaggerating the other way, the problem-solving process could more adequately be referred to as a means-goal process. In a sense, the *knowledge* on the means available—that is, on what a social system is capable of, what resources and capacities it has at its disposal, how it responds to performance pressure, what its shortcomings are, and so on—is *more immediate and more certain*. We will therefore choose goals which, in the light of our knowledge of means and possibilities, we can assume to be achievable. Of course, this does not mean our actual goals will not be set above the achievable mark, for motivational reasons.

One point to consider is that most enterprises (and this also applies to many other social systems) have more variation potential than we would tend to assume. This means that creative speculation about possible new goals may also lead to so far unconsidered usages of the existing potential. It is only with some reservations that we can speak of a means-goal process, and it would make more sense to assume intense interactions between means and goals. Nevertheless, the goal definition process within a complex problem-solving and decision-making process is doubtlessly strongly influenced by assumptions and opinions regarding the options available. From this perspective, independent goal definition is an unrealistic demand and will hardly be found in practice.

Of course, there may be cases where, allegedly or in fact, goals are defined independently of any considerations regarding available means and options, and the means to achieve those goals are determined afterwards. But even when that happens, this does not really speak against the evolutionary approach. Much more likely, it indicates that the protagonist has acted from a very remote perspective, thus having considered a very broad rather than a narrow range of means, or that the protagonist had such unlimited means at his or her disposal that he or she was able to act accordingly, or that it was simply a matter of luck. An approach like this can certainly not be made the subject of a systematic approach. Goal definitions which are obviously made regardless of the options available are more likely to belong in the category of neurotic behaviors.

### 2.455 Restructuring Treatment of Data

Many constructivist-minded writings on decision-making processes demand a detailed analysis of the current situation. As mentioned in the context of determining goals and means, we let ourselves be guided mainly by our views and opinions about actual facts. Yet it is illusionary to think it would be possible to draw up a situation analysis free of other considerations. Any such attempt would clearly fail to clear the relevance hurdle. Any description of facts within a given sector of reality, no matter how small, is only possible in the light of a specific question or perspective, as any description has to be selective. Every fact consists of an unlimited number of realities, and the question as to what is and what is not relevant can only be answered from a specific vantage point.

In the course of a complex problem-solving process, the numerous and diverse thoughts given to possible values and goals, potential alternatives, conceivable consequences, circumstances, and so on can all change to a greater or lesser degree. In processes like these, none of the factors can be considered as given or constant, except for the structures of the process itself. These process structures, however, have to be designed so as to leave all components open to change. In the course of the process they will gradually be narrowed down, amended, and corrected, thus taking on a form that will ultimately permit a decision. Any premature definition of single components would have to reduce the probability of finding a solution as is inherent to the evolutionary process.

### 2.456 Sequential Analysis and Evaluation

The fact that in an evolutionary process only limited numbers of options and consequences have to be considered represents a considerable advantage from a constructivist point of view. On principle it should suffice to point to the unfeasibility of constructivist analyses to rule them out as potential tools for problem-solving processes. The following three sections will show, however, that this advantage can at least be offset.

*Evolutionary problem solving is permanent problem solving.* Many scientific works on the issue of problem-solving processes are based on the fiction that decisions are events that can more or less be isolated. This fiction, however, cannot stand up to realistic assessment. Any real decision is just one instance in a chain of previous and subsequent decisions, or better yet, in a network of previous, subsequent, and adjacent decisions. Except for very few, rather untypical cases, the problem-solving process in social systems must be viewed as an unlimited series of attacks at problems that keep changing under the influence of the process, and which are partly generated by the process itself, and it will only happen occasionally—as a byproduct, so to speak—that partial problems can be considered to have been "solved."

So, every attempt at solving a problem and every decision is embedded in a problem structure and a decision configuration, and the actual decision making contributes to supporting or weakening that configuration. A structure or configuration is absolutely necessary, if the overall behavior of a social system is to have longer-term coherence or meaning. With regard to this problem it was pointed out in the section on spontaneous orders that the necessary coherence results from rule compliance. Factual compliance with behavioral rules is the element that integrates individual problem-solving and decision-making acts that are far apart in terms of time and content. With regard to this problem, Drucker writes:

"We need an integrated decision structure for the business as a whole. There are really no isolated decisions on a product, or on markets, or on people. Each major risk-taking decision has impact throughout the whole; and no decision is isolated in time. Every decision is a move in a chess game, except that the rules of enterprise are by no means as clearly defined. There is no finite "board" and the pieces are neither as neatly distinguished nor as few in number. Every move opens some future opportunities for decision, and forecloses others. Every move, therefore, commits positively and negatively." [284]

As has been mentioned above, decision configurations are not simply a given; they evolve in a process comparable to the growth of a biotope. At least part of the reason why any random decision is taken that particular way

---

[284] See Drucker (Technology), p. 120.

is that *earlier* decisions were taken in a certain way and thus had a predetermining effect; at the same time, every decision taken at present has a certain predetermining effect, as—deliberately or not—it will generate certain expectations. One typical example is that decisions are sometimes justified by pointing to "prevailing practice," in particular in the legal context, where it is customary to cite the "rulings of the federal court." But it is not only the decision rules set by important social institutions, such as courts, which will invariably result in a specific practice of behaviors and decisions—the work of every small committee has the same effect: It generates specific rules for how to handle specific problems, although these rules may be difficult to articulate and their effect on future problems may not always—or at least not exactly— be predictable, as it depends on both the rules themselves and the characteristics of the underlying problem. To sum up, we are talking about a typical evolutionary process: Its inherent structure and crystal-like growth, generated by emerging rules, give it a specific direction which, as the structure itself, is not immediately recognizable, and in particular not perceptible to the senses, but can only be reconstructed mentally. This problem, too, was addressed in the section on spontaneous orders.[285]

Of course, processes like these encompass both dramatic and quiet phases. There are numerous reasons why some of the detail problems occurring may appear important and others unimportant, ranging from existential threats to a social system to pseudo-problems that are blown out of proportion (e.g., by the mass media). Also, it is helpful in some cases to distinguish between an insider's and an outsider's view. What may appear to be a crucial problem to onlookers may have minor importance to the decision maker immediately concerned with it, and vice versa. Of particular importance, however, are invariably those decisions that clearly determine the future direction of the process. Such decisions may have limited impact on the matter itself; however, as they affect the future behavior and decision autonomy to an unpredictable extent, they have importance as means of

---

285 What we are discussing here is a typical sample-producing process, as is increasingly examined by scientists of many disciplines working on questions with an evolutionary focus. See inter alia Bresch (Zwischenstufe Leben), pp. 57 et seq. and passim, in particular p. 60: "A pattern is the result of a *chain* process in which, at any given time, the existing pattern determines the probability that any of the different options encompassed in the following coincidence will transpire. Hence, patterns grow and change by way of random events that are linked together. Patterns are arrangements of modules which develop in 'self-limiting freedom.'"

structuring the process in a meta-systemic sense. Irrespective of these qualifications, the key observation is that problem solving in complex circumstances must be regarded as a permanent process, which also means that the term "problem solution" is of little use. With the exception of fictitious cases, cases used for training purposes, and pure game settings, we hardly ever have the option of solving a problem and then forgetting about it. Instead, we are usually forced to live with the solution we have found, and thus with all further consequences of a so-called solution to a problem. On the one hand, this represents a further obstacle associated with the evolutionary paradigm. On the other hand, this very circumstance offers decision makers repeated opportunities to revisit a "problem solution," modify it, take consequences into account, consider previously unconsidered factors, and closely examine alternatives that have so far been neglected.

Due to decision makers' awareness of this and the actual possibility of addressing resulting problems successively, they actually do not have to find final solutions, as is often claimed (if implicitly) under the constructivist paradigm. Problem solvers are aware that, when faced with high complexity, it is impossible for them to find a final solution, let alone an ultimate and optimal solution; but they will have plenty of opportunities to deal with side effects and consequences as they arise. This way, the breaking down of a problem into partial problems, as is occasionally demanded, is accomplished by the process itself, or its sequential nature.

### 2.457 *Remedial Orientation of Evolutionary Strategy*

Problem solving can happen with two very different goals in mind: Decisions can be aimed at achieving a maximum of positive effects, or at eliminating as many shortcomings as possible.

In the case of social systems, basically both make sense. We have to remember, though, that as matters get more complex it also becomes more difficult to define what is good or what is progress and to identify appropriate criteria, while on the other hand it is relatively simple to determine what the shortcomings are that have to be eliminated. With regard to what is good, in most cases it will be difficult to achieve consensus among a majority of decision makers—except on very general or abstract terms—while it is much easier to reach consensus on what has to be regarded as an evil or deficiency. Popper writes:

"It is a fact, and not a very strange fact, that it is not so very difficult to reach agreement by discussion on what are the most intolerable evils of our society, and on what are the most urgent social reforms. Such an agreement can be reached much more easily than an agreement concerning some ideal form of social life. For the evils are with us here and now. They can be experienced, and are being experienced every day, by many people who have been and are being made miserable by poverty, unemployment, national oppression, war and disease. Those of us who do not suffer from these miseries meet every day others who can describe them to us. This is what makes the evils concrete. This is why we can get somewhere in arguing about them; why we can profit here from the attitude of reasonableness. We can learn by listening to concrete claims, by patiently trying to assess them as impartially as we can, and by considering ways of meeting them without creating worse evils.

With ideal goods it is different. These we know only from our dreams and from the dreams of our poets and prophets. They cannot be discussed, only proclaimed from the housetops. They do not call for the rational attitude of the impartial judge, but for the emotional attitude of the impassioned preacher." [286]

It is hardly surprising, then, that when it comes to dealing with highly complex problems there is a tendency in politics to eliminate the shortcomings identified rather than deal with vague ideas of general welfare, although such ideas keep being addressed rhetorically and have some significance for the disputes between ideologies. The key question, however, is not what decision makers *say* but what they *do*. This does not mean that problem solvers should not be allowed to speculate on a better future for a social system and on the progress toward that target. From an evolutionary perspective, however, the future of a system is *realized* by eliminating the deficiencies identified in the present and by systematically trying to uncover deficiencies yet unknown. Even if the desired progress in the development of a social system can be described very clearly, we must not forget that, at the end of the day, it is the present decisions that determine whether or not the system will come close to that target, and these decisions will often focus on current shortcomings, as they provide a safer target. To put it in anthropomorphic terms, we could say that biological evolution over the past millions of years has not been working towards some concept of humankind; instead it has eliminated the states of adaptation that the different species had reached at each period, thus—unintentionally—generating humankind. Note that human beings themselves must not be considered to be the final point of evolution: This is probably just another transitional stage on a path whose end and outcome no one is able to predict.

---

286 See Popper (Conjectures), p. 361.

Quite possibly, evolution will work in a remedial manner once again, realizing that humans are just another accident and a mistake, and eliminating them in line with its own logic.

This remedial strategy, which is negative in a sense as it is aimed not at generating or creating something positive but at eliminating the negative, thus bringing about the positive, is of crucial significance in many other important areas which I can only briefly touch upon here. As has been mentioned before, we do not have any criteria for social welfare or the general good, but we are certainly able to identify evil, distress, and misery. Likewise, there is no criterion for truth, but in many cases we are able to determine whether an assertion is wrong.[287]

This is why scientific research focuses on uncovering deficiencies and errors in theories, or at least that is what it is supposed to do.[288] Also, we have no criteria for justice, but we do have them for injustice, which is why we should strive to gradually eliminate injustices rather than attempting to create justice in one grand stroke.[289] Finally, there are no general criteria for freedom, but they do exist for unfreedom, and freedom can only be created by successively eliminating unfreedom.[290]

It would clearly not be admissible to conclude from the above that what is true of the areas mentioned has to be true for strategic management as well. Again, it is the arguments relating to the enormous complexity and thus the need for limitation of our knowledge that ultimately permit, even suggest that these observations be transferred. Moreover, the situation in all of these areas, including management, is such that it permits a certain positive orientation with regard to *meta-systemic* structures. Just as it is possible to make statements on how a state's legal and economic system should be designed so as to permit remedial orientation of concrete actions, thus eliminating injustice, unfreedom, distress, and misery—or whatever conditions are required to permit an evolutionary development that will achieve the positive by eliminating the negative—it is equally possible in the field of management to make statements on how the structures of corporate management should be designed to ensure the system will be adaptive, flexible, and capable of learning; in short: viable.

---

287 See Popper (Society), pp. 369 et seq.
288 See Popper (Logik), (Conjectures), (Knowledge).
289 See Hayek (Mirage), pp. 42 et seq., (Studien), pp. 114 et seq.
290 See Hayek (Verfassung), pp. 13 et seq.

As has repeatedly been pointed out, the structure of a viable system, just like evolutionary processes, is aimed at enabling self-organization. Also, it is a key criterion for a theory of self-organization that the positive statements often refer to the *obstacles to be removed*, and that they keep self-organizing capabilities from developing and unfolding. One of the typical practical examples for this way of thinking and acting is the setting up and chairing of a meeting or a permanent work group. It is virtually impossible to list all the key factors of success for a meeting or work group to turn out well because a) we do not know them and b) there are too many of them. It is very well possible, however, to gradually identify and eliminate key obstacles; and of course it is also possible to derive positive rules for handling such systems, which are basically self-organizing. Questions such as "What keeps these people from becoming a real team?" are key heuristics in dealing with complex systems.

## 2.458  Social Fragmentation

In themselves, the sequential nature and the remedial orientation of the evolutionary strategy strongly alleviate the disadvantage that comes with the inevitable restriction to a limited number of options and consequences. An additional factor, however, is that virtually all complex problem-solving processes are also multi-person processes: The fact that a multitude of decision makers, stakeholders, information sources, advisers, and so on are involved considerably increases the probability that at the end of the day a large number of variants, influences, and consequences will be taken into consideration. If the evolutionary process is designed in a meaningful way and if it is impossible for controversial issues to be ignored or covered up, there is a high likelihood that in the course of that process a large number of different viewpoints and opinions will be raised and that they will each have some effect on the decision.

Note that I am not talking about the rather primitive form of majority decisions by vote, least of all open vote. A "social process" is a "gradual evolution which produces better solutions than deliberate design."[291] A majority decision by vote may serve a series of other purposes, but it certainly will not achieve what such a social process can achieve. A social process, no matter whether it takes place in a small group or involves millions of people, is

---

291 See Hayek (Constitution), p. 111.

characterized by extremely intense interaction that influences actions, opinions, ideas, assumptions, and so on, thus causing a variety of modifications,
developments, and mutual adaptations. The deliberate triggering and management of such processes requires the kind of influence that section 2.21
describes as "cultivation." Seasoned policymakers are certainly aware of the
fact that it is part of their set of methodical tools to cultivate opinions and
trends; in much the same way, top managers in many types of social systems
are well aware that it often takes a lengthy opinion-forming process for a
decision to mature.[292]

When that happens, even managers with plenty of experience in this kind
of influencing cannot expect the final result to be what they had hoped for,
or even close to it. Rather, it is very likely that the outcome will not mirror
any of the many opinions put forward in the process. On the other hand, the
outcome is not likely to correspond to the sum of these opinions, at least not
in a simple sense. But even when ultimately a decision is reached that does
not correspond to either any of the viewpoints expressed or the ideas of any
of the persons involved, that decision will still be influenced by all of the
viewpoints, in the sense that it would probably have been different if one of
these views had not been brought to the table. This is a typical example of
how social events can be an outcome of human action without necessarily
being a result of human intention.[293]

In this context, Watkins writes:[294]

"It is our ... hypothesis that decisions shape events, not that those making the
decisions *control* events. It is fully consistent with this hypothesis that the actual result
of a multitude of decisions is very different from what should have happened according to each of the persons involved. Even in the case of a small committee of
equal-minded people, it can easily happen that they will eventually agree on a policy
that differs significantly from any policy which would have been adopted if any one
member could have had his way. And where the number of people involved in a
social situation is large and the decision-makers are dispersed and variegated, it becomes highly unlikely that the collective result of their decisions will be anything like
the large-scale projection of the intentions of any of the individual people. But it will
still be the result of their decisions. Moreover, although it is the result of all their
decisions, which way the result goes may turn on single decisions, in the sense that,

---

292 On this particular point, see the studies by Quinn (Change); also see footnote 146.
293 Here, I remind the reader of the discussion of spontaneous orders in section 2.22.
294 See Watkins (Entscheidung), p. 315 (quote translated by author; emphasis in original), and
(Decision), p. 11.

if one of these had been different, the result would have been very different. (The camel's back was broken by all the straws, but it was the addition of the last straw that made the crucial difference.)"

Therefore, throughout the entire process a policymaker or manager will try not only to exert influence, provide impulses, and determine the direction; he or she will also put intense efforts into sensing what trends, moods, and opinions could become dominant, what opinions will remain chanceless, and so on. Managers, policymakers, and so forth experienced in this field will know, though perhaps intuitively rather than consciously, that they are dealing with a highly complex system that tends to respond in surprising and unpredictable ways; they also know that while there are certain means of control, the system has very strong dynamics that are usually impossible to overcome, but that adept actors can take advantage of. In other words, they try to use the "entropic drift" so often mentioned by Beer: They gauge the general direction of the development that, in line with Ashby's poly-stable system,[295] transfers the process from one state to the next until it comes to rest in a stable zone, at least for the time being.

It is impossible to predict the result of such processes in detail; these are the discovery processes discussed before, which would not be necessary if their result were known or identifiable in advance but which are essential in complex situations. Proponents of the constructivist problem-solving paradigm often try to apply their rationalist methods and techniques in situations like these, in an attempt to replace the "irrationality" of a social process with "better" approaches. Apart from the fact that in most cases their methods and thoughts can only be used in combination with very restrictive conditions and assumptions that are usually far removed from reality in that they lack information, are unable to measure things, and so on, they are often astonished when the social system concerned rejects their "rationality" firmly and with deep conviction. Complex self-organizing systems or spontaneous orders have their own rationality, due to the very fact they are complex, and only an evolutionary or cybernetic paradigm can halfway capture it.

As the example of Bremermann's Limit has shown, even computers are useless when it comes to capturing the details of social processes. The social process, or the spontaneous order, is a computer in itself: It produces the results that we cannot calculate in advance, but that are produced by the operation of the process. Electronic computers are helpful when used to

---

295 See Ashby (Brain), pp. 171 et seq

depict key *structural* or cybernetic characteristics, in order to better identify the direction of the entropic drift and determine the most effective influencing strategies.

It has been mentioned before that majority decisions by formal vote cannot replace the kind of social processes discussed here. They can be carried out at the end of such a social process, after its dynamics have taken it into a stable zone—but their purpose will then be to *determine* the results obtained, not to *generate* them. These two functions of votes are often confused; one could even say that certain forms of modern democracy have institutionalized this confusion. It comes as no surprise, then, that the quality of problem solutions is deteriorating. Even in smaller contexts, such as meetings and the like, votes are—deliberately or not—often used to form viewpoints rather than identify them. It is almost as if a mother believed that by measuring her child's height with a measuring stick she could influence his growth.

## 2.46 Summary

This section's discussion can be summarized in a simple graph.[296] The two coordinates (see figure 2.46(1)) represent the possible scope of understanding of a situation in that situation, and the scope of possible changes. As has been explained, in very complex situations human understanding and human knowledge are bound to be limited. It has also been pointed out that the lack of knowledge in complex situations is not a question of temporary technological limitations; it rather is an unalterable fact that has serious consequences for the design and management of complex systems.

In simple situations it is possible to achieve a rather in-depth understanding of matters, so constructivist (analytical, synoptic) methods can be used. As in most such cases it is also possible to survey the consequences of actions, even large-scale changes can be initiated. By contrast, in complex situations one has to rely on evolutionary strategies: While from a constructivist perspective they may not produce ideal results, they have the clear advantage of being feasible in these situations.

---

296 With reference to Braybrooke, Lindblom (Strategy), pp. 67, 68.

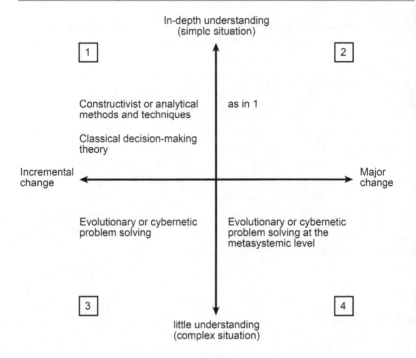

*Figure 2.46(1)*

# 3. Strategies for Managing Complexity

## 3.1 The Reality of Managers' Strategic Behavior

> "An effective general manager
> is an expert juggler."
> *Richard S. Sloma*

> "Science is truth: don't be
> misled by facts."
> Finagle's Creed

A strategy to influence or control complex systems cannot be something as simple as a formula or a series of steps to take. Success in dealing with complex systems requires deep insight into how these systems work and what laws they are based on. Chapter 2 has hopefully provided such insights—in a nutshell:

1. insight into the problem of complexity as such, into the options for dealing with systems characterized by great complexity, resulting from their own momentum and by the dynamics of interaction with other systems;
2. insight into the phenomenon of the emergence and creation of order by means of rules, into the resulting possibilities for orientation, and into the cultivation of orders providing orientation;
3. insight into the attributes of problem-solving and information-gathering processes occurring in complex settings;
4. insight into the options for controlling complex systems, or into why they cannot be controlled.

Part 2 was essentially theoretical in nature, presenting conclusions from theoretical considerations that were primarily based on the consistent acknowledgement of the complexity of real systems. In my opinion it is quite evident, however, that these considerations largely coincide with the findings of recent empirical studies on the observed behavior of managers. Amid the flood of literature mainly dealing with how managers *should* behave, the question of their *actual behavior* is rarely addressed. The results are both surprising and significant.

For instance, Mintzberg[297] published a study back in 1973 where he showed that managers' actual actions greatly differ from the image we tend to have, based on business literature and the recommendations it contains. For the strategic context a work by Quinn[298] is particularly relevant: It deals with the question as to how managers generate strategies—how they tackle the task and what the results are. His studies have produced interesting findings, and they coincide with the observations I have made in my work with larger and smaller companies, with regard to key basic issues of management, such as strategy, corporate structure, acquisitions, and medium- to long-term corporate development.

The following observations are relevant in this context:

1. A major share of management literature that deals with planning, in particular strategic planning, aims to help develop and refine a concept of planning that cannot work the way its inventors and proponents believe, hope, or postulate.
2. Most really important strategic decisions are made outside of formal planning systems, and this is true even for companies with a rather planning-friendly attitude and sophisticated planning systems.
3. In most cases, managers are not immediately involved in strategic decisions. Instead, they are concerned with the conditions of their creation; with the prerequisites for reaching consensus; with balancing opposing and competing groups in the organization; with cultivating the main opinion leaders' awareness of and sensitivity to strate gic issues; with reducing or creating uncertainty, as appropriate (reducing uncertainty by providing preliminary and tentative references to specific directions a decision could take, and creating uncertainty by deliberately leaving major issues open when opinion-building processes seem to be pushed ahead too much); with supporting what seem to be the right opinions by providing various types of encouragement; and with weakening other views by sending contrary signals. Their thinking and acting happens simultaneously over different time periods or time horizons, which they

297 Mintzberg (Nature), passim.
298 Quinn (Change).

sometimes attempt to synchronize and sometimes deliberately keep separate. Contrary to what textbooks stipulate, they rarely operate on clearcut goals. Instead, they work much more with rough paraphrases, or with hints that only indicate directions, tendencies, and general areas; and quite often these hints are negative and excluding in character, such as "I have a feeling this is not a very promising approach," "Perhaps we should stay away from this," and so forth. Many things are in the stage of "thinking aloud," and of tentatively expressing an opinion just to see how others will respond.

Often, this kind of behavior serves no other purpose than to initiate and keep up the process of dealing with strategic issues; to stimulate the dynamics of the system in order to (a) better understand its nature; (b) identify its specific reactions to certain problems, issues, and matters; and (c) create the chance that the system, on its own momentum, will produce favorable constellations that can be taken advantage of.

It would be wrong, however, to assume that these managers know in advance what is right and what they want, that they have already set up their strategy and that it is just for tactical reasons that they are acting this way. There may be cases where the situation is like that. A much more likely interpretation, in my view, is that we are dealing with homeostatic interaction processes of several complex systems whose boundaries, structures, and characteristics cannot be precisely defined. These systems emerge in the very course of the interaction process; in a sense, they keep exploring and understanding themselves better and better as they explore and understand the overall system whose parts they are—a system that, rather than presenting itself in finished form, communicates itself (and can thus be explored) through interaction.

From a cybernetic point of view, the general behavioral pattern of the managers analyzed by Quinn is characterized by their using and stimulating the system's natural momentum for self-organization to create favorable conditions for the generation of strategic decisions, without really interfering with the details. Quinn's study is an excellent example and confirmation of the concept I am proposing here: the concept of meta-systemic management based on thorough and intimate knowledge of the systemic nature of complex social institutions. Quite obviously, these studies have revealed a clear, even blatant mismatch between what text books say and what managers do in practice. The fact that managers' actions deviate from the recommendations given in literature calls for interpretation and clarification. One possible reason could be that these managers have not received enough training on the recommended planning and decision-making methods to be able to master and apply them. Another reason could be that this is one of the (unfortunate) cases where the irrationality of human nature prevails over the rationality of reason.

In my opinion, these managers really understand the true nature of the systems they are expected to control, or at least they understand it better than the scientists who give recommendations from the simplicity and straightforwardness of their study rooms, often without ever having dealt with a complex problem in reality. What may seem rational from the perspective of a simple system may well be irrational in the context of a complex one, which is probably why good managers do things differently from what text books say, yet correctly. In their own way, they overcome the classical-constructivist rationality ideal with all its narrowness and presumptuousness.

Three questions are of interest in this context:

1. Much of what managers do does not seem to lend itself to their own conscious reflection. In other words: They do the right thing systemically but they don't know why. They seem to have developed an intuitive "feel" for the situation based on their experience. So how can this experience be passed on, how can it be learned and possibly taught? In this chapter I will try to suggest a few possible solutions.
2. Even when managers basically act with purpose and deliberation, there will always be certain elements of unpredictability and a lack of systematic structures. What is originally intended as reasonable strategic action when dealing with complex systems can turn into muddled tactics and maneuvering. My feeling is that a good understanding of the Viable Systems Model can be very useful because this model structures and channels complexity. The better a corporate leader gets at understanding his organization in the model's terms, the easier it will be for him to match his actions with actual regulation mechanisms, even when the company is not officially structured after the model.
3. Another series of questions is raised when managers act adequately from a systemic perspective but consider their own actions to be wrong or at least suboptimal, and try to "improve" them in accordance with the usual text book recommendations. Any such attempt will meet all the criteria

for a double-bind situation[299] and thus serious conflicts. It never ceases to amaze me how much relief managers express when they are told that their behavioral tendency, as it were, can actually make a lot of sense and does not necessarily have to measure up to the standards defined in books and management seminars.

## 3.2 Strategic Alternatives

"... the only possibility of transcending the capacity of individual minds is to rely on those super-personal 'self-organizing' forces which create spontaneous orders."
*Friedrich von Hayek*

A major part of part 2 focused on *two kinds of orders or systems and two kinds of problem solving*. While both the system types and the different problem-solving approaches represent methods for dealing with complexity, they differ in efficiency. As I hope to show in the following sections, certain system types and problem-solving approaches are mutually reinforcing. Consequently, we need to examine what basic options exist for combining order/system types and problem-solving processes. Figure 3.2(1) shows all possible combinations. They are also the basic options we have for dealing with systems—basic strategies which also, quite obviously, represent basic ways to organize and control social systems and whose backgrounds are determined by different philosophies and ideologies regarding the nature of humankind and society.

---

299 See Bateson (Ecology), pp. 271 et seq.; and Watzlawick, Beavin, and Jackson (Kommunikation), pp. 194 et seq.

| | | Problem-solving approaches | |
| | | analytical constructivist | evolutionary cybernetic |
| Types of orders (systems) | taxic | 1<br>classical theory of management and administration | 3<br>Attempt to make existing forms of organization more flexible and responsive; organizational development, job enrichment, job enlargement, etc. |
| | polycentric spontaneous, self-organizing | 2<br>actual situation; disimprovement through analytical approaches; degeneration of spontaneity | 4<br>cybernetically oriented, evolutionary management theory |

*Figure 3.2(1)*

Although a lot could be said about each field of this matrix from the perspective of social theory and the history of ideas,[300] we have to limit ourselves to the essential facts here. The combination of *taxic forms of order* (which, as has been pointed out, are based on deliberate design, detailed planning, and commands/instructions) and the *analytic approach to problem solving and decision-making* provides the foundation for the vast majority of management theory, including the different kinds of administrative theory. The underlying assumption is that social systems are deliberately created by humans to meet defined purposes, and that a tight organization—usually in

---

300 In essence, this is about the controversy between classical-constructivist rationa lism in its different varieties and the revisionist, critical rationalism that dispenses with the former's claim to substantiation and certainty, instead orienting itself by in-principle fallibilism. Regarding this matter, see Hayek (Law), (New Studies); and Albert (Traktat).

hierarchical structures—with clear reporting relationships and information/command channels is required to ensure the functionality of a system. Problem-solving processes follow organizational routines and are based on the assumption that the information required for any kind of decision can be obtained through an appropriately designed information system. Processes are characterized by the constructivist concept of rationality; that is, the assumption is that deliberate planning and design and sophisticated calculation methods will produce optimal results.

From the perspective of historic development of social theory, this combination of system design and problem-solving approach is of fundamental, albeit cataclysmic importance.

The following quote from Plato is characteristic of the form of society that corresponds with this combination:

"The greatest principle of all is that nobody, whether male or female, should ever be without a leader. Nor should the mind of anybody be habituated to letting him do anything at all on his own initiative, neither out of zeal, nor even playfully. But in war and in the midst of peace, to his leader he shall direct his eye, and follow him faithfully. And even in the smallest matters he should stand under leadership. For example, he should get up, or move, or wash, or take his meals ... only if he has been told to do so ... In a word, he should teach his soul, by long habit, never to dream of acting independently, and to become utterly incapable of it."[301]

The second field of the matrix results from the combination of *polycentric* or *spontaneous forms of order* with the *analytical problem-solving* paradigm. This setting corresponds to our current social reality. As was pointed out earlier, while we do find taxic forms of order in social systems, their functionality actually results from their polycentric character. The spontaneous form of order in social systems, their tendency toward self-organization, sort of prevails over the intentions of organizers orienting themselves by taxic forms of order. And it is precisely because the actual results of their efforts do not turn out as intended that the resulting forms of order are often considered chaotic, or at least inadequate and inefficient. This is precisely what causes people to try to influence and improve spontaneous orders by applying analytic or constructivist problem-solving and decision-making processes. In most cases, however, all they accomplish is a *disimprovement*, as the system's spontaneous self-organizing tendencies are restrained by constructivist problem-

---

301 Plato of Athens, quoted after Popper (Society), p. 29.

solving processes, to the point where polycentric order degenerates to a taxic form of order with little flexibility and responsiveness.

The content of the third field of the matrix—the combination of taxic forms of order and *evolutionary problem-solving and decision-making processes*—has increasingly been addressed in recent management literature. Concepts that seem to pertain to this combination include organizational development, job enrichment and enlargement, and cooperative leadership style. Almost inevitably, however, evolutionary problem-solving processes cannot really be applied in taxic forms of order because the entire thinking and perception of the members of such an organization, as well as their criteria for organizational efficiency, are aligned with the constructivist problem-solving paradigm. There are examples of polycentric cells emerging within a taxic order, but experience suggests that the evolutionary problem-solving processes in this constellation tend to become increasingly analytical over time. It is probably due to this problem that many serious attempts at reform, both in companies and in social contexts, have eventually failed.

Finally, the fourth field of the matrix combines *spontaneous forms of order* with the *evolutionary problem-solving paradigm*. This combination is an essential part of Neo-Darwinist evolution theory in the areas of both biological and social evolution. In the management realm, it is primarily cybernetic or systems-oriented literature which deals with this combination.

As a general rule, the ideas resulting from the combination of spontaneous forms of order and evolutionary problem-solving processes lead to the following objection: While it is usually admitted that this option might be applicable for certain realms of society, opponents claim that in the case of *purposive* systems, or systems designed to meet specific objectives and/or deliver specific results, things cannot be left to themselves because nothing purposive could come out of it. Following this line of thought, they then point out that enterprises do not just emerge on their own but result from purposeful human action. Looking back at Chapter 2, however, readers will find that these objections have largely been addressed. Even when an order is spontaneous and a problem-solving process evolutionary in nature, this does not mean there cannot be purposive, deliberate action. Quite to the contrary, the question is whether and to what extent the results of such actions match their original purposes.

The apparent paradox is likely to disappear when we consider that self-organizing systems have to be organized, too, although not at the level where self-organization takes place but at a meta-level. So we need to organize the system in a purposeful and deliberate manner by issuing instructions of a certain logical category, to the effect that it will be able to self-organize in the context of another logical category. Beer has expressed this in the following words:

"A self-organizing system is by definition one on which organization is not imposed. And yet it must be designed so that it is self-organizing. There is an apparent contradiction ... But the contradiction is not real; and considered as a technical problem in cybernetics the difficulty is easy to resolve. That is, one designs a free, self-organizing system by using a language of logically higher order than that of the system designed; and our mathematical apparatus for doing this leads us to talk of "metalinguistic" criteria and "metasystemic" regulators."[302]

Put in slightly simplified terms, I would say that the systemic-evolutionary management concept presented here is a mix—or better, perhaps, a gestalt—consisting of both analytic-constructivist and spontaneous-evolutionary elements which appertain to different logical levels.

That is a key reason why the Viable Systems Model is so important in the context of this work: It represents the structurally clearest and most advanced concept of layered logical levels. Systems 3, 4, and 5 (see Chapter 1) are at a meta-level relative to system 1; system 5 is at a meta-level relative to subsystems 3 and 4. Recursive levels of a higher order are meta relative to those of a lower order.

On the other hand, it was quite obvious even when systems methodology was originally developed that it was basically another meta-methodology.

Rather than being aimed at solving problems at the object level, it aims to install control and regulation mechanisms that will address or solve problems. It is a meta-methodology because its immediate subject is the rules and mechanisms determining how problems will be dealt with. As has been shown in Chapter 2, establishing rules and systems of rules will certainly require an analytical-constructivist approach, such that the enforcement of a national constitution will never be left to spontaneous forces of order. Thus, in my view the overall context of a strategic concept for managing complex systems has to integrate all elements discussed so far (as pointed out in Chapter 2) in two ways: The two types of order and problem solving appear in a combination characterized by the differentiation between the object and the meta-level. This approach produces two results—the structure of the viable system and the systems methodology—which have to be

---

302 Beer (Science), p. 2.

seen as interacting very closely: On the one hand, certain principles of systems methodology are required to cultivate the structures of the viable system; on the other hand, these same principles can only be applied effectively in the context and climate of the viable system (see figure 3.2(2)).

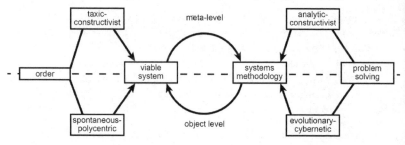

*Figure 3.2(2)*

A very illustrative example of how structures and processes/methods interact and depend on each other has been presented by Vester[303] in the context of the functions of density stress. As soon as a given population grows from a low-density to a high-density group (see figure 3.2(3)) there are only two possible paths of development: Either the group manages to develop new organization methods, behaviors, rules, and so on—in which case it can continue to exist at that higher level—or it fails to develop these procedures— in which case it disintegrates into the earlier, low-density forms of organization.

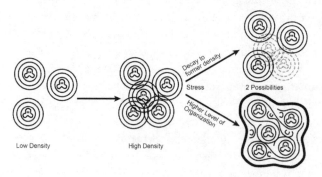

*Figure 3.2(3)*

---

303 Vester (Urban Systems), p. 17.

So, certain procedures and behaviors found in large groups will not be found in smaller ones, and vice versa. These procedures and behaviors are required to organize a high-density population, and they are also a prerequisite for reaching a higher-level organization

In the small group these procedures are not necessary; it also lacks the organization structure they would require.

## 3.3 System and Meta-System; Communication and Meta-Communication

> "1. You can't win.
> 2. You can't break even.
> 3. You can't even quit the game."
> *Ginsberg's Theorem*
> "4. But sometimes you can change the game."
> *My addendum*

At several points in this book, the terms "object language" and "meta-language," "object system" and "meta-system," and "object level" and "meta-level" have been used. While we cannot automatically assume these terms to be sufficiently known, the further discussion on the strategy for managing complex systems is based on them, for in my opinion such strategy will have to be meta-systemic in nature. When we say: "Berlin is a city," this is a statement in object language because it refers to a non-linguistic object: the city of Berlin. By contrast, the statement "'Berlin' has six letters" refers not to the city of Berlin but to an element of language itself—the word "Berlin"—which is why we usually put it in quotation marks for the sake of clarity. So, obviously we can use language to make statements not only about non-linguistic objects but also about language itself. In this case, language functions as meta-language.

The fact that it is important to differentiate between language and meta-language—or object language and meta-language, respectively—has been proven by logical and linguistic studies around such paradoxes or antinomies as the Cretan Liar, the Barber's Paradox, and Russell's Paradox of the set of all sets, which raises the question as to whether it does or does not contain itself as an element. These paradoxes, esoteric as they may be, might have shaken the foundations of logic and mathematics—and thus of science and technology as we know it—had they not been dissolved by the discovery that they result from a confusion of different logical types and will disappear once we carefully distinguish between those types.

Now, as intriguing as these basic problems are, they seem to have little relevance for management practice.

Their practical significance only becomes clear when we remember that, for instance, although grammar is an element of meta-language, it makes a substantial contribution in regulating the correct use of language. We could also say that the rules of grammar are the meta-system of language, and the adequate functioning of language strongly depends on the existence and effectiveness of that meta-system. Interpersonal communication would all but break down if the rules of grammar were no longer valid. Even for the most simple and mundane conversations we depend on following the rules of grammar. Whatever is said in the course of a conversation is usually in object language. But the fact that there is even such a thing as conversation is partly owed to the meta-linguistic regulation that grammar provides. So grammar doubtlessly has significant impact, although we often regard it as self-evident until we cannot help noticing its significance—for instance when we have difficulties making ourselves understood in foreign languages or when, as parents, we try to guide and support our children's efforts at learning how to speak.

As indicated, however, effective communication is much more than compliance with grammatical rules. Research on human communication has provided the important insight that there is not only language and meta-language, but also communication and meta-communication. With every message we send out to someone else, in addition to transmitting information we also define the context: the way in which this information is to be understood and interpreted. We call this the content and relationship aspects of communication. Together with the content, the mutual relationship between the communication partners is defined as well, which gives the content its full meaning. This, however, is information about information, or meta-information or meta-communication. Contrary to conventional wisdom, the meaning of a message is not a quality that appertains to the individual message but a function of the overall repertoire of messages that could have been sent in the same situation, and thus of context.

Now, the problem is that we are often very aware of the content but not of the relationship aspect. The results of normal communication—that is, of permanent or continuous context definition—are generally not in our conscious mind. Not even when communication relations are disturbed are we aware of them, unless we have insight into the basic rules of communication. That is partly due to the fact that meta-information is often transmitted through body language and implied in the interaction itself. This is a cause not only of many misunderstandings but also—as studies by Bateson and the Palo Alto Group have shown—of serious disruptions in the fabric of a social system. In the context of family research, in particular family therapy as well as studies on schizophrenia and alcoholism, it could be shown that many problems that were initially assumed to be personal were actually located in those persons' systemic relationships, and in the interactions determining and determined by these relationships.[304] System and meta-system and communication and meta-communication are the key dimensions of the strategy for managing complex systems. The reason is that many problems arise when the wrong systems or system boundaries are used as a basis and context for one's actions, and that the changes required to solve specific problems are often sought or expedited at the wrong level. These considerations will guide my attempt to set up a methodology for the strategic management of complex systems, as described in the following section.

Instead of adding further theoretical observations, at this point I would like to quote a few examples which Watzlawick and his colleagues of the Palo Alto Group used—in a manner downright inimitable—to illustrate phenomena that are difficult to describe.

1. "The fox population of a certain area of northern Canada shows a remarkable periodicity in the increase and decrease of its numbers. In a cycle of four years it reaches a peak, declines to near extinction, and finally starts rising again. If the attention of the biologist were limited to the foxes, these cycles would remain unexplainable, for there is nothing in the nature of the fox or of the whole species that would account for these changes. However, once it is realized that the foxes prey almost exclusively on wild rabbits, and that these rabbits have almost no other natural enemy, this relation between the two species provides a satisfactory explanation for an otherwise mysterious phenomenon. For it can then be seen that the rabbits exhibit an identical cycle, but with increase and decrease reversed: the more foxes there are, the more rabbits are killed by them, so that eventually food becomes very scarce for the foxes. Their number decreases, giving the surviving rabbits a chance to multiply and thrive again in the virtual absence of their enemies, the foxes. The fresh abundance of rabbits favors the survival and increase of foxes, etc ...

---

304 Bateson (Ecology), part III; Watzlawick, Beavin, and Jackson (Kommunikation), passim.

2. Both American soldiers and British girls accused one another of being sexually brash. Investigation of this curious double charge brought to light an interesing punctuation problem. In both cultures, courtship behavior from the first eye contact to the ultimate consummation went through approximately thirty steps, but the sequence of these steps was different. Kissing, for instance, comes relatively early in the North American pattern (occupying, let us say, step 5) and relatively late in the English pattern (at step 25, let us assume), where it is considered highly erotic behavior. So when the U.S. soldier somehow felt that the time was right for a harmless kiss, not only did the girl feel cheated out of twenty steps of what for her would have been proper behavior on his part, she also felt she had to make a quick decision: break off the relationship and run, or get ready for intercourse. If she chose the latter, the soldier was confronted with behavior that according to his cultural rules could only be called shameless at this early stage of the relationship."[305]

These examples demonstrate that certain phenomena, events, and so on can only be understood when seen in the right context. The distinct bias towards studying things in isolation, in line with the tradition of a certain idea of science, often prevents the deliberate variation of system limits (in order to better understand the system) from being included in standard procedures. As Watzlawick, Beavin, and Jackson go on to explain:

"These seemingly unrelated examples have one common denominator: a phenomenon remains unexplainable as long as the range of observation is not wide enough to include the context in which the phenomenon occurs. Failure to realize the intricacies of the relationships between an event and the matrix in which it takes place, between an organism and its environment, wither confronts the observer with something "mysterious" or induces him to attribute to his object of study certain properties the object may not possess."[306]

Secondly, the examples also show that the events in or behavior of a system are produced by its meta-system: by the "ground rules" determining the mode of interaction. This fact has been extensively discussed in Chapter 2. It is therefore necessary, and an integral part of any strategy for dealing with complex systems, to identify these regulation mechanisms, as in many cases they will have to be changed, or at least taken into consideration for one's own behavior, in order to solve a problem.

When, as in the previous example, English women and American men know about the different courtship rules in their respective cultures, there will hardly be any misunderstandings of the kind described, or at least they

---

305 Watzlawick, Paul (1976). How Real Is Real?. London: Souvenir Press. pp. 63–64.
306 Beavin, Jackson, Watzlawick: Pragmatics of human communication p. 21.

will be amenable to a solution by talking about them: that is, solving or preventing problems through communication about interaction patterns—or meta-communication. So, even if in the individual case it is impossible to say what Jim Brown or Betty Smith will do or say on a given day, as behaviors at the object level of the system can vary greatly, the basic pattern of system behavior is largely predictable and transparent as soon as we know meta-systemic relationships. As a general rule, any insight into meta-systemic regularities will produce the typical light bulb moments: that is, awareness of the immediate and deep understanding of a phenomenon. Furthermore, this insight can lead to a certain form of complete knowledge, and thus foresight and control, even when behaviors at the object level are highly complex and diverse.

The following example may help to illustrate this point:[307] Imagine a system whose activity consists in multiplying random whole numbers, the output being the product of those numbers. This system's behavior is very diverse, as any change in input will lead to a different output. Still, the output features a basic pattern, a regularity that is complete in itself, as we know that

| Even number | × | Even number | = | Even number |
|-------------|---|-------------|---|-------------|
| Odd number | × | Even number | = | Even number |
| Even number | × | Odd number | = | Even number |
| Odd number | × | Odd number | = | Odd number |

Admittedly, this is just a minor share of our knowledge on the system's behavior, but since it belongs to a logically higher level it is complete in itself. When we say "2 x 6 = 12," this is an assertion at the object level. By contrast, "multiplying two even numbers will result in an even number" is an assertion at the meta-level, as it addresses general invariants at the object level. Differentiating between the object and the meta-level also enables us to understand the two different kinds of change that are key in influencing complex systems: change and meta-change, or change of the first and change of the second order. Again, I will use a few examples collected by Watzlawick et al. The first refers to a vehicle with a manual transmission:

"The performance of an engine can be changed in two different ways: either through the gas pedal (by increasing or decreasing the supply of fuel to the cylinders), or by shifting gears. Let us strain the analogy just a little and say that in each gear the car

---

307 Ashby (Introduction), p. 104.

has a certain range of "behaviors" (i.e., of power output and consequently of speed, acceleration, climbing capacity, etc.). Within that range (i.e., that class of behaviors), appropriate use of the gas pedal will produce the desired change in performance. But if the required performance falls outside this range, the driver must shift gears to obtain the desired change. Gear-shifting is thus a phenomenon of a higher logical type than giving gas, and it would be patently nonsensical to talk about the mechanics of complex gears in the language of the thermodynamics of fuel supply." [308]

Here, Watzlawick also points out that Ashby in his theory of the "machine with input" has quite elegantly described this kind of change and its impact. In this context, he quotes from Ashby's *An Introduction to Cybernetics*:

"It will be seen that the word "change" if applied to such a machine can refer to two very different things. There is the change from state to state, … which is the machine's behavior, and there is the change from transformation to transformation, … which is a change of its way of behaving, and which occurs at the whim of the experimenter or some outside factor. The distinction is fundamental and must on no account be slighted." [309]

Another example with immediate relevance for this book, illustrating both its intention and difficulty, is this:

"[The] term method denotes a scientific procedure; it is the specification of the steps which must be taken in a given order to achieve a given end. Methodology, on the other hand, is a concept of the next higher logical type; it is the philosophical study of the plurality of methods which are applied in the various scientific disciplines. It always has to do with the activity of acquiring knowledge, not with the specific investigation in particular. It is, therefore, a metamethod and stands in the same logical relation to method as a class to one of its members. To confuse method with methodology would produce philosophical nonsense." [310]

In line with these explanations, the present book is dedicated to developing a strategy methodology.[311]

---

308 Beavin, Jackson, Watzlawick: Change: Principles of Problem Formulation and Problem Resolution, 2011, p. 10.

309 Beavin, Jackson, and Watzlawick (Change, 2011), p. 11.

310 Beavin, Jackson, and Watzlawick (Change, 1967), p. 10.

311 In the original German version of this book—as well as in the Systems Methodology project mentioned at the beginning—I have chosen to use the word "Methodik" because "Methodology" is a term almost exclusively used in the scientific community. In any case, the objective was to make very clear that methodology and method are not the same thing. "Methodology" refers to the class of relevant methods that are elements of that methodology.

Changes of the second order—that is, changes taking place at the meta-level, thus influencing the object system only indirectly, though often all the more strongly and radically—play a key role in influencing complex systems. Taking influence at the object level often produces the phenomenon described as "plus ça change, plus c'est la même chose," or, as Beer so aptly put it, "change but no alteration." Of course, interventions at the object level do bring about changes—sometimes so many that they are impossible to control because the system's variety fully unfolds at this level. These changes, however, will always be of the same basic type, which remains invariant in itself, as it could only be altered by meta-change.

Results can sometimes even be tragic, when—as superbly described by Watzlawick, Weakland, and Fisch—solutions are attempted by using "more of the same" or when that "'solution' greatly contributes to the problem."[312] In a specific gear, the speed of the vehicle can be increased by pressing down the accelerator pedal. Beyond a certain point, however, this will no longer have an effect and the driver needs to shift gears. To do that, however, he or she will first have to step off the gas—which is the opposite of what was right just a few minutes ago.

The more we consciously try to be spontaneous, the less we will succeed. The more effort we put into going to sleep, the wider awake we will usually be. The more we help an employee, the less independent we usually keep him. In this context, let me cite one last example from Watzlawick, Weakland, and Fisch, which directly illustrates what type of behavior is meant by "strategy of influencing complex systems":[313]

"When in 1334 the Duchess of Tyrol, Margareta Maultasch, encircled the castle of Hochosterwitz in the province of Carinthia, she knew only too well that the fortress, situated on an incredibly steep rock rising high above the valley floor, was impregnable to direct attack and would yield only to a long siege. In due course, the situation of the defenders became critical: they were down to their last ox and had only two bags of barley corn left. Margareta's situation was becoming equally pressing, albeit for different reasons: her troops were beginning to be unruly, there seemed to be no end to the siege in sight, and she had similarly urgent military business elsewhere. At this point the commandant of the castle decided on a desperate course of action which to his men must have seemed sheer folly: he had the last ox slaughtered, had its abdominal cavity filled with the remaining barley, and ordered the carcass thrown down the steep cliff onto a meadow in front of the enemy camp. Upon receiving

312 Beavin, Jackson, and Watzlawick (Change, 2011), pp. 32 et seq.
313 Beavin, Jackson, and Watzlawick (Change, 2011), p. XV.

this scornful message from above, the discouraged duchess abandoned the siege and moved on."

Now, anyone lacking true understanding of the background might refer to this tactical move as a "good idea," a "trick," or—as is often the case—"creativity." In fact, it was based on a very sophisticated thought fully in line with the logic of complex systems, which comprises elements from both cybernetics and games theory, demonstrates true mastery of the rules of communication, and for all these reasons is highly effective.

This might illustrate why Beer defines cybernetics as the "science of effective organization" and how Ashby can state that "[if] the reader feels that these studies are somewhat abstract and devoid of applications, he should reflect on the fact that the theories of games and cybernetics are simply the foundations of the theory of How to get your Own Way."[314]

Contrary to external appearances, this is only partly related to creativity. Changes in systems, in particular the kind that emerge from a variation of system boundaries or from a second-order change, result from insight into logic and into the mechanisms of complex systems. That is why Watzlawick, Weakland and Fisch are able to assert the following:

"But the occurrence of second-order change is ordinarily viewed as something uncontrollable, even incomprehensible, a quantum jump, a sudden illumination which unpredictably comes at the end of long, often frustrating mental and emotional labor, sometimes in a dream, sometimes almost as an act of grace in the theological sense. Koestler, in his *Act of Creation*, has collected an encyclopedic array of examples of this phenomenon, and has introduced the concept of bisociation. According to him, bisociation is "the perceiving of a situation or idea in two self-consistent but habitually incompatible frames of reference", and "the sudden bisociation of a mental event with two habitually incompatible matrices results in an abrupt transfer of the train of thought from one associative context to another". In a brilliant paper, Bronowski deals with the same problem and also assigns to the decisive leap an unpredictable, almost random nature … Despite such combined weight of authority and common perception, it is our experience that second-order change appears unpredictable, abrupt, illogical etc. in terms of first-order change, that is, from within the system. Indeed, this must be so, because, as we have seen, second-order change is introduced into the system from the outside and therefore is not something familiar or something understandable in terms of the vicissitudes of first-order change. Hence its puzzling, seemingly capricious nature. But seen from outside the system,

---

314 Ashby (Introduction), p. 243.

it merely amounts to a change of the premises (the combination rules in terms of Group Theory) governing the system as a whole."[315]

In the following section I will try to use the different elements of the different types of order, of problem solving and of meta-systemic influencing, to shape the components of the methodology.

## 3.4  Cybernetic Systems Methodology: Systemic and Meta-Systemic Strategies

> "… the control function
> is spread through
> the architecture of the system.
> It is not an identifiable thing at all,
> but its existence in some form
> is inferred from the system's behavior."
> *Stafford Beer*

### 3.41  Basic Idea of the Control-Oriented Systems Methodology

To facilitate readers' understanding of the variants of systemic and meta-systemic strategies described below, and which differ by degree of detail, I will start by summarizing the basic idea of the system methodology that was developed in the course of the research project described in the introduction to this book. The starting point was the idea that problem solving can be understood as a learning process or, phrased the other way round, that learning is a problem-solving process. In part A of the treatise on systems methodology[316] I hope to have shown that there are good arguments supporting this view and the dual nature expressed by it. I have summarized the discussion in the graph shown in figure 3.41(1).

In accordance with Popper, the starting point or center of the methodology is a problem. According to Popper, it can be understood as non-fulfillment of an expectation or anticipation (if we refer to knowledge in the subjective or organismic sense) or as inconsistency or incompatibility or as falsification (if we refer to knowledge in the objective sense, as in Popper's world). From a cybernetics point of view, a problem can be interpreted as a

315 Beavin, Jackson, and Watzlawick (Principles, 2011), pp. 23–25.
316 Gomez, Malik, and Oeller (Systemmethodik), part A.

disturbance in a state of adaptation, and the act of solving the problem can be understood as restituting the same or creating a new state of adaptation.

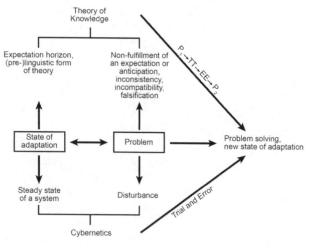

*Figure 3.41(1):[317] Relationships between problem solving, knowledge theory, and cybernetics*

As a consequence, the steps that make up the overall methodology include a methodical claim to identify the control model (control mechanism, controller) causing the problem—or in other words, to model the problem and its potential causes from the perspective of these control mechanisms in hopes of determining possible interventions and influences to (re-)establish the desired state, that is, solve the problem. Now, it was obvious that the diverse nature of real problems cannot be captured by one single category of control mechanisms. Instead, a kind of meta-control mechanism had to be created which would construct or evolve object-level controllers. This idea is expressed by figure 3.41(2) below.

---

317 Gomez, Malik, and Oeller (Systemmethodik), p. 50.

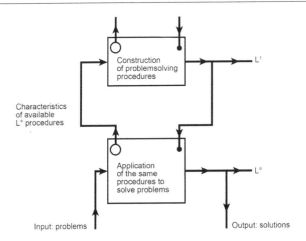

*Figure 3.41 (2):[318] Control as problem solving*

To a specific input, procedures are applied which will change, process, transform, and so on this input to produce solutions as output. This happens in the context and at the logical level of a determined language $L°$. These procedures have determined characteristics which at a logically higher level (Ll) are the objects of constructions of problem-solving procedures.

Of course, the claim to create a control model of the problem situation as a prerequisite for problem-solving and system-influencing interventions is identical to the claim to determine the control-relevant characteristics of the underlying system to be influenced, because, depending on what kind of system it is and what qualities and behaviors it entails, there will be different strategies to influence it.

This thought resulted in the sequence of steps shown in the schema below (figure 3.41(3)).

Figure 3.41(4) contains a more detailed version in which each of the steps is interpreted further.

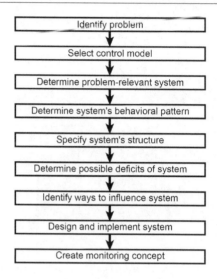

*Figure 3.41(3):[319] Summary of steps of control-oriented systems methodology*

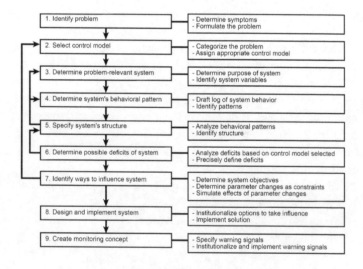

*Figure 3.41(4):[320] Phase schema of control-oriented systems methodology*

319 Gomez, Malik, and Oeller (Systemmethodik), p. 699.
320 Gomez, Malik, and Oeller (Systemmethodik), p. 746.

In these depictions the methodology appears as a *linear* sequence of steps, which obviously does not do justice to its cybernetic nature. If we take into account that a methodology like this can be understood as another control mechanism to control the human thinking process as well as individuals' and/or groups' problem-solving activities (as far as I am concerned, it even has to be understood that way), this will take us to figure 3.41(5), which has to be interpreted as follows:

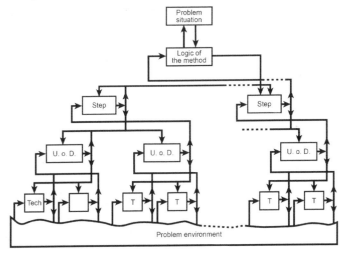

*Figure 3.41(5)[321]*

Contrary to what the linear depiction seems to suggest, there is no predefined sequence of steps. Instead, steps one through nine in figure 3.41(4) form a repertoire from which to select the problem situation. This selection is jointly determined by the logic of the methodology and the characteristics of the problem situation. The most general form of logic of the methodology consists in the basic structure of the trial-and-error process described in part 2. Each step, when understood as a sub-controller, entails its own repertoire of systems of reference (hereinafter referred to as Universe of Discourse, or

---

321 See Gomez (Systems-Methodology), p. 248; this way of depicting the systems methodology as a control mechanism has been discussed extensively in Gomez, Malik, and Oeller (Systemmethodik), part C; part B of the same paper addresses ways to derive control models and their depictions.

U.o.D.), including the respective techniques to process the detailed questions of each step in a meaningful manner.

Even though this depiction has been kept very concise, it should be obvious that a methodology like this operates at various hierarchical levels at the same time. Looking back at section 3.3, it is clear that this has to be the object and the meta-level, or meta-meta-level, and so on.

In the following sections I will show how this concept can be applied in the area of strategy, and in particular what the different applications for different levels of difficulty and complexity can look like. Readers should always remember that the following remarks and the methods described are targeted at the field of very high complexity—that is, at areas where we always suffer from a lack of knowledge and information, where we can never know everything we should know, and where all we can recognize is trends, perhaps patterns, but not causal relationships. Furthermore, complexity in practice is evident in the fact that there are always conflicting goals and intentions, a great degree of ambiguity and uncertainty, and interventions into the system tend to ripple through the network in unpredictable ways we either cannot predict at all, or can predict only in broad categories. Also, any actions in these kinds of systems are characterized by a series of time lags. From the point when an incident occurs, it usually takes a while—and it depends on the type of incident, but also on the system structures how long that will be—until the responsible manager learns about the incident. From then, more time elapses until a relevant decision is made, and even more until appropriate measures are actually launched. Finally, it will take yet more time until measures eventually have an effect with regard to the original incident. Apart from the many filter effects, distortions, and so on that may occur in the course of this chain of events, often there is no more reasonable connection between the effect and the original incident. Sometimes it is not even possible to see that the incident and the effect are parts of what was intended to be one loop.

### 3.42 Evolutionary Overlay of Constructivist Problem-Solving Processes

Under the constructivist paradigm, there is a multitude of normative schemas, or sequences of steps which allegedly lead to a rational approach and thus to an improvement in problem-solving capabilities. In most cases, key problems lie not so much in the contextual design of each step as in the question as to what *extent of knowledge* or information is explicitly or implicitly required and *how* the concrete sequences of steps are to be *applied*. The problem of what information is required and the related difficulties have extensively been dealt with in part 2. At this point I will focus on *the mode of application*, as it immediately leads to the combination of constructivist and evolutionary process elements.

A useful methodology has to do justice to both the nature of the problems to be solved and the functional principles of human thinking. In the area of strategic management, the least to be said about expected problems is that they are likely to be extremely complex; and we know enough about the way the human mind works—related to both the individual and the social system—to be able to tell what a methodology should *not* be. The key requirement is that a meaningful methodology should *not* be *linear*. A procedure is "linear" when each step has to be concluded before the next is launched.

A concrete proposal for a problem-solving methodology might entail the following six steps:[322]

1. Identify problem
2. Determine goals to be reached
3. Analyze current situation
4. Analyze influencing factors and basic conditions
5. Search for alternatives
6. Evaluate alternatives and select one.

This method would be linear if the problem had to be identified in its entirety before any goals could be determined, or if the goals had to be fixed before we could start analyzing the current situation. An approach like this would not be effective, because in solving somewhat complex problems it is impossible, due to that very complexity, to conclusively deal with each individual step.

A substantial number of such step sequences have been extensively dealt with elsewhere, so there is no need to study the numerous variants once again.[323] Also, as has been pointed out above, what matters is not so much the content of each step as the way such a schema is *applied*. It is possible at any time to create a useful methodology from the above-mentioned six

---

322 As mentioned before, there are numerous sequences of steps. This one is used as an example to represent the entire category.
323 See Gomez, Malik, and Oeller (Systemmethodik), part II.

steps, or from any other meaningful approach, when an additional mechanism is used to create a circular or spiraled approach.[324]

*Two basic ideas are crucial:* One is that in the course of a problem-solving process all steps of a schema have to be completed, although their concrete *sequence* is not predetermined but results from the *respective stage* of the problem-solving process. So, the process is not a closed one; it is open. There is not necessarily a predefined initial and end state; instead, it can be begun at any point in the overall schema and its result determines what step will be taken next.

The *second* idea consists in overlaying the rather constructivist step sequences with an evolutionary process. The way to achieve this is by viewing each step as a trial-and-error process, with the content of each step determining the *search area*. This latter idea follows from the basic fact that in complex situations, knowledge is bound to be limited and it takes explorative processes to unearth new knowledge. Figure 3.42(1) shows the structure of such a process, although it cannot provide any insight into its dynamics.

Under this concept, the problem-solving process can begin with any of the steps and continue with any other, allowing leaps between steps and thus taking an irregular course. This allows for the fact that *practical* problems can occur spontaneously in any individual step; that is, practical problems do not follow a predefined sequence. The key point to be considered in this approach, however, is that none of the steps is *systematically neglected.* Systematically omitting individual steps would reduce the probability of finding a solution, or the quality of the solution found, which is rather obvious when we imagine that the search for alternatives is systematically omitted. In that case, the overall structure of the process would be adjusted with the effect of hampering the finding of a solution, and as a result—similar to what happens with a weighted die—certain categories of results would become less probable.

The tool to keep such a process going, which is both teachable and learnable, is a matrix of the kind shown in figure 3.42(2). In principle, all fields of the matrix must be completed for a given problem. This can be achieved either through an individual's thinking processes or through distributing the work among a group of people, with all of them working on all fields or—depending on the situation—individual fields or groups of fields being as-

---

324 Vester (Ballungsgebiete), pp. 30 et seq.

signed to specific members of the group. In cases like those, the matrix allows the determination of the location of the problem-solving process and the estimation of what further activities will be required for the process to come to an end, if a preliminary one. All in all, the methodology serves the purpose of steering the interactions between human brains and a given problem. This is why it has to be designed as a control mechanism, and it needs sufficient control variety to keep interactions under control. A linear approach lacks that variety.

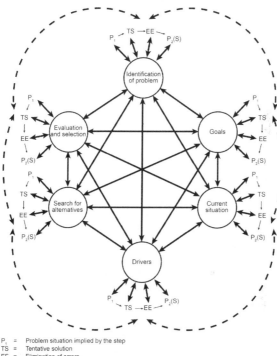

P. = Problem situation implied by the step
TS = Tentative solution
EF = Elimination of errors
P.(S) = New problem situation resulting from the step applied, possibly (solution)

*Figure 3.42(1)*

By contrast, even if we just consistently recognize the fact that each individual step of a methodology will produce results that can only be assumed but not regarded as safe—so we need to make repetitive attempts at exploring things in depth, based on constructive criticism—just this very recognition

will considerably increase variety. These considerations can easily be substantiated epistemologically, which has been done elsewhere, so there is no
need to do it here.[325]

| | | Evolutionary dimension: | | | |
|---|---|---|---|---|---|
| | | Tentative problem P1 | Tentative solution TS | EF = Elimi-nation of er-rors and defi-cits EE | Preliminary solution or new problem P2(S) |
| *Constructivist* | Identification of problem | | | | |
| | Determination of goals | | | | |
| | Determination of current situation | | | | |
| | Identification of drivers | | | | |
| | Search for alternativesSear ch for alternatives | | | | |
| | Evaluation and selection | | | | |

*Figure 3.42(2)*

Instead, I would like to point to an approach often seen in experienced managers. After delegating a problem—such as preparing a decision or setting
up a plan or concept—to an employee, they often reject the results submitted several times, whether with or without reason, demanding that they be
revised. From the employee's point of view such behavior is often difficult
to understand, and in some cases it is perceived as vexatious. From a cybernetic-evolutionary perspective, however, it is a very understandable form of
variety increase by that manager, who has to assume that the first result
handed in cannot be the best achievable under the circumstances. So she will
assume that repeated revisions will lead to improvement, and most likely she

---

325 For more details see Gomez, Malik, and Oeller (Systemmethodik), part A.

will be aware that even repeated revisions might not produce a major improvement. But even this is systemically rational, for she will gain certainty that the job has been done well and needs no improvement. She will risk some degree of frustration on the employee's part, regarding it as an inevitable side effect of this strategy, and try to alleviate or possibly prevent it by giving sound reasons.

Of course this procedure cannot provide ultimate certainty, but it serves well as a heuristic rule for dealing with complex systems. This approach and its cybernetic background will be dealt with in greater detail when we study a practical example in section 3.44.

At this point, however, we need to address a further problem that makes it difficult to apply a process comprising both constructivist and evolutionary elements.

As the methodology itself comprises a total of steps but the concrete sequence has to remain open for several reasons explained above, in a concrete situation the question will be at what point a given step is completed and what step should follow. This depends on two things: One is the stage of the problem-solving process, or the progress achieved so far; the other refers to additional factors such as the time and human and material resources available for the problem-solving process. One of the key evaluation criteria for managing such a problem-solving process is the *increase in information* to be expected from either intensifying the step in question or applying other steps. Often, in the course of a problem-solving process those involved—be they individuals or groups—are increasingly under the impression that additional problem-solving activities, such as a more thorough study of individual steps or the repetitive completion of specific matrix fields, would not provide any additional information that could influence and be relevant for the solutions emerging or already found. In many instances it is this very impression that determines next steps with a view to both the process stage reached and the continuation or discontinuation of the overall process. It has to be noted, however, that this impression can be misleading. In terms of its logical nature, it can be a presumption or hypothesis according to Popper. As intense as the subjective impressions or subjective certainty of those involved may be, there is no reason to assume that they have to be correct. Instead, it will be necessary—and can be observed in actual problem-solving processes—that this presumption is critically reviewed and discussed, thus expanding the argumentative basis for certain control interventions. It will, of course, depend on several factors how thorough such a discussion will be, for instance on the importance attached to a problem (which is a presumption in itself), on the problem-solving activities already undertaken, etcetera. All in all, it must be emphasized that any such discussion on the question of how to manage the problem-solving process has a *"meta" character*. This is illustrated by figure 3.42(3).

Now, before we address these matters in greater detail, another particular point needs to be stressed. People often think that problem-solving exclusively takes place at the linguistic-intellectual level. In other words, they assume that the problem, which is identified in some kind of way, is processed and perhaps solved through intrapersonal thinking processes and interpersonal communication processes, and that its solution is then implemented. Indeed, a somewhat complex problem can hardly be processed effectively in this manner. Instead, we have to assume that a major part of the information required to effectively process the problem can only be gathered by experimenting with the system that has produced the problem: It has to be stimulated to cause it to provide specific information; or in other words, there have to be interventions in reality in order to gain insights. As complex problems cannot be controlled by sheer thinking, the methodology to be applied needs to guide the problem-solver's activities: At certain stages of the process he or she will have to be encouraged to perform a reality check of the ideas he or she has developed so far with regard to the situation. Figure 3.42(4) shows a few typical processes. Figure 3.42(4a) shows the basic situation. The distinction between the two different levels, which is referred to as the "reality limit" here, is based on Popper's "Three Worlds Concept."[326] Figure 3.42(4b) shows a procedure located exclusively in physical reality. With this kind of approach there is no mental simulation phase at the beginning; rather, the problem solver moves in the implementation phase only. Errors are committed in reality; decisions are taken spontaneously and ad hoc, often based on so-called "experience," and have to be canceled just as often when there is unexpected resistance. This approach roughly corresponds to the kind of trial-and-error behavior that is rightly perceived as primitive. Next, figure 3.42(4c) shows a behavior located

---

326 See Popper (Knowledge), pp. 106 et seq., 153 et seq.; this concept was extensively described in Gomez, Malik, and Oeller (Systemmethodik), pp. 34 et seq.; also see Eccles (Reality), pp. 163 et seq., in the context of the state of the art of brain research.

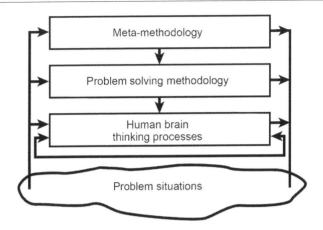

*Figure 3.42(3)*

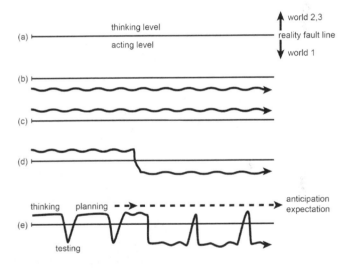

*Figure 3.42(4)*

exclusively at the intellectual level. In this case an effective decision, in the sense of intervening in the physical systemic relationship, is never made. Finally, figure 3.42(4d) shows the variant mentioned before, where problem solving occurs at the mental level only, and after some time—for instance after a "solution" has been identified—it is put into practice. Depending on the situation, the phase of intellectual struggle with the problem can be longer or shorter, and depending on that, the implementation phase can often be more or less difficult. Figure 3.42(4e) then shows the approach to be preferred from an evolutionary or cybernetic perspective. The phase of intellectual struggle with the problem is repeatedly interrupted by real-life tests which help review one's mental concepts of sustainability, realism, feasibility, and so on. When due to meta-systemic interventions the focus of problem solving is shifted from the mental to the real level, thus entering into the implementation phase, the mental concepts so far developed work as anticipations or expectations of the future, and the implementation progress is measured against these expectations. In other words, the problem-solving process does not break off; only its focal point is shifted. Due to the expectations projected into the future, which may repeatedly be corrected depending on the actual course of implementation, we have the possibility—which is key to any control process—of comparing the actual against the expected course. The more complex a problem situation is, the more intense any interaction between mental and real activities must be—both in the phase dedicated to grasping the problem intellectually and in the phase of implementation. Any useful problem-solving methodology therefore has to stimulate and trigger these mutual effects and interactions. This is the only way to find out how complex a situation really is, and the only way to achieve a certain congruence of expectations and the actual course of events; that is, it is the only way to ensure the desired alignment of an evolutionary process.

### 3.43 Taking Account of System Characteristics and Systemic Regulation Mechanisms

The above observation that in complex settings the only way to gain relevant information is usually by *stimulating* or *provoking* the system to yield that information leads us to the next, decisive step in developing a system methodology. This step is of fundamental importance in particular for a systems methodology for strategic management. Its key feature is that in one phase of the process, which is yet to be defined, the methodology requires users to identify the *characteristics of the system producing the assumed problem.* In very simple settings, this would hardly produce additional relevant information. In complex situations, however, this step has great significance. On the one hand, as has repeatedly been pointed out, a meaningful solution must often consist in changing the nature or structure of the underlying system: There is little sense in struggling with problematic outputs themselves, as the system, due to its inherent structure, will tend to produce those same problematic outputs over and over again. On the other hand, the nature of the system determines what the best way is to control the entire process—as there are different ways of obtaining information—and especially how the system can best be influenced and changed.

Simple as this observation may be, in actual problem-solving approaches it is often ignored. This illustrates a fatal dilemma I have pointed out several times before:

Things that seem completely self-evident, as long as they are considered within an area still manageable to the individual, are neglected in the area of complex systems—perhaps even because they are so self-evident in other settings, which can have very problematic consequences. In the individually manageable area it is perfectly clear that people will act differently when, for example, out in the wild they are suddenly faced with an antelope as compared to a lion. Even someone with limited experience in big game hunting will spontaneously adapt his behavior to the vastly different behavioral characteristics of these two animals. Similarly, a mushroom picker will act differently when finding a type of edible mushroom he or she is familiar with and immediately recognizes, as compared to when finding one he or she does not know and which may not be safe to eat. Also, people's behavior towards one another will differ depending on how well they are acquainted, what social status and how much clout they possess, and in what situations they have met. We might even say that the *almost spontaneous and in part intuitive perception of systemic characteristics is the key variable that determines our entire behavior* by selecting a field of behavior in which we move.

Once the situation gets less manageable, however, and especially when we are unable to capture systemic characteristics with our senses and instead need to reconstruct the overall system intellectually, based on key pieces of information, the question of system characteristics is paid little attention, or no attention at all. As a consequence, problem-solving processes are often performed with astonishing naïveté, doing the *nature of the system* no justice whatsoever. Examples abound. Consider the following remarks by Hall:

"Though the United States has spent billions of dollars on foreign aid programs, it has captured neither the affection nor esteem of the rest of the world. In many countries today Americans are cordially disliked; in others merely tolerated. The reasons for this sad state of affairs are many and varied, and some of them are beyond the control of anything this country might do to try to correct them. But harsh as it may seem to the ordinary citizen, filled as he is with good intentions and natural generosity, much of the foreigner's animosity has been generated by the way Americans behave. As a country we are apt to be guilty of great ethno-centrism. In many of our foreign aid programs we employ a heavy-handed technique in dealing with local nationals. We insist that everyone else do things our way. Consequently we manage to convey the impression that we simply regard foreign nationals as "under-developed Americans". Most of our behavior does not spring from malice but from ignorance, which is as grievous a sin in international relations. We are not only almost totally ignorant of what is expected in other countries, we are equally ignorant of what we are communicating to other people by our own normal behavior."[327]

Hall's book is filled with striking examples of how, despite best intentions, people can trigger a series of dysfunctional and even hostile system responses when their own behavior ignores the characteristics of the other system. They represent typical cases in which the *mutually* adaptive behavior required in the context of spontaneous system structures does not work; instead the entire burden of adaptation is shifted to the other system. Another, specifically management-related collection of examples is the book *The Ugly American Businessman in Europe* by L. Gundy,[328] which describes numerous cases in which the failure of U.S. American business and management practices is largely due to the neglect of essential features of the European business system; instead, people had assumed in total naïveté and ignorance that the things that work well in the U.S. had to work in other regions and cultures, too.

The history of conquering peoples and cultures, of colonization, and of the conflict of ideologies also provides excellent material to illustrate this kind of mistake. One persistent admonisher in this context was Peter Drucker, who in his remarks on the problems of multinational corporations kept demanding that systemic characteristics and structures be taken into consideration. Consider this selection of quotes, which are quite straightforward:

"One thing is clear: The multinational tomorrow will be different from the multinational of today. We still, substantially, have the nineteenth-century multinational but use it to do the twentieth-century task of the transnational. We are, in other words, in a transition period. Tomorrow's management structure of the multinational will be different from today. Even within the developed countries the multinational will have to be able to harmonize, in one structure, the need for "polycentric" management with the need for a common business strategy. Where today the tendency in most multinationals is to say, "This is how we do it in Chicago (or Munich, or Osaka,

---

327 Hall (The Silent Language), xiii.
328 Mintzberg (Nature), passim.

or Eindhoven)", they will have to learn tomorrow to say, "This is what we want to achieve; how does one get it done in Pretoria (or Munich, or Osaka, or Amsterdam)?" There is another important problem in top -management structure for the multinational. Top-management structures are not mechanical; they are, above all, cultural. The top-management structure which an American management group accepts as right and proper may appear decidedly odd and uncomfortable to a French, a Japanese, or a German management group. Yet these French, Japanese or German managers have to understand their own local top-management group, have to feel comfortable with it, have to work with it. To be successful, the top-management teams in a multinational have therefore to be different in their structure in different countries, or else they will not make local sense. Yet they have to be compatible at least throughout the company, or else various top-management teams cannot work together. Top-management structure in the multinational, therefore, has to be built on the most complex and most difficult of all design principles: systems management ... every multinational company faces the complexity of business strategy, precisely because it has to be both unified for the entire company and specific for each major product category as well as for each major market. This means that the multinational has complexity built into its very structure. It is multicultural, it is multinational, it is multimarket, and also multi-management."[329]

It is not particularly difficult to see that what Drucker demands goes beyond integrating the respective systemic characteristics: His idea of the structure of multinationals is closely related to the ideas resulting from the Viable Systems Model.

With regard to the basic characteristics of the systems under discussion, we can say that virtually each step of a methodology strongly depends on what attributes the respective systems have. This can be seen in the step sequence shown here, which is used as a typical example representative of many others. Even the question of how *to identify the problem* involves various difficulties, depending on the degree of complexity of the system that generates the problem. If it is a rather limited area within a small company whose basic structure and characteristics are defined by a certain technology, it will probably be much easier to recognize and locate potential disturbances and perhaps even to identify their causes. The situation is very different for, say, the strategic problems of a multinational, the structural and procedural issues of an entire economy, the control of epidemics, the establishment and financing of social security, and so on. But even with small, halfway manageable areas, the overall structure of the respective system strongly affects

---

329 Drucker (People and Performance), chapter 21.

the range of possible solutions. Just think of the questions of marital and family therapy, employee motivation, fair pay, and so forth. With questions and systemic relationships like these, it is often impossible to say whether or not certain states or events must be considered to be disturbances, what the relevant variables are, where the systemic behavioral limits are for these variables, and so on.

The same applies to the question about adequate *goals* to be pursued in the problem-solving process: Answers strongly depend on the degree of complexity of the system under study, on its control structures and systemic characteristics. A factor of particular importance in this context is the quantities of information required to specify goals entailing a greater level of detail than general heuristic guidelines. Ashby[330] used a small graph (see figure 3.43(1)) to make this point, using the management of traffic at an airport as an example.

The control system receives inputs X. It then sends out instructions defining values for the variables Y which are sent back to the airplanes. Of course, a control system like this must be designed so that it will be a "good" control system. The way in which outputs depend on inputs is determined by relation F (the transfer function). It is obviously not necessary, and not to be expected in a case like this, that this transfer function be expressed in arithmetical terms; still it exists, even though it cannot be described either verbally or in any other way, as inputs are de facto transformed into outputs. The goal, a "good" F, does not depend on the transmission from X to Y; instead it depends on the quantity of all possible transfer functions F, so the question is how much information has to be transmitted via channel C in order to solve the problem posed. Note, in particular, that the goal obviously does not depend on the values of Y.

---

330 See Ashby (Setting Goals), pp. 37 et seq.

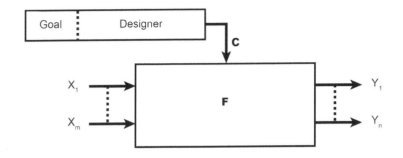

*Figure 3.43(1)*

The question of goal information strongly depends on whether and to what extent there is interdependency between the individual variables. Ashby assumes a complex goal to exist when many variables are given and the relations required show a considerable degree of conditionality between variables, or in other words: when the overall goal is a non-reducible function of several variables. There is an enormous difference in the information volumes required to determine goals, depending on whether they are simple in the sense explained—that is, reducible—or complex/non-reducible. If we assume, for instance, that the traffic at an airport involves only 100 variables, which is probably too little, and that for each variable there are only five values to be distinguished, it will demonstrably take a maximum of 500 bits only to specify the goal—that is, determine the transfer function F—if the goal is reducible. If it is not reducible, the quantity of information required can go to $10^{70}$ bits—a figure far above Bremermann's Limit. It is clear, then, that the system under study, its inputs and outputs, and their characteristics are of crucial importance to the goal definition.

It is similar with determining the current state of a complex system, in particular when it keeps producing new states so it is impossible to predict what aspects will be permanent and what will be subject to quick changes. The search for alternatives follows identical laws in the context of truly complex systems. The number of options basically open is usually enormous, so the entire methodology and its practical application will have to be designed so as to reduce those enormous information quantities. Corresponding curves have been discussed in section 2.

All these considerations show that the attributes of the system producing the problem are of fundamental importance to how the methodology is handled, and that any adequate activities to control the process will be determined by these attributes. The entire set of problems can be illustrated using proverbial experiences from everyday life. Good bait catches fine fish, or so the saying goes. Using good bait also means using the right bait: We use bacon to catch mice, and to fish trout we bait the hook with a worm or fly, not with chocolate—no matter how much we may love chocolate ourselves. The nature and peculiar nature of the system, the question as to what it will respond to—that determines what the best approach will be.

In a communications-theory sense we could say that we need to understand and speak "the language of the system" in order to interact with it, since that is the precondition for being able to influence it. Language obviously must be understood in a very broad sense here, much like a poet—in a rather imprecise manner when viewed from a sciences perspective yet accurately from a systems perspective—speaks of the language of the wind, the leaves, the sea, and so on. So fundamental is the ability to respond to the communication mode of our environment when we are dealing with systems, that it is rather surprising that this has not found its way into our mandatory education and training content.

Of course, many things in this area we do instinctively, without really being aware. Without even having to think, most people will switch to another form of communication when dealing with toddlers or pets. But it takes a special capability when interacting with grown-ups to adapt one's mode of communication to their needs. Most people tend to see everything from their own vantage point and to judge everything by their own standards. Cultivating abilities such as "the art of making friends" or "managing one's boss" is part of the cybernetically relevant strategies to manage complex systems, and so is the "art of diplomatic conduct." To a significant extent, the "nature of the system" relevant here is a question of its regulation mechanisms in the broadest sense. This is why in systems methodology we need to explore the control structures of the systems to be influenced.

Several varieties of control mechanisms have been discussed in detail elsewhere, in particular the simple servomechanism, the ultra-stable system, and the multi-stable system.[331] Rather than recap these rather formal depictions, I will use a few examples to show what kinds of ideas they represent.

---

331 See Gomez, Malik, and Oeller (Systemmethodik), parts B and C; as well as Krieg (Grundlagen).

## 3.431 The Feedback Principle

Human thinking strongly follows a thinking model orientated by *linear cause-and-effect chains*. Causes create effects, which, in turn, are the causes of further effects

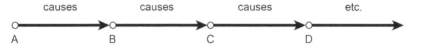

*Figure 3.43(2)*

In the 1940s, however, several sciences found this kind of thinking to be unable to capture and explain a series of phenomena. Virtually all biological, social, physiological, and neurological problems are impossible to explain with linear, cause-analytical thinking. Also, it became increasingly clear that even in technical sciences where linear thinking was particularly prevalent, it was not sufficient.

In those years, scientists from a range of disciplines met for a series of talks organized by the Josiah Macy Foundation to explore the fruitfulness of another, new way of thinking: one based *on circular systems with feedback effects*. Eventually, these conferences resulted in a field of research cutting across classical disciplines, which Norbert Wiener in 1948 called "cybernetics."

In addition to Wiener, further pioneers of the new science include Arturo Rosenblueth, Walter B. Cannon, Julian Bigelow, Warren McCulloch, Walter Pitts, John von Neumann, Ludwig von Bertalanffy, Claude Shannon, Warren Weaver, Margaret Mead, Gregory Bateson, Heinz von Foerster, and Ross Ashby. These people have acquired an almost legendary reputation with experts, as their work produced not only new findings but findings of *a new kind* and we have yet to determine the full scope of their philosophical, technological, and social consequences.

The starting point for these developments was a series of observations—specifically:

- that there are organizations or systems able to strive for and achieve goals on their own accord;
- that they are also able to hit moving targets;
- that they can achieve these targets even when there are disturbances, even when the cause of that disturbance is not known;

– that they can overcome even totally new disturbances that have never occurred before.

Obviously, these observations could not be explained with linear cause-and-effect chains. Furthermore, they had relevance not only for science but for technology, especially military technology.

The closer study of these problems revealed one of nature's most fundamental design principles: the *feedback principle*. Two variants have to be distinguished:

### 1.1 Negative, stabilizing feedback

Very simply put, this variety of the feedback principle means that an organism can take advantage of the feedback it receives regarding the success or failure of its actions to then correct its behavior so it will approach and eventually reach its target. The organism orientates its behavior exclusively by the difference between the actual and the target state. Each correction of behavior is a step to diminish that difference. The behavior of such a system can be described by a typical curve which is referred to as the oscillation curve.

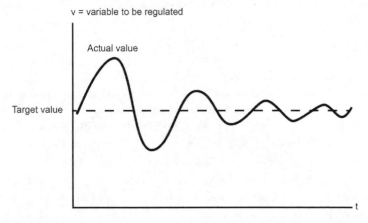

*Figure 3.43(3)*

*1.2 Positive, destabilizing feedback*

Here, the difference between the actual and target state is not reduced, as with the negative feedback, but increased and augmented. The behavior of such a system also shows a typical curve.

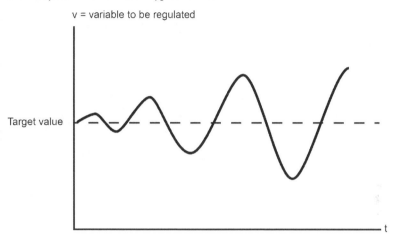

*Figure 3.43(4)*

Quite obviously, positive feedback can work for a limited period only, as it drives the system into increasing fluctuations and eventually ruins it. Hence, positive feedback loops are meaningless or even dangerous for the normal behavior of a system. However, in interconnected systems they often occur together with negative feedback loops.

*3.432 Simple Regulation Systems*

The principle of negative feedback is incorporated into many technical systems today, as illustrated by the example of thermostat-controlled heating.

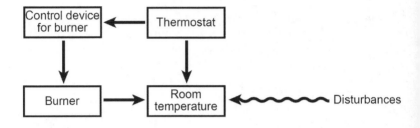

*Figure 3.43(5)*

The key characteristic of this control loop is that the key variable, the room temperature, is influenced not only by the burner but by a multitude of other factors. It changes whenever a door or window is opened, when the external temperature rises or falls, when an open fireplace is lit, when more people enter the room, and so on. Regardless of all those factors, all the thermostat registers is the difference between the target and the actual temperature, based on which it regulates the burner—irrespective of what causes the difference.

This example illustrates very well some of the characteristics of closed control loops, in particular the fact that it is not necessary to know the causes of disturbances to take appropriate corrective measures. This insight alone suffices to refute a century-old dogma upheld by science, according to which appropriate action requires knowledge of causes.

Also, the example contains a few sources of common misunderstandings that have been preventing the widespread use of cybernetic findings. Below I will list some preconditions for this particular example which do not have to be met in all cases, least of all the truly important ones, and indeed are usually not met:

a. The system comprises components that expressly perform the function of controlling or regulating (control unit, thermostat).
b. These components can be identified clearly and easily.
c. The whole system is simple.
d. The goal of the system (e.g., maintaining the room temperature at 69.8°F) is not an inherent system goal—it is set from the outside.
e. The logic of the entire system is clear and obvious to anyone; it can be clearly determined what the purpose of each component is and through what channels information and control signals travel.

f. System relationships and the effects occurring in the system have been determined (a signal from the control unit usually starts or stops the burner).

What this shows is that virtually all technical systems, while they follow cybernetic laws, are basically not suitable for illustrating the true scope and significance of cybernetics. The only exception is complex computer systems.

### 3.433 Higher Forms of Control Systems

#### 3.433.1 Implicit Control

An essential source of misunderstanding in the heating example above is that the control elements are *special* system components added to the system so it will be able to self-regulate. In fact, systems like these—even though they have many advantages compared to non-feedback systems—are anything but perfect, and are subject to a series of disturbances affecting not the variable to be controlled (in this case, temperature) but elements of the system itself. For instance, the temperature sensor may become soiled and thus insensitive, or the control device may fail.

In truly interesting self-regulating systems, such errors are not possible, as the self-regulation of these systems is a result of their structure. The capability to self-regulate through feedback is inherent to them. It is an implicit element of their structure. They *cannot help* self-regulating.

One typical example is the regulation of the total count of an animal population through the availability of food. The more animals the population comprises, the smaller the food supplies available—which causes the number of animals to drop, in turn causing food supplies to recover. Contrary to the heating example, in this case we have no clearly recognizable control components. There is no control unit; instead, the structure of the overall system "animals + available food" produces the regulating effect.

#### 3.433.2 Interconnected Systems

By expanding the animal example, we can delete all simplifications existing in the heating example. As everyone knows, animal populations are not only regulated via food availability. The truth is much more complex.

Let us assume the animals to be rabbits in a biotope undisturbed by humans. What influences their overall number? A structural diagram typical of systems research shows the key connections.

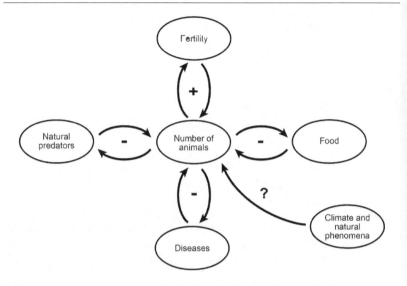

*Figure 3.43(6)*

The following observations are significant for this kind of system:

a. We do not know in advance what the "goal" of the system is. The number of rabbits results from numerous factors and it is impossible to forecast.

b. The goal—the resulting number of animals—is *not predetermined from outside* and indeed cannot be. It is a goal inherent to the system resulting from the numerous interactions mentioned.

c. It is *not a fixed goal*, as the target number keeps changing its steady state under different influences. If the number of animals were constantly recorded, we could probably detect typical cyclical movements of the target.

d. Nobody has *control* of the system. Instead, the overall system self-regulates in the true sense of the word: There is no single or dominant factor decisive for the resulting number of animals. In other words, this system has no identifiable components that could be referred to as regulators or anything of the kind.

e. Contrary to the heating example, where individual system components influenced each other in a way that could be identified and predetermined, in this case we usually *cannot determine what specific effects* individual system components have on each other. We usually do not know how many rabbits per year will be killed by foxes. Perhaps we could work with certain statistical averages, but they have little relevance for a tangible understanding of system relationships. To predict the exact number of rabbits, it is not helpful to have some kind of average—we need the precise number falling prey to predators. However, as foxes do not exclusively feed on rabbits but eat other animals, too, and the number of rabbits killed also depends on the overall number of rabbits and the number of foxes living in the biotope, a quantitative statement will hardly be possible.

f. What can be determined is the *general tendency* of an influence (marked with plus or minus). In other words, the statements we can make regarding such systems are not concrete statements but *statements of a higher order* or a higher level of abstraction. This enables us to determine, for instance, whether the overall system is stable or instable.

g. The individual elements work on each other *not in a determined way* but with a certain probability. This is true for all natural systems and all systems in which human beings are an essential element.

h. The system is *open*. There can be new elements any time, and they can profoundly change the system's overall behavior.

### 3.433.3 The Principle of Homeostasis

The above is an example of what is referred to as *homeostasis*, a mechanism or functional principle of crucial significance. Further examples include the regulation of blood sugar, body temperature, and adrenaline levels. All these parameters depend on an enormous number of other factors which influence each other and this way regulate the state of the parameter in question.

The *key achievement* of a homeostatic system is to keep one or several factors, variables, or parameters within so-called "physiological" limits, that is, stable, and—this is the key point—to do this despite the fact that any influences or disturbances that occur are unknown in terms of their kinds, causes, and effects. "Physiological" means: in line with the system and its specific character. Apart from the feedback principle, the discovery of the phenomenon of homeostasis and its basic principles is one of the greatest achievements of cybernetics. We owe the scientific explanation of this functional principle, or law of nature, to the British cyberneticist Ross W. Ashby.

Not only has Ashby, who is primarily known to experts—contrary to Norbert Wiener—thoroughly studied and explained this principle which is so important for the understanding of animate and inanimate systems; he has also designed a machine that illustrates the principles at work: the homeostat. Accordingly, all natural and artificial systems producing homeostasis are referred to as *homeostats*.

Now, why is the principle of homeostasis so important? Simply put, this principle helps explain all phenomena of stability and adaptation. The principle of homeostasis is the principle of self-regulations by self-organization; the homeostat is the fundamental unit of cybernetic explanation and design. A homeostatic system meets the minimal requirements for autonomy, identity, and survival. Combinations from several homeostatic systems—that is, systems of a higher order consisting of homeostatic subsystems—permit us to explain phenomena such as intelligence, cognition, learning, self-organization, and evolution in a way that is interesting to both science and practice.

One point to consider, however, is that working with this principle requires giving up certain prejudices incorporated into our culture. Also, we have to be prepared to question some very widespread views concerning what science is and is not capable of, and what has to be accepted as "scientific."

In the rabbit example it is clear that the interaction of numerous factors in an interconnected system causes the number of animals to settle at a certain level, or to stabilize. If the system comprised by these factors is left to its own devices for a long while, the resulting number of rabbits will reach a high degree of stability. The animal population, and thus all other factors, will have found their natural equilibrium. The values at which they settle and the ranges in which they oscillate will have adapted systemically—they will be "physiological"—even though they might collide with our own ideas and expectations. How can these matters be represented in a meaningful way, making visible the truly decisive and fundamental connections? The key point in this particular case is the rabbits and their population density. Note that we cannot focus on the rabbits only; we need to take into account the fact that their behavior, and thus their population density, depends on a number of different factors, as has been shown. One way to depict the situation is this:

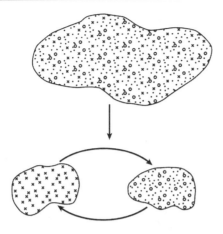

*Figure 3.43(7)*

The upper part of the graph shows the overall system and its possible states represented as dots in an amebic field. In the lower part, the state of the rabbit population has been separated from all other states—the so-called environmental states—and the two arrows indicate that the two interact with each other. Of course, this separation is a purely theoretical one; however, the model—although abstract—contains all elements of the situation that are truly important. All other, also interesting details are left aside; they can be added at any point, if and to the extent that they are important for understanding.

Although in the real world all system components interacting in a homeostatic context form a dense network, almost like a fabric, there are two essential subsystems we can distinguish by mental abstraction: the subsystem that is of immediate interest to us (organization, nation, animal population, etc.) and everything else, gathered in the subsystem "environment."

This way we make sure we will not commit the error of isolating individual subsystems or elements in inadmissible ways. While we do not know precisely what the "environment" comprises, and we will usually not be familiar with all elements of the subsystem in question—as real systems are too complex for that—we have captured all essential relationships, and they can be detailed further, if and as necessary and appropriate, once a specific homeostat is studied.

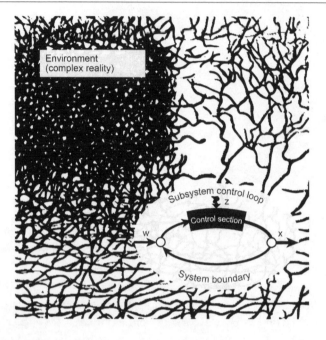

*Figure 3.43(8)[332]*

Just as it is possible to single out one control loop from a network, which remains connected with the "rest of the world" through input and output, it is equally possible to mentally single out larger parts of networks.

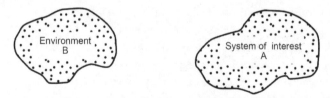

*Figure 3.43(9)*

The dots in both subsystems represent the possible states they can have, or their variety. From our earlier considerations regarding complexity we know that in real systems we have to expect astronomical orders of magnitude. Of all the states a system can potentially assume, usually there are only a few

---

332 See Steinbuch (Maßlos informiert), p. 133.

that represent states of equilibrium (as encircled in the next graph). Due to its inner dynamics, a system that is left alone will always show a tendency towards a steady state.

However, as in a homeostatic context the system is never left on its own, but influences and is influenced by the second subsystem of the overall homeostat, it is not very likely for a steady state of A to also be a steady state of B. As long as B is not in a steady state, however, it will tend to change the state it is in. Due to the linkage between the two systems, this change will affect A as well, possibly throwing it out of balance. These mutual changes keep both sub systems in continuous motion until both have reached their respective states of equilibrium. In other words, one subsystem can sort of "veto" any of the states of the other subsystem, if it is not in a state of equilibrium itself.

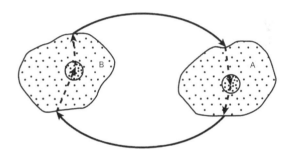

*Figure 3.43(10)*

So, a homeostat will not come to rest until it reaches equilibrium as a whole, that is, with both subsystems (or in detailed, very elaborate cases, with all subsystems). And every time a balance is unsettled—no matter in what way and by what cause—a new balance will be sought. Hence, a homeostatic system is not only able to reach a balance; it also has the higher-level ability to seek a new balance after every disturbance. Ashby calls this type of system ultra-stable.

Probably the best way to recognize and experience the structures and effects of homeostasis is by using the example of the family. Families, no matter whether "healthy" or "broken," show all characteristics of complex systems but are still perceptible to the senses of an individual. The example of the family also shows that homeostasis-controlled and balanced variables do not necessarily have to be physical variables such as temperature, blood sugar, humidity, and so on. Factors like work climate, emotions, organization culture, style, and tradition can also be variables to be considered, and subject to regulation mechanisms. The unfortunate fact that it is difficult to measure variables of this kind does not change anything.

Of particular interest are systems that stabilize their own structure by way of their homeostatic mechanisms, a phenomenon that is currently the subject of intense studies as scientists hope to gain new insights into the phenomenon of life. It is referred to as "autopoiesis." At this point I just remind the reader of the explanations on spontaneous orders provided in chapter 2, as well as the remarks in section 3.3, in particular concerning the different kinds of change and the fact that even a maximum of first-order change will, at best, only strengthen the existing system structure. As has been mentioned before: plus ça change, plus c'est la même chose ...

The following quote may serve to illustrate homeostasis in the social context:

"Many of the things men do take a certain form not so much from instincts as from necessity of adjusting to their fellows ... What characterizes the interactionist approach is the contention that human nature and the social order are products of communication ... The direction taken by a person's conduct is seen as something that is constructed in the reciprocal give and take of interdependent men who are adjusting to one another. Further, a man's personality—those distinctive behavioral patterns that characterize a given individual—is regarded as developing and being reaffirmed from day to day in his interaction with his associates."[333]

### 3.433.4 The Polystable System

The notion that a system can be not only stable but ultra-stable, that is, capable of achieving not only a balance but a new balance after each disturbance, leads to the idea of a polystable system.[334] This also links back to the considerations about first- and second-order change, as discussed in section 3.3. A characteristic feature of such a system is that it can have several, usually even many different states of equilibrium. The field of possible behaviors of a polystable system thus comprises numerous sets of states each of which has one point or cycle of equilibrium. If the system is in one state of a confluent, which does not necessarily have to be a state of equilibrium, its inherent dynamics will drive it towards the state of equilibrium in that confluent. Certain disturbances will cause first-order changes of state only. Other disturbances, however, can lead to second-order changes, causing the

---

333 T. Shibutani, Society and Personality, New Jersey, 1961, pp. 20–23; quoted after Don D. Jackson, Das Studium der Familie, in: Watzlawick and Weakland (Interaktion), p. 21.
334 See Ashby (Brain), p. 185.

system to leave that region and enter another one with different characteristics of equilibrium. Metaphorically speaking, the system overcomes the thresholds of the previous region.

The two graphs below illustrate this type of system. Figure 3.43(10a)[335] shows a field of behavior with 12 confluents. The lines in the confluents indicate that all changes of behavior emerging from any state in that region can only lead to the point or cycle of equilibrium in that region. Figure 3.43(10b)[336] shows how this concept can be interpreted. Here, society as a whole is characterized by only three confluents, or basic modes of behavior, if you like—a somewhat rough model which, however, might suffice for certain purposes. Now the question is under what circumstances, influences, and so on there will be changes from one mode to another. History provides us with a host of examples for this kind of problem.

*Figure 3.43(10a)*

335 See Beer (Decision), p. 476.
336 See Beer (Platform), p. 147.

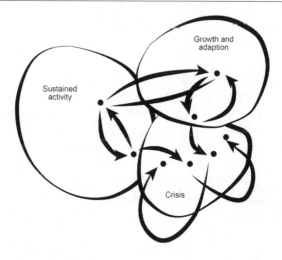

*Figure 3.43(10b)*

The concepts of the polystable system that have been sketched out here, and for which there is a quite precise theory,[337] are useful for systems-methodical and strategic purposes whenever the systems we wish to influence are less structured than in the Viable Systems Model. After all, we must not forget that the Viable Systems Model is based on a very sophisticated structure, whereas there are other types of systems that can better be captured with either the general homeostasis or the polystable systems model. It seems to me that this applies, for example, to what we call ecological systems.

### 3.433.5 Meta-Systemic Regulation

As pointed out above, one of the key requirements—if not the most important one—for influencing strategies so that they are successful is that the character and nature of the respective system, and thus its control and regulation mechanisms, be taken into consideration. Now, the very insight into the way complex systems work—the understanding of their nature—teaches us that we cannot hope to influence a system at the object level, a point that has frequently been made elsewhere.

Successful strategies usually have a meta-character: They concern second-level aspects, criteria, and ways of influencing. Based on my previous explanations regarding regulation mechanisms, it is now possible to outline

---

337 See Ashby (Brain), pp. 177 et seq., as well as pp. 241 et seq.

what this means in practice. Figure 3.43(11) below shows the homeostatic coupling of two subsystems. For illustrative purposes, let us assume this circle to represent a group of employees who jointly try to solve a problem or execute an assignment, which is represented by the ameboid element. This could be, say, a team of IT experts who have been assigned the task of installing certain IT solutions in an organization. For obvious reasons it would not be a good idea for the manager of that team to interfere with the details of the task. His responsibility is the stability of the overall system. So he has to be able to assess the stability or instability of the system and take appropriate action. Consequently, he will have to try to keep abreast of the interactions in this homeostatic system, or "measure" them—as indicated by the symbol M. The purpose of operation M is to collect information about the system, though not about the details traveling through the interaction channels but about whether the overall system is under control. Basically, this is information such as "Everything is okay; we are making progress" or "We are having problems and we don't know whether we will be able to resolve them," or "We are at our wits' end." The details of this meta-information—information about the information flowing through channels—may be expressed in various ways, perhaps even in hints or brief remarks, through good or bad mood, or through any other form of body language. What matters is the actual message. It certainly also takes some degree of experience and sensitivity on the manager's part to read these signs correctly. He has to know his people well. He has to know what it means when John Smith, asked how things are going, just shrugs his shoulders: Perhaps all it means is that everything is okay. On the other hand, when Jack Miller responds to the same question by giving a long-winded and enthusiastic report, he must know that this may not mean too much.

Interpretations of this kind are necessary, and this is a process symbolized by the abbreviation BB for Black Box. The reason this process can be regarded as a Black Box is that usually neither the team members nor the team manager are aware of why they interpret events, information fragments, gestures, and hints in this particular way. Of course, in many instance this Black Box can consist in a specifically designed information filter system, as Beer has shown, which is somewhat comparable to statistical quality control.[338] Its concrete design and manifestation in the individual case is a relevant and often difficult problem. Here, however, we are concerned with

---

338 See Beer (Decision), pp. 299 et seq.; as well as Gomez, Malik, and Oeller (System-methodik), pp. 993 et seq.

STRATEGY FOR MANAGING COMPLEX SYSTEMS

understanding the mechanism as such, so its concrete manifestation is of minor importance.

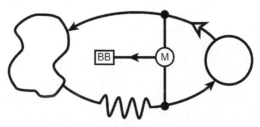

*Figure 3.43(11)[339]*

The basic problem of a meta-authority is to

— establish criteria of systemic stability (which have to be of a meta-systemic nature);
— identify instability, based on these criteria;
— exert stabilizing influence.

Should these attempts fail, it is necessary to

— change the criteria;
— change the system.

In the following sections, we will look at a few examples and discuss appropriate strategies and principles.

### 3.44 Meta-Systemic Control: Strategies and Principles

Meta-systemic control focuses not on the content of the problem-solving
process but on some of its *characteristics*. For instance, meta-systemic variables include the significance of the problem from the broad perspective of
the meta-system, the solution quality desired, the time, material, and human
resources available, the sources of information that can or cannot be made
available in the respective situation, the amount of stress the problem-solving system is expected to withstand, compliance with certain ethical principles and rules, compliance with corporate policies, and, last but not least, the

339 See Beer (Heart), p. 288.

increase in information resulting from the problem-solving process. To illustrate the process of meta-control of complex problem-solving processes in greater detail, I will use an example to show how the systems methodology should be used in this context.

### 3.441   Case #1: Strong Influence

The example has deliberately been chosen so as to represent a system inside an organization, which means that there are only limited possibilities of gathering information, interacting, and exerting influence.

Let us assume that the problem to be solved at the object level consists in designing a product-market strategy for a large-scale enterprise. Let us further assume that this strategy has to be created for a highly specialized segment of the company focusing on medical devices, that it has to take account of the effects of and developments in complicated technologies, and that the management ultimately responsible for creating the strategy does not have detailed knowledge of these things. Finally, let us assume the organization as a whole to comprise a substantial number of qualified staff well-versed in the relevant issues but unable to dedicate their full capacity to the creation of strategic concepts, as they have to work on a variety of problems in a number of different functions across the organization and at various hierarchical levels. In such a situation, what benefits can result from applying control-oriented systems methodology?

### Phase I: Identifying and formulating the problems

The first thing to think about is what system levels should be involved to be able to control the overall process. To solve all the issues likely to occur at the object level—that is, at the level of designing the content of the product-market strategy for medical devices—there is a series of useful approaches and techniques. There is also a number of information sources, including scientific sources, public authorities, and associations or other organizations. On the other hand, there are general concepts to guide the approach to create a product-market strategy. Based on the above assumption that the management of the business is ultimately responsible for the creation and quality of the strategic concept but has no detailed information on the object-level problems, it will only be able to supervise and steer the overall process from a higher level. It will therefore have to regard itself as a meta-system, and due to its lack of detailed information it will not really be tempted to interfere with the object-level processes. The problem that business management faces in its meta-system role is how, under the given conditions, to launch an object-level process that will produce the desired results, how to keep that process going, and how to control and steer it despite the lack of detailed object-level knowledge.

*Phase 2: Creating a control model for the problem situation*

What are the relevant attributes of the system that characterize the overall situation? At the object level we have a highly complex system consisting of a number of people distributed across the organization, from whom we might be able to recruit a core group of people to fully dedicate themselves to the problem. We have to assume, however, that both the members of that core group and everyone else potentially involved in the entire problem-solving process have very different motives, qualifications, experiences, attitudes towards strategic concepts, personal goals, perspectives on problems, and so on. In addition, they have very different tasks to fulfill as well, so they will have different workloads and availabilities. Further, we have to expect that they will have widely differing personal attitudes towards each other: The different hierarchical levels, positions within the status system, and various other factors about which there is usually little information will play a certain role in contributing towards the character of the overall system. Consequently, it is fair to assume we are dealing with a polystable system where stability zones and coupling mechanisms are only loosely defined, where we have limited knowledge of the threshold values marking the transition between stability zones, and where we do not know in advance the relevance that individual variables have.

Also, the task this polystable system has to perform at the object level is very complex: It has to analyze a highly complex market that could be regarded as a polystable system itself, as it is influenced by highly specialized and continuously changing technologies. As with all systems of that kind, it is not immediately clear what relevance the different variables have, where stability limits are, what events determine the transitions between stability zones, and so on. With regard to appropriate forms of control, another relevant factor is the question as to what methods and techniques are available to steer processes at the object level. In view of the complexities existing in the object systems, it is quite important to select a basic framework for developing strategic product-market concepts, for such a framework will strongly determine the rules that support or hinder the development of a self-organizing system.

Another tool to control processes at the object level is the time as well as the material and human resources top management has at its disposal.

In each individual case all factors mentioned will obviously undergo detailed analysis to obtain a clear picture of the relevant system structures. The main focus of this analysis will be on internal developments, the composition of the problem-solving team and the resources that team will need. However, even a very superficial assessment of the object system's complexity—bearing in mind what has been said in part 2 about complex problem-solving processes—is sure to make top management realize that the control of the object system cannot be a single act: Continuous control of the relevant processes will require management, being the meta-system, to be coupled to the object system in a certain way. Also, they will be bound to realize that the sequence of control activities cannot be predetermined once and for all but will have to be determined over and over again, depending on the state the object system is currently in.

*Phase 3: Developing problem-solving control interventions*

As has been indicated above, one of the key control tools is the basic framework to be observed by the object system. The selection of this framework has particular importance at the beginning of the process, that is, when the entire control system is established and the process is launched. Let us assume for this example that the framework is controlled by the system shown in figure 3.44(1) for the formulation of a product-market strategy. Instead of establishing such a framework, it would also be possible, of course, to build on the organization's previous experiences and rely on employees to base their actions on existing habits. Another option would be to get external methodology experts involved. As is easy to imagine, all these approaches will have different control effects.

*Phase 4: Testing and selecting possible problem solutions*

In this phase the fundamental decisions about extrinsic control have to be made, based on intense discussions about the options available to control the object-level process, previous experiences, advice from external advisors, and so on. These decisions must take into account the ideas about the nature of the object systems that have been developed in phase 2, the key challenge being how to balance varieties or, in other words, how to create the variety required to control the object system. As mentioned earlier, let as assume the basic methodological tool to be the framework outlined in figure

3.44(1). Also, for the purposes of this case we have to assume the team members to be familiar with this framework; otherwise a further issue to be solved would be how to familiarize employees with it.

*Phase 5: Introducing and monitoring the selected problem solution*
Based on the previous considerations, the entire control structure should be reasonably clear now. Its basic components are shown in figure 3.44(2). The spontaneous, self-organizing object system, which basically consists of the changing team members, their thinking processes, and their interactions, includes the control methodology as a fundamental meta-systemic control input. It produces two outputs at minimum: strategy proposals at the object level and a number of process characteristics. Both outputs are fed into the meta-system, which also has certain, at least rudimentary ideas about the approach used at the object level. In the graph, these ideas are marked as M for methodology. At the same time, the meta-system has to have at its disposal specific ideas about the structure of a viable system (VS). There are two reasons for this: First, the strategy proposals made at the object level have to be checked as to whether they will promote the viability of the overall system, that is, the organization; second, the object system itself has to operate as a viable system, at least for the duration of the process. The first extrinsic or meta-systemic control measure is the meta-system's disposition of existing resources; the second is that meta-systemic interventions can change methodological rules on which the functions of the object system are based; the third kind of control measure relates to the way in which tasks are formulated (accuracy, precision, etc.), to the socio-physiological characteristics of the team, to the way the team is managed, and so on. Below is a list of questions relating to the process characteristics and sequence, which help to gather the information relevant for meta-systemic control. As is typical of meta-systemic control, these questions do not immediately relate to the creation of the results expected but relate to the *conditions* under which results will be produced. It is the factors of the kind listed here that a manager can use as meta-systemic controllers, in particular when he or she does not know anything, or very much, about the problems to be solved at the object level.

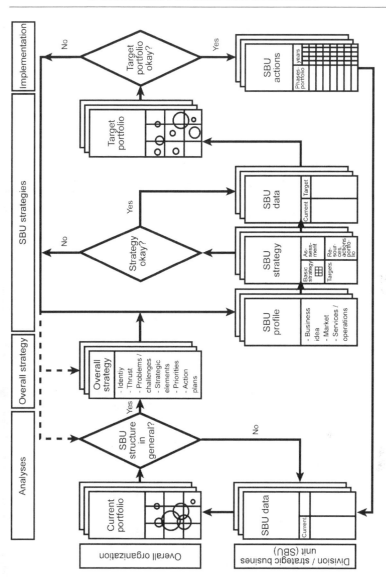

*Figure 3.44(1)[340]*

340 Schwaninger (Software), no. 27055.

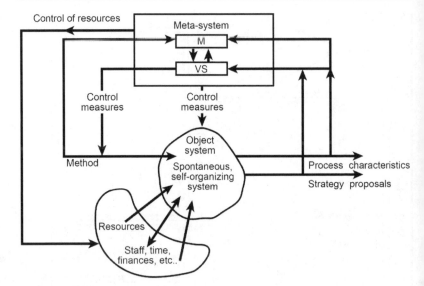

*Figure 3.44(2)*

---

*Sample questions for the meta-systemic control of a problem-solving process*
*(Indicators for a good or bad process)*

1. What is the technical qualification and experience of the people involved in problem solving?

2. Are there any personal tensions, conflicts, or schemes?

3. Are there signs of real team-building (team spirit) or are there any obstacles?

4. Do any of the team members show any signs of fatigue, are they suffering from stress or information overload?

5. Are there enough controversial opinions? How about people's openness to criticism and the way they criticize others?

6. Are there any aversions or shut-offs with regard to specific types of information, specific methods or individuals?

7. How thoroughly and precisely are individual tasks performed? Are there any signs of superficiality?

8. How fierce are the arguments put forward in favor or against certain ideas?

9. Are there any signs of something like devotion to the task?

10. What is team members' motivation based on: earning a salary or serving a cause?

11. Is there any way to find out about people's perspectives, frame of reference, and orientation?
12. Can the distribution of tasks in the group provide any clues?
13. What process monitoring tools are used in the object system? Are there any such tools at all?
14. How consistent are the results?
15. Are there any cognitive shut-offs?
16. How are the proposed methods applied?
17. Is the object system moving in a circular course; how great is the information gain?
18. Are there any clear opinion leaders?
19. Are there any specific dogmas or axioms?
20. How are lines of argument presented?
21. What do group members use for guidance: the maximum that can be achieved or the minimum that will be tolerated?
22. Are there any people in the object system who think not only about the kind of results but also about the way questions are posed? ("The uncreative mind can spot wrong answers, but it takes a creative mind to spot wrong questions.")[341]
23. How does the group act when mistakes are made? Does it look for external causes, or also internal ones?
24. What types of leaders are required in which process stages? Will any leaders have to be exchanged?
25. How sensitive are team leaders and members to feedback? Are they self-critical at all? Are they capable of challenging their own solutions? Do they also have enough confidence in their own results? Would they be ready to take on risks associated with their own suggestions?
26. How does the what-if mechanism work? Has anyone thought about possible failures?
27. How are leadership processes managed? Does the manager have listening skills? Is he or she just? What is his or her own motivation based on? What does he or she use meetings for? Does he or she have a stable personality? What could be a suitable way of testing it? What is his or her preferred way of thinking?

*Figure 3.44 (2a)*

---

341 Jay (Macchiavelli), S. 91

While this list does not claim to be exhaustive, it shows quite well what kind of variables meta-systemic control has to focus on. It can be illustrated using any of the questions as an example. For instance, if a meta-systemic line manager detects any kind of negligence in the way tasks are performed, if things are done superficially, and so on (see question 7), this as such may not justify a massive intervention, in particular as one should always question the appropriateness of one's own standards first. Still, when you discover superficial attitudes this will cause the meta-system to be alert, and you may ask further questions more often and more intensely to find out whether anything might be going wrong. Another example: In some cases, personal tensions and conflicts (question 2) can release creative processes and promote some competition among group members; in other cases, they can be symptoms of deeper problems and might even jeopardize the whole process.

So, asking questions like these helps to monitor the process in order to introduce appropriate meta-systemic measures if necessary. Quite obviously, this monitoring and control cannot consist in single actions; it has to be continuous. Each step of the system methodology has to be applied over and over again at the meta-systemic level. The information gathered by asking appropriate questions often reflects symptoms, thus helping to identify underlying problems. Depending on the type of system and based on the control model that gradually takes shape over time, as experience with meta-systemic process control increases, appropriate problem-solving interventions can be determined, tested under simulated and real conditions, and finally used to control the object system.

Allow me a few additional remarks on this kind of process control.

a.  Often, the only way to determine whether and to what extent a meta-systemic variable might have gotten out of control, or whether it might even indicate deeper problems, is a more or less subjective assessment. Often, the key information channel will be personal inspection by the line manager himself, and based on his personal experience and standards he will have to judge whether or not interventions are called for and what exactly they should focus on. Of course, in this area subjective judgment is not the only source available. In particular where functional problems of groups are concerned, there are scientific findings available. It must be noted, however, that scientific research quite often fails to capture the meta-problems of group processes.[342] In many cases, in particular in monitoring truly complex object-systemic processes, the meta-system will comprise more than one person, thus leaving the option of discussing the issue of meta-systemic control and ensuring a greater degree of certainty in one's judgment.

b. Much of the information that matters for meta-systemic process control cannot be gathered through mere observation or through personal reports from the members of the object system. On the contrary, chances are this information will be filtered or even distorted. It is possible, however, to gain additional information by inducing certain situations. In that case, the question would have to be: What situation or what tests will the object system or some of its members have to be exposed to in order for us to gain the information desired? For instance, to test how thoroughly someone has thought about the arguments, pieces of evidence and considerations he is presenting, one might comment about the fact that until recently he was holding a very different, even contrary view. In many cases this will cause that person to justify his view, and the way he does that will usually provide very valuable conclusions as to how consistent his thinking is, how carefully he proceeds when tackling a problem, what can cause him to change his mind, and so on. In principle, a whole range of tools can be applied which can range all the way to cross-examination-like techniques.

To determine the stability of the overall object system against certain influences, the system can be exposed to certain disruptions. For instance, one way to gather information on the motivation of group members is to demand exceptionally high commitment from that group on short notice (such as weekend work, massive overtime, moving up deadlines). Again, the way in which people respond—their body language, reluctance, and so on—will provide valuable conclusions as to the atmosphere in the group and what to expect in a worst-case scenario. All these tools, which may include more or less infamous tricks, obviously have to be used with some caution, as there can be extreme repercussions if people recognize the intention. But even when they don't realize that they are being tested, any kind of measures will trigger changes in the group. As a result, at each repetition of the situation (perhaps even in a true emergency) the state of the system will be a different one.

---

342 With regard to this topic, see the extraordinary work by Antony Jay (Macchiavelli), (Man).

c. Irrespective of all tools and experiments to test the object system—which is more or less a Black Box—as to its possible behaviors, stability, and so on, a lot of information can only be gained through longer-term interlinkage or collaboration. From a cybernetic perspective, this is due to the enormous quantities of information, and thus variety, that a somewhat complex object system can produce. So great are the wealth of possible behaviors and the range of situations it can be exposed to that the information channels available, which in turn are subject to a number of limitations, will never suffice to learn everything about such a system within a short period of time. So, the information needed to comprehensively assess such a system can only be transmitted through the channels over time, which is why certain activities in the meta-system must be aimed at maintaining the interlinkage as such, and at ensuring that the information exchange between the object and the meta-system will be as intense as it possibly can. After all, you would not expect a dog trainer to complete the task in a matter of hours.

So, formal reporting systems will usually not suffice to keep a successful control process going. Rather, the meta-system as a "participant observer"[343] has to enter into the kind of close interaction with the object system that will provide the communicative basis for successful interventions.

Despite this close interaction, information gathering activities and control measures in the meta-system are always and exclusively directed at the variables relevant to the meta-system. In the example used above, this was achieved by assuming that top management did not have the competence to solve object-level problems concerning the market for medical equipment, and therefore had to leave it to the members of the object system to solve them. In many cases this actually reflects the real situation. But even when management does have technical competence, this does not change the basic structure of process relationships. When members of the meta-system get involved in solving object-level problems, for whatever reasons, they simply operate as members of the object system. In that case they may have to solve meta-system tasks in personal union, which involves the risk that one of the two tasks will be neglected. Of course this focus on the characteristics of the process does not mean

---

343 Regarding the participant-observer concept, see Gomez, Malik, and Oeller (System-methodik), pp. 306 et seq.

that top management has no business whatsoever with object-related issues. As shown in figure 3.44(2), feedback on strategy is also transmitted via the meta-system, and the related control measures are aimed at dealing with any questions the object system cannot resolve on its own, be it due to the distribution of competencies, due to its position in the overall structure of the viable system, or for whatever other reason.

This example should suffice to show how meta-systemic ideas are handled and control-oriented systems methodology is applied in this context. As has been pointed out repeatedly, it is difficult to make general statements about how problems at the object level are solved. What may be valid in the present example (and referring to the market medical equipment) will be very different for strategies to be created for the steel tubes industry, and a medium-sized spaghetti factory serving a local market will have different problems entirely. With regard to the meta-systemic control of this problem-solving process, it seems possible, however, to achieve general, theory-like sets of statements that, while they may need some adaptation in the individual case, do describe some major invariants.

In previous sections I have explained that a text on strategic management would have to focus primarily on the strategy-producing mechanism. At least in part it seems to consist in a coupling between a meta-system and an object system, in such a way that the object system is enabled to develop the necessary strategies at the content level. In any case, strategic management involves the launching of processes and the designing and monitoring of systems that cause the overall system to make the necessary adaptations. The question as to whether this adaptation consists in exiting certain markets, entering others, changing financial arrangements, laying off employees, introducing shorter working hours, and so on, depends on the individual situation and what the system's adaptation mechanisms produce in that situation.

### 3.442  Case #2: Limited Influence

In the above example, in which the object-level problem consisted in creating a strategic concept for a specific product-market segment, the object system was deliberately defined so as to ensure it would be inside the organization. This obviously involves considerable possibilities for the meta-system to exert an influence. Also, there will be ways to gain the information required for control interventions. A structurally similar situation which, however, differs with regard to the scope and effectiveness of the tools available arises when the entire object system or large parts of it are outside the sphere of influence of the meta-system. Referring to the above example, this would be the case if the creation of a strategy for this company not only depended on its own actions but also had to take into account those of its market peers and competitors, of authorities, of associations, and so on. In this case the meta-system nature of the situation is even clearer, for it is obvious that the company's management cannot interfere with internal processes of other organizations. Its focus will therefore have to be on how to use the means and resources available to create conditions in which the processes in those other systems will be influenced favorably. Both its approaches to gathering information and its control interventions will be much less direct; in these cases it is even more important to thoroughly analyze the nature of the object systems in question than it is in cases of direct influence.

The following questionnaire shows what kinds of questions can help to gather the information relevant to the meta-system. It must be pointed out, however, that in many cases the information gained cannot be expected to be very detailed or precise. As is to be expected in the context of highly complex systems, this kind of system analysis can only provide the kind of *orientation* that has been discussed at length in section 2.21, that is, to clarify principles and predict patterns. As was pointed out there, such analyses cannot meet the standards of the "exact" sciences. They do, however, facilitate the orientation of behavior that in strategic management is important to position a socio-technical system in its environment (which, in turn, is made up of other systems).

In human relations, we are used to dealing with such in-principle forecasts and to adapting our own behavior towards our fellow humans accordingly. With regard to other people, this is reflected in expressions such as "He would never do that," "Under certain circumstances, I would trust him to do this," "He would not be capable of doing something like this," and "He would never tolerate this." There is no question we describe large parts of human behavior using such statements, and very often it serves the purpose. The better we know somebody, the more exact the statements we can make with regard to potential or expected actions, or to behaviors that are improbable. But even when people live together very closely and for a long time (as married couples sometimes do) so each of them can gather plenty of information about the other in the course of time, it is highly doubtful whether they will ever transcend the stage of pattern forecasts. Of course, areas will be more closely defined, error rates will decrease, and forecasts about many more facets of behavior will be possible. However, the human is such a complex system that the degree of detail has its limits, as does the precision of descriptions, explanations, and forecasts. Still, we can build *expectations* in this way that are quite reliable and allow us to orientate our behavior strategically, in the sense that certain areas or types of behavior are permitted and some are excluded. This is precisely how meta-systemic system analysis by means of the following questionnaire works.

| List of questions for metasystem analysis |
|---|

- How can the overall system be described?
- Is there anything to indicate where system boundaries are?
- Are any subsystems discernible?
- Are there any indications as to the kinds of elements?
- By what principles is the system structured?
- What kind of relationships hold it together ("unifying principle")?
- What is the system's identity based on?
- How does the system legitimize itself?
- What functions does the system fulfill?
- What interests does it serve? Whose tool is it?
- Are there any clues as to its viability configuration?
- What can/can't it afford?
- Are there any entry barriers to becoming a system element?
- Does the system have:
  leaders (real, pretended ones)
  representatives
  spokesmen?
- Is there a discernible hierarchy?
- Are there any shared functions?
- Are there any clues as to the greater context in which the system operates?
- Are there any discernible trade-offs (inputs, outputs)? What are their ranges; are there any specific patterns? Any interdependencies between inputs and outputs?
- Is the system permanently coupled to other systems?
- Who influences these linkages; what doe they influence? Is decoupling conceivable?
- Would it be possible to integrate representatives of the system in one's own system to couple the two?

- Are there any feedback channels to be recognized through which the system receives information on the impact of its actions?
- Are there any specific environmental characteristics to be recognized which provide orientation for the system and which it is exposed to?
- What are their characteristics?
  Area of changes
  Pace of change
- What other systems influence these environmental characteristics?
- Can any summary behavioral patterns be detected?
- Can stability zones for behavior (confluents) be recognized?
- Are there any clues as to their characteristics?
- Are there any principles marking the transition from one stability zone to the next?
- Are there any discernible threshold values?
- Are they fixed? Do they vary depending on other variables? (if yes: on which)?
- Are there any clues as to the transfer function? Is the transfer function fixed or is it variable depending on other variables (if yes, on which?)
- Are there any indications as to the overall range in which the transfer function can oscillate (or the quantity it originated from)?
- Can any statements be made with regard to the objectives of the system?
- Are there any preconditions that the system has to meet in order to maintain its function? What goals does the system pursue according to its own declaration of intent?

|     |     |
| --- | --- |
| - Are they realistic?<br>- What conclusions can be drawn with regard to other system aspects?<br>What goals are actually achieved?<br>What conclusions can be drawn based on the discrepancy between target and reality?<br>- Are there any discernible procedures? What process concept determines the system processes? What methods are applied?<br>- Are there any discernible principles regulating the system's behavior?<br>    Natural laws; Social regularities; Legal provisions, traditions, habits; Ethnical, religios, moral ties; Legal agreements and ties<br>- What values does the system uphold with regard to its own behavior that of other systems?<br>- How would the system behave in another situation?<br>- Could there be any situations that would put the system under particular stress?<br>- Does this permit any statements with regard to the "physiological" limits of the system?<br>- How does the system respond to stress: Does it bring its variables back into tolerance, or attempt to shift the tolerance limits??<br>- Are there any indications that certain system variables are permanently close to tolerance limits (up-tightness)?<br>- Are there any indications for the system being particularly vulnerable in certain points?<br>- What things are not substitutable? Where does the system lack redundancy?<br>- What resources does the system have at its disposal?<br>- How are resources allocated? What processes are used to control resource allocation? Who controls it?<br>- Are there any indications on internal communicatino flow?<br>– Is it possible to determine what sources of information the system has and what it relies on most? | - Are there any indications as to the social climate in the system?<br>- How does the system respond to changes going on inside or outside? How fast does it respond? In what way does it respond? (defensively, aggressively, routinely, innovatively)?<br>- How well does the information issued by the system match its actual behavior?<br>- Is there any kind of key information the system depends on?<br>- What kind of know-how does the system have?<br>- Are there any discernible power structures in the system?<br>- Are there any coalition tendencies?<br>- Are there any discernible conflicts or symbioses of interest?<br>- In this contect, are any games-theoretical aspects discernible?<br>- Are there any key elements to control the algedonic potential (sacntions, rewards)?<br>- What other systems does the system maintain relationships with? What kind of relationships?<br>- Are there any system that the system in focus is dependent on?<br>- Can we establish any linkages with these systems to influence the system in focus? What would these linkages look like? What advantages and disadvantages would this have?<br>- What measures do the environment and other systems apply to the system in focuse?<br>- Has the system taken on any particular risks?<br>- Are there any indications that its room to maneuver has been limited due to past behaviors and decisions (historicity)?<br>- Are there any indications that its current behavior or decisions might limit its future room for maneuver (futurity)? Is there reason to assume that the consequences of critical behaviors are known to the system? Are they known to us? |

*Figure 3.442*

As should be clear from the way these questions are phrased, we cannot automatically assume we will gain very accurate or precise information. Much of it will have to be deduced from certain clues, and we will often need to ask ourselves what specific situations have to be created to gather the information needed.

Neither can we assume that it will be possible to answer *all* questions in a specific case. But even when we do *not* have a certain piece of information because it is not available or the system under analysis is trying to *withhold* that information from us, that in itself permits valuable conclusions which will help us determine a direction for our own behavior.

Three additional aspects have significance for meta-systemic analysis:

a.  When analyzing a complex system, you have to keep *varying the level of complexity and abstraction*, as your observations and considerations will not make sense at just any level. Once you go into too much detail, you will no longer be able to see the big picture and recognize basic behavioral patterns; on the other hand, you will often need detailed analyses and observations to provide a sound basis for your assumptions about general patterns. So, this is another point where a trial-and-error component exists. It sort of operates in the vertical dimension and, due to the resulting scanning process, increases the probability of gaining significant information.

b.  You also have to *vary the system boundaries* you are taking into consideration. The fluidity of boundaries is a key characteristic of complex systems, and any assumption regarding the possible demarcation of the boundaries has to be repeatedly reviewed. As in the context of the level of abstraction, once again it largely depends on the boundaries of the system whether specific observations are relevant, so to gain a coherent picture it is necessary to sort of move them around mentally.

c.  Often, the observation and analysis of complex system relationships involve an *element of game theory*. Depending on whether the system under analysis is "aware" of its being analyzed and whether it is capable of performing similar analyses itself, this can make the analysis even more difficult. So when applying the above questionnaire, at least *four additional questions* need to be asked which can provide certain clues as to the meta-aspects existing in the system under analysis:

    1.  Is there any reason to assume the system can reflect on its own behavior?
    2.  Does the system itself have any knowledge about systems?

3.  Would it be reasonable to assume it will make similar considerations?
4.  Can you reasonably assume that the system under analysis will expect the observing system to make such considerations?

The answers to these questions often determine whether certain observations make sense and whether certain, mutually dependent behaviors can assumed to be stable.

Stafford Beer has provided an excellent example referring to the Cuban Missile Crisis of 1962. A games-theory analysis of the situation in that period, which cannot be recounted in detail here, leads to the assumption that the actual risk consisted in the Russians' thinking that the U.S. did not know about the existence of nuclear weapons. Now, it is a fact that the Russians did not make any serious attempts to conceal the fact that nuclear missiles were stationed in Cuba. It seems possible, therefore, that the Russians thought it important to let the U.S. know they—the Russians—did not assume the U.S. to be unaware.[344] Analyses like these, which can send you into dizzying thought spirals where homemade logic may desert you, may become necessary when the only way to exert meta-systemic influence on a self-reflexive object system is through information management.

Of course, the above questionnaire has to be adapted to the individual situation. Depending on the context in which meta-systemic analysis is performed, individual sets of questions will have more or less significance. For instance, in analyzing political systems the mechanism of resource allocation will be particularly important, as election campaigns, the forming of coalitions and other political maneuvers are often dominated by those systems or subsystems which are assumed to control the allocation of resources, such as subsidies. Another setting where these questions have particular importance is large corporations where part of the control over divisions and business units is exerted via the allocation of financial resources for investment. In settings like these, the question of *actual control* over resources may be less significant than existing *assumptions* about it. So, a detailed analysis of relevant mechanisms will be useful. It can also be helpful to thoroughly analyze the possible *consequences* of specific lines of action, as well as perform a risk analysis and an analysis of certain *key factors identified in applying the questionnaire.*

---

344 See Beer (Decision), pp. 466 et seq.

In all of these analyses, it is of crucial importance to keep questioning the nature of the information gained. With each piece of information you need to think about which of the categories listed in the following table they fit into (figure 3.44(3)).

| Type of information | Possible interpretations | | | Statements | |
|---|---|---|---|---|---|
| | 1 | 2 | 3 | positive | negative |
| 1. Speculation / imagination<br>"… could be that …"<br>"… it may be possible that …" | | | | | |
| 2. Presumption<br>"… it is probable (for certain reasons) that …" | | | | | |
| 3. Assumption<br>"… I assume that …." | | | | | |
| 4. Information from the system observed<br>"… X has said that …"<br>"… X has assured me that …" | | | | | |
| 5. Information from other systems<br>"… A said that X …" | | | | | |
| Facts<br>"… I know (!?) that …" | | | | | |
| Experience<br>"… I have seen for myself that …" | | | | | |

*Figure 3.44(3)*

As mentioned before, the purpose of this analysis is to gain certainty about the current status of information. When you analyze complex systems it is usually quite difficult to tell what is mere speculation, what is an educated guess, what assumptions you are basing your opinions on (perhaps tacitly and/or unconsciously), and so forth. Particular caution is called for with regard to any information submitted by the system under analysis—no matter through what channels or in what form. In a setting like this you will always have to ask whether it could be a bluff, whether the system under scrutiny is trying to conceal something else, which may be much more important, or whether it could even be downright deception. Deliberate misinformation has always been a key component of strategy.[345]

The same problems can occur with communications from third-party systems referring to the system under analysis; clarification of these questions often requires an additional system analysis of those third-party systems. Another point to be considered is that any information on complex systems can always be interpreted in different ways, so it is highly recommendable to launch a kind of trial-and-error process with regard to possible *interpretations*. Last but not least, it is important to ascertain whether the information gained allows any *positive* statements on system behavior or other relevant aspects, or only *negative* ones. As has repeatedly been pointed out and discussed at length in sections 2.21 and 2.22, any information regarding what can*not* be expected of a system, what it is highly *unlikely* to do, what it is *not* capable of, and so on, is just as important for the strategic orientation of one's own actions as positive information about what the system can or will do.

The analyses described here provide a wealth of knowledge, which will obviously get better as the people performing the analyses gain more knowledge about systems theory and cybernetics, and the more they know about the object sphere. So, the more you know about the structural principles and functions of, say, a polystable system, and the better you know the specifics of, for example, the textile industry in eastern Switzerland or of the Japanese steel sector, or the internal situation in a specific company, the easier it will be to put together the necessary information, and the more productive your analyses will be. The result of all these approaches will be a kind of *mental model* of the system in question. Rather than contents, details, or numbers, it will reflect systemic relationships and cybernetic behavioral options for that system.

Let me emphasize again that this mental model might not be much more precise than what you know about current weather trends. While this comparison may seem peculiar at first, most managers have probably been in situations before where the status of the information available to them, and of the data that were supposed to provide a basis for decisions, was not so different from a weather forecast. It is in the nature of systems consisting in

---

345 This can be the case for many variants, ranging from countless forms of disguise, mimicry, and launching rumors, all the way to sophisticated forms of propaganda and of creating images of the world.

the interactions of hundreds or thousands of variables, like the weather, that their complexity does not permit us to form an accurate, numerically precise picture. Continuous changes, the fluidity of the situation, and the uncertainty of the concrete course of events result from the very structure of the system and form its output.

Faced with this situation, you have a choice between the two basic attitudes discussed in earlier sections: Out of dissatisfaction with this situation, you can try to apply certain techniques to gather more and more "precise" information—which will ultimately lead to the constructivist paradigm. Alternatively, you can accept the enormous complexity of such a system, and think about what options you might have. The weather forecast example illustrates that even a rather rough classification of system states (clear, cloudy, overcast, rainy), together with certain temperature ranges and some information on expected changes from one system state to the other, can certainly provide a sufficient basis for orientation in everyday life. Of course, it all depends on what you need the weather forecast for. If you want to experience a hot-air balloon ride over the mountains, or climb a 13er peak in winter, or go on a sailing cruise for several days, you need a much more detailed forecast with additional information on wind speeds, atmospheric pressures, temperatures, and local weather conditions—which can differ greatly for the same overall weather trend—and above all you will need much more frequent forecasts than you would for everyday life. Rather than inquiring about tomorrow's weather in the evenings, you will probably want to receive weather reports by the hour. One key reason why successful action is possible even with such vague forecasts is that—precisely because your information is so vague—you will try to keep your behavioral variety high. For instance, every mountaineer knows that even with optimal and stable weather conditions it could be a grave mistake not to take your bad-weather equipment. The above-mentioned *mental* model resulting from the analyses discussed here and which provides the basis for any orientation of behavior, as described in the context of strategies for dealing with complexity (see sections 2.21 and 2.22), can sometimes be improved by creating a *formal* model. Once you manage to formalize the content of your mental model, perhaps even computerize it, you will have access to a number of possibilities to a) increase the kind and quantity of the information to be captured simultaneously, and b) improve the application of existing knowledge through simulations. Probably one of the most sophisticated approaches to computerizing such content is Forrester's System Dynamics method;[346] Stafford Beer, too, has presented various examples to illustrate what such models can look like. For instance, in the context of a model on the problem of long-term demand for people with scientific and technical backgrounds, which he describes in great detail, he writes:

"The great discovery of management cybernetics is perhaps that the outcomes of policies are determined more by the macrostructure of the total system, its sub-systemic interactions and the entropic infrastructure of the sub-systems them-selves, than by the particular causal relationships which are activated by particular decisions. The research counterpart of this state of affairs is that very much more is learned about what ought to be done by inference from the system's cybernetics than from the analysis of enormous masses of data. The importance of this conclusion cannot be over-emphasized. Almost the whole of government research is, quite typically, devoted to the collection and analysis of information about what has happened. Hard headed people like to say that these data are the facts of the situation, and are therefore what most matters. On the contrary, they are so much flotsam, floating about on the entropic tides created by the systemic structures below the surface. Given a full understanding of those sub marine structures and of the current at depth, which are the more important facts about the system, it becomes possible to predict effects on the surface using very little data of the former kind."[347]

It is this kind of model, no matter whether mental or formalized, which provides the basis for strategy development. Only the analysis of an object system from a meta-systemic perspective and with meta-systemic means sheds a light on the underlying connections, behaviors, and options for intervening and influencing that ultimately permit the control of a complex system.

Some may argue that this way of analyzing a complex system is much too laborious for anyone to actually take the time to do it—especially when the whole affair must be considered an evolutionary process, kept alive by numerous trial-and-error processes that have to be launched at different stages with different aspects in mind. These people have a point. On the other hand, all the activities going on in all major organizations for the purpose of gathering information, creating extensive statistics, and so on, also involve a lot of work. In addition, let me emphasize once again that this is an analysis of *complex* systems, so according to the Law of Requisite Variety we cannot expect to manage complex matters with simple means. Of course, one factor producing a considerable variety increase in analysis tools is when the focus

---

346 See Forrester (Industrial Dynamics).
347 Beer (Decision), pp. 479 et seq.

of attention is put on meta-systemic regularities, so that the enormous complexity at the object level does not even come into play. But even at a meta-systemic level, variety is still great enough for these analyses to require some degree of effort.

The extent of variety increase to be achieved through the meta-systemic perspective can also manifest itself in the fact that it often takes remarkably little effort to gain truly surprising insights. Just as experienced doctors often need a minimum of time to make a diagnosis, an experienced manager is often capable of diagnosing the situation of a company by asking a few pointed questions.

The above remarks on the meta-systemic analysis of complex systems are summarized in figure 3.44(4).

The graph should be read as follows: The starting point is the scope of knowledge of cybernetics and systems theory. Secondly, the knowledge from various empirical disciplines should be contributed to the extent that it is relevant for the specific object area. The same is true for those insights from management theory that are relevant for the area of management in question. A third component that is necessary includes the "local" knowledge of the object area where the analysis takes place. Of course, particularly useful experiences are those that have been gained in applying insight in one area and may be suitable for transfer to *another* area. That is indicated by the arrows connecting the three areas of knowledge. Cybernetics and systems theory provided the basis for the concept of meta-systemic control, which includes the aspects discussed, such as the different system types, the different types of problem-solving processes, etcetera. The connecting arrows pointing to the other knowledge areas indicate that it might be possible to use certain applications of the concept in individual disciplines, in management theory, possibly even in a similar object area. Every concrete experience in connection with such applications might potentially be useful.

The meta-systemic analysis of the object system in question is now carried out in accordance with the concept of meta-systemic control, and using the insights from other disciplines and/or specific knowledge from

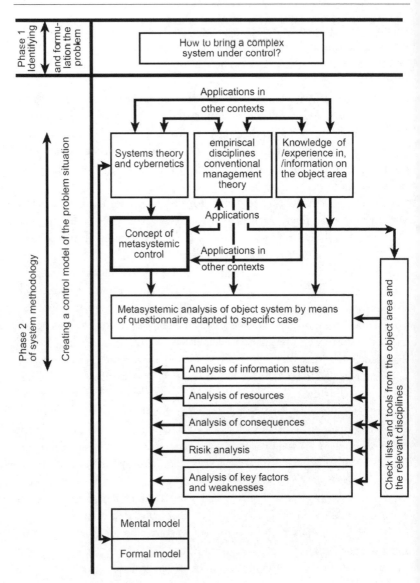

*Figure 3.44(4)*

the respective object area. For this purpose the questionnaire shown here has to be adapted to the specifics of the individual case, based on what is known about the object area. Further detailed information is gathered through information status analysis, resources analysis, consequences analysis, risk analyses, and possibly a special analysis of key factors and deficits of the object system. Whether or not these detailed analyses have to be done depends on the insights gained by evaluating the questionnaire. Usually, in all of these analyses additional check lists and tools have to be used, according to the relevant empirical disciplines, or management theory, and the specific area of the object system. For instance, in analyzing the resources of a system it may be useful to have a check list of the resource categories normally used in that area. The information gathered that way constitutes the mental model of the respective object system, and with the aid of additional methods and modeling techniques from formal and computer sciences it may be possible to create a formal model. The left-hand side of the graph shows the phases of the control-oriented systems methodology. The problem in this case consists in bringing a complex system under control (phase 1); the creation of a control model of the problem situation (phase 2) then follows the concept shown in the graph.

## 3.5    Strategies and Heuristic Principles

> "To think in terms of heuristics rather than algorithms
> is at once a way of coping with proliferating variety."
> *Stafford Beer*

### 3.51 Strategic Principles and Heuristics

Meta-systemic control of a complex system is often comparable to a game for which the rules are not known at first but are determined by the actions of the players, and are of a rather implicit nature. Consequently, it cannot automatically be assumed that players know all the rules. As the actual control measures can be subject to various disturbances emanating from other systems, we have to reckon with an indefinite and constantly changing number of players, all with incomplete information, and who also have to take into account that there is usually yet another player by the name of "Chance" at the table. Just as the rules are unknown, it is not clear what the game is played with. You do not know whether to use cards or dice—it can be either one or the other, in irregular intervals—and, what is more, you cannot even be certain as to what is a card and what is a die. These countless influences, which in the real world determine the behavior of social systems, of individuals, and of groups of people, strongly determine the nature of the game.

That is one reason why systems like these are extremely complex and why, as repeatedly pointed out in this book, certain ideas and methods are not helpful. For all these reasons, the precise, numerical calculations we find in analytical problem-solving play a lesser role in the control of complex systems. They are replaced by a kind of strategic calculus, based on a series of heuristic principles that are designed to instrumentalize the very complexity of the situation. These heuristic principles are often aimed at taking advantage of (or even causing) the deficits existing on the opposing side, the incompleteness of the opponent's information, the specifics of his or her information processing and thinking processes, the distortion of his or her information, etcetera. The moves a player has at its disposal in the process of controlling a system include not only the *conscious elimination* of uncertainty, in the sense of coping with complexity, but also its *conscious creation* through deliberate pretense and deception.

Now, before we look at some of the most important strategic-heuristic principles used to control complex social systems, two problems have to be mentioned that are quite common in this context:

1.  The *first* problem is that certain strategic ideas come from the military sector, and so does the terminology used to describe them. It often happens that people find this irritating, sometimes even to the point where they condemn any kind of strategic thinking and acting and refuse to deal with it at all. Respectable as this attitude may be from a moral perspective, it is incompatible with the realities of everyday life—not only in the military sphere but in human behavior as such. Strategic action and strategic principles serve the key purpose of managing complexity. The way some strategic actions are implemented may be more or less fair in the individual case, or occasionally even fall in the dirty tricks category, which would clearly make them morally wrong. However, one point to consider is that from a meta-systemic viewpoint, customs, morals, codes of honor, and laws are themselves strategic in nature, so they contribute their share to the management of complexity (see Chapter 2) by prohibiting behaviors that would theoretically be possible. This leads to a drastic decrease

in the variety of possible behaviors. Still, even within the limits of customs, morals, and the law there is enough complexity left to require additional strategic principles.

2. The *second* problem is that strategic behavioral principles, once put in words, often seem rather trivial. They are in line with what people do anyway; they are part of their everyday experience. As a result, they often do not seem "science-worthy," as people tend to assume that any science on human behavior or, more generally speaking, on the behavior of complex systems must offer some kind of new insight. As far as the behavior of individuals or small groups is concerned, this is something we surely cannot expect, as such a science could include a few very specific cases at best but not the general picture. Such atypical cases, however, would be of little use to the actors. So, it can certainly be considered a strength of a science—in line with the purpose of science in general—to describe general invariants of human behavior, for even if these correspond to everyday experience, they are not always explicitly formulated and systematically applied. Moreover, it can often be observed that due to the multitude of concrete events and actions and especially because of the countless ways in which strategic principles can be implemented, people fail to recognize the general, or strategic, behavioral patterns. This is all the more true as, in line with certain strategic principles, the actors must be expected to make every effort to conceal the other strategic principles that drive their actions. In the context of influencing and controlling complex social systems, as opposed to the orders of magnitude that individuals can cope with, chances are there will be new insights that are out of sync with everyday experience, so the strategic behavioral patterns of those complex systems would not be amenable to intuition. Examples can be found in Forrester's research on complex urban systems, which has revealed that typical counterintuitive nature of system behavior.[348]

The principles listed below are very general in nature. They regulate the use of a multitude of concrete behaviors which, by following one or several of said principles, obtain an inner logic, coherence, and reason, or in other words: form a pattern. That is why these principles are meta-strategic in nature.

---

348 See Forrester (Social Systems).

At the same time, they represent heuristics. If, following Beer's reasoning,[349] we consider an algorithm to be a set of instructions aimed at achieving a known, fully specified goal, while a heuristic can be defined as a set of instructions aimed at achieving an unknown goal by way of exploration, it will immediately be clear that these are typical heuristic rules.

The strategic principles can be divided into:[350]

1.  Principles for assessing the current situation
2.  Principles for building, using and maintaining the capacity to impose sanctions or, more generally speaking, the coupling between systems
3.  Principles for shaping the availability and flow of information
4.  Principles for shaping the capacity for convincing people.

As we will see shortly, these principles are based on the general options for strategic action to influence systems. To exert the influence required to reach one's goals in a meaningful and effective way, you have to gain an overview of the issues and connections at hand, which has been discussed at length in earlier sections. Another thing is that you need to be able to do something—such as, generally speaking, reward and sanction people, for which there are countless variations. Whether a reward consists in a major payment or a friendly word of recognition depends on the circumstances—but the basic character of these actions is invariant. Sanctions in this sense, whether positive or negative, also determine much of the relationship between systems, or the coupling between them. Without a coupling relationship there is no interaction, so this can be considered a key prerequisite for taking influence. Shaping the information situation is enormously significant, considering that reality is ultimately conveyed through communication and, put in somewhat simple terms, reality for people is what they consider to be real. Of course, this is true for both one's own information and that of the counterpart. After all, the possibility of taking influence and managing complexity also depends on the power of persuasion and the credibility of those acting. A trust-based relationship enormously reduces complexity, while distrust can often lead to unmanageable situations.

---

349 Beer (Brain), pp. 305 et seq.
350 See Grossekettler (Macht), p. 197.

Above all, these principles fulfill three functions:[351] They provide *guidance for plans and actions* and thus help to make sure that from the enormous number of possible strategies and combinations, the variant appropriate for the individual case can quickly be picked out. Secondly, they fulfill a *prohibitive function*, which means they belong in the category of general behavioral rules extensively discussed in part 2. They do this by signaling dangerous thresholds which, when exceeded, may trigger processes that are impossible to anticipate and may be uncontrollable. So, mental recourse to these principles is designed to prevent you from exceeding these thresholds frivolously. The third function, which is just as important, is to *increase variety*, in that compliance with them will take a considerable load of the decision capacity, especially when under time pressure and/or in confusing situations, and due to their rule-like nature they ensure some degree of rationality.

The division proposed does not permit a clear separation between these principles, just some degree of organization. There are obviously many interdependencies, as the boundaries between the individual principles are somewhat fuzzy; some degree of redundancy cannot be avoided. In my view, however, this is not a major issue, as in practice an actor will be guided not by a list of principles, as shown in the table below, but by the overall pattern of principles which he or she will have to keep in view.

*Strategic principles*[352]

| Principles for assessing the current situation |
|---|
| 1.   Principle of meta-systemic assessment of the situation |
| 2.   Principle of making a rounded assessment of the situation |
| 3.   Principle of the open system |
| 4.   Principle of strengths against weaknesses |
| 5.   Principle of selecting ambiguous goals |
| 6.   Principle of avoiding being influenced by biased information |
| *Principles supporting the influencing (sanctioning) capacity and the coupling relationship* |
| 7.   Principle of flexibility |
| 8.   Principle of providing for the future |
| 9.   Principle of reversibility |

---

351 Id., loc. cit., p. 196.
352 According to Grossekettler (Macht), pp. 197 et seq., who, however, does not differentiate between strategy and meta-strategy.

| | |
|---|---|
| 10. | Principle of taking small steps |
| 11. | Principle of keeping the initiative |
| 12. | Principle of occupying sanction centers |
| 13. | Principle of reward motivation |
| 14. | Principle of monitoring all options |
| 15. | Principle of the golden bridge |

*Principles for shaping the availability and flow of information*

| | |
|---|---|
| 16. | Principle of proximity to information |
| 17. | Principle of occupying information interfaces |
| 18. | Principle of explaining one's actions |
| 19. | Principle of disguise |
| 20. | Principle of control |

*Principles for the power of conviction*

| | |
|---|---|
| 21. | Principle of reliability |
| 22. | Principle of rigor |
| 23. | Principle of the rare bluff |
| 24. | Principle of the concealed avenue of retreat |

*Figure 3.51*

Not all of the strategic principles listed here are immediately evident, which is why I will add some comments below. An important preliminary note refers to the *mental* or *formal model* resulting from the meta-systemic analysis of complex systems described above, and the *situation assessment* proposed here: One could assume the two to be identical, which would be wrong. Both meta-systemic analysis and the mental model resulting from it refer to the *basic system* characteristics and the more or less *permanent* behavioral patterns that the structure of the system in focus permits. The model delineates the scope of what is and is not possible in terms of system aspects that can be *ascertained from a meta-systemic perspective* and are *relatively permanent*. By contrast, the situation assessment that forms the starting point for any strategy to influence a system covers the *concrete* and *present state of the system*, which obviously keeps changing within the scope of what is basically possible.

A small example should help to illustrate this. When viewed as a system, a wrist watch has certain general characteristics and basic behavioral options. We know, for instance, that it indicates the time, not the temperature, that its hands have different meanings, that they move within a range from 1 to 12, and that there may be deviations in the range of x seconds per week.

These are all components of the mental system model we have of a watch. Now, a situation assessment would be directed at the current position of the watch hands, permitting us to read the specific time we have this very moment, and its result would be, for example, "It is now 11:45 a.m." How detailed a situation assessment has to be and how frequently it has to be done depends on the permanent system characteristics: If we are dealing with a system that rapidly changes its states within a broad scope of variations, we have to determine its specific state much more often than with a system featuring slow dynamics and a rather stable behavioral pattern.

1. The *principle of meta-systemic assessment of the situation* means that we have to keep asking ourselves at what system level our assessment is taking place. It happens all too easily that we commit the error of shifting from the meta-systemic to the object-systemic level, where the wealth of details blocks our view of the big picture.

2. The *principle of making a complete assessment of the situation* is closely related to that. One of the cornerstones of this work is the view that it is impossible for a complex dynamic system to be captured in its entirety, for the reasons extensively discussed in earlier sections. This refers to the object level, of course; at the meta-level it is much easier to comply with the principle of completeness. Under certain circumstances it may not suffice to focus on the meta-level of the first order; it may be necessary to include meta-levels of higher orders. The principle of making a rounded assessment of the situation refers, last but not least, to the analysis of possible responses from a potential adversary, or from the object system analyzed, as it is impossible to create a promising strategy when key strategic options for the opponent are overlooked. It goes without saying that even at the meta-level, the principle of completeness can only be fulfilled in approximation. One of the key "motors" for fulfilling it is the constant mental scanning of the object system, in the sense of a trial-and-error process that almost works like a radar system. In applying this principle, it is important to ensure that the situation assessment always includes the question as to how the opponent views one's own behavior and situation. Hence the need to cultivate the ability to mentally "step into the shoes" of the opponent to be able to reconstruct the situation

from his or her perspective. This is a key application of Popper's situation logic. Its use for this purpose has been discussed in the book *System-methodik*.[353]

Another aspect I find important is this: Most people tend to think in *causal relationships*. No matter what happens, their first reaction, and often their only one, is to look for a *cause*—which in a social context usually means finding a *culprit*. In complex circumstances, however, events can rarely be understood or explained by causal thinking. They result from the interactions in a network of factors. This is one point to consider in the situation assessment, as otherwise there is a risk of arriving at totally wrong conclusions. It is particularly obvious in those cases where this form of causal thinking leads to a "conspiracy theory" in one of its countless varieties, that is, an event is said to be the result of conscious, intentional conspirative action.[354] No doubt in some cases the possibility of a conspiracy will have to be taken into consideration; the problem here, however, is in *habitually* resorting to this explanation. It is precisely the apparent plausibility of this kind of explanation that often prevents a correct assessment of the situation, especially when it occurs in connection with the so-called "bunker syndrome," that is, the progressive inability to form an objective view of a situation. Of course this does not exclude the possibility of constructing a culprit or conspiracy to take action against, which can be an effective sanction in certain situations. We will come back to this at a later point.

3.  The principle of the open system is a constant reminder that in dealing with complex, dynamic systems you have to be prepared for unexpected developments at all times, and that you need to consider this even in your situation assessment. When a system is open, that does not only mean it keeps exchanging matter, energy, and information with its environment; it also means that the type of relevant variables may keep changing so that new characteristics may emerge. Complex systems keep surprising you, and that is something to keep in mind when assessing the current situation. There is no ceteris paribus clause here.

---

353 See Gomez, Malik, and Oeller (Systemmethodik), pp. 66 et seq., and part C as well as the sources quoted there.

354 Regarding the criticism of conspiracist social theories, see Popper (Gesellschaft II), pp. 119 et seq.

4. *The principle of strengths against weaknesses* is self-explanatory: It indicates that both the assessment of the situation and the choice of interventions have to be based on the specific relative strengths and weaknesses. This also includes the principle that you should never consider your opponent to be less smart than you are. It is dangerous to assume that a strength you believe you have must necessarily be a weakness on your opponent's part.

5. The *principle of selecting ambiguous goals* implies that the interventions selected should have the potential to aim at several targets at the same time. Not only does this increase the variety of means (resembling a missile with multiple warheads); it also means the object system is able to recognize right away what your interventions are aimed at, thus making it harder to circumvent or avoid them.

6. The *principle of avoiding being influenced by biased information.* Your assessment of the situation should be as realistic as possible. This also means you constantly have to be aware that other systems, or "players," are likely to act strategically as well and to be guided by similar considerations to those guiding you. They may also have a vital interest in deceiving you and/or prevent you from gaining relevant information. That is obvious in various areas, from interpersonal relations to business competition all the way to intelligence services. So, while you are considering strategic moves to influence the state of information, as discussed below, and cause confusion and concealment, you have to take care not to fall into the same trap, as you have to assume your opponent to be at least as smart as you are.

7. The *principle of flexibility* is a constant reminder that, whenever possible, unnecessary stipulations and commitments should be avoided, in particular when this can be done at no cost. But even when compliance with the flexibility principle incurs costs, which must usually be expected and leads to the mental concept of a flexibility budget,[355] you should carefully weigh the costs involved and, when choosing a strategy, consider any movements in that flexibility balance sheet.

8. The *principle of providing for the future* is also largely evident; it refers to the necessity of checking strategic measures for their potential "futurity,"[356] or future impact, and of ensuring that the necessary resources and variety potentials/stocks exist. When the principles of flexibility and providing

355 See Bateson (Ecology), pp. 494 et seq.
356 With regard to this term, see Drucker (Technology), pp. 109 et seq.

for the future are complied with simultaneously, it becomes clear what the essential difference is between conscious risk-taking and a hazard game. Rommel has outlined his views on this as follows:

> "It has been my experience that audacious solutions promise the greatest success. Operational and tactical audacity must be distinguished from military hazard playing. An operation is audacious when it may lead to the desired outcome but, if it fails, leaves enough means at hand to master any situation. A hazard game, by contrast, is a move that may either lead to victory or to the destruction of one's own units." [357]

9. The *principle of reversibility* demands that in any specific case you think about whether and under what conditions a step you have taken can be reversed and what state or position this would lead to. Of course, irreversible decisions can never be completely avoided; however, from a strategic perspective it is important to get a clear picture of the context in which you have made, or are about to make, irreversible decisions and the context in which your decisions are reversible. Reversible decisions can be made differently and, above all, more quickly than irreversible ones, for which you should always take your time. Specifically, it is important to think through the consequences, in terms of accompanying measures, actions to ensure legal security, and so on.

10. The *principle of taking small steps* supports the principles of flexibility and of reversibility: It implies that in each step you should carefully think about what intermediate results you will use to gauge the impact of a strategic action, and that these intermediate steps should be completed before the next step. In other words, you need deliberate "point-of-no-return management" to avoid situations where you realize with hindsight, and to everyone's surprise, that the point of *no return* has long passed. Again, admittedly there can be situations requiring major steps to be taken. You should always ask yourself, however, whether there is no alternative, as the risks involved are usually rather large and the line between reasonable risk-taking and mere hazarding can be rather thin.

11. The *principle of keeping the initiative* means that you should always try to (co-)determine the course of action, and not be pushed or pressured by others. This means there might be situations in which you have to stay very active in order not to lose the prerogative of acting. Based on his studies of state-determined systems, Ashby has found out, among other things,

---

357 Quoted after Grossekettler (Macht), p. 200.

that the variables that vary most, and most frequently, determine the behavior of all other variables.[358]

That is nothing other than one manifestation of the principle "Keep them busy." Keeping a system under a certain amount of pressure at all times—by issuing assignments, keeping everyone busy, and so forth—reduces that system's leeway and increases one's own. This also includes the principle of making time your ally, remaining the master of your agenda, and controlling the course of events (as far as you possibly can). Finally, I should add that in most cases it is the person taking deliberate and resolute action who keeps the upper hand, if only because most of the others are rather undecided.

12. The *principle of occupying sanction centers*. It is obvious that the capacity to issue effective sanctions, to reward and punish, largely determines one's options for intervention. This principle means that you should try to occupy existing or recognizable centers of potential sanctions, at least in part. Its significance is quite obvious in the political arena, where it is usually linked to the control over finances and positions. Here, the principle of occupying sanction centers also implies that you need to identify key positions and, above all, key people in a system, seek access to them, and build your avenues for influence.

Every system has its own forms of sanctioning, along with procedures to determine and set sanctions. If you manage to influence those, you may also be able to influence to some degree the aspiration levels that regulate the system. The reason why I think this is encompassed in this principle is that the decision of when to reward or punish someone largely depends on the standards or reference variables the respective system has.[359] Although in most cases these standards and variables are not fixed but variable, they are often controlled quite rigidly or are difficult to modify (requiring qualified majorities and things like that). So, being able to influence sanction centers also requires an influence on sanctioning mechanisms and the conditions for sanctions. When in this position, you may decide to follow ground rules such as "Never tolerate mediocrity" or "Never be satisfied with results,"[360] which both contribute to defining aspiration levels. By the way, this is where the heuristic nature of these principles is particularly apparent: They produce a certain

358 Ashby (Psychiatry), p. 115.
359 Regarding this point, see Powers (Behavior), pp. 44 et seq.
360 See Sloma (Management), pp. 11, 81 et seq.

attitude, a drive to keep seeking even better solutions, which in entrepreneurs often manifests itself as "creative unrest" of some sort.

The last aspect I would like to address in the context of this principle is the "scapegoat" problem. Problematic as it usually is to build the situation assessment on mono-causal explanations (the cause, the culprit, etc.), it can be very effective to sanction a scapegoat, if only a constructed one. There are so many examples to prove the mechanisms at work here, and it is a principle applied so frequently that there is probably no need for further explanations at this point.

13. The *principle of reward motivation* is of utmost significance for influencing systems and especially for maintaining the coupling relationship, that is, the precondition for having any possibilities to intervene at all. From a meta-systemic view it is clear that the fundamental, abstract possibilities to influence an object system basically consist in changing its structure and steering its behavior the algedonic way, that is, according to the pain-and-pleasure principle. However, interventions following the punishment principle have considerable disadvantages compared to applying the reward principle. On the one hand, you always have to be prepared for a social system to do anything to avoid being punished—not only by exhibiting the desired behavior but also by searching for ways around it. And since the behavioral variety of social system is usually so great you will never be able to anticipate and control all circumventions, there is always a possibility the system will find a loophole to slip through and evade a control measure. Another point that becomes very clear in this context is what meaningful *variety engineering* can be: If the intervention is a reward, the burden of proof is usually with the object system; that is, it has to prove that it actually deserves the reward. If the intervention is a measure of punishment, the burden of proof usually is with the meta-system—the punishing system—as it has to prove that a) it is entitled to deal out punishments and b) the object system's behavior is consistent with the offense incurring punishment. So the principle of reward motivation takes enormous strain off the meta-system, while the principle of punishment would charge it with the entire burden of proof. There are examples from the legal field to illustrate this kind of strategic behavior and the way this strategic principle works, as the positions of prosecutor and defense in a court case strongly depend on where the burden of proof lies. At this point, a principle attributed to Machiavelli fits quite well: If you do good, do it slowly; if you do evil, do it at once.

A special variety of the principle of reward motivation consists in dangling a utopian reward—one that may exist in the constructed reality of the system but does not require any real achievements. Utopian rewards can be surprisingly effective, which illustrates very well how the laws of communication work.

14. The *principle of monitoring all options*. Here, you strive to shape your opponent's behavioral options in such a way that each of them will be to your advantage—or to influence the way he or she thinks of his or her own options. The latter case reflects a key element of this principle: the fact that what really matters to people is not the options they actually have but those they believe they have. For instance, since ancient times it has been a strategy of military leaders to tell soldiers on the day before a major battle that they only have two options: being executed or fighting bravely—and that the latter is the smaller evil. Some people use this strategy even to influence their own behavior, thus closing down any avenues for retreat they may have. The phenomenon discussed here is the true nature of the so-called double bind. This type of situation is probably best illustrated by the following example:[361] The prosecutor asks the defendant, "Have you stopped abusing your wife at last? Answer my question! Yes or no?!" Whichever answer the defendant chooses, he will not be able to show that he has never *never* abused his wife. To do that, he will have to step out of the overall situation, uncover its underlying structure and thus try to change it, in order to escape this narrow choice that is detrimental to him either way. So the solution in this case is not to choose one or the other—it is to refuse the choice as such, and thus the options at hand. This, however, is the key problem in many situations: People do not see the way out. The control of options through communication, including the creation of a set of options where they actually do not exist, will have to be addressed in the context of influencing the state of information, as these things are closely connected.

Another form is the principle of equitable sharing, or the fixation of options. In a negotiation you suggest to your opponent something he or she will consider to be just, and indicate with your actions that you are not prepared to negotiate.

15. The *principle of the golden bridge*, the last of the principles in this category, says that interventions and control measures should never be designed

---

361 Watzlawick, Beavin, Jackson (Kommunikation), p. 213f.

to drive the object system into an impasse; rather, it should be offered a "golden bridge" permitting it to save face. As is quite obvious, this principle is closely related to the principle of controlling all options, as in the majority of cases the opponent will choose the option permitting him or her to save face.

Of course, this line of action is often like laying traps. Another form of it is "Divide et impera." The "golden bridge" then consists in letting the opponent have a share of the power to one's own power even more.

16. The *principle of proximity to information* calls for information paths to be as short and direct as possible in order to avoid distortions, unintentional and uncontrolled filter effects, and things like that. Since information paths in complex and strongly intertwined social systems tend to become longer, we should at least think about what options we have for planned redundancy and how we can establish cross checks between independent information channels.

17. Next, the *principle of occupying information interfaces* or relays indicates that these are the weakest points in both one's own and the opponent's information network, and thus the best points to gain access to information. It is a principle that the intelligence services have developed to a high level of perfection, and even if you are basically skeptical with regard to intelligence operations as such, you will have to admit that intelligence services often have considerable knowledge about systems and an excellent understanding of systemic behavior and structures.

18. The *principle of explaining one's actions* is a warning signal, reminding us to keep thinking about how our strategic actions might be understood and interpreted by other systems that perhaps are not directly involved. There will always be strategic situations in which you have to take great care to avoid misinterpretation, and you will need to make respective arrangements and declare your intentions. Such declarations can take very subtle forms, as illustrated by diplomats' professional activities. Further means to find out what the opponent party is saying, and what it may actually mean by it, include the careful analysis of press releases, mutual declarations, and so on.

In this context, a few other aspects are significant as well. Changes of behavior often serve the purpose of *reinterpreting* situations. For instance, people may declare that they *regard* a matter as very or hardly significant. At this point, let me repeat once again that in the social and communication context we are not dealing with objective realities but we are able to create realities. A matter can be made significant or insignificant, it can be said to be simple or complicated—under certain circumstances, the mere act of making an assertion, even if it is an invention or a lie, can create precisely the reality that is asserted, or at least put the opponent under pressure to furnish proof of things that cannot be proved. Irrefutable assertions, which in most cases only permit unprovable justifications, are one element of exerting influence that involves the conscious creation of realities.[362]

Finally, there is one further point to consider. Social processes are *punctuated* by their participants; that is, the latter arrange the sequences of events according to specific, but possibly different aspects. This may result in very peculiar situations. Remember the example of the courtship behavior of British women and American soldiers as described in section 3.3: In that example, the courses of events were punctuated very differently by the two parties, and it is obvious that this was a question not of correct behavior but of the way the two parties understood the other's behavior and how they responded to it. In most cases, the punctuation of courses of events happens subconsciously, but of course it can be used very deliberately to shape a situation and influence others' thoughts and actions. If one party succeeds in making the other party's behavior appear threatening, it thus establishes a reason to take measures which would otherwise not be tolerable, but are adequate by way of defense. A somewhat dramatic example is that of the cuckolded husband who shoots and kills his rival in alleged self-defense, maintaining that he thought it was a burglar threatening him.[363]

19. The *principle of disguise* is largely self-explanatory. Rather than contradicting the principle of explaining one's actions, it complements it in various ways. While explanations of one's actions are sometimes aimed at those systems or parties that are not immediately involved in strategic processes but, due to misunderstandings or expected own advantages, might feel the need to intervene as soon as they find a good excuse, the principle of concealing is usually aimed at the systems immediately involved, which in most cases are not supposed to know about one's actual intentions. Of course, explanations of one's actions can be just that: a disguise.

---

362 Watzlawick, Beavin, Jackson (Kommunikation), pp. 166 et seq.

363 On the analysis of the punctuation of social courses of events and their consequences, see Watzlawick, Beavin, and Jackson (Kommunikation), pp. 92 et seq.

This ambiguity is characteristic of many strategic and meta-strategic actions, making them both effective and dangerous at the same time. Disguise comes in many forms. Apart from the obvious varieties of keeping
things confidential and concealing them, it includes the strategy of faking
ignorance or pretending not to notice. Some problems arise only from
the fact you realize things and let the other party know you have realized
them—that is what often creates the urgency.

20. The *principle of control* says that you should think carefully about what information you will use to check the impact of interventions. Interventions, especially the threatening to take certain measures, are not necessarily ineffective just because they cannot be controlled—but it is realistic
to assume that an intervention will be more effective when the chance
of making appropriate checks is greater, and when both parties are aware
this possibility exists. Some self-explanatory aspects of this principle
should be regarded as heuristics to be complied with. It is better to check
a bit too much than to lose control. It is easier to eliminate or loosen
checks than to install new ones. The shorter the control cycles, the better
results will usually be.[364]

With all the twists and turns often found in strategic thinking and acting,
it is important to observe some basic rules concerning the meta-system's
*power of conviction* or *trustworthiness*. One point to keep in mind is that strategic actions are perceived in very specific ways—in particular by people
with limited knowledge of meta-systemic thinking and who are therefore
less likely to take account of possible strategic actions. One common
response is to refer to strategic actions as shabby tricks, mean and unfair
methods, and declare them to be beyond any set of valid rules. Even
though it is often no more than the outrage and revenge of naïveté, it
can put the strategic actor under so much social pressure he or she cannot stand it. Another frequent response from people affected by strategic
actions is that they tend to feel powerless and inferior, thinking there was
no way for them to win this game as they had no chance from the outset.
Results can be either open rebellion or inward emigration and passive
resistance. Both responses can erode the very foundation of control, thus
undermining the coupling relationship between systems. This can culminate in an almost complete loss of mutual trust. We might even say that

---

364 See Sloma (Management), pp. 29 et seq.

*smart* strategic behavior rooted in a deep understanding of systemic relationships and also of human behavior, often based on long-standing and
rich experience, can be distinguished from actions perceived as *unfair* and
*immoral* in that a good strategist will always take into account the principles of maintaining his or her power of conviction. By observing these
principles, one will usually manage to gain a reputation as someone who
is a serious opponent, not to be underestimated, and familiar with all
kinds of intricacies, but who deserves a lot of respect and whose fairness
is appreciated, even when it can be assumed that he will use the whole
range of strategic levers available. So, strategic behavior is characterized
by the use of the total power of individual and social intelligence, not by
any crude attempts to trick each other.

21. The *principle of reliability* requires that any obligations accepted have to be
    met. What kind of obligations they are and whether any obligations have
    been accepted at all depends on how the strategic principles discussed
    here are ultimately applied. Once such obligations exist, however, they
    should be taken seriously in order not to risk one's power of conviction,
    future trustworthiness, and sound reputation.

22. The *principle of rigor* refers to the consistency by which you stick to your
    own plans and strategies, as nothing will undermine your credibility more
    quickly and more effectively than when you deviate from measures you
    have previously announced. This does not mean you must rigidly cling
    to each and every principle you have ever set; rather, it is important to
    make sure you only announce or threaten with measures you are actually
    willing and able to implement. There is nothing as ineffective as a threat
    that cannot be carried out. On the other hand, the most effective threats
    are those that are bound to transpire and that cannot be prevented when
    the conditioning factors occur. In a sense, what you do here is create
    anticipated realities.

23. The *principle of the rare bluff* is evident: Even if the occasional bluff, smartly
    conceived, cannot be avoided, this is something that you should only
    resort to in very rare and inevitable cases.

24. The *principle of the concealed avenue of retreat.* When you do decide to use the
    tool of bluffing, you must be quite clear that there is nothing more det-
    rimental or embarrassing than having your bluff called. Consequently,
    this principle says that you need to think in advance about how you are
    going to get out of a situation like that and save face. It is not only in the
    bluff situation that this principle is meaningful, but as a general rule. As

has been pointed out several times in this book, in particular in the context of the open system, you need to be ready for surprises at all times when dealing with complex systems. You should never assume things to develop as planned and expected. It is therefore important to give some thought to how, in general terms, you will get out of a situation while limiting the damage or even creating advantages. Hence, it should be part of any strategic approach to consider what is currently happening and what might happen, and what to do if the situation develops differently from what you expect. This includes thinking about your line of argument, how you will present it, and what excuses you will use, which obviously have to be credible in line with the principle of maintaining your power of conviction. In this context it will often happen that you construe realities, interpret matters accordingly, and generally describe things as you want them to be seen. Even if your opponent sees through your strategy, he or she will have no choice but to accept your arguments and excuses, as long as your avenue of retreat has been well prepared.

As I have mentioned in the introduction to this section, some of the principles discussed here are so closely interlinked that any distinction between them is rather arbitrary, in particular as they exist in a range of variations. However, what matters more than a faultless structure is that you know and observe the principles described, whether for the purpose of obtaining advantages for yourself or avoiding disadvantages. As mentioned several times before, even if you are unwilling to apply one or several of these principles, you have to be prepared for others applying them.

## 3.52 Strategic Behaviors

Next, I would like to address some strategic behaviors that are closely related to the strategic principles discussed above. They represent typical behavioral patterns, some of which have gained historical significance, while others are patterns frequently observed in everyday life. The historical references are evident from their names, which have become standard usage over the years.[365]

---

365 Readers may notice that some of these examples are referred to as tactics, such as in "fait accompli tactics." This is because these names have become common, sometimes even in everyday language. However, in the sense that they are used to influence complex systems, they certainly represent strategies.

However, the historical contexts that gave these patterns their name and made them famous should not lead anyone to believe they have lost relevance. As will be easy to see, for each of these strategic behaviors there are countless examples from modern business and politics, as well as numerous applications. They are timeless, that is, invariant, and that is what makes them so important.

1. *Napoleonic strategy of successive attacks:* This strategy consists in destroying the adversary alliance's combat power by successively defeating the enemies one by one. Generally speaking, this is about breaking down a complex system into simpler subsystems that are easier to handle. One variety, or real-life application, of this strategy is the principle of doing one thing after the other, or completing a task before tackling the next one. Drucker has tirelessly pointed out the significance of this principle in terms of management efficiency and effectiveness. Another application is a question that often emerges in legal contexts: whether several aspects of a case should be prosecuted in one or more suits. In decision-making processes, too, the question keeps arising as to what should be addressed, submitted for approval, and decided upon jointly or separately.

2. *Fabian strategy of attrition:* In the second Punic War against Hannibal, Fabius made a point of evading larger battles and instead chose small, surprising attacks to wear down the enemy. This strategy is still applied by modern-day guerilla fighters, and is doubtlessly very common in business. The concept of "keeping them busy," as discussed earlier, is one variety. The weaker party is often strongly guided by the principle of maximum flexibility, while the stronger party is led—by its very strength—to give up its flexibility, which makes it even more vulnerable to attacks. Achieving many small victories, the weaker party can make this seem like a trend in its favor, thus demoralizing the other party.

3. *Periclean strategy of exhaustion and exploiting the opponent's vulnerabilities:* This strategy, too, is designed to produce a series of small victories by taking advantage of the opponent's vulnerabilities, thus creating a perception of strength or a tendency that will translate into a self-fulfilling prophecy. As an additional component, Pericles's approach included the strategy of choosing one's arms or battlefield. He avoided ground warfare and attacked Sparta by sea, where the Athenian fleet of ships was clearly superior. So the success of Pericles's strategy was based not only on a perceived trend but also on the opponent's recognition of the actual balance of power.

4. *Fait-accompli tactic:* This approach is well-known and needs no further explanation. Together with other strategic approaches yet to be discussed, such as the incremental increase of impetus or the Fabian Strategy, it forms what is commonly known—and in numerous variations—as the "salami technique." Just like all the other approaches, this tactic is not without risk: It can cause the opponent to build up enormous emotional tension because it remains just below the threshold point that would require counteraction. That is why it often has to be combined with appropriate cover-up measures. One of them is the strategy of "benevolent sabotage":[366] Under the pretense of being helpful, it creates a disadvantage for the opponent. All the time, you act as though you didn't know anything, then pretend to be awfully sorry—although unable to change anything—or outraged because you wanted nothing but the best for the other party.

5. *Tactic of playing the fool:* Again, this is a very common strategic approach: You play stupid in order to make your opponent give up caution or provoke him or her into trying to prove things, in which case you may have further opportunities to gain "salami technique" advantages. Machiavelli called this tactic a manifestation of great wisdom. Quite frequently, it comes with a sophisticated questioning technique which is aimed at a) keeping the initiative and b) causing the other party to report contradicting versions of a situation. Not only is this a key technique for gaining information, but it can also provide valuable clues as to where your own actions should focus.

6. *Ratchet strategy:* This course of action is grounded on the fact that both people and social systems, once they have achieved an (absolute or relative) position, tend to hold on to it—an attitude that often causes them to defend their vested rights with all their might, and to form coalitions with whoever has conceded these rights to them or is basically able to. So, by conceding a certain advantage to the system to be influenced, you cause it to sort of snap into place, thus creating a situation where your counterpart would have to concede an even greater advantage to you in order to win. Due to the decline in incremental benefit, this advantage might even have to be disproportionate, thus incurring disproportionate costs, so your opponent will not be able to enjoy the victory.

---

366 See Watzlawick, Weakland, and Fisch (Lösungen), pp. 168 et seq.

7. *Gambetta's ratchet tactic:* Despite the similarity in names, this is a different strategic approach. The Gambetta tactic is based on the principle of constantly keeping sight of your strategic objectives without ever mentioning them. Under this principle, you do not really need to develop a proactive plan—you just remain watchful and wait for social systems' natural dynamics to produce situations that will enable you to secure advantages for yourself. In view of all we know about the course of social processes, social dynamics can certainly be expected to produce new situations over and over again, some of which will certainly be favorable. So, with a maximum of flexibility you just keep prepared to take advantage of positive circumstances, or to eliminate or diminish the effects of negative ones. To an external observer this may seem like you are randomly hitching onto accidental events, and the strategy will not become obvious until you reveal your underlying intentions. Hence it is key to conceal your objectives.

8. *Moltke tactic of focusing on breakpoints:* Under this strategy, you first try to find out what points of attack the opponent seems to find particularly relevant, to then deliberately weaken these points on your own side. This is supposed to make the opponent attack at a point that is predictable and therefore known, thus giving you the advantage of being able to prepare your counteraction very carefully, based on your superior state of information. Of course this strategy is often combined with laying traps.

9. *Belisarius's tactic of defensive offense:* This strategy can be considered one variety of the tactics of Gambetta and Moltke. Rather than waiting for an opportunity to arise based on natural dynamics, you provoke the opponent into lowering his or her guard. This is usually done by hinting at a weak point you supposedly have.

10. *Strategy of deliberate confusion:* The more you stick to habits, traditions, principles, and the like, the more predictable you become to your opponent—which will enable him to determine his own lines of action based on this quite reliable information. In other words, by observing principles you restrict your own behavioral variety and force it into an anticipatable pattern. On the other hand, the less predictable your actions are, the less your opponent will be able to form the anticipations that provide an essential basis for any kind of pre-planned action. Consequently, it can be very useful in the context of certain phases or moves to do things

you would "normally" never do, so as to deliberately confuse your opponent. As a side note, the technique of brain-washing is based on this very principle.

11. *Bazaar tactic.* This kind of behavior is almost ubiquitous in everyday life. As the name indicates, the bazaar tactic is one of countless varieties of bargaining, with player X making certain concessions or providing anticipatory services, thus acquiring a right, so to speak, to equivalent concessions from player Y. This is also a good example of how certain rules can be introduced implicitly, without requiring any formal negotiations. The "voluntary" gesture of one player maneuvers the other into a situation where he or she cannot reject this gesture but has to respond with a similar act. This process tends to continue and reinforce itself, which can even lead to a situation where everything happens in a climate of pronounced mutual sympathy and possibly trust. One perfidious variety of the bazaar technique consists in pretending to make concessions or in providing anticipatory services that do not really demand any sacrifices, then pocketing the opponent's genuine services. This way of acting can also be regarded as a combination of the bazaar technique and the Belisar strategy, the difference from Belisar being that you start out negotiating in a peaceful climate.

12. *Strategy of the mutual example.* This approach has certain commonalities with the bazaar tactic, although it is much more general. You very ostentatiously act in a certain way to signal to the other party that there are rules and standards. This strategy can work extremely well if the other party is in a reporting relationship, or one of dependency. Without needing many words, thus avoiding unpleasant or embarrassing conflicts, you can signal to the other party that "this is the way we do it here." This strategy is often applied in the management of small groups. Unfortunately, it sometimes comes with strange, partly even grotesque spirals of behavior where one party tries to commit the other to its own behavioral style with extremely pronounced and ostentatious acts. This can result in downright ridiculous contests of rituals, and it often happens that opponents lose sight of their original purpose, turning these mutual demonstrations of style into an end in themselves.

13. *Strategy of choosing means and battlefields.* Similar to how in the above strategy each party tries to force its own styles onto the other, in this version you try to make your opponent use the means you have chosen, and a battlefield you have determined. An astute strategist will always be striving to

secure for him or herself the initial advantage of being able to make an active choice; at the same time he or she will try to prevent any attempt by the opponent to regain the initiative. One key application of this strategy, of course, is to refuse or avoid fighting. This has been discussed in the passage about heuristic principles, when dealing with the control of options and the double-bind theory. Too often, managers let themselves be maneuvered into situations where they feel pressed to make a decision, rather than wonder whether a decision is required at all.

14. *Nip-in-the-bud tactic*: Under this strategy, even minute deviations from an existing or alleged standard are immediately sanctioned. This approach is very common in everyday life and needs no detailed description. It is also referred to as taboo technique. It should be noted, however, that it can cause the other party to build up negative emotions, as it does not do justice to the fact that fluctuations around a mean level are a natural thing in complex systems. On the other hand, it is worth considering what aspects the strategy is focused on. At the object level, certain fluctuations are not unusual and should largely be tolerated; at the meta-level, however, it can certainly make sense to sanction even minute deviations from certain rules and principles.

15. *Repressive tolerance*: To put it somewhat pointedly, the strategy consists in carrying any kind of exploitation just to the point where those exploited are not aware of it. In more general and less ideological terms, it is about keeping the load on a social system—no matter in what sense—within certain limits while trying to approach those limits as far as possible. This situation can easily be described by using the concept of the ultra-stable system and the physiological limits to its essential variables. In this context you usually face the—sometimes rather difficult—problem of finding out where the limits actually are and what load a system can effectively take.

16. *Incremental increase, or variation, or improvisation of impetus*: One possible strategy to determine physiological limits of a system, or its load capacity, is an incremental increase in impetus. You increase the load on the system step by minute step, with the actual size of those steps obviously depending on the characteristics of the respective system. Each intervention is first checked on its impact before the next is launched. Along with this incremental increase in impetus, there can also be a variation of the impetus in terms of both kind and direction. As the individual effects, or chains of effects, are impossible to predict in most of these cases, the

strategy usually has to be combined with one of smart improvisation—which, by using the latch technique according to Gambetta, attempts to take advantage of the system's behavioral variety in seizing opportunities to improve one's own situation.

17. *Common "enemies" or goals*: A majority of people usually become a tight-knit community, and thus a social system, when confronted with a common enemy—an aggressor who represents a collective threat, and whom they can only defeat by joining forces. So, one very effective strategy of integration is to create this joint point of attack, either in reality or in the perception of those involved. Of course, the aggressor can also be replaced with a common goal. In an analysis that might not be entirely valid in every detail, but it still represents a very interesting approach. Anthony Jay points out that the cornerstone of every social organization is a group of four to approximately fifteen people, with a cluster in the range of around ten, and that the key factor linking them together is this common goal. He writes: "The first condition for a ten-group, therefore, is that there must be a common objective, a single criterion of success by which all succeed or fail."[367] One variety is to spread a vision, or even a utopia. This is a very significant and effective management principle: As different as past leaders (also present ones) have been, the common basis for their power and effectiveness was the ability to communicate a higher ideal which was not related to them as a person, and in the interest of which they could demand sacrifices and eliminate opponents.

18. *Creating outlets for emotions*: Some of the strategies described here put considerable strain on social systems and/or cause an accumulation of negative feelings which, in turn, are a stress factor and thus have "revolutionary" potential. To keep this potential under control and channel the emotions, an appropriate strategy can be to enable substitute responses that provide emotional outlets. Typical examples range from sports events—or in more general terms, any kind of ritualized competition—all to way to festivities, parades, and such. Combining this with the strategy of the common enemy, you can create artificial points of attack to deflect the emotional potential.

19. *Infiltration*: When strategies of direct confrontation do not promise much success, the infiltration strategy can often help. Historically there have been countless examples of the application of this pattern, all in line with

---

367 Jay (Man), p. 49.

the motto, "If you can't beat them, join them." A much more subtle and almost ubiquitous variety consists in assuming seats and votes in other systems' decision-making and sanctioning bodies in order to be able to influence them. All modern-day societies have developed this strategy to great levels of maturity, providing a series of official mechanisms for implementation.

20. *Coupling.* The sublimated form of infiltration is immediately followed by the coupling strategy: You integrate influential representatives of other systems in the decision-making and sanctioning centers of your own system in order to a) ensure a connection of interests, b) using any of a series of strategies discussed—such as the strategy of setting mutual examples—establish certain rules, and c) be able to influence them directly. Another factor to be considered is that these mutual interconnections lead to a significant increase in information. One variety consists in coupling subsystems, along the lines of the old proverb that "when two dogs fight over a bone, the third runs away with it."

21. *Deliberate indiscretion.* As has been pointed out before, the chances of succeeding with a specific strategy, or combination of strategies, increase as information management improves, in particular with regard to confidentiality. The obvious counter-strategy is to deliberately provide the other system with information about yourself or third-party systems. This can either be a genuine indiscretion, in the sense that you leak information on actual or planned details to the other party, or it can be deliberate disinformation—a strategy that has been developed to great perfection by international intelligence services. The latter kind is based on the fact that at the end of the day it is not actual truth but perceived truth that counts. The strategy of deliberate indiscretion, by the way, is something the press and other mass media frequently apply. A newspaper report may be wrong, offensive, biased, or whatever—but once it is published there is usually nothing to compensate for its impact, be it a counterstatement or a lawsuit. Launching rumors is a tried and proven scheming technique. It should not be overlooked, however, that the forms of indiscretion discussed here can not only be applied in their negative, harmful varieties—there are positive applications as well: Experience has taught that you can influence people toward a positive and cooperative attitude by letting them know how much you appreciate and respect them.

A few aspects warrant special emphasis: First, we need to take into account that the strategic behaviors listed here can be *implemented in countless varieties and combinations of behaviors*. For instance, with Belisarius's strategy of defensive offense you often need to threaten the opponent to make him or her do a specific thing. Now, the act of threatening as such can be accomplished in various ways: They range from a certain way of looking at people, or of smiling at them, all the way to certain kinds of advertising campaigns or even military maneuvers. How a specific behavior is interpreted depends on the specific context, and also on how well opponents know each other's system. Also, the strategy behind a particular action is often not immediately obvious, so the variety you may face in pursuing a specific strategy can easily keep you from seeing the essential point, which is the underlying structure, and, as has been mentioned before, it can even be created on purpose based on additional strategic considerations.

A second point that has to be made is that the strategies listed above are often pursued in *various combinations*, not only in their pure forms. After all, it often happens that a strategic approach has to be accompanied by another or that strategic behaviors have to be combined in certain ways to support each other. For instance, one combination can consist in the Belisar strategy of defensive offense plus the tactic of playing the fool to make the opponent act in a certain way. If this fails to produce the desired effect, you could combine the Gambetta ratchet tactic with a deliberate indiscretion (e.g., leaking information to the press) and, once that information has spread, make the respective medium look like the joint enemy, thus creating an outlet for built-up emotions. As the press are usually committed to not divulging their sources, chances are this strategy will lead to the desired result without the opponent's ever finding out what actually happened. Another combination of strategies is this: Applying the technique of playing naïve, you commit deliberate indiscretions (pretending not to be aware), then increase the effect using both the Fabian strategy of attrition and the repressive tolerance strategy—that is, you take care to remain just below the response point, then use the Belisar approach to increasingly provoke your opponent, building in a break point (according to Moltke) where you finally—when your opponent has fallen into your trap—use the nip-in-the-bud technique to teach him or her a lesson. These examples may appear extremely perfidious; however, depending on the means you use and precisely how you implement these strategies, they may actually remain within the limits of fairness.

The above remarks on strategic behaviors and principles mainly refer to phases 3, 4, and 5 of the systems methodology, and of course at the meta-systemic level. This closes the circle of exploring and shaping, or of information and influencing, and at the end of the day these kinds of closed circles provide the foundation for the cybernetic paradigm of controlling complex systems. Closed-circuit loops like these make for the stability of events, situations, and processes, thus leading to the formation of invariants.

This complete and closed circle of analysis and design, information and influence, has been addressed from a very generic perspective in this chapter, in particular as these considerations were based on the very basic cybernetic model of the polystable system—a system for which no specific assumptions are made except one: that it has a very broad repertoire of possible states, many of them stable, the transition from one state to the next being marked by threshold values. That is why existing insights on strategic behaviors, information, and influencing are broadly applicable, as ultimately very large parts of reality are in line with this type of system, even if their concrete manifestations vary widely.

Matters are very different when we assume the structures of the viable system apply. Here, we know much more about structural details, functional relationships, and so on than we normally do. The next section therefore discusses ways to combine the Viable Systems Model with the concept of meta-systemic management described here.

## 3.6  Applying the Viable System in Systems Methodology

> "Control is the attribute of a system which tends to sustain its structure ... Control is the dynamics of structure"
> *Stafford Beer*

Strategic management has been identified as the meta-systemic control of complex systems. The paradigm of meta-systemic control is based on object systems largely organizing themselves, and on object-level processes regulating themselves. The fact that events at the object level cannot be organized in detail is due to their complexity, which makes it impossible to ever feed to a designing or controlling authority the knowledge and information required for detailed organization and control. Starting from this central hypothesis, the only way to achieve effective control is to design—from a higher level, as it were—the principles governing self-organization and self-regulation. The reason this kind of indirect detail control can be effective is that it permits taking advantage of a reinforcing effect: Rules and principles will be applicable not to one specific case but to all the cases of a category or type. This way an indefinite number of particular events can be regulated, which means that the control variety increases. Note that this kind of control applies not to every detail of these individual events, just to certain characteristics—that is, the attributes captured by said principles. The "higher level" mentioned above, from which this control is carried out, is "higher" not necessarily in a power sense but in a logical sense, which is what makes it a meta-level. Of course, the principles governing the particular circumstances can in turn be subject to yet higher-level principles, so in effect we have a concept of a hierarchy of meta-levels. However, as each level follows the same laws of control in the sense defined here, it is basically sufficient to address a principle just once, and it can then be applied over and over again. The only trouble is that the content aspects to which the principle is supposed to be applied will keep changing, which means that there has to be some kind of adaptation; also, due to the varying content there is a risk of losing sight of the oneness of the control paradigm.

Key meta-system control principles include those by which the events and processes at the object level are structured, categorized, and sub-categorized, or in other words: organized. In view of the arguments put forward in part I, the structure of the viable system is particularly suited to controlling this organizing activity. While control-oriented systems methodology is geared towards helping the problem solver or manager read symptoms and their implications for management (that is, filtering out the control-relevant characteristics of the systems causing problems and developing and monitoring appropriate interventions), the Viable Systems Model can now be built into the relevant phase of the systems methodology as a basic analysis and design grid, enabling the problem solver to align management-related ideas along the model and express them in its terms.[368]

These operations first address the question as to what degree and in what concrete forms a socio-technical entity has the structure of a viable system, then derive from the results of that analysis a system development program to determine along what lines the present structures can be migrated to a viable system. So, whereas—as shown in the previous section—the analysis

---

368 Regarding the following, see figures 1.6(1) through 1.6(10).

of complex systems works with general cybernetic system concepts such as the general polystable systems model to create a system-adequate basis for interventions, at this point it is replaced by the Viable Systems Model with its highly differentiated structure.

Once the structure of the viable system has been established, it goes without saying that within its subsystems there will be systems-methodological processes going on that are aimed at a) maintaining the system structures themselves, b) solving internal problems in the subsystems, and c) anchoring the viable system in its environment. In the course of these system-internal processes, to create a control model of specific problem situations you can use both general cybernetic system concepts such as the servomechanism, ultra-stable system, and multi-stable system and, of course, the Viable Systems Model (although related to another level of recursion).

The following example should help to illustrate this point: We know from part I that the function of system 4 is to safeguard the external stability and position of the overall enterprise by gathering and processing information. To ensure it will be appropriately embedded in its environment, the first thing to analyze under the systems methodology is the system characteristics of that environment. In most cases this issue requires very differentiated analyses. The segment of the environment referred to as "market" may show typical system characteristics of a poly stable system, with no specific intrinsic structure apart from the respective stability zones, their thresholds, and their transition criteria. So, to capture the systemic characteristic of this part of the environment it will be a good idea to use the model of the polystable system. Besides that, the environment of an organization contains a series of other elements with distinct and differentiated structures. Above all, the system environment is "populated" by other systems as well, the structures of which are very similar to that of the enterprise itself. It will be best if related problem-solving processes and control-relevant interventions directed at these other systems are based on the Viable Systems Model.

Of course, the question as to what cybernetic model to use cannot be answered by a priori stipulations. Rather, in the course of problem-solving processes under the systems methodology you have to keep asking yourself whether the model you use for guidance is really the right one for the particular problem, and it may well be that in the course of your thinking process you decide to change the underlying model. Based on cybernetics' isomorphism theorem, however, it is to be expected that all cybernetic models—which invariably address the problem of control—have fundamental commonalities at a certain level of abstraction, so the insight gained by using one model can often be used in other models as well. Consequently, the entire process can be regarded as the mental toying with or testing of different models from the same category: the category of control models. Once again we have a typical trial-and-error process here. It is not a random process—otherwise it would permit any kind of model to be used—it is aligned in the sense that all trials will have to remain within a more general, but strictly limited search area: the category of control models.

Once it is clear how to use models, and especially how to mentally toy with those of the same category, it should also be reasonably clear what the next steps will be. The analysis of system-specific characteristics in phase 2 of the methodology is done not by means of a general list of questions, as has been shown in section 3.4, but by using a special question toolkit directed at the analysis of the viable system. Key aspects to be addressed can be found in the appendix of this section. To apply this kind of questionnaire well, and thus to analyze a complex system (e.g., an entire business organization) effectively, you need comprehensive knowledge about the viable system, what it looks like, and how it works. Just applying it schematically, without that knowledge, you would be bound to fail. The main reason is that the degree of detail of the questions can vary widely. Depending on the specific case and the purpose of the analysis, it may suffice to do a rough analysis to filter out the basic system structures, that is, subsystems 1 through 5, and help to identify how they work. Even a rough analysis enables you to determine whether there are any major flaws in the structures of a socio-technical system, in which case a more detailed analysis would be called for. Another thing that can happen is that in the course of using the analysis tool, particular problems arise that call for a very detailed analysis of specific system parts, subsystems, or system functions. Therefore the analysis tools have to be adapted to the individual situation. These adjustments, however, are only possible if you have the necessary knowledge about the structure and functions of the viable system.

In this context it is important to note that a systems-methodological analysis like that can never be a clean-sweep exercise—it always has to start from the given situation. As pointed out in part 1, the socio-technical system under analysis exists in a certain form, and the mere fact it has survived to date suggests that there must be certain rudimentary system forms. So, the art in applying the analysis toolkit is in looking at the abundance of specifications, job descriptions, functional diagrams, organization charts, and tasks and activities identified through interviews and personal observation and filtering out those activities and structures that are relevant from the viable systems perspective. Figure 3.6(1) shows a schematic overview of how this analysis can be set up. Its purpose is to identify and allocate those activities that, from the perspective and logic of the elements of the Viable Systems Model, belong together.

| Tasks Functions, Activities | Subsystems of the Viable System | | | | |
|---|---|---|---|---|---|
| | System 1 | System 2 | System 3 | System 4 | System 5 |
| Activity $x_1$ | – – ├ – –●– – – – – – – – –● | | | | |
| Activity $x_2$ | – – ├ – – – – – – – –●– – – – – – – – – –●– – – – ● | | | | |
| Activity $x_3$ | – – ├ – – –● | | | | |
| Activity $x_4$ | – – ├ – – – – – – –●– – – – – – – – –● | | | | |
| etc. | | | | | |

*Figure 3.6(1)*

In this context it is very important not to focus exclusively on the official tools an organization has (i.e. those that exist in writing and/or have been institutionalized) but, as suggested by the questionnaire, to also pay attention to what goes on "below the surface," which often says much more about how a system actually works.

Similar to the approach shown in figure 3.4(23), this analysis also permits you to form a mental, possibly even formalized or semi-formalized model of existing structural matters that are relevant from the viable systems perspective. The content of that model then determines your next steps, again in accordance with the following phases of the systems methodology. As mentioned above, at this point a system development program can be set up which contains all the measures required to shape the necessary system structures. Here, a key point is that an analysis like this is simply not possible unless certain conditions apply. The system development processes required may call for serious interventions in an existing system, in which case there may be considerable resistances. So we are clearly dealing with a problem of a strategic nature, and all strategic behaviors and principles described in the previous section are relevant.

In addition to the basic strategic principles that are of general importance for influencing complex systems, in the specific case of implementing a viable system the following three principles have to be observed:

- the principle of recursion
- the principle of completeness of structures
- the principle of viability.

1. The *principle of recursion* has been exhaustively discussed in part l. The only point that remains to be emphasized here is that this principle is essentially about defining the limits of a system in such a way that the Viable Systems Model can be implemented in each of the resulting areas, thus creating the typical system-subsystem relations that have also been discussed earlier, and which are comparable to Chinese boxes or Russian nesting dolls. Dividing a complex socio technical system into subsystems—that is, smaller, easier-to-handle units that are still able to interact within the framework of a greater whole—is something that will obviously not be accomplished by a purely schematic or mechanistic approach. The recursion principle can be a valuable help here, as it reminds you to go by the following consideration: "If boundaries are set like this, will each of the resulting areas cover the basic structural elements of the viable system, at least in rudiments, and/or is it possible or conceivable to shape these areas in accordance with the Viable Systems Model?"

2. The *principle of the completeness of structures* is closely related to the principle of recursion. It says that you should strive to establish the complete viable systems structure at each of the recursion levels. In other words, the principle is designed to prevent design efforts from producing nothing but a torso of the viable system. Remember that according to this cybernetic model, partial structures are not viable, so at best they can be appendices of another system that is viable. That, in turn, would mean that a genuinely viable system might have to support or even maintain a number of fragmented and thus artificially viable systems—which is usually impossible to do on a permanent basis, or if it is possible, only at considerable cost. Of course the principle of structural completeness does not imply that all five subsystems of a viable system have to be elaborate and refined to the very last detail. I have repeatedly pointed out that we find different levels of structural detail in the different development phases of a system; we might even say that this is precisely why there are

different system development or maturity phases: because the development of a structure happens in phases. There are a number of analogies, for instance from embryology, that could provide valuable insights into system development processes. Also, Piaget's works on the developmental psychology of the child can provide valuable hints, by analogy, as to the general course of system development processes.

3. Finally, the *principle of viability* means that in all system-analysis and system-design activities we should think about what the specific viability constellation is, that is, what variables or values of variable the state of viability requires. Both in the design of a complex system and in the creation of concrete strategies, this principle will play a key role, since it permanently reminds you not to transgress the limits to a system's functionality. Every single action and every project you can think of in the context of concrete strategies may be fascinating and even promising. The key challenge, however, lies is weighing the different aspects and factors against each other to achieve a state of dynamic (or steady-state) equilibrium for the overall system.

In this context, Drucker notes:

"There are three kinds of balance needed in setting objectives. Objectives have to be balanced against attainable profitability. Objectives have to be balanced as to the demands of the immediate and the distant future. They have to be balanced against each other, and trade-offs have to be established between desired performance in one area and desired performance in others. Setting objectives always requires a decision on where to take the risks, a decision as to how much immediate results should be sacrificed for the sake of long-range growth, or how much long-range growth should be jeopardised for the sake of short-run performance. There is no formula for these decisions. They are risky, entrepreneurial, uncertain—but they must be made. There are few things that distinguish competent from incompetent management quite as sharply as performance in balancing objectives. There is no formula for doing this job. Each business requires its own balance—and it may require a different balance at different times. Balancing is not a mechanical job. It is risk-taking decision."[369]

At another point, Drucker writes about this important topic:

"Success, like failure, in business enterprise is *multi-dimensional*. This, however, brings out another important need: a rational and systematic approach to the *selection and balance among objectives* so as best to provide for survival and growth of the enterprise. These can be called the "ethics" of business enterprise, in so far

---

369 Drucker (Management), pp. 117 et seq.

as ethics is the discipline that deals with rational value choices among means to ends. It can also be the "strategy" of entrepreneurship. Neither ethics nor strategy is capable of being absolutely determined, yet neither can be absolutely arbitrary."[370]

Drucker's brief remarks illustrate why the viability principle has to be included in our set of strategic principles, and in which way the continuous urging and warning that is immanent to this principle as well as others can unfold its heuristic effects.

In addition to the compliance with strategic principles and behaviors, as well as with the principles specifically resulting from the viable system, there are two strategic "thrusts" to be derived from the viable systems concept: One is the *internally oriented* design and maintenance of system structures and system processes; the other is the *externally oriented* positioning of the overall system in its environment. This distinction is perfectly compatible with an approach by Ansoff, as shown in the following table (see figure 3.6(2)).[371] While Ansoff's terms and categories may be influenced by the period, culture, and context, his basic ideas are highly valid in that the problems of a system's relationships to the outside world, its internal configuration, maintaining its flexibility, and cultivating its "awareness" are permanent problems that have to be solved time and time again.

These two strategic "thrusts," or dimensions, cannot capture the strategic problem in its entirety, which is why they do not suffice to set a new direction for a socio-technical system's overall behavior.

---

370 Drucker (Technology), p. 136; also see Ulrich (Unternehmung), passim.
371 See Ansoff (Weak Signals), pp. 137 et seq.

| Domain of Response | Direct Response | Flexibility | Awareness |
|---|---|---|---|
| **Relationship to Environment** | *External Action*<br><br>- Optimize timing of response<br>- Seize Opportunity<br>- Enter New Product Market<br>- Convert a Threat to Opportunity<br>- Change competitive Strategy<br>- Share Risks with other Firms<br>- Secure Supply of Scarce Ressource<br>- Diversify Threatened Ressource Technology<br>- Reduce Commitment to Threatened Area<br>- Divest from a Threatened Market | *External Flexibility*<br><br>- Portfolio of Strategic Area<br>- Life-cycle Balance<br>- Balance of near/long term Profi tability<br>- Balance of Strategic Ressources<br>- Valance of Power Relations<br>- Diversification of Discontinuities<br>  - Economic<br>  - Technological<br>  - Social<br>  - Political<br>- Each Strategic Area<br>- Optimal Product Market Niche<br>- Product-Market-Diversification<br>- Diversification of Business Risk<br>- Limitation on Size of Risk–Long Term Contracts<br>- Negotiation with Environment | *Environmental Awareness*<br><br>- Extrapolative Economic<br>- Forecasting<br>- Sales Analysis<br>- Sales Forecasting<br>- Monitoring of Environment Structural, Techno, Econo, Socio Forecasts<br>- Modelling of Environment Threats and Opportunities Analysis |

| Internal Configuration | Internal readiness | Internal flexibility | Self awareness |
|---|---|---|---|
| | - Pre-plan<br>- Adapt Structure and Systems<br>- Acquire Technology<br>- Preposition Resources<br>- Acquire Skills<br>- Build Facilities<br>- Develop New Products Services<br>- Develop Operational Capability | - Managerial Managers<br>  - Future Awareness<br>  - Enbvironment Awareness–Facing Unpleasant/Threatening Altern.<br>  - Unfamiliar Prolem Tacking<br>  - Risk-responsive Behaviour<br>  - Creative Problem Solving systems and Structure<br>  - Multi-Alternative Strategic Planning<br>  - Threat/Opportunity Anticipation<br>  - Responsiveness to unfamiliar Problems<br>  - Speed of Managerial Response<br>  - Expeditions Management of Change<br><br>- Logistics<br>  - Diversifi cation of Skills<br>  - Diversifi cation and Critical Ressource<br>  - Ressource Liquidity<br>  - Convertibility of Capability<br>  - Elasticity of Volume<br>  - Modularity of Capacity–Multi-Purpose Capacity<br>  - Speed of Convertibility | - Performance Diagnosis (DuPont Ratio Analysis) Value Analysis Critical Resource Audits Capacity Audits Strenghts Weakness Analysis Capability Profiles Financial Modelling Strategic Modelling |

*Figure 3.6(2)*

*Two further dimensions* are shown in figure 3.6(3). They result from the fact that every socio-technical system, in particular a business organization, has to pursue its current activities and simultaneously develop its future ones, which can be considered to be two dimensions of the same problem. The overlapping sigmoid curves shown in figure 3.6(3) can have different meanings: Often they can be seen as depicting two very different basic technologies, but they can also refer to different leadership styles, management concepts, and so forth. The existence of every socio-technical system at any given point in time is based on specific technologies, marketable products, ways of thinking and acting, a specific management concept and leadership style, and so on. The *viability* of a system, however, fundamentally depends on its ability to exploit its current potential to build its future one. As the beginning and end of each development are unknown and often buried under a host of more or less relevant details, these situations usually involve enormous challenges in terms of coping with complexity. In most cases the situation is aggravated even further by the fact that while the management of a social system usually knows what the system's *current existence* is based on, there are usually several conceivable curves for its *future development*. This situation is illustrated by figure 3.6(4). In this context, Stafford Beer notes:

"In either case, we should know, two serious conditions apply. Firstly, we have to overcome a host of practical difficulties associated with mammoth change—while keeping everything running at full blast. The second difficulty, strangely enough, is even more serious because it is conceptual. If the people concerned regard the change as "a new venture", as some "diversification", or as a means of giving their quiescent patient a shot in the arm, they will fail. They have to stand back and take a much larger view. They have to see and to understand that the new growth curve is superimposed upon the old growth curve in order to create part of an envelope curve which will drive upwards to higher and possibly quite other things. They are not enhancing an old technology but embracing novelty. They are not improving the business they have known and loved, they are devising a new business of unknown characteristics."[372]

Ansoff also distinguishes two basic types of activities of a system relative to its environment:

---

372 Beer (Brain), p. 24.

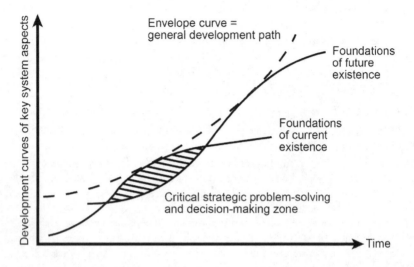

*Figure 3.6(3)*

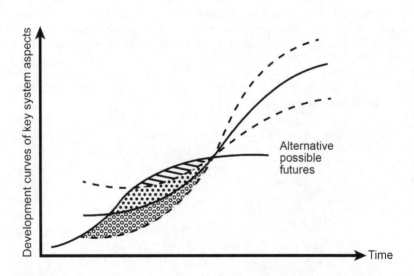

*Figure 3.6(4)*

1. competitive or operative behavior and
2. entrepreneurial or strategic behavior.[373]

Both types of behavior can largely be identified with the curves shown in figure 3.6(3). The core of the problem seems to be not in distinguishing these activities and curves, but in the fact that from a strategic management perspective both these dimensions—the present-focused, competitive behavior and the future-focused one, which is entrepreneurial in an innovation-related sense—have to be permanently balanced. In the viable system structure, this problem is located in systems 3 and 4 and their interactions. These interactions are monitored and steered by system 5, which largely happens by allocating resources to the two types of activities.

As indicated above, the dimensions of *present-focused or competitive and of the future-focused or innovative behavior are superimposed onto the dimensions of inward and outward orientation.* So, the entire design, maintenance, and development work in the context of the viable systems structure as a meta-systemic design tool has to be geared toward this superimposition, and thus the simultaneous and continuous balancing of these strategic dimensions.

The following table summarizes key principles in applying the Viable Systems Model. Each principle has been explained in earlier sections: Some of them also represent general and evident principles of cybernetic thinking, in which case no explanation is required.

---

373 See Ansoff (Strategy), pp. 42 et seq.

| Summary of key principles in applying the Viable Systems Model |  |  |
| --- | --- | --- |
| General cybernetic principles[374] |  |  |
| - Principle of intense interaction<br>- Principle of negative feedback<br>- Principle of dense networks<br>- Principle of the spontaneous order<br>- Principle of symbiosis<br>- Principle of the judo effect<br>- Principle of independence of growth<br>- Principle of independence of the product<br>- Principle of multiple use<br>- Principle of recycling<br>- Principle of the biological basic design |  |  |
| Principles of design and application for the Viable System |  |  |
| - Pinripcle of five subsystems<br>- Principle of connectivity & interaction of the five subsystems<br>- Principle of completeness of structures<br>- Principle of recrusion<br>- Principle of relative autonomy<br>- Principle of viability |  |  |
| Inward:<br>differentiation according to the recursion principle and te five subsystems<br>integration according to the recurision principle and system connectivity | Outward<br>Positioning in the environment, according to general cybernetic models and the Viable Systems Model, applied to environmental systems |  |
|  | Internal readiness<br>Internal flexibility<br>Self-awareness | External action<br>External flexibility<br>Enwironmental awareness |
| Competitive / present-focused |  |  |
| Innovative / future-focused |  |  |

*Figure 3.6(4)*

In concluding this section I want to point out a very important aspect. A major part of the comments made so far have been written in a positive sense or intention. The perspective has always been on creating or achieving something positive. However, as has been pointed out in describing the course of complex social processes, there is often a distinct *remedial focus*, for

---

374 See also Vester (Ballungsgebiete), pp. 24 et seq.

example a focus on the elimination of deficits or at least on preserving what has been achieved. Such a focus is obviously only possible and meaningful if a deficit or shortcoming has been identified, or if there is a clear view and agreement on what is worth preserving. Here, the Viable Systems Model seems to have particular significance. If the model helps to determine what subsystems a viable system should entail and what functions have to be fulfilled, it should also be possible to establish a *pathology* of the viable system. In other words, it is safe to assume that as our understanding of this kind of structure and our experience in dealing with it grows, so does our knowledge of what the typical shortcomings—diseases, as it were—the system could have and how they could typically be healed. It seems that certain approaches are suggested by studies attempting to identify the typical course of company breakdowns or—in a more general sense—of system break downs. Above all, studies dealing with the collapse of systems and its preconditions are likely to offer significant insights. In the social systems realm, we are still at a very early stage here, although we can certainly learn a lot from the collapse of major cultures and world empires.

What were the systemic causes of the collapse of the Roman Empire? How could it happen that stable cultures such as those of the Central and South American Indians could be brought down by just a handful of conquistadores? What systemic functions failed there; what subsystems of a viable system were missing; what was the process understanding for problemsolving activities? These are just a few of many questions that could be asked in this context, and from which we could probably learn quite a lot, also with regard to modern socio-technical systems.

It seems that in the context of managing business organizations, the analysis of pathological system states and of system collapses—or bankruptcies—was long blocked by the fact that managers' self-image was, and still is, closely linked to the notion of success. Nobody likes to talk about failures or mismanagement, although we could probably learn much more from them than from reported successes. One of the very few exceptions is an analysis by Agenti, who identified three typical patterns of business failures. While it would exceed the scope of this chapter to address these patterns in detail, I will quote just one passage from Argenti's analysis, where he summarizes 12 key factors which he believes to form the overall pattern for a business failure.

"… I think it is possible to see that these items have formed into a pattern, an embryonic story line is already emerging and the items in the list are not just in a random order. Put as briefly as possible, the twelve elements (in italics) are linked together in a mechanism that operates as follows: If the management of a company is poor then two things will be neglected: The system of accountancy information will be deficient and the company will not respond to change. (Some companies, even well-managed ones, may be damaged because powerful constraints prevent the managers making the responses they wish to make.) Poor managers will also make at least one of three other mistakes: They will over trade; or they will launch a big project that goes wrong; or they will allow the company's gearing to rise so that even normal business hazards become constant threats. These are the chief causes; neither fraud nor bad luck deserve more than a passing mention. The following symptom will appear: Certain financial ratios will deteriorate but, as soon as they do, the managers will start creative accounting which reduces the predicting value of these ratios and so lends greater importance to nonfinancial symptoms. Finally the company enters a characteristic period in its last few months."[375]

Quite obviously, some of the factors mentioned here (such as overtrading, launching big projects, and no response to change) are closely related to the viable system principles, while other factors are related to the problem of systemic information.

Although the subject cannot be explored any further here, it is clear that any analysis of the typical course of system crises will gain increasing importance in the future for what we call *prophylactic management*.

Figure 3.6(5) provides a graphical summary of the explanations provided in this section. It shows that the systems-methodological application of the Viable Systems Model at the meta-level follows both the dimensions of "inward" (differentiation and integration) and "outward" (positioning in the environment) and the dimensions of "present-focused" and "future-focused." In addition, all problem-solving processes required in this context are based on the strategic principles and behaviors previously developed, usually applying object area-related perspectives (such as the typical product-market strategies) as well. Furthermore—as already mentioned—the pathology of systems, the problem of system crises, and, along the same lines, some sort of prophylactic management will gain importance.

---

375 Argenti (Corporate Collapse), p. 122.

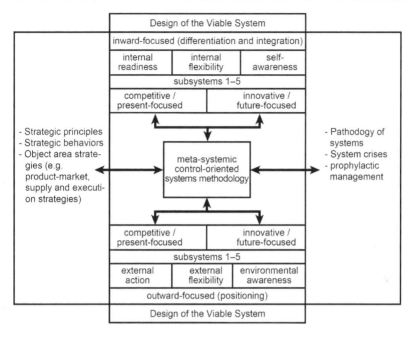

*Figure 3.6(5)*

| **Appendix/Questionnaire for the analysis of the viable system[376]** | |
|---|---|
| **System 1** | |
| – Are there any clues as to the appropriate course of recursion levels?<br>  – Who is able to influence whose rules of behavior?<br>  – Who makes the rules?<br>  – Would a spin-off of individual areas be possible, and und what conditions?<br>  – Are there any relationship clusters, and what are they based on?<br>– How can identifiable avtivities and existing structures be allocated to the five subsystems?<br>– How many potential systems 1 can be identified? | – What are their behavioral characteristics?<br>– What are their mutual relationships (inputs, outputs etc.)?<br>– How do the systems 1 interpret their own autonomy?<br>– In what aspects is either lack or an abundance of autonomy complained about?<br>– Are there any clues as to partial environments of systems 1 and their characteristics?<br>– Are there any aspect requiring considerable local knowledge?<br>– How do the systems 1 perceive/interpret their fellow systems? competitive/cooperative condescending/respectful |
| **System 2** | |
| – Where do perceived shortcomings in overall coordination exist?<br>  – Are there any ideas for improvement?<br>  – How are they to be judged? Will they just increase the proponent's own autonomy, or do they reflect a company-wide perspective?<br>– Are there any connections and relationships between the partial environments of systems 1 causing congruent/diverging behavioral characteristics?<br>– What activities are coordinating the systems 1?<br>  – Are there any common behavioral or fairplay rules etc?<br>  – Are there any common approaches?<br>  – Are there any plans, programs etc. with common features?<br>  – What are the main points of friction?<br>  – To what extent do the systems 1 contribute to coordination by anticipating the behavior of other systems 1?<br>– Where would the systems 1 locate their own interfaces–what do they | – What formal coordination tools can be identified? Are there any clues as to the varieties of both the factors to be coordinated and the coordination tools?<br>– Are there any informal coordination mechanisms? What aspects are they aimed at? Are those involved familiar with the way they work?<br>– Do people from the different systems 1 have seats in the key bodies of the other systems 1 (meetings, planning rounds, etc.)?<br>– What formal reporting systems exist? How are they actually used? How can they be characterized? (central line of command, sympathetic and parasympathetic branch)?<br>– What systemic aspects can be identified in objectives, means and processes? What inherent coordination activities can be identified in this context? What autonomy aspects do they include? What coordination requirements result from them?<br>– Do objectives, means and processes match the tentative delineation of the recursion levels and systems 1? To what degree do they need to be revised? |

376 See figures 16(1) through 16(10).

| | |
|---|---|
| perceive to be an organic delineation of their activities? | – How can/must objectives, means and processes be restructured to match tentative delineations? |

### System 3

| | |
|---|---|
| – What current activities are in line with the System 3 function? What activities make a contribution?<br>– Based on what information are these activities carried out?<br>– What process characteristics can be identified in the execution of these tasks? What process understanding (constructivist, evolutionary) do they reveal?<br>– Are these activities carried out irrespective of each other, or is there an internal coordination of System 3 functions?<br>– Do System 3 activities also take into account any non-stereotypical information (parasympathetic information channel)?<br>– What characterizes the central/vertical communication path–commands, persuasion, or selling?<br>– Are any formal tools used? Which are considered useful, which are perceived as a burden?<br>– Is there an overall plan underlying the System 3 activities?<br>– How are deviations from internal stability perceived? | – How is internal stability defined? what tools are used to detect deviations?<br>– What time lags can be identified between interventions in systems 1 and the check of effectiveness?<br>– Are there any signs of contradictions between system-3 and System 2 activities?<br>– What impact do possible personal unions between systems 1, 2 and 3 have on the way systemic functions are perceived?<br>– Are there any analogs to arousal filters?<br>– How is the interaction between systems 3 and 4 accomplished? What current activities can be considered to be a contribution? What institutionalized bodies belong in this field?<br>– What typical conflicts occur?<br>– What standard arguments are put forward regarding deficits, obstacles, and/or conflicts in systems 3-4 interaction?<br>– In what social climate does this interaction occur?<br>– How is systems 3-5 interaction accomplished? |

### System 4

| | |
|---|---|
| – What current activities correspond to System 4 functions? Which could be seen as a contribution to it?<br>– Based on what information are these activities carried out?<br>– Do these activities occur in isolation, or is there any internal coordination of System 4 activities to be noticed?<br>– What process characteristics can be identified? Welches Prozessverständnis (konstruktivistisch, evolutionär) charakterisiert die System 4-Aktivitäten?<br>– What kind of environment information channels does System 4 have?<br>– Are there any personal relationship that fulfill a similar function?<br>– In what environment systems (political parties, associations of government-level and local authorities, professional<br>– What are the standard arguments used in this context? | organizations, interest groups, clubs and societies, supervisory and administrative boards) are system members represented?<br>– About what environment factors can you gain information using these connections?<br>– To what extent is this information relevant?<br>– Are any representatives of other systems present in your own system; what information can they contribute?<br>– What consultants are being used? Are representatives of other systems, consultants, etc. used the right way?<br>– How can the interaction between systems 3 and 4 be described (from the perspective of system 4); what are permanent causes of friction and conflict? |

| | |
|---|---|
| – In what social climate does this interaction take place?<br>– What are common views about other systems?<br>– What views about one's own system are other systems believed to have?<br>– What formal tools are used to fulfill the respective function?<br>– How well is system 4 informed on the overall enterprise; are the individual subsystems and their relationships and tasks represented adequately?<br>– Is system 4 aware of its function? | - How can the interaction with system 5 be described? (formal, personal, frequency, atmosphere, kind, etc.)<br>– What information is passed on to system 5? What information is required from system 5?<br>– Are there any instances of personal union with other subsystems?<br>– How are controlling interventions by system 5 into the interaction of systems 3 and 4 perceived?<br>– Is there anything like arousal filters?<br>– Are there any formal models that are used to fulfill system 4 functions? |

| **System 5** | |
|---|---|
| – What current activities are in line with the system-5 function? What activities contribute?<br>– Based on what information are these activities carried out?<br>– What process characteristics can be identified in the execution of these tasks? What process undrstanding (constructivist, evolutionary) do they reveal?<br>– Are these activities carried out irrespective of each other, or is there an internal coordination of System 3 functions?<br>– Are there any personal unions with other functions?<br>– How are the activities of systems 3 and 4 perceived and interpreted by system 5?<br>– How are interactions with systems 3 and 4 carried out (from the perspective of system 5)? | – Based on what considerations and with what tools and means are resources allocated to present (System 3) and future activities (system 4)?<br>– How is systems 3-4 interaction monitored and steered?<br>– Are there any signs that a distinct "what if" mechanism exists? How does it work?<br>– What does system 5 dedicate more of its efforts to–analying past matters or creating alternative futures?<br>– What signs can be observed that indicate an experimental climate in that sense?<br>– How is the system-5 decision-making process organized? |

| **General questions** | |
|---|---|
| – How is information processed?<br>– Are there any starting points for thinking about potentials and capabilities?<br>– Are there typical variety patterns?<br>– What can generally be observed about modes of interaction?<br>– What are prevailing opinions about other subsystems? | – What means are used to influence the respective *logically* subordinate system and modify its behavior?<br>– What behavioral and process characteristics does the superordinate system use for guidance? |

| Comments on how to use the questionnaire | |
|---|---|
| Using a questionnaire will only make sense if there is a profound understanding of the Viable Systems Model. Based on the enormous wealth of structures under the model, it is impossible to phrase all the questions that could conceivably be asked. An analysis tool like that would comprise a large number of pages. | Rather, the exploration (analysis, diagnostic) of a complex system, with the model serving as a thought framework, has to be done in a typical open process where one question leads to another. The only thing to resembling a formal analysis tool is a set of key questions, providing starting points from which you inch forward in any direction that appears promising based on the present state of knowledge. |

*Figure 3.6.(6)*

## 3.7 Synthesis

> "There are many possible manifestations: there is one cybernetic solution."
>
> *Stafford Beer*

Keeping in mind the basic hypothesis of cybernetics, according to which the central problem of all living organisms as well as all social institutions is the management of complexity, in this chapter I have tried to present a concept for coping with complexity and to show how it can be used to resolve the strategic problems of a system. The strategic problem to be solved was defined as the overall positioning of a system in its environment. It is obvious that this position depends on the systemic characteristics of both the institution in question and its environment. This entire issue—the essential characteristics of a system determining the way it is embedded in its environment—was discussed in the context of two basic types of order: the taxic and the spontaneous order. This "theory of order," which may be considered a general systems theory or at least part of it, forms the basis for more specific types of systems, in particular the basic cybernetic models that range from the simple servomechanism to the ultra- and polystable system, all the way to the Viable Systems Model. All these systems are based on a combination of taxic and spontaneous forms of order, in the sense that certain aspects of a system are taxic—that is, organized in detail by way of command and instruction—while the taxic forms of order as such are aimed at enabling spontaneous forms of order and promote their further development. This resolves an ancient paradox which plays a key role in many views on the management of social institutions, mostly manifesting itself as some variety of an "either-or" philosophy. In addition to the variety of system forms and structures as one tool for coping with complexity, another key tool that was addressed here is the different processes—mainly problem-solving and decision-making processes—to be considered in the context of strategic issues. Here, too, I made an effort to take the general discussion of two fundamentally different concepts—the constructivist and the evolutionary one—further and form a synthesis that combines the clarity of constructivist approaches with the variety-increasing effect of evolutionary processes, thus evading both the rigidity of constructivist processes and the vagueness of evolutionary ones. Together with the notion that the issue of systemic characteristics has to be taken into account methodically, this synthesis leads to the systems methodology.

These relationships were summarized in figure 2.11(4), which is repeated here to provide a complete overview.

As the graph shows, another synthesis—integrating system structures (in particular that of the viable system) with systems methodology—will lead to the concept of strategic management. On the one hand, this synthesis refers to the thought that system structures and systems-methodological processes are linked together in some sort of autopoiesis, or symbiosis, and are mutually dependent. In a sense, this is the internal strategic component that leads to the variety potential required to achieve the second strategic component: the embedment of the system in its environment.

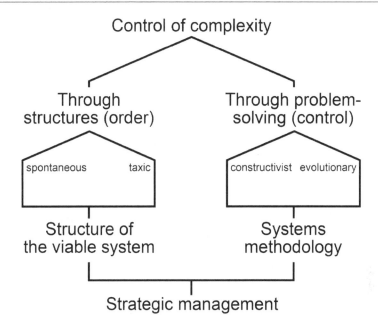

*Figure 3.7(1): identical to 2.11(4)*

As the environment of a system also consists of systems, it makes sense to apply the very same considerations and tools to this problem as well—that is, use system-methodological processes to identify the basic system characteristics of those environmental systems, then initiate appropriate interventions and control measures. Similar to the structural recursion principle in the viable system, we could speak of a recursion principle in our methodology, and it may indeed be beyond mere speculation to assume that at the end of the day, it may be this and perhaps several other recursion principles that are yet to be discovered that form the basis of the much-discussed oneness of systemic relationships that has captivated humankind's curiosity throughout history. This double connection between system structures and systems methodology is shown in figure 3.7(2). The subsequent summary allocates the tools of strategic management to the phases of control-oriented systems methodology.

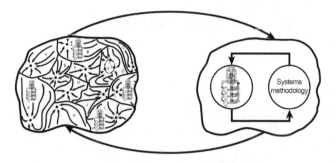

*Figure 3.7(2)*

| Significance of control-methodological phases in the strategic management context | |
|---|---|
| Identifying and formulating the problem | General problem How can you get a complex system under control? <br> Specific problems: <br> - Establishing/maintaining/improving a viable system <br> - Establishing/maintaining/improving individual subsystem of the viable system / a systemic connection <br> - Launching/maintaining the necessary systems-methodological processes- Launching/maintaining specific systems-methodological processes in the subsystems |
| Creating a control model for the problem situation | Metasystemic analysis <br> - of internal system structures <br> - based on the Viable Systems Model and within the subsystems <br> - based on other cybernetic models (general feedback/feed-forward model; ultra-stable/poly-stable model) unless the recursion principle permits using the Viable Systems Model. <br> - of the environment <br> - based on the Viable Systems Model, to the extent that other socio-technical sytems are concerned <br> - based on other cybernetic models (feedback, feed-forward, ultra-stable, poly-stable model) where the Viable Systems Model is not applicable (e.g., consumer markets) |

| | Metasystemic control: |
|---|---|
| - Developing problem-solving interventions | - based on semi-permanent models of the relevant internal and external systems |
| | - in line with the current assessment of the situation |
| - Testing and selecting possible solutions | - in line with the algedonic principle |
| | - in line with strategic principles and behaviors |
| -Introducing and monitoring the selected solution | - in line with object-area strategies that experience has shown to be useful (e.g., Golden Banking Rule and the like, which have usually resulted from one or several of the strategic principles) |

*Figure 3.7(3)*

In addition to the two aspects of system structures and system methodology mentioned above, a third aspect is of crucial importance for this work: the observation that the only way to have a meaningful discussion about strategic management issues is by keeping it at the meta-systemic level. This is the aspect most difficult to understand and explain.

The tasks to be fulfilled within each subsystem, required activities, and so on are located at the object level. By contrast, questions such as what criteria and principles should guide the creation of these subsystems as well as the activities occurring in them are typical meta-level questions. However, the distinction between the object and the meta-level should not lead anybody to conclude that these are matters of differing importance. They are equally important, although the meta-level has received far less attention to date than the object level has.

To sum up, the three areas mentioned—system structures, system methodology (processes) and the meta-perspective—constitute the essence of this work. They permit a deep understanding of the nature of systems and systemic nature.

# 4. Epilog: When the End is a Beginning

## 4.1 Experiences with Complex Corporate Development Processes

Toward the end of their manuscript, many authors would probably wish to be able to be at the start again; at least that is the impression many forewords and introductions convey. Ever since 1977, I have tried to test in practice the position laid down in this book. My primary concern was not so much the empirical testing of a hypothesis in the usual sense; rather, I was trying to find out whether it is possible at all to work with the underlying ideas, whether the conceptual models presented here help to understand what happens in business organizations, and whether any specific techniques and methods can be developed to make them applicable to concrete situations.

In these years there have been several publications that have helped me to better interpret this approach and to better understand what I had initially sensed and presumed in mere outlines. Foremost among them are two books by Stafford Beer: "The Heart of Enterprise", 1979, and the greatly expanded edition of "Brain of the Firm" that was published in 1981. Further important writings include those by Rupert Riedl: "Die Ordnung des Lebendigen", 1975, and "Die Strategie der Genesis", 1976 (both having come to my attention rather late) as well as "Biologie der Erkenntnis", 1980, which has considerably enriched my understanding of evolution theory. Next, the third volume of Friedrich von Hayeks "Law, Legislation and Liberty", published as late as 1979–six years after the first and three years after the second volume–as well as Röpke's "Strategie der Innovation", 1977, have also been significant eye openers. Finally, Gregory Bateson's "Mind and Nature", 1979, Hans Albert's "Traktat über rationale Praxis", 1978, and James Brian Quinn's "Strategies for Change", 1980, have made for very enlightening readings.

In addition, in the course of this period I tried to better understand the Theory of Autopoietic Systems. The writings by Maturana and Varela were long known to insiders only, their key paper having been published in Spanish in 1972. It was not until the publicationof the English translation in 1980 that I actually had access to them, although some fragments of manuscrips and essays about them had been in circulation.

Last but not least, some works by my St. Gallen colleagues have contributed to my better understanding, specifically Gilbert Probst's paper "Kybernetische Gesetzeshypothesen als Basis für Gestaltungs- und Lenkungsregeln im Management", 1981, and Thomas Dyllick's essay "Gesellschaftliche Instabilität und Unternehmungsführung–Ansätze zu einer gesellschaftsbezogenen Managementlehre", 1982. The numerous discussions with them, as well as with others that had read my manuscript for this paper in its 1977 version, helped me to recognize major errors, open issues and poor lines of argument.

What helped me most of all, though, were my attempts at applying the theory in practice when working on consulting issues, as well as the related discussions with client executives and with my own peers and employees, some of whom worked on these client projects with me. In revising the manuscript I was able to integrate some of what I had learned by adding comments and footnotes, but the majority did not fit in the framework. For all these reasons, I thought it might be helpful to use a case example to illustrate what the practical application of my approach can look like.

The consulting situations I faced were without exception complex projects dealing with corporate development. Although their focus sometimes appeared to be on individual or even partial issues, at the end of the day they were always about the development of overall organizations with widely varying sizes, histories, and from a broad range of fields.

At this point you may find it helpful to go back to Chapter 2 and view the examples described in sections 2.23 and 2.24. Just like the variety of soccer is of astronomical proportions because every game takes a different course and the resulting number of possible, rule-conforming tactics and approaches is unlimited, it is the same with consulting projects focusing on corporate development: they take a different course each and every time. In essential aspects, the variety situation is the same as in soccer, with an enormous number of possible constellations and courses. The complexity is further increased–and this is where the analogy has its limits–by the fact that there is no such thing as a set of invariant rules known to all players, as in soccer; instead, a specific set of rules will evolve and be defined in the course of each individual project. What may be perfectly possible and in order in one organization may well cause resistance in another.

No doubt there are conventions accepted everywhere, and over time some invariants–rules and principles–will emerge that seem to characterize all projects, or at least a majority, and which could be compared to the rules of the soccer game; i.e., compliance with them seems to increase the chances of success while non-compliance is likely to cause difficulties. This includes the principle of a neat and clearly structured project documentation, to name just one example, which enables project members to access current project status information any time they wish, irrespective of disruptions, deadline shifts, or staff changes in both the consultant team and the client organization. However, even if the principles established on grounds of theoretical considerations and practical experiences are complied with, the variety of each individual project is still great enough to raise a serious control problem, not to mention the variety of all projects you could theoretically be faced with. This very complexity is the reason why the concepts and methods of strategy management, as laid down in this paper, are necessary. In them, the power of cybernetic control models, in particular the Viable Systems Model, is clearly evident. As the first of two guiding principles concerning the "final structure" of a system, they help steer the complex process of their implementation by starting not from the system's initial state but from its purpose–a principle without which there is no control of complex systems. The second guiding principle of control is the profound knowledge about the course of such processes, about what can and cannot be expected based on the nature of complex systems.

One essential insight is that disruptions are natural components of such projects. It makes no sense and is unnecessary to try to determine an optimal course in advance. Complex systems have 1001 ways of achieving their objectives. They are equifinal; i.e. contrary to the predetermined systems found in physics, the achievement of objectives and the results are not determined by the initial state and conditions but by the nature of the process. Different initial states may lead to the same final states, while identical initial states are no guarantee that the same final states will be reached.

So, since disturbances are inevitable and become even less predictable as both their likelihood and variety increase with growing complexity, and considering that "many roads lead to Rome", project management clearly has to strive to keep identifying *new* promising roads over and over again rather than rely on a predetermined plan–no matter how carefully developed and optimal it may seem. This type of project management focuses on anticipating future developments, based on continuous information on any changes in the current state of the system. Starting from the insights gained this way, it seeks to neutralize potential disruptions proactively by keeping and deploying reserves, determining new paths and approaches, rearranging indivdiual tasks, and revising the system's subsequent behavior. During all that time it simultaneously operates with several time horizons, as has been explained several times in this paper. It is the precondition for being able not only to deal with the present effects of past causes, as in the classical causality concept, but to plan for future causes based on expectations formed concerning probable system behavior ("probable" to be understood in the propensity theory sense). This may but does not necessarily have to lead to "self-fulfilling prophecies", or to a situation where the anticipation of future events will render itself ineffective. When a bad weather situation is forecast, this will cause a group of mountaineers to revise their route but it will not change anything about the weather. In much the same way, the insight that due to various production delays–whether already occurred or to be expected– a set delivery date cannot be met will also cause a change of plans (e.g., outsourcing, overtime, using substitute items, etc.) that will not prevent the disruption as such but define another of many possible routes to the destination.

This is also in accordance with latest research on the way the human brain works. Sommerhoff notes:

"...the activities of the organism must be matched to the objective features of the environment rather than to the subjective qualities of the stimuli impinging on the senses. The efficiency with which the organism can effect this control depends on the degree to which it can *anticipate the outcomes of its actions* and can build up *expectations regarding the manner in which the sensory inputs transform* as a function of time, or more importantly, *as a function of its own activities*. Metaphorically speaking, the effective power of the brain therefore hinges on its knowledge of what depends on what in what sort of way at any one time."

In the context of what the *internal* models postulated by cybernetics consist of, he explains:

"...these models consist in the main of aggregates of expectations of how the sensory inputs will transform (a) in consequence of the movements of the eyes, head or body, and (b) in consequence of the subject's active interference with or manipulation of the objects of the outer world."[377]

Compare this to Stafford Beer's remarks on the essence of planning from a cybernetic perspective:

"There are two points that a number of real thinkers have been making about planning ... The fi rst is that planning is a *continuous* process. This notion confl icts violently with the stereotype of a plan based on the next month, the next year, the next five years, or 'the year 2000'. Nature does not have a calendar ...

The continuity arises from the *constant readjustment* of *rational expectations against shifting scenarios*–in circumstances where some sorts of expectations are more rational than others, and some sorts of scenario are more credible than others . . .

Secondly, ... what needs to be reiterated is that planning happens only when there is an *act of decision*. This act commits *resources now*, so that the future may be different from what would otherwise have simply happened to us." [378]

This is another example of the isomorphism theorem of cybernetics, according to which it is possible to identify structural and behavioral identities for all complex systems, provided we regard them from an appropriate perspective, which means we have to model their systemic and cybernetic regularities. Insights gained on the function of the brain have been applied in the planning process, and we can also use them to control a complex project. We also see the extremely tight relationships between planning (expectation building), decision making and acting, and how they incorporate the fact that different time dimensions have been integrated, i.e. events at different time levels are part of the purpose of present management.

The current dispositions steering future system behavior are based on current expectations regarding the future system states likely to evolve from present actions (or omissions), which we seek to explore based on current information about current system states, as well as past experiences.

Of course, when I talk about "control" or *management* here I am not referring to the project manager or leader but to the self-organization mechanisms of the overall system, where the project manager plays a key role which, however, he could not replace in a centralistic sense. Self-organization results from the state of information in the system. Any

---

377 Sommerhoff (Brain), p. 30; emphasis added by author.
378 Beer (Heart), pp. 336 and 337.

knowledge about the current state of the system, disturbances that occurred, alternative ways to goal achievement, available resources and, most importantly, the objective pursued have to be accessible to as many system elements as possible. That is why a clear, simple, system-adequate language is essential. As everyone knows, the degree of control you can have over a system is in proportion to the degree of effective information existing in the system.

Once again, we can use soccer as an example. Every player, provided he remains focused, knows about the current state of the game at any point in time. If he had to be notified about the other players' current positions from the coaches' bench it would be impossible to play soccer. The same is true for the musicians in an orchestra. Likewise, if the speeds of cars in a city would have to be reported to police headquarters, which would then tell each driver to drive slower or faster, all traffic would break down. By letting each driver control his own speed, he can keep self-organizing according to the constantly changing flow of traffic. This, by the way, is an example I owe to professor Alois Gälweiler. It illustrates quite nicely the absurdity of some regulations in business and administration.

As mentioned above, consulting projects in the field of corporate development are projects of that kind. Controlling and managing them requires a strategy for managing complexity, its main elements being cybernetic control structures and systems-methodological approaches. Before we proceed to a case example, the next section will offer some practical hints for the interpretation of the Viable System because it plays a key role in the case to be discussed.

## 4.2 Interpretations of the Viable Systems Model

As mentioned in the introduction to this book, Chapter 1 is no longer entirely satisfactory from a current point of view. While the model structure presented there is formally sound and builds on the theory Stafford Beer has laid down in the first edition of "Brain of the Firm", his later book "Heart of Enterprise" dispenses with all the neurophysiologic analogy and terminology used in "Brain of the Firm", instead developing the model from scratch for a managerial context. In addition, there is now a much greater wealth of detail and a different graphical convention, in that the book depicts several recursion levels at once and uses a more expressionist mode of depiction that, in my view, clearly facilitates the understanding of the model.

Irrespective of that, in my experience the key difficulty is in *interpreting* the model, i.e. relating real-world phenomena to the elements of the model or, put the other way around, perceiving reality in the terms of the model. This mapping process in both directions is extremely important and has to be done the right way; otherwise the model is useless or even misleading. In particular when as a result of modeling you suggest new design approaches to the further development of a company, you risk serious aberrations if you misinterpret the model. The situation would be comparable to choosing the wrong route based on a misinterpretation of your map.

Another reason why the correct interpretation is so important is that this is not simply another, more or less random approach but in my view a genuine theory, perhaps even the only one we have in management. Beer considers his model to be *necessary and sufficient* for the modeling of viable systems, and I find his arguments to be both conclusive and compelling. Also, my own experiences in applying the model have convinced me of its effectiveness. The sustainability of this theory, however, depends on its correct interpretation. In this sense, I find that it presents much greater challenges than commonly found in management literature. Part of the reason is that the term 'model', as used by Beer, and the corresponding model theory are very different from what the majority of business authors understand it to be. There is no denying that it has become very common to use the term 'model' in a very casual manner, which is further supported by the undisciplined use of the term in everyday language.

In this context I should also point out, however, that there are some difficult problems to be solved with regard to the model itself, and that we are far from having clarified all the questions it raises. Having said above that Beer's model represents a genuine theory in my opinion, I should add that this may not be fully in line with the author's own views. Beer remains vague and ambiguous in these matters, perhaps due to different understandings of the term "theory." Also, I have to admit that an empirical test of the theory involves certain difficulties. This is not because it could not be falsified—I could certainly think of events or observations that would be incompatible with the model. The problem, rather, is that the conventional methods for testing hypotheses and theories would probably not work here. No: it cannot be that the quality of a theory depends on the current state of empirical test methods; rather, these methods have to be developed further for that purpose, as happens in many other disciplines as well. Cybernetic theories have always challenged the imagination.

Below I will try to sketch out my current understanding of Beer's model, as it has formed in many attempts at applying it in practice, one of which will be described in the following section. Above all, what I am hoping to demonstrate is how great the scope of applications is for this model and how great the variety of phenomena to be captured with it. Whether it leads to a *better* understanding in each case than you would have without the model is a question that, in my opinion, can only be answered from a very individual and personal perspective. Depending on how familiar a person is with a very concrete system, he may consider a certain modeling approach and interpretation to be trivial, in the sense of "long known." However, in surveying the entire spectrum of phenomena to be captured with the model, we will quickly see that it is an extremely universal tool, which is why it serves us in precisely the way we would expect of a *general* systems theory: by improving our understanding of any kind of systems, including those on which we must not consider ourselves to be experts, based on our training which is inevitably disciplinary.

Another thing I am trying to show with the following outlines is that the model is anything but technocratic, mechanistic or deterministic. In addition, I am trying to provide at least a vague idea of how, using this model, we can discover design and control options we would otherwise fail to see, or at least not have available in this concentrated form as a pool of insights.

Unfortunately I cannot spare you from going back and forth between this chapter and chapter 1–depending on how well you remember its contents–to look at graphs or compare my views of those times with my current thinking.

## 4.21 Basic Thoughts on Establishing Structures in Organizations

Some preliminary remarks on the ideas underlying the model seem warranted because here, too, my practical trials have caused certain shifts of emphasis that may facilitate readers' understanding.

### 4.211 *Viability of the Whole*

Contrary to the efficiency criteria used in business organization theory, most of which are focused on economics, the following structural ideas are based on the thought that the main characteristic an enterprise should have is "viability." This has been explained at several point in this paper, so a few general remarks should suffice here.

In the greater scheme of things, the fundamental purposes of an enterprise are not economic in nature. The point is not to maximize profits, optimize costs, and all these things–the point is to stay in business. So the key concern is to secure the enterprise's existence, which is a parameter that cannot be expressed in financial or accounting terms such as balance sheets and the like. To this date, business theory fails to thoroughly deal with the concept of a "healthy enterprise"

### 4.212  The Whole and Its Parts

As a general rule, every company consists of three parts. Whereas in classical organization theory it was assumed that practically just any operation could be defined to be a part of the enterprise, and as a consequence any part even remotely appropriate has been used as a base element of organizational alternatives, my considerations are based on the notion that only very specific elements can be considered appropriate parts of the whole thing. To be part of an entity, an element must be an entity in itself. For instance, a Swiss canton is both a part of Switzerland and an entity in itself. The total of all the parts form the entity of Switzerland, without giving up their identity and autonomy. They give up just enough autonomy to jointly form a new entity, but they keep enough autonomy to be able to exist as independent entities, each with its own identity.

Whereas for the nation the relationship between the parts and the whole is largely fixed, in an enterprise it has to be considered variable because companies are under much more pressure to continuously adapt.

### 4.213  Structure and Organization

What conventional organization describe usually has very little to do with an organization's ability to function, or its character. Yes, organization charts are needed to express things like direct reporting relationships. But they leave much to be desired when it comes to describing how an organization really functions. It is the structures "behind" the or charts that determine an organization's options for action. I call them "deep structures", as opposed to the superficial structures visible in organization charts.

The fact that official organization charts, including the regulations required for "organization" in a broader sense, have little to do with how the enterprise actually functions becomes very obvious when you consider that in many organizations, full compliance with these rules and regulations would come close to a general strike. When "work to rule" rules, nothing works. In my view, this is a significant–although not very popular–indicator that companies often function *despite* their organization regulations, not because of them.

## 4.22 The Basic Components of a Viable System: System 1

Fundamental entities in a viable system are all operations or activities enabling the organization to perform and fulfill its purpose. Usually these are all areas which in principle could or should form an enterprise of its own. A basic component in this sense, which Beer refers to as "operational element", has to have its own external environment; i.e. a market, economic region, etc. with which it interacts in rendering its services. The environment of such a basic component comprises everything required for the viability, or sustainable success, of the operation–current and potential customers, competitors, suppliers, potential employees, etc.–in all relevant dimensions: economic, cultural, technological, social, political, etc. If such an environment cannot be identified, this warrants considerable doubt as to whether an operation proposed as a basic unit can truly be an element of System 1.

The operations have to comprise everything required to secure viability, i.e. all services to be provided to the environment to secure sustainable success. The management of this operation has to ensure the dynamic equilibrium between the environment and the organization.

Consequently, in real-life situations these considerations focus on the question as to what parts of a company can be considered to be elements of System 1. For certain types of enterprises there are a few rather simple interpretations. When we are dealing with a divisionalized group with rather independent subsidiaries, it is evident what its basic components are. It gets trickier when no relatively autonomous parts can immediately be identified, when we have a traditional, essentially function-based corporate structure. Depending on the industry, there are different options for interpretation. If we imagine a typical industrial company structured by functions, there are basically just two possible System 1 candidates: Manufacturing and sales (and very rarely, marketing).

Now the decision as to whether to define manufacturing *and* sales or *only* manufacturing or *only* sales as System 1 is a point that illustrates an essential aspect of the model's interpretative power. If we define System 1 to comprise both manufacturing and sales in equal measure, this will immediately raise the question as to their concrete forms of interaction, the trade-offs made, and especially the forms of coordination required so the system as a whole will be viable. It is known from practice that these two central functions very rarely exist as equals, but one or the other will strive to dominate. In practice, this confronts management in such structures with typical problems.

If we choose any of the other forms, it is equally clear that the nature of the enterprise will completely change, depending on the choice we make. If we assume manufacturing to be System 1, we will be dealing wit a typically manufacturing-driven, thus usually technology-dominated organization where very specific mentalities prevail and certain personalities with typical educational backgrounds and attitudes are in the majority. Consequently, the permanent viability of such an organization will be a very particular type of issue and it is almost safe to predict that its effectiveness in solving marketing issues is limited, and that it will always be inferior to companies with different structures when it comes to serving and penetrating its markets. Whether or not this is tolerable in individual cases, whether or not resulting problems are acceptable, is something that cannot be decided once and for all. It requires very thorough analysis of the specific situation and, above all, appropriate arrangements with regard to other subsystems. As a board member in such an organization, the questions I would worry about would be completely different compared to a company where Systems 1 are represented by sales. (The reason I keep speaking of "Systems 1" in the plural form is that in companies like that, there are usually several manufacturing or sales units distinguished by product groups, regions or still other criteria, which is why we rarely deal with one completely homogeneous System 1. This parlance slightly differs from that of Stafford Beer, but that should not cause any problems or misunderstandings.

"System 1" here refers to all the subsystems that Beer calls "operational elements", and which jointly form System 1. Also, I have chosen the term "operative", not "operational", in order to avoid any association with the problem of operationalizing, operationalism, etc. We are dealing with completely different questions here.)

When the sales units represent System 1, and define the criteria for the overall system's viability, it is obvious that the practical forms of existence of such an organization are very different from that of the manufacturing-focused type. Again, executives will have still other thinking patterns and educational backgrounds, set other priorities, etc. The whole corporate culture, work climate, etc., i.e. all the things that are so difficult to capture but matter so much for the management of an organization, will be very different in this type of company.

As practical examples for each of the two forms, I refer to two manufacturers of machine tools. Company A started back in the early 60s to make market dominance the key criterion to take priority over all other factors. In line with this principle, in the mid-60s the company began to build a direct sales organization and install market units, thus giving so much dominance to all sales issues that all other questions were pushed to the background. This is in sharp contrast to company B, which offers rather similar product lines but, being much more traditional in character, has remained very manufacturing-focused. The products relevant in this context are distributed through the traditional retail trade. To this date, both companies have proven their viability and it would exceed the scope of this paper to attempt any forecasts regarding their future development. Irrespective, it is obvious that two companies structured differently have to be very different in character. A company's viability can be safeguarded in different ways; however, in the light of this criterion any basic decision will involve very different consequences in the remaining divisions.

What Beer's model also shows is that other units to be found in functional organizations, such as HR, finance, R&D, IT and administrative services, generally *cannot* be Systems 1 as they do not serve the key purpose of that system. Rather, they represent support functions and the only reason they are needed is to the company to manufacture and sell. At this point we are faced with the question of meaning, which is often said to have no place in Beer's model. The meaning of a company is in its purpose, which is judged based on criteria lying outside the organization. In my view, societal relevance–the ability to permanently render a set of services that are useful to society–makes up 90 percent of the meaning a company can have. Now, the question of meaning is determined by what we consider to be System 1 and what activities, functions, etc. are part of it.

This is the second question frequently raised: Is social reality truly real, i.e. given, or is it a collective construct? I believe it is both. There are certain "givens" we have to take into account in certain situations, no matter whether we like it or not. Then there are things we can shape, or "construct." When working with the Viable Systems Model, we also have both factors to consider. However, in the context of constructivist argumentation another factor that matters is that we have some leeway in determining what we want to be System 1. Consequently, in many cases the given realities such as market structures, potential customer groups, existing technologies, etc. will not necessarily provide a sufficient basis for deciding what to choose as Systems 1- So, in a sizeable number of cases it will be necessary to *make a decision* in the true sense, i.e. choose the foundations on which to build the viability of the overall enterprise. Of course this choice may be wrong, or what was originally right may turn out wrong over time because conditions have changed.

To determine the operative elements of System 1, the following questions can be useful: Would the unit or operation proposed be able *in principle* to operate as an enterprise in its own right? Would it have the appropriate size, in view of the conditions given in the environment and especially the market? Do its environment and activities justify its being equipped with the entire infrastructure (staff, know-how, machinery, space, resources, etc.) as would be required based on the current state of information. Does the unit render appropriate services? What is its viability based on? How much autonomy will it need? What relationships will be necessary? What support will the unit need from the overall system? What ties it to the whole? Questions of this kind have to be discussed very thoroughly. Mistakes or poor trade-offs invariably lead to structural or operational problems.

To gain an even deeper understanding of the operative units equipped with Systems 1–with relatively high degrees of autonomy–that also determine much of the overall system's purpose and meaning, it will be helpful to look at entirely different kinds of systems which have nothing to do with business. For instance, the individual members of a family are also systems. In general, modeling a family is a truly interesting application of the Viable Systems Model. Everyone knows the typical forms of behavior, in particular pathological ones, occurring in families. The hypothesis is that in sound families we should be able to find all functions implied by the model. Any familiar deficiencies, pathological structures and the like should be identifiable through corresponding deficiencies in the model's structure and functions. I have made several attempts to interpret, e.g., the works on family theory by *Watzlawick* and the *Palo Alto Group* in the light of *Beer*'s model, and I find these interpretations to make a lot of sense. Of course, children up to a certain age are only potential System 1 candidates: while they are viable based on their biological structure, i.e. at a lower recursion level, it is usually only after puberty that they reach that state in a socio-cultural, economic etc. sense. The problems that a family faces during the children's puberty illustrate in a particularly drastic manner what it means when potentially viable systems now claim their autonomy. In this phase, a family needs to adjust its different forms of control in various ways to avoid falling apart. It needs new forms of mutual understanding, new forms of mutual consideration, and in many respects a redefinition of the roles that the individual members play, in particular of the system functions each of them has to assume or give up.

Another example of typical Systems 1 is the Swiss cantons or the states of a federation. The degree of autonomy relative to the federation is a question solved in different ways in different countries. We know from both history and political science, however, how difficult it can be to solve this problem both in general and with regard to the detailed issues. Another thing that this example nicely shows is what it means to be a part of a greater whole, yet maintaining both wholeness and oneness within the partialness. Interestingly, in this case the quality of being part of a whole strongly influences the wholeness of a part. In Switzerland, it is particularly interesting to see how the canton of Jura was established. Here, the key question was par excellence what infrastructure, rights and obligations, etc. one part needed to be viable in its own right–without being completely autonomous, i.e. the requirement was for the unit to remain a part of the whole.

Similarly, we might regard the nations in the European Community or the United Nations as Systems 1. Contrary to a genuine federation, in these cases we have very loose ties, their main foundation being the fact that the individual states regard themselves not as parts of a whole but as autonomous entities. So great is each state's autonomy that it clearly jeopardizes the existence of the total, as is evident from both the EC's frequent problems and also the UN's situation. In the light of the model, both the EC and the UN lack structural features that make them viable overall systems. As long as these structural features (Systems 2, 3, 4 and 5) are missing, it is safe to predict that the effectiveness and efficiency of these systems will not get better and we will continue having to live with the problems already known.

To provide an example from a totally different realm of life, let us proceed to the field of music. The members of an orchestra (i.e., the individual instrumentalists) are its Systems 1. The same is true for the members of a jazz band. However, as they are parts of totally different kinds of system, their individual understanding will differ greatly, and so will their actions. In other words, the oneness of an orchestra is based on different factors compared to the oneness of a jazz band. Consequently, the output of the respective system–the music produced by both ensembles–is equally different. Still, once again we can clearly see the phenomenon of the relative autonomy of parts in a whole.

In all these examples, when we speak of viability we are never referring to viability in the biological sense, except perhaps at a very specific level of recursion. The viability of a musician playing in a renowned orchestra such as the Berlin Philharmonic is not a matter of his biological structures, although these are certainly required for him to be viable as a biological entity at another recursion level. His "survival" as part of the orchestra, is based on entirely different things, such as his virtuosity in terms of mastering his instruments, his willingness to comply with the rules of the system, or in short: his acceptance of being part of a whole. Still, we will strive to maintain some kind of identity within this ensemble–the kind that makes him an individual musician with very specific ways to interpret his score, with a very specific range of expressions on his instrument, etc. While ordinary orchestra musicians, such as the members of the second violin or string bass sections, etc., have to subordinate much of their musical identity to the orchestra's overriding purpose and reason (which represents a genuine problem for many musicians), the soloists in each section or the concertmaster have much more leeway in adding an individual touch. The real instrumental soloists, of course, for whom the orchestra is more of a supporting tool than a purpose in itself, can act out their individuality almost to the maximum; however, depending on the musical piece, they may more or less have to subordinate themselves to the orchestra during certain parts of the composition. Similar considerations apply to the musicians in a jazz band. As a general rule, the relationship between the individual jazz musician and his band differs greatly from that of an orchestra musician with the overall orchestra. Both are Systems 1 in an overall system. In both cases, the whole becomes effective through its parts and the parts make up the whole. Their respective mutual relationships–the question as to what autonomy, identity and meaning are based on–have different solutions. That is the very reason, however, why these two examples superbly illustrate the entire spectrum of what Beer's model is able to capture.

## 4.23 Several Parts–Chances for a Greater Whole: System 2

### 4.231 Plurality of Parts

Every business organization, just as every other social institution, usually has several parts that can be considered to be operative elements. Contrary to how they are depicted in organization charts (provided they appear there at all) they are not identical. Rather, each of the operative units has its own nature, particularities, its own self-understanding, its past development–in short: its own story. As in most families there are tall and short people, fat and skinny ones, calm and spirited ones, etc., and all of them have to get along.

The individual operative elements usually have contact and interact with each other. These can be extremely diverse modes of contact, and its is worth thinking them through in detail as they have a strong influence on the nature of the overall enterprise. When the divisions of a company have mostly competitive mutual relationships, the overall situation will be very different compared to a setting where mutual relations are cooperative in nature, or when they are rather loose and perhaps only consist in the legal affiliation to a common parent company.

The mutual relationships between the parts are where potential synergy effects lie. Is it possible to use competitive relations constructively to increase performance? What needs to be done to transfer know-how, experiences, expertise, etc. from one area to another? In what way can the individual parts benefit from each other? Where can they support each other? How can one unit help out the other–e.g., by leveling out peak loads, exchanging staff, etc?

### 4.232 Oscillationes and Coordination

When several units must or want to collaborate, there will usually be conflicts. Each unit's mission is to exploit is environment and the economic opportunities it holds. In every environment (market, etc.) there may be very different rules to be considered. So each unit absolutely needs its relative autonomy to be able to do business.

Even with the best mutual intentions there will inevitably be friction, potential misunderstandings, and very tangible conflicts of interest. The stronger individual units and their local management are, the more likely is it that situations of conflict will arise. To a considerable extent, these conflicts result from the fact that each individual unit knows too little about the others, thus failing to fully understand the reasons why other units act in a certain way. This may even lead to the widespread opinion that other units act on intentions that are detrimental to one's own unit. This can lead to a kind of competitive attitude where the main motive is not sportsmanship but fending off perceived machinations.

When the different units maintain exchange relations with each other there will also be various coordination needs. For instance, when larger projects require cross-functional collaboration it will be necessary to exchange staff in order to buffer peak loads; or if there are any questions concerning joint customers and projects there will be a need for coordinating systems. In Beer's model, this coordination task is assigned to System 2. It is interesting to see the great variety of ways in which Systems 2 can be manifest. Below I will just give a few example without much commenting, as I believe that these examples speak for themselves.

A typical System 2, for instance, is the flight controller system at large airports. A flight controller is not the supervisor of all the pilots of arriving and departing airplanes. Yet every flight captain will not hesitate to follow the flight controller's instructions, in order to ensure orderly traffic at the airport and prevent accidents. It is this form of coordination (in this case, in a so-called tightly controlled system) that Beer refers to when he describes System 2. Flight controllers are primarily responsible for giving pilots the information they need to successfully complete their operations. They have to do this in reference to each individual case and based on their knowledge of all other cases, for each movement of an aircraft can only be judged, corrected and controlled in consideration of all other aircraft's movements. Other typical Systems 2 include the radio control systems used by taxi cab companies, school or university curriculums, timetables at schools, or restaurant menus. Also, most auction-type markets–in particular the stock exchanges–fulfill System 2 functions; so do price signals in a market economy. Apart from these, in every system there are lots of other components that jointly fulfill the task of overall coordination. Consequently, it would be wrong to assume that the price system is the only coordination mechanism in the field of business.

Another typical System 2, for instance, is the habit often found in companies or departments to have a joint coffee break at certain hours of the day. In many cases this is the only chance for all or most employees to get together. It is obvious that these breaks represent an important hub of information; this is where direct interpersonal coordination takes place. Also, things such as meetings, pin boards and the like fulfill typical System 2 functions. Anyone that has grown up in a small village, in particular in catholic regions, will know that after Sunday morning mass the men of the village usually stand in small groups to discuss all kinds of matters. Again, this is a social institution that fulfills System 2 functions. Anyone familiar with these mechanisms knows very well that they often provide the only opportunity to gather certain kinds of information. In this context it depends on your being part of the community, or being admitted to it, whether you are accepted as System 1 and thus can benefit from the coordination provided by System 2.

In business organizations, typical Systems 2 are certain parts of financial controlling, certain operative planning units—such as certain forms of PPS—as well as in some cases production planning and the like. Also, certain production modalities (line production, shop production, etc.) actually perform coordination and can thus be considered to be Systems 2.

## 4.24 Operational Corporate Management: Optimization, Synergies and Resource Allocation: System 3

Can the whole really be more than the sum of its parts? If yes, under what conditions?

As such, mutual interactions among several, basically autonomous units are not enough to guarantee that the sum will be more than its parts. Coordinating mechanisms cannot accomplish this either. In the longer run, for a unit to feel part of a whole it must partake of advantages it would otherwise not have. Just as each Swiss canton draws certain advantages from belonging to Switzerland, for which it is willing to make certain sacrifices in return, business enterprises are in a similar situation.

Hence, a function is needed which, based on its knowledge of the whole and in view of the concerns of the whole—in particular its internal coherence—is able to assume certain controlling and regulating tasks. In a family, you sometimes have to hold back one child to allow another to come out of his sibling's shadow. Everyday experience in child rearing has taught us, however, that this kind of balancing function has to be performed with great care and caution.

The task of balancing the interactions of the units in a company is similar to some extent. This task is carried out by System 3 and it is referred to as "operational corporate management" or "operations directorate." It represents the total of all operational line management functions we find in traditional organization charts. As such, it exerts the central power of intervention that is in a position to enforce the directives issued, if and as needed. It is of utmost importance, however, that this central power of command be used very sparingly, as each of the quasi-autonomous units will naturally tend to regard any such intervention as an improper interference with their autonomy. While the need for such a function is generally accepted, nobody cares to gather first-hand experiences with it.

So, the clearer the boundaries between individual autonomous units are, the cleaner the logic of breaking down the whole in its components and the more effective the coordinating mechanisms of Systems 2, the higher the probability that System 3 can afford the "luxury" of intervening very sparingly.

In any case, interventions should provide help and support rather than constraint and regulation. Key tools to be used by System 3 in exerting its function are the resources the overall system has at its disposal.

What immediately comes to mind here are financial resources. And indeed these are of utmost importance, as the allocation of funds to the individual units is a key measure to support or restrain them, depending on how their development potential is assessed (which is the deeper sense of meaningful portfolio management). It is important to remember, however, that it does not suffice by far to allocate finances. There are further resources of great significance, such as the time that operative management can dedicate to each unit, the brainpower made available for controlling them, the attention given to them, etc.

A point of key importance is the correct understanding of the relationship between divisional management (Systems 1) and operations directorate (System 3). On principle, divisions and their management operate with a view to the local interests of each division. It is their noblest and most prominent duty to do anything in its might to ensure the division's viability. The individuals responsible for the management of a division are not entitled to consider any other interests as long as they are wearing the division manager's hat. On the other hand, the overall organization requires a totally different view. From the corporate management perspective, the interests of each individual unit always have to be regarded in relation to the interests of all other units, and thus restricted in line with the interests of the total organization.

In many organizations, System 3 is set up as a body of peers and staffed (at least partly) from the collective of System 1 managers. It is anything but safe to assume, however, that this personal union of very different functions will actually render satisfying results.

Again, it will facilitate a deeper understanding of the matter if we consider how Systems 3 are set up in other institutions. Take, for instance, the public administration: here, federal and national governments are usually System 3 components. This may seem strange at first because at a superficial glance we tend to consider governments to be parts of System 5. Without doubt, however, a government is not the superior normative authority of a system; it rather performs internal stabilization and optimization functions in the System 3 sense. This is not altered by the fact that it often contributes to System 5 functions.

In some systems, however, it is not necessarily people that fulfill this function. For instance, in certain families there are traditions much stronger than any of the family members or even the family as a whole.

Neither the UN nor the EC have truly functional Systems 3. The existing rudiments of this function are clearly unable to cope because they also lack efficient Systems 2, and also because the Systems 1–as explained earlier–have a very autonomous self-concept.

Similar to what has been said for System 2, once again the examples listed do perform the entire Systems 3 function on their own. For instance, the Federal Council of Switzerland does not operate as a System 3 on its own accord; it is aided by the administration. The key question for all Systems 3 is linked to the integration of its parts. Most Systems 3 are split in partial functions that can no longer be integrated, due to disastrous misunderstandings with regard to the principle of the division of labor. Hence, the key problem in interpreting Systems 3 is not so much in identifying its parts as it is to integrate those parts in a complete System 3 which is capable of acting in a coordinated manner.

Optimizing the overall organization may require individual units to be adjusted to settings far from the local optimum. The sum of divisional optima does not guarantee an overall optimum.

In this context, some difficult problems arise. To make the right decisions from the System 3 perspective, System 3 relies on the divisions to receive information. According to figure 4.24(l) this information arrives through the vertical command and communication line, coming from the divisional managements, and through System 2 via the coordinating mechanisms. Ultimately, decisions made by System 3 can never be better than the information the system has. Now every divisional manager (System 1) tends to present his division in the way he wants it to be seen. Even leaving aside extreme forms of intentional deceit, even the most objective divisional manager will hardly be free of personal interests, career goals, etc. Even if he strives hard to provide objective information, it will always be *his* division-related objectivity.

Also, only very specific kinds of information travel through the coordinating mechanisms. In a company, these are certain kinds of planning and financial controlling activities usually carried out by staffers or relatively young people. It would be unreasonable to assume that the information they have is complete enough in all aspects for System 3 to be able to make truly balanced decisions and take account of all relevant factors.

This is why another information channel is required, which in most companies is also inadequate and often completely misunderstood. In figure 4.24(1) it is represented by bold lines.

This information channel provides direct access to the operations, permitting an unadulterated view of the true realities. It is like the entrepreneur who begins eac of his working days by taking a walk through the plant, just to to gain an overview of where things currently stand. He will chat with employees, check how this or that machine works, walk the production hall, have a conversation with one person here and give advice to another one there, offer encouragement and criticism. The information he gains this way cannot be replaced by any kind of tables, charts, or reports—not even face-to-face ones. When afterwards he meets with his executives for a 9 or 10 o'clock meeting, he often knows more—or in any case, different things—than they do, which enables him to put their reports in a specific context.

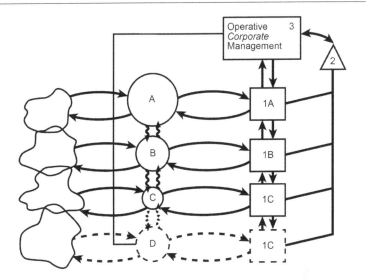

*Figure 4.24(1)*

In multi-layered and complex organizations, however, this possibility has shrunken to a minimum. The function is performed by the internal audit, but also by managers working on projects (at the "front end"), maintaining direct customer contacts, and getting involved in important purchasing negotiations. This enables them to make operatiional management decisions for the total company not only based on reports and numbers but also in consideration of first-hand experience and immediate contact with reality.

It goes without saying that this channel is often understood to be a tool for spying on people and bypassing line manager competencies. It is therefore of utmost importance that all employees have a maximum of information on the functional significance of this channel. Only based on optimal insight into the relationships and structural effects of viable systems will they be able to understand that this channel is essential.

All systems and components interacting in the way described are aimed at keeping a grip on *current business*. This is to ensure a certain degree of internal stability by constantly balancing all parts in the light of optimal and truthful information. However, the current business and internal stability are not enough to guarantee the viability of an enterprise. It requires an additional function whose basic purpose it is directed to the outside and the future.

## 4.25 Strategic Development: System 4

As a general rule, the sum of all markets served by a company does not equate the totality of its environment. For instance, the totality of the environment relevant for an automotive company comprises far more than the individual markets currently served. Above all, this relevant environment also includes all the technologies and their development which may substitute the automobile at some point. In many industries, the excessive fixation on momentary relevant parts of the environment has proven disastrous. Examples include the Swiss watch industry or the office machinery sector.

It is the function of System 4 to make and actively maintain the contact to this extended environment. This is the only way to gather all the information that ultimately enables the company to readjust even in very fundamental ways.

In practice this includes everything usually referred to as strategic management. This system component entails all the staff units or employees dealing with longer-term considerations, the products and services of tomorrow, possible technology substitutes, new value systems, aspirations, customer needs, etc. There are clear limits to how far this can be formalized, so it is important to keep in mind that system 4 includes but is *not limited to* such components.

One factor of key importance in this context is the entire network of relationships and contacts that managers maintain and cultivate. Above all, this includes mutual supervisory board functions as well as memberships in associations and service clubs (Rotary, Lions, etc.), academic fraternities/sororities, political parties, and in Switzerland also existing linkages to the Army.

Experience has shown that managers attach great importance to these networks, which serve as a kind of seismograph. The reason they do this is not the sheer enjoyment of power, as some ideologists are fond of insinuating. Above all, it is because their instinct tells them that the formal planning and adaptation systems in companies are usually incapable of capturing the abundance of vital, critical information. For general management–in particular for determining the company's fundamental positioning, for building prompt responsiveness, etc., these networks are of much greater importance than formal planning mechanisms.

It is extremely regrettable, yet somehow very typical that there is hardly anything in business management literature about this phenomenon and that it is not really understood how these relationship networks, which often span entire continents, actually work. It is true—and this is a point where some of the critics are actually right—that these networks involve a potentially dangerous power potential that can also be misused. At the same time, however, they are an enormously important element of stabilization, of anticipatory adaptation and coordination of business and society.

This is a point, however, where a crucial problem arises in the organization: In most cases, the collaboration between members of Systems 3 and 4 is rather poor. System 3 is focused on the present and on day-to-day business. Here, we find the mentality and short-term focus of the typical line manager who, fully aware of his significance, often refuses to deal with anything related to the future on grounds of it being irrelevant and mere theory. He knows he is responsible for the present cash-flow, for current products and services, and that without the cash he makes it would not be possible to work out any strategies at all.

This is in sharp contrast to System 4 people, who typically have a very different attitude and mentality. They are fully aware that the main reason why companies fail is an excessive focus on current operations, and they think about what products and services the company needs to do business tomorrow. What problems and needs will tomorrow's customers have, what technologies and approaches are needed to solve these problems?

The result is some kind of schizophrenia in the organization. System 3 and System 4 people virtually live in different worlds. So, in order to enable an enterprise to adapt smoothly to its entire environment and to make sure the future will evolve from the present in a harmonic manner, it must be ensured that there will be intense interaction between Systems 3 and 4.

## 4.26 Normative Management: System 5

Ensuring that the functions of Systems 3 and 4 are designed appropriately and effectively is the central task of the actual top management, or System 5. The challenge here is to solve the problems resulting from interaction of systems 3 and System 4—i.e., balancing the present and the future, the company's internal and external environment—by making overriding, normative decisions (cf. fig. 4.26(1)).

Often there is a tendency to assign this role to the company's board. No doubt it does have a specific responsibility here, but it is not the only body that performs System 5 functions.

In addition, the so-called souvereign–i.e., shareholders or, in the case of the state, the people–plays a role, not only in the context of ballots and elections. No doubt the members of a parliament (which is part of System 5) perform their tasks with a view to the people's voting. This does not necessarily mean, however, that they actually represent the people and act in its interest. No matter how they see their own function–be it for the good of the people or their own–they will try to anticipate and take into consideration the voters' behavior, if only to be reelected. Of course, parliaments' de-facto role is far from being as clear as it may appear based on the individual nations' constitutions. Instead there are diverse mixtures of executive and legislative powers, with political parties and all forms of interest groups, along with their lobbies, playing key roles. Not long ago, Friedrich von Hayek presented a very interesting analysis and a proposal for constitutional realignment which in many respects would do justice to the cybernetic needs of System 5 as well as the interactions between Systems 3 and 4, 4 and 5, and 3 and 5.[379]

---

379 Cf. Hayek (Lw), Vol. III.

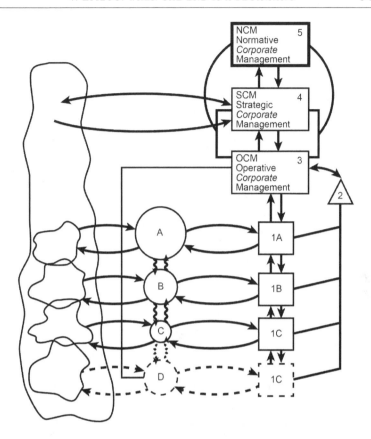

*Figure 4.26(1)*

For practical applications of this model, one case of particular relevance is that of the owner-entrepreneur, or as one variety of it, the family business. What functions does an owner-entrepreneur actually have? What functions should he have? What roles do the individual family members play, with their often complicated interconnections based on ownership rights, management functions, and family ties? Obviously, important functions that are to be distinguished from a systemic perspective are often largely performed in personal union. Can we hope to build enough variety this way in the company's interactions with its environment?

## 4.27 Top-Structure of Interfaces

Systems 3, 4 and 5 have to be able to interact in a very distinct way implied by the model. To a substantial extent, this interaction is accomplished by the existence and function of work groups, committees, and the like. In addition, private, semi-official and official events and mutual invitations among executives clearly serve this function. Many firms make a point of organizing executive-level meetings at certain intervals, e.g. once or twice per year. These meetings and the discussion on (or occasionally just announcements of) corporate goals, basic issues and future developments play an essential role in linking together the different system components, though this role is sometimes difficult to define in detail. Further examples include events such as the "jour fixe" or other society events hosted by, e.g., the CEO: in terms of their cybernetic function, they also form part of the model.

Note, however, that it is often extremely difficult to determine what recursion level the different activities, bodies, etc. belong to. After all, many of these system functions are not directed at integration and regulation toward the internal or external (i.e., recursion-relevant) environment–rather, they represent links to other, super- or subordinate levels of recursion.

If we begin to model the different systems in this way, we will often find that this act of modeling is highly effective in helping us understand what really happens in companies and other institutions. We will be able to put structural or behavioral characteristics that in classical thinking are difficult or impossible to categorize in a totally different context, thus giving them new meaning. These interpretations may not necessarily suffice to solve structural problems, cure pathological features, etcetera. However, it will usually help to know what kind of problem you are facing and what questions you need to clarify. The broader the range of possible interpretations, the greater the chances that you can transfer experiences from other systems in solving certain problems.

Of course it will not be clear from the start which of several possible interpretations is "right" in the individual case, or which permits the best possible understanding. Some observations you can make in companies may first seem rather inexplicable, especially from the perspective of the Viable Systems Model; you may not immediately identify a relevant, model-adequate function for each organizational body, and above all you may find the word of the bible "… for they know not what they do…." to be extensively valid. In the sense of the model, many executives in fact do not know what their true function and impact are. On the other hand, it never ceases to amaze me that there are managers who have never heard of cybernetics or systems theory, not to speak of the Viable Systems Model, yet instinctively do the right thing in accordance with the model.

In most cases, it is necessary to experiment with different interpretations of the same enterprise or institution in the light of the model. What may appear as System 2 under one interpretation may be part of System 3 from another perspective, to name just one example. Again, this is only partly due to the fact that we construct social wealth by way of interpretation, rather than simply perceive it.

Based on such interpretations, above all one thing is often possible: predicting possible future behaviors, forming expectations regarding probable problems, etc. It is amazing how accurately we can often predict the responses of a system that has been modeled that way. This comes as no surprise when we take seriously what general systems theory postulates: that systems have their own laws, that their structure determines their options and that, based on this knowledge, we can make correct forecasts in areas that so far have eluded any anticipation. This is not to say that any old thing is predictable. What is predictable, though, are the systemic behaviors whose structural causes we have truly understood based on such a systemic modeling process.

Based on the interpretations of the model as discussed here, in the next section I will describe a real-life case that had all the attributes of a highly complex development process and in which the modeling approaches according to the Viable System played an important role. As mentioned in the previous sections, there is an infinite number of course such projects can take. Still, I would argue that the following case has many typical attributes, which is why it does not only have singular significance but can be generalized in several respects.

## 4.3  The Practice: A Case Example

### 4.31  Historiography Versus Keeping a Diary

The problem with the following reconstruction is that it is not based on a journal kept in the course of the process. It is an ex-post description based on the superior knowledge a historian invariably has.

Hindsight enables us to structure a complex process in larger sections or epochs that would not have been recognizeable this clearly before or during the process. As a young student, in history class I used to wonder how people of earlier times knew they were living in the age of antiquity or feudalism...

It seems to me that in order to truly understand processes and systems like those dealt with in this book, it is of fundamental importance that we clearly distinguish between two settings: writing a diary and writing history. In some way, these two perspectives illustrate quite nicely the constructivist and the evolutionary paradigm.

The writer of a journal or diary lives *in* the process. He is in the midst of events, which makes him a "participant observer." As far as the future course of the process is concerned, he can only take the usual guesses; apart from that the future is hidden from his view. Events keep unfolding in new ways over and over again. It is full of surprises, and it is precisely from this perspective that it reveals its evolutionary nature–not only because new things keep happening but also because the things that happen result from the actions of those involved but not from their intentions. From the log writer's perspective, it is usually rather clear that any control over events is highly problematic, that no one can *truly* control things and that those involved are far from being mere subjects: more than anything they are also objects of events.

By contrast a historian, acting as an "external observer", describes events from the big-picture perspective enabled by that very distance, as well as based on his knowledge of process results and the roles some or all parties played, and he can draw completely different conclusions compared to the diary writer. The ex-post structuring of a process in sections and event patterns, the assigning of names and terms to epochs, and in particular the act of dealing with what I metaphorically refer to as "frozen complexity" are bound to lead to systems and processes being regarded in very distinct ways.

I am aware that the historian faces a complex problem, too, in having to build his reconstruction and interpretation from fragments of information, which is not an easy thing to do. However, while his question primarily focuses on what really happened, the problem of the diary writer–being an acting party himself–is tightly linked to what could be.

The historian only has to deal with *one* constellation of varieties, with one of the countless courses of things that are possible, i.e. with the one that actually happened, even if he does not know this yet, which means he may initially be faced with the many courses of events that are possible in principle. The journal keeper, by contrast, is faced with the entire variety that unfolds from day to day and is continuously altered by its own past.

This difference should be taken into consideration when reading the following description. I will try to avoid the typical mistake committed in so many management books, case studies and journalistic reports on management problems, which is to not only render a reconstruction of events but–with a view behind the scenes of events–also draw conclusions, offer recommendations, and make demands regarding what else could have been done or considered, which fails to do justice to the actors' situation.

## 4.32 Phase 1: Gaining a First Impression

A medium-sized electromechanics company that had been very successful in the past faced the need for numerous measures to increase profitability, due to both the general economic conditions and an increasingly fierce competition. In the course of several years, it cut back much of its staff–from initially almost 700 down to 500–while generating increasing business volumes year after year, not only nominally but in real terms. In all these years the company was successful economically, achieving positive financial results. However, it turned out that its extensive efforts at realignment had been designed very one-dimensionally, focusing on the cost side only, without taking into account the difference between costs in the sense of unnecessary resource consumption and costs that represent potential resources. In some divisions, streamlining and "rationalization" was taken a point where it led to a real erosion of assets and diminished the company's performance. Together with the uncertainty felt by employees in view of the general economic situation, this led to a change in "climate", in working atmosphere, and in employees' attitude towards the company, which was noted by management and increasingly became a cause of concern. Although the phenomena observed were not analyzed with empirical means, board members said there was no way of overlooking them, so they felt the need to do something.

There was, however, no consensus in management as to what exactly should be done. The situation was further affected by the fact that top management was in the midst of a generation change. The company's sole owner, a typical pioneering entrepreneur who had established and built the company, over time had assigned an increasing share of his responsibilities to his three sons, aged between 25 and 35 and very different in character, without actually retiring from business. This put the remaining board members, as employees, in a not so easy situation vis-à-vis the members of the owner family. As could be expected, they started forming different camps or blocks which, however, differed by issue or question, thus leading to new coalitions every time. This spread all the way to the shop-level workforce, some of which were remnants of the "old school" who had built the business together with its founder and, of course, had a very special relationship with him. The company had an amazing number of what appeared to be excellent management tools at its disposal which, however, turned out to be rather technocratic upon closer analysis, promoting considerable bureaucratization tendencies in people's behavior. Above all, much effort had been put into meticulously regulating the company's organization. There were detailed organization charts, as well as job descriptions for most employees. Many processes were regulated one way or the other.

Now, increasing efficiency pressure seemed to cause employees to defend their institutionalized "vested rights", pointing to and insisting on formal regulations. As a result, the ability to self-coordinate seemed to decline at all organizational levels.

To counteract these tendencies, management in a quasi-sovereign act declared all organization charts and job descriptions invalid. At the same time, managers appealed to people's common sense and general willingness to cooperate. It goes without saying that this was met with mixed responses. By and large, however, positive reactions seemed to prevail and it seemed as though this step would lead in the right direction.

In the following weeks, management increasingly was under the impression that it had caused even more uncertainty. Where there had been certain points of orientation before, though rather bureaucratized ones, now people had no clue as to what structures were desirable. Some people with rather "imperialist" tendencies kept expanding their areas of responsibility, others kept withdrawing further and further. In some areas, technology and manufacturing processes made for de-facto structures, on other areas that was not the case.

Management felt that something had to happen, for the to regain control of the situation. There was consensus, however, that it was impossible to return to the old org charts—if only to save face and maintain their credibility.

This view was shared even by those board members who had initially opposed the abolishment of organization charts and job descriptions.

Interestingly, the recount of the situation I was presented with when I was called in to help improve the work climate and solve organizational problems, was strongly influenced by lines of arguments reflecting conspirative theories. It was assumed–although, again, there were widely varying opinions on this–that this was a case of deliberate scheming, aimed at undermining the company's work climate, eroding the trust base among employees and towards management. All in all, the board members' attitude reflected that they basically believed an oppositional "us and them" divide to exist between management and staff, their thinking being characterized by clear enemy images. Typical phrases included: "... people just don't work hard enough ..."; "... these days, nobody knows what it means to deliver truly great performance..."; "... nobody really uses their brains ..."; "...everyone is just interested in their paychecks ..." etc.

One board member referred to the problem I was called in to solve as "improving the organizational culture." I was under the distinct impression that this man had recently picked that term up and did not really know what it meant. Another, who had been with the company for many years and did not know any other employer, so he had no way of making comparisons, kept talking about "rationalizing" and "restoring order."

## 4.33 Phase 2: "Feeling" Complexity

It was not difficult to see that this was a rather complex situation, almost an impasse, characterized by how people in the company treated each other and the experiences they had made (e.g., concerning what the boss did and did not "want to hear" ). It was also my impression that some of the five members of the executive board were rather anxious to be proven right rather than get the problem solved.

At that point I naturally knew very little about the company. The situation explained here could be derived from two conversations, each lasting around two hours. One was a preliminary discussion with the eldest son, who had initiated my engagement; the other was with the entire board. It was obvious that some of the board members regarded me with skepticism, or at least reserve, also due to my academic activities.

In line with my views on complex systems, I worked on the assumption that we never know enough about a company to be able to fully justify and substantiate the approaches we suggest. You always start on a very insufficient base of understanding of a system, and you have to take many steps without being able to provide a rationale for them.

In traditional management consulting, you would work from the assumption that you could accumulate sufficient knowledge for the task ahed by going through a phase of information gathering (or business analysis). However, anyone seriously dealing with the issue of complexity of any real system will quickly see that these hopes are an illusion. As a general rule, the only way to obtain the truly relevant information that we need, or achieve the necessary understanding of the complex system, is by working in and with the system. Only intense interaction with a system will offer the opportunity to achieve the kind of familiarity with the specifics of the system–which are often unique and apply exclusively to that system–that is crucial for designing measures that will have an impact. Depending on the dominating theoretical concept, you will arrive at very different "therapy approaches" in such a situation. Lat but not least, your approach will depend on the experience you bring to the project. One and the same matter, the same facts, the same remarks made by employees, etc., will be read differently depending on what theoretical concept and experience you enter into the equation.

Both aspects discussed above–the inevitable incompleteness of our knowledge of the situation and the fact that our understanding of the problem is subject to interpretation–have to be kept in mind at all times while devising measures of organizational or corporate development.

## 4.34 Phase 3: Making the System Talk

When you do not know everything you should know about a system, you have to try to discover it. Based on my previous state of knowledge and the experience I had gathered with other clients, the following was clear to me:No one really knew what the problem was; perhaps there was only one, perhaps there were many–in any case, everyone assumed it was only one problem but each of the people I had talked to thought it was something else.

That is why I had to rely on the system itself to "tell" me whether it had problems and what they were, not its would-be representatives.

If for no other reason, the system had to be involved not only because it was the only way to identify the problem but because it had to solve its own problems.

But what was the system anyway? Who or what belonged to it, who or what did not? Where were its limits? What were its essential subsystems? What were the points with the greatest influence? Who was for or against whom? I would have to find a way to make the system define *itself*, and I would have to make it talk so it would tell me where its problems were.

It is with good reason that I am choosing these anthropomorphic expressions. I was looking for an analog to the "conversation situation" [380] according to Gordon Pask, which permits a system to express itself in a way that comes natural, thus externalizing things it might not be aware of our could not describe in the usual sense.

For the above reasons, it did not seem useful in this particular case to choose a conventional approach. First off, it did not seem to be a good idea to use an approach in which the organization in the usual sense (as recorded in organization charts and the like) would play any kind of role. This subject had become so controversial in this company that it seemed more sensible to leave it aside.

At the same time, this gave me an opportunity, from a theoretical perspective, to question the purpose, meaning and value of organization charts as such, which continue to play a prominent role in organization theory. The way in which a company's organization is depicted in organization charts may prevent precisely the kind of understanding of corporate matters that employees need in order to act the right way. Part of the reason is that this kind of depiction promotes certain ways of thinking, behaviors, expectations and dispositions.

Different depictions are likely to result in different dispositions, for it is safe to assume that, just as information flows in a company are channeled through its structures, the perception and interpretation of events is strongly influenced by an organization as the analogon of a cognitive schema. This is all the more valid when structures are formed around job profiles, and thus constellations of specialization, or–vice versa–when professional specializations result from organizational regulations. Simply put, employees will see the world through the lenses of their understanding of the organization, which, in turn, will lead to further entrenchment of these same

---

380 Cf. Pask (Cybernetics) and (Group).

structures. In other words, what we have here is a process of cognitive homeostasis in which *one* (!) reality is constructed and, in a continuously self-reinforcing loop, this reality then presents itself as the only possible one.[381]

For all these reasons I chose the approach described below, for which I had the board's approval. In this phase it was particularly important not to propose a large-scale project to management. Instead I explained to them that it was better to start modestly, at one corner point of the problem, to quickly achieve visible results that, if they turn out to be useful, might lead us to further steps.

This was no tactical trick. I was deeply convinced that this was the only way to get anywhere. Incidentally, it was not difficult at all to make board members–all of them seasoned managers, albeit with partly one-sided backgrounds–that we needed to see how people would react.

This probing strategy is typical when you deal with complexity, and used in many situations and variations. It never fails to amaze me how quickly practitioners, due precisely to their own experience, recognize and accept the usefulness of approaches like these. It also helps to build trust and cooperative spirit, as people realize you have chosen an approach that does not jeopardize their control.

This is what we did: Some 35 managers from the company, including the board, got together in two groups for a two-day workshop meeting. The assignment was basically for *each of them to draw up a system diagram, or process flow diagram,* placing their current activity at the center and including all relevant links to other people or units–irrespective of hierarchical levels, departments and the like.

In developing the diagram, they were to think about questions such as: What can *I* do in order for the overall system to work? What is *my contribution?* What services do I need to receive from others in order to be able to render *my contribution?* What services do I have to provide to others so they can render *their contributions?*

Answering this set of questions, which Drucker has been recommending for many years[382], is much more difficult than you would think. In most cases, managers are virtually unable to provide satisfactory answers. What you will typically hear–and Drucker himself has described this–are things like: "I head Materials Management" or "I manage Sales." It goes without saying that answers like these are far from expressing what particular

---

381 Von Foerster (Reality).
382 Cf. e.g., (Führungskraft), pp. 88 et seq.

contribution a manager has to make in order for the whole system to function.

So, to find an answer to this question, each individual has to think carefully about his or her specific situation and occupation. In day-to-day business and the hectic that usually comes with an enterprise's operative needs, it is difficult to imagine how anyone could attempt to ask and answer questions like these, unless they are given a special opportunity for that.

Even the opportunity provided here, for which two to three hours were allowed, permitted a depth of individual analysis that would not be feasible on regular working days. For most people, situations like these provide the first opportunity to really think about the deeper meaning of their work. This is not done in an unstructured way, but based on a specific perspective that is crucial for effective and efficient management. An experienced facilitator can provide valuable help, urging everyone to take their time and not be satisfied with convenient or bland answers.

Now, it is largely common practice in organizational development projects to have employees make their own situation analysis. That is not enough: it depends on *how* you do it. Although the different organizational development concepts have generated hosts of methods and techniques, there seem to be certain shortcomings in linking organizational development and management principles to systemic strategies for dealing with proliferating variety, as is invariably found in situations like these.

One key factor for the system's self-definition is that this analysis is first done on an individual basis. However, those involved are encouraged to think not primarily *about themselves* but about the people (and their activities) they need to cooperate with in order to make their contributions. So, the *point of reference* is everyone's *own* activities, everyone's *own* contribution–but their *focus* is on the *others:* everyone whose services they depend on and to whom they deliver services, or in other words: a relevant system or subsystem. Supported by methodical instructions from the facilitator, participants will begin to apply the method of subjective *reenactment*–putting yourself in other people's shoes–that the historian and philosopher Collingwood recommends. According to him, it helps to achieve the kind of understanding that, from a hermeneutic viewpoint, is considered so important in a social systems context.[383]

---

383 Cf. Collingwood (History), p. 146. The methodological and epistemologic significance of this method is an entirely different matter, as extensively discussed by Popper in Objective Knowledge, London 1972, pp. 183 et seq. I agree with Popper's views in this

Thinking about one's own contribution and how it is embedded in the overall context, is something everybody usually has to start for himself; however, in most cases there will be questions he can only answer by *directly* asking the colleague or employee concerned. Thanks to the permanent physical presence of all persons involved, this mutual exchange and coordination is possible at any time. As a general rule, this also helps improve people's cooperative attitude.

After just a few hours, each participant will have a process-flow or system diagram containing the input-output relationships he considers relevant, based on his own contribution to the whole as the central reference point. It is in the nature of things that there will be better and worse results, but that does not matter so much at this point. What matters is the thought process, the mental occupation with the subject that led to the result. A typical example is shown in figure 4.35(1).

Next, everyone involved presents his results to everyone else in plenary discussion, and this is where the system's self-definition process enters its crucial phase. In most cases there will be very intense discussions, causing participants to complete or modify their diagrams, but above all the issues arising in the different units' collaboration will surface.

Experience has shown that in the course of such discussions, which can last several hours, there will hardly be a relevant question that remains untouched. Mind you, these discussions are not limited to organizational issues, although they may be a starting point. In the course of the talks, unhindered by any kind of agenda, almost every aspect of the much-discussed corporate reality (or realities) is touched upon. The way in which these things are discussed largely depends on the facilitation. In most cases the discussion can be guided to the extent that, though far from keeping dispassionate (which would not be desirable anyway) it will produce actual results. Discussions like these usually reveal much more relevant information about the company, in the sense of a business analysis, than any other method could. Keeping minutes of meeting will help to make sure this information is available for further processing.

At the end of that process, every participant has a process flow diagram he has finalized with everyone's input, including all the materials from the discussion that are relevant to him. These can have various contents: some

---

respect. However, applying the Collingwood method in organizational development serves another purpose: it is about developing people's ability to understand the situation, rather than achieving a truthful or correct description of it.

may address unsolved problems from the perspective of his colleagues, staff members and superiors; some may include suggestions for possible solutions, and it happens quite often that some group members draft concrete solutions right then and there. Note that this also solves the relevance problem in a new, systemic way. Nobody has to actually decide or determine what is relevant and what is not. It is usually clear enough from the intense discussion everyone is involved in. Systemic interaction replaces authoritative stipulations. Of course, there is always the possibility that something might be overlooked or forgotten. The risk is small, however.

What can happen, though, is that the discussion gets stuck–or the system locks in place, so to speak–as a result of corporate inbreeding. Systems tend to externalize modes of interaction that keep causing double-bind situations in companies, a typical characteristic of complex systems repeatedly described in this paper. What matters is not what the actors say in this situation, but the way they interact–not content but relationships. There is hardly another way to identify these phenomena, least of all through the bilateral interviews and questionnaires so common in business analysis. A key prerequisite, of course, is that the facilitator is aware of this phenomenon and able to recognize it. It is an example of mentally modeling a situation by means of governance structures.

Compared to ordinary restructuring projects, which often also include self-diagnostic elements, this approach has the major advantage of focusing on procedural aspects at two levels–what happens in the company and how the individual acts–so that hierarchical relations have practically no significance. The numerous presentations and discussions can also help to build a very high degree of mutual understanding and goodwill. Some of it is certainly due to the involvement of those concerned, as is common on organizational development, but in particular the approach of having people draw up a process flow diagram from the perspective of their own individual contribution plays a key role, which is going to be studied in greater detail.

Each participant has his *his* own system diagram, and the company as a whole has an entire set of these diagrams which have been agreed on by everybody. These individual diagrams can now be joined together in a complete graph, which is usually done at the end of the workshop. In other words, you end up having a system description at two levels of recursion. It is important to carefully record the outputs of the entire process, as they represent the tangible manifestation of what has been mentally reconstructed. These diagrams are very different from an organization chart, in that they express something that matters much more for the functionality of a system than the hierarchical relationships depicted in an organization chart.

At this point it would certainly be interesting to explain the effects resulting from a sound understanding of the processes and relationships determining a company's operations, as opposed to an approach that generates a conventional organization chart. Suffice it to say that the questions asked are completely different in each case, thus triggering different thought processes, and as a result the whole context in which organizational issues are addressed is another one.

The question now is whether an org chart is dispensable for choosing a process flow variant. At present I tend to answer this with yes, although my position is not yet final. The basic principle of structuring organizations by tasks are rather controversial, as are the underlying questions, and they have clear downsides from an organization psychology point of view. Combined with the notion that hierarchical relations should not be based on logical connections in the object- and meta-level sense, rat her than power and competencies, this suggests that the process-flow-based approach may indeed be better. In my experience, it also facilitates the linkage to general management questions, such as the structure of planning systems, goal-setting and control processes. However, further analyses will be required to validate these presumptions.

### 4.35  Phase 4: What the System Told Me

The key point is that as participant or facilitator in such a process, you constantly identify and record the systemic structures that emerge, almost like the driftwood in a stream is whirled up by eddies. In addition to the double-bind phenomena mentioned before, a wealth of systemic and subsystemic groups of relationships and regulation mechanisms will emerge. At this point, the true positions of the individual participants in the company's relationship network will crystallise, and they will often be very different from their official ranks. The process reveals who the opinion-leaders are, who favors and who opposes something and why, what coalitions are conceivable on what subjects, what positions are put forward and what arguments are used to support them, what issues are discussed openly and which are swept under the rug. In most cases, people's true dispositions come to the surface. All in all, you can expect this procedure to bring you closest to the truth–unless the process gets out of hand or is managed incompetently–because even skilled tacticians will find it difficult, if not impossible, to keep their cover for two whole days. Any attempt at tactical maneuvering will quickly be visible to everyone in the group, and thus ineffective, and the individual concerned will risk losing credibility and thus authority and acceptance. But even if someone succeeds, his responses will provide you with valuable insights into how the system really works. The objective is not to insist on complete frankness and honesty.

After all, camouflage, disguise, evasive maneuvers and the like are part of the system. A further output to be expected of the process is that it will provide extraordinary insights into the question as to whether the structures of the Viable System exist, and how distinct they are. Provided, of course, you are very familiar with these structures so you will recognize them.

As a conclusion or preliminary output from the process so far, I was able to make the following diagnosis:

1. It was not clear what operative elements were forming System 1. The first to come to mind were manufacturing and sales, both structured by five geographic markets for each of which a sales area manager was responsible, as well as three product groups that were strongly mixed in manufacturing and materials management because, despite all differences, they have considerable similarities in technological aspects.
   The interaction between sales and manufacturing was rather conflict-ridden. A topic that kept coming up in many different facets throughout the workshop was the company's constant delivery problems. Of ten delivery dates confirmed to customers, on average six were actually kept; with some customers requesting customized product versions, it could happen that throughout a whole business year none of the lots was delivered on time. The process-flow/system diagrams developed were not confined to internal relations; they also included the problems of each of the System 1 elements that began to crystallise. By definition, customers and competitors were parts of the sales people's diagrams, just like unions, labor market regulators etc. had to appear in the HR head's diagram and supplier relations in those of the manufacturing and materials people.
   This way it became very obvious that the permanent delivery problems in some areas were beginning to threaten the viability of the elements at that recursion level. It often took almost superhuman efforts to maintain

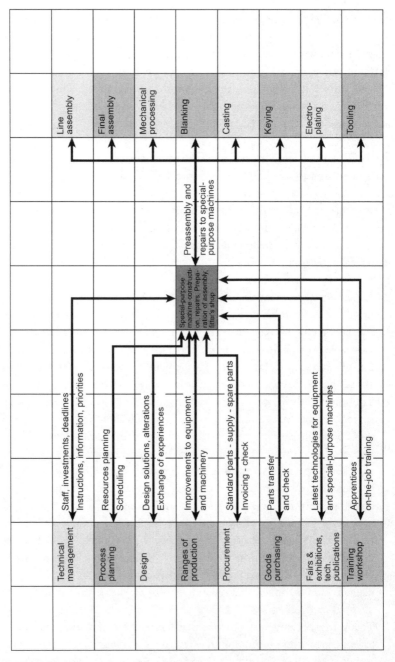

*Figure 4.35(1)*

or restitute the homeostasis between operations and their environments. This, in turn, put the System 1 elements concerned under permanent stress. They often operated at the limits of their performance capacity, which was massively aggravated by the one-sided streamlining efforts mentioned befoe.

As a result of these problems, the systems kept going out of control temporarily and requiring emergency measures; that, in turn, led to disruptions in other areas which were often affected to uncontrollable degrees. Typically, disturbances were "coped with" by shoving them from one area to the next so they would reverberate in the system's processes for weeks–a clear sign of systemic instability which, as I assumed based on various systems, largely originated in the way that sales and manufacturing interacted with each other.

2. At the same time, these were significant clues with regard to System 2. What mechanisms did the company have to cope with these oscillations? There was a series of tools: parts of the planning system, in particular sales and production planning, although a later analysis revealed that the way the planning was done made it completely impossible to have any kind of coordination. There was a financial controlling system that worked reasonably well. In particular process engineering, production scheduling and warehousing were permanently busy fire-fighting to buffer these permanent disruptions, which put them under enormous strain. The rate of modifications was much higher than the rate of possible adjustments.

In other words, System 2 was poorly developed and some activities that should have been collaborating to perform System 2 functions actually operated against one another, making System 2 a source of disruptions rather than an attenuator. As a consequence of all this, the number of ad-hoc interventions by board members and the old chairman seemed to keep increasing, so there was a risk of generating the kind of paralysis and lethargy in the operative elements that will inevitably occur when officials issue contradictory and uncoordinated instructions.

More precisely, take a situation where a certain sequence of tasks had been set in manufacturing, based on process schedule considerations, capacity utilization and cost patterns. When a customer would call his sales agent to complain about a delayed delivery, the sales person would go to talk to the old chairman because he himself had no way of incluencing the production schedule. Based on his account of the situation–in other words, on biased information–the boss would directly contact the machine operator, thus bypassing the production manager, and demand that he complete the order and shift his schedule accordingly.

It would be premature to conclude that all these people were incapable or did not know anything about management. That would not do justice to the complex nature of a system. Each of them acted reasonably from his individual perspective. The problem was in the way they interacted, or rather: in the lack of interaction, the disintegration of things that should have been coordinated, while processes that should have been kept separate were integrated.

3. These factors also permit several conclusions concerning System 3. The advantages of a functionally focused organization become very obvious here. The staff in the individual functions–engineering, manufacturing, sales, materials management, finance, administration–tried to serve their units' interests as best they could, and in doing so generated dangerously suboptimal results, not least because certain structural elements were missing or failed. Put in extreme terms, it sometimes reminded me of the way cerebral palsy patients move. To the extent that any coordination of System 3 functions existed at all, it happened through the board meetings held every Monday, although the three hours available for those meetings were far from enough to generate the regulation variety required, what with the dramatically proliferating variety of operative elements and the functional deficits of System 2.

In the course of several weeks, a vague impression I had had during that process phase was confirmed: the old chairman, though formally no longer a board member, continued to be the heart of the business, the focus and locus of control, which was due above all to his habit of maintaining intense contact with his "old pals", the employees that had built the company with him. When he was on site he would be on the shop floor, usually donning a blue work coat. This way he embodied the parasympathetic channel, and he had the information required, as well as the expertise, since he really knew a lot about his operations–in some ways more than anyone else. These habits made it hard for the executive board, above all his own sons, to fulfill their functions.

For the record, family relations were far from broken. On the contrary, an outside observer had to perceive them as enormously intense, warm-hearted and full of mutual respect. The father obviously loved both his sons and was proud of them, and vice versa. But what exactly was he proud of?

His sons were capable, well-educated, hard-working, and doing an excellent job for their company. However, they were not doing what their father thought they should be doing, or at least not in the way he wanted it done. Of course, their father kept saying that they were right, that times had changed and new ways of thinking and acting were required–but he did not walk the talk. In other words, while he constructed his own version of reality about his sons, praising them to the extent that he seemed virtually uncritical to the external observer and giving them all the support they needed, at the same time he made sure the things that seemed truly important to him were done exactly as he felt they had to be done–and he could be certain to have the allegiance of his buddies in the firm.

In short, a difficult situation that no organization chart could reflect, and which is not addressed in any business management textbook, but which represented the reality that was truly relevant to that company.

4. As you can imagine by now, Systems 4 and 5 were non-existent. They were embodied in the "old man's" omnipresence, even more so when he was not physically present. They were also embodied in the juniors' efforts to lead the company into what they thought to be a "new era." Paradoxically, the wedge between both were the "good family relations" which made it impossible to talk about the core problem, which was exactly that: that they were unable to talk about this without putting their good relationship at risk. At least that is what everyone thought.

This situation, by contrast, was seen perfectly clearly by everyone involved–a second-order paradox, if you will. This was very evident from a series of individual talks I had, some of them happening incidentally and some arranged on purpose. After taking a while to gain some trust, each of them would tell me their woes, more or less along the lines of, "... you know, to be very honest, I have to tell you that ..."

In his own way, the old man also saw the situation very clearly. He knew he should talk to his sons about his views but feared he would have to disappoint them and los credibility, for he would have had to destroy the reality construction he had created and perpetuated himself.

## 4.36 Phase 5: Learning to Become What You Can Be

After the system had defined itself and in the process produced a wealth of information on its own nature, and it seemed to me I had a fairly valid interpretation of the cybernetics of this company that was reasonably supported by my observations, the question was what should be done.

On the one hand, the workshops had created a very positive mood in the organization. Some of the participants were downright excited that something like this had been done at all, as well as about the results achieved.

I had to assume, however, that this was the kind of euphoria you will typically see when an experience is still fresh, and much of it would be put into perspective once they returned to day-to-day business. Nevertheless, at least it was a promising start and the system had been moved into a state of receptiveness. Now it was time for concrete next steps. Both the executive board and the old boss, who had been to part of the workshops, were aware of this.

On the other hand, in the light of the Viable Systems Model my analysis did not give me cause for much optimism. Nevertheless, I wanted to reinforce the positive trend and try to create situations that might offer opportunities to introduce fundamental changes. Above all, I was thinking about gradually familiarizing some people with the Viable Systems Model in order to get the concept of evolutionary corporate development entrenched in the company itself.

At the moment they were far from that point. For the time being, the challenge was to stabilize their readiness for change and score some more quick wins.

In a *short* report of no more than four pages, I summarized my opinion on how the workshop had turned out. A long, academic or professionally produced report would not have been read by anybody. I tried to make my communication very action-oriented.

My report addressed three key issues: The first was the problem of having delivery dates under control. This was something that immediately affected the system's viability and therefore needed to be addressed quickly, even though a genuine solution was not in sight. Rather, one component of a "solution" had to be to make all employees concerned understand that they were facing a permanent control problem. (Interestingly, a common view repeatedly expressed was that it would only take certain methods or tools, such as a different computer system, for the problem to disappear.)

The second issue I had identified was that main causes of existing difficulties in manufacturing lay in the company's production range. From a few hundred parts it had grown to more than 3,000 items in just five years. This was basically the company's response to changed market conditions. Faced with increasingly difficult times as well as market and competitive pressures, the sales people had practically taken every order received. As a result, the company had to deal with an exploding number of special requests, with unpredictable consequences for the entire materials management, for tool making, engineering, documentation of items, etc. As a result, inventories went up, turnover rates deteriorated, and so did capital lock-up and the company's cost situation–which then led to sever streamlining on the cost side.

However, these streamlining efforts–important as they were, as long as they remained in proportion–were only directed at the symptoms. It seemed to me that the root of the problem was in production variety. Quite understandably, customers had first responded very positively to the company's willingness to produce special designs even in small lots. So, the situation was fine sales-wise, but profit contributions were declining. However, it was natural for customers not to put any limits to their demands; instead they increasingly took advantage of the situation by "blackmailing" the firm.

They did not do this for the fun of it; rather, in the course of those five years a peculiar but typical systemic effect had materialized that nobody had foreseen. The components manufactured by the company went to the production of their corporate clients, which were mechanical engineering firms. Now when the company started taking more and more special requests, manufacturing methods were adjusted accordingly, making the clients themselves dependent on the company. Special designs and special parts were no longer just a convenient thing; they were a necessity. Deleting these components from the product range offered would have had disastrous consequences for many of its corporate clients. Of course, this was also the sales people's justification for taking on such orders, which the manufacturing people were strongly opposed to for underandable reasons. However, even manufacturing would ultimately understand clients' desperate situation and make more and more complicated efforts to manage incoming orders. Somehow this vicious circle had to be broken.

As a third point, I suggested installing Management by Objectives across several hierarchy levels in the company. I did this for various reasons: It seemed an appropriate way to ensure that the individuals that had defined individual systems and subsystems could control those subsystems themselves. Furthermore, I was hoping to mitigate the shortcomings existing in the System 2 and 3 functions in this way, especially since I had a specific object-setting approach in mind.

My suggestions were approved of. Two task forces were established to work on the delivery dates issue and on product range streamlining. I agreed to support these teams in terms of methodology, and together with top management I was to work on the issue of management by objectives. These were the activities immediately understandable to employees and considered useful by them. It was my intention, however, in addition to addressing these doubtlessly important issues, to get the company on a development path where the structures of the Viable System would take shape. It was my concern to enable the system to be what it ultimately had to be: a system that was viable of its own accord. I am deliberately expressing it this way because, contrary to what may be the popular view, it is not a matter of *becoming* what you can possibly be but, on the contrary, of implementing the potential that already exists by acting–living–it on a daily basis.

In this context it is of crucial significance that from a cybernetic perspective it is completely impossible to achieve this with the usual organizational approaches. A viable system cannot be built like you would build a machine, by manufacturing and assembling individual parts. Rather, from the existing reality and its latent variety you select the states that represent the Viable Systems structure and try to increase the probability they will occur. In other words, reality is selectively shaped by leveraging its own momentum in line with the Jiu Jitsu principle. In doing this, many of the strategic principles and behaviors discussed in part 3 can be applied. One of the is the strategy of stimulating the system to make changes, in order to sort of snap into a target configuration of states at a given point.

At this point it seems warranted to moot a comment by Beer regarding this design concept:

"A particular design of anything at all ... involves the SELECTION of one configuration out of a vast population of configurations. That is, the invention of the design is best regarded as the annihilation of a myriad alternative design. For instance, in carving the *Pieta* out of a block of stone Michelangelo PREVENTED his statue from being anything else...." [384]

Another issue I wanted to solve in a separate process, or at least get something moving there, was the intra-family interaction relationships that played a crucial role, of course. This was doubtlessly a sensitive issue and I did not know whether I would have an opportunity.

## 4.37 Phase 6: The Journey is the Reward

Things then happened at various levels at once. On the one hand, the task forces worked on the issues mentioned, which I will comment on at a later point. On the other hand, I tried to grasp an opportunity to enter into an interaction of another kind with the family members. In the weeks that followed, there were several contacts of a more private nature which gave me an opportunity to explore their willingness to address the subject of family relations at all. At these occasions, the dual paradox mentioned in my description of phase 4 became very clear, as did some possibilities for (perhaps) achieving a solution.

On the other hand, these occasions gave me several opportunities to make a few remarks, almost in passing, on the viability of a company, and thus to raise their interest in these questions.

Next–and I have to tell this story in fast-forward mode, as it would take a book of its own to do justice to the variety of events–in a dedicated closed meeting I presented the Viable Systems Model to the executive board and the old company boss, then sketched out my interpretation in the light of this model of what was going on in their company. After that, each board member took on the "homework" of trying, based on his naturally much better detailed knowledge of the company and his specific area of responsibility, to work out his own interpretation that would then be discussed and finalized in another closed meeting. As a result, the model is well understood and represented in the company today.

Its credibility was considerably strengthened by the fact that at another level–in one of the task forces–remarkable results were achieved that could nicely be interpreted in the light of the model; in addition, the subproject "management by objectives" was making good progress.

It was particularly important in all these discussions to avoid promoting the constructivist notion that the Viable Systems Model could now simply be "introduced." My greatest worry was that someone would suddenly say: "You have convinced us. Please organize our company exactly like that." What helped enormously was that all of us, being members of the Christian culture and heritage, had a common understanding of several factors, such as that the goal of being "a good Christian" was something quite different from, say, the goal of becoming a home owner. In the latter case it is possible to achieve the goal in the sense that you will then be able to say, "Look, this is my house." But can we expect the same for that other goal? Can we "achieve" it in the same way?

### 4.38  Phase 7: Yes, Why Don't You Set Up a Plan …

Of course things did not evolve in this straightforward manner. As anyone can imagine, the company had to keep operating at full blast, irrespective of all these activities, and all the problems continued to exist and to put employees under enormous stress. It took enormous efforts to make the time for meetings or monitoring progress–on both sides, for this project was not the only one that kept me busy.

Innumerable deadlines were postponed or missed, detail tasks and preparations could not been delivered on time, employees fell ill, had to give priority to special tasks, had family issues–from births to deaths–and last but not least some people left and some new ones joined, as the process stretched over more than a year.

Disruptions of this kind can be anticipated, however, though not in the sense that we are able to know who will get sick when, which customer will cause all priorities to be turned upside down, etc. However, as has been said in section 4.1, this kind of disruptions is in the nature of the system and therefore has to be taken into account by process management by including blank positions, in the sense of having an open program.

In real-life situations you are usually able to foresee certain things in the sense that certain developments seem probable. After all, the birth of a child has a lead time of nine months, and even though we do not know exactly what day it will happen, we do know that Mr. Miller might not be free for appointments in the first half of October. We do know that employees are busy finalizing the budgets in, say, November and that this usually happens under great time pressures; that in April we have to expect a special delivery peak because this is how the client firms have set up their production schedules; that we need to attend major industry fairs at such and such date, and so on.

In addition, you can improve your ability to assess the probability of events by intensifying your monitoring activities. As I knew that some members of the "delivery dates" task force had almost inhuman work loads to cope with and, although they showed enormous commitment, there was a possibility that this subproject might occasionally get out of hand, I made a habit of calling those people in certain intervals to ask about progress, offer help, provide tips, and simply lend them a sympathetic ear for their concerns.

Besides, the intense collaboration with people provided me with plenty of opportunities to personally give them tips for improving their work approach, scheduling, etc.

It never ceases to amaze me how easy it is to achieve results here, when you are familiar with people's work situation as opposed to teaching such techniques in a formal training setting. Working together also helped everyone involved to assess their own capabilities better, i.e. more realistically. While at the start of the project the time estimates given for completing specific tasks would sometimes be unrealistic in my view, this happened less and less frequently after a while.

Finally, everyone on the project adopted a specific habit: As soon as they realized that missed deadlines and other disruptions would not incur any sanctions (such as complaints to management) but that the information on actual or expected disruptions was needed to make corresponding plan changes, they would proactively call me as soon as they realized that a milestone was not feasible. This anticipatory linkage, a cybernetic approach, does wonders for project management. It was further supported by a very specific kind of project documentation and job scheduling that was available to everyone involved at any time, so they all had a complete overview of the state of things, their own tasks, their significance for the whole, and the consequences of postponing their completion.

This was particularly important and effective for the "delivery dates" task force. In addition to many suggestions for improving details of production control, templates used, etc., the cross-functional team gained significant insights related to the core of the problem.

During the workshops described in phase 3 I gained the impression that one essential cause of the specific difficulties in the coordination of delivery dates was the interaction between manufacturing and sales. The individual talks I had with key people confirmed that impression.

What was the situation? I have already commented on this case in the introductory chapter, although in a different context (cf. section 0.44) and will now describe it in some more detail and from another perspective. I said then that the company had organized its operations reasonably well by all business management criteria. Production planning, together with a unit specializing in operations control and deadline monitoring, was responsible for making sure that order throughput was constantly monitored and controlled. However, this did not prevent the precarious situation described above. The permanent difficulties experienced over the years caused the company to introduce a computer-aided production control system which, however, rather increased the problems because it eliminated certain means of improvisation that had existed before.

The increasingly difficult and tough market conditions caused customers not only to raise their demands, as mentioned before, but also to plan at increasingly short notice. While many clients, especially large ones, placed blanket orders stretching over six to twelve months, they would submit the technical details such as performance standards, material variants, etc. at the latest possible point in time. In addition, they increasingly demanded that the company take on further services, such as warehousing and delivering small amounts on a weekly basis instead of larger amounts in biweekly intervals.

This way, corporate clients that were under pressure from their own markets tried to gain more flexibility and leeway at the expense of their suppliers. Metaphorically (but also systemically) speaking, we could say that the clients were eating away the company's flexibility. It turned out then that with the way the company's planning system worked, sales had to propose a sales plan for the coming year no later than four months before the current business year ended. This sales plan served as a basis for the annual production planning. Now, faced with changing customer behavior it was completely impossible for sales to provide more than very general skeleton plans. Nevertheless, the planning system forced them to submit plans for each individual product group. In the given situation this could not be much more than a guessing game, based on the previous year's plan or actual figures.

Incoming orders, be it for specification or call-off, were then passed on directly to manufacturing–without changing the original sales plan. As a result, production planning still relied on the original sales plan, so the current plan changes that reflected market reality had to be perceived as a nuisance. In many cases, the ad-hoc measures taken to meet delivery dates failed to really improve the company's delivery readiness, instead causing the turbulences and instabilities described.

This, in turn, led to a general tendency to blame individuals for the mistakes that happened. More and more often, people were said to be incapable or unrealiable. There was growing distrust and ultimately downright hostility between both functions. The sales people said manufacturing was unable to meet deadlines, which caused major difficulties for them because they kept having to inform clients of delivery delays and then had to listen to their complaints. Manufacturing said that sales were unable to offer realistic delivery dates to their clients, and instead agreed to any kind of terms just to maximize their short-term sales, and on top of everything one could not rely on the delivery dates agreed because they were constantly changed.

While there were weekly coordination meetings between both functions, they were used as a vehicle to cast blame and justify one's own actions rather than to solve problems. It was obvious that a major cause of difficulties was the patterns of interaction between sales and manufacturing. Manufacturing learned about market-driven changes too late and therefore *could not* respond appropriately; on the other hand, they did not warn sales about imminent deadine problems. As a result, sales people were unable to forewarn their clients or, knowing about the situation, change their plans.

As a consequence of holding on the original plan, which was partly due to the computer system, manufacturing was focused on an illusory world that, as explained, kept being disturbed by reality. On the other hand, sales managers managed their units based on production and delivery lists. It was not until that point that they learned about missed deadlines—unless they had already been called by furious clients, which did happen quite often.

It was perfectly clear, of course, that inside the manufacturing and the sales system there was much more information on the respective situation than was obviously passed on to the other function. This information could have done a lot to enhance control; however, as the interaction between both functions was rather poor they did not know about each other's information and thus did not even have the chance to assess its usefulness.

The sales people usually knew some time in advance how clients would act. After all, each sales rep maintained rather intense relations with his clients and was familiar with their manufacturing, so he was able at a relatively early point in time to at least give certain probabilities of a client's future actions with regard to a given order. In many cases this could have done the manufacturing people a valuable service. The earlier they knew about the probability of certain plan details, the better their chances of responding appropriately.

The same was true the other way round: In many cases it would have been possible, once manufacturing realized they would not meet a deadline, to let clients know right away so they would have been able to modify their plans, or else the company could have taken alternative measures such as replacement deliveries, outsourcing, etc. Quite often the problems could have been mitigated or even neutralized that way.

This type of information on the latest developments in the market and in manufacturing which represented anticipations, often no more than presumptions and indicators for possible or probable states, could neither be captured by the computer system nor entered in any of the templates circulating in the subsystem. There was basically no way to communicate about these things because the official system did not offer any kind of code or language that would have been appropriate.

Once this situation was on the table and everyone realized that the difficulties at hand were not caused by their colleagues' evilness or lack of capability but by the structure of the system itself, it was easy to see possibilities for improvement. In systemic terms–though the task force members did not know that–the objective was to install an effective System 2. Instead of thinking about even more computers and more templates and procedures, we started seeking the solution in the social realm. A steering committee was established which, in place of the original weekly coordination meetings, met twice a day for very short, usually half-hour talks. Both the drastically reduced intervals (remember: planning is something continuous and planning is decision ...) and the personal interaction helped to bring more variety to the coordination process, specifically the variety that consisted in vague assumptions and anticipations, or often in just a gut feeling that something would happen. This, however, sufficed to enable the other function to enhance its efforts at anticipatory coupling–setting aside reserves, looking for alternative routes to the target, etc.–, thus creating the conditions for responding in an appropriate way.

All of a sudden, the different time horizons were synchronized much better, and when efforts were made to very systematically identify the indicators responding most promptly, in order to get better and better control of the early and advance warning process, the situation improved considerably.

Of course this did not mean that all difficulties were eliminated. But that was no longer expected by anyone. People had learned to better manage a complex system by means of cybernetic control.

## 4.39 Phase 8: A System Is a System Is a System

The concepts underlying these efforts at improving delivery performance have probably been understood. Two systems that only appeared to interact, and whose pseudo-interaction actually kept driving them further apart, were to be coupled in such a way that true interaction would ensue, that their current states would continuously influence one another, and that each of them would immediately be modified by the other system's state–as a result of which the meta-criterion of stability (in this case delivery dates and the ability to modify plans and use all of the system's inherent options for action) would be within "physiological" limits. Abstractly speaking, the goal was to install an effective homeostat. Meanwhile the plan to introduce "management by objectives" had gotten farther ahead. The timing was right, too. Object setting and coordination could be tied to the budgeting process and the passing of the annual plan.

I managed to convince the board to have a meeting for all managers to inform them about their foremost objectives and intentions. You do not need cybernetics to know that this can have an enormous effect in terms of anticipatory coordination, if it is done the right way. "Right" in this case simply means "convincing." Top management must come across as sincere and honest. It must be clear to see that it is their foremost concern to enable each individual, by means of the information provided, to fulfill his task better and more easily. Objectives set must not come in the guise of power-based commands or instructions but as a help to the individual, enabling him to better understand and take advantage of the torrent of events.

It is remarkable to what extent bilateral goal setting and coordination are still common practice. For reasons of variety this is a completely unsuitable approach.

In this particular company, I suggested a joint goal-setting workshop. This required careful preparation. All employees involved in the process received comprehensive instructions, along with written guidelines and concrete examples aligned with their area of competence. As the goal was to gather 35 to 40 people for a joint activity, we also agreed on carefully crafted schedule of which we had to expect that it would be met.

The procedure stipulated that the managers of large departments attend the workshop jointly with their staff, and all participants were to present their own objectives. This put participants under some pressure to prepare really well, for it could be assumed that nobody wanted to make a bad impression.

It was also fair to assume that each department head would put some effort into making his team look good, so they would all spend the preparation phase identifying well-thought-out and agreed-on objectives jointly with their staff.

The agenda for the actual workshop had to be very dense, due to the large number of presentations. Each participant had a timeslot allocated to his presentation; the time available for the subsequent discussion, which was to identify, not solve pending questions of coordination, was limited as well.

In the context of our joint project, the company's employees had previously had numerous opportunities to improve their presentation skills. Before they had usually talked around a subject forever; now the concept of "effective communication" had grown into a true value for everyone. Not only had they understood that they were winning time (which also meant leisure time) this way; they had also learned to differentiate between those just talked and those who actually said something. The system began to independently cultivate its capability of self-definition and selection. For me, the object-setting workshop also served the purpose of establishing a connection between the very first workshop we had held, and the system diagrams developed there, and the objectives and criteria governing the control of these systems. This intention was based on the fact that cybernetic systems must always form closed loops.

A factor of particular significance in this context was that in the course of the project the board had made great progress in understanding the Viable Systems Model. Of course there were still differing interpretations, critical distance in one of them and uncritical adoption in the other, but their ability to interpret the goings-on in their company from this perspective was well-established. It should be emphasized here that it is the process of *dealing* with the model that matters, the process of mentally experimenting with it, not its simple acceptance.

Above all, thinking in terms of the model had led them away from the hierarchy and rank focus that had previously characterized their discussions. This enabled the board members to see the objective-setting workshop in all its multi-dimensionality. As was to be expected, the object-setting activities mainly focused on annual targets for the following business period. However, it is factually and logically impossible to coordinate annual targets in a meaningful way without making the connection to longer-term plans.

It was not surprising, then, that many considerations, questions and suggestions emerged at that workshop which concerned the company's fundamental issues, such as its future product policy, market opportunities, technology, and so on. Despite the necessity, resulting from the circumstances, to manage the discussion very tightly and focus it on the company's annual objectives, it was striking how the system kept shifting across all the dimensions of systems-2-4-5 interaction.

Its systemic results were these: The employees realized that they had very different possibilities for anticipatory coordination compared to what they had known and experienced. Together with other insights on control by anticipating future events, it created a basis of conviction that this was the right way to go.

In addition, participants came to realize once again that they really formed a system. While the former, chiefly bilateral relationships totally fragmented the connections in the system, now, in addition to me-you relationships they could also experience we-relationships. The system began to be conscious of itself, to experience itself as an entity. It began to learn how to deal with complexity, and thus with itself.

Moreover, a major share of employees, and above all the board members, realized that some fundamental questions of product-market strategy had to be addressed very urgently. This insight was primarily triggered by the still very diffuse character of the operational System 1 elements, as well as the progress made by the "product range streamlining" task force. Its structural analyses had revealed enormous disproportionalities, as had to be expected. A minimal share of products generated the major share of sales and profit contributions. It turned out that the company consisted of at least two homogenous parts: one that operated in the mass market and one that produced custom products. It was obvious that they had to find answers for the question as to the balance between them.

Another result that seemed particularly important to me with regard to the company's future activities was that this workshop provided board members with a live example of how certain subareas of the Viable System work, which became very clear in the course of the extensive discussions we had after the workshop. This was the first occasion for board members, having learned about the structures of the Viable System, to watch a larger group of employees at very specific activities. It seemed to me we had managed to establish a kind of variety generator for spreading these ideas in the company. To use a historical analogy, the Viable Systems Model had found its disciples; they had understood its message and were ready to evangelize.

At another level, several weeks before the objective-setting meeting the members of the owner family had had a constructive conversation, which went back a long way and opened up tangible new opportunities to bring about a second-order change in their relationships.

All in all, the prospects for further positive development of the company were quite good at that point. Mind you, I do not wish to create the impression that all problems had been solved. The strategy for dealing with complex systems is a constant caution to be ready for surprises at all time

## 4.4 Enlightenment or Clarification?

> "Complex systems tend to produce complex responses (not solutions) to problems"
> *John Gall*

Irrespective of the differences between the historian and the journal keeper, as mentioned in the introduction to the previous section, both have one thing in common: their task does not come to a natural end; it is terminated at will. So when does a corporate development process end? When does the description of a complex system end?

The purpose of this chapter was to illustrate possible applications for the ways of thinking, the methods and models described in this book. Above all, I wanted to show that this approach can be applied "unarmed", so to speak– without aids, computers, statistics, and even without a host of graphs, as useful as they may generally be.

The strategy of dealing with complex systems, the cybernetics of controlling open, evolutionary processes, has its own methods. We are not at the mercy of that complexity, provided we accept it and, as we would do with many everyday things, make it a fixed element of our thinking and actions; provided by gaining insight into the nature of complex systems we learn to recognize what is impossible in order to better implement what is possible and feasible.

In his recollections of a conversation he had with Marion Gräfin Dönhoff,[384] Rupert Riedl formulated a very compelling thought: Man's belief

---

384 Riedl, R. (Evolution und Erkenntnis), pp. 339 et seq., p. 541.

in the limitlessness of his mind and reason–which, with all its naïve optimism, confidence, presumptuousness, and overestimation of its own abilities, is a true product of Enlightenment–will have to make room for the kind of wisdom we refer to as worldly wisdom.

# References

Albert, Hans (Traktat) *Traktat über rationale Praxis*, Tübingen, 1978

Albert, Hans, Topitsch Ernst. (eds.) (Werturteilsstreit) *Werturteilsstreit*, Darmstadt, 1971

Ansoff, Igor H. (Strategy) *Corporate Strategy*, New York, 1965

— (Weak Signals) "Managing Surprise and Discontinuity – Strategic Response to Weak Signals", in: *Schmalenbachs Zeitschrift für betriebswirtschaftliche Forschung*, 28, 1976, pp. 129–152

Ansoff, Igor H., Hayes, Richard L. (Introduction) *"Introduction"*, in: Ansoff Igor H., Declerck Roger P., Hayes Richard L., *From Strategic Planning to Strategic Management*, London 1976

Ansoff, Igor H., Declerck Roger P., Hayes Richard L. (Strategic Management) *From Strategic Planning to Strategic Management*, London 1976

Argenti, John (Corporate Collapse) *Corporate Collapse – The Causes and Symptoms*, London, 1976

Ashby, Ross W. (Brain) *Design for a Brain – The Origin of Adaptive Behaviour*, 3rd edition, London, 1970

— (Bremermann) "Some Consequences of Bremermann's Limit for Information-Processing systems", in: Oestreicher, Hans, Moore, Darrell (eds.), *Cybernetic Problems in bionics*, New York, 1968, pp. 69–76

— (Informational Measures) "Systems and their Informational Measures", in: Klir, George (ed.), *Trends in General systems theory*, New York, 1972, pp. 78–97

— (Intelligent Machine) "What is an Intelligent Machine?" in: *Proceedings of the Western Joint Computer Conference*, Los Angeles, CA, pp. 275-280

— (Introduction) *An Introduction to Cybernetics*, 5th Ed., London 1970

— (Modelling) "Modeling the Brain," in: *Proceedings IBM Scientific Computing Symposium on Simulation Models and Gaming*, IBM Watson Research Center, New York: NY, pp. 195-208

— (Models) "Mathematical Models and Computer Analysis of the Function of the Central Nervous System", in: *Annual Review of Physiology*, 38, 1966, pp. 89–106

— (Setting Goals) "Setting Goals in Cybernetic Systems," in: *Cybernetics, Artificial Intelligence and Ecology*, Robinson, H. W. and Knight D. E. (eds.), Spartan Books: New York, NY, 1972, pp. 33-44

— (Cybernetics) *An Introduction to Cybernetics*, 1st ed., London, UK, 1956

Bateson, Gregory (Ecology) *Steps to an Ecology of Mind*, New York, 1972
— (Nature) *Mind and Nature*, New York, 1979
— (Ökologie) *Ökologie des Geistes*, Frankfurt a. M., 1981
Beer, Stafford (Automation) "The Irrelevance of Automation", in: *Cybernetica*, I, 1958, pp. 280, 295
— (Brain) *Brain of the Firm – The Managerial Cybernetics of Organization*, London, 1972
— (Crisis) "Immanent Forms of Imminent Crisis", in: Infor Journal, Vol. 12, No. 3,1974
— (Cybernetics) *Cybernetics and Management*, London, 1959
— (Decision) *Decision and Control – The Meaning of Operational Research and Management Cybernetics*, London, 1966
— (Development) "Cybernetics of National Development", The Zaheer Lecture, New Delhi, 1974
— (Factory) "Towards the Cybernetic Factory", in: Von Foerster H., Zopf G. G. (eds.) *Principles of Self-organization*, Pergamon Press, Oxford, 1962, pp. 25–89
— (Freedom) *Designing freedom*, London, New York, 1974
— (Governors) "On Viable Governors", in: Discovery 23, 1962, pp. 38–44
— (Heart) *The Heart of Enterprise*, London 1979
— (Laws) Laws of Anarchy, The Irvine Memorial Lecture, University of St. Andrews
— (Plan) "The Aborting Corporate Plan", in: Jantsch E., *Perspectives of Planning*, OECD, Paris, 1968, pp. 395–422
— (Platform) *Platform for Change*, London, 1975
— (Prerogatives) "Prerogatives of System in Management Control", United Kingdom Automation Council, 8th Annual Lecture, 1969
— (Science) "On Heaping Our Science Together", Keynote Address to the Second Meeting on Cybernetics and systems Research (Internal Paper), Wien, 1974
— (Systems Approach) *A Systems Approach to Management*, in: Personal Review, 1972
Bircher, Bruno (Unternehmungsplanung) *Langfristige Unternehmungsplanung*, Bern/Stuttgart, 1976
Braybrooke, David, Londblom, Charles E., (Strategy) *A Strategy of Decision*, London, 1963
Bremermann, Hans J. (Optimization) "Optimization Through Evolution and Recombination", in: Yovits Marchall C., Jacobi, George T., Goldstein, Gordon D. (eds.), *Self-Organizing systems*, pp. 93–106
Bresch, Carsten (Zwischenstufe Leben) *Zwischenstufe Leben – Evolution ohne Ziel?*, München, 1977
Brown, Spencer (Laws) *Laws of Form*, New York, 1972 in German: Gesetze der Form, Frankfurt a. M., 1972

Campbell, Donald T. (Blind Variation) "Blind Variation and Selective Survival as a General Strategy in Knowledge Processes" in: Yovits M., Cameron S. (eds.), *Self Organizing Systems*, New York, 1960, pp. 205–231
— (Epistemology) "Evolutionary Epistemology" in: Schilpp P.A. (ed.), The philosophy of Karl R. Popper. The library of living philosophers. Lasalle, IL: Open Court Publishing Company, Vol. 14-1, 1974, pp. 413–463
Collingwood, Robin G. (History) *The Idea of History*, Oxford, 1946


Dickson, Paul (Rules) *The Official Rules*, New York, 1978
Drucker, Peter (Changing World) *The Changing World of the Executive*, New York, 1982
— (Führungskraft) *Die ideale Führungskraft*, Düsseldorf/Wien, 1967
— (Großunternehmen) *Das Großunternehmen*, Düsseldorf, 1966
— (ed.)(Leaders) *Preparing Tomorrow's Business Leaders Today*, New Jersey, 1969
— (Management) *Management-Tasks, Responsibilities*, Practices, London, 1974
— (People and Performance) *People and Performance*: The Best of Peter *Drucker on Management*, London, 1977
— (Praxis) *Praxis des Management*, 6th ed., Düsseldorf, 1969
— (Technology) *Technology, Management and Society*, London, 1970
Dyllick, Thomas (Unternehmungsführung) *Gesellschaftliche Instabilität und Unternehmungsführung*. Ansätze zu einer gesellschaftsbezogenen Managementlehre, Bern, Stuttgart, 1982


Eccles, John. C. (Human Mystery) *The Human Mystery*, Berlin, Heidelberg, New York, 1979
— (Psyche) *The Human Psyche*, Berlin, Heidelberg, New York 1980
— (Reality) *Facing Reality*, Berlin, Heidelberg, New York 1970
Eigen, Manfred, Winkler Ruthild (Spiel) *Das Spiel*, München, Zürich, 1985


Fischer, Hans R. (Management) "Management by Bye?", in: Schmilz, C., Gester, P.W., Heitger, B. (eds.), Managerie, *1. Jahrbuch für Systemisches Denken und Handeln im Management*, Heidelberg, 1992
Foerster, Heinz v. (Biological Computers) "Some Aspects in the Design of Biological Computers", in: Proceedings of the 2nd International Congress on Cybernetics, Namur, 1958, Paris, 1960
— (Memory) "What is Memory that It May Hindsight and Foresight as Well?" in: Bogoch S. (ed.), *The Future of Brain Sciences*, New York, 1969, pp. 19–63
— (Objects) "Objects:Tokens for Eigen-Behaviors", ASC Cybernetic Forum 8, Vol 3-4,1976, pp. 91-96
— (Reality) "On constructing reality", in: Preiser, F. E. (Ed.) *Environmental Design*, Stroutsbourg, 1973
— (From Stimulus to Symbol) "From Stimulus to Symbol: The Economy of Biological Computation" in: Buckley W. (ed.), *Systems Research*, 1966, pp. 170–185

— (Gegenstände) "Gegenstände: Greifbare Symbole für (Eigen-) Verhalten", in: Foerster, H. v., *Wissen und Gewissen*, Frankfurt, 1993, pp. 103 et seq

Forrester, Jay W. (Industrial Dynamics*) Industrial Dynamics*, 6th Ed., Cambridge Mass, 1969.

— (Social Systems) "Planning under the Dynamic Influences of complex social systems", in: Jantsch E. (ed), *Perspectives of Planning*, OECD, Paris, 1969, pp. 235–254

Friedman, Yona (Utopien) *Machbare Utopien*, Frankfurt a. M., 1977

Gall, John (Systementics) *Systemantics: How systems work and especially how they fail*, New York, 1977

Gälweiler, Aloys (Marketingsplanung) *Marketingplanung im System einer integrierten Unternehmensplanung*, Luchterhand, Neuwied 1979

— (Unternehmenssicherung) "Unternehmenssicherung und strategische Planung", in: Zeitschrift für betriebswirtschaftliche Forschung (zfbf), 28, 1976, pp. 362–379

Gomez, Peter, Malik, Fredmund, Oeller, Karl Heinz (Systemmethodik) *Systemmethodik: Grundlagen einer Methodik zur Erforschung und Gestaltung komplexer soziotechnischer Systeme*, Bern, Stuttgart, 1975

Gomez, Peter (Operations Management) *Die kybernetische Gestaltung des Operations Managements*, Bern, Stuttgart, 1978

— (systems-Methodology) "The systems-Methodology for Organic Problem Solving, Part B", in: Malik F., Gomez P., Oeller K. H., "Organic Problem Solving in Management", 3rd European Meeting on Cybernetics and systems Research, Wien, 1976

Goodstein, Reuben L. (Recursive Number Theory) *Recursive Number Theory*, Amsterdam 1957

Grossekettler, Heinz (Macht) *Macht, Strategie und Wettbewerb*, Diss. Mainz, 1973

Gundy, Leo (Businessman) *The Ugly American Businessman in Europe*, 1975

Hall, Edward T. (Language) *The Silent Language*, New York 1973

Harrison, Jeffrey P., Stevens, Colin F. (Forecasting) "A Bayesian Approach to Short-Term Forecasting", in: Operational Research Quarterly 22, 1971, 4, pp. 341–362

Hayek, Friedrich. A. v. (Individualismus) *Individualismus und wirtschaftliche Ordnung*, Erlenbach, Zurich, 1952

— (Constructivism) "The Errors of Constructivism and The Pretence of Knowledge" in: *New Studies in Philosophy, Politics, Economics and the History of Ideas*, London, Chicago, 1978

— (Konstruktivismus) *Die Irrtümer des Konstruktivismus und die Grundlagen legitimer Kritik gesellschaftlicher Gebilde*, Muenchen, 1970

— "Kinds of Order in Society", in: New Individualist Review, vol.6, ed. Ralph Raico, Indianapolis 1964, pp.495 - 504

— (Law) *Law, Legislation and Liberty*, Vol. I–III, London 1973–1979

— (Mirage) *Law, Legislation and Liberty*, Vol. II, The Mirage of Social Justice, London, 1976
— (New Studies) *New Studies in Philosophy, Politics, Economics and the History of Ideas*, London, 1978
— (Order) *The Sensory Order: An Inquiry into the Foundations of Theoretical Psychology*, London, Chicago, 1952
— (Phänomene) *Die Theorie komplexer Phänomene*, Walter Eucken-Institut, Vorträge und Aufsätze, Vol. 36, Tubingen, 1972
— (Political Order) *Law, Legislation and Liberty*, Vol. III: The Political Order of a Free People, London, 1979
— (Primacy) "The Primacy of the Abstract", in: Koestler, Arthur, Smythies, John R., (eds.), *Beyond Reductionism*, London, 1969
— (Primat) "Der Primat des Abstrakten", in: Koestler, Arthur, *Das neue Menschenbild - Die Revolutionierung der Wissenschaften vom Leben. Ein internationales Symposium*, 1970
— (Rules) *Law, Legislation and Liberty*, Vol. I: Rules and Order, London, 1973
— (Studien) *Freiburger Studien*, Tübingen, 1969
— (Studies) *Studies in Philosophy, Politics and Economics*, Chicago 1967
— (Verfassung) *Die Verfassung der Freiheit*, Tübingen 1971
— (Vernunft) *Missbrauch und Verfall der Vernunft*, Frankfurt 1959
— (Serfdom) *The Road to Serfdom*, London, 1944; in German: *Der Weg zur Knechtschaft*, München, 1971

Jackson Don, D (Familie) "Das Studium der Familie", in: Watzlawick, Paul, Weakland, John H. (Eds.), *Interaktion*, Bern, 1980
Jantsch, Erich (Perspectives) *Perspectives of Planning*, Paris, 1969
— (Selbstorganisation) "Erkenntnistheoretische Aspekte der Selbstorganisation Natürlicher Systeme", Konferenz über Wahrnehmung und Kommunikation, Univ. Bremen 1977
Jay, Antony (Man) *Corporation Man*, London, 1972
— (Management) *Management and Macchiavelli*, Harmondsworth, 1970

Kami, Michael J. (Opportunity) "Business Planning as Business Opportunity", in: Drucker, Peter F. (ed.) *Preparing tomorrow's business leaders today*, Englewood Cliffs NJ, 1969
— (Planning) "Planning in the Age of Discontinuity", Seminar Weiterbildungsstufe Hochschule St. Gallen, 1976
— (Strategies) *Manual of Management Assumptions for Planning Business Strategies*, Lighthouse Point, 1976
Klir, George, (ed.) (Trends) *Trends in General systems Theory*, London 1972
Kneschaurek, Francesco (Unternehmer) *Der Schweizer Unternehmer in einer Welt im Umbruch*, Bern, 1980
Koestler, Arthur (ed.) (Menschenbild) *Das neue Menschenbild*, Wien, 1970

Koestler, Arthur, Smythies, John R., (eds.) (Beyond Reductionism) Beyond Reductionism, London, 1969

Korzybski, Alfred (Science) *Science and Sanity*, New York, 1941

Krieg, Walter (Grundlagen) *Kybernetische Grundlagen der Unternehmungsorganisation*, Bern, 1971

Lindblom, Charles E. (Intelligence) *The Intelligence of Democracy*, London, New York 1965

— (Muddling Through) "The Science of Muddling Through, in: Public Administr. Review 19, 2, 1959, pp. 79–88

Lorenz, Konrad (Rückseite) *Die Rückseite des Spiegels – Versuch einer Naturgeschichte menschlichen Erkennens*, Muenchen, 1973

Malik, Fredmund (Unternehmungsentwicklung) "Sichere Unternehmungsentwicklung in turbulenten Zeiten" in: Bücher-Perspektiven, Sondernummer anlässlich des Kongresses "Management-Revolution – Perspektiven 2000. Von der Weisungs- zur Selbstkultur", Österreichische und Deutsche Gesellschaft für Baukybernetik, Salzburg, 12,13.9.1991

Malik, Fredmund, Gomez, Peter (Entscheide) "Evolutionskonzept für unternehmerische Entscheide" in: Industrielle Organisation 45, 1976, 9, pp. 308–312

Malik, Fredmund, Gomez, Peter, Oeller, Karl Heinz (Organic Problem Solving) "Organic Problem Solving in Management", 3rd European Meeting on Cybernetics and systems Research, Wien, 1976

Maturana, Humberto R. (Autopoiesis) Varela, Francisco, J., *Autopoiesis and Cognition*, Dordrecht, 1980

McCulloch, Warren, S. (Mind) *Embodiments of Mind*, MIT Press, 1965

Mintzberg, Henry (Nature) *The Nature of Managerial Work*, London, 1973

Oeller, Karl H. (Cybernetic Process Control) Organic Problem Solving in Management, Part C: Cybernetic Process Control, Paper presented at the 3rd European Meeting on Cybernetics and systems Research, Wien 1976

— (Kennzahlen) "Grundlagen und Entwicklung kybernetischer Kennzahlen Systeme", unpublished, 1978

Oestreicher, Hans L., Moore, Darrell R. (eds.) (Cybernetic Problems) *Cybernetic Problems in Bionics*, New York, l968

Pask, Gordon (Approach) An Approach to Cybernetics, London, 1961

— (Cybernetics) *The Cybernetics of Human Learning and Performance*, London, 1975

— (Cybernetic Theory) *Conversation, Cognition and Learning: a Cybernetic Theory and Methodology*, Elsevier Press, 1974

— (Group) "The Self-Organizing System of a Decision Making Group", in: *Association Internationale de Cybernétique* (ed.), Proceedings 3rd Congress, Belgium, 1961, pp. 814–826

— (Human Learning) *The Cybernetics of Human Learning and Performance*, London, 1975

— (Organic Control) "Organic control and the cybernetic method", in: Cybernetica, vol 3, 1958, pp. 155-173

Peters, Richard S. (Motivation) *The Concept of Motivation*, London, 1959

Polanyi, Michael (Logic) *The Logic of Liberty*, London, 1951

Popper, Karl (Autobiography) "Intellectual Autobiography", in: Schilpp, Paul (ed.), *Philosophy of Karl Popper*, Illinois 1974, pp. 3–181

— (Conjectures) *Conjectures and Refutations – The Growth of Scientific Knowledge*, 4th Ed., London, 1972

— (Gesellschaft) *Die offene Gesellschaft und ihre Feinde*, 2 Vols, Bern, 1958

— (Gesellschaft II) *Die offene Gesellschaft und ihre Feinde*, Vol 2, *Falsche Propheten;Hegel, Marx und die Folgen*, 2nd ed., Bern, 1970

— (Historizismus) *Das Elend des Historizismus*, 3rd ed., Tuebingen, 1971

— (Knowledge) *Objective Knowledge – An Evolutionary Approach*, London, 1972

— (Logik) *Logik der Forschung*, 4th ed., Tuebingen, 1971

— (Propensity)"The Propensity Interpretation of Probability", British Journal for the Philosophy of Science, 10, 1959, pp. 25–42

— (Replies)"Replies to My Critics", in: Schilpp, Paul (ed.), *Philosophy of Karl Popper*, Illinois, 1974, pp. 961–1197

— (Society) *The Open Society and its Enemies*, Vol. II: *Hegel, Marx and the Aftermath*, 5th Ed., London, 1974

Popper, Karl, Eccles John C. (Self) *The Self and its Brain*, Berlin, Heidelberg, New York, 1977

Powers, William T. (Behaviour) *Behaviour: The Control of Perception*, Chicago, 1973

Preiser, Siegfried (Kreativitätsforschung) *Kreativitätsforschung*, Darmstadt, 1976

Probst, Gilbert (Gesetzeshypothesen) *Kybernetische Gesetzeshypothesen als Basis für die Gestaltungs- und Lenkungsregem im Management*, Bern, Stuttgart, 1981

Quinn, James B. (Change) *Strategies for Change: Logical Incrementalism*, Irwin, Homewood, IL, 1980

Riedl, Rubert (Biologie der Erkenntnis) *Biologie der Erkenntnis*, Hamburg, Berlin, 1980

— (Evolution und Erkenntnis) *Evolution und Erkenntnis*, Muenchen, Zuerich, 1982

— (Genesis) *Die Strategie der Genesis*, Muenchen, Zuerich, 1976

— (Ordnung) *Die Ordnung des Lebendigen*: Systembedingungen der Evolution, Hamburg, Berlin, 1978

— *Order in Living Organism*: A Systems Analysis of Evolution, New York 1978

Roepke, Jochen (Innovation) *Die Strategie der Innovation*, Tuebingen, 1979

Schilpp, Paul (ed.) (Philosophy) *Philosophy of Karl Popper*, Illinois, 1974

Schwaninger, Martin (Strategische Plannung) *Software Strategische Planung*, Nr. 27055, unpublished, Management Zentrum St. Gallen, 1982

Shibutani, Tamotsu (Society) *Society and Personality*, New Jersey, 1961

Siegwart, H., Probst G. (eds.) (Mitarbeiterführung) *Mitarbeiterführung und gesellschaftlicher Wandel, Festschrift für Charles Lattmann*, Bern, Stuttgart, 1983

Sloan, Alfred P. (General Motors) *My Years with General Motors*, New York, 1964

Sloma, Richard S. (Management) *No-Nonsense Mangement*, New York, 1977

Sommerhoff, Gerd (Brain) *Logic of the Living Brain*, London 1974

Steinbruch, Karl (Maßlos) *Maßlos informiert: Die Enteignung unseres Denkens*, Muenchen, Berlin, 1978

Steinbruner, John. D (Cybernetic Theory) *The Cybernetic Theory of Decision*, Princeton 1974

Streissler, Erich (ed.) (Freedom) *Roads to Freedom*, London, 1969

Tarr, Graham (Problem Solving) *The Management of Problem Solving*, London, 1973

Taylor, Gordon R. (Future) *How to avoid the Future*, London, 1975

Tobinson, H. W., Knight D. E. (eds.) (Cybernetics) *Cybernetics, Artificial Intelligence and Ecology*, Proceedings of the Fourth Annual Symposium of the American Society for Cybernetics, New York, 1973

Tullock, Gordon (Corporations) "The new Theory of Corporations", in: Streissler, Erich (ed.), *Roads to Freedom*, London, 1969, pp. 287–309

Ulrich, Hans (Unternehmung) *Die Unternehmung als produktives soziales System*, 2nd ed., Bern, 1971

Ulrich, Walter (Kreativitätsförderung) *Kreativitätsförderung in der Unternehmung*, Bern, 1975

Varela, Francisco J., Maturana Humberto R., Uribe Ricardo (Autopoiesis) "Autopoiesis: The Organization of Living systems, its Characterization and a Model", Bio systems, 5, 1974, pp. 187–196

Vester, Frederic (Ballungsgebiete) *Ballungsgebiete in der Krise*, Stuttgart, 1976

— (Neuland des Denkens) *Neuland des Denkens*, Stuttgart, 1980

— (Sensitivitätsmodell) *Sensitivitätsmodell*, Frankfurt, 1980

— (System) *Unsere Welt ein vernetztes System*, Stuttgart, 1978

— (Urban Systems) *Urban Systems in Crisis*, Munich 1983.

Watkins, John W.N., (Decision) *Decision and Belief*, in: Audley, R.J. (ed): Decision making, 1967

— (Entscheidung) "Entscheidung und Überzeugung", in: Albert, Hans, Topitsch Ernst (eds.), *Werturteilsstreit*, Darmstadt, 1971

— (Unity) "The Unity of Popper's Thought", in Schilpp, Paul (ed.), *Philosophy of Karl Popper*, Illinois, 1974, pp. 371–407

Watzlawick, Paul, Beavin, Janet H., Jackson, Don D. (Kommunikation) *Menschliche Kommunikation*, Bern, Stuttgart, Wien, 1974

Watzlawick, Paul, Weakland, John H. (eds) (Interaktion) *Interaktion – Menschliche Probleme und Familientherapie*, Bern, Stuttgart, Wien, 1980

Watzlawick, Paul, Weakland John H., Fisch Richard (Lösungen) *Lösungen: Zur Theorie und Praxis menschlichen Wandels*, Bern, Stuttgart, Wien, 1974

Weinberg, Gerald M. (General Systems*)* *An Introduction to General Systems Thinking*, New York, 1975

Wöhe, Guenter (Betriebswirtschaftslehre) *Einführung in die Allgemeine Betriebswirtschaftslehre*, 13th ed., Muenchen, 1978

Wolff, Harald (General Motors) "Das große Erfolgsgeheimnis von General Motors" Fortschrittliche Betriebsführung 1964,4, pp. 97–107

Wynne-Edwards, Vero C. (Dispersion) *Animal Dispersion in Relation to Social Behaviour*, Edinburgh 1962


Yovits, Marshall, Cameron, Scott (eds.) (Systems) *Self-Organizing systems*, Oxford, 1960

Yovits, Marshall, Jacobi, George T., Goldstein, Gordon D. (eds.) Self-Organizing systems) *Self-Organizing systems*, Washington, 1962

# Index